D0123590

FITZ-GREENE HALLECK

At about the age of sixty-five.

From a photograph by M. B. Brady.

Fitz-Greene Halleck

An Early Knickerbocker

Wit and Poet

BY

NELSON FREDERICK ADKINS

Washington Square College, New York University

New Haven · Yale University Press

LONDON

HUMPHREY MILFORD · OXFORD UNIVERSITY PRESS

1930

TO

MY MOTHER

THE OLIVER BATY CUNNINGHAM
MEMORIAL PUBLICATION FUND

THE present volume is the tenth work published by the Yale University Press on the Oliver Baty Cunningham Memorial Publication Fund. This Foundation was established May 8, 1920, by a gift from Frank S. Cunningham, Esq., of Chicago, to Yale University, in memory of his son, Captain Oliver Baty Cunningham, 15th United States Field Artillery, who was born in Chicago, September 17, 1894, and was graduated from Yale College in the Class of 1917. As an undergraduate he was distinguished alike for high scholarship and for proved capacity in leadership among his fellows, as evidenced by his selection as Gordon Brown Prize Man from his class. He received his commission as Second Lieutenant, United States Field Artillery, at the First Officers' Training Camp at Fort Sheridan, and in December, 1917, was detailed abroad for service, receiving subsequently the Distinguished Service Medal. He was killed while on active duty near Thiaucourt, France, on September 17, 1918, the twenty-fourth anniversary of his birth.

PREFACE

THE basis of the present biography of Fitz-Greene Halleck was a doctoral dissertation presented in 1925 to the faculty of the Yale Graduate School. Since then, the work has been fully revised and enlarged. No apology has been thought necessary for presenting thus minutely the personal and literary career of an American man of letters who can claim but a minor place in the development of our literature. Believing with Longfellow that ''a life that is worth writing at all is worth writing minutely,'' the author, from a careful and, as he believes, adequate examination of the sources of Halleck's life, has sought to re-create the picture of one of the most brilliant and charming literary amateurs that America has produced. The work may further be regarded as a study in early Knickerbocker letters. The writings of Halleck amply illustrate a local literary tradition set in motion by the *Salmagundi* (1807–8) and the *Knickerbocker's History of New York* (1809), and persisting in New York literature for the next thirty years. We find in Halleck's work not only the inevitable contrast between the worlds of romance and reality, which the early New York writers felt so keenly; but also the spirit of good-fellowship which found expression through the channels of *bonhomie,* gallantry, and conviviality. It was of this spirit that New York literature was born in 1807; it was this spirit that gave it its vital force for the next three decades.

The sources of Halleck's biography are perhaps more numerous than one would at first suspect. An examination of the newspapers and periodicals of Halleck's day has yielded much authentic information which has frequently assisted the biographer to a marked degree in determining the state of the poet's reputation during his lifetime. The many references to Halleck's name to be met with in the magazines prior to 1835 have amply revealed the extent to which the poet endeared himself to the public both through his works and personality.

If the newspapers and periodicals of the period are the best means of throwing light upon Halleck's reputation as a writer, it is the poet's personal letters to which we must turn for the most perfect reflection of his character. A very significant collection of these letters is contained in James Grant Wilson's *Life and Letters of Fitz-Greene Halleck,* published in 1869 by D. Appleton & Company, for many years Halleck's publishers. After Halleck's death in 1867, General Wilson gathered both from the residents of Guilford and from other sources all the letters and other documents relating to the poet which he could find. By far the most valuable part of this material was contributed by Miss Maria Halleck, the poet's sister, who had kept the greater part of the family correspondence with her brother. Of the letters preserved by Miss Halleck and later turned over to General Wilson, the most important are those of the poet's early years in New York. Without this material it would be impossible to trace in any detail Halleck's life during those years, prior to 1819, in which the poet was establishing himself in the metropolis. But all these documents once owned by General Wilson have now vanished. The author's repeated attempts to locate the manuscripts through Wilson's relatives and friends have met with no success; and he has been forced to content himself with the transcripts which Wilson left in his volume.

Notwithstanding the large group of letters which are to be found in General Wilson's life of Halleck, a considerable collection of unpublished manuscripts has been newly gathered, and is now presented for the first time both in the body of this biography and in the Appendix. Of this new material, very important are the documents relating to Halleck collected by Evert A. Duyckinck, the friend of the poet, and now preserved in the Duyckinck Collection of the New York Public Library. A few extracts only of these letters were printed by Duyckinck in his article on Halleck in *Putnam's Magazine* for February, 1868. These documents have been placed at the author's disposal by that genial friend of scholars, Mr. Victor Hugo Paltsits, Keeper of Manuscripts at the New York Public Library. To Mr. Paltsits the present biographer is also indebted for much friendly advice regarding biographical problems which have presented themselves in the course of his work.

Other libraries have also generously furnished hitherto unpublished manuscripts. Among these institutions may be mentioned the Yale University Library, whose Collection of American Literature, presented by Mr. Owen F. Aldis, is one of the most complete of its kind in the country; the Brown University Library, whose Harris Collection of American Poetry contains, in addition to Halleck

manuscripts, two unique editions of the poet's *Fanny;* the Henry
E. Huntington Library and Art Gallery of California; the Historical Society of Pennsylvania; the Massachusetts Historical Society;
the Connecticut Historical Society; the New York Historical Society; the Boston Public Library; and the libraries of Columbia
University, the University of Chicago, the University of Amsterdam, and Haverford College. To several individual owners of Halleck manuscripts the author is also indebted either for the privilege
of examining the original documents or copies: Mrs. Edward
Jenkins of New Haven, Connecticut; Miss Lilly G. Foote of Hartford, Connecticut; Captain Frank L. Pleadwell of the United
States Navy; Mr. W. W. Lange, President of the Southside Malleable Casting Company, Milwaukee, Wisconsin; and Mr. Alfred E.
Hammer of the Malleable Iron Fittings Company, Branford, Connecticut. Mr. Thomas F. Madigan, dealer in autographs; and the
proprietor of the Pegasus Book Shop both generously allowed the
biographer to make copies of Halleck manuscripts in their possession; and Mr. Walter R. Benjamin, another New York autograph
dealer, kindly copied for the author a Halleck letter in his stock.

Many other individuals have been of material assistance in the
preparation of this volume. Of special help in the work have been
Prof. Stanley T. Williams of Yale University, and Prof. Thomas O.
Mabbott of Hunter College, New York. It was Professor Williams
who suggested to the author the field of early Knickerbocker literature from which developed the present study of Halleck's life and
literary career. Professor Williams' kindly and sound advice has
also been of inestimable value throughout the preparation of this
biography. Soon after the author began his researches on Halleck's
life, he became acquainted with Professor Mabbott, whose intimate
knowledge of American literature has been freely placed at his
disposal. Professor Mabbott kindly read the proofs of the work, and
offered many helpful suggestions.

Special mention should also be made of librarians whose assistance has proved of great value. Mr. Clarence S. Brigham of the
American Antiquarian Society aided in the interpretation of an
obscure passage in one of *The Croakers* by generously furnishing
detailed information regarding an early New York newspaper. Mr.
William C. Lane of the Harvard University Library kindly located
in the files of the *Pandora* a Greek rendering of "Marco Bozzaris."
Mr. A. J. Wall of the New York Historical Society also performed

special services in connection with Halleck material to be found in that institution. To the Librarian of Congress and his assistants special thanks are given for frequent reference work undertaken for the author. Of particular help in determining the sources of the Eliot genealogy were the researches of Mr. F. S. Hellman, Acting Chief Bibliographer of the Library of Congress. Gratitude for special favors is further expressed to the late Miss Caroline M. Hewins, for many years librarian of the Hartford Public Library. Finally, for frequent help in his work the author would thank the assistants of the Yale University Library and the New York Public Library, where most of his research on the life of Halleck has been conducted.

Among the other individuals who have aided in the preparation of the present volume may be mentioned Mrs. Mary L. Ferris, Miss Lita Rice, Mrs. Emma A. Wyckoff, Miss Claire K. Hague, Miss Clara V. Leonard, Mrs. Annie G. Davis, Miss Adelaide Rudolph, Mr. Charles De Kay, Prof. Julius Goebel, Prof. Carl F. Schreiber, Prof. James T. Hatfield, and the late Prof. Henry A. Beers. Of those abroad who have been helpful in establishing Halleck's reputation in England should be named Mr. William Will, Managing Editor of the London *Graphic;* and, particularly, the late Dr. D. McNaught, whose letter on Halleck's "Burns" appears in the Appendix of this volume.

To the *New York Herald-Tribune,* the *New York Times,* the *Saturday Review of Books,* and the *Boston Transcript* the author wishes to express his thanks for publishing appeals for Halleck material. Further thanks should be expressed to the following publishers who have courteously granted permission to make quotations from their books: Houghton Mifflin Company; G. P. Putnam's Sons; Charles Scribner's Sons; J. B. Lippincott Company; Dodd, Mead & Company; D. Appleton & Company; and Harcourt, Brace & Company. Permission for the use of quotations has also been generously granted by the editors of the *Atlantic Monthly,* the *North American Review, Harper's Magazine,* and the *Brooklyn Daily Eagle.*

To these and others who have kindly furnished information which has aided the author in his researches, many thanks are given.

N. F. A.

New York City,
  January, 1930.

CONTENTS

PORTRAITS OF HALLECK

FITZ-GREENE HALLECK

I

ANCESTRY

TRADITION has connected Peter Hallock, the probable ancestor of Fitz-Greene Halleck, the poet, with a band of twelve men, who, in company with their minister, John Youngs, sailed from England about 1638 in pursuit of religious liberty. The group landed at New Haven, Connecticut; and, according to Augustus Griffin,[1] settled in 1640 on the northeastern shore of Long Island, at a spot which they called Southold.[2] As a special distinction accorded by lot, Peter Hallock was allowed first to set foot on the new soil, and subsequently gave his name to the spot, which as late as 1856 was known as "Hallock's Landing."[3] At Southold, Hallock remained not more

[1] The sketch of Peter Hallock here given has been taken from Augustus Griffin's *Griffin's Journal* (Orient, Long Island, 1857), pp. 13 ff. The accuracy of Griffin's record, among the earliest accounts of the founding of Southold, and one to which subsequent historians have been indebted, has been questioned by Epher Whitaker [see *History of Southold, L. I.* (Southold, 1881)]. The Reverend Mr. Whitaker has presented evidence that the thirteen traditional founders of the town "never came from England in company; that they never were together in New Haven, either in 1640, or before or after this date; that they never came to Southold in the same vessel and at the same time" (p. 35). "Peter Hallock," Whitaker says, " . . . may have come to Southold; but there is only traditional evidence of it" (p. 30). Lucius Hallock, however, in a recent work called *A Hallock Genealogy* (Orient, Long Island [1928]) is inclined to believe that Peter Hallock had more than a traditional existence, and was, in fact, the first of the Hallock family in America.

[2] The early historians disagree regarding the dates of Youngs's coming to America, and of the founding of Southold. See Benjamin Trumbull, *A Complete History of Connecticut* (New Haven, 1818), I, 119; Benjamin F. Thompson, *The History of Long Island* (New York, 1843), I, 374; and the critical examination of the facts in Epher Whitaker, *History of Southold, L. I.*, pp. 28 ff.

[3] Griffin's account of Peter Hallock, here and in several other places, differs slightly from that given in a *Brief Sketch of the Hallock Ancestry in the United States*, by William Hallock, which occupies pages 389–404 of Cyrus

than a year. Traveling east to a neck of land named by the Indians *Pequatuck*,[4] he purchased from the natives that tract which was later called Oyster Ponds, now Orient. Peter soon went back to England to get his wife whom he had left behind, but he remained there so long that upon his return to America he found that the Indians had resold his land. "It is believed he subsequently settled some twenty miles west of the village of Southold, near what is now called Acquebogue."[5]

Tradition gives way to certainty as we come to Peter's probable son, William, whom Epher Whitaker regards as "the ancestor of all the Hallocks and Hallecks in this country."[6] William Hollyoake,[7] as he spelled his name, was a resident of Southold, and left a will dated the "10th of february [1682] in the thirty fouth yeare of the Reigne of our Soveraigne Lord Charles the Second." His bold royalist stand suggests the beginning of that Cavalier spirit which found so significant a place in the personality of Fitz-Greene Halleck, the poet. In the will, forfeiture of property is assigned as penalty to any of his heirs who "shall Apostate from the protestant Doctrine and faith of the Church of England." This clause William probably inserted with his eldest son in mind, for to the father's great sorrow and indignation John had married a Quaker lady, and joined the Society of Friends. In consequence, the father disinherited John, whom in the will he designates "an Obstinate Apostate." He so far relented, however, as to "give Unto him his heirs and Assignes forever my Second Lott att the Wading Creeke with

Yale's *Life of the Rev. Jeremiah Hallock of Canton, Conn.* (New York [1865]). The *Brief Sketch* was also issued separately as a pamphlet, a copy of which is preserved in the New York Public Library.

4 See Benjamin F. Thompson, *The History of Long Island*, I, 385. This work, which antedates Griffin's, makes but one mention of Peter Hallock: "Oyster Ponds was originally purchased from the Indians by Peter Hallack [*sic*] in 1647, who afterwards admitted as joint owners with himself, Young, Tuthill and Brown" (I, 386).

5 *Griffin's Journal*, p. 18.

6 *History of Southold, L. I.*, p. 30. The family of Hallocks is very numerous. For the various branches and members see Charles Hallock's *Hallock-Holyoke Pedigree and Collateral Branches in the United States* (Amherst, Massachusetts, 1906). Among the more famous members may be noted Gen. Henry Wager Hallock.

7 The family name has undergone several variations in spelling. See Charles Hallock, *op. cit.*

the Appurtenances thereunto belonging which is all that he is ever to have of my Estate."[8] William died on September 28, 1684.[9]

It is probable that by the turn of the century William's son[10] had left the township of Southold. "The Westbury Monthly Meeting of Friends record [sic] the death of John Hallock, the grandson of Peter of 1640, and that of his wife Abigail at Setauket in Brookhaven, in 1737, 'both very ancient and in unity with Friends.' . . . The neat dwellings of John Hallock *first* and *second* still remain (1863) in Setauket, where they were a committee on a Friends' Monthly Meeting held for more than a century, but now discontinued."[11]

Peter,[12] John's second son, removed about 1750 from Brookhaven to Nine Partners, a Quaker settlement in Dutchess County, near Poughkeepsie.[13] Peter's eldest son, who bore the same name, settled in Union, Clinton County, New York. His wife was Anna Greene, a Quaker lady,[14] and the sister of Israel Greene, who was descended from a member of the distinguished family of that name in Rhode Island.[15] Peter's wife, from whom, it is said, the poet took his baptismal name, has been described as "a woman of unusually

8 See will in office of Surrogate, Hall of Records, New York City.

9 *Brief Sketch of the Hallock Ancestry*, p. 390.

10 In the list of the residents of Southold, made probably prior to 1700, and contained in *The Documentary History of the State of New York* (Albany, 1850), I, 447–456, no mention of John Hallock is made, although the names of several other members of the same family are given.

11 *Brief Sketch of the Hallock Ancestry*, p. 398.

12 Born 1689; died July 20, 1772.

13 *Brief Sketch of the Hallock Ancestry*, p. 399.

14 In William Hallock's *The Hallock Ancestry, for the Memoir of Rev. Jeremiah Hallock of Connecticut and Rev. Moses Hallock of Massachusetts, 1863*, a thin pamphlet in the New York Public Library, Peter Hallock is mentioned as having "married out of meeting" (p. 393); but this statement was not retained in the revised *Brief Sketch of the Hallock Ancestry in the United States*, to which we have already referred as a source in this chapter. James Grant Wilson, however, makes a similar assertion in the *Life and Letters of Fitz-Greene Halleck* (New York, 1869), where he says that Peter Hallock "who had abjured the Quaker faith, adopted that of the Church of England" (p. 19). In the absence of further evidence it is, of course, impossible to determine precisely Peter Hallock's religious affiliations. It may be, however, that Peter was in early manhood a Quaker, but as time went on he inclined more and more toward the Anglican faith. That Peter Hallock had royalist leanings is highly probable in view of the fact that his son, Israel, was a staunch adherent to the British cause.

15 Louise B. Clarke, *The Greenes of Rhode Island* (New York, 1903), p. 162.

bright intellect,'' who ''never lost her mental vigor although ninety-nine years of age at the time of her death,[16] which occurred in the little settlement of Union, N. Y., in 1830. She is buried there in the rural graveyard of the Quakers.''[17] The second son of Peter and Anna Hallock was Israel, the father of Fitz-Greene Halleck, the poet.[18]

Thus in spite of the Puritan proclivities of old Peter Hallock, the alleged follower of John Youngs and the founder of the family in America, the Puritan strain did not long continue in his descendants. Peter's son, William, we have seen, was an avowed Royalist, and the line of the family to which Fitz-Greene belonged, for the next two generations professed the Quaker faith. With Israel Hallock we again find strong royalist leanings.

Israel was born on December 25, 1755, at Nine Partners, also the birthplace of James K. Paulding, the early literary collaborator of Washington Irving. At the outbreak of the Revolution, Peter Hallock and his son adhered to the British cause. Leaving his father's farm, Israel now ''made his way, with several comrades of loyalist tendencies, to New York City, after it was occupied by the British in 1776.''[19] What part Israel played in the Revolutionary War, it is difficult to say; even the poet himself was in doubt concerning his father's status in the English army. ''My father,'' Fitz-Greene once told Frederic S. Cozzens, ''was a British Commissary. But I am inclined to believe that this high-sounding title was a fiction. British and other commissaries, in the army, usually accumulate fortunes; but, as my father made nothing out of the war, I think he must have been a *sutler*. And my opinion is that, as a sutler transacts his business upon his own capital, and a commissary draws his funds from the military chest, the chances of being an honest man *are greatly in favor of the sutler*.''[20] Whatever Israel Hallock's precise relation to the British forces may have been, it is evident that throughout the Revolution he remained loyal to England. ''Early in the war,'' we are told, ''he became acquainted with

[16] Wilson in his *Life and Letters of Fitz-Greene Halleck*, also says that Halleck's grandmother ''lacked but three days of having lived a century'' (p. 35).

[17] L. B. Clarke, *The Greenes of Rhode Island*, p. 163. Here this passage is given as coming from a ''family letter.''

[18] *Brief Sketch of the Hallock Ancestry*, p. 399.

[19] Wilson, *Life*, p. 19.

[20] F. S. Cozzens, *Fitz-Greene Halleck. A Memorial* (New York, 1868), p. 4.

Colonel Tarleton, and accompanied that fiery *sabreur* in his various campaigns." It is probable that "Tarleton, becoming attached to him as a friend and companion, made him a member of his military family. Tarleton's mess-table was enlivened by Halleck's songs and stories, and by his remarkable conversational gifts and charming manners."[21] "The poet's father was deeply attached to the daring and dashing Tarleton, and, in his conversations regarding the events of his early life, often spoke admiringly of the smooth-faced, dark-complexioned, and active young soldier, with the small, piercing black eye, and pleasant smile."[22]

Young Hallock is also reported to have been much in the company of the Duke of Clarence, later King William IV of England, "who now and then came, in his midshipman's roundabouts, to Tarleton's quarters to dine, and who lived with Admiral Digby in the old Beekman House, in Hanover Square."[23] "The Prince," we are told, "manifested, when on shore, a decided fondness for manly pastimes. One of his favorite resorts was a small fresh-water lake in the vicinity of the city, which presented a frozen sheet of many acres; and was thronged by the younger part of the population, for the amusement of skating."[24] "Many a skating-bout did the Dutchess-County boy have with the young Duke, . . . and on one occasion saved him from a watery grave, by helping his Royal Highness out of a hole in the ice through which he had fallen."[25]

Little of the Puritan tradition, in fact, clung to Israel Hallock. The lively song and merry jest that had so enlivened Tarleton's mess table were never laid aside. In later life, he is said even to have surpassed in wit and vivacity the conversational powers of his son.[26] Though something of a reveler,[27] he was "punctiliously polite, with a well-bred, high-born courtesy,"[28] which his son amply inherited. Many years after his death[29] he was remembered in Guilford "as a man fond of books, a great reader, of extraordi-

[21] Wilson, *Life*, pp. 19–20.

[22] *Ibid.*, p. 20.   [23] *Ibid.*, p. 20.

[24] See John Watkins, *The Life and Times of "England's Patriot King," William the Fourth* (London, 1832), p. 65.

[25] Wilson, *Life*, p. 20.   [26] *Ibid.*, p. 20.

[27] An old resident of Guilford has informed me that Israel Hallock in jest used to call his bottle "Jeroboam," for, he explained, it was Jeroboam that made Israel to sin.

[28] Wilson, *Life*, pp. 20–21.   [29] He died in 1839.

nary memory, full of wit and anecdote, and of most courteous manners."[30]

After the Revolution, Israel Hallock returned to the place of his forbears in Southold, Long Island; and joining with a certain James Peters, became a country merchant. A few years later, we find him making a trip to the West Indies. Returning in a vessel bound for Guilford, he stopped for a time at the village. Hallock's fine figure[31] and engaging manners pleased the inhabitants of Guilford, with whom he remained longer than he had at first expected. One young lady in particular claimed his attention—Mary Eliot, the great-great-granddaughter of John Eliot, the Apostle to the Indians.[32]

The Eliots were of stern Puritan mold. The Apostle to the Indians, born in 1604[33] and educated at Cambridge University, took orders in the Church of England; but his opinions, which were at variance with those of the Established Church, led him in 1631 to emigrate to New England. After remaining in Boston for about a year, he became in 1632 the pastor of the church at Roxbury. His duties now became numerous. With Richard Mather and Thomas Weld he aided in the preparation of *The Whole Booke of Psalmes*[34] (usually known as *The Bay Psalm Book*), which was the first book printed in America. Early in his ministry he became concerned for the spiritual welfare of the Indians, and spent two years in acquiring their language. In 1646 he began preaching to the natives in their own tongue; and in 1651[35] established at Natick the first Indian church.[36] "Thus, in the spirit of piety and good order," writes Convers Francis, Eliot's biographer, "a town of 'praying Indians' was established, with such religious, civil, and economical

[30] Evert A. Duyckinck, *Putnam's Magazine*, XI, 232 (February, 1868). During his residence in Guilford, Israel Hallock worked as a tailor (see *ibid.*, XI, 232).

[31] Wilson says that Israel Hallock was six feet in height (*Life*, p. 34).

[32] *Ibid.*, pp. 21–23.

[33] In preparing this sketch of John Eliot I have relied much on the carefully documented account of the divine by H. R. Tedder in the *Dictionary of National Biography*.

[34] Printed at Cambridge in 1640.

[35] The date given by Convers Francis. Tedder gives 1660, but fails to note his authority.

[36] This church "continued until the death of the last native pastor in 1716" (Tedder).

regulations as seemed to give promise of a prosperous issue. It was natural that the founder should wish some of the leading men of the colony to take note of the settlement. On the 8th of October, which was the next lecture day, Governor Endicot, the Reverend Mr. Wilson, and many others visited Natick, to see for themselves what the pious industry of Eliot had done for the natives. Soon after their arrival, the usual religious service was attended. One of the best instructed of the Indians discoursed to his brethren. The Governor and others were so much interested in his manner and appearance, that they desired Mr. Eliot to write down the substance of his remarks."[37]

In addition to *The Bay Psalm Book,* Eliot's name is remembered as the author of many books,[38] chief among which is the famous *Up Biblum God,* a translation of the Scriptures into the Indian tongue. One of the most noted of the early Puritan divines, Eliot has long been honored as a preacher and missionary. His strong Puritan bias is evinced in the opening sentence of a letter he once sent to Oliver Cromwell in behalf of New England: "Envy itself cannot deny that the Lord hath raised and improved You in an Eminent manner to overthrow Antichrist, and to accomplish, in part, the prophecies and Promises of the Churches Deliverance from that Bondage."[39] John Eliot was also a friend of Cotton Mather, who in his *Magnalia Christi Americana* left a lengthy sketch of the Apostle to the Indians. The figurative diction of the following passage from the *Magnalia,* descriptive of Eliot's eloquence, will amuse not a little the modern reader:

To his congregation, he was a preacher that made it his care "to give every one their meat in due season." It was *food* and not *froth,* which in his publick sermons he entertained the souls of his people with; he did not *starve* them with empty and windy speculations, or with such things as *Animum non dant, quia non habent;* much less did he *kill* them with such poyson as is too commonly exposed by the Arminian and Socinian doctors that have too often sat in Moses's chair. His way of preaching was very plain, so that the very *lambs* might wade into his discourses on those texts

37 *Life of John Eliot, the Apostle to the Indians* (Boston, 1836), pp. 173–174.

38 See the list of Eliot's works in *The Cambridge History of American Literature,* I, 390–392.

39 *Genealogy of the Descendants of John Eliot* [New Haven, 1905], p. 284. This work was edited by Wilimena H. Eliot Emerson and others.

and themes, wherein *elephants* might swim; and herewithal, it was very powerful; his delivery was always very graceful and grateful; but when he was to use reproofs and warnings against any sin, his voice would rise into a warmth which had in it very much of energy as well as decency.[40]

John Eliot died in 1690 at the age of eighty-six.

Somewhat dim is now the reputation of Joseph Eliot,[41] son of the Apostle, though toward the close of the seventeenth century he, too, was famed as a divine. He graduated from Harvard in 1658, and for a few years was minister of the church at Northampton, Massachusetts.[42] In spite of the protests of his Northampton parishioners, however, he was finally induced to settle in Guilford, where he remained as pastor until his death. In the words of the Reverend Thomas Ruggles, an early Guilford pastor, it was "about the year 1664 or 1665" when "the renowned Mr. Joseph Eliot, son of the famous and pious Mr. John Eliot of Roxbury, (the Indian New-England apostle) was called and introduced, and by the laying on of the hands of the presbytery, was ordained to the pastoral office in the church. Mr. Mather[43] of Northampton, with whom Mr. Eliot had lived some time before he came to Guilford, being the chief in the ordination. The church and town greatly flourished under his successful ministry."[44] Joseph Eliot's "great abilities as a divine, a politician, and a physician, were justly admired," we are told, "not only among his own people; but throughout the colony, where his praises are in the churches."[45] As here suggested, Eliot was much in demand as preacher outside of his Guilford pastorate. Samuel Sewall in his *Diary* several times mentions Eliot's preaching, as in the quaint entry for October 18, 1687:

[40] Hartford, 1855, I, 547–548 (Book III).

[41] 1638–1694.

[42] *Genealogy of the Descendants of John Eliot*, p. 22.

[43] The Reverend Eleazer Mather.

[44] "Extracts from Ruggles' MS History" in the *Massachusetts Historical Society Collections*, X, 93–94 (1809). A condensed statement of this passage may be found in "A Sketch of a History of Guilford, in Connecticut, from a manuscript of the Rev. Thomas Ruggles." *Massachusetts Historical Society Collections*, IV, 188 (1795).

[45] Thomas Ruggles, *The Death of Great, Good, and Useful Men Lamented. A Discourse . . . on the Lamented Death of . . . Dr. Jared Eliot* (New Haven, 1763). A somewhat mutilated copy of this rare book is in the Yale University Library. Jared Eliot, the eldest son of Joseph, was a friend of Benjamin Franklin, and distinguished as a divine and physician. See William B. Sprague, *Annals of the American Pulpit* (New York, 1857), I, 270–272.

Carried Mother Hull behind me to Roxbury-Lecture; Mr. Joseph Eliot preached. . . . House not very full because of the rawness and uncertainty of the day. Got home about ½ hour after Three. . . . Mr. Eliot said the King was turn'd a Puritan, and he was ravish'd at it; supose 'twas from something he had heard as to som Nonconformists, Aldermen and Lord Mayor. . . . [46]

Joseph Eliot also appears to have enjoyed the company of Sewall:

Nov. 21, 1692. Mr. Joseph Eliot, of Guilford, visited, supped and prayed with us, went not away till half an hour after nine at night.[47]

"After this burning and shining light had ministered to this good people about thirty years," writes Mr. Ruggles, "he deceased May 24, 1694, to the inexpressible grief of his beloved flock, whose memory is not forgotten to this day."[48] His grave, unmarked, is said to be "upon the east side of the Guilford Green."[49]

By his second wife,[50] Mary Wyllys, daughter of Samuel Wyllys of Hartford, Connecticut, Joseph Eliot had four children. Abial, the last, who was born about 1692,[51] was the great-grandfather of the poet.[52] With Joseph Eliot, the clerical strain in this branch of the family vanished. Abial, who was a Guilford farmer, is said to have had some skill in versification, and "was in the habit of amusing his friends by making rhymes with any word they might mention."[53] Abial Eliot in 1726 married Mary, the daughter of John Leete of Guilford, a descendant of William Leete, one time gov-

[46] *Diary of Samuel Sewall* (Boston, 1878), I, 192.

[47] *Ibid.*, I, 369. Another entry worthy of note is the one for May 30, 1688: "Mr. Joseph Eliot here, says the two days wherein he buried his Wife and Son, were the best that ever he had in the world" (*ibid.*, I, 215).

[48] *Massachusetts Historical Society Collections*, X, 94 (1809).

[49] *Genealogy of the Descendants of John Eliot*, p. 25. For other references to Joseph Eliot, see *The Public Records of the Colony of Connecticut from 1665 to 1678* (Hartford, 1852), pp. 84, 99, 389, and *The Public Records of the Colony of Connecticut, May, 1678–June, 1689* (Hartford, 1859), p. 93. For three letters which Joseph Eliot wrote to Increase Mather, see *Collections of the Massachusetts Historical Society*, XXXVIII, 374–379 (1868). Joseph Eliot's will is printed in William H. Eliot's *Genealogy of the Eliot Family* (New Haven, 1854), pp. 145–147.

[50] "About 1675–6" Joseph Eliot married Sarah Brenton of Rhode Island. His second marriage was "about 1684–5." See *Genealogy of the Descendants of John Eliot*, pp. 27 and 32.

[51] For discussion of the date of Abial's birth, see *ibid.*, p. 35.

[52] *Ibid.*, p. 46.   [53] Wilson, *Life*, p. 33.

ernor of Connecticut.[54] Of their son Nathaniel, who was born in
1728, nothing is known except that he was a farmer. In 1754 he
married Beulah Parmelee, a native of the town.[55]

Little evidence has survived to aid the biographer in recapturing
the personality of their daughter, Mary. To General Wilson, the
mother of the poet was once described by a person who had seen
her at her wedding[56] as "plump as a partridge, and as pretty a girl
as there was in Guilford."[57] "Miss Eliot," we are further told,
"was a lady of superior intellect, and was noted for her love of
reading, with a particular fondness for poetry, of which, both before and after marriage, she read everything that came in her
way."[58] Of this "excellent lady, of irreproachable worth,"[59] no
other memorials have survived.[60]

Such was the lineage of Fitz-Greene Halleck, the poet. From his
father, the old Cavalier, Halleck, we shall find, inherited the spirit
of the English gentleman, curiously preserved in the New World.
And it was this inheritance that gave to the poet in later life the
engaging manners and charming quaintness observed by all who
knew him. Something of the English gentleman always clung to
him. It may in a sense be said that Halleck never quite threw off
his Old World traits; he never thoroughly became habituated to
the world and age in which he lived. He moved, in fact, somewhat
in the past; a little bewildered at the growing commercialism of
America, despite his identification with it. He never entered quite
whole-heartedly into this "bank-note world"; yet he felt constantly
its heavy and inevitable pressure. Fleeing from a too close, too enduring contact with the material present, he sought an escape in

[54] *Genealogy of the Descendants of John Eliot*, p. 46.

[55] *Ibid.*, p. 78.

[56] Mary Eliot was married to Israel Halleck on September 30, 1787. Their
children were Maria (b. 1788; d. 1870); Fitz-Greene (b. 1790; d. 1867); and
Nathaniel (b. 1792; d. 1793).

[57] Wilson, *Life*, p. 33.   [58] *Ibid.*, p. 33.

[59] She is so described by the Reverend Lorenzo Bennett in a letter to E. A.
Duyckinck (dated December 11, 1867), now in the Duyckinck Collection of the
New York Public Library.

[60] Regarding the church affiliations of Halleck's parents, little is known.
Among the parish records of Christ Church in Guilford is a notice of Mrs.
Halleck's burial in 1818 at the age of fifty-seven, but of Israel Halleck, who
died in 1839, no mention is made.

Cavalier gallantries, in complimentary verses, in convivial meetings, which carried him for the moment into the realms of sentiment.

But despite the convivial spirit and devotion to romance which Halleck undoubtedly received from his father, the environment of the poet's boyhood may be more accurately represented by the life and character of his mother. From Mary Eliot, we have found, Halleck derived an inheritance in strict accord with the Puritan tradition. As a lineal descendant of the Apostle to the Indians, she unquestionably retained much of the austerity of character and love of religion which was the life and breath of the Puritan. Unfortunately, Halleck has left us no observations on the life and personality of his mother. Yet we may well believe that from her he received the reverence for religion and love of the Bible,[61] manifested to a marked degree in his later life.

Nothing is known of the early home life of the poet. Whether Cavalier or Puritan influences prevailed there it is now impossible to say. Yet both attitudes to life were without doubt present in the Halleck home, and each must have contended for mastery over the boy. Both influences probably worked in silent antagonism, molding, as we shall see, a mind torn between a life of freedom and imagination and one of inhibition and practicality.

Whatever may have been the dominating influence within the Halleck household, there can be no question of the spirit at work outside the home in the small town of Guilford. Guilford possesses a strictly Puritan ancestry. Founded in 1639 by the Reverend Henry Whitfield[62] and a band of dissenters from the Church of England, Guilford may be regarded as a typical Puritan settlement of New England. "The first settlers were most of them gentlemen of some rank and estate in their native country, and came over for the purpose of enjoying the exercise of their religious feelings in their own way, as well as what they considered political and moral freedom."[63] It was not until 1643, however, that a church was formally instituted. In pursuance of a plan of church government followed some time before in the colony of New Haven, "seven pillars" were

---

[61] See pp. 197–198.
[62] For a biographical sketch of Henry Whitfield, see William B. Sprague, *Annals of the American Pulpit* (New York, 1857), I, 100–102.
[63] Ralph D. Smith, *History of Guilford* (Albany, 1877), p. 54.

chosen of those in the community deemed the most godly. ''These Christians in the wilderness,'' observes one historian, ''had cut loose from the ancient foundations. They were feeling for the simplicity of the early Church which gathered about Christ as the only foundation, and practically attained it. Yet, members as they were of the ancient Church of England, it must have satisfied their imagination and filled a void in their hearts, *to have something to join*. These seven godly, Christian men, choicest of the whole band —these seven pillars, in some unconscious way and with a sort of Scriptural sanction[64] stood to them, we cannot doubt, in the place of the goodly battlements of that historic Church from which they never separated, but from which they were now cutting loose.''[65]

Such were the religious pioneers, the religious radicals of their day, who were responsible for the founding of New England; and for their noble work we can but do them reverence. Yet they laid upon the shoulders of their descendants burdens grievous to be borne, and obligations that frequently warped the spirit and hardened the heart. Although the people of most New England towns by the first decade of the nineteenth century had put aside the sterner principles of Calvinism, yet much of the old bigotry and intolerance remained and found expression in the daily life of the people. Guilford is situated some twelve miles from New Haven, and in the days of the poet's childhood the inhabitants had no easier means of traveling to New York than by stage. Thus Guilford, a typical rural community, found difficult any access to the outside world. Hemmed in geographically, the village naturally underwent mental and moral restraint. Early prejudices remained, and daily life, although possessing a native vigor characteristic of a farming community, lacked a broad and comprehensive outlook on life.

But despite the severity which Halleck in later life came to feel so much a part of the New England temper, he was always proud of the place of his birth. Picturesquely situated inland about two miles from Long Island Sound, Guilford is an ideal spot for one seeking the repose of country life. ''The southern shore of Connecti-

---

64 This manner of church organization was founded on the text in Prov. 9.1: ''Wisdom hath builded her house, she hath hewn out her seven pillars.''

65 The Reverend Cornelius L. Kitchel in his ''Historical Sermon,'' to be found in *Proceedings at the Celebration of the 250th Anniversary of the Settlement of Guilford, Conn.* (New Haven, 1889), pp. 52–53.

cut, bordering on the Long Island Sound,'' once wrote William Cullen Bryant in commenting on the poet, ''is a beautiful region. I have never passed along this shore, extending from Byrom river to the Paugatuck, without admiring it. Here the somewhat severe climate of New England is softened by the sea air and the shelter of the hills. Such charming combinations of rock and valley, of forest and stream, of smooth meadows, quiet inlets and green promontories are rarely to be found. A multitude of clear and rapid rivers, the king of which is the majestic Connecticut, here wind their way to the Sound among picturesque hills, cliffs and woods.''[66] General Wilson asserts that ''the poet on more than one occasion playfully boasted . . . that there were none but gentlemen born in his native town of Guilford, their mechanics and labourers all being importations from New Haven and elsewhere.''[67] And, indeed, for the natives of the village Halleck entertained a due respect. To Charles J. Hoadly, for many years librarian of the Connecticut State Library, Halleck once wrote in response to a request for his autograph: ''I well remember your grandfather and grandmother, as among my earliest acquaintances, and am glad to claim you as, to some extent, a brother townsman. Your wish to preserve my Autograph makes me quite proud.''[68]

[66] W. C. Bryant, *Some Notices of the Life and Writings of Halleck* (New York, 1869), p. 6.

[67] James G. Wilson, *Bryant and His Friends* (New York, 1886), p. 245.

[68] From an unpublished letter, dated November 15, 1857, in the Hoadley Collection of the Connecticut Historical Society, Hartford.

II

EARLY LIFE IN GUILFORD

1790–1810

GUILFORD, like many New England towns, is pleasantly situated about a square or "green." This green, originally the common property of the townsfolk and used for many years as a burying ground, was in Halleck's day, as now, the center from which the streets of the village radiated. Israel Hallock, the poet's father, owned land on the street forming the west boundary of the green, and it was probably in a house on this property[1] that Fitz-Greene was born on July 8, 1790.[2]

[1] It is now impossible to ascertain definitely the portion of Guilford where the poet was born.

[2] The date of Fitz-Greene Halleck's birth was for many years in dispute, and still remains in some doubt. William Leggett, the poet and journalist, in writing a biographical sketch of Halleck for the *New York Mirror* of January 26, 1828 (V, 226), stated that he was born in August, 1795. This date appeared invariably in every study of the poet's life down to a few years before his death in 1867. Many, however, believed this date to be incorrect. Bryant, for example, at the time of Halleck's death, was uncertain regarding the poet's age. In writing to R. H. Dana, Sr., on November 30, 1867, Bryant said: "You speak of Halleck's age. The telegram which came from Guilford announcing his death said that he was eighty, but it was corrected to correspond to the printed biographies of him, and made seventy-two; yet I am by no means certain that this is right. There was always a suspicion that Halleck's age was not rightly stated." [Parke Godwin, *A Biography of William Cullen Bryant* (New York, 1883), II, 266.] After the poet's death, effort was made to ascertain the actual date of Halleck's birth. Evert A. Duyckinck, who was preparing a memoir of Halleck, wrote to Dr. Lorenzo Bennett, Rector of Christ Church in Guilford, asking for the correct date (see Dr. Bennett's letter dated December 20, 1867, and preserved in the Duyckinck Collection of the New York Public Library). Dr. Bennett gave the date as July 8, 1790, and indicated that his information was derived from the "Eliot Genealogy." In turning to William H. Eliot's *Genealogy of the Eliot Family* (New Haven, 1854), page 78, we find the date actually given to be July 8, 1760. It is obvious, of course, that the "6" had been inverted, and should have read "9." The *Genealogy of the Descendants of John Eliot*, a revised edition of the preceding book, published in 1905, gives the date as July 8, 1790. Duyckinck's memoir appeared in *Putnam's Magazine* for February, 1868 (XI, 231), giving the date indicated by Dr. Bennett. In the same month James Grant Wilson

The earliest event of real importance in Halleck's[3] life occurred when the boy was two years old. ''Two drunken militiamen,'' the story goes, ''on a 'training-day,' passing by his father's door, near which they saw him at play, thought they would astonish the little fellow by discharging their guns, loaded only with powder. They did so, one of them, unfortunately, placing his piece so near the side of the child's head, that it ruined the hearing in his left ear for life.''[4] In manhood Halleck tried several proposed cures to restore the hearing to his deaf ear, but all proved ineffectual. The deafness which resulted from this accident remained always a source of annoyance and embarrassment to the poet.

Halleck's formal education consisted only of what the Guilford schools had to offer. But this education was perhaps the best any small New England town of that day could afford. The Puritans who settled America found in learning and scholarship an effective means of furthering the cause of religion, and from the beginning they put due emphasis upon the educational training provided by the schools. ''The schools of Guilford,'' says Bernard Steiner, ''have been good from the very first. In 1674 the town defined the duties of its school teacher as 'to instruct all sorts and that from their ABC, and to be helpful in preaching when required.' ''[5]

Most of the events recorded of Halleck's school life are founded on tradition gathered by General Wilson, after the poet's death, from the residents of Guilford. Thus it is a fanciful, idealistic picture that we have of Fitz-Greene as a boy. He was, indeed, quite

published a biographical sketch of Halleck in *Hours at Home* (VI, 362), which gave the same date. Wilson undoubtedly consulted Miss Maria Halleck regarding the date of her brother's birth, for Wilson was intimate with the family, and was soon to bring out the poet's biography.

All attempts to trace the date of Halleck's birth to its source have proved futile. The town records of Guilford make no mention of his birth. The parish records of Christ Church in Guilford, although giving the date of the poet's confirmation by Bishop Jarvis as 1809, are silent as to his birth and baptism. The family records of the Hallecks also cannot be traced. In view of the absence of proper records, we must regard the date given by Duyckinck and Wilson as the reliable one, with the probability of its correctness.

[3] All the town records in Guilford which have reference to the family spell the name *Hallock*. The poet and his sister, however, always preferred the form *Halleck*.

[4] Wilson, *Life*, pp. 40–41.

[5] *Proceedings at the Celebration of the 250th Anniversary of the Settlement of Guilford, Conn.* (New Haven, 1889), p. 180.

precocious as a lad—"so good a little boy and so attentive to his
studies," we are told, "as to be the pride of his schoolmaster, who,
when he wished to display to visitors the proficiency of his pupils,
would place little Fitz on a chair to pronounce the piece,

> You'd scarce expect one of my age
> To speak in public on the stage."[6]

The heart of the poet's sister, who was two years older than he, is
said to have "fluttered with pride and delight to see her brother so
honored."[7] General Wilson tells of a very old lady who was present
on an occasion when the boy recited this poem, and who said that
Fitz "was the brightest and sweetest-looking boy [she] ever saw,
and so intelligent and gentle in his manner, that everyone loved
him."[8] If one is to credit tradition, Fitz-Greene was a model pupil.
"He invariably knew his lessons, and was never on any occasion
called up for misconduct or delinquency of any description."[9] The
same refined and studious habit of mind also followed him outside
of school. The boy "had no taste for the rough sports and adventures in which most boys find delight, but preferred to wander
alone in the fields and woods, by the river's banks, or on the shores
of Long Island Sound, with a copy of Campbell's poems or some
other favorite volume."[10] The only sport in which the boy would
allow himself to indulge was "a mild game of marbles," or "a
quiet fishing excursion."[11] Tradition has, in fact, made of Fitz
a "teacher's pet." He was greatly beloved by his schoolmaster,
whose name was Samuel Johnson, "a real 'Blue Light Federalist,'" it is said, "such as could be found only in Massachusetts,
Connecticut, and Delaware." On a day when party feeling ran
high in politics, he set his pupils the copy, "Demons, demagogues,
democrats, and devils."[12] It may have been in part the influence of
this master that made Halleck in later life a political conservative.
At any rate, as a boy Halleck was devoted to his teacher. "Many a

6 From a letter of Dr. Bennett to Evert A. Duyckinck, dated December 11,
1867, and preserved in the Duyckinck Collection of the New York Public
Library. Duyckinck relates this incident in his article on Halleck in *Putnam's
Magazine*, XI, 232. Wilson relates the same anecdote in his *Life*, p. 42.

7 From the letter cited above.

8 *Bryant and His Friends*, p. 249.   9 Wilson, *Life*, p. 52.

10 *Ibid.*, p. 51.   11 *Ibid.*, p. 51.

12 *New England Magazine*, I (N.S.), 421 (December, 1889).

pleasant ramble did the master and scholar take together after school-hours, the gentle and diffident boy drinking in with eagerness the teacher's conversation about poetry and other literary topics."[13]

Idealistic and romantic as is the picture of Halleck's boyhood, there is probably reason for the belief that he was a youth of thoughtful, studious disposition. John P. Foote, a native of Guilford, asserts that Halleck was "a young lad of very modest and pleasing demeanor, and of remarkably precocious talents."[14] Halleck's reading undoubtedly began early. The inhabitants of Guilford have always been "a reading people";[15] and the village library at the beginning of the nineteenth century is said to have contained "most of the standard histories and other works of the highest class in English literature."[16] General Wilson reports that the poet once told him that he had read every volume in the public collection[17]—a fact which, if literally true, shows how few volumes the Guilford library must in reality have contained. Halleck's early love of reading may also be gathered from a remark to a friend to whom the poet was speaking of his youth, "I fastened like a tiger upon every romance and collection of poetry that I could lay hands on."[18]

The boy's studious habit of mind, however, is most authentically shown by his first poetical efforts. The earliest extant attempts of Halleck at verse-making are preserved in a manuscript written in ink on both sides of six 16mo leaves and dated 1803.[19] This manuscript contains three poems, entitled respectively "A View of the United States,"[20] "The History of New England," and "The For-

13 Wilson, *Life*, p. 52.
14 *Memoirs of Samuel E. Foote* (Cincinnati, 1860), p. 28.
15 See the Reverend James L. Willard's "Address. Education in Guilford and Madison" in *Proceedings at the Celebration of the 250th Anniversary of the Settlement of Guilford, Conn.*, p. 66.
16 J. P. Foote, *op. cit.*, p. 29. See also B. Steiner, *A History of the Plantation of Menunkatuck* (Baltimore, 1897), pp. 410–411.
17 *Life*, p. 53.
18 *Ibid.*, p. 53.
19 See catalogue of the fifth part of the William F. Gable Collection, sold at the American Art Galleries on November 24–25, 1924 (item 326).
20 The title, as well as some of the contents of this poem, was perhaps suggested by a school book which the boy may have used: Jedidiah Morse's *American Geography; or a View of the Present Situation of the United States of America*. A second edition of this book appeared in 1792.

tunate Family.''[21] In spite of the date given on the manuscript, Wilson believes that these verses were written prior to 1800.[22] Such may have been the case, for the events referred to in the lines,

> Fair peace continued till a bloody train
> Of Gallia's traitors crossed the Western main,[23]

occurred in 1798, and may have been fresh in the boy's mind as he wrote the poem.[24] This reference to recent naval engagements between the Americans and French indicates at least the interest which a boy of eleven or twelve took in the events of the day. These early pieces in subject matter and diction are obviously the work of a boy just becoming conscious of his mental powers, and are noticeably more crude and untutored than any of his later work. The subject matter of the first two was derived from a zealous application of the boy to his books of geography and history; while the meter and some of the thought of the poems show the probable influence of Oliver Goldsmith:

> From wild Canada's cold and frozen shores
> To where the gentle Mississippi pours
> Along the tide, as through the woods it bends,
> So far the seat of liberty extends:
> Here all the gentle virtues are combined
> Which form the pure and the enlightened mind.[25]

"The Fortunate Family," written in tetrameter couplets, is a tissue of banalities, and may have been suggested by some of Wordsworth's *Lyrical Ballads*.[26] Two other poems written at about this period should be mentioned. The verses "Inscribed with all reverence to Miss Maria Halleck, by her brother, Fitz-Greene Halleck,"[27] which are dated May 20, 1803, and the lines addressed to "Evening," "written in the poet's twelfth year,"[28] show a slightly higher

---

[21] Printed by Wilson in the *Life*, pp. 43, 47, and 49.

[22] *Ibid.*, p. 42. [23] "A View of the United States."

[24] See John Spencer Bassett, *A Short History of the United States* (New York, 1918), p. 281.

[25] "A View of the United States" (Wilson, *Life*, p. 43).

[26] The *Lyrical Ballads* appeared in 1798. The first American edition was published at Philadelphia in 1802. See Albert H. Smyth, *The Philadelphia Magazines and their Contributors 1741–1850* (Philadelphia, 1892), p. 109.

[27] Wilson, *Life*, p. 54.

[28] *Ibid.*, pp. 54–55.

stage of development both in the selection of subject matter and in the metrical treatment.

In his fifteenth year Halleck completed the education which his native village had to offer, and entered the employ of Andrew Eliot, a kinsman, who kept a store in Guilford. In accordance with the custom of that day, the boy left his own home, and resided with his employer.[29] Halleck soon learned to keep accounts by double entry,[30] and during the next six years, must have trained himself with unusual care, for in 1811 he was fully prepared to enter the business office of Jacob Barker in New York. One of the ledgers kept by Halleck, while he was in the employ of Mr. Eliot, is now preserved in the Yale University Library. It is inscribed "Day Book No. 10 / R. Elliot & Co.[31] / Guilford, Conn. / from June 1809 to May 1810." Although not all of the entries are in Halleck's autograph, a great number are in the neat hand written by the poet at this time. With the possible exception of a few manuscript verses, this ledger is the most tangible memento that has come down to us of Halleck's life in Guilford before his going to New York. Mr. Eliot kept a typical country store where everything needed by the household could be bought. The names of many prominent Guilford people of the day are preserved in the ledger. We find, for example, Maria Halleck, the poet's sister, on August 28, 1809, buying coffee, sugar, and Poland starch; and another well-known lady of Guilford on August 1 purchasing a quart of rum. During the period of Halleck's employment in Guilford, it is said that

---

[29] *Ibid.*, p. 57.   [30] *Ibid.*, p. 57.

[31] Wilson asserts that the store was kept by Andrew Eliot, but the inscription on the ledger reads "R. Elliot & Co." The doubling of the "l" in the name has, of course, no significance, for both spellings were used interchangeably. The difference in the Christian names, however, needs comment. The "R" in the inscription on the ledger undoubtedly stands for Reuben, who was the brother of Andrew (see *Genealogy of the Descendants of John Eliot* [1905], p. 82). Probably the brothers were in partnership. As Reuben was the elder of the two, the business was, of course, in his name. The Eliot genealogy (*op. cit.*, p. 117) states that Reuben Eliot was a merchant in Guilford, and for several years Judge of Probate and Postmaster. It is probable that Reuben's official duties in the town made it impossible for him personally to attend to his store, so that the business was practically in the hands of Andrew.

he was often confined in the store fifteen hours a day.[32] Frequently he took complete charge of the store, while Mr. Eliot was on his farm, which was situated not far from Guilford.[33] How much this work in the country store contributed to the formation of the boy's character we may well imagine. Besides affording him experience in the more practical matters of meeting customers and keeping ledgers, his fifteen hours a day doubtless provided him plenty of time for reading and writing; and the few of his early poems that have been left us show he was not idle.

It was during the spring of 1808 that Halleck made his first visit to New York, on business for Mr. Eliot. While there, the youth attended a performance at the Park Theatre of Morton's comedy *The School of Reform.*[34] Whether or not this was the first theatrical performance which Halleck ever attended is only a matter for conjecture. In any case, he here saw two actors who, some years later, he mentioned in satirical sketches. Thomas A. Cooper, then manager of the Park Theatre, and a popular actor, was humorously introduced into "The Dinner Party";[35] and Mr. Olliff was mentioned in two of *The Croakers.*[36] While on this trip, tradition says, Halleck caught a glimpse of the two men who were later to be his employers in the great city. A companion pointed out to the poet the young Quaker banker, Jacob Barker, and the merchant, John Jacob Astor.[37]

The following summer Halleck joined the state militia. Not long after his enlistment he became a sergeant, and is said to have filled the position "with credit to himself and to the general satisfaction of his comrades."[38] The next winter he opened an evening school. Here Halleck taught writing, arithmetic, and bookkeeping—subjects in which he had trained himself in the village store.[39] Halleck at this period wrote a beautiful hand—in sharp contrast to the almost illegible scrawl of his later life. The few of Halleck's early

[32] See Wilson's memoir of Halleck in *Hours at Home,* VI, 363 (February, 1868).

[33] Wilson, *Life,* p. 58.   [34] *Ibid.,* pp. 61–62.

[35] *Poetical Works of Fitz-Greene Halleck* (New York, 1869), p. 342.

[36] *Ibid.,* pp. 266 and 289.

[37] Wilson, *Bryant and His Friends,* p. 251.

[38] Wilson, *Life,* p. 64.   [39] *Ibid.,* p. 64.

manuscripts which have been preserved are perfect specimens of calligraphy.

Halleck's circle of intimate friends, confined to the young people living in the town of Guilford, was necessarily limited. We now catch only a faint echo here and there of what the social life of the poet must have been. Yet these hints afford us a pleasant picture. Among Halleck's male acquaintances was a handsome young Cuban, named Carlos Menie, who had been sent to Guilford by his father, a West Indian merchant, to learn the English language. Upon Menie's return to his own country, Halleck addressed to him some verses which bear the date, 1809.[40] Halleck, however, seems to have been especially popular in the village with the young ladies, for many of whom he wrote verses. Lydia Cezanne, the daughter of a French merchant in Guilford, was at one time a special favorite whom the poet, after leaving Guilford, mentioned in two letters to his sister.[41] But perhaps the scene of Halleck's greatest social enjoyment was Nut Plains, where was situated the home of the Footes. Harriet Beecher Stowe, who at the age of three or four, just after her mother's[42] death, spent much time with her aunt at Nut Plains, has left her early impressions of the old home:

Among my earliest recollections are those of a visit to Nut Plains immediately after my mother's death. . . . At the close of what seemed to me a long day's ride we arrived after dark at a lonely little white farm house, and were ushered into a large parlor where a cheerful wood fire was crackling.[43]

Halleck often accepted of the hospitality of the Footes. The special attraction was two of the Foote sisters. The elder, Mary Ward, who had married in 1803 J. J. Hubbard, son of the Reverend Bela Hubbard of New Haven, had gone to live with her husband in Jamaica;

[40] *Ibid.*, pp. 65–68.

[41] *Ibid.*, p. 65. For the letters in which Halleck mentions Lydia, see *ibid.*, pp. 114 and 140–141. The original manuscript of the quatrain which Halleck addressed to Lydia (printed by Wilson, p. 65) is in the possession of the present biographer.

[42] Mrs. Lyman Beecher, Harriet's mother, was Roxanna Foote, sister to Mary, Catherine, and George, who were friends of Halleck.

[43] Charles E. Stowe, *Life of Harriet Beecher Stowe* (Boston, 1890), pp. 5–6.

but, shocked at the social conditions among the planters, soon returned to Guilford. Her younger sister, Catherine, of delicate
health,[44] and a brother, George,[45] were also of the household. A
cousin, Sarah Redfield,[46] who often visited the Foote home, completed this group of young people with whom Halleck appears to
have spent at this time many of his leisure hours. Intimate evidence
of the good times which Halleck had at Nut Plains is provided in
a rhymed invitation which Mary Hubbard wrote to Halleck, asking him to spend an evening with the family.[47] Here her sister,
Catherine, and her cousin, Sarah, are fittingly mentioned. Halleck's
gallant reply is in the same meter. An acrostic and a sleigh-ride
invitation written to the vivacious Sarah have also been preserved.[48]
A hint of the encouragement which the Footes undoubtedly gave
Halleck's genius is derived from a remark of J. P. Foote, an older
brother: ''His earliest poetical efforts were submitted to the critics
of Nutplains, and highly commended. Many pieces, which he did
not consider as possessing sufficient merit to be included among
his collected works, were preserved, and some of them published
many years afterward. They were more highly estimated by the
public than by the author.''[49]

Halleck in these early days was carefully cultivating his literary and artistic taste. Limited in formal education, he yet appears
to have had an instinctive desire for self-improvement—an incli-

[44] For references to Catherine Foote in Halleck's letters, see Wilson, *Life,*
pp. 110–112, 114.

[45] For a letter which Halleck wrote to George Foote in 1828, see p. 228.

[46] Married later William Todd. For a portrait of Mrs. Todd, see Henry
Robinson, *Guilford Portraits* (New Haven, 1907), p. 113.

[47] A copy of the invitation, with Halleck's reply, has been furnished me
by Mrs. Edward Jenkins of New Haven, and as they have never been published, they now appear in the Appendix, p. 426. Halleck's poem ''Trifles
'Light as Air' '' (Wilson, *Life,* pp. 93–95) also seems to have occasioned an
exchange of verses between the poet and Mrs. Hubbard.

[48] Wilson prints the acrostic in the *Life,* pp. 99–100, under the title ''Rebus
No. 2.'' Miss Lilly Gillette Foote of Hartford, Connecticut, has also furnished
me with a copy of the acrostic from Halleck's manuscript. To Miss Foote I
am also much indebted for many of the details here given regarding the
Foote family at Nut Plains. The sleigh-ride invitation to Mrs. Todd is printed
by Wilson, *Life,* p. 60. A variant form of the invitation appeared in *Harper's
New Monthly Magazine,* XXXVI, 676 (April, 1868). Still another set of
verses addressed to ''dear Sarah'' may be found in Wilson's *Life,* p. 59.

[49] *Memoirs of the Life of Samuel E. Foote,* p. 28.

nation which was later to manifest itself in the artist's love of perfection. The exactness to which he brought his handwriting at this early period is tangible evidence of his innate artistic temperament. Halleck, of course, at this time had no literary ambitions; even in later life he was curiously indifferent to fame. Yet his youthful interest in literature was certainly strong for a boy of his age. With the money derived from his evening school, Halleck bought copies of the poems of Campbell and Burns, and also Addison's "Spectator" papers.[50]

Halleck's attempts at verse-making while he was a clerk in Andrew Eliot's store are naturally of more value as reflections of the boy's interest in literature, than as specimens of poetic art. Although distinctly superior in verse-technique to those poems written at an earlier time, they give almost no evidence of poetic genius. Their chief excellence lies in a smoothness of versification. They are of genuine importance, however, in reflecting the character of the boy's reading at this period. One of the strongest literary influences both in Halleck's youth and manhood was the Bible. Six of the boy's early poems are religious in character, four being founded directly upon the Bible.[51] This interest in the Holy Scriptures was probably due in large part to the influence of his mother. Before he reached manhood Halleck had read the Bible through several times, and during his residence in New York he is said to have read several chapters almost every day.[52]

In Halleck's early poems we may note other literary interests. The works of Thomas Moore exerted a marked influence on the metrical efforts of the poet, as may be seen by the verses, "No Rose

[50] Wilson, *Life*, p. 64.

[51] These poems are as follows: (1) "I Samuel xviii, 6, 7, Paraphrased," printed in Wilson's *Life*, p. 73. (2) "The Lamentation of David over Saul and Jonathan," printed in the *Life*, p. 76. The original manuscript of this poem is owned by Mrs. Edward Jenkins of New Haven, Connecticut. (3) "Versification of Job, 14th Chapter," printed in the *Life*, p. 90. (4) "Vision of Eliphaz, Paraphrased from Job," printed in the 1869 edition of Halleck's poems, and dated 1809. (5) "Religion, Written on a Blank Leaf of My Prayer Book," printed in the 1869 edition, and dated 1810. (6) "Lines Occasioned by the Perusal of a Late Publication entitled 'The Star in the East,' " printed in the *Life*, p. 74.

[52] Wilson, *Life*, pp. 72–73. For further influence of the Bible on Halleck, see pp. 197–198.

Without a Thorn,''[53] and the song, ''How sweet at that hour, when
the moon mildly beaming.''[54] ''Matilda''[55] is an ''imitation'' of Allan
Ramsay's ballad ''Lochaber No More.'' Ossian was the inspiration
of two poems, ''Malvina's Dream'' (''Paraphrased from Ossian's
Croma, 'It was the voice of my love' '')[56] and ''Lines, Written on
a Blank Leaf in Ossian's Poems.''[57] Evidence of the poet's reading
of Mrs. Anne Radcliffe appears in a ''Paraphrase of an Extract
from the Italian by Mrs. Radcliffe.''[58] ''Trifles 'Light as Air' ''[59]
had its origin in Richard Cumberland's novel, *Arundel.*

Two of Halleck's poems found their way into print before his departure for New York. His first published verses, so far as is known,
appeared in an important New York newspaper entitled the *Columbian,* and edited by Charles Holt. The poem was printed in the
issue of August 22, 1810, and was headed ''Native Poetry.'' A preface commented briefly on the poem:

> The versification of the annexed translation of Mrs. Radcliffe, is the
> performance of an obscure, uneducated country boy. It is certainly a very
> brilliant specimen of uncultivated genius; and many a master poet would
> be proud to own this production of an humble apprentice. B.

The paraphrase from Mrs. Radcliffe to which we have already referred, followed this introduction.

The second of Halleck's youthful verses to meet the approval of
an editor was ''The Indian Warrior.'' Wilson relates that Halleck,
while in the employ of Andrew Eliot, spent many of his evenings
with a servant of the Eliot household, named Leah Norton. ''Not
wishing to be disturbed in his reading by the visitors who were
frequently in the parlor and sitting-room,'' Halleck ''sought refuge
in the kitchen,'' where many of his youthful poems were written.[60]
Miss Norton, to whom he read his poems as soon as they were completed, took an unusual interest in the boy's work. She committed
to memory ''The Indian Warrior,'' and, after the poet's death, repeated the verses to General Wilson.[61] The poem was first printed in

[53] Wilson, *Life,* p. 82.   [54] *Ibid.,* p. 84.
[55] *Ibid.,* p. 88.   [56] *Ibid.,* p. 85.
[57] First published in the 1869 edition of Halleck's, and dated 1810.
[58] Wilson, *Life,* p. 86.
[59] *Ibid.,* p. 93. For Halleck's comments on Cumberland's death, see *ibid.,*
p. 102.
[60] *Ibid.,* p. 61.   [61] *Ibid.,* p. 62.

the *Columbian* for September 28, 1810, with the heading, "For the Columbian." It was unsigned, and bore the date "Sept. 1810."[62]

[62] Of the compositions written before Halleck's departure from his native village in 1811, seven were included in the final collected edition of the poet's works, published in 1869. These poems, some of which have already been mentioned, are as follows: (1) "The Tempest" (1804), published in part in *Hours at Home*, VI, 363 (February, 1868). (2) "Memory" (1810), first published in the *Connecticut Herald* for August 27, 1811, and later printed in the *New York Times* for February 2, 1868. (3) "Lines, Written on a Blank Leaf in Ossian's Poems" (1810), first published in the *Connecticut Herald* for September 3, 1811. (4) "The Vision of Eliphaz." (5) "Religion" (1810). (6) "The Bluebird, on Its First Appearance in the Spring of 1810." (7) "Ode to Good Humor" (1811), first published in the *Connecticut Herald* for June 18, 1811. The *Connecticut Herald* was a New Haven paper.

III

FIRST YEARS IN NEW YORK

1811-18

I<small>N</small> May, 1811, Halleck left Guilford to seek employment in New York.[1] He had, of course, no thought of entering upon a literary career. New York literature in the first decade of the nineteenth century was merely in its infancy, and its writers were amateurs and gentlemen of leisure. Literature as a profession was then unknown. Such fame as was accorded the authors of *Salmagundi* (1807-8) and *Knickerbocker's History of New York* (1809) was most unusual; and however attractive, could never be attained by a young man inexperienced in the varied life of the great city. Knickerbocker literature for the next twenty-five years can hardly be said to have rested on a sure financial basis. The man who would write must first enter a regular profession, and thereby earn a livelihood. With the possible exception of Washington Irving, none of the important men who later became Halleck's literary associates in New York, could be regarded as a professional man of letters. Gulian C. Verplanck, upon graduating from Columbia College in 1801,[2] was admitted to the bar; Robert C. Sands, after leaving college in 1815, also entered a law office,[3] although he appears not to have remained long in the profession; while James K. Paulding, the early literary partner of Irving, for many years held government positions. Others of the early Knickerbocker group were less fortunate in their pecuniary arrangements. Samuel Woodworth, whose chief occupation was editing periodicals and writing verses for the newspapers, was twice relieved from financial want by benefit theatrical performances.[4] McDonald Clarke, who had little to do but promenade Broad-

---

[1] Wilson, *Life,* p. 101.

[2] Evert A. and George L. Duyckinck, *Cyclopaedia of American Literature* (New York, 1856), II, 68.

[3] *Ibid.,* II, 271.

[4] See the *Critic,* I, 292 (March 7, 1829), and the *New York Mirror,* XV, 144 (October 28, 1837).

way and fill several volumes with his hopeless doggerel, was repeatedly reduced to utter penury. And even Washington Irving, during his residence abroad, found himself under the necessity of seeking assistance of his friend, Brevoort.[5]

Relying upon his experience as clerk and bookkeeper in a country store, Halleck now sought work in the city. It is small wonder that his services were not at once accepted. On June 11, 1811, Halleck wrote to his father: "I am still on the wing; but whenever I get settled once more I will write you longer letters."[6] A month later he was still without employment. "I am preparing to bid New York farewell to-morrow," he wrote home at this time, "and the place that knew me shall know me no more. No vacancies appearing in this city, and some prospects opening in Richmond, Virginia, I am on the point of embarking for that place."[7] But the trip to the South was luckily prevented by Halleck's meeting with Jacob Barker, then a young Quaker banker in New York, whose counting-house was situated at No. 84 South Street. "In my last I informed you of my expectation of going to Richmond," wrote Halleck to his father on July 22, 1811, "and, as I fear that that plan, for various reasons, did not meet your approval, I am pleased now to remove your apprehensions, by informing you that Jacob Barker has offered me a salary, and that I have accepted his terms and engaged for one year."[8]

There is no doubt that Halleck found in New York a freer moral and intellectual atmosphere than in his native village. From his father, the old Cavalier, the young man had inherited a breadth of imagination and fulness of life that clashed harshly with the restraint and bigotry imposed by his New England environment. Now freed from the narrow yoke of prejudice, Halleck at once found in the freer life of the city the liberty for which his heart yearned. Frequent echoes of the restraint that he had undergone as a boy come to us as we examine carefully the records of the poet's early life. A few months after Halleck arrived in New York he wrote to his sister, Maria, a letter describing some of his fellow boarders. Several of his comments in this letter reflect with accu-

[5] George Hellman, *Letters of Washington Irving to Henry Brevoort* (New York, 1915), II, 153 ff.

[6] Wilson, "Halleckiana" in the *Independent*, February 29, 1872.

[7] *Ibid.*, February 29, 1872.   [8] Wilson, *Life*, p. 102.

racy his attitude to the New England Puritanism of his day. One boarder is described as "a member of the Presbyterian Church," but "very social and no bigot."[9] Another is "a member of the church," who "has disposed enough of his Connecticut principles to go to the theatre occasionally."[10] Even more revealing of Halleck's attitude to Connecticut and his native village is the following passage from a letter written three years later to a friend in regard to a young man in Guilford who had been guilty of moral indiscretion:

I am sorry that his libertinism has been made so public in G. as such is the great regard of the good people there for morality and virtue at least for the appearance of them, that I fear this character which he has recently acquired will prevent him from obtaining their good graces which the Conduct of Miss G—— has proved.[11]

Such were Halleck's early reactions to the Puritan manners of his native town. And as time went on, he found himself more and more estranged from the environment of his youth. When, a few years later, Halleck was enjoying the friendship of Joseph Rodman Drake, the two poets were wont to amuse themselves by writing sermons in answer to the Calvinistic discourses of a certain Dr. Cox, an eminent preacher of the day.[12] In 1826, when Halleck had become fully at home in New York, and could look back quietly upon those people among whom his boyhood had been passed, he recalled humorously in his verses on "Connecticut" what he deemed the narrowness and bigotry of his native state.

Halleck's correspondence during the months immediately following his arrival in New York reflects with a curious nicety the emergence of the young man, long narrowed by the monotonous pursuits of a country village, into a world of gaiety and fashion. The self-consciousness with which a youth first meets the world is well suggested in a letter written to the poet's sister, four months after his arrival in the city:

9 Wilson, *Life*, p. 117. The letter is dated August 20, 1811.

10 *Ibid.*, p. 119. Same letter.

11 *A Letter* [dated April 26, 1814] *Written by Fitz-Greene Halleck to Joel Lewis Griffing in Guilford, Connecticut, in 1814.* Thirty-one copies printed for Charles F. Heartman and his friends, Rutland, 1921. This letter is valuable throughout in reflecting the freedom of the new life into which he had now entered and become a part.

12 Wilson, *Life*, p. 226.

The foundation of an extensive acquaintance with the world did not fall to the lot of my early years, and the novelty attendant on the acquisition of new friends—friends in a certain sense of the word, I mean—opens a source of pleasure hitherto unknown. True, it is not a real pleasure, but 'tis gratifying to trace the endless variety of man, to mark the different propositions, passions, and pursuits, as well as situations, of our fellow creatures; and it will not, perhaps, be unproductive of benefit to learn that a proportionate degree of happiness is allotted to all, that those states in life to which we naturally attach felicity are not without their cares and anxieties, and that although our path may not appear so thickly strewed with roses, yet it is far less choked with thorns.[13]

Influenced as this passage obviously is by Goldsmith's *Traveller* and Johnson's *Rasselas,* it shows the distinct trend of Halleck's mind at this period. The bookish, abstract diction reminiscent throughout of the eighteenth-century periodical essay, was soon abandoned, as his acquaintance with life and literature broadened. The poet's sketches of his fellow employees in the countinghouse of Jacob Barker,[14] and similar detailed descriptions of those who inhabited the same boarding house with him[15]—all written a few months after Halleck left Guilford—illustrate his interest at this time in tracing "the endless variety of man."

Excursions to places not far distant from the city and the witnessing of frequent theatrical performances further widened Halleck's experience. In a letter of August 7 he tells of a trip to New Jersey;[16] and also mentions several plays which he has attended.[17] His *blasé* comment on a circus performance is amusing. "It affords but little variety," he observes, "and is always much alike. The riders display a great deal of agility and dexterity, and certainly deserve applause, which is generally given by the audience indiscriminately and without hesitation."[18]

A few months after Halleck's arrival in New York, several of the poems which he had written in Guilford appeared in a New Haven newspaper.[19] Of these poems he wrote to his sister:

[13] *Ibid.,* p. 104. The letter is dated August 3, 1811.
[14] *Ibid.,* pp. 105 ff. Same letter.
[15] *Ibid.,* pp. 115 ff. The letter is dated August 20, 1811.
[16] *Ibid.,* p. 110. The letter is dated August 5 [1811].
[17] *Ibid.,* p. 112. Same letter.   [18] *Ibid.,* p. 113.
[19] The following poems, some of which have already been mentioned, were published in the *Connecticut Herald:* "Ode to Good Humor" (June 18, 1811);

I received yesterday, through Horace Elliot, a letter from George,[20] in which he mentions the success of my "poetry." I have requested him to send me the newspapers which contain it, but, lest he should not, wish you to send them to me, if you can conveniently do so.[21]

Before many months had elapsed, Halleck had so gained the confidence of his employer, Jacob Barker, as to be advanced to a more responsible position.[22] After a year's service, he returned to Guilford for a brief vacation. Halleck took with him as a present for those at home, a miniature of himself done on ivory by an English artist then in New York, popularly known as "Mysterious Brown."[23] While enjoying his vacation in his native town, Halleck entertained at the public inn five of his village friends, two of whom were still alive when General Wilson wrote the poet's biography, and could recall the merry meeting.[24] Halleck remained in Guilford about two weeks. Upon his return to New York, he wrote to his sister of his journey on the stage, and of the greeting which he received from his associates. The young man's popularity among his fellow clerks is well shown by the description which he then gave of his reception at the office. "I was received with a welcome the most cordial and ardent I could wish," wrote Halleck enthusiastically, "and, indeed, far beyond my expectations. Sam. shook my hand with a grasp which, though rather unpleasant, bespoke the honest disposition of the heart. McCarthy received me with that finished politeness of which his education and country had made him perfectly master, and seemed earnestly pleased with me. Tom welcomed me with a burst of frantic laughter, and seemed overjoyed; and Jacob appeared to be as glad to see me as if I had been his own son, and returned after an absence of twenty years."[25]

As a result of the Embargo Act of 1807, and of the subsequent War of 1812, Jacob Barker found his commercial affairs so badly involved as to demand his whole attention. He therefore handed

---

"Lines on the Rainbow" (August 13, 1811); "No Rose Without a Thorn" (August 20, 1811); "Memory" (August 27, 1811); "Lines on Reading Ossian's Poems" (September 3, 1811).

20 George Foote; see pp. 22 and 228.
21 Wilson, *Life*, p. 114. The letter is dated August 14 [1811].
22 *Ibid.*, p. 122.
23 *Ibid.*, pp. 125–126. See also the present work, p. 384.
24 Wilson, *Life*, p. 126.
25 *Ibid.*, pp. 127–128. The letter is dated June 12, 1812.

FITZ-GREENE HALLECK
At the age of twenty-two.
From a photograph of a miniature.

over to a relative, Thomas Barker, and to Halleck ''all the Commission business which was under [his] care when war took place.''[26] In a letter to his father written on July 8, 1812, Halleck explained the state of his employer's affairs, and said that Barker had ''transferred his commission business to his nephew, Thomas Barker, and myself, who have accordingly entered into a partnership, under the firm of Halleck & Barker. This arrangement, although from circumstances attending it not such as to be very profitable immediately, will, however, be useful to me in the future, by giving my name some celebrity in the city, which while a mere clerk, I could not obtain.''[27] But Halleck was unsuccessful in this business attempt. In writing to General Wilson in 1868, Jacob Barker said: ''The embargo, non-importation laws, blockade, and War of 1812 interrupted business to such an extent, that I could not afford to pay accustomed compensation to my employés, when Halleck associated himself with a relation of mine in the ship-chandlery business, but, being unsuccessful, they soon abandoned that pursuit, and Mr. Halleck returned to my employ, without ever again embarking in any commercial business on his account.''[28]

As a relief from the duties of business during his first year in New York, Halleck spent much of his spare time in reading and study.[29] A natural reserve and sensitiveness of disposition at first made it difficult for the young man to seek friends and companions. Soon after settling in New York he wrote to his sister of the difficulty he experienced in finding ''among the numerous fellow-mortals I meet with, a person whose disposition and ideas are congenial with my own, and whose friendship I might cherish as a valuable acquisition, nor do I expect to find one.''[30] It was not long,

26 *Ibid.*, p. 129. A letter written by Jacob Barker, and dated ''7th mo. 7, 1812.''

27 Wilson, *Independent*, February 29, 1872.

28 Wilson, *Life*, p. 337. Two years later (1814), Jacob Barker, through complications resulting from government loans, became insolvent. Halleck was one of the three assignees appointed to adjust the affairs of the estate. In a rare pamphlet preserved in the New York Society Library, and entitled *Memorial, &c. To the Honourable the Senate and House of Representatives in Congress Assembled*, the three assignees state at length the claims of Barker against the United States Government. At the close of the pamphlet are printed the names of Richard R. Ward, Fitz G. Halleck, and Jacob Little.

29 *Ibid.*, p. 122.

30 *Ibid.*, p. 121. The letter is dated August 20, 1811.

however, before he met two young men of his own age whose friendship proved worthy of the name. These were James E. De Kay and Joseph Rodman Drake. In the summer of 1812 young De Kay, who was then a medical student in New York, spent his vacation in Guilford, Connecticut. While there, he was introduced to Halleck's sister, who, upon his return to the city, gave him a letter of introduction to her brother.[31] In this way the two young men met. De Kay later became distinguished throughout America as a physician and naturalist. He was perhaps best known in the literary world of his day by his *Sketches of Turkey*,[32] which were written after his travels abroad in 1831 and 1832. "In De Kay, Halleck found a good friend—one who could appreciate intellectual worth and sympathize with the poet's feeling."[33]

Through De Kay, Halleck met Joseph Rodman Drake. Probably no more picturesque friendship has been recorded in the annals of American letters than that of Drake and Halleck, who found in poetry a common bond of fellowship. From the start, the spirit of romance favored the two young poets, and made of their meeting a legend which, in its idyllic simplicity, was symbolic of the naïve faith that was later to characterize their friendship. On a September afternoon in 1813, so the story runs, Drake and Halleck, who had previously been introduced, were sailing down the New York Bay on an excursion. It was after a shower that Halleck, in commenting to his companion on the "delights of another world," ventured to remark that "it would be heaven 'to lounge upon the rainbow and read Tom Campbell.'" The idea responded so forcibly to Drake's imagination that from that moment he found in Halleck a lasting friend. Halleck, too, discovered in the sensitive and poetic Drake the true companion for which he longed.[34] In writing of Drake in 1815 Halleck remarked:

[31] See article on Halleck by James Lawson in the *Southern Literary Messenger* for April, 1842 (VIII, [2]43). For an interesting reference to De Kay, see *A Letter Written by Fitz-Greene Halleck to Joel Lewis Griffing in Guilford, Connecticut, in 1814* (Rutland, 1921).

[32] New York, 1833.

[33] *Southern Literary Messenger*, VIII, [2]43.

[34] Various versions of this meeting between Drake and Halleck have been preserved. I have selected the present account by Wilson (*Life*, p. 163) because he seems to have been the only one to assign to the meeting a definite date. Another version of the story says that the famous meeting occurred on the Battery (Duyckinck, *Cyclopaedia of American Literature*, II, 204); and

Even to the most common and trifling subjects he will give an interest wholly unexpected and unlooked for. His manner of reading Shakespeare is unique, and to the bombast of our old friend, ancient Pistol, he will give a force beyond description. He has a taste for music, and plays the flute admirably. As I owe to his acquaintance many a pleasant hour, he has become endeared to me, and I must apologize for dwelling so long upon the picture.[35]

Halleck further widened the range of his acquaintanceship at this period by joining the newly formed "Ugly Club."[36] The earliest available reference to this organization occurs in a letter addressed to Mr. Holt, editor of the *Columbian.* The style of the epistle is amusing, and must have mystified not a little those unacquainted with the group. "I have always conceived it a selfish principle," comments the writer, "that would tend to prevent the world from participating with us in the enjoyment of any humorous discovery; this, sir, must be my apology for introducing to the notice of my fellow-citizens, a quizzical society, called 'The Ugly Club' —the avowed object of whose institution is independently to advocate ugliness in all its hideous forms; to collect portraits and profiles of all the distinguished ugly men in the United States, whether civil, military, or ecclesiastical; and to assist such members as may labor under age and deformities.'"[37] The officers, which consisted of "a president, secretary, two censors, and a treasurer," are then described by the writer. The portrait of the president, perhaps the most engaging description the author presents, will bear quoting. "First, then, for the president—his lily-livered, lanthorn-jaws, and his face beautifully and fancifully variegated with small protuberances, would assimilate him to the renowned knight, Don Quixote, did not a keen black eye relieve in some measure, his notorious ugliness. His shape is good and (perhaps were he not associated with such choice spirits) might be esteemed handsome, if a most un-

---

yet another relates the incident as occurring at the time of a beautiful sunset instead of a rainbow, and as happening in a purely fortuitous fashion, without a previous introduction. This last version occurs in an unpublished letter of J. N. Mead to E. A. Duyckinck, dated November 29, 1867, and preserved in the New York Public Library.

[35] Wilson, *Life,* p. 164. Exact date of letter is not given.

[36] There is no evidence whether or not Halleck was a charter member of the club.

[37] November 27, 1813.

seemly gait, resembling, as it were, the ambling of a spavined jade, did not happily interfere.''[38] This letter is signed ''X.'' Another, with the signature ''Z,'' apparently in answer to ''X's'' communication, although obviously by the same hand, appeared in the *Columbian* several days later. Pretending to have no connection with the organization, ''Z,'' however, expresses a friendly interest in the group. He then speaks of a friend who is well acquainted with the club, and who has furnished him with information concerning its members. For the benefit of the readers of the *Columbian*, ''Z'' quotes from his friend's description of an acquaintance who is a member of the club. It is in this description that the real character of the organization begins to leak out.

A particular friend of mine, who had run some danger of late of *degenerating into a beau of the first water,* who may, it is to be hoped, owe his reformation to the club, was too remarkable a character to escape their observation. Almost on their first organization, his ugliness attracted their attention, and, indeed, I do not know a person, in all respects better qualified to hold a distinguished situation among them. *His features, it is true, are pretty regular, and his person, I believe, what the ladies call rather pretty;* and these objections might have been urged against his admission, with fatal effect, had not a pair of wall eyes, as expressive as two snowballs, *a walk affected, finical, and mincing,* an awkwardness of address, *more conspicuous from its aiming at excessive politeness,* and a general uncouthness of manners, which might rival a Calmuck's, more than counterbalance them, and at first glance, precluded the possibility of his bringing disgrace upon the institution by his beauty.[39]

This description, particularly the italicized portions, reveals a more whimsical and farcical character to the club than was suggested by the first epistle. The fact is that the members, in true Knickerbocker style, were satirizing and burlesquing their own position; that instead of admitting to their number only those qualified by extreme ugliness, they were extending the privileges of the club only to those deemed the most handsome and foppish. Another letter, this time with the signature ''A,'' continues a description of the members. The writer refers to a ball which he had lately attended, where he observed a most finely dressed infantry lieuten-

---

[38] The *Columbian*, November 27, 1813.
[39] *Ibid.*, December 7, 1813. The italics are mine.

ant,[40] "formed," as he says, "in the prodigality of nature; his manly form resembling the famed Apollo Belvedere." "While I was thus contemplating with admiration this model of manly beauty," the writer continues, "my friend stopped me short, and informed me that this was the person to whom the famed 'Ugly Club' had presented the freedom of their institution in a tin box."[41]

The remaining references to the Ugly Club extend over the two succeeding years, and consist for the most part of paid advertisements of club meetings. Three of these are in rhyme, and present the same characteristics displayed in the letters already quoted. One which appears in the *Columbian* for June 16, 1814, begins:

> Ugliest of created races,
> Hither bring your ugly faces,
> Show ugly mouths with hairlips [*sic*] cleft
> Inclining to the right and left.

The announcement closes with the lines:

> On eve of Thursday next repair
> To Ugly Hall, 4 Wall Street, where,
> Midst scenes of usual glee and sport
> You'll hear your committee's report
> On subject of the celebration,
> Of day which gave birth to the nation.
> Your committee have published this
> By order of his Ugliness.

It was probably in October, 1814, that Halleck was elected "Poet Laureate" of the club. In a letter, written by Halleck on January 2, 1815, to Abraham S. Fowler, a native of Guilford, the poet informs that gentleman of his recent election to the club, and speaks of himself as having recently been chosen "Poet Laureate of the 'Ugly Club.'"[42] On January 19, 1815, appeared an advertisement in the

[40] There is probably an attempt at personal satire here. Several blanks in the same narrative also suggest this.

[41] December 11, 1813.

[42] Wilson, *Life*, p. 157. On the following page of the *Life*, Wilson prints another letter addressed to Mr. Fowler, announcing his election to the club, signed "By order of his Ugliness.—Thomas J. De Lancey." Although there is no direct evidence, we may assume, without doubt, that Drake was also a member of the club. In a letter to Maria, Halleck once said of Drake, "He is, perhaps, the handsomest man in New York—a face like an angel, a form like an Apollo" (*Life*, p. 184).

Columbian, announcing a ''Quarterly Election of Officers,'' to take place the following day. Halleck, it will be remembered, was already ''Poet Laureate'' at the time this meeting was called, and it is probable that he had been chosen to that office at the previous election in October, 1814.

In the *Columbian* for December 15, 1814, appeared a rhymed advertisement of a club meeting, which may have come from the pen of Halleck. The versification of the lines is smoother than that of the rhymed advertisement already quoted, and, considering the occasion for which they were produced, they are not unworthy of Halleck. The reference to the ''Poet Laureate'' is, without doubt, to Halleck.

> The poet Laureat for fame
> Will also offer there his claim,
> In numbers musical and terse,
> With sweet, harmonious, flowing verse,
> Like Poets all for fame he'll pant,
> On Ugliness will he discant.
> Ay, there's a subject that could raise
> A Milton or a Homer's lays;
> A subject there that might inspire
> The pen of Scott or Byron's fire.

The advertisement appearing the following month, to which we have already alluded, consisted both of verse and prose. The rhymed portion, one may feel confidently certain, was the work of Halleck. The obvious attempt to lift the verse above the doggerel of the two preceding notices, and the curious literary polish of the lines, mark them as unmistakably Halleck's.

> Vain flatterers in Beauty's beam!
>   Away!—'tis not on you we call;
> Glide on, down Folly's idle stream,
>   Nor dare to seek our Hallowed Hall.

> But ye! whose Ugly forms and faces,
>   In Nature's frolic mood designed,
> Have taught to shun the tinsel graces,
>   And court the treasures of the mind;

Ye, who ne'er basked in "Ladye's bower,"
Whose lips were ne'er by Beauty kiss'd,
For you it comes—the welcome hour!
List! list!—O list![43]

A brief prose advertisement, appearing in the *Columbian* for April 5, 1815, is the last available reference to the Ugly Club, and it is likely that about this period the club dissolved. Formed on a whimsical and superficial basis, the club, whose novelty alone had once held the members together, now undoubtedly began to pall on the members, and in time simply died a natural death.

Returning to the close of 1813, we find that Halleck that year published a poem anonymously in the *Columbian* for December 22. Mr. Holt prefaced the verses with these words: ''The following lines possess such singular beauty and excellence, that one almost doubts their being original. The future favors of our correspondent, we hope, will remove all suspicions on the subject.'' The poem, which begins with the lines,

When the bright star of peace from our country was clouded,
Hope fondly presaged it would soon reappear,

was written when the War of 1812 was at its height, and is but one of the innumerable lyrics which the conflict produced. Plainly influenced by the style of Halleck's favorite, Thomas Campbell, the lines possess a smoothness of diction and meter which was characteristic of Halleck's later lyrics.[44] The poem was signed ''Y.H.S.''[45]

Another war lyric, similarly signed and addressed to the American flag, was published in the *Columbian* for July 14, 1814. These verses are upon the whole inferior to the preceding, and have perhaps justly been forgotten. Because of their general inaccessibility, however, they have been reprinted in the Appendix of this volume.[46]

[43] *Columbian,* January 19, 1815.

[44] These lines were reprinted by Wilson in the *Life,* pp. 144–145. Compare the meter of the poem with that of Campbell's ''Exile of Erin'' and the ''Soldier's Dream.'' The same meter was also used by Thomas Moore. Both poets were Halleck's early masters.

[45] The significance of this signature, if indeed it has any, is unknown. It was used on three lyrics written by Halleck at this period, and was not employed again, so far as is known, until the last year of his life (1867), as the signature of a letter to Thurlow Weed (see *Life,* pp. 551–553).

[46] This poem is mentioned neither by Wilson nor by any other Halleck biographer.

The year 1814 brought with it all the gloom occasioned by a war with no hope of peace in sight. Worn out by their ill success, the New England states for a time threatened to withdraw from the Union. As the year progressed, the conflict grew more intense. Toward the latter part of the summer it became known that Sir George Prevost was making preparations for an invasion of New York. The defense of the city now became uppermost in the minds of the people; and for the purpose of assisting in a possible crisis, a troop of volunteers from New York was organized called "The Iron Grays." This military company, which Halleck at once joined, was composed of men from the best families of New York. "Many of them," wrote Halleck to his sister, "were in the habit of coming to the parade preparatory to marching to camp, a distance of three miles, in their coaches and curricles."[47] Samuel Swartwout was captain of the regiment; Henry Brevoort, Jr., first lieutenant; Henry Carey, Philip Rhinelander, and Gouverneur S. Bibby, the remaining lieutenants.[48] Their encampment lay "adjacent to the Hudson River, and near Fort Gansevoort, on Governor George Clinton's farm."[49] A letter of Halleck addressed to Edward Greene, and written in 1863, describes in the humorous, whimsical style characteristic of the poet's last years some of his experiences in the Iron Grays.

I am very sorry to learn from your letter the death of our friend Palmer.[50] He was a man of exemplary energy of character, and his general intelligence and various acquirements made him an agreeable and instructive companion. We became known to each other in 1814, as brother soldiers in Swartwout's corps of "Iron Gray," a band of one hundred or more, mostly, like Palmer, young lawyers without clients. That we did not beat the enemy on a field of battle was no fault of ours; but simply because, like Tom Thumb in Fielding's farce, we "found no enemy to fight with"; for our reputation as "sharpshooters," having reached the ear of England soon after our organization, induced her to make peace, which we condescendingly allowed our Government to accept.

[47] Wilson, *Life*, p. 153. The letter is dated December 28, 1814. A very old gentleman once told Wilson: "Halleck was the best fellow in the Grays, and by God, sir, the world never saw a finer body of men. Every man of them was a gentleman, sir!" (*Life*, p. 147).

[48] *Ibid.*, p. 145.

[49] *Ibid.*, p. 145.

[50] Aaron H. Palmer, for many years a resident of Washington, had previously lived in New York.

We had no major-generals among us, costing the country we were defending $1,787,626.15 per annum, and *fighting each other*. On the contrary, we received $8 per month and a ration each, and spent in *feasting each other* $5 per day regularly, besides extra "wine and women" bills for dinners and dancing.

We mutinied but once, and that for a laudable purpose—namely for clean straw. The unclean in our tents we moulded into an effigy of our contractor, a striking likeness of him, and burnt it in great glee. General Picton would have hanged the fellow, and "served him right." I have forgotten the contractor's name. The race to which he belonged is, I understand, not yet extinct.[51]

While at Fort Gansevoort toward the close of October, Halleck composed an ode entitled "The Iron Grays." He intrusted the poem to a friend, Charles W. Sandford, "under the most sacred promises of secrecy."[52] Sandford, who was a member of the Iron Grays and an excellent elocutionist, frequently recited poems to his fellow campers for their amusement. The recitation of Halleck's verses is said to have produced the greatest enthusiasm, not only among the Iron Grays, but throughout the entire encampment of soldiers of which this regiment was a part.[53] The morning after the recitation of the poem Halleck commented enthusiastically to his friend, "Why, Charlie, I had no idea I was a poet until last night, when you repeated my lines."[54] The verses were subsequently published in the *Columbian*[55] over the signature "N. Y. October—Y.H.S."[56]

Toward the close of November, 1814, the Iron Grays broke camp at Fort Gansevoort, and took up winter quarters on the Battery.[57] At the withdrawal of the British troops, however, the organization soon disbanded, and the gentlemen who composed the company returned to their several employments. A letter which Halleck addressed to his sister on December 28, 1814, after the Iron Grays

[51] *Independent*, February 29, 1872. The letter is dated "Guilford, Conn., May 5th, 1863."

[52] Wilson, *Life*, pp. 145–146.   [53] *Ibid.*, p. 146.

[54] *Ibid.*, p. 146.   [55] October 29, 1814.

[56] A manuscript containing the three war poems written at this period with the signature "Y.H.S." is preserved in the Yale Collection of American Literature. The manuscript may not be strictly contemporary, as the dates given by Halleck of the appearance of the poems in the *Columbian* are only conjectural. The manuscript, however, is probably of early date, and may have been written shortly after the poems were published.

[57] Wilson, *Life*, p. 146.

had disbanded, describes intimately the poet's experiences in camp. His motives in joining the Iron Grays, it appears, were not unmixed. After mentioning the spirit of patriotism which had in part prompted him to assist in the crisis, Halleck observed: "Leaving that enthusiasm, however, out of the question, other motives actuated me at the moment, not quite so consistent with honor and patriotic feeling, but comformable to true worldly wisdom and a regard for the opinion of others. I was conscious that the dictates of duty were in favor of defending one's country, one's fireside, wife, children, etc., in the hour of danger. By volunteering, in a moment of peril and alarm, to die for their defence, I have discharged that duty, and stand acquitted not only at the bar of my own conscience (if there is any such thing in the case), but also at that of the world's opinion, and am now resolved to volunteer no more."[58]

To the year 1814 Wilson assigns two other compositions by Halleck.[59] "The Pilgrim Fathers" was printed, probably for the first time, in the 1869 edition of Halleck's works.[60] The verses beginning,

> The heart hath sorrow of its own, and griefs it veils from all,
> And tears that hide them from the world, in solitude will fall,[61]

were many years later incorporated, with but few verbal changes, in the poet's "Young America" (1864). The address to "Lady" in the final stanza is a probable indication that the verses were originally written for a lady's album.

Halleck's sphere of activity was now more and more widened,[62] and his interests varied and diversified. He had by this time thrown

[58] Wilson, *Life*, p. 152. The Reverend Lorenzo Bennett in a letter (dated December 11, 1867) to E. A. Duyckinck says that after Halleck was mustered out, he "received at the proper period the land bounty" (Duyckinck Collection). The Iron Grays were mentioned by Halleck in two of his poems—the "Croaker" beginning, "When Bony fought his hosts of foes," and *Fanny* (stanza 64, 1839 ed.). For other references to the Iron Grays, see the letter of Washington Irving to Henry Brevoort, dated September 26, 1814 (Pierre Irving, *Life and Letters of Washington Irving*, New York, 1862, I, 314). See also *ibid.*, I, 325.

[59] *Life*, p. 155.

[60] Under the title, "The Pilgrims" (p. 245).

[61] Printed in full in the *Life*, pp. 155–156.

[62] It may here be noted that Halleck in the spring of 1815 made a short visit to Boston, probably on business for Jacob Barker. On his return he stopped off for a few days at Guilford. See Wilson, *Life*, pp. 159 ff.

off much of his sensitive reserve which had at first made his stay in New York lonely and unsocial. He now, as we have seen, sought fresh contacts with the world. It was also at this period that Halleck determined to acquaint himself with the French language. He already possessed what he called a "smattering" of French, and he now changed his lodging from Mrs. Buchanan's, where he had lived for some time, to Madame Berault's, in the hope of finding an atmosphere more conducive to his learning the language. Here he joined his friend De Kay and several other acquaintances. But he found "too many Americans at Madame Berault's," who, he thought, would interfere with his mastering the language, and about the first of February, 1817,[63] he left these lodgings for "Mons. Villagrand's, in Chambers Street."[64] Here the poet appears to have perfected his knowledge of French to a marked degree. "I now speak it with facility," he remarked in one of his letters, and added with perhaps a touch of humor, "and have been often taken, or mistaken for a Frenchman by Frenchmen themselves."[65]

In June, 1816, Halleck had the opportunity of making a trip to the South, whither he was called on business for his employer. In a letter written probably to his mother, Halleck described his experiences both on shipboard and on land. He found the whole trip "an irksome business, nor is there anything in that part of the country," he added, "in the smallest degree connected with ideas of gratification or of pleasure. I had long passages going and coming. The packets in that trade are not very commodious, and I was everything but comfortable on board of them."[66] The storms were unusually violent while Halleck was aboard. A curiously romantic description of the poet's feelings during these natural disturbances is preserved in a letter from which we have already quoted, and is of interest in showing the way in which Halleck's imagination responded to the mighty forces of nature. The passage is colored with a Byronic exultation at finding himself momentarily a part of an unfathomable vastness.

[63] Probably in 1817, although it may have been February of the preceding year. The letter (*Life*, pp. 169 ff.) from which these facts have been taken, as well as the accounts of the poet's two southern trips which follow, is a fragment and undated.

[64] *Ibid.*, p. 175.

[65] *Ibid.*, p. 175.

[66] *Ibid.*, pp. 175–176.

My feelings were rather those of pleasure—that pleasure derived from the view of scenes of sublimity and grandeur, which the attendance of dangers serves but to heighten. I watched the mountain-wave as it rolled far above the masts and burst in air. I listened to the mingled conflicts of winds and waters, and the creaking of the masts at the rush of the billows. I marked the sheets of volleyed lightning that gleamed and played around me in almost a constant glare till my eyes were blinded with the gaze, and owned a feeling, indistinct and undefinable, but far removed from terror or dismay.[67]

In November, 1816, Halleck made a second trip to the South. Although this was undertaken ostensibly for business reasons, he was in part "actuated," as he said, "by a desire to see (or rather to say that I had seen) some of the Southern cities."[68] This trip, made by land, proved far more entertaining to the poet than the one of several months before. He traveled as far south as Alexandria, Virginia, stopping some days at Philadelphia, Baltimore, and Washington. In his picturesque manner, Halleck described in a letter several of the cities which he had visited. Baltimore the poet found most like New York of any of the cities through which he passed. Washington, which had recently been burned by the British, Halleck found a "mere desert." "The capitol and President's house were in ruins. They had commenced repairing them, but it must take many years to reinstate them in their former splendor."[69] The poet failed to see the President, who was ill at the time, but at a theater performance he was gratified with a sight of "Dolly" Madison, whom he described as "handsome and dignified looking."[70] He later made a trip to Mount Vernon, which he mentioned in enthusiastic terms. Toward the middle of January Halleck returned home.[71]

Halleck now spent more and more time in the company of his friend, Joseph Rodman Drake, whom he had met three years before. "Drake was the handsomest man in New York," once remarked Charles P. Clinch, a contemporary Knickerbocker. "He had a fine figure and was much larger than Halleck. I once described them in some lines beginning,

[67] *Life*, p. 176. [68] *Ibid.*, p. 170.
[69] *Ibid.*, p. 171. [70] *Ibid.*, p. 172.
[71] *Ibid.*, p. 183. A letter addressed to Halleck's sister and dated January 29, 1817.

'There comes big D—— and little H——.' "[72]

Whether or not, however, Halleck contributed to the inspiration of "The Culprit Fay" cannot be known. In any case, the traditional story of the meeting of Drake, De Kay, Cooper, and Halleck, and of the subsequent discussion which, we are told, led to Drake's writing "The Culprit Fay"—a legend repeated by every biographer of Drake—is entirely without foundation in fact. In communicating with Evert A. Duyckinck on May 13, 1866, when that gentleman was considering a new edition of his *Cyclopaedia of American Literature*, Halleck remarked: " 'The Culprit Fay' was written in 1816. De Kay was then in Europe. Drake was never acquainted personally with Cooper. The whole paragraph is a fiction.' "[73] But Halleck was a great admirer of the poem, and made at least two manuscript copies which he presented to friends. In January, 1817, he sent one of these[74] to his sister with the comment: "I send you herewith two manuscript poems, written by a friend of mine, Mr. Drake, whose name, I believe, I once mentioned to you. He is a young physician, about twenty. 'The Culprit Fay' was written, begun, and finished in three days. The copy you have is from the original, without the least alteration. It is certainly the best thing of the kind in the English language, and is more strikingly original than I had supposed it possible for a modern poem to be."[75]

On the other hand, Drake's faith in the poetic ability of Halleck cannot be denied. He is said on one occasion to have advised his friend to give up the business office, and "to embark upon the career of a man of letters."[76] It was probably in 1817 or the fol-

[72] Wilson, *Bryant and His Friends*, pp. 395–396. The intimacy of the friendship existing at this time between the two is well reflected in a letter which Drake wrote to Halleck, telling him of the death of a mutual friend, Walter Franklin, who had committed suicide. See Wilson, *Life*, pp. 191–193. The original letter in Drake's hand may be found in the New York Public Library.

[73] In a letter preserved in the Duyckinck Collection of the New York Public Library. Duyckinck had repeated the well-known anecdote in his *Cyclopaedia*, II, 203. See present work, p. 355.

[74] This copy was indorsed thus: "The following lines were written by Joseph Rodman Drake in New York, North America, August, 1816, and copied from the author's manuscript in January, 1817, by Fitz-Greene Halleck" (*Life*, p. 169). Another copy similarly indorsed was sent to George A. Foote of Guilford, a friend of Halleck.

[75] Wilson, *Life*, p. 183. The letter is dated January 29, 1817.

[76] Wilson, *Harper's New Monthly Magazine*, XLIX, 68 (June, 1874).

lowing year that Drake addressed his well-known lines to Halleck, in which he urged his friend to devote himself more conscientiously to poetry. This poem was first published in the *New York Mirror* for March 3, 1832,[77] under the title "To Fitz-Greene Halleck, Esq.," with the note that it had been written some fifteen years before.[78] The exact circumstances under which the poem was composed are unknown. But the verses show the obvious influence of William Collins' famous "Ode," addressed to Mr. Home, the author of *Douglas*, and might well enough have been called an "Ode on the Popular Superstitions of America."

The appropriateness for poetic treatment both of America and of American scenery was at this period and somewhat later a frequent subject of discussion among Knickerbocker writers. Now completely freed from the political domination of England, America soon began to look for independence in letters; and in this growing national consciousness, the New York school, then the most important literary group working in this country, played a characteristic part.[79] This tendency toward nationalism in literature took the form of an unorganized controversy in which each side argued for or against the fitness of America and her traditions as subject matter for poetic inspiration. We have already shown that the traditional story of the composition of "The Culprit Fay" had no basis in fact. But fictitious though it be, it reflects the trend of popular thought at this period. Drake, it will be remembered, had maintained against the contention of Halleck and Cooper, that the beauties of our own natural scenery possessed sufficient romantic associations to render them fit subjects for poetry; and to sustain his case he produced "The Culprit Fay." A few years later we find Washington Irving, although drawn irresistibly to Europe, "rich in the accumulated treasures of age," admitting that "never need an American look beyond his own country for the sublime and beautiful of natural scenery."[80] Robert C. Sands, a New York poet of the time and

[77] IX, 273. The poem was later published in Drake's collected works (1835) under the title "To a Friend."

[78] *New York Mirror*, IX, 278. The poem was reprinted in the *New York Evening Post* for March 22, 1832.

[79] The part played in this movement by James F. Cooper and James K. Paulding—the former in his *Leatherstocking Tales*, the latter in such works as *The Backwoodsman* (1818) and *Westward Ho!* (1832)—is worthy of note.

[80] See in *The Sketch Book* "The Author's Account of Himself" (1819).

editor of the *Atlantic Magazine,* undertook further to defend the
American cause against a previous writer for his periodical who
had asserted that "the history, superstitions, and natural and moral
features of our country are inadequate for the purposes of poetry
and fiction."[81] In Drake's poetic epistle to his friend, we find expressed a similar appeal in behalf of the American tradition.

> Shame! that while every mountain, stream, and plain
> Hath theme for truth's proud voice or fancy's wand,
> No native bard the patriot harp hath ta'en,
> But left to minstrel of a foreign strand
> To sing the beauteous scenes of nature's loveliest land.[82]

In Halleck, the poet visions the birth of a national bard.

> Arouse, my friend,—let vivid fancy soar,
> Look with *creative* eye on nature's face,
> Bid "goblin's damn'd" in wild Niagara roar,
> And view in every field a fairy race.[83]

But in spite of this eloquent appeal, Halleck appears to have
produced little poetry at this period. But one lyric, so far as is
known, was written in 1817. The verses beginning,

> I turned a last look on my dear native mountains,
> When the dim blush of sunset grew faint on the sky,

were composed for Miss Eliza McCall, a singer of Halleck's acquaintance. In a letter to his sister, Maria, Halleck said: "I annex
some lines I wrote one Sunday morning lately. They were written
for a Miss McCall, who sings, as the phrase is, divinely, in order
to go to the tune of 'Jessie of Dunblane,' the original words of
which are miserable."[84] The poem later found its way into a commonplace book owned by Francis R. Tillou, Drake's brother-in-law.
After Halleck's death, C. Graham Tillou, the son, sent a copy with
three other poems by Halleck to Evert A. Duyckinck,[85] who pub-

---

[81] *Atlantic Magazine,* I, 130 (June, 1824). Sands (1799–1832) in collaboration with his friend, Dr. James Eastburn, wrote a poem "Yamoyden" (1820)
founded on the history of Philip, the Indian Chief.

[82] Stanza 3. Drake is here referring to Thomas Campbell's "Gertrude of
Wyoming."

[83] Stanza 9.

[84] Wilson, *Life,* p. 186. The letter is dated July 14, 1817.

[85] The letter, dated December 6, 1817, which accompanied the poem, as well
as the poem itself, is preserved in the Duyckinck Collection of the New York
Public Library.

lished it in *Putnam's Magazine*[86] under the title "A Farewell to Connecticut." Though couched in personal phraseology, the poem has probably little autobiographical significance.

The following year Halleck wrote the poem, "There is an evening twilight of the heart." These verses are of special interest in being the earliest of the poet's work to find a place in the collected edition of 1827. They were composed, says Wilson, "on a lovely moonlight evening in the summer of 1818, while passing upon Long-Island Sound to New Haven, *en route* for his native town. Miss Halleck very distinctly recalls the fact of her brother, on his arrival at home, asking for pen, ink, and paper, when he immediately wrote the lines almost *verbatim* as they now appear."[87] Later in the same year Halleck offered the verses to Mr. William Coleman for publication in the *Evening Post*. The extremely fastidious editor of the *Post* is said to have given the verses "to the printer without comment"—a fact which was regarded as an evidence of his favorable opinion of the poem.[88] It is also of significance to note that Halleck's was the only poem published in the *Post* during October.[89]

That Halleck produced so few poems at this period was probably due to the fact that he was constantly engaged in work for Jacob Barker. Knowing Halleck to be of strict integrity of character, his employer more and more relied upon him as a personal agent and representative. The following extract from a letter written November 9, 1817, shows how at least some of Halleck's time was occupied, and illustrates to what extent Barker trusted his employee. In October, 1817, Halleck had made a short business trip to Lake George concerning which he wrote to his sister: "My excursion to the north was not one of pleasure. Had I the privilege of making such excursions, my steps would be turned in a different direction. I went to Lake George purely on business. Being the (nominal) director of a bank near there, my presence was necessary previous to the commencement of its operations. I shall be obliged to go again, probably, in a few weeks."[90]

86 XI, 235–236 (February, 1868).　　　87 Wilson, *Life*, p. 207.

88 Wynne, *Harper's New Monthly Magazine*, XXIV, pp. 637–638 (April, 1862).

89 The poem, which was published in the *Post* for October 13, 1818, was signed "F.G.H." and dated "October, 1818." It was again printed in the *Post* for May 8, 1819.

90 Wilson, *Life,* p. 188.

In October, 1816, Halleck had officiated as groomsman at the wedding of Drake, who married the daughter of Henry Eckford, a wealthy shipbuilder of New York.[91] In a letter from which we have already quoted, Halleck commented on the marriage. Since the Eckfords are rich, observed Halleck, ''I imagine he will write no more. He was poor, as poets, of course, always are, and offered himself a sacrifice at the shrine of Hymen to shun the 'pains and penalties' of poverty. I officiated as a groomsman, though much against my will. His wife is good-natured, and loves him to distraction.''[92] Viewed in the light of Halleck's comment, Drake's marriage appears at best but mercenary—an attempt to evade the responsibilities imposed by poverty. Such, however, could hardly have been the case. George P. Lathrop has supposed that Halleck's condemnation of his friend's marriage proceeded from a ''singular coldness, indifference, rigidity'' of character.[93] To be sure, there is frequently discernible in the poet's work a curious practicality and even cynicism which destroys the spirit of romance. But while this note of disillusionment is often struck in his writings, there is evidence enough that Halleck was in reality warm-hearted; and although he once characterized the ''female sex'' as a ''rattle-headed set,''[94] there is more than one occasion on which he displayed marked gallantry and tenderness toward women.[95] Whatever may be said of Halleck's remarks in regard to Drake's marriage, it should be kept in mind that the poet was distinctly ''bachelor-minded,'' and undoubtedly found it difficult to see life from the standpoint of the married man. Halleck's growing intimacy with Drake, however, may perhaps be regarded as the chief reason for his disappointment at his friend's marriage. Halleck, we may be sure, wished Drake to remain unmarried if for no other than the freedom which unmarried life affords to companionship.

Dr. and Mrs. Drake in the spring of 1818 made a trip to Europe, accompanied by James De Kay and another friend named Langstaff, who kept an apothecary shop at number 34 Park. Although

---

[91] The following notice appeared in the *New York Evening Post* for Thursday, October 24, 1816: ''Married—on Monday Evening last, by Rev. Doctor Milledollar, Dr. J. R. Drake to Miss Eckford.''

[92] Wilson, *Life,* pp. 183–184.

[93] *Atlantic Monthly,* XXXIX, 726 (June, 1877).

[94] Wilson, *Life,* p. 117.   [95] See, for example, pp. 267 ff.

of a gruff, eccentric personality, often at variance with itself, Langstaff was a good-hearted soul, and a devoted friend to Drake. After Drake returned to America, he joined Langstaff in the drug business, as is evidenced by the New York directory for 1820 which mentions the firm of "Drake and Langstaff."[96] Langstaff is described by Halleck in a letter to Maria, as "a nondescript. He is something like Lord Byron's 'Lara,' for nobody knows where he came from, or who he is. He says he is from somewhere near London, and there his history ends."[97]

Two poetic memorials of Drake's European trip are of the greatest interest in the light they throw upon the friendship between Drake and Halleck. These poems consist of epistles written in pseudo-Scotch dialect, and addressed to Halleck. Composed in a stanza-form familiar to Burns, and full of allusions to the Scottish bard, the first of these letters, written on May 1, 1818, must indeed have filled Halleck with a glorious longing to be with his friend. In the opening stanza Drake frankly admits his ignorance of the Scotch dialect.

> Well, Fitz, I'm here, the mair's the pity,
> I'll wad ye curse the vera city
> From which I write a braid Scotch ditty,
>   Afore I learn it;
> But if ye canna mak it suit ye,
>   Ye ken ye'll burn it.[98]

Drake comments further in the concluding stanza upon his curious hodgepodge of English and Scotch:

> But pouk my pen—I find I'm droppin'
> My braw Scotch style to English loppin',
> I fear a'maist that ye'll be hoppin'
>   I'd quite it quite.
> If so, I e'en must think of stoppin'
>   And sae gude night.[99]

The second epistle, written in the meter of "Tam O'Shanter," and dated "Irvine, 10th May 1818—10 P.M." is similar in spirit

[96] An anonymous letter is published by Wilson (*Bryant and His Friends*, pp. 288–289), in which the writer describes from memory the old house at 34 Park.

[97] Wilson, *Life*, p. 196. The letter is dated January 24, 1818.

[98] *Ibid.*, p. 198.   [99] *Ibid.*, p. 200.

to the preceding. Here Drake alludes pleasantly to his tour of the places famed in Scottish lore. But amid all these romantic scenes, he catches sight of Hesper in the western heavens, and his heart returns instinctively to "my bonny Bronx" and to his friend.

> Ah! Fitz, my lad, I'm thinking, aye,
> How blithe and happy'll be the day
> When we shall meet again together
> I' the land of freedom and fine weather;
> How we shall talk of all that's past
> Since you and me forgathered last,
> And, fecks! ye'll crack a dainty kernel
> When ye get hold of Wully's journal.[100]

[100] *Ibid.*, p. 207. These two poetic epistles were originally to be included in the 1835 edition of Drake's poems. A review of this edition from proof sheets in the *American Monthly Magazine* for September, 1835 (VI, 65), prints portions of the two poems, but they never appeared in the final printed edition. The reason for this deletion is unknown, although Halleck may have objected to their inclusion because of their personal character.

IV

"THE CROAKERS"

1819

The year 1819 was the *annus memorabilis* in the literary life of Fitz-Greene Halleck. He now entered upon a new stage of his career, characterized by a sudden realization of his poetic powers. This fresh impetus given to his genius was in part the result of his natural growth as an artist. For ten years he had served a poetic apprenticeship, and with varying degrees of success had imitated the poets of the English school of sentimental verse. But this period of training was now largely at an end, and Halleck was ready to draw more confidently upon the resources of his own imagination. A second, and perhaps more potent reason for this sudden flowering of poetic talent lay in the inspiration afforded by his companion, Joseph Rodman Drake. It is perhaps doubtful whether Halleck would have come to a full appreciation of his powers as a poet, had it not been for Drake.[1] We have already seen how Drake called to his friend's mind the importance of the national scene and tradition as the subject matter for his poetry;[2] and he is said to have urged Halleck to leave Jacob Barker, and devote himself wholly to the pursuits of poetry.[3] Such was the mutual harmony existing between the minds of the poets that there can be little question of the reciprocal influences at play. Naturally inert and somewhat desultory in poetic composition, Halleck needed the added stimulus of working for a time with a friend who had explicit confidence in his genius. Halleck was now ready to assert himself in all the pride of authorship, and in the space of ten years was to step from almost total obscurity into a fame that was nation-wide.

Viewed in the light of early Knickerbocker literature, the inti-

[1] Bayard Taylor believed that Drake's friendship "was the spell which awoke his true powers, and gave him a swift and delightful fame" (*North American Review*, CXXV, 60).

[2] See pp. 44–45.

[3] Wilson, *Harper's New Monthly Magazine*, XLIX, 68 (June, 1874).

mate friendship of Drake and Halleck, and the resultant series of poetic sallies on local characters and institutions were but expressions of a town spirit which had already begun vigorously to declare itself in letters. The so-called "Knickerbocker School" may be said to have had its beginning in the publication of *Salmagundi*, a small periodical issued from January 24, 1807 to January 25, 1808, which had for its aim "to instruct the young, reform the old, correct the town, and castigate the age."[4] These light, satiric papers, the work of Washington Irving and James K. Paulding, could have attained popularity only in the New York of the early nineteenth century—a city, with a population of less than 125,000,[5] which occupied the lower part of Manhattan. Marked by frequent references to local characters and customs, the *Salmagundi* papers were obviously addressed to the inhabitants of a town with a fully developed *esprit de corps*—a community relatively unified in thought and action. From such a town consciousness a taste for personal satire invariably springs; and *The Croakers*, coming ten years after *Salmagundi*, thus found a fertile soil in which to flourish.[6]

These satires, thirty-five in number, were produced, some by the individual poets, others in collaboration. All but three, which appeared in the columns of the *National Advocate*, were published in the *New York Evening Post*. They derived their name from the signatures which the poets appended to their work. In general, Drake signed his productions "Croaker," and Halleck, "Croaker, Junior"; whereas to their combined work they gave the pseudonym, "Croaker & Co."[7] The latter signature, however, was in many cases a misnomer: not infrequently the poems so signed were virtually the work of a single poet—the collaboration consisting only in some slight verbal change or suggestion made by the other poet.

---

[4] See the first paper of the series.

[5] The population in 1810 was 96,373; in 1820, 123,706.

[6] Literary collaboration played a significant part in early Knickerbocker literature, and reflects something of the friendly spirit unifying the group of authors then working. "Yamoyden" (1820), a poetic romance based on the life of Philip, the Indian chief, was the work of two friends, Robert C. Sands and the Rev. James W. Eastburn. *The Talisman*, a literary miscellany issued for three successive years (1828–30), was edited by William C. Bryant, Gulian C. Verplanck, and Robert C. Sands.

[7] This signature was, of course, suggested by the character of Croaker in Goldsmith's *Good Natured Man*.

It is now difficult to ascertain precisely how *The Croakers* came
to be written. Indeed, the origin of these sketches is so clouded by
tradition and marred by conflicting anecdote, that it is almost impossible to trace their source with exactitude. In general, however,
the stories regarding the composition of *The Croakers* are two. The
first of these, told by James Lawson, gives to Drake alone the credit
of originating this clever series of *jeux d'esprit*. "Dr. Drake, a
poet of lively imagination and brilliant wit," wrote Lawson in the
Southern Literary Messenger, "sent in March, 1819, to the Evening Post some verses 'To Ennui,' under the signature of Croaker.
. . . They attracted so much attention that Drake communicated
his secret to Halleck, and asked his assistance to amuse the town.
With characteristic modesty, he pleaded inability, but was at length
prevailed upon to make the attempt—in which, succeeding under
the signature of Croaker, Jr., the two friends wrote afterwards, in
most instances, as Croaker & Co."[8]

The second story, related by James Grant Wilson, differs from
the first in making *The Croakers* the outcome of a merry meeting,
one Sunday morning, of Drake, Halleck, and Langstaff. Drake and
Halleck were amusing themselves by writing verses, when the former composed lines "To Ennui" which Halleck is said to have answered with stanzas on the same subject. "The young poets,"
continues Wilson, "decided to send their productions, with others
of a similar character, to William Coleman, the editor of the *Evening Post*. If he published them, they would write more; if not,
they would send them to M. M. Noah, of the *National Advocate*."[9]

A careful comparison of the two stories shows that the second
has on its side the greater probability. Of course, it is undoubtedly
true that from Drake came the idea of the series, for he it was
who wrote the first poem, and at the start was more active in publishing than Halleck.[10] And yet, as we have already observed,
Drake and Halleck were at this time the most devoted of friends,
and it is scarcely probable that Drake would have kept his secret

---

[8] This article, one of the earliest biographical sketches of Halleck, appeared
in the *Messenger* for April, 1842 (VIII, [2]41).

[9] *Life*, pp. 215–216.

[10] That the suggestion for the series probably came from Drake is further
indicated by the fact that his contributions were signed "Croaker"; whereas
Halleck's were signed "Croaker, Jr." Halleck was, of course, older than
Drake, so that the "Junior" could not have referred to age.

for any length of time from his companion. What could be more natural than for Halleck to spend a Sunday morning at Drake's lodgings, and for *The Croakers* to be an outcome of the merry meeting? That the weight of evidence tends to support Wilson's version is further shown by a careful examination of the dates on which the first of *The Croakers* appeared. "To Ennui," by Drake alone, appeared in the *Post* for March 10, 1819. On the following day another was published from the pen of Drake in the same paper. It should now be noted that Halleck made his first contribution to the series on the twelfth of the month in the *National Advocate*. On the twelfth and thirteenth two more *Croakers* by Drake were printed in the columns of the *Post*. On the fifteenth three new poems were contributed to the series—the first, by Halleck in the *Post;* the second and third, by Drake in the *Advocate* and *Post*. From the relation of the respective contributions of the two poets, it may be seen that the early numbers of *The Croakers* must have been composed at approximately the same period, and that Halleck was probably a copartner with Drake in the project from the very start.

The manner in which the two poets collaborated in many of these sketches has been described by Frederic S. Cozzens, the famous humorist and author of *The Sparrowgrass Papers,* to whom Halleck once imparted the secret of the composition of *The Croakers*. Cozzens writes that either Halleck "or Drake would furnish a draft of the poem, and that one or the other would suggest any alteration or enlargement of the idea; a closer clipping of the wings of fancy; a little epigrammatic spur upon the heel of a line."[11] To Cozzens we also owe the charming anecdote, related to him by Halleck, of Drake's joy at receiving the proof from the printer of one of his poems. Drake "laid his cheek down upon the lines he had written, and looking at his fellow-poet, with beaming eyes, said, 'O, Halleck, isn't this happiness!' "[12] Thus were *The Croakers* born in the enthusiasm of intimate friendship, and a closeness of collaboration resulted rare in literary history. Only two kindred spirits could have produced work following so closely a single, dominant tone. Bryant believed he could detect in the laughter of *The Croakers* the racier note of Hal-

[11] *Fitz-Greene Halleck. A Memorial* (New York, 1868), p. 14. An address delivered on Halleck before the New York Historical Society on January 6, 1868.

[12] *Ibid.,* p. 14.

leck, and once remarked that Halleck "drove home his jests with the sharpest percusion."[13] But in vain does the modern reader, without the help that Halleck has given,[14] attempt to solve the mystery of this literary partnership.

The Croakers, as we have already seen, were contributed to the *Evening Post* and the *National Advocate.* William Coleman, a lawyer from Massachusetts, had founded the *Post* in 1801. He was a man of peculiarly sensitive disposition, firm in his own opinions, and ready always to maintain his rights. In those days when the newspaper was largely the tool of party hatred, Coleman, who was Federalist, found a competent rival in Mordecai Noah, editor of the *National Advocate,* a Democratic paper. Coleman, we have noted, possessed a reputation for great fastidiousness in the selection of literary material for his paper. Imagine then the surprise of the two poets when they read in the *Evening Post* for March 9 that the lines "To Ennui" had been received, and would "have a place to-morrow." Coleman further praised the poem by calling it the production of "genius and taste"; and suggested that "a personal acquaintance with the author would be gratifying." Another contribution, however, submitted by Drake at the same time, which poked fun at Trumbull's painting "The Declaration of Independence," was rejected by Coleman.[15]

The following evening[16] Drake's verses "To Ennui" appeared. It should here be noted that in general the subject matter of *The Croakers* was drawn from the topics of the day that had acquired either local or national importance. "To Ennui" was scarcely an exception to this rule. It was fashionable at this period to be afflicted with a species of melancholy which took all hope from life, and left

[13] *Some Notices of the Life and Writings of Fitz-Greene Halleck,* p. 11.

[14] It may here be noted that the original signatures "Croaker," "Croaker, Junior," and "Croaker & Co." represent very inaccurately the exact authorship of the poems. Far more reliable is the designation in the 1869 edition of Halleck's poems where *The Croakers* have been marked "H," "D," and "H and D." These initials, though assigned by Halleck in all probability late in life (see p. 79), and subject to all the inaccuracies incident to memory, present a fairly correct statement of the authorship. With a few exceptions, this designation will be followed in the present account of *The Croakers.*

[15] "'*The declaration of independence,*' from the same pen, is declined; for we hold with Lavater, that it is more honorable to crush a jest between the teeth than hurt the feelings of a good man" (the *Post,* March 9, 1819).

[16] Wednesday, March 10, 1819. Signed "Croaker."

one at odds with himself.[17] Halleck at this time appears to have been the victim of some such distemper, although in his case it was hardly the fashionable weariness of body and mind of which we have spoken. In a letter to his sister dated November 19, 1818, Halleck tells how for a time a "total indifference" to life possessed him. "I was not miserable," he says, "but my mind felt a kind of indifference toward everything like emotion, whether of pain or pleasure; in short, I was a complete stoic, and could have received the most unlooked-for stroke of ruin without a pang." Hoping for relief, Halleck consulted a physician, who pronounced his trouble the "hypo." The doctor refused to prescribe anything, and, Halleck significantly added, "I find I am since getting better."[18] Drake in his lines "To Ennui" alludes to Halleck's curious attack.

> And F * * *[19] is almost hpy'd to death,
> And L * * *[19] has got the blues.

In the same issue of the *Post* which contained the stanzas "To Ennui," appeared an editorial note from the pen of Coleman, which informed the "unknown correspondent, Croaker," that two more contributions had been received, and should soon have a place in the paper.

On February 23, 1819,[20] General Jackson had been honored with a gold box, "presented by the Mayor, Aldermen, and Commonalty of the City of New York," which granted the general "the freedom of the city, as a testimony of respect for his high military serv-

---

[17] For example, in Holt's *Columbian* for March 5, 1814, we find a poem entitled "Ennui." I quote the first stanza:

> What demon pours these shadows round,
> Chills with drear horror every nerve,
> And checks the generous sallies of the soul?
> What fell despair doth me possess,
> What mad distrust of e'en my friends,
> And loathing of the very name of faith?
> 'Tis Ennui.

[18] Wilson, *Life*, p. 211.

[19] So printed in the original version, but changed to "Fitz" (Halleck) and "Lang" (Langstaff) respectively in the Bradford edition. This edition of *The Croakers*, published by the Bradford Club in 1860, was the first complete collection of the satires in book form. See p. 336.

[20] "The freedom of the city, voted to major gen. [*sic*] Andrew Jackson by the common council, will be presented to him this day in the large court room of the City Hall, at one o'clock" (*National Advocate*, February 23, 1819).

ice.''[21] In the next *Croaker*[22] Drake celebrated this event. The poet's disgust at this affair of empty pomp is well summarized in the concluding lines of the poem:

> Dear General! though you swallow all,
> I must confess it sickens me.

The freedom with which Drake had exposed the vulgar *entrée* of the general into the city began plainly to disturb Coleman, who now knew scarcely what to expect from his mysterious correspondent. He had already rejected one contribution which he thought too personal,[23] although admitting another which might well have been censured on similar grounds. He probably believed his position as an editor unsafe; yet it would not do to refuse to print the poems, as ''Croaker'' would at once turn to Coleman's rival, Noah, and offer him the remainder of the verses. He consequently sought, through his paper, ''a personal and confidential interview with our friend Croaker.'' ''If he declines,'' Coleman went on to say, ''will he inform me how he may be addressed by letter? In the meantime, whatever may happen, (he, at least, will, before long, understand me) I expect from him discretion.''[24]

On the following day[25] Halleck contributed his first poem to the series. It was accepted for publication by Mordecai Noah, editor of the *National Advocate*. Noah under President Madison had acted as United States consul to Morocco, and upon his return to America, in addition to founding the *Advocate*, had published his *Travels in England, France, Spain, and the Barbary States from 1813 to 1815*. As the editor of a paper with contrary political principles, Noah was the natural opponent of Coleman and, although not of so irascible and defiant a nature as his rival, was by no means free from party prejudice and hatred. Halleck's rather innocuous verses, entitled ''When Bony Fought His Hosts of Foes,''[26] were composed in celebration of the sudden growth of mushroom officers in the

[21] These words formed part of the inscription on the box. See notes to the Bradford edition, p. 138.

[22] ''On Presenting the Freedom of the City in a Gold Box to a Great General'' appeared in the *Post* for March 11, 1819, and was signed ''Croaker.''

[23] ''The Declaration of Independence.''

[24] The *Post*, March 11, 1819.

[25] March 12, 1819. The Bradford edition of *The Croakers* gives the date incorrectly as the eleventh.

[26] Signed ''Croaker, Junior.''

state militia, as a result of the liberality of Governor Clinton, who had bestowed his favors with none too discriminating a hand.

On the same evening the *Post* printed another of Drake's humorous sallies on General Jackson. "The 'Secret Mine' Sprung at a Late Supper"[27] satirized Jackson's indiscreet toast to "De Witt Clinton, the Governor of the great and patriotic State of New York," made much to the confusion of Clinton's political opponents at Tammany Hall, whither the general had been invited to dine.[28] These verses, like many which were to follow, were full of personal references to politicians then in the public eye.

Coleman continued to be disturbed by the personalities indulged in by the "Croakers," and in a prefatory note to the verses on General Jackson made it plain that the "witty idea and the flowing lines" were their "principal recommendations with the editor," and that he entered "not into the merits of the personal satire." With the publication of the next *Croaker*[29] on the following day Coleman praised the new poems which had been submitted as "gems of such brilliancy that we shall hasten to set them with all possible expedition." "Croaker will find, by applying to the right place," Coleman went on to say, "that we have pursued the hint communicated in a private note, and addressed a letter through the post-office to his fictitious name. A similar communication will be kept up."

On March 15 three new satires were added to the series. Coleman had already publicly rejected "The Declaration of Independence." But the poem was straightway submitted to Noah under a new title. It is not improbable that the editor of the *National Advocate* saw in the acceptance of this satire which Coleman had refused, a way of defying his rival. In any case, "The National Painting" appeared in the *Advocate* for March 15.[30] John Trumbull had recently completed his well-known painting for the rotunda of the Capitol at Washington, so that the topic was not an untimely one for the

27 Signed "Croaker."
28 See 1869 edition of Halleck's poems, p. 378.
29 "To Mr. Potter, the Ventriloquist" (signed "Croaker") by Drake alone, appeared in the *Post* for March 13. See in the same issue of the *Post* an advertisement of a performance given by Potter. Hereafter most of *The Croakers* in which Halleck had no part will not be discussed in detail.
30 Signed "Croaker."

satirist.[31] Drake published another *Croaker* in the *Post* of the same day, entitled "The Battery War."[32]

The third *Croaker* to appear on the fifteenth was one by Halleck, the first of a series of four addressed "To Mr. Simpson," the manager of the Park Theatre. Following the title was printed a note relating the occasion of the poem. Simpson that evening was to take his benefit, and the poet intimates that "notwithstanding the following croaking lines," the manager "has the wishes of the bard that it may prove a *bumper*." The second stanza of the poem is typical of the playful personal satire in which both Drake and Halleck often indulged.

> Poor Woodworth! his Chronicle[33] died broken-hearted;
>   What a loss to the drama! the world and the age!
> And Coleman is silent since Philipps[34] departed,
>   And Noah's too busy to think of the stage.
> Now the aim of this letter is merely to mention
>   That, since all your critics are laid on the shelf,
> Out of pure love of you, it is my kind intention
>   To take box No. 3, and turn critic myself.[35]

Halleck's two contributions to the series—"Bony's Fight" and "To Mr. Simpson"—had each borne the signature "Croaker, Junior." Drake, therefore, on the evening of March 16 addressed his partner in a poem "To Croaker, Junior,"[36] opening with the sprightly lines,

> Your hand, my dear Junior! we're all in a flame
>   To see a few more of your flashes;
> The Croakers forever! I'm proud of the name—
> But brother, I fear, tho' our cause is the same,
>   We shall quarrel like Brutus and Cassius.

[31] Cf. Halleck's ridicule of Trumbull's painting in *Fanny*, stanza 51 (1839 ed.).

[32] The first of the poems to be signed "Croaker & Co.," although credited to Drake alone in the 1869 edition.

[33] The *Republican Chronicle*, a semiweekly newspaper, was established in 1817. In March, 1818, the *Republican Chronicle and City Advertiser*, a daily, was also established under the editorship of Samuel Woodworth. Its run was indeed short, for there is no record of any number issued after October, 1818. For the information regarding this rare newspaper I am indebted to Mr. Clarence S. Brigham, librarian of the American Antiquarian Society.

[34] Thomas Philipps, the actor. See George Odell, *Annals of the New York Stage* (New York, 1927), II, 499 ff.

[35] Signed "Croaker, Junior."   [36] Signed "Croaker."

These verses show better than any others the spirit of comradeship from which *The Croakers* sprang. Almost entirely free from personal animus toward those whom they were lampooning, the two were exulting in the momentary sensation they were causing. In the same issue of the *Post*[37] also appeared Halleck's verses entitled "A Very Modest Letter from One Great Man to Another."[38] Purporting to be an epistle from Alexander Hamilton to De Witt Clinton, the governor of New York, the poem introduced a bit of political gossip then on the public lips.

Halleck's next contribution[39] to *The Croakers* was another epistle "To E. Simpson, Esq.,"[40] written "on witnessing the representation of the new tragedy of Brutus."[41] What could be more calculated to win popular applause for *The Croakers* than the brisk style of banter in which these verses were written! Take, for example, the third stanza in which Mr. Simpson is addressed by name.

> In your dresses and scenery, classic and clever!
> Such invention! such blending of old things & new!
> Let Kemble's proud laurels be withered forever!
> Wear the wreath, my dear Simpson, 'tis fairly your due.

Drake and Halleck had, during all this time, carefully kept their own identity a secret, and the mystery of the authorship of *The Croakers* had consequently become the talk of the town. They felt, however, that their secret would soon be revealed unless they took immediate measures to prevent discovery. They therefore addressed a letter to Coleman, suggesting a new method of communication. The editor replied most courteously to *"Croaker & Co.'s* private

---

[37] March 16, 1819.   [38] Signed "Croaker & Co."

[39] On the three preceding evenings Drake had published poems in the *Post*. "To the S*rg**n G*n*r*l of the State of New York," signed "Croaker & Co.," was addressed to Dr. Mitchill, a distinguished physician and scientist of the city, whose learning and pedantry served as an excellent butt for the satire of the Croakers (March 17). The poetic epistle "To John Minshull, Esq." (signed "Croaker") is of interest for its mention of Samuel Woodworth, the author of "The Old Oaken Bucket," and James K. Paulding, an original partner with the Irvings in the *Salmagundi* papers. Paulding in 1818 had just published a poem called "The Backwoodsman" (see the present work, pp. 94 ff.). "To John Minshull, Esq." appeared in the *Post* for March 18. The lyric beginning, "The man who frets at worldly strife" (signed "Croaker & Co."), was published in the *Post* for March 19.

[40] Signed "Croaker, Junior." Published in the *Post* for March 20.

[41] The subtitle of the poem.

letter," saying that "we are inclined to believe his apprehensions that the post office is watched at certain hours, are not without foundation. Agreeably to his suggestion, therefore, we shall in the future deposit our notes at a certain coffee-house designated by him; and expect his by the same conveyance we received the first."[42]

So popular, indeed, had *The Croakers* now become that numerous imitations of the satires were daily received in the newspaper offices. As early as March 15 Mordecai Noah promised that he would soon print an imitation called "A Pill to Croaker,"[43] and added that "we have always a corner for Croaker himself."[44] Coleman also commented briefly on the imitations he had received, but declared that "none of them partake in any degree of the inspiration which marks every effort of his [Croaker's] muse."[45] Coleman in time became thoroughly irritated at these inane and vapid attempts to rival the fame of the "Croakers," and issued what he believed would be a decisive notice to the "imitators of Croaker & Co.," declaring that "if they do not appear to reclaim" their productions "before three o'clock to-morrow, they will one and all, without the least remorse, be consigned to the chimney with a fire in it."[46] But the rhymesters about town were in no wise disturbed by this grim threat, and continued to ape the clever sallies of the "Croakers." Coleman, at length, was forced to yield ground, and finally consented to the publication of one of the imitations which he deemed "a nearer approach to the spirit of the original than any yet received."[47]

The tone and workmanship of the imitation which Coleman first admitted to his paper were perhaps slightly above the average of those which were to follow. It possessed a liveliness of movement which in a measure identified it with the originals, but it was almost wholly lacking in that characteristic quality of humor that made

---

[42] The *Post*, March 17, 1819. Wilson says that *The Croakers* "were copied from the originals by Dr. Langstaff or Mr. Clinch [Charles C.], that the hand-writing should not divulge the secret of the authorship, and were either sent by post, or more frequently taken to the office by Clinch or Winthrop [an associate of Halleck at Barker's]" (*Bryant and His Friends*, p. 397).

[43] Noah published this imitation in the *Advocate* for March 17. He later asserted, however, in the issue for March 20, that "none of the 'Croakers' will answer, and for the very best reason—none writes like the original."

[44] *National Advocate*, March 15, 1819.

[45] The *Post*, March 15, 1819.

[46] *Ibid.*, March 17, 1819.   [47] *Ibid.*, March 22, 1819.

the genuine *Croakers* so charming. As an example of the many parodies of *The Croakers* which appeared during the subsequent weeks, I quote two stanzas from the first one printed by Coleman. It was addressed

TO THE CROAKERS

My dear lads, you're immortal, if croaking can make ye,
You're the wits of the day, and the pride of the age;
May the devil take him who can ever forsake ye,
As long as ye copy from Nature's great page.

In England they've writers, some bad and some good,
And many but middling (that is, but so so),
But I doubt very much if among them they could
Find one to excel Messrs. Croaker & Co.[48]

From now on, imitations and parodies of *The Croakers* appeared in the daily papers side by side with the genuine poems. Little critical acumen is demanded to distinguish the originals from their crude imitations. Heavy in wit and lame in meter, they lacked distinctly the polish and grace of the originals; and although they attained a certain popularity at the time of their publication, they shone only in the reflected light of the more finely cut gems of Drake and Halleck.

Returning to the publication of *The Croakers*, we find the next contribution to the series was from the pen of Halleck. John Lang, editor of the *New York Gazette*, a newspaper specializing in commercial and shipping news, was, like Coleman, a man of sensitive disposition. In spite of many names of local fame which *The Croakers* had touched upon, no mention had as yet been made of Lang. Some one of the many imitators of the satires, however, apparently submitted a poem for his consideration, signed "Croaker & Co." But Lang declined the contribution, asserting that "the poetic effusion of Croaker & Co. is too personal for this Gazette."[49] An evening or two later, Coleman, in mentioning several "Croaker" imitations he had received, commented on a poetical communication from "A Friend to Croaker" advising Croaker "to beware of Mr. Lang."[50]

[48] *Ibid.*, March 22, 1819. References to other Croaker imitations appeared in the same issue of the *Post*.
[49] *New York Gazette*, March 20, 1819, as quoted in the Bradford edition of *The Croakers*, p. 150.
[50] The *Post*, March 22, 1819.

All this gossip concerning Lang aroused the interest of Halleck, and the following evening he published his lines "To John Lang, Esq."[51] Coleman, no doubt to obviate any possible trouble with Lang, penned a letter to himself as if from Croaker, and prefixed it to the poem. He asserted that the purpose of the poem is "to convince Mr. Lang that I have been among the most attentive of his readers and admirers for years." Halleck's innocuous verses should have given no offense.

> We've twined the wreath of honor
>   Round Doctor M–tch–ll's brow[52]
> Though bold and daring was the theme,
>   A loftier waits us now.
> In thee—Immortal Lang!—have all
>   The Sister Graces met—
> Thou Statesman! Sage! and *"Editor"*
>   Of the New-York Gazette.[53]

In spite of the obvious playfulness of Halleck's lines, Mr. Lang was irritated. Coleman, in his issue of the following evening, printed an editorial comment, with the view to placate the injured feelings of his rival. Coleman now confessed himself the author of the epistle that had preceded the verses, and declared his regret that Lang should wince "so much under the anguish which the poet has, unconsciously, inflicted."[54] Lang apparently made no reply to Coleman's defense, and the affair was dropped.

On the evening of March 24 Coleman printed Drake's lines "To Domestic Peace,"[55] and on the following night Halleck's third poetic letter "To E. Simpson, Esq."[56] The latter treated of various matters of local interest at the Park Theatre, where Simpson was manager. From the pen of Halleck also came "A Lament for Great Ones Departed,"[57] which celebrated in a mildly satiric vein the departure for a time of several of the city officials, to take their places in the state legislature.

Halleck's excitement over the popularity of *The Croakers* was

---

[51] The *Post*, March 23, 1819. Signed "Croaker & Co."
[52] See p. 59 (note).   [53] First stanza.
[54] The *Post*, March 24, 1819.   [55] Signed "Croaker & Co."
[56] The *Post*, March 25, 1819. Signed "Croaker, Junior."
[57] *Ibid.*, March 27, 1819. Signed "Croaker & Co."

now at its height. On April 1 [58] a lull in the publication of the poems gave him an opportunity to write home to acquaint his sister with the success of the project, and to express his own enthusiasm at the part he was playing in it.

Can you believe it, Maria, Joe and I have become authors? We have tasted all the pleasures and many of the pains of literary fame and notoriety, under the assumed name of "The Croakers." We have had the consolation of seeing and of hearing ourselves praised, puffed, eulogized, execrated, and threatened as much, I believe I can say with truth, as any writers since the days of Junius. The whole town has talked of nothing else for three weeks past, and every newspaper has done us the honor to mention us in some way, either of praise or censure, but all uniting in owning our talents and genius. . . . [59] As luck would have it, Joe was under the necessity of going to Albany, and I have been compelled to carry on the war alone for ten days past, during which time I furnished Coleman with one piece each day. Langstaff is at work copying them from the newspapers into a book, which I shall soon send you. The subjects are, many of them, purely local, and will, of course, be unintelligible to you. They are well understood here, however. Joe has not yet returned, and, having now set the whole town in a blaze, I have thought best to give them a "resting-spell" for a while.[60]

Precisely what Halleck could have had in mind, when he said that he had "been compelled to carry on the war alone for ten days," it is difficult to say. Judging from the date of Halleck's letter, Drake must have left for Albany about March 21. During the ten days that followed but four genuine *Croakers* appeared, two of which were the work of Drake. If Halleck "furnished Coleman with one piece each day," as he says, the editor must for some reason have withheld several from publication. To be sure, Halleck's reference to giving the town a "resting-spell" is borne out by the fact that from March 28 to April 8 Coleman printed no *Croakers*.

[58] Between March 19 and April 1, appeared four imitations and parodies of *The Croakers*. Two of these have already been commented upon. In the *Post* for March 23 were also printed lines "To Major-General Croaker, Commander of the Forces Attacking Gotham," signed "Crow, Brigadier-General, Commanding corps de reserve." On March 27 Coleman published an announcement, stating that "*Falstaff to Prince Croaker* was punctually received, and we owe him an apology for postponing him till our next; for in him we recognize the true blood of the Croakers." As promised, the poem appeared on the following Monday evening (March 29).

[59] Wilson's omission.   [60] Wilson, *Life*, pp. 218–219.

A certain mystery, too, appears to have been connected with this lull in publication. That there was a sufficient number of poems on hand which for some unexplained reason were being kept from the public, may be inferred from a notice which Coleman printed in the *Post* for April 5. The editor stated that he was waiting "for permission to go forward with the stock of manuscript which we have on hand," and explained that, "on account of the public," he was "a little impatient for some intimation to that effect."

The series was soon resumed with the publication of Drake's verses "To Captain Seaman Weeks, Chairman of the Tenth Ward Independent Electors,"[61] which reviewed humorously several political parties then in vogue in New York. A joint paper by Drake and Halleck then made its appearance in the *Post*.[62] Dr. Samuel Mitchill, a professor at Columbia College, and at that time Surgeon General of the state, whom Drake had addressed in a *Croaker* on March 17, was again honored by a skit on his recent report, which has been described as filling "eight folio pages of the Senate journal."[63] The two poets cleverly burlesqued the doctor's tedious pedantry, and parodied without reserve his pompous display of learning. Mitchell, for example, was thus made to define "Grog":

> Grog—I'll define it in a minute—
> Take gin, rum, whiskey or peach brandy,
> Put but a little water in it,
> And that is Grog—now understand me,
> I mean to say, that should the spirit
> Be left out by some careless dog—
> It is—I wish the world may hear it!
> It is plain water, and not Grog.

Mrs. John Barnes, a well-known actress of the day, was made the subject of the next *Croaker* by Drake and Halleck.[64] She had made her *début* at the Park Theatre in 1815, and had almost

---

[61] The *Post*, April 8, 1819. Signed "Croaker."

[62] *Ibid.*, April 10, 1819. Signed "Croaker & Co."

[63] *The Croakers* (Bradford ed.), p. 155. It was this same Dr. Mitchill whose volume *The Picture of New York*, published in 1807, set Irving to writing *A History of New York.*

[64] On April 15, 16, and 17 respectively Drake published in the *Post* "To an Elderly Coquette" (signed "C"), "To —— ——, Esquire" (signed "Croaker & Co."), and "Ode to Impudence" (signed "Croaker & Co.").

immediately secured a public regard which remained undimmed
throughout her long professional career of twenty-five years.[65] The
epistle "To Mrs. Barnes"[66] embodied both a compliment and a rebuke to the actress.

A second joint composition appeared the following evening.
Simon Thomas, a caterer of New York, was frequently called upon
by the *élite* of the city to assist at their fashionable entertainments. "To Simon"[67] was prefaced by a few words, ostensibly by
the poets themselves, indicating that the verses were "a lick at a
fashionable folly which reigns among the sons and daughters of the
higher order, in the renowned city of Gotham, at this present writing."[68]

Halleck next contributed to the series "A Loving Epistle to Mr.
William Cobbett, of North Hempstead, Long-Island."[69] Cobbett,[70]
a native of England, was early in his career forced to leave his
native country because of difficulty with the government. He made
his way to America in 1793, and was soon drawn into politics. His
indiscreet personal attacks in *Porcupine's Gazette* now involved
him in several suits for libel, which finally resulted in his return to
England in 1800. Seventeen years later he reappeared in America,
but instead of identifying himself with political issues, settled this
time on a farm at North Hempstead, where he lived for two years,
tilling the soil, and writing books and pamphlets.[71] At one time
during his second visit Cobbett appears to have kept a shop on
Fulton Street, where he offered for sale books, seeds, and "black
pigs for ten dollars each."[72] Cobbett, notorious alike in England

[65] *The Croakers* (Bradford ed.), p. 156.

[66] *National Advocate*, April 19, 1819. Signed "Croaker & Co."

[67] The *Post*, April 20, 1819. Signed "Croaker & Co."

[68] This preface Evert Duyckinck quoted in commenting on the poem in his
Cyclopaedia of American Literature, II, 208. Halleck, in writing to Duyckinck,
who in 1866 was contemplating a new edition of his *Cyclopaedia*, explained
that "the preface 'To Simon' was Coleman's nonsense," and desired it
omitted from any future edition (see the letter to Duyckinck, dated May 13,
1866, preserved in the Duyckinck Collection of the New York Public Library).

[69] The *Post*, May 1, 1819. The poem is signed "Croaker & Co."

[70] For biographies of Cobbett, see the sketch in the *Dictionary of National
Biography*, and C. D. H. Cole, *Life of William Cobbett* (London [1924]).

[71] While in America Cobbett continued to publish his famous *Register*, each
week sending the copy to England.

[72] *The Croakers* (Bradford ed.), pp. 157 and 159.

and America,[73] now became a fitting target for the Croakers. Coleman in the *Post* for April 27, stated that "An Epistle from Croaker to Cobbett" had been received and should soon appear. But Halleck was not the only rhymester at that moment at work on the subject. Before inserting Halleck's satire, Coleman reprinted[74] from the *Baltimore Federal Gazette* verses "Inscribed to Wm. Cobbett, Author, Farmer, Seeds-Monger, and Anti-Borough Monger." This he introduced with the promise that the satire of "Croaker & Co." on Cobbett should appear the following day, and suggested that the reader might amuse himself with the comparison of the two poems. On May 1, Halleck's verses were printed. As usual, Halleck's lines both in meter and other phases of verse-technique, excelled those of his rival. The crudity of the latter's work may be readily perceived.

> Ring the bells of Christ Church steeple!
> Listen, all ye market-people!
> Cobbett here his servant sends,
> Horse-dealers, clear the Market space,
> To Hamme ton [*sic*] give up the place,
> While "the seeds" for cash he vends.

Halleck's satire in this case is not unmixed with a certain bitterness which is largely absent from the work of the Baltimore rhymester. Halleck's final stanza sums up his attitude to Cobbett.

> In recompense, that you've designed to make
> Choice of our soil above all other lands,
> A purse we'll raise to pay your debts, and take
> Your unsold Registers all off your hands.
> For this we ask that you, for once, will show
> Some gratitude, and, if you can, be civil;
> Burn all your books, sell all your pigs, and go—
> No matter where—to England, or the devil!![75]

[73] In 1797 Cobbett had aroused Philip Freneau who attacked the editor of the *Gazette* in a satire. See E. Duyckinck, *Cyclopaedia of American Literature*, I, 332.

[74] The *Post*, April 30, 1819. The poem is signed "Croak." Other Croaker imitations published during April included lines "To Croaker, the Witty Satirist in the New-York Evening Post" (The *Post*, April 7). In the *Post* for April 20, Coleman expressed irritation that a correspondent in the *Utica Patriot* should sign his effusions "Croaker"—a step he designated as "very improper and indelicate." For other imitations of and references to *The Croakers* during April, see the *National Advocate* for April 5 and 21, and the *New York American* for April 9.

[75] Cobbett is several times mentioned in Horace and James Smith's *Re-*

It was undoubtedly during the latter part of April or the first week in May that the identity of "Croaker & Co." was revealed to Coleman. In republishing on May 8 Halleck's stanzas to "Twilight,"[76] Coleman gave among his reasons for reprinting the verses the fact that he had just discovered the poem to be the work of Croaker. As "Twilight" had originally borne the initials "F.G.H.," it is evident that by May 8 Coleman was aware of at least one of the parties in the Croaker project, and there is no reason to suppose that he was unacquainted with the other.

Wilson has related the story of the first meeting of Coleman and the two poets. When Drake and Halleck had at length decided to reveal their secret to the editor, they called at Coleman's residence in Hudson Street. After the door had been "closed and locked," Drake said, " 'I am Croaker, and this gentleman, sir, is Croaker, Junior.' Coleman stared at the young men with indescribable and unaffected astonishment,—at length exclaiming, 'My God, I had no idea that we had such talent in America.' "[77] Bryant, who was associated with Coleman on the *Post* for some years before assuming complete charge of the paper, has further described the interview between the editor and the poets. Coleman once told Bryant that when Drake and Halleck came before him, he "was greatly struck by their appearance. Drake looked the poet; you saw the stamp of genius in every feature. Halleck had the aspect of a satirist."[78] But the two poets charged Coleman not to reveal their identity,[79] and the authorship of *The Croakers* continued to remain a secret to the general public.

During the month of May, Coleman printed but two *Croakers*. Of "A Loving Epistle to Mr. Wm. Cobbett" mention has already been made. Drake's famous poem to "The American Flag"[80] was the next *Croaker* to be published. These verses illustrate very well the manner in which Drake and Halleck collaborated on these sketches. When Drake had finished the poem, he was unsatisfied with the four concluding lines,

---

jected Addresses. In the same authors' *Horace in London* "Ode XIX" (Book II) is addressed to Cobbett. For the Smith brothers' influence on *The Croakers*, see pp. 83–84.

[76] Appeared originally in the *Post* for October 13, 1818.

[77] *Life*, p. 217.

[78] *Some Notices of the Life and Writings of Fitz-Greene Halleck*, p. 11.

[79] Wilson, *Life*, p. 217.

[80] The *Post*, May 29, 1819. Signed "Croaker & Co."

> And fixed as yonder orb divine
> That saw thy bannered blaze unfurled,
> Shall thy proud stars resplendent shine,
> The guard and glory of the world.

"Fitz, can't you suggest a better stanza?" he asked. Whereupon Halleck sat down and composed at once the lines as we now have them in the poem.[81] For some years subsequent to the publication of the verses the poem passed as Halleck's in literary circles. William Leggett, a poet and journalist of some distinction in New York, was among the first to restore to Drake the credit of writing "The American Flag," as well as to indicate Halleck's precise share in the poem. In the *Critic*,[82] one of the many short-lived periodicals which the early Knickerbocker school produced, Leggett published a sketch of Drake in which he asserted that he had it "from Halleck's own lips, that all his share in" "The American Flag" was "the four concluding lines."[83] Leggett's statement is further substantiated by the original manuscript, which is preserved in a notebook called *Trifles in Rhyme*, owned for many years by Drake's nephew, C. Graham Tillou.[84] This manuscript shows distinctly the last four lines of the poem canceled, and below in Halleck's hand the verses as they were finally printed.[85]

All of *The Croakers* which now followed were composed either wholly or in part by Halleck. "The Forums"[86] presented a humorous picture of a local debating society, mildly satiric in its exposure of the empty bombast of the members.

> Heaven bless 'em—for their generous pity
> Toil'd hard to light our darken'd city,

---

[81] Wilson, *Life*, p. 225.   [82] Founded by Leggett in 1828.

[83] *Critic*, I, 353 (April 4, 1829).

[84] Tillou tells of his possession of this notebook in a letter to Evert A. Duyckinck, dated December 6, 1867, in the New York Public Library. *Trifles in Rhyme* is now in the Henry E. Huntington Library and Art Gallery.

[85] A facsimile of the manuscript of this poem was printed in the *Century Magazine*, LXXX, 442 (July, 1910), in an article on Drake by J. G. Wilson.

[86] By Halleck in the *Post* for June 4, 1819. Signed "Croaker & Co." A notice of a meeting of the Forum appeared in the *National Advocate* for March 12, 1819: "Forum—An interesting question is to be debated this evening; and as the forum [sic] is principally attended by those who do not visit the theatre, there is reason to expect a crowded audience." For another reference to the Forum, see Halleck's *Fanny*, stanza 54 (1839 ed.).

> With that firm zeal that never flinches;
> And long, to prove the love they bore us,
> With *more last words* they linger'd o'er us,
> And like a tom-cat, died by inches.[87]

"The Ode to Fortune,"[88] beginning with the lines,

> Fair lady with the bandag'd eye!
> I'll pardon all thy scurvy tricks,

which was the result of collaboration, was published by Coleman on June 9. A few days later Halleck's verses on "The Love of Notoriety" appeared in the *Post*.[89] As the original title was followed by the designation "No. 1," the poet obviously intended another satire on the same subject; but a second installment was never printed.

A joint sketch by the poets was contributed to the *Post* of June 17. "An Ode to Simeon De Witt, Esquire, Surveyor-General"[90] embodied a clever hit at the indolence and pedantry of this public official. The naming of the western district of the state had been left to De Witt's judgment. "Finding the Indian appellations too sonorous and poetical, and that his own ear was not altogether adapted for the musical combination of syllables, this gentleman hit upon a plan. . . . It was no other than selecting from Lemprière and the British Plutarch, the great names which those works commemorate. This plan he executed with the most ridiculous fidelity, and reared for himself an everlasting monument of pedantry and folly."[91]

The fourth and last of Halleck's poetical epistles "To E. Simpson, Esq."[92] appeared in the *Post* of June 29. In these verses the suggestion was made to Mr. Simpson that he employ certain gentlemen of politics, then famous in the public eye, for the important *rôles* in his plays. For example, the poets[93] remark

> How nicely now would S—— [94] fit
> For "Overreach" and "Bajazet,"

[87] Last stanza.
[88] Signed "Croaker & Co."
[89] June 15, 1819. Signed "Croaker & Co."
[90] Signed "Croaker & Co."
[91] From the preface to the poem, possibly from the pen of Coleman.
[92] Signed "Croaker & Co." The Bradford edition gives the date of appearance of this poem incorrectly as June 20.
[93] Drake also had a hand in this paper.
[94] The Bradford edition undertook to fill in the dashes. "S——" stands for Judge Ambrose Spencer [see *Appletons' Cyclopaedia of American Biography* (New York, 1898), V, 627].

V—— B——,[95] tricky, sly, and thin,
Would make a noble "Harlequin."
C——[96] would play King Dick the surly,
The learned "Pangloss," and grave "Lord Burleigh";
——[97] (whose name the Muse shall hallow),
Is quite at home in "Justice Shallow,"
And slippery, smooth-faced T——[98] stands
A "Joseph Surface" at your hands.

This method, frequently practiced in *The Croakers*, of indicating the names of important persons by the initial and dash served, of course, a double purpose. It freed the poets and Mr. Coleman from any accusation of libel; and at the same time gave the public, in an attempt to solve the riddle, an opportunity to exert its ingenuity.

Like Drake's "American Flag," Halleck's verses "To *****"[99] beginning with the lines,

> The world is bright before thee,
> Its summer flowers are thine,

were among the few serious poems included in the *Croaker* series. The poem shows the obvious influence of Thomas Moore, as was observed by Coleman, who, in the prefatory note, suggested that "the reader of taste" would undoubtedly recognize in the stanzas "the plaintive tenderness of the author of Lalla Rookh." The poem was addressed to Miss Eliza McCall,[100] a singer of Halleck's acquaintance, for whom in 1817 he had written some lines to the tune

---

[95] Van Buren.   [96] De Witt Clinton; see p. 158.

[97] John Woodworth, according to the Bradford edition. Woodworth was a well-known jurist of New York state. See Francis S. Drake, *Dictionary of American Biography* (Boston, 1872), pp. 1004–1005.

[98] James Tallmadge, a New York state politician (see *Appleton's Cyclopaedia of American Biography*, VI, 26).

[99] The *Post*, July 7, 1819. Signed "Croaker & Co." Several imitations of *The Croakers*, published in the *Post* during June, may be noted. "To Mr. Croaker," signed "Joker," appeared on June 3, and on June 10 "To Croaker & Co.," signed "Fortune." Verses "To Croaker," with the signature of "Jew Venal, Jun.," were also printed on June 23; and another series of verses on the same subject, without a title but signed "Butler," appeared on June 26. The *National Advocate* (June 18) published lines in ridicule of Drake's "American Flag," but in an editorial note asserted that "ridicule is not the test of truth, and Croaker's American Flag is a very superior production."

[100] Wilson, *Life*, pp. 184 ff.

of "Jessie of Dunblane."[101] This *Croaker* to Miss McCall was Halleck's second published poem to be included in the collected edition of 1827.

"The Council of Appointment," a *Croaker* in which Drake and Halleck each had a share, appeared next in the columns of the *Post*.[102] As a piece of political machinery, this council readily lent itself to the humorous and satirical thrusts of the young poets. Halleck's sketch "Curtain Conversations"[103] was the last[104] of the published *Croakers*. This poem, which appeared in the 1827 edition under the title "Domestic Happiness," and the lines to Miss McCall to which we have already referred, were the only *Croakers* that Halleck deemed worthy of a place in the early collected volumes of his works.

In September, 1819,[105] a collection of *The Croakers*[106] was published in New York. This small pamphlet of thirty-six pages was issued surreptitiously, and had the sanction neither of Coleman nor of the two poets. Halleck once said of the volume that it was "more or less imperfect, although generously improved by additions from other and unknown sources."[107] The poet here did not refer to additions made to the text itself, as the reprinting of the poems from the *Post* was, for the most part, accurately done. His

[101] "Drake also wrote two songs for the same young lady, whom both the young poets greatly admired . . . " says Wilson. "The songs are included in Drake's poems, where they appear with the titles 'To a lady on hearing her sing "Cushlamachree"' and 'To a lady with a withered violet'" (*Life*, p. 185).

[102] July 16, 1819. Bradford edition gives the date incorrectly as July 19. Signed "Croaker & Co."

[103] The *Post*, July 24, 1819. Signed "Croaker & Co."

[104] The remaining poems printed as *Croakers* in the Bradford edition and in the 1869 edition of Halleck's poems, so far as can be ascertained, were not published at this period. Many of them are in the spirit of *The Croakers*, and were for that reason obviously printed as such in the editions named; but most of them do not belong to that series of poems which began in the *Post* on March 10, 1819, and closed on July 24. A few of the poems which are contained in the final pages of the Bradford edition may date from the *Croaker* period, but the manuscripts of these are now inaccessible, and no early printed versions have been discovered.

[105] Wilson, *Bryant and His Friends*, p. 300.

[106] The title-page reads, "Poems by Croaker, Croaker & Co., and Croaker, Jun. As published for the Reader . . . New York, 1819." A copy of this rare book is in the Yale Collection of American Literature. The poems from this edition were reprinted on pp. 498–507 of Waldie's Octavo Library, No. 22, for May 31, 1836. A copy of this reprint is in the New York Public Library.

[107] Wilson, *Life*, pp. 390–391.

reference was to two poems, not genuine *Croakers,* which were
added to the collection. The first of these was the imitation addressed "To Prince Croaker"[108] and signed "Falstaff." The other
was Halleck's poem to "Twilight," which, we have seen, Coleman
had revealed as the work of Croaker. Only twenty-five out of the
thirty-five genuine *Croakers* were here preserved. The satires were
not arranged in chronological order, nor does any conscious plan
of classification appear to have guided the unknown editor. No
contemporary reference to this pirated edition has come to light,
and the chances are that it had almost no circulation.

In addition to the publication in the daily papers of innumerable imitations of the satires, the genuine *Croakers* were frequently
reprinted in newspapers and periodicals of the period. As early as
April 5 Coleman reported that the poems had begun to make their
appearance in the *Washington Gazette.*[109] About a month later another Washington paper, the *National Register,* in reprinting some
of *The Croakers,* described them as "possessing much nerve and vivacity," and the author as holding "a pen quite as satirical and more
chaste than Peter Pindar."[110] The *National Intelligencer,* wishing
to acquaint its readers with *The Croakers,* introduced a specimen
with the remark that "the New-York Wits have for some time employed themselves in beguiling the tedious time, enlivening the dul-
ness of the newspapers, and blunting the point of electioneering vio-
lence, by a series of Pindaric Odes not inferior in style to the best
of Peter Pindar's, nor less caustic in their application."[111] But contemporary comment was not all so gracious and laudatory. A critic
in the *Hudson Whig* expressed his indignation that "The American Flag" should have been so widely "republished throughout the
United States," and further intimated that the most respectable
newspapers of the day were printing "compositions, both native
and exotic, in the *extremest* style of tumid fustian."[112] During the
early part of May appeared what was probably the first book to

---

[108] Printed in the *Post* for March 29.　　[109] The *Post.*
[110] *Ibid.,* May 1, 1819.　　[111] *Ibid.,* May 3, 1819.
[112] *Ibid.,* July 9, 1819. The *Port Folio,* a periodical published in Philadelphia, also reprinted three of *The Croakers.* "To ——, Esquire" and "An Abstract of the Surgeon-General's Report" appeared in the number for May,
1819 (VII [fourth series], 439); "A Loving Epistle to Mr. William Cobbett"
in that of the following month (VII, 524). The *Analectic Magazine* published
"The world is bright before thee" in the issue of August, 1819 (XIV, 168).

contain a reference to *The Croakers*. Henry T. Farmer, a native of England, who was studying medicine in New York at this time, published in 1819 a volume called *Imagination; the Maniac's Dream and Other Poems*. The collection included "An Essay on Taste: Dedicated to Dr. J. W. Francis, Professor of the Institutes of Medicine and Forensic Medicine in the University of New York,"—a work which a reviewer in the *New York Evening Post* called "the master poem of the volume," and added significantly: "This is a poem. It is, indeed."[113] These verses to Dr. Francis introduced near the beginning an address "To Croaker."[114]

> When last I saw your elfin muse,
> She smiled, and gaily beckon'd;
> And begg'd that I would not refuse
> Forthwith to be her second.
> I bow'd, and undertook the task,
> No whispering fiend was nigh;
> 'Tis hard when gentlewomen ask,
> For poets to deny.
> Oh! there was rapture in her laugh,
> Her eye—old Nick was in it;
> That intellectual telegraph
> Spoke volumes in a minute.[115]

The author at the close of his poem reverted to Croaker.

> All things must end, the poet says,
> But it excites my sorrow,
> To end my solitary lays,
> And leave New-York to-morrow.
>
> May she be blest with bright renown
> No jealousy provoke her,
> Unrivall'd as a trading town,
> Immortal for her Croaker.[116]

[113] May 4, 1819.

[114] A footnote in this curious work explains the word "Croaker" thus: "A satirical writer, whose poetical effusions are, at the time, enriching the gazettes and chronicles of the day; much to the merriment of our worthy 'Knickerbockers.'"

[115] *Imagination; the Maniac's Dream*, pp. 120–121.

[116] *Ibid.*, p. 143. A reference to Dr. Farmer may be found in Halleck's *Fanny*:

> Of Woodworth, Doctor Farmer, Moses Scott—
> Names hallow'd by their reader's sweetest smile.
> (Stanza 60; 1839 ed.)

The references to *The Croakers* during the five or six years after
their publication are of value in reflecting the sensation which these
satires produced in the heyday of their popularity. For a year or
more after the poems had ceased to appear, the newspapers continued to allude in various ways to the series of satires. Coleman
in the *Post* for August 3 complained of "some foolish lines in the
Columbian of last evening, signed Croaker & Co." which, he adds,
"we merely notice as an imposition." Again in the same paper we
find a brief mention of Croaker in an "Ode to the Sable Regiment
Who Daily Sweep Our Streets."

> Friends of the world! around your brows divine
> Immortal Croaker shall a wreathe entwine.[117]

Another curious allusion to Croaker was made in an issue of the
same paper during the following year. In a whimsical letter to Mr.
Coleman, an anonymous Blue-Stocking, who signed her name as
"Judith Tippit," railed rather bitterly against the male sex in
general, but concluded her epistle with a statement of her intention
to propose for election to her society at the next meeting, the name
of "Croaker, Esquire, as an honorary member."[118]

Opinions of *The Croakers* expressed by the American *literati*
from 1820 to 1825 include those of Paulding, Cooper, and Neal.
James K. Paulding, whose attention for some years had been directed almost wholly to satire and burlesque, in 1818 attempted a
serious narrative poem. "The Backwoodsman," the story of a man
who sought in the West the rehabilitation of health and fortune,
was at once derided by the critics. A certain reference to "a stately
cabbage,"[119] introduced into the poem as a "Homeric simile," gave
the critics of Paulding untold delight. The passage naturally served
as a ready target for the Croakers. In the verses "To John Minshull" Paulding was mentioned as "the poet of cabbages";[120] and
in the address "To ——, Esquire," we find the lines,

> Rogers shall hash us an olla podrida
> And the best of *"fat cabbage"* from Paulding we'll buy.[121]

---

[117] August 12, 1819.   [118] March 14, 1820.

[119]
> So have I seen in garden rich and gay
> A stately cabbage waxing fat each day;
> Unlike the lively foliage of the trees,
> Its stubborn leaves ne'er wave in summer breeze.
>
> *The Backwoodsman* (New York, 1818), p. 40.

[120] *The Croakers* (Bradford ed.), p. 26.

[121] *Ibid.*, p. 48. Both these poems were the work of Drake.

But these jests, penned in the spirit of innocent fun, appear to have given to Paulding no little annoyance. In a letter to Washington Irving, Paulding alluded bitterly to the clever sallies of Croaker.

My unfortunate poem has been over and over again attacked by the combined powers of wit and dullness, the former led by a wicked wag called *Croaker,* the latter by our old friend H.,[122] who I believe can't forgive me for beating him with his own weapons.[123]

James Fenimore Cooper by 1822 had written two novels, *The Precaution* and *The Spy*. In arranging for the publication in England of his next work, *The Pioneers,* he employed his friend Halleck, about to set sail for Europe, to convey a portion of the manuscript to Mr. Benjamin W. Coles, who was to oversee the publication of the work abroad. In writing to Washington Irving, who was then in Europe, and whose guidance Cooper sought in adjusting the final details with the publisher, the novelist referred to Halleck as "the admirable Croaker."[124] This brief phrase summed up what pages could scarcely have done, the esteem in which Cooper held *The Croakers* and one of their authors.

John Neal, an American author of several novels, desiring to try his literary fortunes abroad, went to England in 1824. To *Blackwood's Edinburgh Magazine* he subsequently contributed a series of articles on American writers, which were perhaps the most egotistical, inaccurate, and slovenly pieces ever admitted to a reputable journal. At the close of the series the author boasts of having prepared his sketches without the aid of a single note (except in one or two instances)—a thing, he ingenuously adds, "which was never attempted before."[125] Neal's comments on Croaker exhibit the same inattention to truth which characterizes his estimates of other American writers. He describes the satires as possessing "more unaffected pleasantry, and real wit, by far, than any transatlantic rhymer of whom we have heard." The following passage, taken from the author's succeeding remarks on Croaker, would be difficult to match for hopeless inaccuracy and unabashed egotism.

[122] This probably refers to Halleck. See pp. 94 ff.
[123] William Paulding, *Literary Life of James K. Paulding* (New York, 1867), p. 95. The letter is dated January 20, 1820.
[124] Pierre Irving, *Life and Letters of Washington Irving* (New York, 1862), II, 74. The letter is dated July 30, 1822.
[125] XVII, 204 (February, 1825).

We do not know this writer's [Croaker's] true name. Near the same time, too, another person appeared, in the same paper, (much to the credit of Dr. Coleman, whose paper was one of the last, into which we should have looked for anything of the kind) and threw off, somehow or other, in conjunction with Croaker, a magnificent piece, to an American Eagle. Would that we knew *his* name! He is dead, we believe; we have been promised a manuscript of his[126] by John M'Lean, a judge of New York, who, we hope, will take the hint. Extravagant as the piece was; and although some of the Eagle part was taken from Neal's Battle of Niagara[127]—which is made up, as he himself owns, of "eagles, rainbows, plumes and stars,"—yet was it enough to prove that the author of it had more poetry in his blood, than forty thousand Pauldings, Eastburns, Bryants, Percivals, and Spragues of the day.[128]

Public opinion regarding *The Croakers* from 1825 to the time of Halleck's death in 1867 presents little change in critical attitude. A few of these comments, however, as made by Halleck's friends, are worthy of note. William Leggett, in an article on the poet in the *New York Mirror,* a periodical edited by George P. Morris, expressed merely the conventional view, when he said that *The Croakers* were "a series of Pindaric odes, in which the follies and extravagances of society were lashed with infinite pleasantry and humour."[129] Little is added to this estimate by Bryant's slightly more elaborate comment on the series. These poems he described in 1836 as examples of the "happy use of the familiar topicks of the day," and added that without a consideration of *The Croakers,* "we might miss some of the peculiar characteristicks of his [Halleck's] genius."[130] Edgar Allan Poe alone departed from the beaten track of convention in calling "Halleck's *Croakers* local and ephemeral."[131] On another occasion he characterized them as satires whose "political and personal features" "gave them a consequence and a notoriety to which they are entitled on no other account. They are not without a species of drollery, but are loosely and no doubt carelessly written."[132]

[126] Probably a copy of "The Culprit Fay" which was being circulated in manuscript at this time.

[127] Neal's articles were, of course, published anonymously. His *Battle of Niagara and Other Poems* had appeared in 1818.

[128] XVI, 565 (November, 1824).   [129] V, 226 (January 26, 1828).

[130] *New York Mirror*, XIV, 97 (September 24, 1836).

[131] *Southern Literary Messenger*, XV, 189 (March, 1849)—from a review of Lowell's *Fable for Critics*.

[132] *Godey's Magazine and Lady's Book*, XXXIII, 13 (July, 1846).

Such was the vague and wholly uncritical attitude expressed toward *The Croakers,* after their contemporary popularity had begun to fade. This was in part the result of the low ebb of American criticism during the first part of the nineteenth century. With the single exception of the work of Poe, there was almost nothing that could be called at this period rational criticism. But even Poe, in estimating the literary value of *The Croakers,* failed in fundamental appreciation of the poems. Like others, he appears to have relied more or less upon traditional evidence and garbled versions instead of examining the satires for himself. But Poe's negligence in this respect was not entirely his fault. The texts of the poems as a whole were at this period practically inaccessible. Files of the *New York Evening Post* were then, as now, not easy to obtain; and the pirated edition of the satires published in 1819 had long since become an unknown book. It was not until 1860 that the Bradford Club issued the first complete edition of *The Croakers.*

The question may well be asked, When was the authorship of *The Croakers* first made known to the general public? Never, so far as we know, did the poets reveal themselves as the authors, except to their most intimate friends. Bryant once remarked of the satires that they were "never publickly acknowledged," but were "attributed to him [Halleck] by universal consent."[133] The poets chose from the beginning to conceal their names from the public; and we have noted how even Coleman was for a time mystified by his unknown correspondents. But it is not impossible to understand the reason for this reticence on the part of the poets. The early years of the century in American literature were a period when anonymous publication was fashionable. The authors of the *Salmagundi* papers (1807–8) had withheld their names from the public. Many of Paulding's works were printed without his name on the title-page;[134] and during the years 1819–20 Washington Irving was publishing his *Sketch Book* under the pseudonym of Geoffrey Crayon. Drake and Halleck, then, in signing their work "Croaker and Co." were simply following a fashion which in their day had become well established. At the same time, much of the thrill in publication both for the authors and the public was derived from the fact that the authors were unknown. Judging from

---

[133] *New York Mirror*, XIV, 97 (September 24, 1836).
[134] For example, *The Lay of the Scottish Fiddle* (1813) and *Letters from the South, Written during an Excursion in the Summer of 1816* (1817).

a remark which Halleck made to his sister,[135] it may be supposed
that at least one of the poets fancied himself emulating the fame of
the mysterious Junius. But a second, more powerful motive mili-
tating against a disclosure of the authorship, may be found in the
extremely personal character of much of the satire. Even Coleman,
we have seen, found it best to mitigate the irritated feelings of his
rival editor, Lang; and doubtless others were smarting under the
lash of *The Croakers.*[136] Then, too, Halleck who was of a retiring
disposition, was naturally reluctant to disclose his name to those
whom he had successfully ridiculed.[137]

But in spite of the precautions which were taken to conceal the
names of the poets, the secret eventually leaked out. It is undoubtedly true that the occasion which witnessed the first interview between Coleman and the young poets, carried with it the seeds of a
complete revelation of the mystery. The editor himself appears, indeed, to have shown little discretion in keeping his part of the secret.
Coleman, it will be remembered, reprinted Halleck's lines ''To Twilight,'' which had previously appeared with the initials ''F.G.H.,''
and referred the poem definitely to Croaker. Thus the secret was
revealed to those who had ever associated with Halleck; and the
news was then in a way to spread quickly throughout the whole
town. It was perhaps this attention which Coleman drew to Halleck
that gave to that poet much of the credit for *The Croakers,* and
lessened the importance, in the public eye, of the part which Drake
had played in the project. By 1827, whatever doubt remained,
touching at least one party in the enterprise, was entirely removed
by the inclusion of two of *The Croakers* in Halleck's first volume

---

[135] In a letter, already quoted, dated April 1, 1819. See p. 63.

[136] Samuel B. H. Judah actually spent a period in the city jail for his
libelous statements in an anonymous pamphlet, *Gotham and the Gothamites*
(New York, 1823). See Thomas R. Lounsbury, *James Fenimore Cooper* (Boston, 1882), p. 60.

[137] The following anecdote, related by Henry T. Tuckerman, illustrates at
once the sensitive and kindly disposition of Halleck: ''A venerable and life-
long friend of the poet told me, with much feeling, that, at the time of the
Croaker effusions, one hit him rather hard: thirty years after, Halleck called
on him to disclaim the authorship. 'I knew you gave me the credit of the satire,' he said, 'and it pained me that you should think me capable of wounding
the feelings of an old friend; but I bore the imputation silently till to-day,
when for the first time, I felt at liberty to right myself with you: the author
of that squib is just dead!' '' (*Lippincott's Monthly Magazine,* I, 210 [Feb-
ruary, 1868]).

of collected works. *Alnwick Castle with Other Poems* appeared anonymously, but by the year 1827 many of the poems included in the volume had become well known as the work of Halleck, and there was no doubt concerning the authorship of the book.[138]

Uncertainty continued, however, as to the relative distribution of the work done on *The Croakers*, as well as to the authorship of the individual papers. Owing both to Coleman's indiscreet exposure of Halleck and to the rapid rise of that poet's reputation after the death of Drake in 1820, Halleck received by far the greater honor for the satires. William Leggett, we have noted, sought to restore to its rightful author "The American Flag," which was fast becoming identified with the name of Halleck.[139] But Poe, like many other critics, appeared ignorant of the general situation of authorship when he claimed for Halleck the chief responsibility for the series.[140] Besides restoring the original signatures to the satires, the Bradford edition did little to distinguish between the work of the two poets.[141] Halleck, in fact, was always reluctant to reveal the authorship of the individual papers. On one occasion, he wrote to a friend that he had never deemed his "portion of them worthy of recollection."[142] To the urgent request of another friend, however, Halleck yielded in so far as to indicate in pencil on the table of contents of the Bradford edition the precise authorship of the papers, but added that he had done so for his friend's "exclusive information."[143] In 1869 the final collected edition of Halleck's works was published. Here a complete text of *The Croakers* was printed, and the initials "H" and "D," probably supplied by the friend for whom seven years before he had disclosed the authorship, identified the individual papers.

The care taken by the authors of *The Croakers* to insure secrecy for themselves reflects well the nature of the contemporary popu-

[138] Bryant, for example, in reviewing this volume for the *United States Review and Literary Gazette* for April, 1827 (II, 8), referred directly to Halleck as the author.

[139] *Critic*, I, 353 (April 4, 1829).

[140] *Graham's Magazine*, XXIII, 166 (September, 1843).

[141] Halleck was much disturbed at the inaccuracies contained in the notes of this edition. See Wilson, *Life*, p. 221.

[142] Letter from Halleck to R. Lawrence, dated August 4, 1858 (*ibid.*, p. 391).

[143] Letter from Halleck to B. Winthrop, dated December 29, 1862 (*ibid.*, p. 223).

larity which they attained. It was, of course, a reputation based rather on clever wit and persiflage than on any essential poetic merit. Dealing in the material of personal jest and innuendo, *The Croakers* naturally responded to the libelous and scandalous instincts of the popular mind. But it is also true that however corrupt may have been the pleasure which the public derived from these pieces, the satires were penned in the spirit of ingenuous playfulness. That nonchalant, carefree manner that we find in *Salmagundi* and in *Knickerbocker's History of New York* had already become a prevailing mood in early New York literature.[144] If folly and pretense could not be exposed by serious denunciation, they might for a time be dispelled by laughter. If not by laughter—then why disturb the mind by philosophic meditation? Critical to a marked degree was the Knickerbocker mind, but not reflective. It sensed evil with acumen, but found no remedy for it in rational speculation. It recognized a moral obligation, but was unwilling to fulfil that obligation except in terms of merriment and laughter. The early Knickerbocker writers were in short "laughing philosophers."[145] Thus Drake and Halleck saw the pseudo-great man, marked the sly, scheming politician, looked blandly on at party wrangling, and eyed the empty pomp and vulgarity of the *nouveau riche*. And the laughter of *The Croakers* was the result—pure, hearty, wholesome laughter.

> There's fun in everything we meet,
>   The greatest, worst, and best;
> Existence is a merry treat,
>   And every speech a jest.[146]

*   *   *

[144] Even as late as 1863, when much of the youthful exuberance of the Knickerbockers had faded, we find in one of the leading New York magazines these significant words: "*Carpe diem!* I prefer the Horatian to the ascetic philosophy, always. Because we have to die, is that a reason why we should not live? It is common, at sunrise, to moralize upon the night that is to come. Why not exult in the more immediate joys of noontide?" (Editor's Table in the *Knickerbocker*, LXI, 185 [February, 1863]).

[145] "We are laughing philosophers, and clearly of opinion, that wisdom, true wisdom, is a plump, jolly dame, who sits in her arm-chair, laughs right merrily at the farce of life and takes the world as it goes" (*Salmagundi*, January 24, 1807).

[146] "The Man Who Frets at Worldly Strife," stanza 2. *The Croakers* (Bradford ed.), p. 27.

> For us, enthron'd in elbow chair,
> Thy foes alone with ink we sprinkle,
> We love to smoothe the cheek of care,
> Until we have no furrow there
> Save laughter's evanescent wrinkle.[147]

But this characteristic disposition of the Knickerbockers was not wholly responsible for *The Croakers*. The verses may be said to have had their prototypes and models in the work of two English satirists of the late eighteenth and early nineteenth centuries.[148] That critical age that gave to England Alexander Pope, produced toward the close of the same century a much less gifted satirist in Dr. John Wolcot, who wrote under the pseudonym of "Peter Pindar." Vain and scurrilous, Wolcot found much to mock and ridicule in the England of his day. The range of his satire appears to have been unlimited, and included even George III among its objects of attack. *The Croakers*, we have seen, were frequently compared to the work of Peter Pindar; and the comparison was not inapt, for both Drake and Halleck were undoubtedly steeped in the burlesque and satire of the period. Echoes of Wolcot appear occasionally in *The Croakers*. In the course of his notorious career as a satirist, Wolcot produced several series of "Odes" to the "Royal Academicians," which lampooned the work of well-known painters of the day. It may be that these satires suggested to Drake his lines on Trumbull's painting of "The Declaration of Independence."[149] But it was in the methods of satire rather than in subject that Peter Pindar influenced *The Croakers*. Occasionally Wolcot, in attacking an individual, would suggest some ridiculous or incongruous occupation as more fitting than the one in which he now engages. Take, for example, the stanza:

> Fie, Cosway! I'm ashamed to say
> Thou own'st the title of R.A.—

[147] "To Domestic Peace," stanza 5. *The Croakers* (Bradford ed.), p. 34.

[148] A. H. Smyth in his *Bayard Taylor* (Boston, 1896) says, "Imitation was the life and breath of the Knickerbocker literature" (p. 65).

[149] Take, for example, the following stanza from Wolcot's "Ode VI" (*Lyric Odes to the Royal Academicians, for the Year MDCCLXXXII*):

> Thy portraits, Chamberlin, may be
> A likeness, far as I can see;
> But faith! I cannot praise a single feature:
> Yet, when it so shall please the Lord,
> To make his people out of board,
> Thy pictures will be tolerable nature.

> I fear, to damn thee 'twas the devil's sending;
> Some honest calling quickly find,
> And bid thy wife her kitchen mind,
> Or shirts and shifts be making, or be mending.[150]

This method Drake and Halleck frequently employed, as in the lines "To Mr. Potter," "To Simon," and "To E. Simpson, Esq."[151] Again in the mock salutation prefacing Wolcot's lines to James Boswell[152] we note a slight similarity to the opening verses of Halleck's epistle to Cobbett:

> O Boswell, Bozzy, Bruce, whate'er thy name,
> Thou mighty shark for anecdote and fame;
> Thou jackall, leading lion Johnson forth,
> To eat M'Pherson 'midst his native North;
> To frighten grave professors, with his roar,
> And shake the Hebrides, from shore to shore—
> All hail![153]

But these echoes of Wolcot are after all but occasional, and one looks in vain in the work of Peter Pindar for the "laughing philosopher." His verses, on the whole, are bitter and abusive, and seem to have had their source rather in spleen than in genuine mirth. His satire is usually of a coarser grain than Drake's and Halleck's, and his wit heavier and often flatter. *The Croakers* took what they needed from the work of Wolcot, and rejected those elements that made Peter Pindar one of the most despised and hated men of his day.

---

[150] From "Ode VIII" (*Lyric Odes to the Royal Academicians, for the Year MDCCLXXXII*).

[151] The last epistle to Mr. Simpson which was printed in the *Post* for June 29, 1819.

[152] "A Poetical and Congratulatory Epistle to James Boswell, Esq."

[153] "A Loving Epistle to Mr. William Cobbett":

> Pride, boast, and glory of each hemisphere!
> Well known and loved in both—great Cobbett, hail!
> Hero of Botley there, and Hempstead here,
> Of Newgate, and a Pennsylvania jail!

Of Drake's and Halleck's debt to Wolcot, G. P. Lathrop has said: "They rhymed as easily as Peter Pindar, whom they were thought to rival. Perhaps it would be nearer the truth to say, they imitated. Something of their free-hand drawing they probably learned from that too industrious doctor; but they had wit enough of their own to give all the flavor of originality. At least they deserve great respect for not emulating the English satirist in the tenacity with which he maintained the habit of doggerel through a long life-time" (*Atlantic Monthly*, XXXIX, 720 [June, 1877]).

Nearer to the laughter of *The Croakers* is the work of James and Horatio Smith,[154] the authors of *Horace in London*.[155] The harmony existing between the two brothers that made possible these parodies of Horace was paralleled by the friendship of Drake and Halleck. The Smith brothers, who at first published their satires anonymously in the *Monthly Mirror*,[156] also appear to have been moved by a purpose similar to that of the authors of *The Croakers*. Unlike the coarse and scurrilous Peter Pindar, James and Horatio Smith produced work, for the most part, in a light, facetious vein. A town consciousness, too, pervades the poems of the Smiths. What Drake and Halleck did for New York in touching lightly the pretenses and follies of the town, the authors of *Horace in London* had done some years before for the English metropolis. Dealing with local institutions and characters, touching upon passing events of public interest, alluding intimately even to streets in the great city, *Horace in London* frequently suggests the satirical method which the Croakers were later to employ.[157]

The Smiths' "Tributary Stanzas to Grimaldi the Clown" sum up well the spirit in which the satires were written, and illustrate the closeness of feeling between *Horace in London* and *The Croakers*. The first stanza, for example, might well have served as a model for the opening lines of the verses "To Ennui":

> Facetious mime! thou enemy of gloom,
>   Grandson of Momus, blithe and debonnair,
> Who, aping Pan, with an inverted broom,
>   Can'st brush the cobwebs from the brows of care.[158]

[154] The Smith brothers were perhaps better known for their famous *Rejected Addresses* (1812). These *Addresses*, parodies of the work of famous writers of the day, probably had little influence on *The Croakers*.

[155] In a letter to his sister dated August 31 [1813], Halleck mentions sending home several books, one of which is *Horace in London* (see Wilson, *Life*, p. 143). These were books which undoubtedly he had read, and was passing on to his sister.

[156] The satires were collected in 1813 under the title of *Horace in London*.

[157] Epes Sargent's comment on *Horace in London* might, with almost equal truth, be applied to *The Croakers*: "Possessing but a fugitive interest, though sometimes the Latin text was ingeniously adapted to the characters and occurrences of the passing hour, these papers, in their collected form, had but a limited sale. They were re-published in this country on their original appearance, but the allusions in them have become obscure, and their merit would hardly justify their reproduction with the notes necessary to make them generally understood" [see *Rejected Addresses and Other Poems*, edited by Epes Sargent (New York, 1871), p. xiii].

[158] *Horace in London* (London, 1815), fourth edition, p. 42.

And in the last stanza of the same lyric we have an English statement of the philosophy of laughter.

> Long may'st thou guard the prize thy humour won,
> Long hold thy court in pantomimic state,
> And to the equipoise of English fun
> Exalt the lowly, and bring down the great.[159]

Further illustrations serve to point out an identity of mood between the two works. Chancing suddenly upon the verses "The Bumper Toast," one might well think he were reading *The Croakers.*

> Away with dull politics! prythee let's talk
> Of something to set all the club in a titter
> The aim of convivial meetings we baulk,
> When thus we our sweetest enjoyments embitter.[160]

The allusions to local characters and institutions in the following stanza at once suggest some of the clever felicities of *The Croakers:*

> Come, too, *Mendoza,* foe to ham,
> Whose fame no bruize can sully!
> Come, wary *Crib,* Batavian *Sam,*
> And last, not least, come *Gully.*
> Assuming the dictator's seat,
> Late to thy Plough in *Carey Street,*
> Return to end thy halcyon days:
> Long may'st thou rally, hit, and stop,
> And may no envious Newgate-drop
> Put out thy glory's blaze.[161]

Only uncritical enthusiasm would call *The Croakers* genuine poetry; and it is probable that their authors never thought of them as products of poetic genius.[162] *The Croakers* are memorable as constituting an engaging episode in early American journalism;[163] and

---

[159] *Horace in London,* p. 43.

[160] *Ibid.,* p. 85. Compare a similar idea developed in Drake's lines "To Domestic Peace."

[161] "Hurly Burly" in *Horace in London,* p. 21. A study of the verse-forms both of Peter Pindar and of the Smith brothers reveals possible metric and stanzaic influences on *The Croakers.*

[162] For Halleck's opinion of *The Croakers* as expressed late in life, see the letter addressed to S. Austin Allibone, p. 406.

[163] Of Coleman's exclamation when he first met Drake and Halleck, "My God, I had no idea we had such talents in America!" G. P. Lathrop has per-

as essentially journalistic work must they be judged. To the age
that produced them they were brilliant—far superior in wit and
workmanship to the verses usually admitted to the daily newspapers. To us, far removed from the events and characters which
they celebrate, the verses seem dull, often monotonous in tone; and
only as we reconstruct for ourselves the life of New York during
the early days of the nineteenth century, do we begin to catch
something of the flashing wit and wholesome good humor that so
pleased the contemporaries of Drake and Halleck. In the words of
Charles F. Johnson, "Light satire has never been written in America with more spirit and fluency."[164]

haps correctly said, "Only in the infancy of American journalism could so
ardent an expression have been wrested from a managing editor" (*Atlantic
Monthly*, XXXIX, 719).

[164] See *Proceedings at the Celebration of the 250th Anniversary of the
Settlement of Guilford, Conn.*, p. 103.

V

"FANNY"

1819

I

THE novelty of *The Croakers* had scarcely begun to wear off when Halleck turned with marked success to another form of satire. Purporting to be an imitation of Byron's "Beppo," *Fanny* retained enough of the town atmosphere of *The Croakers* to delight a New York audience. The story proper, which concerned the rapid rise into society of a poor merchant and his daughter, Fanny, gave the author ample opportunity to discourse lightly on the follies of the *nouveau riche;* while frequent digressions permitted crisp comments on contemporary politics and literature of local interest. Following in the wake of *The Croakers, Fanny* was well calculated to meet with immediate success.

The last twelve numbers of *The Croakers,* it will be remembered, were in large part the work of Halleck. The fact that the responsibility for the series had devolved more and more upon Croaker, Junior, was due, no doubt, to the declining health of Drake, who, toward the close of the year, undertook a horseback trip to the South.[1] Thus Halleck was deprived for a time of the companionship of Drake, and was obliged to turn his attention elsewhere. A second factor tending to change the mode of life to which Halleck had become accustomed in the city, was the sudden outbreak, early in September, of an epidemic of yellow fever.[2] The Corporation of the city soon passed a resolution providing for the removal of persons from the infected area.[3] Halleck, who was touched by this edict, retired to Bloomingdale, whence on October 11, 1819, he wrote to his sister:

The alarm about the fever has almost subsided. There are few cases, and the citizens generally would have long since returned to their original

[1] Wilson, *Life,* p. 241.
[2] *New York Evening Post,* September 6, 1819.
[3] *Ibid.,* September 14, 1819.

places of abode but for the interdiction of the Corporation. I imagine that the interdiction will not be taken off before the frosts of November. At any rate, it is probable that I shall continue at Bloomingdale till that time.[4]

Fanny, which had apparently been started in the summer, was now completed in the autumn during the period of Halleck's enforced idleness at Bloomingdale.[5] "To render my solitary hours less irksome," wrote the poet to his sister on January 1, 1820, "I have spun out the poem which I repeated to you last summer into a book of fifty pages. . . . I had no intention of publishing it, but the bookseller[6] who brought out Irving's 'Sketch Book,' offering to publish 'Fanny' in a style similar to that work, I consented to his doing so. . . . The bookseller stated to me that I was the only writer in America, Irving excepted, whose works he would risk publishing. This opinion was founded, of course, upon the popularity of 'The Croakers.' "[7]

Fanny appeared on December 27, 1819.[8] Halleck had little confidence in the success of his new poem. "I have, of course, heard nothing of its fate since I left New York," he wrote in the same letter to Maria, "but as the publisher seemed very sanguine in his expectation of its popularity, I hope, for his sake, as well as my own pride, though the author is unknown, that he will not be disappointed. He is binding a copy for you, which I shall forward immediately on my return. For my own part, I do not think much of the merits of the work, the plague of correcting the proof-sheets, etc., having put me out of conceit with it, and I fear that its localities will render it almost entirely uninteresting to you." After alluding to the popularity of *The Croakers,* Halleck continued, "I do not anticipate the same popularity for this work. 'The Croakers'

[4] Wilson, *Life,* p. 230. The quarantine was lifted on October 18, 1819 (see the *Post,* October 19, 1819).

[5] Wilson, *Life,* p. 231. William Leggett's assertion in the *New York Mirror,* V, 227 (January 26, 1828) that "it was but three weeks from the time the work was commenced until it issued from the press," appears to have no basis in fact.

[6] Charles Wiley.

[7] Wilson, *Life,* pp. 231–232. Written from Sandy Hill.

[8] The following advertisement appeared in the *Post* for that date: "C. Wiley and Co. No. 3 Wall Street, have this day published, Fanny, a poem, price 50 cents."

cost the public nothing, this costs them fifty cents, which will have, no doubt, an effect in limiting the number of readers.''[9]

On the same day that *Fanny* appeared, the *New York Evening Post* promised to review the poem in its columns.[10] The expected notice, which was printed about a week later, was profuse in its praise of the new work. After noting a similarity in the style of *Fanny* to that of ''Beppo,'' the reviewer[11] observed that ''the imitation will be found in most respects superior to the original. If the definition of wit, that it consists in bringing together unexpected resemblances in things supposed to be remote, is just, as I think it is, Fanny leaves Beppo at a very perceptible distance.'' The critic at once caught the likeness of *Fanny* to *The Croakers*. ''Although the author is not designated,'' he significantly remarked, ''few readers of the Evening Post, the past year, can be at much loss to conjecture that it comes from the same quarter that furnished the *petit morceus* [*sic*] that appeared under the signature of Croaker.'' ''I confine my remarks to the literary merit of this poem alone,'' concluded Coleman in his customary, cautious manner, ''and do not mean to be understood as lending the sanction of the E[vening] P[ost] to one word of the satire, further than to say, that I think it sportive but not malicious.''[12]

The similarity in style between *Fanny* and *The Croakers* was recognized even by critics outside of New York. A reviewer in the *Analectic Magazine*, a periodical published in Philadelphia, of which Washington Irving had once been the editor,[13] commented on the relationship of *Fanny* to the earlier series of satires.[14] The poem, wrote the critic, ''is attributed to the pen of one of those gentlemen who have amused the public with the lively *jeux d'esprit* in the newspapers under the signature of *Croaker & Co.* The present production is only a more prolonged effort, or rather a more prolonged indulgence in the same humorous style. The total absence of the appearance of effort, and the graceful ease and vivacity of the versification, forms, indeed, one of its most pleasing characteristics.'' It is natural, however, that the Philadelphia critic should have failed

---

[9] Wilson, *Life*, p. 232.
[10] December 27, 1819.   [11] Probably William Coleman.
[12] January 6, 1820.   [13] From 1812 to 1815.
[14] The *Analectic Magazine* for August, 1819, had reprinted the *Croaker*, ''The world is bright before thee.''

to appreciate the "local allusions," which, he remarked, "are frequent, and appear (we understand) extremely piquant and diverting to those who comprehend their full force."[15] Among several extracts from the poem were the lines on Weehawken, which the reviewer reprinted with the comment that "the author forgets himself sometimes and betrays the true poet in spite of his levity."[16]

By some odd chance a copy of *Fanny* found its way to Lexington, Kentucky, where appeared in the *Western Review*[17] a four-page article on the poem. The reviewer, unfavorable to the Knickerbocker taste for lampooning, complained that the satire was "much too rough," but admitted that "the spirit is good and the execution also. Stateliness and dignity he [the author] certainly does not possess, but they, who read with eagerness and ingenuous satisfaction the salt of Peter Pindar, will find Messrs. Croaker & Co. (if they are the authors) no less pointed and witty." The critic believed that "our author's imitation of Byron's style is admirable" but deplored the taste of an age that seeks its poetic pleasures rather in the "halting, hobling [sic] lines" of "his Lordship"[18] than in the harmonious numbers of "Milton, Thompson, and Pope." "The poem is in all respects deserving of commendation," concluded the reviewer, "except when it descends to personalities. That kind of writing is beneath an high-minded and honorable man, and superior genius seldom condescends to such meanness. We advise the author of Fanny to employ his muse upon subjects more worthy of her and we have no doubt she will do them ample justice."[19]

If the western reviewer found much to condemn in the personal quality of the satire, it was, of course, this very characteristic which gave "Fanny" its great local popularity—a popularity, indeed, far above the expectations of Halleck.[20] It was not long, if we may believe common report, before the first edition was entirely sold. "In a very short time," wrote an early biographer of Halleck, "there was not a single copy for sale; yet the demand was by no means

15 I (Second Series), 76 (January, 1820).

16 *Ibid.*, I, 80.

17 This periodical, edited by William Gibbes Hunt, ran from August, 1819, to July, 1821. For a history of the magazine, see Ralph L. Rusk, *The Literature of the Middle West* (New York, 1925), I, 165–167.

18 The lines on Weehawken were quoted as especially Byronic.

19 April, 1820. The review is signed "B."

20 Wilson, *Life*, p. 236.

exhausted. Halleck, however, would not consent to republish. In consequence, the book was lent by friend to friend; its scarcity made it equally sought for, and those who could not borrow, paid five dollars, and even more, for a single copy."[21] "Applying to my bookseller for a copy," wrote a contemporary of the poet, "he informed me that it was out of print and suppressed by the author,[22] as some of his friends suspected it of being personal, and perhaps vindictive—so, at least, understood in certain bankrupt circles."[23] The popular mind naturally attempted to attach a personal significance to Halleck's satire on the merchant and his daughter; but there is little evidence that Fanny and her father were drawn from models, although it is plain that both were drawn from life. "Everyone imagined that he knew the original, while in fact it was purely ideal,"[24]—a generalized picture based upon many instances of the kind that had doubtless come within the range of the author's personal experience.[25]

Not long after the publication of *Fanny*, Halleck was called away to Albany on business for Jacob Barker. While stopping at a hotel in the city, Halleck was surprised one evening by the announcement of Governor Lewis that there was a satirical poem which he wished to read to those present. The governor straightway read *Fanny* to the people assembled in the lobby. "I laughed with the rest, as in duty bound," wrote Halleck to his sister, "till a Mr. Livingston, a senator with whom I was acquainted, came in. He believed me to be Croaker, and had heard that 'Fanny' was by the same pen. I observed him whisper to his neighbor, whose eye was then turned

---

[21] James Lawson in the *Southern Literary Messenger*, VIII, [2]42 (April, 1842).

[22] There is no evidence that this statement is correct.

[23] From a letter by "one of Halleck's contemporaries" (otherwise unnamed) written to J. G. Wilson, and published by him in the *Independent* for February 29, 1872.

[24] The *Southern Literary Messenger*, VIII, [2]42 (April, 1842).

[25] Halleck's note on *Fanny* in the 1869 edition of his poems (p. 371) is undoubtedly a bit of the poet's quaint humor so characteristic of his old age. "Of this young lady and her worthy father, to whose exemplary and typical career the author was indebted for the theme of his story, we are not permitted to reveal more than that they wish to be known and remembered only in the words from Milton, on the title-page, among

'Gay creatures of the element,
That in the colors of the rainbow live,
And play in the plighted clouds.' "

upon me, and I thought best to beat a retreat. On my entering the supper-room I was honored with the stare of every one, and seemed to attract as much attention as a Hottentot Venus. I left Albany next morning."[26] "Since my return," continued the poet, "I have hardly walked out at all, but am informed that among the nobility I am to be pointed out as a lion of the winter."[27] Halleck's shy and sensitive nature shrank instinctively from all public acclaim. "I have felt flattered only in one instance," he wrote at another time. "A person who could have no motive in deceiving me says that Brevoort told him that he should be prouder of being the author of *Fanny* than of any poetical work ever written in America. Brevoort was one of the original 'Salmagundi' concern,[28] and has deservedly the character of a man of extensive literary taste and knowledge. From him, therefore, a compliment is worth having."[29]

The curiosity of the public over the authorship of *Fanny* is further reflected in the publication of an inane and banal pamphlet entitled *Frank; or Who's the Croaker?* which was issued in 1820.[30] Apparently basing his halting verses on current rumor, the anonymous author discussed the activities of the Croakers, whom he designated as "Mr. Frank and Crony Tom."[31] Frank, we are told, is a broker, residing in Wall Street.[32] But aside from this hint of Halleck's occupation, there is nothing to indicate that the author possessed the slightest knowledge of who the Croakers really were. The general plan of the poem was undoubtedly suggested by *Fanny*, for frequent digressions on political and literary topics intrude themselves into the attenuated narrative. The verses conclude with a brief reference to *Fanny*:

> From *Tom* we soon may hear again,
> He has a most prolific brain;

[26] An anonymous contemporary of Halleck repeats substantially the same story in the *Independent*, February 29, 1872.

[27] Wilson, *Life*, pp. 233–234. The letter is undated.

[28] This is an error; no part of *Salmagundi* is now credited to Brevoort.

[29] Wilson, *Life*, p. 236. Letter to Miss Halleck, dated February 7, 1820.

[30] Published by George S. Wharam of New York. Copies of this rare pamphlet may be found in the library of the New York Historical Society, and in the Harris Collection of American Poetry at Brown University.

[31] *Frank; or Who's the Croaker?* p. 19.

[32] *Ibid.*, p. 8.

And better verses writes than many
For he the author is of Fanny.

It is not without interest to note that early Knickerbocker literature was conspicuously the work of young men who turned instinctively to satire as a means of amusing themselves and others.
Irving was twenty-six when he produced *A History of New York*
(1809); Samuel Woodworth twenty-seven when he published *Quarter Day* (1812). *The Lay of the Scottish Fiddle* was written by
Paulding at the age of thirty-five; and Halleck was about thirty
when *Fanny* was at the height of its popularity. It is significant
that the youthful exuberance of *Fanny* found an appreciative audience of young men even outside of New York. In 1818 several
young gentlemen of Boston, of whom William H. Prescott, later
the historian, appears to have been the leader, formed a social and
literary club. Wishing to display their literary talents, the members determined to issue a small periodical called the *Club-Room*,[33]
to which Halleck was also asked to contribute. *Fanny,* Prescott declared, was "of a higher order" than *The Croakers,* and he further asserted that "for its easy conversational wit, and poetry of
descriptions," *Fanny* "must go alongside of Lord Byron's and
Mr. Rose's productions in the same way." "It is the admiration
of your poetical talents," added the editor, "which has led me to
make this communication to you."[34] As the poet soon after remarked in a letter to Miss Halleck, "This is what one may call the
puff direct."[35] Halleck, however, who was usually indifferent to
contributing to periodicals at the request of editors, never availed
himself of the opportunity of writing for the *Club-Room*.[36]

Halleck received another "puff" in the form of verses addressed
"To Mr. Croaker of New York," and signed "Rob Raven." These
lines were written in the verse-form of *Fanny*, and affected something of the colloquial ease of Halleck's poem. *Fanny*, as it originally appeared, broke off abruptly at the close of the 124th stanza,
and was virtually without an ending. To this fact "Rob Raven"
alluded in his opening lines.

[33] George Ticknor, *Life of William H. Prescott* (Boston, 1864), pp. 52–53.
[34] Wilson, *Life*, p. 239. Prescott's letter is dated Boston, March 15, 1820.
[35] *Ibid.*, p. 237. Letter is undated.
[36] The periodical was discontinued after the fourth number.

I took up little "Fanny" t'other day,
   And with a deal of pleasure read it through—
And now, dear Sir, I feel concern'd to say,
   Just in a friendly manner, *entre nous,*
That tho' 'tis clear it was by genius penn'd,
It seems a thing most truly *without end.*

Begun entirely in a humorous and nonchalant vein, the verses ended in a serious attempt to arouse the muse of Halleck to more sustained and lofty flights.

Go to thy native glens—thy mountain scenes—
   And there seek inspiration—they shall tell
Where Nature o'er her silent glory leans,
   The fragrance and the might of feeling dwell,
There breathe in air thy "native wood-notes wild,"
And be, what thou may'st be, the Muse's favor'd child.[37]

These lines pleased Halleck who referred to them in a letter as "very pretty verses."[38]

Opinions of *Fanny* as expressed by Samuel Woodworth and James K. Paulding are of value in throwing further light upon the contemporary popularity of the poem. Woodworth had in 1819 started a periodical which he called the *Ladies' Literary Cabinet.* Halleck's sentimental lines "To the Horse Boat,"[39] placed in setting at once satiric and comic, attracted the editor's attention, and he selected the lyric for republication in his new magazine. In introducing the poem to his readers, Woodworth observed that "satirical poems are generally made up of local matter, and, of course, altogether uninteresting to persons remote from the scene of action. Its circulation is, therefore, principally confined to those who are acquainted with the popular and leading characters of the day, as

[37] The *New York Evening Post,* February 16, 1820, as reprinted from the *Philadelphia American Daily Advertiser.* The verses probably had a rather wide circulation, for they also appeared in the *National Advocate* for February 16, reprinted from the same Philadelphia paper.

[38] Wilson, *Life,* p. 237.

[39] A portion of this song, says Wilson (*ibid.,* p. 228), appeared in pencil on the flyleaf of a London edition of Coleridge's poems, dated 1803, and once owned by Halleck. It is probable that this lyric, and possibly others in *Fanny,* were composed at an earlier date than the body proper, and later incorporated in the poem. The edition of Coleridge's poems to which Wilson refers appeared as Item 71 in Halleck's library, sold on October 12, 1868.

relating to them alone. But it not infrequently happens that we find interwoven with the keenest satire, passages of the most beautiful poetry, and even these often pass off unnoticed because we seldom think of looking for anything exquisite in the pages of books of this stamp. We do not recollect of ever seeing the following lines from *Fanny* inserted in any public prints, although they merit the encomiums of the best of them.''[40]

Paulding's opinion of *Fanny* presents a complex problem, and involves, in fact, the whole question of the literary relations between the two poets. In discussing Paulding's attitude to *Fanny*, it will be necessary to refer again to his letter to Washington Irving in which he alludes to his poem of ''The Backwoodsman,'' published in 1818. ''My unfortunate poem,'' he writes, ''has been over and over again attacked by the combined powers of wit and dullness, the former led by a wicked wag called *Croaker*, the latter by our old friend H., who I believe can't forgive me for beating him with his own weapons.''[41] The cryptic reference to ''our old friend H.'' involves the question whether or not Halleck is the author meant, and whether *Fanny* is the work alluded to as the product of ''dullness.'' Considering *Fanny*, first of all, from the standpoint of the author of ''The Backwoodsman,'' one may discover in Halleck's poem sufficient basis for Paulding's resentment. The passing reference to ''cabbage head'' in stanza eight,[42] although in itself innocuous, was not well calculated to please an author who was seeking for his new work the commendation of the critics. But Halleck's most vigorous attack upon the poem is contained in the following stanzas:

LXIII

Alas! for Paulding—I regret to see
    In such a stanza one whose giant powers,
Seen in their native element, would be
    Known to a future age, the pride of ours.

[40] III (N.S.), 13 (November 18, 1820). In another number of the same periodical we find a curious ''Parody on the 'Lines to the Horse Boat,' '' signed ''Ecce Homo.'' It is addressed ''To William C * * * * y'' [see III (N.S.), 111 (February 10, 1821)]. Still another parody on this lyric, entitled ''To the Steam Boat,'' and signed ''Uncle Adam'' was published in the *Cabinet* [V (N.S.), 100 (April 27, 1822)].

[41] William Paulding, *Literary Life of James K. Paulding*, p. 95. The letter is dated January 20, 1820.

[42] The stanza references are to the first edition of *Fanny* (1819).

There is none breathing who can better wield
The battle-axe of satire. On its field

LXIV

The wreath he fought for he has bravely won.
  Long be its laurel green around his brow!—
It is too true, I'm somewhat fond of fun
  And jesting; but for once I'm serious now,
Why is he sipping weak Castalian dews?
The muse has damn'd him—let him damn the muse.

Indeed, if we are to reject Halleck, it is difficult to select from among Paulding's contemporaries any to whom the author of "The Backwoodsman" might have referred by "our old friend H." Paulding's letter to Irving was written at a period when the public interest was being directed to *Fanny*, and it is probable that at that time Halleck's attack on "The Backwoodsman" was uppermost in Paulding's mind. When Paulding called "H." a rival, "who I believe can't forgive me for beating him with his own weapons," he undoubtedly had in mind not a particular literary controversy in which Halleck and he were involved, but rather the general weapon of satire. It appears probable that in using the term "weapons" Paulding was alluding to Halleck's lines,

There is none breathing who can better wield
The battle-axe of satire. . . .

Two apparent difficulties with this interpretation do not, upon further consideration, seriously affect its validity. Washington Irving, to whom Paulding's letter was addressed, had at this time no personal acquaintance with Halleck. Writing from Madrid to his friend, Henry Brevoort, in 1827, Irving said: "I have been charmed like-wise with what I have seen of the writings of Bryant and Halleck. Are you acquainted with them? I should like to know something about them personally."[43] Irving's second residence abroad had begun in 1815, and continued until the year 1832. There is no evidence that Halleck had met Irving before the latter's departure for Europe; nor had Halleck met the author of *The Sketch Book* during his own brief tour of Europe in 1822.[44] And yet

[43] *Letters of Washington Irving to Henry Brevoort*, edited by George Hellman (New York, 1915), II, 200. Quoted by courtesy of G. P. Putnam's Sons.
[44] See Wilson, *Life*, p. 284.

Paulding spoke of Halleck as "our old friend." One explanation of the difficulty suggests itself. Paulding had undoubtedly been a regular correspondent with Irving, and may from time to time have mentioned Halleck in his letters. Assuming at least a slight acquaintance between Irving and Halleck, Paulding might well have referred to the author of *Fanny* as a common friend. Irving, on the other hand, probably had no distinct recollection of Paulding's remarks on the poet, and when Halleck's first volume of collected poems appeared in 1827, wrote to Brevoort for further information regarding the author.

The second difficulty lies in the fact that Paulding, in his remarks to Irving, appears unaware that the author of *Fanny* was also a partner in the Croaker project. Drake, to be sure, had been the sole author of the two *Croakers* which had ridiculed "The Backwoodsman," but there is no likelihood that either Paulding or anyone but the most intimate friends of the poets knew at that time of the authorship of the individual papers. Indeed, the authors of the satires were in many quarters regarded as a single person, Croaker. At first, it seems incredible that Paulding should not have known what was then common literary gossip, that Croaker was, without doubt, the author of *Fanny*. But this difficulty is easily obviated by noting that Paulding ceased to be a resident of New York on April 28, 1815, when he was appointed secretary of the newly appointed Board of Naval Commissioners.[45] From 1815 to 1832 Paulding resided in Washington. He was consequently out of touch with affairs in New York; and in those days when communication was difficult, and newspapers few, the separation of 200 miles from New York would undoubtedly result in an almost total ignorance of what was going on in the great metropolis, at least in the then minor pursuits of literature and art. It is therefore not to be wondered at that, although Paulding knew that *Fanny* was the work of Halleck, he should have been ignorant of the exact situation touching the authorship of *The Croakers* and *Fanny*.

But in spite of Halleck's acrimonious comments on Paulding's poem of "The Backwoodsman," his hostility did not include Paulding's other works, or, indeed, the man himself. Paulding's literary work had for the most part been in the fields of burlesque and satire.

[45] William Paulding, *Literary Life of James K. Paulding*, pp. 69 and 182.

And here Halleck recognized Paulding's strength to lie. The couplet,

> Why is he sipping weak Castalian dews?
> The muse has damn'd him—let him damn the muse,—

obviously alludes to Paulding's recent excursion into the realm of serious narrative verse, which Halleck regarded as a failure. If Paulding, however, had been in an appreciative mood, he would not have missed the compliment paid him in the lines,

> There is none breathing who can better wield
> The battle-axe of satire. . . .

At the close of his life Halleck was again to pay his respects to the satirical powers of Paulding. In commenting on the *Literary Life* of the author, Halleck wrote in 1867: "A glance over its passages gladdens me with the view of many of my earliest literary favorites, especially of the one entitled 'The Idea of a True Patriot,'[46] which I remember admiring exceedingly on a first perusal, and now find well worthy of my continued admiration. It is, in thought and expression, peculiarly characteristic of its author's writings and conversation, making, as it so pleasantly does, the sportive playthings of irony and raillery powerful in the battle of honest and honorable indignation against dishonesty and dishonor."[47] But the clearest and most definite estimate made by Halleck of Paulding's character is that contained in a letter, also written in the last year of the poet's life, in acknowledgment of a picture of the satirist which Mr. Evert A. Duyckinck had sent him.

The likeness of Mr. Paulding does not remind me of him either in his youth or age. I saw him for the first time in, I think, 1813. He was then one of the literary Lions of my admiration. In his later life, he honored me with his acquaintance and hospitality.

I am glad to hear that his collected writings are soon to appear. He had great honors as a writer, and great merit as a man. He thought

---

46 See *ibid.*, pp. 56 ff.

47 Letter to Paulding's son upon receipt of a copy of the *Literary Life*. Quoted in an article on Halleck by Duyckinck in *Putnam's Magazine*, XI, 238 (February, 1868). A copy of Paulding's *Lay of the Scottish Fiddle* (1813), both a burlesque of Scott's poem and a satire on the burning of Havre de Grâce by the English in the late war, Halleck sent home to his sister with the comment, "I am quite sure [it] will make you laugh" (Wilson, *Life*, p. 143). No other records are available of Halleck's early reactions to Paulding's works.

clearly and bravely, and spoke as he thought. His two lines alluding to our revolutionary soldiers, wherein he says they "Saved this good land and when the tug was o'er, Begged their way home at every scoundrel's door," are a specimen of his manner of expression when indignantly battling for the right against the wrong.[48]

The couplet here quoted by Halleck is, curiously enough, from "The Backwoodsman,"[49] although more nearly in Paulding's usual satiric vein of which Halleck approved. Since Halleck was here viewing Paulding's poem through a vista of almost fifty years, it is probable that its defects had largely receded into the background, and that only the moral power and force of the poem presented themselves to his memory. But even allowing for all the cheerfulness and indulgence characteristic of the poet's old age, we are no doubt justified in crediting Halleck's statement of his deep regard in early manhood for the author of "The Backwoodsman."

Returning to our discussion of *Fanny*, we may note for the sake of completeness, the opinions of several other friends and contemporaries of Halleck. These comments, most of them of little value, reflect what the post-contemporary reputation of *Fanny* must have been, after its novelty had in large measure worn off. *Fanny* "is an exquisite compound of playful humour, light satire, and tender sentiment," wrote William Leggett in 1828; "no one has ever read it without according to the writer a high rank among the poets of this country."[50] William Cullen Bryant, never a keen literary critic, in an address before the New York Historical Society, just after Halleck's death, characterized *Fanny* as "a satire upon those who, finding themselves in the possession of wealth suddenly acquired, rush into extravagant habits of living, give expensive entertainments, and as a natural consequence sink suddenly into obscurity from which they rose. But the satire takes a wider range. The poet jests at everything that comes in his way; authors, politicians, men of science, each is booked for a pleasantry; all are made to contribute to the expense of the entertainment set before the reader."[51]

---

[48] The letter, dated March 29, 1867, is preserved in the Duyckinck Collection of the New York Public Library.

[49] *The Backwoodsman* (New York, 1818), p. 76.

[50] *New York Mirror*, V, 227 (January 26, 1828).

[51] *Some Notices of the Life and Writings of Fitz-Greene Halleck*, p. 12.

Poe, on the other hand, recognizing the ephemeral quality of the satire of *Fanny*, found little to admire in the poem, which he believed to be "constructed with [no] . . . great deliberation. . . . If we except a certain gentlemanly ease and *insouciance*, with some fancy of illustration, there is really very little about this poem to be admired."[52] Fanny Kemble, the English actress who made her *début* on the American stage in 1832, read Halleck's poem during her first year in New York, but naturally found the satire difficult to understand. "The wit being chiefly confined to local allusions and descriptions of New York manners," she wrote in her diary, "I could not derive much amusement from it."[53] About a month later Miss Kemble met the author of *Fanny*.[54]

We must close this section on the reputation of *Fanny* with the story of John Randolph's lively appreciation of the poem. On one of Randolph's voyages to England, Jacob Harvey, a fellow traveler, found among the statesman's books a copy of *Fanny*. Questioned as to the poem and its author, Randolph said: "I always admire talent, no matter where it comes from; and I consider this little work as the best specimen of American poetry that we have yet seen. I am proud of it, sir; and I mean to take it to London with me, and to present it to that lady whose talents and conversation I shall most admire."[55] Harvey further relates the great delight which Randolph took in reading the poem aloud.

He proposed, one fine morning, to read Fanny to me aloud, and on deck, where we were enjoying a fine breeze and noonday sun. It was the most amusing "reading" I ever listened to. The *notes* were much longer than the poem; for, whenever he came to a well-known name, up went his spectacles and down the book, and he branched off into some anecdote of the person or of his family. Thus we "progressed" slowly from page to page, and it actually consumed three mornings before we reached—

> "And music ceases when it rains
> In Scudder's balcony."[56]

[52] *Godey's Magazine and Lady's Book*, XXXIII, 13 (July, 1846).
[53] *Journal* (Philadelphia, 1835), I, 69. Entry for September 10, 1832.
[54] See pp. 255–256.
[55] The poem was later given to Miss Maria Edgeworth.
[56] Hugh A. Garland, *Life of John Randolph of Roanoke* (New York, 1851), II, 173–174.

II

In considering the origin of Halleck's interest in the serio-comic it is well to keep in mind the two contrasting strains that mingled in his character. Israel Hallock, the engaging, shiftless Royalist took to wife the lineal descendant of John Eliot, the Apostle to the Indians. And thus began that struggle in the son between a love of romance and a sound, Yankee practicality. Never did the two strains find complete harmony. In the romantic kingdom of the "quiet mind" where the seventeenth-century Cavalier sought a safe retreat from the pressing cares of the world, Halleck too would have found repose, but for the invading enemy of the "common sense." With a simple, childlike trust he could write that

> in deceiving
> Lies the dear charm of life's delightful dream;
> I cannot spare the luxury of believing
> That all things beautiful are what they seem.[57]

But like Hosea Biglow in Lowell's shrewd appraisal of Yankee character, Halleck inevitably returned to

> the plain all-wool o' common-sense,
> Thet warms ye now, an' will a twelvemonth hence.[58]

Between these two poles he moved with increasing restlessness. A Puritan distrust of romance, an instinctive fear of all that logic cannot prove, became with Halleck a cause of disillusionment, but at the same time a source of the keenest pleasure. In the warring of the ideal and the practical he took a curious delight. And in this inherent love of the incongruous lay the fundamental source of the poet's interest in the serio-comic. "The shrewdness and worldly wisdom of Mr. Halleck's choice in life," once wrote N. P. Willis, "are marked strongly upon his works. He is that remarkable production of nature, 'a born poet' with a powerful under-current of common sense. We have often thought he was what Byron would have been with a stern Connecticut education, and the same circumstances of life altogether.'"[59]

Halleck's instinctive love of the serio-comic was materially

---

[57] *Red Jacket*, 1869 ed., p. 49.
[58] *Biglow Papers* (Second Series), No. VI, ll. 297–298.
[59] *Athenaeum*, February 7, 1835.

strengthened by his early coming under the influence of the
Knickerbocker school. The almost abnormal fascination of the early
New York writers for parody and burlesque seems in part to have
had its origin in Diedrich Knickerbocker's *A History of New York*
(1809). If Shandyism be "die Unmöglichkeit über einen ernsten
Gegenstand zwei Minuten zu denken,"[60] we may observe at work
in Irving's production the mind of a Laurence Sterne, somewhat
at war with itself—the scholar and the jester subtly blended. But
Irving's jests derive from a more wholesome air than Sterne's, and
his scholarship in the *History* consists in a boyish playing with
learned books. Here the ancient and modern worlds meet in happy
incongruity. "Irving instinctively divined and admirably illustrated in his 'Knickerbocker,' " writes James R. Lowell, "the humorous element which lies in this nearness of view, this clear, prosaic daylight of modernness, and this poverty of stage properties,
which makes the actors and the deeds they were concerned in seem
ludicrously small when contrasted with the semi-mythic grandeur
in which we have clothed them, as we look backward from the
crowned result, and fancy a cause as majestic as our conception of
the effect."[61]

Irving's *History,* with its mock scholarship and its delightful
sporting with heroic subjects, set the tone of New York literature
for the next twenty years. It became, for example, the life and
breath of Paulding's style. His parody of Sir Walter Scott in *The
Lay of the Scottish Fiddle* (1813) illustrates the influence of the
History upon a mind lacking the genial, boyish temperament of
Irving. Harsher in his critical judgments than Irving, Paulding
in his writing became so much the heavier and duller. Yet he possessed a natural love of parody, which frequently overcame his
better literary judgment. Irving himself, about ten years after
the publication of the *Knickerbocker,* counseled Paulding to
give more time to the correction of his work, and to abstain from
jesting in serious composition; but Paulding, although promising
to try, offered the apology that "it seems to me that uniform
sweetness and sentiment is [*sic*] tiresome at last, and that a little
occasional rugged carelessness is no blemish when taken into view

[60] *Goethe's Werke* (Berlin, 1883), X, 430 ("Sprüche in Prosa").
[61] "New England Two Centuries Ago" in *Among My Books* (Boston,
1870), p. 231.

as part of a whole.''[62] What statement could have been more in accord with the Knickerbocker literary tradition!

It is not without a touch of irony that we find Gulian C. Verplanck, who scored Irving for his ridicule of the Dutch fathers,[63] influenced by the *History* in his early political satires. *The State Triumvirate, a Political Tale; and The Epistles of Brevet Major Pindar Puff*,[64] satires on De Witt Clinton and his political clique, was printed in 1819 with an elaborate mock-critical apparatus by Scriblerus Busby, LL.D. The authority of Alexander Pope is unmistakable in the scholastic annotations; but that Verplanck found his chief inspiration in Cervantes and Irving is quite apparent from the following passage:

I call upon the muse, and thus proceed:

The Age of Chivalry Revived in 1819

For a long age, while dead to honour's flame,
Our chiefs no more the Muse's tribute claim,
Heroic valour and chivalric pride
Have lain entomb'd by gallant Quixote's side;
There doom'd to lie, till some high-minded knight
Once more should call them to the fields of light—
Should bid them, clad in ancient glories, rise,
And this chill age with knighthood's deeds surprise.
That day hath come.—O thou, my verse inspire,
Muse of Romance, with thine heroic fire!
Such as erst glow'd in great Cervantes' page
Or such as, in our colder, baser age,
Fired Knickerbocker's soul, what time he told
The high exploits of Stuyvesant the bold.[65]

Thus Halleck in writing *Fanny* found himself on familiar literary

[62] Letter, dated January 20, 1820. See William Paulding's *Literary Life of James K. Paulding*, p. 96.

[63] Pierre Irving, *Life and Letters of Washington Irving* (New York, 1862), I, 241.

[64] This work, though published anonymously, has always been attributed to Verplanck [see Duyckinck, *Cyclopaedia of American Literature* (New York, 1856), II, 68]. The volume was issued at the close of the year 1819, so that it could have had no influence on Halleck's *Fanny*. It is noted here, however, as indicating something of the general influence of the *History*, as well as showing the Knickerbocker appetite for burlesque at this period.

[65] Pp. 105–106.

ground. Like Irving,[66] he seems to have delighted in parodic and serio-comic works. His humorous assertion in *Fanny*,

> I hate your tragedies, both long and short ones
> (Except Tom Thumb, and Juan's Pantomime),[67]

is curiously enough supported by another reference to Fielding's farce in a letter to a friend,[68] and in cursory allusions to the work of Cervantes,[69] Samuel Butler,[70] and Samuel Foote.[71] *A History of New York* Halleck regarded as "a work superior . . . to the 'Sketch Book' ";[72] and in a letter addressed to the humorist, Frederic S. Cozzens, who had sent the poet a copy of his volume, *The Sayings of Dr. Bushwhacker,* Halleck wrote: "Since the dropping of the Swan's quill that wrote 'The Knickerbocker' (a bolder and a funnier book than that of 'The Sketch Book'), there has not appeared among us a quill equal to yours in its rare Rabelaisian power and pathos, purified for modern libraries by a delicate sense of propriety."[73] The *Knickerbocker History* and Halleck's *Fanny* are essentially akin in the spirit of jest in which they were conceived —in the conscious desire to shock the feelings of the unsuspecting and ingenuous reader. As Irving cleverly heralded his mock *History* as the work of Diedrich Knickerbocker, an eccentric Dutch historian; so Halleck aimed at a similar hoax in innocently prefacing *Fanny* with a romantic quotation from Milton.

[66] For Irving's indebtedness to the mock-heroic writers, see *A History of New York,* edited by Professor Stanley Williams and Tremaine McDowell (New York [1927]), pp. xxxviii ff.

[67] Stanza 164 (1839 ed.).

[68] To Edward Greene, dated May 5, 1863. The *Independent,* February 29, 1872. See p. 38.

[69] "Like Sancho in his island reigning." See "The Recorder" (1869 ed.), p. 167.

[70] "We have Hudibras and Milton." See "The Rhyme of the Ancient Coaster" (1869 ed.), p. 208.

[71] "There was Captain Cucumber, Lieutenant Tripe, Ensign Pattyman and myself" (motto following title, "Bony's Fight" [1869 ed., p. 261]). Samuel Foote (1720–77) was an English writer of comedy and farce.

[72] Letter of Halleck to General Wilson, dated September 11, 1867 (*Life,* p. 262).

[73] Dated August 21, 1867. This letter is preserved in the Yale University Library. Cozzens in *Fitz-Greene Halleck. A Memorial* (p. 23) has recorded Halleck's opinions of Irving's *Knickerbocker* thus: "There was no book like it; it was the only original book of the kind. A travestie of history! a travestie of what history! It is original, and full of Irving's genius."

> A fairy vision
> Of some gay creatures of the elements,
> That in the colours of the rainbow live,
> And play in the plighted clouds.

Upon the incongruity between motto and poem Halleck especially prided himself.[74] In speaking of *Fanny*, the poet once remarked: "I do not pride myself upon anything in it except the quotation. You know the subject is not elevated. The story of a bankrupt, dry-goods merchant is not a poetical theme. But the motto is the very opposite of such a story, and therein lies the wit."[75]

Halleck's literary interest in the serio-comic had yet another source in the work of a group of English writers who flourished at the opening of the nineteenth century. George Colman, the Younger, John H. Frere, William S. Rose, and Lord Byron in several of his later productions represent an important reaction from the super-romantic and sentimental literature of the day. The Younger Colman (1762–1836), known chiefly as a comic dramatist, took an exceptional delight in ridiculing false sentiment. Of Colman's serio-comic style the Smith brothers,[76] whose work we have already noted as influencing the tone of *The Croakers*, made occasional mention in *Horace in London*.

> From grave to gay he loves to fly,

the Smiths remark in an "Ode" "To the Comic Muse";[77] and in the same poem we find this quatrain descriptive of Colman:

> By either sister lov'd, caress'd,
> He, gay deceiver, picks and chuses;
> To serve two masters is no jest,
> But he contrives to serve two muses.[78]

A fair specimen of Colman's work may be found in a volume entitled *My Nightgown and Slippers*, first published in 1797, but bet-

---

[74] Wilson, *Life*, p. 231.

[75] F. S. Cozzens, *Fitz-Greene Halleck. A Memorial*, pp. 14–15.

[76] Occasionally we find a serio-comic note in *Horace in London*. Take, for example, the following stanza from "Brighton":

> Alas! how short the span of human pride!
>   Time flies, and hope's romantic schemes, are undone,
> Cosweller's coach, that carries four inside,
>   Waits to take back the unwilling bard to London.
>   (*Horace in London* [London, 1815], p. 27.)

[77] *Ibid.*, p. 97.   [78] *Ibid.*, p. 96.

ter known under a later title *Broad Grins* (1802). Here Colman sums up his dislike of the pseudo-romances of the day, and states succinctly his philosophy of the serio-comic:

> Now, a Romance, with reading Debauchees,
>   Rouses their torpid powers, when Nature fails;
> And all these Legendary Tales
> Are, to a worn-out mind Cantharides.
>
> But how to cure the evil? you will say:
> My *Recipe* is,—laughing it away.
>
> Lay bare the weak farrago of those men
>   Who fabricate such visionary schemes,
> As if the Night-mare rode upon their pen
>   And troubled all their ink with hideous dreams.
>
> For instance—when a solemn Ghost stalks in,
>   And, thro' a mystic tale is busy,
> Strip me the Gentleman into his skin—
>   What is he?
>
> Truly, ridiculous enough:
> Mere trash;—and very childish stuff.
>
> Draw but a Ghost, or Fiend, *of low degree*
> And all the bubble's broken: Let us see.[79]

In the "Water-Fiends," which follows, he admirably illustrates his theory.[80]

---

[79] *Broad Grins*, London, 1811 (fifth edition), pp. 9–10.
[80] A few odd stanzas from the "Water-Fiends" will illustrate the nature of Colman's serio-comic style.

> Ah! not averse from love was she;
>   Tho' pure as Heaven's snowy flake;
> Both lov'd: and tho' a Gard'ner he,
>   He knew not what it was to *rake*. (p. 16)
>
> 'Twas a tall youth, whose cheek's clear hue,
>   Was tinged with health and manly toil;—
> Cabbage he sow'd; and, when it grew,
>   He always cut it off, to boil. (p. 14)
>
> All in the flower of youth I fell,
>   Cut off with health's full blossom crown'd;
> I was not ill—but in a well
>   I tumbled backwards, and was drown'd. (pp. 21–22)

More akin, however, to the spirit of Halleck's *Fanny* is the work of John H. Frere (1769–1846), who published in 1817 his "Prospectus and Specimen of an Intended National Work, by William and Robert Whistlecraft, of Stowmarket in Suffolk, Harness and Collar Makers. Intended to comprise the most Interesting Particulars relating to King Arthur and his Round Table."[81] Frere adopted a stanza-form in imitation of the *ottava rima* of the Italian poets, Pulci, Berni, and Casti. This form has never been surpassed in English as a medium for serio-comic expression. The couplet at the close naturally segregates itself from the rest of the stanza, and may be used by the humorous poet as a means of summing up with comic after-tone what has heretofore been conveyed with tolerable seriousness. The double and triple rhymes, frequent in the final couplet, although natural and effective in the native Italian, are difficult of management in English for purposes of serious writing, but are excellent when adapted to the ends of humor and burlesque.[82] Frere's poem was for a long time believed a political allegory, but the author himself firmly denied any such intention. His real purpose in writing the poem he later put in words which I here quote for the light which they throw on the serio-comic method employed in *Fanny*:

I wished to give an example of a kind of burlesque of which I do not think that any good specimen previously existed in our language. You know there are two kinds of burlesque, of both of which you have admirable examples in Don Quixote. There is the burlesque of the imagination, such as you have in all the Don's fancies, as when he believes the wench in a country inn to be a princess, and treats her as one. Then there is the burlesque of ordinary uninstructed common sense, of which Sancho constantly affords examples, such as when he is planning what he will do with his subjects when he gets his island, and determines to sell them "at an average." Of the first kind of burlesque we have an almost perfect specimen in Pope's "Rape of the Lock," but I did not know any good example in our language of the other species, and my first intention in the "Monks and Giants" was merely to give a specimen of the burlesque treatment of lofty and serious subjects by a thoroughly common, but not necessarily low-minded man—a Suffolk harness maker.[83]

[81] A second part was later added, and both published in 1818 with the title *The Monks and the Giants*.

[82] George Saintsbury, *A History of English Prosody* (London, 1910), III, 99–100.

[83] *The Works of John Hookham Frere* (London, 1872), I, clix.

Halleck's method is closely allied to that of the Whistlecrafts. The author of *Fanny* may pretend to be a poet to whom "banknotes . . . are curiosities," yet he poses at times as hardly less vulgar than the ingenuous Whistlecrafts. Halleck is, in fact, attempting to describe how high life seems to the ignorant Fanny and her father, who possess sufficient ambition, but through want of education lack the intellectual power to sustain the vision. Viewed in another light, the poem represents the reaction of hopelessly crass and material minds to idealistic impressions. The mind plays restlessly between the world of vision and that of vulgar practicality, never able completely to realize the one or the other, and in the end experiencing utter disillusionment. The serio-comic form, where the ideal is constantly being created only to be lost in the practical, is thus admirably suited to the subject of Halleck's poem. Fanny and her father finally receive the only possible reward for their ill-grounded ambitions.

> . . . on my hopes, and those of my dear daughter,
> These rascals throw a bucket of cold water![84]

Several other points of contact between Frere's poem and *Fanny* may be noted. Frere's frequent use of the digression, in burlesque of the old metrical romances, found favor both with Byron and Halleck in their humorous attempts to entangle the reader in a maze of matter foreign to the story. Frere's methods of satire also at times suggest those used by Halleck; as in the ironic contrast produced by placing in juxtaposition customs and characters of ancient and modern times, with cursory, sarcastic comment.

> And certainly they say, for fine behaving,
>   King Arthur's Court has never had its match;
> True point of honour, without pride or braving,
>   Strict etiquette forever on the watch:
> Their manners were refin'd and perfect—saving
>   Some modern graces, which they could not catch,
> As spitting through their teeth, and driving stages,
> Accomplishments reserv'd for distant ages.[85]

---

[84] *Fanny*, stanza 150 (1839 edition).
[85] Canto I, stanza 10. Compare stanza 106 of *Fanny* (1839 ed.):

> Of these enlighten'd days at evening crowd,
>   Where fashion welcomes in her rooms of light,
> The "dignified obedience; that proud
>   Submission," which, in times of yore, the knight
> Gave to his "ladye-love," is now a scandal,
> And practised only by your Goth or Vandal.

Frere's manner of introducing contemporary allusions is occasionally similar to Halleck's;[86] as also his reference to his "bookseller."

> Beginning (as my Bookseller desires)
> Like an old Minstrell with his gown and beard.[87]

John Frere passed on the torch of serio-comic verse to William Stewart Rose and to Lord Byron. Like Frere, William Rose early became fascinated by the Italian poets, and in 1819 translated the "Animali Parlanti" of Giambattista Casti.[88] Each canto of this free adaptation of Casti's poem was prefaced by an address to one of Rose's friends. A single stanza of a group addressed to Frere will illustrate Rose's use of the Italian verse-form.

> O Thou, that hast reviv'd in magic rhyme
> That lubber race, and turn'd them out, to tourney,
> And love, after their way; in after time
> To be acknowledg'd for our British Berni;
> Oh! send thy Giants forth to good men's feasts:
> Keep them not close.—But I must to my Beasts.[89]

It may readily be seen that Rose reduced the original *ottava rima* to a six-line stanza, probably to facilitate rhyming. It was in this adaptation of the Italian stanza to his own uses that Rose definitely influenced the verse-form of *Fanny*.[90] Beyond this single influence on Halleck, Rose's poem did not reach. The translation of

---

[86]
> In form and figure far above the rest,
>   Sir Launcelot was chief of all the train,
> In Arthur's Court an ever welcome guest;
>   Britain will never see his like again,
> Of all the Knights she ever had the best,
>   Except, perhaps, Lord Wellington in Spain:
> I never saw his picture nor his print;
> From Morgan's Chronicle I take my hint. (Canto I, stanza 13)

[87] Canto I, stanza 1. Compare the concluding couplet of stanza 170 of *Fanny* (1839 ed.):
> And if I've wrong'd her, I can only tell her
> I'm sorry for it—so is my bookseller.

[88] *The Court and Parliament of Beasts Freely Translated from the Animali Parlanti of Giambattista Casti. A Poem in Seven Cantos* (London, 1819).

[89] Canto II, stanza 7.

[90] The six-line stanza is, of course, very old, being used by Shakespeare in his "Venus and Adonis." Following the publication of *Fanny*, the New York newspapers published frequent verses in this stanza (see the *Evening Post* for February 19, 1820, and March 8, 1820; the *American* for April 1, 1820). It is also interesting to note that Edward C. Pinkney in his Byronic fragment,

the "Animali Parlanti" is stilted and monotonous beside the crisp, fresh stanzas of *Fanny*.

To Lord Byron we turn as the final important influence in shaping *Fanny*. The appeal of Byron in America in the early nineteenth century was widespread,[91] although the literary expression of that appeal was narrowed generally to the minor writers.[92] The shock with which America met the news of Byron's death reflects something of the romantic feeling which his name inspired.[93] Halleck, upon hearing the news while visiting friends, is said to have "walked up and down the drawing-room, wringing his hands" and exclaiming, "What a terrible loss to literature!"[94] Yet Halleck's enthusiasm for Byron appears to have been genuine.[95] It was undoubtedly "Beppo," undertaken by Byron in deliberate imitation of the Whistlecraft style, that served as the immediate inspiration for *Fanny*. During Halleck's lifetime *Fanny* passed in general for an imitation of "Don Juan," as we have already noted in contemporary reviews, which frequently suggested by way of comparison the name of Byron's poem. After Halleck's death, however, Frederic S. Cozzens came forward with the claim that Halleck was unacquainted with "Don Juan" at the time he wrote *Fanny*, and further quoted from the poet that *Fanny* "was published before Don Juan had crossed the Atlantic, and that he [had] adopted the versification of *Beppo*, one of Byron's minor poems."[96] It seems reasonable to suppose that Halleck was set to writing *Fanny* from an interest in "Beppo," which was published in 1818;[97] but there is also evidence that the first two cantos of "Don Juan" came into his hands while *Fanny* was in the process of composition. *Fanny*, we have seen, was

"Cornelius Agrippa," modified in the same way the *ottava rima* [see Prof. T. O. Mabbott and Capt. F. L. Pleadwell, *The Life and Works of Edward Coote Pinkney* (New York, 1926), pp. 174 ff.]. Halleck later turned to the unmodified *rima* in "Connecticut."

[91] See William E. Leonard, *Byron and Byronism in America* (Boston, 1905), pp. 19 ff.

[92] *Ibid.*, p. 39.

[93] *Ibid.*, p. 32.   [94] Wilson, *Life*, p. 305.

[95] For a further discussion of Halleck's attitude to Byron, see pp. 195–197.

[96] *Fitz-Greene Halleck. A Memorial*, pp. 25–26. Wilson also relates that Halleck made the same statement to him (see *Life*, p. 231).

[97] A portion of "Beppo" was published in the *New York Evening Post* for June 26, 1818, as copied from the *London Literary Panorama*.

completed and the earlier part probably revised during Halleck's retirement in Bloomingdale, which began about September 15, 1819.[98] "Don Juan"[99] had appeared in England in July, 1819.[100] On September 14 a notice was published in the *New York Advertiser*[101] that "Don Juan" had been reprinted in the city. Thus Halleck might well have bought a copy of Byron's new poem, and taken it with him to Bloomingdale. Halleck was frequently inaccurate in referring to matters pertaining to his poetry, and his statement to Cozzens, probably made many years after the composition of *Fanny,* was undoubtedly due to inadvertence.

Prof. William E. Leonard has pointed out in two instances Halleck's probable indebtedness to Byron's "Don Juan."[102] Halleck's lines beginning,

> In all the modern languages she was
> Exceedingly well versed,[103]

suggest immediately the description of Lady Inez in "Don Juan";[104] and the stanzas in *Fanny* beginning,

> Dear to the exile is his native land
> In memory's twilight beauty seen afar,[105]

echo Byron's lines,

> 'Tis sweet to hear the watch-dog's honest bark
> Bay deep-mouth'd welcome as we draw near home.[106]

It may also be observed that Byron's manner of referring to himself in "Don Juan" is curiously paralleled in Halleck's poem. One

---

[98] The ordinance requiring the removal of persons from the infected district was passed on September 14.

[99] The first two cantos.

[100] See article on Byron in the *Dictionary of National Biography.*

[101] "A new poem has been recently published in England, under the title of *Don Juan,* and within a few days past, we observe it is advertised as having been reprinted here, and is for sale in this city."

[102] *Byron and Byronism in America,* p. 40 (note).

[103] Stanza 121 (1839 ed.).

[104] Canto I, stanzas 13 and 14.   [105] Stanzas 25 and 26 (1839 ed.).

[106] Canto I, stanzas 123 ff. These passages should be compared in detail to get the full resemblance.

knowing anything of the details of Byron's private life would smile at the lines,

> For my part, I'm a moderate-minded bard,
>   Fond of a little love (which I call leisure):
> I care not for new pleasures, as the old
>   Are quite enough for me, so they but hold.[107]

Those who knew of Halleck's employment in the countinghouse of Jacob Barker, would understand well enough the allusion in

> Money is power, 'tis said—I never tried;
>   I'm but a poet—and bank-notes to me
> Are curiosities.[108]

But in spite of Halleck's obvious indebtedness to the work of Lord Byron,[109] *Fanny* can hardly be called a pure imitation of either "Beppo" or "Don Juan." Halleck, it should be remembered, adopted not the original *ottava rima* used by Byron, but the modified form employed by Rose. But it is in the spirit rather than in the form of *Fanny* that Halleck's poem differs most perceptibly from "Beppo" and "Don Juan." There is an obvious universality particularly in "Don Juan" which is lacking in Halleck's work. "Half jest, half superstition, the world's face is" seen in Byron's poem "in all its incongruous phases."[110] In *Fanny* we feel instinctively a lack of human perspective. As the satire of Irving's *Knickerbocker* "is diffuse and tepid compared with the terrific in-

---

[107] Canto I, stanza 118.

[108] Stanza 6. In noting the cumulative evidence in favor of the assumption that "Don Juan" came into Halleck's hands while he was completing *Fanny*, one may well include Byron's absurd rhyme of *grief* and *pockethandkerchief* (I, 157), which Halleck appears to have adopted in stanza 26 of *Fanny*.

[109] Two verbal echoes of "Childe Harold" should not be forgotten. The line, "There was a sound of revelry by night" (stanza 126), which Halleck acknowledged by quotation marks, was taken *in toto* from Canto III, stanza 21, of "Childe Harold." The verses,

> Fanny! 'twas with her name my song began;
> 'Tis proper and polite her name should end it; (Stanza 170)

were obviously adapted from those of Byron,

> My daughter! with thy name this song begun—
> My daughter! with thy name thus much shall end. (Canto III, stanza 115)

[110] Thomas Powell, *The Living Authors of America* (New York, 1850), p. 245.

dictment of mankind'"[111] in Swift's *Gulliver's Travels;* so *Fanny*
is local and provincial beside the bitter appraisal of society life to
be found in "Don Juan." But Halleck was living in America, not
in England—and this difference in environment suggests the truth
of N. P. Willis' remark that Byron would have been like Halleck,
had he been born in Connecticut.[112] Halleck's early Puritan environment was largely responsible for a difference in moral tone to
be found in the two poems. When James R. Lowell characterized
Halleck as

> a pseudo Don Juan
> With the wickedness out that gave salt to the true one,[113]

he put his finger on an essential point of departure from the serio-
comic standard set by Byron. If the human implications of *Fanny*
are less universal than those of "Don Juan," the moral atmosphere
of Halleck's poem is more healthy. The worldly wisdom of Byron's
poem is replaced in *Fanny* by a youthful buoyancy—somewhat vulgar, to be sure, but without scorn. One of the special felicities of
Fanny is its freedom from cynicism. Bryant[114] was keen to catch
this difference; as also Charles F. Johnson who once remarked:
"If his [Halleck's] rhymed rhetoric is not so copious and powerful as Byron's, it is never cynical with a shallow and ill-natured
contempt of mankind. Such self-knowledge as he had did not under-
mine self-respect nor regard for his brothers. If his songs have not
quite the musical quality of Moore's, their gaiety is more simple
and natural and echoes a less conventional sentiment."[115]

The device of interspersing lyrics in the course of his narrative
poem Halleck probably derived from "Childe Harold," as no lyrics
appeared in either "Beppo" or the first two cantos of "Don
Juan."[116] Professor Leonard is perhaps right when he says that the

[111] *Knickerbocker's A History of New York,* edited by Williams and
McDowell, p. xliii.

[112] *Athenaeum* for February 7, 1835.

[113] *A Fable for Critics* (New York, 1848), p. 69.

[114] *Some Notices of the Life and Writings of Fitz-Greene Halleck,* pp.
12–13.

[115] "Fitz-Greene Halleck" in *Proceedings at the Celebration of the 250th
Anniversary of the Settlement of Guilford,* p. 100.

[116] Canto III of "Don Juan," in which appeared the famous lyric, "The
Isles of Greece," was not published until August, 1821 (see *D.N.B.*), after the
second part of *Fanny* had been issued.

lyric manner of these songs suggests Moore rather than Byron.[117]
The song, "To the Horse Boat," probably written at an earlier
date than the rest of *Fanny*, illustrates well the influence which
Moore exerted on Halleck's lyric style. Indeed, at times we note a
sincerity about the "serious" portions of *Fanny* for which we look
in vain in the first two cantos of "Don Juan." One contemporary
reviewer noted that Halleck "seems at times to be struggling with
the natural bent of his mind, and to forget himself into sentiment
and pathos."[118] No better illustration of this tendency can be found
than in the song which completes the second half of *Fanny*, "Young
thoughts have music in them." This lyric is most of it in Halleck's
best style of sentimental verse, yet the occasional introduction of
"Scudder's balcony" leaves the reader troubled and disillusioned.
Of so deliberate a hoax perpetrated on the reader Byron was never
guilty. But this was more than mere empty jest; it suggests at once
the instinctive fear of romance inherent in Halleck's nature. It
suggests too why he parodied Moore's absurdly sentimental lyric in
Lalla Rookh, "There's a bower of roses by Bendemeer's stream."[119]
But Halleck's humor was perhaps more subtle than the public of
his day entirely understood. Else why should editors have innocently
quoted the lines on Weehawken, and thought them of surpassing
beauty? Applied to their subject and viewed in the light of their
setting, these verses become a mere Byronic affectation of which
Halleck could hardly have been unaware.

> Amid thy forest solitudes, he climbs
>   O'er crags, that proudly tower above the deep,
> And knows that sense of danger which sublimes
>   The breathless moment—when his daring step

[117] *Byron and Byronism in America*, p. 40.

[118] *Literary Gazette*, I, 209 (April 7, 1821).

[119] Phoebe Cary also parodied Moore's lyric [see *Poems and Parodies* (New York, 1856), p. 196]. Verplanck in *The State Triumvirate, a Political Tale; and The Epistles of Brevet Major Pindar Puff*, p. 156, introduced a parody of Campbell's "Lochiel's Warning."

> My Clinton, my Clinton, beware of that day
> When the bucktails shall meet thee in civic array. Etc.

Verplanck's volume and *Fanny* were published at approximately the same time, so that there is little chance of the one influencing the other.

Is on the verge of the cliff, and he can hear
The low dash of the wave with startled ear.[120]

Excellent imitation, this, of passages in Byron's "Childe Harold,"
yet as a description of Weehawken hopelessly absurd. And we may
believe that Halleck realized this incongruity, and inwardly laughed
at those who insisted upon wresting from their settings the lyrical
passages. Curiously dramatic and ironic the lyric portions become
when viewed in the light of the rest of the poem. That Halleck conceived of this incongruity as an essential felicity of *Fanny* may
be seen from his remark to Cozzens[121] regarding the dissonance of
motto and poem. Only, then, as we take a comprehensive view of
Fanny, and feel the intimate relation of the serious to the comic do
we begin to glimpse the humor which sparkled in Halleck's eye as
he wrote the poem.[122]

Thus we have seen that *Fanny* had its origin both in a warring
of the ideal and the real within Halleck's own nature, and in an
almost abnormal interest of the period in the serio-comic style.
Of the literary influences at work in the case of *Fanny* that of
Byron in "Beppo" and "Don Juan" was undoubtedly the most immediate and compelling. The others we may note as showing the host
of secondary influences which silently but with subtle force affected
the literary taste not only of Halleck, but of the whole Knickerbocker school. That *Fanny* suffers as a literary production when
compared with Byron's work of the same kind, we have already
seen. Yet we can hardly hold the view of the critic who believed
Fanny "the flattest, tamest, dreariest of comic poems that have
won any note";[123] or with another who characterized the poem as a

---

[120] Stanza 95. Stanza 98 in the same description suggests Scott.

> Tall spire, and glittering roof, and battlement,
> And banners floating in the sunny air.

The lines on Weehawken were used as the subject of a humorous poem addressed "To Fitz-Greene Halleck, Esq.," which appeared in the *Morning Courier and New York Enquirer* for November 22, 1831.

[121] Quoted on p. 104.

[122] George B. Cheever recognized something of the dramatic necessity of
keeping the songs of *Fanny* in their settings when he reprinted the verses
beginning, "Young thoughts," with several of the preceding lines, which explain the reference to "Scudder's balcony." See *The American Common-Place
Book of Poetry* (Boston, 1831), p. 362.

[123] G. P. Lathrop in the *Atlantic Monthly*, XXXIX, 721 (June, 1877).

"feeble and discursive satire on the social climber."[124] There is, of course, no disputing tastes when humor is the question at issue, and in such cases we must allow for the personal equation. Yet one should invariably judge a secondary work of art with reference to the time and place of its birth. To appreciate the wit of *Fanny*, like that of *The Croakers*, we must understand the life of the people to whom the poem was addressed. We must know the literature of the age; we must know something of its politics. To fail to read *Fanny* in the light of the times in which it was written is inevitably to rank the poem far below its true worth as a literary product.

[124] Vernon Parrington, *Main Currents in American Thought* (New York, 1927), II, 202.

THE DEATH OF DRAKE AND A TRIP ABROAD

1820–22

THE years that immediately followed the publication of *The Croakers* and *Fanny* were for Halleck ones of comparative self-confidence and assurance. The poet had now found himself, and was at ease in the world. He knew well the world about him with its superficial flutter and its endless train of vanities. He was able to look on with the humorous detachment of one who sees and silently appraises. He recognized too his powers as a satirist; and he knew he could command the respect and admiration of men. Already master of the French language, he was now, as a man of fashion, to see something of Europe, with its quaint splendor and mellowed tradition. Returning from abroad, he was soon to publish several of the poems for which his name later became a household word in America. It was, indeed, during these years of early manhood that the writer of "Alnwick Castle" and "Marco Bozzaris" laid the foundation for his fame as a poet.

Perhaps these years would have been for Halleck ones of supreme happiness as they were of achievement, had it not been for the loss of his friend, Joseph Rodman Drake. Halleck's own gloomy prophecy, "There will be less sunshine for me hereafter, now that Joe is gone," seems in large measure to have been fulfilled. For a time able to assert his will amid the gaieties of a gay world, he later felt with deepening sadness the shadow cast by the death of his friend. The mood of the famous elegy on the death of Drake was in later life frequently to return. Many years afterward, he recalled in verse the happy days he had spent with Drake—

[1] During the middle of June, 1820, Halleck made one of his customary business trips for his employer, Jacob Barker. This was probably the poet's first extended journey to the North. On his way to Canada, he stopped at Niagara Falls. To his trip the poet briefly referred in a note to his sister dated York, Upper Canada, June 12 [1820] (see Wilson, *Life*, p. 241).

FITZ-GREENE HALLECK
At about the age of thirty.
From an engraving by Burt after a miniature by Nathaniel Rogers.

He the most
Honored and loved, and early lost—
He in whose mind's brief boyhood hour
Was blended, by the marvellous power
    That Heaven-sent genius gave,
The green blade with the golden grain;
Alas! to bloom and beard in vain,
Sheafed round a sick-room's bed of pain,
    And garnered in the grave.[2]

The first hint that we have of Drake's declining health is the horseback journey which he took to the South in the autumn of 1819, in the hope of conquering the consumption in its incipient stages. Here he remained during the winter. In Louisiana he spent some time with his sister, and appears to have shown improvement in health. "We heard from Drake yesterday," wrote Halleck to Maria. "He was on the seventh of March within about a week's journey of New Orleans; his health is much improved. He will probably return in May."[3] But Drake's assurance was doubtless founded on the hopeless optimism peculiar to the disease, for in the spring he returned home "fatally smitten."[4]

The loving attentions shown to Drake by his friends, De Kay, Halleck, and Langstaff, during the closing weeks of his illness, have been touchingly described by General Wilson.[5] Death finally came to the young doctor on Thursday, September 21, 1820.[6] A curious account of the funeral procession has been preserved, which reflects something of the popularity Drake must have had. "I remember very distinctly," says an unknown writer, "witnessing the funeral *cortège* as it proceeded up Chatham Street, in the direction of Hunt's Point, and of counting thirty carriages which formed the procession. . . . The coffin was borne on the shoulders of men, and it was followed by the mourners and the friends of the deceased on

[2] From verses written at the request of Mrs. Rush of Philadelphia, and accompanying a letter to her, dated March 8, 1842 (see Wilson, *Life*, pp. 434–435).

[3] *Ibid.*, pp. 237–238. Letter undated.   [4] *Ibid.*, p. 241.

[5] *Bryant and His Friends*, pp. 304–305.

[6] "Died—this morning after a lingering illness, Doctor Joseph Rodman Drake. His friends and acquaintance, and those of his father-in-law, Henry Eckford, are requested to attend his funeral to-morrow morning, at 10 o'clock, from No. 34 Park" (*Evening Post*, September 21, 1820).

foot.''[7] The grave at Hunt's Point, and the tombstone[8] originally erected to mark the final resting place of Drake, had, in the early years of this century, become much neglected, and were threatened with being overrun by the growing city. In 1915, through the efforts of the Bronx Society of Arts and Sciences, the ground adjoining the grave was set apart and dedicated as the Joseph Rodman Drake Park, and a bronze tablet, inscribed with lines from Halleck's elegiac poem, was placed upon the tombstone.[9]

Tradition says that as Halleck was returning from the funeral, he remarked sadly to De Kay, ''There will be less sunshine for me hereafter, now that Joe is gone.''[10] A more imperishable memorial of his grief is preserved in the touching lines,

> Green be the turf above thee,
> Friend of my better days!
> None knew thee but to love thee,
> Nor named thee but to praise.

The poem was written probably soon after the death of his companion, and may never have been intended for publication.[11] De Kay, it is said, handed a copy of the lines to the editor of the *Literary*

[7] Wilson, *Bryant and His Friends*, p. 290. From a letter to Wilson by an anonymous correspondent.

[8] A curiously romantic description of Drake's grave was written by William Leggett in the *Critic*, I, 354 (April 4, 1829). ''As I approached the little mound, I saw that 'the graveyard bore an added stone,' by which I was too surely informed that death had sent another tenant to the dreamless abode, and my fluttering heart seemed to thrill with presentiment of the individual. Conjecture was soon made certainty; for as I approached the neat marble monument which mourning kindred had erected over his remains, I read by the moonlight, the name of Joseph Rodman Drake, and underneath, as a fitting epitaph, a couplet from Halleck's beautiful lines,

> None knew him but to love him
> Nor named him but to praise.''

[9] See *Papers and Proceedings of the Drake Memorial Celebration, May 29, 1915. Together with a Bibliography of the Writings of Dr. Joseph Rodman Drake by Victor Hugo Paltsits* (New York, 1919).

[10] Wilson, *Life*, p. 242.

[11] Of this poem Wilson says, ''It was composed on the day of his friend's death, and was originally written on a blank leaf of a manuscript collection of Drake's poems in the possession of his wife'' (*ibid.*, p. 242). The only notebook of Drake now extant is the one entitled *Trifles in Rhyme,* to be found in the Henry E. Huntington Library. The lines on Drake appear in this notebook, but are written as if in prose and in a hand not absolutely identified as Halleck's. Whether or not it is this version to which Wilson refers cannot be determined.

and Scientific Repository, and Critical Review,[12] where they appeared in the January number for 1821.[13] The poem, which was
unsigned, appeared under the title "Lines on the late Doctor Joseph R. Drake," with the following preface:

The following stanzas, for beauty and exquisite finish, are infinitely
superior to the verses generally afforded on similar occasions. They were
written by a friend of the late Dr. J. R. Drake of this city.

To commemorate the virtues and talents of a departed friend, or to
weigh with impartiality his claims to public attention, is indeed no easy
task; but the subject of these lines was worthy of all the commendation
and all the sorrow here so beautifully expressed. A devotion to the muses
marked his early life; and many of his unpublished productions would
not discredit (we speak it confidently) the pen of a Moore, or a Campbell.

He fell an early victim to the *Consumption*,—a disease which seems
peculiarly to select for the objects of its attack, the amiable, the intelligent, and the virtuous.[14]

In addition to the lines "On the Death of Joseph Rodman Drake,"
Halleck composed in 1820 several poems which may be found in
the collected edition of 1869. The lines beginning,

> Within a rock, whose shadows linger
> At moonlight hours on Erie's sea,[15]

Halleck is said to have written for Miss De Kay, presumably the
sister of Dr. James De Kay.[16] De Kay himself, then unmarried, was
made the subject of some clever verses entitled "The Tea-Party,"
which was to be held at the doctor's bachelor apartment at the

---

[12] Wilson, *Life*, p. 242.   [13] II, 85–86.

[14] The lines to Drake were reprinted from the *Repository* in the *New York
American* for February 9, 1821. The poem also appeared in the *Evening Post*
for February 21, 1821.

A translation of the poem made into the French by the Rev. Adrien Rou-
quette may here be noted (see Wilson, *Life*, pp. 243–244).

Prof. T. O. Mabbott has pointed out an interesting parallel between Halleck's poem and lines in E. C. Pinkney's "Rodolph" (1823). See *The Life
and Works of Edward Coote Pinkney* (New York, 1926), edited by T. O.
Mabbott and F. L. Pleadwell, p. 148.

[15] Capt. Frank L. Pleadwell of the United States Navy owns what is
probably the original manuscript of this poem, and has kindly provided me
with a copy of it. It is dated October 6, 1820. The poem was not collected
until the 1869 edition of Halleck's work, where the lines are called "Album
Verses."

[16] Wilson, *Life*, p. 246.

invitation of two ladies[17]—Mrs. Joseph Rodman Drake and Miss Eliza McCall.[18] The poem pictures in lively fashion the preparations going on,—

> For the first time these six months, a broom has been there,
> And the housemaid has brushed every table and chair.

But the two ladies, the poet hints, are

> mistaken for once, as they'll presently see,
> For D. K.'s drinking whiskey with Langstaff and me:
> They'll find the cage there, but the bird is away—
> Catch a weasel asleep, and catch Doctor D. K.[19]

As may be seen in these lines, Halleck, who was naturally of a somewhat shy and reserved disposition, was fast gaining ground as a man of society. This increasing love of good company and sprightly conversation, coupled with the literary facility which the composition of *The Croakers* and *Fanny* had given him, made him, as time went on, a master of society verse. Another poem, written at this time, and in a similar vein, is "The Dinner-Party,"[20] which is this time held at the home of John R. Livingston (the "Johnny R——" of the poem), "a wealthy gentleman, who dispensed liberal hospitalities both at his city residence and at his countryseat on the Hudson."[21] In the manner of *The Croakers*, names of local interest are freely introduced. A fourth poem, written probably at the close of the same year, is "The Great Moral Picture,"[22] a playful skit on a painting by Rembrandt Peale of Baltimore. As the picture, which was then on exhibition in New York, had excited little interest,[23] the Common Council resolved to "visit the Academy of Arts, for the purpose of viewing" the painting, and they

---

[17] "To-night we take tea with you, Doctor D. K." (line 16 of the poem).

[18] For Miss McCall both Drake and Halleck wrote poems. See pp. 45 and 70–71.

[19] First published in the *Home Journal* for June 7, 1856. Signed "F.G.H. 1820." Whether this poem was written before or after Drake's death cannot be determined.

[20] Published in the *Home Journal* for June 7, 1856. Though bearing no relation to the *Croaker* series, these poems, along with others having something of the style and spirit of the earlier verses, were printed in the Bradford edition of *The Croakers*.

[21] See 1869 edition of Halleck's poems, p. 383.

[22] First printed in the 1869 edition, p. 359.

[23] See the *New York American*, December 18, 1820.

"recommended to our fellow-citizens to go also."[24] Halleck's satire on this resolution is happily summed up in the lines,

> Hide your diminished heads, ye sage Reviewers!
> Thank Heaven, the day is o'er with you and yours;
> No longer at your shrines will Genius bow,
> For mayors and aldermen are critics now.[25]

In November, 1820, appeared a thin pamphlet in the format of *Fanny*, entitled "Fanny Continued."[26] The excitement over Halleck's poem was at once renewed. "This morning," wrote Coleman in the *Post*, "my eye was caught by a label on a bookseller's window, giving notice that a continuation of this little favorite poem was just published, and for sale there; so stopping in I asked for a copy, which was handed me, price, 3s. Casting my eye over the first verse I laid it down, and left the shop under a strong suspicion it was not genuine. In a few minutes, I met the author of *Fanny*, who handed me the following note for insertion:

'We are requested to say that *The Second part, or continuation of Fanny* this day published, is not written by the author of the first part.' "[27]

Thus Halleck definitely disclaimed the authorship of "Fanny Continued."[28]

The booksellers evidently anticipated for "Fanny Continued" the same success that had attended the original poem. Five advertisements of the pamphlet appeared in the same issue of the *Post* for November 15, 1820. The critics and reviewers, however, at once detected the forgery. The *Literary and Scientific Repository* for January, 1821, noted "Fanny Continued" in their "List of late Publications," but added the bracketed phrase, "A stranger to the original Fanny."[29] "The poetry is not bad," wrote Woodworth in

[24] Quoted from the "Extract from the minutes of the Common Council Dec. 26, 1820," which Halleck reprinted below the title to his poem.

[25] 1869 edition, p. 361.

[26] An advertisement of the poem was printed in the *Post* for November 15, 1820. Copies of this rare pamphlet are preserved in the Yale University Library, and in the New York Public Library.

[27] November 15, 1820.

[28] The *Advocate* (November 16, 1820) also observed that they had been authorized to say that "Fanny Continued" was not "by the author of the former sketch."

[29] II, 259.

the *Ladies' Literary Cabinet,* "but it is evidently not from the same
pen with Fanny. It is a good imitation, and no doubt will become
popular."[30] Noah, writing in the *National Advocate,* noted that
the new poem lacked the "sprightliness, vivacity, and naivete" of
the original, but observed that "this Fanny possesses considerable
merit—a smoothness of versification not unmixed with choice, and
sometimes elegant language, proves the author, if not a master, at
least, a promising scholar."[31] But these prophecies of fame for the
author of "Fanny Continued" were never fulfilled, and the writer
of the poem still remains a mystery. Halleck once told General Wilson that the author of the poem "was unknown to him, but that
it had been attributed to Isaac Starr Clason, who wrote a continuation of 'Don Juan.' "[32] Clason later produced a series of satirical
sketches, one of which introduced Halleck.[33]

In certain of its formal characteristics "Fanny Continued" resembled the earlier poem. The modified *ottava rima* used by Halleck
was, of course, retained. An extended digression near the opening
again helped to suggest the original poem, although the subject of
the digression—the fickleness of woman—was foreign to Halleck's
manner of thought. Curiously enough, the author of "Fanny Continued" visioned with almost uncanny accuracy the ending which
Halleck was later to give his story. Fanny's father, Halleck eventually showed, ended a bankrupt, but not in debtor's prison, as the
author of "Fanny Continued" foresaw his fate.

LIII

Thy[34] poor old ruin'd father, who acquir'd,
    Some of the world's breadth, for his ready name,
Lent to those airier merchants, that, inspired
    By modern commerce, destitute of shame,
Declare insolvent, as the readiest way
To ride in coaches—creditors must pay:—

LIV

He now, deceiv'd, derided and unknown,
    To stylish bankruptcy, must sad resume
Former obscurity, and sigh alone,
    Darkly encompass'd in the prison's gloom,

---

30 III (N.S.), 16 (November 18, 1820).
31 November 16, 1820.   32 *Life,* p. 234.
33 See pp. 178–179.   34 Fanny's (the heroine).

> Mourning more deeply, in his shelter rude,
> Thy wants, than *his* false world's ingratitude.[35]

The ultimate fate of Fanny, after her father's failure, is, indeed, alarming, for the author suggests that she must now undertake the duties of governess, or descend to the still more degrading profession of actress!

It is in the essential qualities of thought and style, however, that "Fanny Continued" departs most noticeably from its prototype. The penchant for serious moralizing displayed by the author robs the poem of the genuine Knickerbocker spirit that pervades *Fanny*. The brisk and often saucy way which Halleck had of treating local characters and institutions the new author either could or would not imitate. Probably the serio-comic style was completely beyond his grasp. There are in "Fanny Continued" almost no surprising modulations from grave to gay; no conscious attempts, as in *Fanny*, to carry the reader far away on a wave of sentiment and to leave him suddenly startled and disillusioned on the sandy shore of common sense. Heavy, serious, and moral, with but here and there a glimmer of that dashing brilliancy that had characterized Halleck's work, "Fanny Continued," so far as can be known, found but few readers and fewer admirers.

This spurious edition of *Fanny* and the fact that the original poem was now out of print, probably suggested to Wiley, the publisher, the possibility of a new edition by Halleck. He finally made the proposal to the poet, offering him $500 for a second canto.[36] "The bookseller had long been bothering me for a continuation of 'Fanny,'" wrote Halleck to his sister, "and I at last wove on fifty stanzas or so, and the second edition has appeared. It sells, which is saying the best that can be said."[37] The new edition was issued on March 26, 1821.[38]

---

[35] Stanza 56, which introduces Tammany, is worth quoting as another specimen of the author's style:

> No more, High Tammany! thy echoes cheer,
>   With *war-whoop* answer'd back, his patriot breast,
> While turgid periods o'er his charmed ear
>   Fall, from the imitators of the best
> And purest style of Indian eloquence,
> Full of short words, wild figures, and small sense.

[36] Wilson, *Life*, p. 234.
[37] *Ibid.*, p. 247. Letter dated March 31, 1821.
[38] See the *New York Evening Post* for that date.

On the whole, the new *Fanny* was favorable received. The *New York Evening Post* remarked that the additions made by the poet "are no way inferior in poetic merit to what appeared in the first. An impotent attempt was made last summer to foist off a spurious edition upon the public, but the deception was discoverable in the first page; of the genuineness of this before me no doubts can remain, after reading the short specimen we now present."[39] A dashing, sprightly review of the volume, in perfect keeping with the spirit of the poem, was printed in the *Literary and Scientific Repository*. "Who has not read *Fanny?*" asked the critic, "both the first and second editions of it—that delightful *bagatelle,* which some unknown but highly favoured *protégé* of the Muses has brought out, to turn care into mirth, gravity into lightheartedness, ennui into self-complacency, and pride, pedantry, affectation, extravagance, folly and 'the first society'—into fun." The reviewer concluded by quoting the lines on Weehawken, which he called "a picture that exhibits powers of description; an ease and sweetness of versification, and a poetic sensibility, which, if spread over a larger work, and applied to subjects less fleeting than the local evanescent follies of the day, would secure to their possessor that enviable reputation of taste and genius, which receives its stamp in the temples of muses."[40] Something of the same doubt as to the permanent value of Halleck's satiric manner, and a desire to wrest from their setting and preserve as gems of "purest ray serene" the sentimental passages throughout the poem, are to be found in a review, probably by Woodworth, in the *Ladies' Literary Cabinet.* "Though we are offended," commented the reviewer, "by the incongruity which exhibits a mind wedded to all the associations and habits of mere traffic, and consequently limited to the low ambition of vulgar vanity, mingling the bitter thoughts of defeated triumph with the fate of 'Marius,' &c., and alive to that sweet and deep feeling of nature and beauty, which dictated the verses to the Boat; we are, notwithstanding, much interested in the talent which combined these discordancies, which . . . has perverted exquisite perceptions, and a fine descriptive faculty." "In our recollections of 'Fanny,'" he went on to say, "we separate all thoughts of censure and distaste,

[39] March 27, 1821. The following evening Coleman reprinted from *Fanny* the song, "Young thoughts have music in them, love."
[40] II, 397 (April, 1821).

and disencumbering the gems scattered through the poem, from all that clouds their beauty, or contrasts with it, we admit them into that constellation of poetic lustres, that gild the dull prosaic path of vulgar days.''[41]

In contrast to this fulsome review, the criticism of the poem given in the *Literary Gazette* deserves attention as coming from a pen outside of New York. The observations of this Philadelphian reviewer present an important commentary not only upon *Fanny*, but in general upon the stylistic idiosyncrasies of the Knickerbocker school. '' 'Fanny,' in the first edition, was very amusing,'' affirmed the critic, ''—had many good hits and piquant jests, and evinced a genuine vein of poetic talent. The additional stanzas now appended, are not so entertaining, being written with much less spirit. There is, throughout the whole, an odd mixture of the droll and the serious, which is not always pleasing. The author seems at times, to be struggling with the natural bent of his mind, and to forget himself into sentiment and pathos.'' The critic finally presented this Philadelphian estimate of the Knickerbocker temperament: ''In New York they make a man jocose in spite of himself—at least, whether he be so inclined or not. An excellent, amiable, and intelligent set of people, they certainly are in that town, but ever since they have had to boast of 'Salmagundi' and 'Knickerbocker,' as indigenous productions—a propensity to satire and burlesque has been their besetting sin; the passion has been a perfect *mania*, and they have laughed at their own caricature in every variety of shape. No wonder, therefore, if a poet should find it difficult either to escape the infection (*contagion* it would be called there), or to resist the current.''[42]

Turning from the formal reviewers, it is refreshing to catch a glimpse of *Fanny* through the eyes of one of Halleck's intimate friends. The following letter, written by Ogden Hammond from Savannah, Georgia, bears the date, May 14, 1821.[43]

"Fanny" is the only thing that has brought me to the vulgarity of a hearty laugh since I first made a track in the sands of Georgia. I am glad

[41] IV (N.S.), 5 (May 12, 1821).

[42] I, 209 (April 7, 1821). This periodical formed ''a third series of the *Analectic Magazine*.'' Another notice of the poem appeared in the *Commercial Advertiser* for March 31, 1821.

[43] Printed by Wilson in an article on Halleck in the *Independent* for February 29, 1872.

Wiley's eloquence had at last the effect. From all I hear, the second edition goes off well, and there will probably be a demand for another. Whether my being from home gave me an improved taste for your facetious conceits and fantasies I know not; but certainly I enjoyed them much more than before. I like your additions and alterations, and think you have shown your usual good judgment throughout. My old acquaintance is craftily introduced as a finale. . . . [44] I hope soon to set off (as we Americans say) for home, and shall have the gratification of once more taking you by the hand—I trust before the middle of June. . . . [45] Pray, who wrote "Sukey,"[46] published in Boston? The newspapers say it is good, and in the style of "Fanny" and "Don Juan." *Apropos,* tell Eastburn, if you please with my compliments, to send me the new cantos of "Don Juan" as soon as possible, as I notice they are published. Remember me kindly to De Kay and the rest of our coterie.

It was probably the attempted imitation of Byron's "Beppo" and "Don Juan" that attracted to *Fanny* the attention of some of the English publishers and reviewers. A few months after the publication of the poem in New York, *Fanny* is said to have been reprinted in full in a London periodical,[47] but unfortunately this version, if it exists, has not been recovered. In the following year, however, Whittakers published in London a reprint of the second American edition.[48] At least two English periodicals noticed this volume in their columns. "It is certain . . .," commented the *Monthly Review* for November, 1821, "that we can discover no high beauty in the poetry, nor any great poignancy in the satire; though

[44] The omission is Wilson's.   [45] The omission is mine.

[46] "Sukey," an imitation of *Fanny,* but longer and heavier than the original, was from the pen of William Bicker Walter (see Duyckinck, *Cyclopaedia of American Literature,* II, 284). The satire was published in Boston and Baltimore in 1821. Another imitation of *Fanny,* the *National Advocate,* quoting from the *Charleston Courier,* noted in its issue for July 14, 1821. "In *New York* they have 'Fanny,' in *Boston* 'Sukey,' and why should we not have 'Kitty' in *Charleston?*" An extract from "Kitty" follows. Another excerpt from the same poem was printed in the *Advocate* for July 28.

[47] Wilson in the *Independent* for February 29, 1872.

[48] No copy of this edition has been located either in America or England, but a notice of the volume in the *Monthly Review* (XCVI, 323) appeared with the following heading, which indicates clearly that such an edition was issued: "Art. 17. *Fanny,* 8vo. pp. 67. Printed at New York, and republished in London by Whittakers. 1821." The preface to *Fanny* in *Specimens of the American Poets* (London, 1822) states that "an English edition of 'Fanny' has been published, but does not appear to have had a very extensive circulation."

we have often met with worse versification.''[49] A more patronizing
tone was adopted by the *New Monthly Magazine*, which confessed
that "some of the stanzas possess wit," but complained that the
poem as a whole "is wire-drawn, and wants originality. As a transatlantic performance, however, we wish not to judge it fastidi-
ously." "We are sorry," the reviewer also observed, "that the
Americans are so early beginning to indulge in a propensity for
this kind of satire, of which we have unfortunately had too much
of late in our country."[50] In 1822 a portion of *Fanny* was again
published in England in a small volume entitled *Specimens of the
American Poets*,[51] which also included some of the work of Paulding, Sands, and Eastburn. A prefatory note praised *Fanny* as
"one of the cleverest efforts of the American Muse." The editor
believed the author "to have been very successful in catching" the
spirit of the serio-comic, and, he added, "it will perhaps be thought
that in some passages he fully equals his English prototypes." As
this volume of *Specimens* received considerable attention from British reviewers, *Fanny* came in for frequent mention. The critic for
the *Literary Gazette* called *Fanny* "a sprightly thing in the
Whistlecraft way," and regarded it "as a favourable specimen of
Transatlantic talent," although he discovered a "want of polish in
many parts."[52] A *Blackwood* reviewer spoke of *Fanny* as "a beautiful little poem";[53] while the *Monthly Magazine, or British Register*
mentioned its being written "in the manner of 'Don Juan,' and not
without effect."[54] Two other periodicals, however, which had previously reviewed the London edition of *Fanny*, now mentioned the
poem with small favor.[55] Again in 1837 Halleck's poem was pub-

49 XCVI, 323. Four stanzas of *Fanny* were also quoted.
50 III, 579 (November, 1821).
51 Published in London by T. and J. Allman.
52 VI, 307 (May 18, 1822).
53 *Blackwood's Edinburgh Magazine*, XI, 686 (June, 1822).
54 LIII, 315 (May, 1822). This review was reprinted in the *New York Mirror*, II, 300–301 (April 16, 1825).
55 The *Monthly Magazine*, VI (Second Series), 269 (June, 1822); and the
Monthly Review, C, 33 (January, 1823). In the *Retrospective Review* for 1824
(IX, 312) *Fanny* is mentioned thus: "The poem called 'Fanny' is for the
most part jocose; but we like the following serious stanzas better, we confess,
than the author's humour, which, however, is *naïve* at times, if not very pun-
gent." The lines on Weehawken follow. The *Kaleidoscope*, III, 249 (February
4, 1823), also commented briefly on the poem as it appeared in *Specimens* [see
Willliam B. Cairns, *British Criticisms of American Writings, 1815–1833* (Madison, Wisconsin, 1922)], p. 167.

lished in England in separate form, but no reviews of the volume have come to light.[56]

It should be noted that Halleck's literary work at this period occupied but a small part of his time. It was done at intervals of leisure, with often no other apparent purpose than to eschew idleness. Drake, it is said, had counseled Halleck to leave the employ of Barker, and to give his whole time to writing.[57] But this advice, had it been followed, would probably have yielded little success. Even if the financial prospects had been assuring (which they were not),[58] the name of *poet* in New York during these early days was not sufficiently respected to invite the man of letters. "There is a vulgar Dutch notion, very prevalent in this metropolis," observed the *Atlantic Magazine* in its first number in 1824, "that no person who has a fondness for literature can be competent to discharge the duties of his profession. This is a very gross superstition, but has great currency, and deters many from exercising their wits in any way at all, notwithstanding the illustrious examples in all ages and countries that confute this absurd theory."[59]

Thus Halleck gave his chief attention to the work of his employer, Jacob Barker. Much of his leisure, however, during the early twenties, which he did not devote to poetry, was spent in travel. Halleck's enthusiasm for the poetry of Thomas Campbell made especially dear to him the Vale of Wyoming. This "paradise of America," as he once described it to his sister, he had visited several years before, while on a trip to the South.[60] In June, 1821, he again

[56] A perhaps unique copy of this rare edition is in the Harris Collection of American Poetry at Brown University. It was published in London by T. Tickler & Co., Piccadilly.

[57] Wilson, *Harper's New Monthly Magazine*, XLIX, 68 (June, 1874).

[58] Philip Freneau, the American poet, wrote to Dr. J. W. Francis on May 15, 1819: "After all, as I take it, the genius of the City of New York is so entirely commercial, that I suspect it swallows up all ideas of poetry, or refuses any attention to poetical productions, further than what is calculated for the fly market stalls, or to be sung at some Tammany Convivial Meeting or the Bacchanian Sons of the Hotels." See the catalogue of the Dormitzer Collection of Americana, sold by the American Art Association, Inc., on January 30, 1925.

[59] I, 3-4 (May, 1824). Even as late as July, 1850, we find *Fraser's Magazine* (XLII, 15) remarking, "Fashionable as writing is in America, it is not considered desirable, or, indeed, altogether reputable, that the poet should be *only* a poet."

[60] Wilson, *Life*, p. 174.

made a pilgrimage to the scene of Campbell's celebrated poem.[61] The length of his stay in the valley is unknown, and almost the only reminder which has survived of this trip is the poem, "Wyoming," which was not published until 1827.[62]

Later in the summer, Halleck's friend, Dr. James E. De Kay, was married to Miss Eckford, the sister of Mrs. Drake.[63] Halleck acted as groomsman at the ceremony,[64] as he had done, five years before, at the wedding of Drake. After the ceremony, Halleck accompanied the De Kays and Mrs. Drake on a trip to Canada. Of this journey the poet wrote to his father upon his return to New York: "De Kay was married to Miss Eckford this day three weeks, at ten o'clock in the morning. I accompanied him, his wife, and Mrs. Drake to Quebec, from which pleasant journey we have just returned."[65]

It was probably during the summer of 1821 that Halleck amused himself by writing, in the manner of The Croakers, "An Address for the Opening of the New Theatre, to be Spoken by Mr. Olliff."[66] The Park Theatre had been destroyed by fire in July, 1821, and a new building had subsequently been erected in its place. A prize medal, for which many of the poets of New York were contesting, had been offered for the best poetical address to be spoken at the re-opening of the theater. Among the contestants for the prize were several of Halleck's friends—Samuel Woodworth, McDonald Clarke,[67] and Charles P. Clinch.[68] Halleck, who apparently had no desire to compete for the prize, wrote a burlesque address which was published in the Post.[69] The poem, which was obviously suggested by Horace and James Smith's Rejected Addresses, was accompanied by the following note, presumably by Coleman:

61 Ibid., p. 248.   62 See pp. 180–181.

63 In the New York Evening Post for July 30, 1821, appeared the following notice: "Married—this morning, Dr. J. E. De Kay, to Miss Eckford, daughter of Henry Eckford, Esq." Eckford was a wealthy shipbuilder of New York.

64 Wilson, Life, p. 249.

65 Ibid., p. 249. The letter is dated August 20 [1821].

66 In 1808, on his first visit to New York, Halleck saw Olliff, the actor, who was then very young (see Wilson, Life, p. 62).

67 See pp. 242 ff.

68 One of the lesser known Knickerbocker writers, who produced in 1822 a drama entitled The Spy, founded upon Cooper's novel of that name.

69 August 28, 1821. The Bradford edition of The Croakers gives the date incorrectly as August 21.

We do not know whether the above address was among the number presented to the literary committee for the premium, at the opening of the Theatre, and rejected; but one thing we will venture to say, there was none offered half so well calculated to produce dramatic effect. And we should hope the managers will present the author with the freedom of the Theatre, by way of encouraging him to make a second effort.

Later in the year, a small book was issued containing all the addresses produced for the occasion.[70] Among the rest appeared Halleck's humorous lines.[71]

Several other minor compositions of Halleck were written in 1821. The lines "To Walter Bowne, Esq.," later published in the *New York Mirror*,[72] bore the subtitle, "Senator of the State of New York, Member of the Council of Appointment, &c., &c., &c., at Albany in the Spring of 1821." Halleck's *Croaker*, "The Council of Appointment,"[73] had satirized at length this piece of political machinery. The poet again made the Council the subject of satire, but this time pointed his darts directly at the figure of Walter Bowne, one of the most influential members of the organization. The sudden descent from office of numerous prominent politicians of the day is here cleverly described. Another poem written at this period, and harking back to the *Croaker* series, is the burlesque of Moore's song in "The Fire Worshippers," "Farewell, farewell to thee, Araby's daughter." "Farewell, farewell to thee, Baron Von Hoffman," published in the *National Advocate*[74] and signed "Poker," was directed at a bogus Dutch baron, who but a short time before had captivated New York society.[75] His numerous creditors, who lament with mock solemnity his late departure, are humor-

---

[70] *Rejected Addresses; Together with the Prize Address Presented for the Prize Medal Offered for the Best Address, on the Opening of the New Park Theatre in the City of New York.* The prize was awarded to Charles Sprague of Boston.

[71] Halleck's poem was introduced with the words, "The following burlesque is taken from the *New York Evening Post*, and is now republished for the amusement of our readers."

[72] January 26, 1828.   [73] The *Post*, July 16, 1819.

[74] November 16, 1821. Printed in the 1869 edition of Halleck's poems on p. 354. A manuscript of the poem, now inaccessible, was sold with Halleck's library [see *Catalogue of the Private Library of the late Fitz-Greene Halleck* (New York, 1868), item 62].

[75] Halleck had mentioned the Baron in the *Croaker* entitled, "Love of Notoriety" (see the notes on the Baron in the 1869 edition [pp. 382 and 385]).

ously described by Halleck.[76] The lines entitled "The Rhyme of the Ancient Coaster"[77] are mentioned in a note accompanying the poem as "written while sailing in an open boat on the Hudson River, between Stoney Point and the Highlands, on seeing the wreck of an old sloop, June, 1821." The discursive character of this half-humorous, half-sentimental meditation on the old wreck suggests the improvisatory composition of the verses, which add little to Halleck's reputation as a poet. Some complimentary verses called "A Valentine," which are described as "given to Miss Caroline Drake (Mrs. F. N. Tillou) the evening before her wedding, 14 February 1821," have for their opening lines the first stanza of Halleck's *Croaker*, "Curtain Conversations."[78] The remaining stanzas, which in the original *Croaker* played lightly with the theme of domestic infelicity, are now addressed personally to "Cara" with assurances of future happiness.[79] The following six poems were also probably written during the year 1821.[80] (1) "Music—To a Boy of Four Years Old, on Hearing him Play on the Harp." (2) "Psalm CXXXVII."[81] (3) "Love."[82] (4) "A Sketch."[83] (5)

[76] The title of the poem in the 1869 edition is "To the Baron Von Hoffman, Morrison's Hotel, Dublin, June 20, 1823." The poem, however, was first published, as noted, in 1821. The original text differs somewhat from that which was printed in the collected edition.

[77] First published in the *New York Mirror* for January 15, 1831.

[78] Published in the collected edition of 1827 as "Domestic Happiness."

[79] This poem with three others was sent by Drake's nephew, C. Graham Tillou, to Evert A. Duyckinck on December 6, 1867. These verses were written in a commonplace book once owned by Mr. Tillou's father. Concerning this poem Mr. Tillou said that it "was given to my mother the evening before her wedding, at which ceremony Halleck acted as groomsman." The poem, with accompanying letter, is preserved in the Duyckinck Collection of the New York Public Library. These verses, which were printed in the *Independent* for March 7, 1872, but which have never been collected, appear in the Appendix.

[80] Assigned to that year by Wilson (see *Life*, p. 249).

[81] A late manuscript copy of this poem in Halleck's hand is owned by Capt. F. L. Pleadwell of the United States Navy, who has kindly furnished me with a transcription of it. The copy is dated May 18, 1845.

[82] C. G. Tillou informed Mr. Duyckinck that this poem, like "A Valentine," was written for his mother. (In the letter already referred to in discussing "A Valentine.")

[83] These four poems were not published, so far as I am aware, until the edition of 1827. "A Sketch" reflects the popular interest of the day in the "Blue Stocking" or "Azure Hose," as the female intellectual of that day was sometimes called. The poem was reprinted from the 1827 edition in the *New York Mirror* for April 21, 1827, under the title of "A Blue Stocking."

Halleck composed the lyric, "The summer winds are wandering free," says Wilson, "for a young girl of fourteen, while spending a few days in the same hotel with her at Schooley's Mountain."[84] (6) The verses "In her Island Home" were written for the album of a Miss Bronson.[85]

Another interesting bit of writing which Halleck did in 1821 was the inscription for the monument of the English tragedian, George Frederick Cooke. Cooke had died in America in 1812,[86] and was buried in a vault beneath St. Paul's Church. Edmund Kean, while traveling in this country in 1821, caused the remains to be removed to the churchyard, where he erected a monument over the grave.[87] At Kean's request, "that fat, jolly little tar," Jack Nicholson, the friend of Washington Irving,[88] wrote the following letter to Halleck asking him for an inscription:

I have wished to see you for some time, and, not knowing your address, I take the liberty of leaving this to the care of Mr. Eastburn,[89] who has been polite enough to say that he will deliver it. Mr. Kean has written me from Baltimore, that he intends to raise a monument over the remains of his predecessor, Cooke, the Tragedian. His remains are now in the strangers' vault in St. Paul's. It is an act which will redound to Kean's praise, both on this side as well as across the Atlantic. The monument, I understand, will be a handsome and tasty one. I am desirous that the inscription should emanate from our countrymen, and at the same time give to our friend Kean the credit for his generosity, which he certainly deserves for this act of liberality. Am I taking too great a liberty in asking you to think on the subject, and, if you can, honor his memory by committing to

[84] *Life*, p. 249. This poem is not extant, but may have been, with some variations, the one incorporated many years later in "Young America" (see 1869 ed., pp. 187–188).

[85] *Life*, p. 249. This poem was first published in the collected edition of 1869.

[86] Wilson says that Halleck attended the funeral of Cooke. See "Halleck and His Theatrical Friends" in *Potter's American Monthly*, IV, 218 (March, 1875).

[87] Arthur Hornblow, *A History of the Theatre in America* (Philadelphia, 1919), I, 280–281.

[88] See Pierre Irving, *Life and Letters of Washington Irving*, II, 399.

[89] "A New York bookseller, and an elder brother of the late Bishop of Massachusetts, referred to by Dr. Francis, in his 'Old New York' as 'that intelligent publisher and learned bibliophile, James Eastburn'" [Wilson's note].

the marble a few lines, which will exist even longer than the tablet on which they may be inscribed.[90]

With the inscription[91] which Halleck furnished, Kean was greatly pleased.

At the beginning of the following year, 1822, Halleck was called upon to act as witness in a lawsuit in which his employer was involved. With the exception of a brief period during which Halleck was engaged in business for himself, the poet since 1811 had been in the office of Jacob Barker, and had come to share the utmost confidence of the financier. After the failure of the Liverpool House, a business organization with which Barker was intimately associated at this period, violent protestations were made against the banker. One of Barker's opponents named Rogers grossly insulted him.[92] Keenly sensitive to the least affront to his personal honor, Barker replied to the gentleman in a sharp note, demanding satisfaction.[93] As the financier persisted in his demands, Rogers complained to the Grand Jury, testifying "that Mr. Barker had challenged him to fight a duel."[94] Barker was at once indicted for the offense, and a trial followed. During the suit, "the district attorney called on Mr.

[90] J. G. Wilson in *Potter's American Monthly*, IV, 218–219 (March, 1875).
[91] The inscription as recorded by Arthur Hornblow, *op. cit.*, I, 281, is as follows:

Erected to the Memory
of
George Frederick Cooke
by
Edmund Kean
of the
Theatre Royal, Drury Lane
1821
Three kingdoms claim his birth,
Both hemispheres pronounce his worth

In spite of the fact that the inscription has been several times retouched, it is now almost illegible.

For the sake of completeness, it may be noted that Halleck's authorship of the concluding couplet has been challenged. W. Alfred Jones claimed for Dr. John Francis the authorship of the lines [*Characters and Criticisms* (New York, 1857), I, 271]. A mock inscription for the monument was published in the *New York American* for June 8, 1821.

[92] *Incidents in the Life of Jacob Barker* (Washington, 1855), p. 139. No author's name appears on the title-page of this work, but it is probably for the most part from the pen of Barker himself. The work is very biased, and exceedingly inaccurate as to dates.
[93] *Ibid.*, p. 139. The note is dated January 29, 1822.
[94] *Ibid.*, p. 140.

Halleck and other friends of Mr. Barker, in the expectation of establishing from his confidential conversations what he meant Mr. Rogers should understand from'' the letters which had been sent him.[95] The exact nature of Halleck's testimony on this occasion is unknown. In spite, however, of his own vigorous protestations Barker was found guilty.[96] This was among the first of those lawsuits in New York which finally led to the financial ruin of Jacob Barker, and to the retirement of Halleck from his employ.

The year 1822, however, was of particular significance in Halleck's life because of his trip to Europe. What should have induced the poet to undertake the journey at this time is not entirely clear. Of course, he had always wished ''to see the world,''[97] and he may now have taken advantage of a probable lull in the business of Barker which followed the lawsuit. Halleck's health at this time also appears to have been affected. For some time past he had been troubled by mental depression, and in April he wrote to his sister of ''another attack of the complaint in my head.'' ''I am so low-spirited when the 'dark hour' is on me,'' he went on to say, ''that I can attend to nothing.''[98] It is probable then that Halleck undertook the voyage largely with the view of restoring vigor both to body and mind. The first mention of the intended trip to Europe is contained in a letter to Maria, in which he speaks of having ''taken passage in the packet-ship Amity, Captain Maxwell, for Liverpool,'' which is to ''sail on Monday, the 1st of July.''[99] On June 30, the eve of his departure, he again wrote to his sister, giving her a few directions for the disposition of his property, should he fail to return.[100]

On July 21, 1822, Halleck arrived at Liverpool. Writing home on the following day, the poet said:

We arrived here yesterday morning, after a pleasant passage of twenty-one days. I was sea-sick for an hour or two on the first day, and in perfect health during the remainder of the voyage. We had some severe weather, which made all hands sick except myself, so that I passed for an

[95] *Incidents in the Life of Jacob Barker*, p. 141.

[96] *Ibid.*, p. 142.

[97] This he said in a letter to his sister, dated December 28, 1814 (see Wilson, *Life*, p. 153).

[98] *Ibid.*, pp. 249–250. The letter is dated April 8, 1822.

[99] *Ibid.*, p. 250. The letter is dated June 25 [1822].

[100] *Ibid.*, p. 251.

old sailor. . . . [101] There is little at this place worth seeing, and I shall start for London at one o'clock.[102]

Halleck reached London on July 25. From thence he visited Bath, Bristol, Cheltenham, Stratford-on-Avon, and Oxford.[103] Crossing the Strait of Dover, he arrived at Calais, and two weeks later wrote to his sister, "I have seen nearly all the lions of Paris and Versailles, and shall proceed to Bordeaux to-morrow."[104] The following fragment of a letter, addressed to a friend from Paris, is the only intimate evidence which we have of Halleck's stay in France.

Our poor friend Jones is dead. We buried him yesterday in Père la Chaise. The Protestant priest, Mr. Maro, made a most impressive prayer over his grave, sympathizing with his friends and congratulating him on having died in this most hospitable country, where, he should have said, we had to pay a prodigious price for his six feet of earth. An interesting incident of our visit to the city of the dead was the chance meeting with the poet Beranger, who was also following a friend to the grave.[105]

The poet was again in London on September 26, whence he sent home a letter. "I wrote to you from Paris on my return from Switzerland," he said. "Since that time I have been at Brussels, Waterloo, Ghent, etc., and returned to England by way of Calais and Dunkirk."[106] During Halleck's stay on the Continent he also visited Germany.[107]

On his way to Scotland, Halleck directed his course to the north of England, visiting the districts of Yorkshire, Durham, and Northumberland. It was on the occasion of a visit to the Percy Castle

[101] The omission is Wilson's.

[102] Wilson, *Life*, p. 252. The letter is dated July 22 [1822].

[103] *Ibid.*, p. 252. From a letter dated August 3, 1822.

[104] *Ibid.*, p. 252. The letter is undated. Wilson merely says a "fortnight later" than the date of the previous letter.

[105] *Independent*, March 7, 1872. Wilson gives the date as "October, 1822," but this date fails to tally with that of the letter in which Halleck says he is again in London on September 26. There is no evidence that he was again on the Continent.

[106] Wilson, *Life*, pp. 254–255.

[107] The successive steps of Halleck's tour may be minutely traced from the detailed list of places visited by the poet while on his travels. This itinerary, which is printed by Wilson in the *Life* (pp. 265–269) is unfortunately without dates, so that it is not always possible to trace his travels accurately with respect to time. This list, originally contained in a memorandum book of the poet's, probably passed, with Halleck's other manuscripts once owned by his sister, into the hands of General Wilson, and is now inaccessible.

at Alnwick that he wrote his famous poem "Alnwick Castle," which was later published in the *New York Evening Post*[108] with the title, "Lines written at Alnwick Castle, the seat of the Duke of Northumberland, October, 1822." A romantic story of the composition of the poem has been related by General Wilson. Halleck visited the "Home of the Percy's high-born race" on the last day of September. "The evening of the following day," affirms Wilson, as the poet "sat alone beneath the shadows of Melrose Abbey, he arranged the thoughts that had filled his mind during the day, and on returning from his moonlight excursion to the Melrose inn, when long past midnight, the poet wrote with a pencil a rough draft of the beautiful poem of 'Alnwick Castle.' "[109] Whether this story rests purely upon traditional evidence cannot be known. There is, of course, the possibility that Wilson received it in substance from the lips of the poet.

The days spent in Scotland were in after years among the poet's most cherished memories. In Edinburgh, where Halleck passed much of his time, he dined with the publisher, Blackwood, who also had as guests James Ballantyne, the intimate friend of Scott, and James Hogg, whose eccentric manners are said to have delighted Halleck.[110] One of Halleck's favorite haunts in Edinburgh was the bookshop kept by Stevenson, where it is said Brougham and Sydney Smith first considered the project of the *Edinburgh Review*. Here Halleck again saw the "Ettrick Shepherd" and also "Christopher North."[111] The theaters of Edinburgh were another source of delight to Halleck. The poet saw there the celebrated comedian, Charles Mackay, in his famous *rôles* of Baillie Nichol Jarvie and Edie Ochiltree;[112] and was also fortunate enough to be present at a

---

[108] December 6, 1823. See pp. 145–146.

[109] *Life*, p. 270.   [110] *Ibid.*, p. 255.

[111] *Independent*, March 7, 1872.

[112] Several plays which retold Scott's novels in dramatic form were published and performed during the novelist's lifetime. *The Antiquary; a Musical Play in Three Acts*, the author of which is given in the British Museum Catalogue as Daniel Terry, was first issued in London in 1820. An Edinburgh edition of the same play, published probably in 1823, with the title *The Antiquary; a National Drama*, and with the text altered from that of 1820, is preserved in the New York Public Library. In this edition the part of Edie Ochiltree is assigned to "Mr. Mackay." The drama *Rob Roy*, in which Mackay played with marked success the *rôle* of Baillie Jarvie, is mentioned at length by John Gibson Lockhart in *Memoirs of the Life of Sir Walter Scott* (Boston and New York [1901]), III, 314 ff. No bibliographical information

performance at which appeared "in one of the boxes, Sir Walter Scott, surrounded by several members of his family."[113] Only one record of Halleck's stay in Glasgow has been preserved. While he was inquiring of a dealer concerning some recent poetry, the bookseller handed him a volume which he said was "just published, a capital poem, and destined to be quite popular."[114] The work was *Fanny*, which had been reprinted at Greenock.[115] Halleck also visited the places famed in Scottish song. On October 10 he made a pilgrimage to the birthplace of Burns, and two days later "stood by his grave." Near Alloway Kirk in Ayrshire, Halleck plucked a rose which later served as the inspiration for his famous verses to Burns.

> Wild Rose of Alloway! my thanks;
>   Thou 'mindst me of that autumn noon
> When first we met upon "the banks
>   And braes o' bonny Doon."[116]

The poet also visited the scene of Scott's "Lady of the Lake," which he mentions at some length in his stanzas "To Ellen."[117] Another brief record of Halleck's sojourn in Scotland is preserved in a letter written a short time before the poet's death to Donald G. Mitchell, the author of the well-known *Reveries of a Bachelor*. "While sight-seeing in Scotland many years ago," remarks the poet, "I was particularly charmed with the beauty of Torwood-lee,

---

concerning the play is given by Lockhart. See, however, the editions listed in Charles D. Yonge's *Life of Sir Walter Scott* (London, 1888), bibliography, p. xxxiii. It is of interest to note that Halleck mentions Baillie Jarvie in "Alnwick Castle."

[113] *Independent*, March 7, 1872.   [114] Wilson, *Life*, p. 240.

[115] Duyckinck in *Putnam's Magazine*, XI, 235 (February, 1868). No copy of this edition has been recovered.

[116] Wilson, *Life*, p. 274. There is no evidence for Wilson's statement that "Burns" was "written and published anonymously in Great Britain before his departure for the United States" (*Life*, p. 274), or for the remark that a copy of the poem "has ever since hung on the walls of the principal room of Burns' birthplace" (*Life*, pp. 274–275). See the letter of Dr. D. McNaught printed in the Appendix; and a discussion of the publication of the poem, p. 180.

Charles A. Davis has related his meeting in Ayr, years later, with an old native who spoke warmly of Halleck's "Burns." See the *Knickerbocker*, XXVI, 575 (December, 1845). Wilson reprints the account in his *Life*, pp. 276–280.

[117] The edition of 1869, p. 228. See p. 269.

the seat of the Pringle family, and with the added beauty of its then Lady Proprietress.''[118]

Halleck's brief trip to Wales was of peculiar interest because of an unexpected encounter with one of his poems in a newspaper. During the previous March the poet had read an article in the *Quarterly Review* which thoroughly aroused his resentment.[119] While in this agitated frame of mind, he had composed some verses called ''Yankee Ravings,'' which he addressed ''To the Critics of England.'' Halleck gave the poem to a friend before leaving for Europe, but did not intend that it should appear in print. The verses, however, were published in New York, and later found their way into the London papers. While in a country tavern in Wales, Halleck thus chanced upon his ill-fated poem.[120] Little is known of the poem beyond the facts given by Wilson,[121] and the original printings of the poem have not been recovered. Many years later, in talking to James Grant Wilson, Halleck remarked, ''By the way, speaking of the British, did you ever hear my growl at the *Quarterly Reviewers*, written in 1822, before going to Europe?'' and he repeated to Wilson several of the stanzas.[122]

> Growl, critics of England, growl on, ye hired hounds
> Of a pitiful court! at America's name,
> For long as that name through your vassal-air sounds
> It must crimson your cheeks with the blushes of shame.[123]

After making a short stay in Ireland, where the poet visited Blarney Castle,[124] he returned to England where ''from the second week

[118] Mitchell, *American Lands and Letters* (New York, 1897), I, 292. A portion of the letter from which this extract was taken, is reproduced on p. 291.

[119] In the *Quarterly Review* for April, 1822, appeared a review of four books of American travels, published in London. The reviewer displayed a curiously hostile attitude to certain phases of American life, and it was probably this article which aroused Halleck's indignation.

[120] Wilson, *Life*, pp. 256–257.

[121] Substantially the same incidents relating to the publication of the poem are stated by Duyckinck (*Putnam's Magazine*, XI, 235; February, 1868). This account may be the source of some of Wilson's statements in regard to the verses. Wilson, however, gives the entire poem, whereas Duyckinck presents only four lines, which he says the poet ''recalled from memory.''

[122] Printed by Wilson in the *Life*, pp. 257–258.

[123] These verses were cleverly rewritten, probably by Halleck, and made to apply to a political situation before the public in 1834. The new title read, ''Ode to the Pensioned Presses.'' See the Appendix.

[124] Wilson, *Life*, p. 256.

of November to the 10th day of December'' he remained in London.[125] Here he saw the Duke of Wellington, the Duke of Clarence, and other celebrities.[126] He also ''visited the India House, and saw Charles Lamb's desk, but missed a meeting with the gentle Elia, whom he really wished to see face to face.''[127] Wilson has pointed out in how many ways Halleck resembled the English essayist. ''He had Lamb's delicate organization,'' remarks the biographer, ''like him, he was wedded to an accountant's desk; like Lamb, Halleck was a bachelor, and for a portion of his life lived with an unmarried sister; like Lamb, he was poor; and he possessed Lamb's love of humor, his passion for reading, and the same genial, social, and loving traits that endeared Charles Lamb to so many admiring friends.''[128] Halleck was always shy and retiring in manner, and invariably shunned a meeting with the great. Before leaving America, he wrote to his sister that he possessed ''letters of introduction to Byron, Campbell, Moore, Scott, Southey, Wordsworth, and Washington Irving,[129] now in England, and to Lafayette, Talleyrand, and many other great persons in France.'' ''Whether I shall deliver them or not,'' added the poet, ''will depend upon circumstances.''[130] But circumstances were unfavorable, and he made no special effort to deliver the letters. General Wilson once asked Halleck why he had not availed himself of the opportunity of meeting ''these literary magnates,'' to which he replied that since he had been ''described in the letters as 'one of the most intelligent men in America,' 'a poetical genius,' etc., he thought it prudent not to deliver them.''[131] Samuel Rogers, who later became a great admirer of Hal-

---

125 *Ibid.*, p. 258.   126 *Ibid.*, p. 258.
127 *Ibid.*, p. 258.   128 *Ibid.*, pp. 258–259.
129 The letter of introduction to Irving, furnished by William Coleman, has fortunately been preserved, and may be found in the New York Historical Society. It is here reprinted as an expression of Coleman's friendship for Halleck.

New York June 30th 1822

Dear Sir

PERMIT me to introduce to your personal acquaintance, in the bearer, Mr. Halleck, the author of Croaker, Fanny & some other miscellaneous pieces which I have herefore sent you. You will receive him with the courtesy due to a fellow countryman, a respectable & estimable man; but bid him welcome *for he is your brother*, treat him with distinguished kindness *for he is your kindsman* [*sic*].

From your sincere friend & ardent admirer

Wm Coleman

[Postscript, which does not concern Halleck, omitted.]
Washington Irving Esq.

130 Wilson, *Life*, p. 251. The letter is dated June 30, 1822.
131 *Hours at Home*, VI, 364 (February, 1868).

leck's poetry, was frankly disturbed that the poet had not called to see him. In writing to Irving in 1837, Rogers said of Halleck, "When he comes here again, he must not content himself with looking on the outside of my house, as I am told he did once—but knock and ring, and ask for me as an old acquaintance."[132] In London Halleck spent much of his time at the bookstores and theaters. At one bookshop kept by Robert Triphook, a favorite meeting place for literary men of the day, Halleck enjoyed many hours, talking with the proprietor and seeing various notables who chanced to drop in. Here he was introduced to Hobhouse, a friend of Lord Byron, and could have met Coleridge, but "after a careful survey of the author of the 'Ancient Mariner,' and having heard him utter a few sentences, he diffidently withdrew."[133] While in the city, Halleck enjoyed theatrical performances at Drury Lane and the Haymarket, and saw such actors as Charles Mathews[134] and Edmund Kean.[135] By a curious coincidence, while making an earlier stop at London in July, the poet had attended the funeral of Mrs. David Garrick.[136]

Halleck, who was always ready to lend assistance to his friends, was of material aid to James Fenimore Cooper, in conveying the proof sheets of the novelist's *Pioneers* to Mr. Benjamin Coles, who was to arrange for the publication of the volume in England. It was in a letter to Washington Irving relating to this arrangement that Cooper referred to Halleck as "the admirable Croaker."[137]

On December 11, Halleck set sail from Liverpool on his homeward voyage. "We are now dropping out of the harbor," wrote the poet to his sister on the same date, "and, although the wind is not quite as fair as we could wish, we still hope to get out to sea in a day or two. You must not be alarmed if you do not hear of us for ninety days or even more, for at this season of the year the winds on the Atlantic are generally west, and, of course, ahead for us."[138] But in spite of Halleck's warning, Maria was much concerned for her brother's safety. In writing home soon after his arrival in this coun-

[132] *New York Mirror*, XIV, 359 (May 6, 1837).

[133] Wilson, *Life*, pp. 264–265.   [134] *Ibid.*, p. 261.

[135] *Ibid.*, p. 261. Wilson says that Halleck "twice had the pleasure of gazing upon Mrs. Siddons" (*Life*, p. 258), who had retired from the stage in 1812.

[136] *Ibid.*, p. 261.

[137] Pierre Irving, *Life and Letters of Washington Irving*, II, 74–75.

[138] Wilson, *Life*, p. 265.

try, Halleck said: "I am sorry you were induced to despair of my arrival after the sixty days allowed me had gone by. . . . [139] As soon as I get my affairs a little in order, and the weather becomes more desirable, for a traveller, I intend coming to see you. 'The gay lilied fields of France' have ruined the climate of this cold country in my opinion, and I am afraid of another attack of my whirligig in the head if I expose myself much at this season. I am now perfectly free from it, except that I do not hear with my left ear; but at Liverpool I was tortured with it for three weeks, and I fear the cold and the rainy weather still. Please tell my father that I am well and intend visiting Guilford before long. I did not see the personages you mentioned. Washington Irving was not in England while I was there. Had I seen him, I probably should have formed more acquaintances than I did, but I went to see things, not men, and it did not comport with my plans or my pocket to mix in society."[140]

In addition to "Alnwick Castle" three short lyrics were produced by Halleck during the year 1822.[141] The song beginning,

> The harp of love, when first I heard
> Its song beneath the moonlight tree,[142]

was composed for Charles P. Clinch's drama, *The Spy*, written in 1822, and based upon Cooper's novel of the same name, which had just appeared. Clinch was a friend of Halleck, and undoubtedly requested the poet to write this lyric as an added distinction for his new drama. The lyric was sung by Miss Johnson in the *rôle* of Frances.[143] A translation from the French of General Lallemand, a political refugee, beginning with the line

> Sweet maid, whose life the frost of destiny,

[139] The omission is mine.   [140] Wilson, *Life*, pp. 283–285.

[141] Wilson (*Life*, p. 281) asserts that these three poems were written before Halleck's departure for Europe, but fails to state his reasons for assigning the last two to the year 1822.

[142] First collected in *Fanny with Other Poems* (New York, 1839), p. 115. It is here dated "1822." When and where this lyric was first published has not been determined, although it had apparently found its way into print by 1831. The *New York Evening Post* for June 25, 1831, printed the lines, with some accompanying verses signed "W.H.W."

[143] The manuscript of Clinch's drama is in the New York Public Library, and is dated 1822. Halleck's song, however, is not in the manuscript. The lyric was probably sung at a fitting point in the play, without ever being in-

was written in the album of a Miss Denning;[144] and a translation from the Italian of Lorenzo Da Ponte entitled "Eyes Blue and Bright and Beautiful as Thou" was made for Miss Eliza Livingston,[145] probably the daughter of John R. Livingston,[146] who owned a beautiful summer home on the Hudson. In 1825 Da Ponte went to reside with Livingston, whose three daughters he was instructing in Italian.[147] Da Ponte, Mozart's celebrated librettist, who had been exiled from Austria, came to America in 1805, where in New York he taught the Italian language and engaged in literary work. In 1828 he became Professor of Italian at Columbia College. Halleck was among Da Ponte's pupils, and "often spoke feelingly of his former *maestro.*"[148] It is probable that the lines "From the Italian," published in the 1827 edition of Halleck's poems, were first written as an exercise in translation. They are not in Halleck's usual style, and suggest a restraint imposed by a language unfamiliar to the translator.[149]

serted in the prompt-book. *The Spy* was first performed at the Park Theatre, March 1, 1822 (see A. H. Quinn, *A History of the American Drama,* New York, 1923, p. 455). An advertisement of the first night of *The Spy, or a Tale of Neutral Ground,* in the *New York American* for March 1, 1822, assigns the *rôle* of Frances to Miss Holman. The Miss Johnson mentioned by Wilson may have assumed the *rôle* at a later date. The play apparently had a considerable run. An advertisement of a performance for November 22, 1822, is printed in the *Albion* for November 15. Another performance of *The Spy,* to be given at Chatham Theatre on June 1, 1826, is advertised in the *New York American* for the same date. The drama does not appear to have been published.

[144] Wilson, *Life,* p. 281. First published in the collected edition of 1869, p. 217.

[145] Wilson, *Life,* p. 281. These verses, so far as may be ascertained, have never been printed; nor is the manuscript available.

[146] See the account of Halleck's poem, "The Dinner-Party," p. 120.

[147] Joseph L. Russo, *Lorenzo Da Ponte* (New York, 1922), p. 118.

[148] Wilson, *Life,* p. 282.

[149] No earlier printing or manuscript of this poem has been discovered.

VII

MARCO BOZZARIS AND OTHER POETRY

1823–26

THE first piece of writing done by Halleck after his return from Europe in 1823 was the "Lines on the Death of Lieut. Allen." William Allen, a young naval officer, has been described as possessing "strong and vigorous intellectual powers," a man who "mastered the sciences with ease and laid a solid foundation for future usefulness. He always availed himself of every opportunity that offered for distinguishing himself, and as occasion required he evinced both skill and courage."[1] Allen had been killed, while Halleck was still abroad, "in a gallant attack upon the pirates on the coast of Cuba."[2] It is not improbable that Halleck was a personal friend of the lieutenant. Born in the same year as the poet, Allen was also an intimate associate of Jacob Barker, and played an important part in the lawsuit in which the financier was engaged during the early months of 1822.[3] Another probable point of contact between Halleck and Lieutenant Allen was the father-in-law of Drake and De Kay, Henry Eckford, who was instrumental in calling a public meeting of the citizens of New York after Allen's death for the purpose of expressing the regret of the nation, and of raising a subscription for the relatives of the deceased.[4] Various monodies were written on the death of Allen. "An Apostrophe to the Island of Cuba" appeared in the *New York Spectator*,[5] and a Latin poem to Allen's memory, together with an English translation, was printed in the *Albion*.[6] Owing to Halleck's absence in Europe, his lines on

---

[1] *Incidents in the Life of Jacob Barker*, p. 147.

[2] *Albion*, November 30, 1822. The *Albion* was a weekly paper devoted to foreign news. Halleck was an enthusiastic reader of the paper. Toward the close of his life, the poet said, "I look forward to it weekly" (Wilson, *Bryant and His Friends*, p. 264).

[3] See pp. 133–134.

[4] This meeting was held on December 28, 1822 (see the *Post*, December 30, 1822, and the *Albion*, December 28, 1822).

[5] December 3, 1822.

[6] December 14, 1822. "A Tribute to the Memory of the late Lieut. Wm.

the naval officer were not published until March 4, 1823.[7] This elegy attracted almost no attention at the time of its appearance.

Two months after the publication of Halleck's verses on Lieutenant Allen, the poet made his annual trip to Guilford. This was probably the first visit to his home since his voyage abroad, and one may imagine the eagerness with which the family listened to his many delightful anecdotes. He remained in Guilford about ten days.[8] On his way back to New York, Halleck had the opportunity of meeting the poet, James G. Percival. "I spent two or three hours with Percival in New Haven the day I left you," wrote the poet to his sister. "Mr. Fowler, now a tutor in the college there, formerly a classmate of George Elliot,[9] met me in the street and very politely showed me the lions, that is to say, the colleges, library, pictures, minerals, Professor Silliman, and Mr. Percival. I found the latter an agreeable companion after his embarrassment at being introduced had subsided. He is wonderfully timid, and hardly spoke for the first half hour."[10] Many years after this event, Professor Fowler in a letter to Julius Ward, the biographer of Percival, described the meeting of the two poets. The account is of special importance in the vivid picture which it paints of Halleck's appearance and personality at this period. "Not very long after Percival became known to the country as a poet," wrote Professor Fowler, "I happened to meet in New Haven my old friend, Fitz-Greene Halleck, the poet, who had just returned from his travels. I proposed to him to call upon Percival, who was personally a stranger. To this he readily consented. Accordingly we went to Percival's room, a retired chamber in the house of Mr. Johnson in Chapel Street. When the two poets met, there was certainly a great contrast between them. The one was a man of the world, polished and fashionably dressed, fresh from foreign travel, of warm manners, ready sympathies, fasci-

Howard Allen'' appeared in the *Olio* (New York, 1823). The author of the volume is said to have been William B. Gilley. A brief biography of Lieutenant Allen may be found in William Raymond's *Biographical Sketches of the Distinguished Men of Columbia County, Including an Account of the Most Important Offices They Have Filled, in the State and General Governments, and in the Army and Navy* (Albany, 1851).

[7] *New York Evening Post.* Four lines from Halleck's poem were placed on the monument erected to the memory of Lieutenant Allen at Hudson, New York (see the *New York Evening Mail,* January 9, 1868).

[8] Wilson, *Life,* p. 286.

[9] One of Halleck's Guilford friends.   [10] Wilson, *Life,* p. 290.

nating address, and graceful conversation. The other was Percival, such as I have described him to be. During the first part of the interview they were still apart, though in the presence of each other. After a while, Percival became responsive, the coldness passed off, and the souls of the two poets, in full and free communion, flowed on in a delightful stream of conversation.''[11] Many years later Halleck's early impressions of Percival were sharpened, and his admiration for the poet greatly deepened, by a perusal of Julius Ward's *Life and Letters of James Gates Percival.* ''Have you read the Life of Percival?'' asked Halleck of Evert A. Duyckinck in 1866. ''It has added greatly to my previous high opinion of his genius and acquirements. Had his career been more in Europe, especially on the Continent of Europe, he would have been ranked among the ablest of her learned and lettered men. Even here in America, where a Geologist[12] is the embodied wonder and wisdom of the home, the man whom Sir Charles Lyell pronounced to be 'one of the most remarkable men he had ever seen' ought to be known and esteemed wherever Sir Charles himself is.''[13]

The year 1823 closed with the publication of Halleck's poem ''Alnwick Castle,''[14] which was printed in the *New York Evening Post* for December 6. It was preceded by a note, probably from Coleman's pen:

In the following lines, our readers will find themselves engaged with no ordinary poet. The third stanza contains one line exquisitely beautiful, but

[11] Ward, *Life and Letters of James Gates Percival* (Boston, 1866), p. 139. Judging from a letter regarding Percival that Halleck himself wrote to Professor Fowler, it is evident that this was not the first meeting which he had had with the New Haven poet. ''I was introduced to him [Percival] for the first time as far back as 1821 or 1822 in New York, where he was passing a few weeks, and was a frequent guest of Mr. Cooper, the novelist, and of a circle of gentlemen delighting in literature and its specialties, all of whom appreciated and admired him alike as a man and a man of letters, and were very desirous that he should become a resident of New York, and make authorship a pursuit as well as a pastime'' (Ward, *Life and Letters of James Gates Percival*, p. 141. The letter is dated August 13, 1863).

[12] Percival had almost as great a reputation as a geologist as a poet. ''In my opinion,'' wrote Prof. James D. Dana of Yale, ''no one in the country has done better work in geology or work of greater value to the science'' (Ward, *Life and Letters of James Gates Percival*, p. 418).

[13] The letter from which this extract is taken is preserved in the Duyckinck Collection of the New York Public Library.

[14] Signed ''C.''

I shall leave him or her who duly appreciate [*sic*] it to find it out. Probably the reader of taste and sagacity, who has been conversant with the poetry which has heretofore adorned the columns of the Evening Post, will not long conjecture in vain as to the fortunate author.

There is no indication that the verses attracted more than momentary attention at the time of their first publication in the *Post*. Few opinions regarding the poem have been recovered which antedate its appearance in the collected edition of 1827. About a week after the publication of the lines in the *Post,* they were reprinted in the *New York American.*[15] They were here described in the sentimental idiom of the period as "exquisitely poetical. Those who have visited the scene where they are laid, will be not less struck with the graphic fidelity of the picture than by the taste and finish of its execution, while none can fail to respond to the enkindling sentiments of the poem generally." But an age whose conception of poetry rested so confidently upon sensibility and romance found the note of disillusion struck in the second part of the poem difficult to understand.[16] Only the first half[17]—the romantic description of the castle and the historic memories it evoked—found its way into *The Album,* a book of selections from the American poets, compiled by an unknown hand[18] in 1824.

We may note at this point a translation of "Alnwick Castle" into the French, made by Monsieur de Chatelain in 1858 or 1859. The French translator gave the poem to John Bigelow, the American ambassador to France, who in turn forwarded it to Halleck.[19] At once amused and annoyed by this ill-advised attempt to render his poem into a foreign tongue, Halleck answered Mr. Bigelow in a note dated May 24, 1860. "Much of 'wild and wonderful' you have doubtless met with in your 'sight-seeing' pilgrimages abroad," wrote the poet in a whimsical mood, "—pilgrimages which, I hope, have proved pleasant and profitable to you; but pray tell me candidly if, in all the sights detailed in Murray's hand-books, those you have seen, and those you have wisely refrained from seeing, in all the museums you have visited, from the British to Barnum's, have you met a greater curiosity than the document which, to my infinite instruction and delight, you have done me the kindness to

---

[15] December 13, 1823.   [16] See pp. 210–211.
[17] Ending with the line, "The Norman's curfew-bell."
[18] Published in New York.   [19] Wilson, *Life,* p. 521.

forward with your letter.''[20] This translation, which is now unfortunately lost, continued to amuse Halleck for some years, and in 1866 it was sent to his friend, Evert A. Duyckinck. The accompanying letter, from which the following extracts are taken, is sparkling with the quiet, playful humor characteristic of the closing years of the poet's life.

In order to prove myself entitled to the exclamations of Peter Quince in the Midsummer Nights Dream, "Bless thee, bless thee, Bottom! thou art translated!" and to gratify your love of literary curiosity, I send you herewith not only the promised Greek translation of Marco Batzaris, but a French translation of "Alnwick Castle." . . . The French translation was sent me some five or six years since, from London by Mr. Bigelow, our present ambassador at Paris, "at the request," as he says in his letter enclosing it, "of its author, Monsieur de Chatelaine [sic], a French gentleman of some distinction in the world of letters as the translator of Chaucer." You will observe that I am indebted to the translator's genius for many ideas exclusively his own.[21]

It was also in 1823 that Halleck wrote the poem ''Magdalen,'' which was not published, so far as can be ascertained, until the edition of 1827. Nothing is known of the verses beyond the cryptic note in that volume which describes them as written ''for a love-stricken young officer on his way to Greece. The reader will have the kindness to presume that he died there.'' In the edition of 1836 the date of composition, 1823, was added to the note.

Halleck's social life at this period has been preserved for us in a series of interesting documents. It was in 1824 that the poet first met William Cullen Bryant at the home of Robert Sedgwick, a lawyer and brother of the novelist, Catherine Sedgwick. Bryant had made his first visit to New York, and soon after his arrival wrote to his wife, ''I dined yesterday at Mr. Robert Sedgwick's in a com-

20 A copy of this letter is preserved in the Duyckinck Collection of the New York Public Library. It is substantially the same as that printed by Wilson (*Life*, pp. 521–523). In endeavoring to procure this copy, Duyckinck wrote to Bryant, and the resulting correspondence may be found in the New York Public Library.

21 The letter, dated May 23, 1866, is in the Duyckinck Collection of the New York Public Library. Chevalier de Chatelain (usually so spelled) translated portions of the work of Chaucer and Longfellow. See *Contes de Cantorbéry, traduits en vers français* (London, 1857–60), 3 vols.; and *Évangéline; suivie des Voix de la Nuit; poèmes traduits de H. Longfellow* (London, 1856).

A parody of ''Alnwick Castle'' appeared in Jacob Bigelow's *Eolopoesis*, New York [1855].

pany of authors,—Mr. Cooper, the novelist; Mr. Halleck, author of 'Fanny'; Mr. Sands, author of 'Yamoyden.' ''[22] Many years later, Bryant recalled pleasantly his first meeting with Halleck.

It was in 1825,[23] before Halleck's reputation as a poet had reached its full growth, that I took up my residence in New York. I first met him at the hospitable board of Robert Sedgwick, Esq., and remember being struck with the brightness of his eye, which every now and then glittered with mirth, and with the graceful courtesy of his manners. Something was said of the length of time that he had lived in New York, "You are not from New England?" said our host. "I certainly am," was Halleck's reply. "I am from Connecticut." "Is it possible?" exclaimed Mr. Sedgwick. "Well, you are the only New Englander that I ever saw in whom the tokens of his origin were not as plain as the mark set upon the forehead of Cain."[24]

The home of Robert Sedgwick and that of his brother, Henry, at whose advice Bryant finally settled in New York, were the meeting places of many of the *literati* of the period. Here Bryant again mentions having seen Robert C. Sands, James Hillhouse,[25] Samuel F. B. Morse,[26] and Halleck, "then in the height of his poetical reputation."[27]

It was about 1830, just after the writing of Halleck's sentimental tribute to Bryant in "The Recorder,"[28] that the two poets became a frequent subject of comparison by critics. "Mr. Bryant," wrote the *American Monthly Magazine,* "is beyond competition the most finished poet of our country. With less inborn poetry than Percival, less force and originality than Halleck, and less invention and graphicism (if we may make a word) than Hillhouse, he has written better poetry than either, and will probably be longer read and remembered."[29] "Without the lyric fire and brilliant fancy and versatile genius of Halleck," remarked another Bryant enthusiast,

---

[22] Parke Godwin, *A Biography of William Cullen Bryant* (New York, 1883), I, 189.

[23] This date refers, of course, to Bryant's final settlement in New York, and not to his first meeting with Halleck, which was earlier.

[24] *Some Notices of the Life and Writings of Halleck,* pp. 13–14.

[25] The poet, mentioned by Halleck in ''The Recorder'' (1869 ed., p. 171).

[26] The distinguished artist and inventor. He painted a portrait of Halleck (see p. 226).

[27] See Bryant's ''Reminiscences of Miss Sedgwick'' in Mary E. Dewey, *Life and Letters of Catherine M. Sedgwick* (New York, 1871), p. 441.

[28] 1869 ed., p. 171.   [29] II, 350 (August, 1830).

"—as a poet, as a classical scholar, an orator and prose writer of the first class—Bryant occupied a position to which Halleck had no pretensions."[30] But Halleck had his adherents who rallied to his support. Philip Hone, at one time mayor of New York, wrote in his *Diary*, "Bryant may be considered the best of American poets, with the exception of Halleck";[31] and the *New York Herald*[32] expressed displeasure that the name of Bryant should be so widely published at the expense of Halleck's. Frederic S. Cozzens was also warm in his praise of Halleck, to whom he wrote in 1864: "Oh you will have a wreath of laurel when that old Puritan who has more brain than heart, will fade away in the effulgence of Wordsworth's fame. Did you ever read Wordsworth, and after him Bryant? Why it is a penny trumpet after a full orchestra."[33] George W. Curtis, in reviewing the early Knickerbocker writers in 1884 when the name of Halleck was slowly being forgotten, thus placed the two poets side by side:

But while many of the noted writers in the Knickerbocker circle of half a century since are no longer famous nor even much known to the New York readers of to-day, yet the great Knickerbocker names are great still, and Irving, Cooper, and Bryant, and perhaps Halleck, although Halleck is fading, still hold the place they held with our fathers.[34]

Further light is thrown upon the society in which Halleck moved in the twenties by a letter of Catherine Sedgwick, the novelist, whose first work, *A New England Tale*, had been published in 1822. The excerpt here presented is of peculiar interest because of the description which it gives of Halleck's personal appearance at this period.

I went to Mr. Sewall's in one of those horrid fits of depression when one would cut one's throat, if (as Jane said about killing a chicken) it would not hurt. But when I got there I found the rooms full of agreeable

[30] William A. Jones, essayist and critic, in a letter to Wilson [Andrew J. Symington, *William Cullen Bryant* (New York, 1880), p. 253].

[31] *The Diary of Philip Hone* (New York, 1889), I, 44. Entry for January 19, 1832.

[32] May 12, 1837.

[33] This letter is owned by Capt. F. L. Pleadwell. It is dated January 24, 1863. The year, however, should be 1864, as allusions in the letter plainly indicate. See pp. 346–347.

[34] *Passages from the Correspondence and Other Papers of Rufus W. Griswold* (Cambridge, 1898), p. 75.

people, and before the evening was over I thought this quite a holiday world. Halleck, alias Croaker, was there. I have never seen him before. He had a reddish, brown complexion, and a heavy jaw, but an eye so full of the fire and sweetness of poetry that you at once own him for one of the privileged order. He does not act as if he had spent his life in groves and temples, but he has the courtesy of a man of society. He dances with grace, and talks freely and without parade.[35]

Halleck's love of the theater was gratified in 1825 by the first performance in New York of Italian opera. On November 29 Rossini's *Barbiere de Seviglia* was presented at the Park Theatre by Manuel Garcia,[36] whose daughter, Maria Malibran,[37] captivated the city with her beautiful voice. Conspicuous among the fashionable audience[38] that assembled to enjoy the opera was Halleck's Italian master, Lorenzo Da Ponte.[39] Others present included "Joseph Bonaparte, the ex-king of Spain, and the friends Fenimore Cooper and Fitz-Greene Halleck, who sat side by side."[40]

Joseph Bonaparte, who attended the performance of *Il Barbiere,* had sought refuge in America after the defeat of his brother, Napoleon I, and for some years resided in New Jersey. During this period of exile, Halleck formed an acquaintanceship with Joseph. The poet once described to General Wilson a wedding party, held at Villagrand's in Warren Street, in honor of a member of the Bonaparte family, at which he was the only American present.[41] The guests included Marshal Grouchy, "Generals Renaud, St. Jean d'Angely, Van Dam, Desnouettes, Lallemand," and other followers of Napoleon who had been exiled. Joseph Bonaparte, says Wilson, "talked to Halleck on this and other occasions without reserve, referring to his former situation as 'Quand j'étais roi d'Espagne,' or 'Dans mes belles affaires.' In the course of the

---

[35] Dewey, *Life and Letters of Catherine M. Sedgwick,* p. 171. The letter is dated January 20, 1825, and is addressed to Charles Sedgwick.

[36] J. Russo, *Lorenzo Da Ponte,* pp. 126–127.

[37] Halleck mentioned Signorina Garcia in "The Recorder" (see 1869 ed., p. 173).

[38] *Evening Post,* November 30, 1825.

[39] Russo, *op. cit.,* p. 127.   [40] Wilson, *Life,* p. 282.

[41] *Ibid.,* p. 519. The affair is undated by Wilson; nor does George Bertin in *Joseph Bonaparte en Amérique 1815–1832* (Paris, 1893) supply the missing information. Bertin apparently knew nothing of the party except what he learned from Wilson's book. In the *Albion* for July 27, 1822, we find the following cryptic note: "M. Joseph Buonaparte, Comte de Survilliers, arrived in this city a few days ago."

evening the party became quite hilarious, and enjoyed themselves
as no other men on the face of the earth but Frenchmen could
have done under similar circumstances. The ex-king made a trumpet of a newspaper, and blew it vigorously; the marshal sang
songs, all present joining in the chorus; the famous cavalry leader,
Lallemand, jumped about on all fours, with a four-year-old boy on
his back; while another Waterloo general gave laughable imitations
of a stuttering French soldier, and other comicalities. They romped
and played like children, and although some of the party were old,
others elderly, they were all full of youthful spirit. Halleck modestly refrained from stating in what manner he contributed to the
enjoyment of the evening, which he characterized as the 'raciest
and most amusing night I ever passed.' ''[42]

An intimate friend of Halleck at this time was James Fenimore
Cooper, who by 1824 had published four novels,[43] and had acquired
a literary reputation both in this country and in England. Cooper
was described to Washington Irving in 1827 as a man with ''a rough
& confident manner of expressing himself'' but ''a right good
fellow at bottom.''[44] Added to a certain social instinct which Cooper
undoubtedly possessed, was a love of associating with literary men.
It was probably soon after the novelist's coming to New York in
1822 that Halleck met him.[45] In the early twenties we find Cooper

[42] Wilson, *Life*, pp. 519–520. A very curious footnote in Bertin's book (p.
209) translates into French Wilson's account of the dinner party. It was also
at this period that Halleck met Lafayette, who visited the country in 1824, and
the Prince of Saxe-Weimar, who came the following year (Wilson, *Life*, p.
480).

[43] *Precaution* (1820); *The Spy* (1821); *The Pioneers* (1823); and *The
Pilot* (1824).

[44] *Letters of Henry Brevoort to Washington Irving*, edited by G. S. Hellman (New York, 1916), I, 160–161. Quoted by courtesy of G. P. Putnam's Sons.

[45] The date of Halleck's first meeting with Cooper is uncertain. Halleck
once said, ''I met Cooper soon after his marriage'' (Wilson, *Bryant and His
Friends*, p. 236). As Cooper was married in 1811, this would make the date of
meeting 1812 or 1813. Wilson, however, asserts that Halleck became acquainted
with him in 1815 (*Life*, p. 490). But it is doubtful whether either of these
dates is correct. That Halleck should have met Cooper prior to the publication
of his first novel in 1820 is extremely unlikely. Cooper did not come to live in
New York until just after the publication of his second novel, *The Spy*, in 1821
[Thomas Lounsbury, *James Fenimore Cooper* (Boston, 1882), p. 63]. It was
then in all probability that the two became acquainted. The first indisput-
able evidence of their acquaintanceship is preserved in the letter Cooper wrote
to Irving on July 30, 1822, in which the novelist says that Halleck, ''the admi-

frequently at Charles Wiley's bookstore, gathering about him such men as Paulding, Halleck, Verplanck, and Morse.[46] The meeting place of these men was a small back room of Wiley's store, which Cooper in those days of good-fellowship christened "The Den." Here too Richard Henry Dana, author of "The Buccaneer," first met Cooper, Percival, and Halleck, soon after Wiley had published the second edition of *Fanny*.[47]

This literary group which gathered about Cooper in "The Den" may be regarded as a forerunner of the famous Bread and Cheese Lunch, organized by the novelist in 1824. Of the founding of this club Cooper once declared, "It is one of the acts of my life . . . in which I take great pride."[48] The Lunch in its insistence upon good-fellowship was truly representative of the social spirit prevailing in the early Knickerbocker school. New York at this period, we have had occasion to observe, possessed a town literature much of whose power depended upon the social propensities of its members. Authorship rested lightly on the shoulders of these young men who found in the amenities of brisk conversation and good eating quite as alluring a pastime as in the felicities of the pen. One of the most intimate pictures which have survived of the Bread and Cheese Club is that by Cooper's daughter, Susan Augusta, who once wrote her "Memories" for her "nephews and nieces."[49]

It was about this time my Father planned and founded a Club to which he gave the name of "The Lunch." It met every Thursday evening, I think at the house of Abigail Jones, a colored cook, famous at that day, who kept the Delmonico's of the date. Most of the prominent men of ability and character in New York belonged to the club, which also, through its members, invited strangers of distinction. Conversation was the object; I do not think there was any card-playing. The evening closed with a good

rable Croaker," is to convey a portion of *The Pioneers* to Mr. Benjamin Coles in England (see p. 140). During the early years in New York, Cooper's house appears to have been a rendezvous for literary men of whom Halleck was one. See Mary Phillips, *James Fenimore Cooper* (New York, 1913), pp. 89–90; *Correspondence of James Fenimore-Cooper* (New Haven, 1922), I, 56; and Julius H. Ward, *Life and Letters of James Gates Percival*, p. 141.

[46] J. C. Derby, *Fifty Years among Authors* (New York, 1886), p. 293.

[47] Wilson, *Bryant and His Friends*, p. 190.

[48] *New York American*, May 30, 1826.

[49] "Small Family Memories" in the *Correspondence of James Fenimore-Cooper* (New Haven, 1922), I, [7] ff.

supper, one of the members being caterer every Thursday, while Abigail Jones carried out the programme to perfection in the way of cooking.[50]

The meeting place of the club "at the house of Abigail Jones," or at what was perhaps her restaurant at No. 300 Broadway,[51] was probably during the early days of the Lunch. In 1827, it appears, the club changed its meeting place to Washington Hotel or Washington Hall, as it was sometimes called, located at the corner of Broadway and Chambers Street.[52] It is this place that is described as the club's rendezvous by Dr. John Francis, whose volume, *Old New York,* a valuable commentary on New York life and letters for more than half a century, throws further light upon the business procedure and social activities of the organization. "The selection of members for nomination to this fraternity," wrote Dr. Francis who belonged to the club, "rested, I believe, entirely with him [Cooper]: bread and cheese were the ballots used, and one of cheese decided adversely to admittance, so that in fact a unanimous vote was essential to membership. This association generally met at Washington Hall, once, if I remember rightly, every fortnight, during the winter season. It included a large number of the most conspicuous of professional men, statesmen, lawyers, and physicians. Science was not absent. I cannot in this place attempt anything like an enumeration of the fellows. Our most renowned poet was Halleck, our greatest naturalist was De Kay; William[53] and John Duer[54] were among the representatives of the bar; Renwick,[55] of philosophy; letters found associates in Verplanck[56] and King;[57] merchants, in

[50] *Correspondence of James Fenimore-Cooper,* I, 49.

[51] Abigail Jones's address is given as such in an early advertisement of a club meeting which appeared in the *New York American* for April 13, 1826.

[52] Advertisements of meetings of the Lunch appearing in the daily papers after 1826 give the place as Washington Hall. Parke Godwin in *A Biography of William Cullen Bryant* (I, 208) states the club as meeting "in Washington Hotel, on the site of Stewart's late wholesale store."

[53] William Duer, president of Columbia College from 1829 to 1842; author of *New York as It Was during the Latter Part of the Last Century* (New York, 1849).

[54] John Duer, brother of the president.

[55] James Renwick, professor of Natural and Experimental Chemistry at Columbia from 1820 to 1854.

[56] Gulian C. Verplanck, author and lecturer, editor of Shakespeare's works (see also pp. 222–223 and 397–398).

[57] Charles King, newspaper editor, and president of Columbia from 1848 to 1864.

Charles A. Davis[58] and Philip Hone;[59] and politicians, who had long before discharged their public trusts, were here and there chronicled in fellowship.''[60]

Susan Cooper, we have seen, described the object of the club as ''conversation'' and further showed how the impulse to conversation was materially aided by the culinary art of Abigail Jones. In spite of the exclusive and restricted character accorded the club by Dr. Francis, it may readily be seen from the wide range of professions from which members were taken, that in reality no rigid test of admittance could have been exacted. No official records of the organization have come down to us, if, indeed, such records were ever kept, and we are forced to rely solely upon the memoirs and reminiscences of members and friends, in an effort to reconstruct the activities of the club. One of the primary objects of the society was, no doubt, to invite men of eminence and distinction to dine at the club, so that the members might have the privilege of meeting and conversing with them. Thus Susan Augusta mentions Bishop Hobart[61] as ''a frequent guest,''[62] and Dr. Francis records that ''the meetings of the Club (or Lunch) were often swelled to quite a formidable assembly by members of Congress, senators, and representatives, and in this array were often found Webster,[63] and Storrs,[64] W. B. Lawrence,[65] and the French Minister, Hyde de Neuville.''[66]

The more dignified and serious character of the club, however, received at times a needed modification in the introduction of hu-

[58] Charles A. Davis, an intimate friend of Halleck. See letter from Davis to Halleck in Wilson, *Life*, pp. 447–448; and one from Halleck to Davis in the present work, pp. 329–330.

[59] Philip Hone, at one time mayor of New York, and author of the famous *Diary*.

[60] Francis, *Old New York; or Reminiscences of the Past Sixty Years*, edited by Henry T. Tuckerman (New York, 1865), pp. 291–292.

[61] John Henry Hobart, a distinguished Episcopal bishop; founder of the *Churchman's Magazine* in 1808.

[62] *Correspondence of James Fenimore-Cooper*, I, 50.

[63] Presumably Daniel Webster.

[64] Henry Randolph Storrs (1787–1837), a distinguished lawyer and judge in New York state [see *Appletons' Cyclopaedia of American Biography* (New York, 1898), V, 708–709].

[65] William Beach Lawrence (1800–1881), a Columbia graduate, and in early life a prominent New York lawyer. In 1845 he removed to Newport, Rhode Island.

[66] Francis, *Old New York*, p. 292.

morous and even burlesque elements. The manner of voting by
means of bread and cheese reflects a marked tendency to break
away from the formalities of ordinary club life, and to indulge in
pure and unadulterated fun. This penchant for the mock-serious,
so habitual with the early Knickerbockers, and persisting to a less
noticeable degree in their immediate descendants, is best illustrated
in the "official" correspondence sent to Cooper, while the novelist
was traveling in Europe. The formal opening of a letter addressed
to Cooper as the "Constitution of the Club," and dated New York,
November 25, 1826, is of unusual interest, burlesquing, as it does,
the formal procedure customary in letters of this character.

To

"J" the Constitution of the "Bread and Cheese."

We your dutiful and affectionate Commissioners, most graciously nomi-
nated, appointed, authorized, and enjoined by our dear and ever vener-
ated *Constitution,* to convoke and convene the Great Diet of the Bread and
Cheese Lunch, deem it our bounden duty promptly to communicate to
Your Patriarchal Highness, an account of the measures and proceedings
touching our momentous charge.[67]

The letter continues in a similar vein, playfully suggesting to
Cooper, who was then touring France, that "His Most Christian
Majesty," the King of France be elected an honorary member of
the club, and that a *Branch Lunch* be established in Paris.[68]

Of Halleck's intimate relations with the club little has been preserved. That he was a charter member of the organization we may
infer from his literary reputation at this time, and from his intimacy with Cooper. Dr. Francis, in naming him among the members
of the Lunch, called him "that most adhesive friend."[69] In 1827
he was also mentioned along with Bryant by Henry Brevoort who
was writing to Washington Irving, then abroad. "You mentioned
in your letter Halleck & Bryant," wrote Brevoort, "—they are
both members of 'The Lunch,' a social club which has been in existence here for several years.—When you come to us, I know you
will have great enjoyment in their society & in that of the Lunch.
They are shy men & are very little seen in society. Halleck is Sec-

---

[67] *Correspondence of James Fenimore-Cooper,* I, 105–106.
[68] *Ibid.,* p. 108.
[69] *Memorial of James Fenimore Cooper* (New York, 1852), p. 94. Dr. Francis in a letter to the anthologist, Rufus Griswold, dated October 1, 1851.

retary of an Ins: Comp^y.—Bryant lives by his pen. They are undoubtedly men of very high endowments. Halleck regretted that he did not meet you some years since—I gave him a letter to you, but I believe you were in Germany.''[70] As a matter of fact, the Lunch had not waited for Irving's return from Europe, before enrolling him in their ranks. At a farewell dinner given to Cooper just before his departure for Europe in 1826, Irving had been elected an honorary member of the society. It was a gala occasion, this on which Cooper received his ovation at the City Hotel. Surrounded by his many friends and guests—several notables were present— Cooper was made to feel the warm regard in which he was held by his fellow citizens. Charles King, who many years later became president of Columbia College, made the address of welcome to the novelist, and, in mentioning several of the distinguished people who were present, thus referred to Halleck:

As a lyric poet there is now before us one, whose genius and fine taste have graced with laurels the laurelled flag of his country—who has in verse as beautiful as the beautiful scene that inspired him, added something even to the "storied Percy's pride";[71] and in the glowing lines of Marco Bozzaris, given to liberty another battle-cry.[72]

Halleck's tribute to Cooper that memorable evening took the form of a toast: ''The Navy of our Country has nurtured many heroes who merit immortality, and one poet historian who can give it.''

It is probable that the Bread and Cheese Club did not continue after 1830. Wilson in his biography of Halleck states that it lasted for almost ''fifteen years,''[73] but it is doubtful whether the Lunch maintained so long an existence. Prof. Thomas Lounsbury intimates that it died not long after Cooper's departure for Europe in 1826.[74] The novelist, in writing to De Kay from Florence on May 25, 1829, speaks as if he had heard nothing from the club for a long time. ''What has become of the Lunch,'' asks Cooper, ''of Dunlap,[75] of

---

[70] *Letters of Henry Brevoort to Washington Irving*, II, 6. The letter is dated November 19, 1827. Quoted by courtesy of G. P. Putnam's Sons.

[71] One of the few references to ''Alnwick Castle'' before the publication of the poem in the collected edition of 1827. It is the only extant reference of this period that associates the poem definitely with its author.

[72] *New York American*, May 30, 1826.

[73] *Life*, p. 401.

[74] *James Fenimore Cooper* (Boston, 1883), p. 64.

[75] William Dunlap, the dramatist.

Cooper,[76] of the Academy,[77] of Moore,[78] and the other strange fish, Francis[79] included?''[80] A final dated reference to the Bread and Cheese Club occurs in General Wilson's *Life and Letters of Fitz-Greene Halleck*, and consists of an invitation dated January 5, 1830, addressed to the poet, and informing him of ''the next meeting of the Lunch.''[81]

This social life to which the poet was now becoming habituated is further exemplified in an event in which Halleck participated in 1824. A dinner was given at Washington Hall in honor of Judge John Trumbull, author of the famous poem, *M'Fingal*. This dinner, ''intended as a mark of respect for the professional, personal, and literary character of the distinguished guest,'' was largely attended by literary and professional men of New York. Among the toasts that were offered on the occasion one is worthy of especial note. By the death of Byron which had occurred a few months before, Halleck, we have seen, had been profoundly affected. His admiration for the late English poet is well reflected in the toast which he proposed to Lord Byron's memory:

> For him the voice of festive mirth
> Be hush'd—*his name* the only sound.[82]

Leaving this picture of Halleck's social life in the early twenties, we may now turn to several literary works which the poet produced in 1824 and 1825. Some time during the former year Halleck wrote the poem ''Woman,'' which appeared in print, probably for the first time, in the collected edition of 1827.[83] These lines, which were further described in the title as ''Written in the Album of an Un-

---

[76] Probably Thomas A. Cooper, the actor.

[77] The New York Academy of Fine Arts was organized in 1801, and incorporated in 1808 as the American Academy of Fine Arts. ''With the downfall of the American Academy, the National Academy of Design took its rise about 1828.'' See Dr. John Francis, *Old New York*, pp. 277–279.

[78] Clement C. Moore, author of the famous ''Night Before Christmas.''

[79] Dr. John Francis, an eminent New York physician, already referred to in connection with the Lunch.

[80] *Correspondence of James Fenimore-Cooper*, I, 166.

[81] *Life*, p. 401.

[82] *New York American*, July 16, 1824.

[83] The date of composition, 1824, was given for the first time at the close of the poem in the 1836 edition.

known Lady,'' were in reality addressed to a Miss Devens, who resided at or near Boston.[84]

The only extant poems written by Halleck in 1825 are ''Mr. Clinton's Speech, January, 1825,''[85] and ''Marco Bozzaris.'' In 1812 De Witt Clinton had run for the presidency on the Federalist ticket against James Madison, and was defeated. In 1816, however, he was elected governor of New York State, and was reëlected in 1820 and 1824. In this poem Halleck cleverly burlesqued the formal speech made by Clinton in addressing the legislature in January, 1825.[86] The style obviously harks back to the days of *The Croakers*, as may be noted in the concluding stanza, in which the poet alludes to the desire, still in the mind of Clinton, of becoming head of the nation.

> This is my longest speech, but those
> Who feel, that, like a cable's strength,
> Its power increases with its length,
> Will weep to hear its close.
> Weep not—my next shall be as long,
> And that, like this,—embalmed in song,
> Will be, when two brief years are told,
> Mine own no longer, but the Nation's,
> With all my speeches, new and old,
> And what is more—the place I hold,
> Together with its pay and rations.[87]

The death of Marco Bozzaris on August 20, 1823, an episode in that brilliant struggle for liberty begun by the Greeks in 1820, soon became an object of public interest in the United States. The *Albion*, a New York weekly paper specializing in foreign news, recorded in its issue for January 10, 1824, the performance of ''an appropriate and attractive melodrama'' ''entitled *Greece and Liberty*, written in New-York, founded on the last exploit of Marco Batzari, the Grecian chief who fell in storming the Turkish camp

---

[84] This information was furnished me by Miss L. A. Rice of Springdale, Connecticut, a niece of Miss Devens.

[85] First published in the Bradford edition of *The Croakers*. A manuscript of this poem was offered at auction in a sale of Americana held by the American Art Association on January 30, 1925.

[86] Much of G. C. Verplanck's pamphlet, *The State Triumvirate, a Political Tale; and The Epistles of Brevet Major Pindar Puff* (1819), satires the pedantry of Clinton's literary style. See also Halleck's *Fanny*, stanza 82 (1839 ed.).

[87] *The Croakers* (Bradford ed.), p. 121.

in July last.'' In the same issue of the *Albion* also appeared a poem addressed ''To the Memory of Marco Botzari, the Greek hero, who fell storming the Turkish Camp with 400 Suliotes. Translated from Modern Greek.'' It is not improbable that Halleck's poem was written as early as 1824, although there is no available evidence to that effect.

In 1825 William Cullen Bryant and Henry James Anderson began a new periodical, the *New York Review and Athenaeum Magazine,* which was issued in continuation of an earlier periodical, the *Atlantic Magazine,* conducted for a time by Robert C. Sands. Bryant states that Halleck brought his poem, ''Marco Bozzaris,'' to the new periodical.[88] The verses, which appeared in the first number,[89] were prefaced by a sketch of the hero's exploit,[90] and concluded with an expression of unqualified praise for the poet's work. ''It would be an act of gross injustice to the author of the above magnificent Lyric,'' wrote one of the editors, ''were we to withhold the expression of our admiration of its extraordinary beauty. We are sure, too, that in this instance, at least, we have done what is rare indeed in the annals of criticism,—we have given an opinion from which not one of our readers will feel any inclination to dissent.'' This editorial comment was from the pen of Henry Anderson, as may be seen from a letter which Bryant wrote to Richard H. Dana, whose poem to ''A Dying Raven'' was published in the same issue of the *Review* with ''Marco Bozzaris.''

You will appear in our magazine in company with Mr. Halleck. The poem entitled ''Marco Bozzaris'' was written by him, and I think it a very beautiful thing. Anderson was delighted with it—he got it from the author after much solicitation—that he could not forbear adding the expression of his admiration at the end of the poem. For my part, though I entirely agree with him in his opinion of the beauty of the poem, I have my doubts whether it is not better to let the poetry of magazines commend itself to the reader by its own excellence.[91]

[88] *Some Notices of the Life and Writings of Fitz-Greene Halleck,* p. 14.
[89] I, 72 (June, 1825). Signed ''H.''
[90] ''The Epaminondas of modern Greece.—He fell in a night attack upon the Turkish Camp at Lapsi, the site of the ancient Plataea, August 20, 1823, and expired in the moment of victory. His last words were 'To die for liberty is a pleasure and not a pain.' ''
[91] Godwin, *A Biography of William Cullen Bryant,* I, 216–217. The letter is dated May 28, 1825. The following story of the composition of the poem is

"Marco Bozzaris," dealing as it did with a subject uppermost in the public mind, attracted more attention on first publication than did "Alnwick Castle." The lines were soon reprinted in the *New York Observer;*[92] and in the *American* they also appeared along with a review of the first number of Bryant's periodical. "This is to be a monthly publication," wrote the reviewer, "and the first number gives promise of a good sequel. If, indeed, it contained nothing but the stirring and 'magnificent lyric' with which we this day grace our columns, it would make good its claim to immortality; for nothing certainly within the compass of our reading, that Greece, her wrongs, her sufferings and her heroism, have inspired, can at all be compared to this ode to Marco Bozzaris. He who can read it without emotion, would pass over the fields of Marathon and Plataea as though they were common to earth. We will not wrong our readers so much as to suppose it necessary to name the author; within that circle *none* dare walk but he.''[93]

To what extent the poem was reprinted in England we have no means of knowing. In any case, it found its way into the columns of the *New Times,* and was thence published in the *Edinburgh Literary Almanack*. As the poem had appeared in America without the author's name, it was naturally printed abroad anonymously. The editor of a Philadelphia magazine, *The Museum of Foreign Literature and Science,*[94] seeing the verses in the *Almanack,* copied them for insertion in his periodical. Before the number of the magazine finally went to press, however, it is probable that he discovered

related by Henry T. Tuckerman: "Among his [Halleck's] fellow-clerks in Jacob Barker's counting-house was a young man of literary culture and disciplined taste, to whom he used to confide his effusions, to be read overnight and reported on at the first interval of leisure the next day. One evening, having missed the usual opportunity of quietly slipping into his friend's hand the latest 'copy of verses,' he left them at his lodgings, with *'Will this do?'* written on the margin: the poem was Marco Bozzaris and the fortunate owner of the unique and precious autograph related the incident as he showed me the original manuscript" [*Lippincott's Magazine*, I, 214 (February, 1868)]. Halleck's inability to hand the verses in the usual manner to his friend is possibly explained by the tradition that "Marco Bozzaris" was written at a house "on the western side of the Harlem River," now located at 160th Street and Edgecombe Avenue [see Charles Hemstreet, *Literary New York* (New York, 1903), pp. 123–124].

92 July 9, 1825.

93 June 7, 1825.   94 IX, 459 (November, 1826).

the authorship of the lines, and inserted on another page of the same issue a note stating the poem "was written by our accomplished countryman, F. G. Halleck, Esq., and first appeared in the *New York Review,* about two years ago. We are glad of this opportunity of publishing it in the Museum, without infringing upon our plan, and copy it exactly as it appeared in Edinburgh. It is proper to mention, however, that in attempting to amend it, the British editor has interpolated a line,

'Like forest pines before the blast!'

in the third stanza. This was not required by the rhyme or measure, and is not in accordance with the sense."[95]

This reprinting of the poem from a British source at once directed the attention of New York citizens to what was regarded as a gross piece of plagiarism on the part of England. The charge was, of course, wholly absurd, but stands as a curious commentary on Halleck's local reputation at this time. A correspondent of the *New York American* appears to have started the fracas by asserting himself "peculiarly tenacious in regard to our literary honours, and more especially as to everything that belongs to the limited stores of American poetry." "I cannot but exclaim," he continued, "at the meanness of the English Editor, in attempting to rob us of the little claims we make to good poetry."[96] At least one New York newspaper, however, found little incriminating in the action of the British editor, and was inclined to excuse the alleged plagiarism.[97] But the *New York Evening Post,* a staunch adherent of Croaker, returned to the attack by condemning the liberal attitude assumed by the *Enquirer,* asserting that "it would certainly be better to give some sort of credit, for it will be admitted on all hands that it is not quite fair, knowingly and purposely to republish the articles of another journal without mentioning the source from which they are derived."[98] Brief though the excitement was, the incident was remembered for some years. In 1831 William J. Snelling

---

[95] *Ibid.,* p. 480.   [96] November 16, 1826.
[97] *New York Enquirer,* November 18, 1826.
[98] November 18, 1826. On the previous day (November 17) the *Post* had published a brief notice commenting on the reprinting of the poem from the *Edinburgh Literary Almanack* and the *New Times.*

introduced in his satire, "Truth: A New Year's Gift for Scribblers,"
the line,

> One of the few who are not born to die,

with the following comment:

I trust Mr. Halleck will excuse me for altering and using two of his
noble lines. As the English journals attempted to purloin the whole piece
from him, I hope he will pardon a smaller freedom in his countryman.[99]

Strangely enough, Halleck's sister, Maria, appears to have known
nothing of "Marco Bozzaris" until almost two years after the
poem's appearance in print. In a letter to his sister, dated March
26, 1827, the poet expressed extreme surprise that she had never
heard of "Marco Bozzaris." "Why," exclaimed Halleck, " 'Bozzaris' is here considered my *chef d'œuvre,* the keystone of the arch
of my renown, if renown it be. It has been published and puffed in
a thousand (more or less) magazines and newspapers, not only in
America, but in England, Scotland, Ireland, etc. It has been translated into French and modern Greek. It has been spouted on the
stage and off the stage, in schools and colleges, etc. etc. It has been
quoted even in the pulpit, and placed as mottoes over the chapters
of a novel or two. It was published in a Philadelphia magazine of
foreign literature as selected from an Edinburgh work, and all the
newspaper editors in town accused all England of plagiarism, etc.,
for a whole week (a long time for one subject to live, as times go),
and the editor of the Philadelphia magazine came out with a puff
and an apology, and something about 'our accomplished countryman, F. G. Halleck, Esq.' "[100]

Several translations of "Marco Bozzaris" have been made, although none survives of so early a date as those mentioned by Halleck. In Eugène A. Vail's *De la littérature et des hommes de
lettres des États-Unis d'Amérique,* published at Paris in 1841, appeared a verse translation of the poem into French.[101] The trans-

[99] P. 30 (see p. 251 of the present work).

[100] Wilson, *Life,* pp. 293–294. Halleck was not always exact in stating facts.
The note in the *Museum* appeared in the *same* issue with the poem, and was
not in the nature of an apology (see "Early History of the Publication of
Marco Bozzaris" in *Living Age,* C, 642 [March 6, 1869]).

[101] A German translation of "Marco Bozzaris" appears in Karl Bleibtreu,
Geschichte der Englischen Litteratur im Neunzehnten Jahrhundert (Leipzig
[1888]), II, 401–403.

lator's name, however, is unknown. Two modern Greek paraphrases
of the poem are also extant. One, made into Greek prose by George
D. Canale, a Zacynthian, and dedicated to Washington Irving, was
published in Cambridge, Massachusetts, in 1859.[102] It was probably
to this Greek rendering of his poem that Halleck humorously referred in a letter to Evert A. Duyckinck to whom the poet sent a
copy of the translation. The paraphrase, Halleck explained, "has
to-day been returned to me by a Yale College Professor of Greek to
whom I had lent it. I presume from the cudgelled appearance of its
outside that its inside must have cudgelled his Brains not a little, a
proof that he knows little of the ancient Greek he professes, or that
my Greek born friend, Mr. Canale's favorite theory, that the difference between the ancient and the modern is very slight, cannot
be as he fancies sustained."[103] Another Greek translation, but this
time in verse, was made in March, 1868,[104] by A. R. Rangabe, the
Greek ambassador, and issued in a thin pamphlet.[105] Of "Marco
Bozzaris" Mr. Rangabe said in writing to Wilson: "After the receipt of your letter, thinking that the beautiful poem should be
known and considered as a poetical and sympathetic link between
our two countries, nations devoted equally to the worship of freedom, I attempted myself a metrical translation of the ode. I sent
it yesterday to Athens, and I presume that it will be published in
the May number of the *Pandora*,[106] the most important of our
periodicals."[107]

[102] A copy of this rare pamphlet is available in the New York Public
Library. What was probably an enlarged and improved edition of the translation was published at Athens in 1870 under the title, "A Memorial of the
American poet, Fitz-Greene Halleck, with a translation of Marco Botzares also
in modern Greek by Prof. George D. Canale." No copy of this edition is available.

[103] From a letter in the Duyckinck Collection of the New York Public
Library, dated May 23, 1866.

[104] Wilson, *Life*, p. 295.

[105] A copy of this translation may be found in the Yale Collection of American Literature. The author's name has been added in ink, thus: A.P. ΡΑΓΚΑΒΗ.

[106] Appeared in the *Pandora* for April 1, 1868 (XIX, 21–22). The translation was located in a rare file of the periodical in the library of Harvard University, through the kindness of the librarian, Mr. William C. Lane.

[107] Wilson, *Life*, p. 295. The letter, addressed to Wilson, is dated March 31,
1868. Echoes of appreciation from Greece were, of course, rare. Two, however,
have been preserved. Two nephews of Marco Bozzaris sent Halleck a picture,
accompanied by highly complimentary letter (Wilson, *Life*, pp. 303–304).

Almost without exception, the contemporary opinion of "Marco Bozzaris" was distinctly laudatory. Bryant's praise of the poem, which we have noted in a letter to Richard H. Dana, author of "The Buccaneer," may be supplemented by a remark made to Wilson in 1878, that "the reading of 'Marco Bozzaris' and some other of Halleck's best poems stirs up my blood like the sound of martial music or the blast of a trumpet."[108] Dana himself, although never intimately acquainted with Halleck, undoubtedly had "Marco Bozzaris" in mind when he said to General Wilson, "Your friend Halleck has produced the best lyric poem yet written in this country."[109] "To be permanently admired," said William Leggett in the *Critic,* "an author must write on the universal truths of morals, or describe the invariable and immutable features of nature. The Sketch Book and Marco Bozzaris will be read with delighted attention when Salmagundi and The Croakers are forgotten."[110] James Lawson, in writing on Halleck in the *Southern Literary Messenger,* mentioned in particular the third stanza of the poem, calling it "beautiful, its language nervous and spirit-stirring; it is indeed worthy of high praise. On reading it, especially the closing lines, we feel as Sir Philip Sydney said he did on reading Chevy Chase."[111] Poe, however, dissented from the popular opinion, though approaching nearer to soundness of judgment, when he said: " 'Marco Bozzaris' has much lyrical, without any great amount of *ideal* beauty. Force is its prevailing feature—force resulting rather from well-ordered meter, vigorous rhythm, and a judicious disposal of the circumstances of the poem, than from any of the truer lyric material. I should do my conscience great wrong were I to speak of 'Marco Bozzaris,' as it is the fashion to speak of it, at least in print. Even as a lyric or ode it is surpassed by many American and a multitude of foreign compositions of a similar character."[112]

The recitation of "Bozzaris" not only by the untutored schoolboy, but by accomplished elocutionists became popular in Halleck's

---

The daughter of Bozzaris is said to have studied English so that she might read Halleck's poems in the original, and come to America to express her gratitude to the poet [see J. Benton, *Frank Leslie's Illustrated Newspaper,* XXV, 243 (January 4, 1868); and Wilson, *Life,* p. 291].

[108] *Bryant and His Friends,* p. 113.　　　[109] *Ibid.,* p. 224.

[110] I, 119 (December 20, 1828).　　　[111] VIII, [2]47 (April, 1842).

[112] *Godey's Magazine and Lady's Book,* XXXIII, 14 (July, 1846).

day. Bryant has related the story of Mrs. Nichols' dramatic rendering of the lyric in the presence of Halleck at the home of Robert Sedgwick.[113] The *New York Mirror* for May 10, 1828, reported that "Marco Bozzaris" "was recited at the Park Theatre the other evening by Mrs. Hilson." "We are totally at a loss which to admire most," the reviewer concluded, "the poem itself, or the lovely being by whom it was spoken. We hope Mrs. Hilson may be induced again to repeat 'Marco Bozzaris.' "[114]

In March, 1826, Halleck contributed to the *New York Review and Athenaeum Magazine*[115] his poem "Connecticut."[116] These verses, though perhaps less popular than "Alnwick Castle" and "Marco Bozzaris," are among Halleck's more substantial and enduring compositions. With the detachment of an outsider who has found in New York a natural and pleasing environment, Halleck has here given a curiously judicial appraisal of the Connecticut character. The poem, of course, contained sufficient delineation of the harsher elements of the New England mind to make it acceptable to a New York audience, without, however, venturing upon a caricature of the Yankee disposition, which would undoubtedly have given the poem a greater local popularity.[117] The verses, as originally published, were signed "H," and bore an explanatory subtitle, "From *Minute-Men*, an unpublished poem." By this designation, Halleck probably had in mind a poem which he intended some day to write, and of which the fragment entitled "Connecticut" should be a part. But the poet, yielding to the mood of literary inertia which was to grow

[113] *Some Notices of the Life and Writings of Fitz-Greene Halleck*, p. 14. See also Mary Dewey, *Life and Letters of Catherine M. Sedgwick*, p. 441.

[114] V, 351. Several parodies of "Marco Bozzaris" may be noted. One entitled "John McKeon," was written by Miss Sandford, daughter of General Sandford (Wilson, *Life*, p. 515). The poem is not extant. Another parody called "New Year's Calls" is preserved in an unidentified clipping now in the Manuscript Division of the New York Public Library. It is signed "Charles Hallock." It may be that this is a pseudonym, although several Charles Hallocks, distant kinsmen of Fitz-Greene, are noted in *The Hallock-Holyoke Pedigree* (Amherst, Massachusetts, 1906). A third parody, "Poet Dreams," may be found in Grace Greenwood's *Greenwood Leaves* (Boston, 1850), p. 292.

[115] II, 319. Bryant alludes to the fact that Halleck contributed this poem to the *Review* in *Some Notices of the Life and Writings of Fitz-Greene Halleck*, p. 15.

[116] The poem was reprinted in the *New York Evening Post* for March 13, 1826, and in the *New York Mirror* for March 18, 1826.

[117] See also Chapter VII.

with the coming years, never found a fitting opportunity to carry out his plan. The "Minute-Men," however, soon became a subject of gossip in the literary world, and critics derived no little pleasure from anticipating the advent of the new poem. Several times the poem was reported virtually finished and about to be published. The first hint that we get of the publication of the new poem comes from an English periodical, the *Literary Gazette and Journal of the Belles Lettres,* which mentioned Halleck as "one of the most popular and sweetest bards of America," who "is about to give the world a new poem. The subject is supposed to be the 'Minute-Men,' from which, it is hinted, his lines on Connecticut are extracted."[118] The following month, the *New York Evening Post* gave its readers the confidential information "that the Messrs. Carvill are about to publish 'Ledyard, or the Minute Men'; a poem in three cantos, by Mr. Halleck;"[119] but a few days later the same paper expressed great surprise at finding they had been anticipated by the British periodical already noted.[120] Another reference to the poem at this period may be found in a manuscript of Halleck's lines to "Burns," dated August 28, 1830. Following the text of the poem in Halleck's autograph, is an indorsement in another and unknown hand, which mentions briefly the poet's reputation in England and states that Halleck "is now publishing in England 'The Minute Men,' a poem in three Cantos."[121] In 1834 the *New York Mirror* printed a "Literary Report" which rather sarcastically described Halleck as having "almost made up his mind to commence his long-talked-of poem, 'The Minute-Men.' "[122] A final reference to the poem occurred in the *Southern Literary Messenger* for November, 1841. In mentioning a new edition of Halleck's works which had just been announced, the reviewer stated that "this collection will embrace all Mr. Halleck's more serious poems, hitherto published, and 'The Minute Men' and other original pieces."[123] Except for these random references, little else is known of the poem.[124] In the year 1852, when Halleck wrote another poetical fragment on Connecticut, which he related to his

---

[118] April 10, 1830.
[119] May 20, 1830.   [120] May 27, 1830.
[121] Manuscript in the Yale Collection of American Literature.
[122] XII, 39 (August 2, 1834).   [123] VII, 816.
[124] No mention of the poem is made by Wilson.

earlier poem, he wisely refrained from any mention of "The Min-ute-Men."[125]

During the year 1826 the financial affairs of Jacob Barker, for some time in a precarious state because of a series of litigations in which he had been involved, came to a culmination in the famous Conspiracy Trials. In June of that year several important insurance companies and banks in which Mr. Barker was a shareholder, failed. The managers of these companies were at once indicted by Hugh Maxwell, the district attorney, on the charge of defrauding the public. Maxwell exerted every means before the grand jury to have Barker's name included in the indictment. At first he was unsuccessful, and the grand jury denied his request. But "the district attorney refused to bring the persons indicted to a trial until another grand jury was formed, in the hope that they could be induced to include Mr. Barker."[126] In this, Maxwell succeeded, and the financier soon found himself involved in a series of lawsuits. Barker always insisted upon Maxwell's dishonesty, asserting in his usually vigorous and emphatic manner that the district attorney had "arbitrarily and unlawfully deprived [him] of [his] documentary proofs," and further charging him with "refusing to comply with the solemn promise he made to the Grand Jury, to allow [him] to benefit by their use, on the trial."[127]

It was probably at this time that Halleck, always faithful to his employer, wrote and circulated among a small group of friends his slashing denunciation of Hugh Maxwell. The name of the public

125 See *The Poetical Works of Fitz-Greene Halleck* (New York, 1852), pp. 80 and 217. In the final edition of 1869 the two fragments appeared in succession. In *Richardsiana; or Hits at the Style of Popular American Authors* (New York, 1841), which was published anonymously, occurs a parody on "Connecticut," entitled "Extract from an Unpublished Poem."

126 *Incidents in the Life of Jacob Barker*, p. 150. This life, probably in large part by Barker himself, is, we have noted, extremely inaccurate in regard to dates, and is very biased in favor of the banker. Barker's business integrity was one of the freely discussed questions in New York at this period. Barker, as well as many of his friends, stoutly maintained his own honesty, and insisted that he was being unduly persecuted. The problem is, indeed, very complex, and cannot be dealt with adequately in this work. I have attempted merely to summarize Halleck's part in the trials. Barker was a powerful personality and a man of amazing business ability. A critical life of the banker is really a desideratum.

127 *Jacob Barker's Letters, Developing the Conspiracy Formed in 1826 for His Ruin* (n.p., n.d.), pp. 39–40.

functionary was but thinly veiled in the appellation "Billingsgate McSwell," which served as the title of the poem. Two stanzas will illustrate the glib, but cutting style in which the satire was written.

> Ye gentlemen and ladies all
>   That reverence the law,
> Come, listen to the law's own bird,
>   That holds it in his claw.
> I who am famed for turning tail,
>   And have a tale to tell,
> Am a tale bearer, and my name
>   Is Billingsgate McSwell.
>
> . . . .
>
> And now I'm master of the law,
>   Its hangman and its rope,
> And in infallibility
>   His Holiness the Pope;
> And since that kind protecting power,
>   *Impunity*, was mine,
> I've been a wholesale dealer in
>   The Inquisition line.[128]

In the trials which followed the indictment of the parties concerned, Jacob Barker, the most prominent and influential of the accused financiers, became the center of attention. "Mr. Barker relying on the integrity of his cause and his own capacity to establish his freedom from offence, declined the aid of his professional friends, conducting the defense himself, until near the close of the first trial."[129] The details of court procedure during the trials are too complex for analysis at this point. It will be necessary, however, to note in general the part which Halleck played as witness. In 1822 Halleck had become secretary of the Dutchess Insurance Company, "which," Mr. Barker once affirmed, "was managed and controlled by me, he [Halleck] assisting me at the same time in my

---

128 Wilson, *Life*, pp. 313–315. A manuscript of this poem is preserved in the Henry E. Huntington Library. Another satire on Maxwell, which, unlike Halleck's, actually found its way into print during the Conspiracy Trials, is contained in Isaac S. Clason's *Horace in New York* (New York, 1826). Curiously enough, this brochure, in addition to the satire on Maxwell, included skits on Halleck (see pp. 178–179 of this work) and Jacob Barker. The three satires were printed consecutively: section VI (p. 22), dealing with Maxwell; VII (p. 26), with Halleck; VIII (p. 31), with Barker.

129 *Incidents in the Life of Jacob Barker*, p. 150.

other business.''[130] This secretaryship was probably but a nominal one, so that Halleck acted in all cases merely as Barker's agent.[131] But the responsibility for the business affairs of the concern doubtless rested heavily upon his shoulders, and it may have been at the poet's request that the *New York American*, before the affairs of the company had become seriously involved, informed its readers ''on authority, that the Dutchess Insurance Company have received no money save that which has been loaned them, and for which they pay an interest.''[132]

During the first trial, which took place in September and October, a minor named St. John testified against Jacob Barker in such a way as to involve Halleck. The boy said that he had been directed to give a sum of $10,000 to Mr. Barker at the office of the Dutchess Insurance Company, and that Barker had pointed out ''Mr. Halleck, the secretary of the Dutchess, as the person to receive it.''[133] St. John alleged that he had then handed over the money to Halleck. Halleck's testimony in this particular involved the statement of many business details, but in general, although affirming that the money had been paid him, he failed to recollect that St. John had delivered the sum.[134] While entirely consistent with personal honesty, Halleck in this trial, as in succeeding ones, insisted upon the integrity of Barker. He said that he frequently copied Barker's letters for him,[135] and freely admitted the financier

130 Wilson, *Life*, p. 337. From a letter dated April 12, 1868, presumably addressed to Wilson, who had inquired of Barker regarding Halleck. Advertisements of the Dutchess County Insurance Company, signed ''F. G. Halleck, Secretary,'' were common in the newspapers of 1826. See, for example, the *New York American* for May 2, and the *New York Evening Post* for July 3, 1826. The advertisement in the latter paper announces a dividend of 4 per cent which has just been declared.

131 It was customary for Halleck to act as Barker's agent in transacting the business affairs of the concerns which the latter controlled. In a letter of Halleck dated November 9, 1817, the poet tells his sister of his being ''the (nominal) [*sic*] director of a bank'' near Lake George, whither he was obliged to go on business (Wilson *Life*, p. 188).

132 January 21, 1825. The Dutchess Insurance Company in the first indictment was not named as one of the institutions defrauded. In all probability its funds were still intact at the opening of the first trial. As time went on, however, and Barker's business affairs became more and more involved, the Dutchess was seriously affected.

133 *Incidents in the Life of Jacob Barker*, p. 171.

134 *Ibid.*, p. 171.

135 See Supplement to the *New York American* for October 20, 1826.

a "personal friend."[136] At the close of the first trial, Barker's lawyer, in summing up the case, thus mentioned Halleck:

And here he would turn aside to notice the evidence given by Mr. Halleck. The District Attorney had expressed great surprise that he had not recollected the signing his name to the certificates of Tradesmen's Bank stock. The District Attorney may in his summing up bear upon this fact as an uncommon instance of forgetfulness. And lest the name of Halleck, with which so many sweet ideas are inwoven, should go down to posterity sullied by a single surmise against the purity and truth of him who bears it; lest that name which will hereafter be ranked among those of the brightest ornaments of our country; which will call forth the admiration of all who speak the English language, and will be repeated with the same emotions which those of Milton, and Shakespeare and Byron now excite—should suffer by any unjust imputation, let me call your attention to the testimony of Mr. Catlin, Mr. Fleming, Mr. Worth and Mr. Bucknor. They all have stated that it was impossible for them to recollect the various papers to which they had signed their names.[137]

The jury, however, disagreed, and found it impossible to come to a decision. A second trial was, therefore, held in November. Halleck's testimony, as well as the comments made concerning the poet, on this occasion, adds little to our study of his life.[138] The jury formed for the second trial rendered the verdict of guilty. A few days after the trial, several of the insurance companies with which Mr. Barker was connected issued statements exonerating the banker. Among these was a letter from the Dutchess Insurance Company, dated December 6, 1826, which claimed Barker's innocence as touching the business affairs of that company. The statement was signed by the President, and countersigned by "F. G. Halleck, *Secretary*."[139] During the year 1827 Barker underwent a third trial,[140] at the close of which a verdict of guilty was again

---

[136] See Supplement to the *New York American* for October 20, 1826.

[137] *Ibid*.

[138] For references to Halleck during the second trial, see the *New York American* for November 29, 1826; and *The Speeches of Mr. Jacob Barker and his Counsel on the Trials for Conspiracy, with Documents Relating Thereto* (New York, 1826), pp. 187, 233, 237–238.

[139] *Incidents in the Life of Jacob Barker*, pp. 178–179.

[140] References to Halleck during this and subsequent trials may be found in *Trial of Jacob Barker, Thomas Vermilya, and Matthew Davis for Alleged Conspiracy* (New York, 1827), pp. 249–250; and *Jacob Barker's Letters, Developing the Conspiracy Formed in 1826 for His Ruin*, p. 27.

rendered. The following year the financier was engaged in a chancery suit. In this litigation the District Attorney accused Mr. Barker of attending a certain meeting which resulted in the selling of the Tradesmen's Bank.[141] Halleck, however, testified that "Mr. Barker left New-York for Nantucket on the 10th June 1826, and was gone about a fortnight."[142] The poet thus established an alibi which was considered of importance in freeing Barker from the charges of fraud relating to the Tradesmen's Bank.

By his untiring efforts Mr. Barker finally discovered, he believed, that a conspiracy had been "formed immediately after the first trial, by a portion of the accused and others connected with the incorporations in question, in which transactions Mr. Barker had no part or lot, to shield the innocent and make Mr. Barker answerable for the errors of the guilty."[143] "Mr. Barker, having obtained what he considered sufficient evidence of that conspiracy, went before the grand jury and made a formal complaint against some of the parties."[144] It was Richard Riker, the Recorder of New York City, whom the financier believed particularly instrumental in the fraud. In making certain accusations at an earlier trial Mr. Barker had pressed his claims too closely, and was charged in two instances with libel.[145] Barker appealed, but the Recorder, Richard Riker, sustained the charges, and the financier was forced to pay the fines.[146] During the chancery suit, several facts had also been brought to light which appeared to reflect unfavorably upon the character of the Recorder. But Barker was unsuccessful before the grand jury in bringing Riker and his fellow conspirators to trial. As a final move, however, to establish his own innocence, Mr.

---

141 *Disclosure of the Real Parties to the Purchase and Sale of the Tradesmen's Bank* [n.p., n.d.], p. 4. This pamphlet was published by Barker sometime during the early part of December, 1828. It is referred to in the *Evening Post* for December 10, 1828.

142 *Ibid.*, p. 15.

143 *Incidents in the Life of Jacob Barker*, p. 183.

144 *Ibid.*, pp. 183–184.

145 See the *New York American*, March 14, 15, and April 10, 1827.

146 Of Barker's behavior in court, the *New York American* said: " 'Mr. Barker's manner,' says our Reporter, 'was highly reprehensible—he appeared to have lost all command of himself. And, throughout all our attendance upon courts, we never remember to have seen a more marked instance of contempt' " (May 9, 1827).

Riker.[154] "I had the honor of a personal acquaintance with him [Riker]," wrote the poet in acknowledgment of the present, "before making him the theme of the sportive lines you allude to, and that acquaintance became afterward more and more cordial, as he learned how highly—

'In his happier hour
Of social pleasure ill exchanged for power'—

I respected and esteemed him; and he kindly bore with me for selecting one in his high position as an 'office holder,' to do duty as a vicarious sufferer for the sins of the whole 'class,' in the consciousness of my knowledge of his own individual blamelessness."[155] And at another time Halleck wrote to his friend, Evert A. Duyckinck, who had just reviewed his "Young America," "In the words of our old and gentlemanly acquaintance, Mr. Recorder Riker, addressed to me on a certain occasion, 'You have made me immortal.' "[156] These words reflect only a spirit of generosity and good will toward the Recorder. Bryant in addressing the New York Historical Society after the poet's death, expressed much the same opinion respecting the spirit of Halleck's verses. Although acknowledging the "assault" as "somewhat disrespectful" to Riker, Bryant considered it "by no means ill-natured," and believed that "the man in office, who was the subject of it, must have hardly known whether to laugh or be angry."[157] Barker himself, when accused by the public press of displaying undue animus toward the Recorder, declared, "I am neither the personal nor the political enemy of the Recorder, but . . . I am the enemy only of the conduct in question."[158] But no one who has examined, with care, Barker's protestations against the Recorder can doubt that the financier's atti-

[154] Wilson, *Life*, p. 325. The letter is dated July 13, 1863.

[155] *Ibid.*, pp. 326–327. The letter is dated July 21, 1863. The original letter I have examined through the courtesy of Thomas Madigan of New York City. For a further statement of Halleck's feeling toward Riker shortly before the poet's death, see the note on the ex-functionary (p. 29) in the edition of the *Recorder* privately printed in 1866 by William L. Andrews. Here the Recorder is described as "a gentleman of great merit, who had previously filled, and continued to fill through life, offices of the highest trust."

[156] From a letter, dated February 2, 1864, in the Duyckinck Collection of the New York Public Library.

[157] *Some Notices of the Life and Writings of Fitz-Greene Halleck*, pp. 16–17.

[158] The *Post*, December 24, 1828.

tude was far more personal than he was willing to admit. Halleck, it should be remembered, was always a loyal friend to his employer, and, so far as we know, upheld Barker's position throughout the Conspiracy Trials. It is thus reasonable to suppose that Halleck's feeling toward the Recorder was distinctly hostile at the moment the satire was published, and that the poem may be regarded as a defense of Barker's innocence. That the poem was published as a piece of propaganda is self-evident from even a cursory examination of the notice which accompanied the poem in the *American*. Halleck's letter to Mr. Hall, from which we have quoted, was written four years before the poet's death. After a lapse of thirty-five years, the real causes which had inspired the famous lines had largely receded into the background, and little of the hostility of earlier years remained.

Internal evidence indicates, with little doubt, Halleck's true position in regard to Richard Riker in the year 1828. The attributing of the poem to the mysterious Thomas Castaly was, of course, merely a clever ruse on the part of Halleck to avoid the responsibility of authorship. Bryant also deemed it proper, in printing the lines, to make light of the satirical aspects of the poem, noting in his preface that "the sportive irony of the piece will amuse our readers and offend nobody." The opening lines of the poem present no hint of the sting lying beneath the bland and easy verse.

> My dear Dick Riker, you and I
>   Have floated down life's stream together
> And kept unharmed our friendship's tie
> Through every change of Fortune's sky,
>   Her pleasant and her rainy weather.[159]

The poet then proceeds to draw a comparison between the Recorder and Julius Caesar. Suddenly we find ourselves in the midst of trenchant satire.

> Both eloquent and learned and brave,
>   Born to command and skilled to rule,
> One[160] made the Citizen a slave,
>   The other[161] makes him more,—a fool.

[159] The text of these quotations from "The Recorder" is that which originally appeared in the *Post* and in the *American*.
[160] Caesar.   [161] Riker.

> The Caesar an imperial crown,
>   His slaves' mad gift, refused to wear,
> The Riker put his fool's cap on,
>   And found it fitted to a hair.

Throughout the poem we find this curious alternation between apparently innocent jest and bitter mockery. But behind the playful humor of the verse, the irony is unmistakable. One of the most revealing examples of the poet's attitude to Riker is that given in the following lines. Halleck is here asking the Recorder for permission to make him the subject of a poem,—

> A poem, in a quarto volume—
> Verse, like the subject, blank and solemn,
>   With elegant appropriate bindings,
> Of rat and mole skin, the one half
> The other a part fox, part calf.

One other important example of the poet's irony may be noted.

> Oh for a Herald's skill to rank
>   Your titles in their due degree!
> At Singsing—at the Tradesmens' Bank,
>   In Courts, Committees, Caucuses:
> At Albany, where those who knew
>   The last year's secrets of the Great,
> Call you the golden Handle to
>   The earthen Pitcher of the State.

It is altogether patent that these passages proceeded from a mind charged with indignation against the public official. To be sure, the easy playfulness which is ever and anon coming to the front helps in a measure to mitigate the harshness and asperity of the satire. These qualifying lines were doubtless the result of expediency,— the desire to disarm any accuser who would be inclined to produce a charge of libel against the writer. Thus Halleck sought to protect both himself and Bryant. The satirical writer of Halleck's day must have had clearly before him the example of Samuel B. H. Judah, who, five years before, spent a period in the city jail for publishing his libelous "Medley," *Gotham and the Gothamites.*[162]

[162] Wilson, *Life,* p. 309. See also Thomas R. Lounsbury, *James Fenimore Cooper,* p. 60.

But Halleck's real purpose in writing the lines on the Recorder stands forth clearly. The epistle was distinctly more than the mere *jeu d'esprit* which the poet and some of his friends claimed for the lines in later years. And whatever Halleck's subsequent attitude to the Recorder may have been, the satire at the time of its birth undoubtedly sprang from a spirit of hostility and indignation.

VIII

THE MAN OF LETTERS

1827

I

I<small>N</small> 1826 Isaac Starr Clason, a New York actor, who during the previous year had written a continuation of "Don Juan," produced a series of satirical sketches called *Horace in New York*, suggestive in title of the Smith brothers' *Horace in London*. Halleck had now attained sufficient eminence in the poetical world of New York to merit an entire section of the satire devoted to him. The author began his sketch, entitled "A *Bumper* to Fanny," by lamenting the death of poetry in America, and then indicating Halleck as a possible means of resuscitating the art.

> Halleck, awake! shake off this drowsy sleep.
> Nay man, no modesty—no shocks of shame:
> I'll have a starling, Sir, shall speak thy name.
> Must eagles hide, while owls their dull wings rear?
> Shake off this sleep! Halleck, I say, appear!![1]

After enumerating other poets of the time, including Bryant,

> within whose mind a crystal shines,
> With adjectives and fustian fills his lines;

and Percival,

> so pleased with painted things,
> Buoys in the air with tinsel, tawd'ry wings;

Clason suddenly exclaimed,

> Faugh! thin small beer! Halleck—Halleck, come forth!
> Come like the 'borealis of the North,
> A beaut'ous wonder. 'Rise and wildly shine!
> Rise like a comet in the night's bright mine;
> Making the upturned eyes of mortals gaze,
> And leave the galaxy to track thy blaze.

[1] *Horace in New York* (New York, 1826), p. 26.

A volunteer within Thalia's train,
Duty decides you still should there remain.
The British Critic justly sneers to see,
A pitchy void within our melody:
Let not the scribe full fairly point his dart,
But shew a flame can from bitumen start.
Wait not for rules which Horace made of yore;[2]
Snatch up your manuscript; unbar your door;
Put in bold *pica* your own neat *italic;*
And be no longer *"Secretary Halleck."*
    You've found the silver nib of Byron's pen;
Prove that its iron stem can plough again.
The last touch of the chissel [*sic*] you have shown;
Prove that the block you work on is your own.
'Wake every nerve; and let us something view,
As smooth as marble, and as lasting too.[3]

These extracts from "A *Bumper* to Fanny" describe with some truth the state of Halleck's reputation at the close of 1826. They reflect a popularity resting in part, of course, upon *The Croakers,* but more especially upon *Fanny,* which the public had from the first identified with Byron's "Beppo" and "Don Juan," and which has ever since been described, with more persistency than accuracy, as Byronic. That is, Halleck's reputation to the year 1827 was, in large part, that of a satirist. Yet as a lyrist he was slowly gaining ground. "Alnwick Castle" and especially "Marco Bozzaris" were coming more and more into universal favor, and the time was now ripe for a published collection of Halleck's serious poems. Still, the body of his work was small, and the public, whose opinion found expression in the verses by Clason, was constantly looking to Halleck to give to American letters a richness and dignity which should silence the captious critics of England. In 1827 the first collected edition of his works appeared. No moment in Halleck's literary career could have been more propitious for the publication of the new book. Halleck had given to the world no volume since 1821, and in the six years which had elapsed, while his reputation was steadily growing, he had greatly matured both as an observer of life and as a poet. *Fanny* had been published as a humorous and

---

[2] "Nonumque prematur in annum." (Clason's note to the line.)
[3] Clason, *op. cit.,* pp. 28–29.

satiric poem. *Alnwick Castle with Other Poems* contained only the serious pieces which Halleck had written.

Two poems, printed early in 1827, preceded the publication of the new volume. The lines on "Burns" were contributed to the *United States Review and Literary Gazette,*[4] of which Bryant was editor. Wilson believed the poem to have been "written and published anonymously in Great Britain" prior to the poet's return to this country, and to have "attracted much attention in England and in Scotland."[5] There is no other evidence, however, that "Burns" was either written abroad; or published in England or in Scotland, until after its appearance in the *United States Review.* Bryant evidently possessed no knowledge of a previous version of the poem, when, in his memorial address on Halleck before the New York Historical Society, he stated that it had been "contributed by Halleck in 1827 to the *United States Review.*"[6] Internal evidence also argues against the assumption that the verses were written and published in Great Britain. The poem, as originally printed in the *Review,* bore the date "April, 1823," which was two or possibly three months after Halleck's return to America. There is, moreover, in the collected edition of 1827 no mention, as in the case of "Alnwick Castle," that "Burns" was written abroad. The subtitle[7] to the poem, as well as the opening stanza, clearly indicates that the verses were written after Halleck's return to the States, and were the product of "emotion recollected in tranquillity."

> Wild Rose of Alloway! my thanks;
> Thou 'mindst me of that autumn noon
> When first we met upon "the banks
> And braes o' bonny Doon."[8]

It will be remembered that in June, 1821, Halleck had visited Wyoming, and while on this trip had written his lines on the fa-

---

[4] I, 277 (January, 1827). The poem was signed "F.G.H."
[5] *Life,* p. 274.
[6] *Some Notices of the Life and Writings of Fitz-Greene Halleck,* p. 15.
[7] "To a Rose, Brought from near Alloway Kirk, in Ayrshire, in the Autumn of 1822."
[8] The poem was at once reprinted in the *New York American* (January 11, 1827), the *Evening Post* (January 15), and the *New York Mirror* (January 20). In the same issue of the *Mirror,* and following the text of "Burns" appeared a poem signed "Sigma" and addressed "To Fitz-Greene Halleck, Esq. On His Poem 'Burns.'"

mous Valley,[9] immortalized by Campbell. The poem was not published, however, until February, 1827, when it appeared in the *United States Review and Literary Gazette*.[10] Concerning these verses and their publication Bryant once said: "Halleck had been led by his admiration of the poetry of Campbell to pay a visit to the charming valley celebrated by that poet in his Gertrude of Wyoming. In memory of this he wrote the lines entitled Wyoming which he handed me for publication in the same magazine" [*United States Review*].[11]

The first collected edition of Halleck's poems, which included the verses on "Burns" and "Wyoming," was issued in February, 1827.[12] The work was received with universal acclaim. The *Post* believed the collection "what the author has long owed to his distinguished reputation as a poet, and to the literature of his country"; and regretted that "so little of his leisure has been devoted to a species of composition in which he is eminently successful."[13] The *New York Literary Gazette and American Athenaeum* opened a review of the collection with extravagant praise both for the author and his work. "The only regret we feel with regard to this volume," commented the critic, "is that it is not more voluminous. Everything from the pen of its accomplished author attracts admiration and imparts delight. Mr. Hallock [*sic*] possesses more versatility of genius than any other poet in America. He has tried the gay and witty, the pathetic, and the sublime, and in all he has been eminently successful. . . . 'Alnwick Castle,' the 'Death of Marco Bozzaris,' and the tribute to the memory of Robert Burns are the

---

9 See pp. 128–129. 10 I, 376.

11 *Some Notices on the Life and Writings of Fitz-Greene Halleck*, p. 15. The poem was dated "June, 1821," and signed "F.G.H." It was at once reprinted in the *New York Evening Post* for February 10, 1827, and the *New York American* for February 12.

12 The volume contained the following poems. For those marked with an asterisk no previous printing has been discovered. "Alnwick Castle," "Marco Bozzaris," "Burns," "Wyoming," "On the Death of J. R. Drake of New York, Sept. 1820," "Twilight," "Psalm CXXXVII,"* "To ****" ("The world is bright before thee"), "Love,"* "A Sketch,"* "Domestic Happiness," "Magdalen,"* "From the Italian,"* "Woman. Written in the Album of an Unknown Lady,"* "Connecticut. From an Unpublished Poem," "Music —To a Boy of Four Years Old, On Hearing Him Play on the Harp,"* "On the Death of Lieut. William Howard Allen of the U. S. Navy."

13 February 20, 1827. Another review of the volume appeared in the *Post* for April 5, 1827.

longest pieces in this collection. We refrain from extracts, solely
because they are familiar to the reader of poetry, and shall not comment on their beauties, because they are universally appreciated
and extolled.'' ''In conclusion,'' said the reviewer, ''we have to
express a hope that the present volume may be a prelude to more
from the pen of a writer so deservedly popular, and who writes
with the worth of a man of genius, the feelings and the manners
of a gentleman.''[14]

Another review of the volume in the *New York Mirror* voiced
the same general opinion, registering, indeed, disappointment that
Halleck had written so little, but commending the poet in extravagant terms for having written that little so well. This attitude we
shall find from now on reiterated with increasing frequency, until
it becomes a tiresome commonplace in all critical discussions of the
poet. ''Wherever poetry is prized,'' asserted the reviewer in the
Mirror, ''not only throughout the wide extent of our country, but
in England also, and in places where his name is unknown, the productions of Halleck have been read and admired; and yet we must
confess, we closed the work with feelings somewhat akin to disappointment. Let it not be supposed, however, for a single moment,
that our disappointment arose from any deficiency of merit in what
the poet has done—it resulted entirely from his having done so
little. . . . In relation to 'Marco Bozzaris' we have not one word to
say: every reader of the Mirror doubtless has perused and repe-
rused that truly noble lyric, with glowing admiration: if there be
any who have not, we could almost find in our heart to envy them,
for their pleasure is *all* to come—but we advise them to defer it no
longer.''[15]

[14] III, [2]97–[2]98 (February 24, 1827).
[15] IV, 263 (March 10, 1827). In the *Mirror* for March 24, 1827 (IV, 280),
appeared a tribute in verse ''To the Author of Alnwick Castle,'' signed ''Isa-
bel.'' To realize the increase in popularity which Halleck's poetry underwent
with the publication of the 1827 volume, one has but to observe the great number of his poems which were reprinted in the current newspapers and periodicals. A few of these may be noted. The *New York Mirror* printed ''Love''
(April 7, 1827); ''The Blue Stocking'' (April 21, 1827—called ''The Sketch''
in the 1827 edition); and ''Domestic Happiness'' (September 13, 1828). The
New York American published ''Magdalen'' (February 21, 1827; see also the
issue for February 22); and the lyric, ''Young thoughts have music in them''
(March 3, 1827. Reprinted from *Fanny*, not from the edition of 1827).
''Psalm CXXXVII'' appeared in the *New York Observer and Religious
Chronicle* (March 24, 1827). A stanza from ''Woman'' was used as a motto
for a sketch in the *Casket* for December, 1827 (I, 457).

In the memorial address on Halleck delivered before the New York Historical Society, Bryant recalled the pleasure he had taken many years before in "saying to the readers" of the *United States Review and Literary Gazette* how greatly he admired the poet's new collection.[16] "The author of these poems," asserted Bryant in the issue of April, 1827, "is understood to be Mr. Halleck, a name already too well known in the literature of this country, and moreover, too closely associated with many of these compositions to justify us in affecting to speak of this collection as an anonymous work." Unlike other reviewers of the edition, Bryant sought to analyze the sources of beauty in Halleck's poetry. "Some of the principal characteristics of this author's poetry," he wrote, "are the great grace and freedom of the style, and the apparently unlabored melody of the numbers. It is not that the highest degree of correctness is in all cases given to the diction, nor that the most severe judgment is invariably applied to the imagery: an occasional instance of negligence in the one, or of doubtful brilliancy in the other, only serves to set off, in a more striking light his power of happy expression, the sweetness of his versification, and the beauty of his conceptions. Touches of pathos, and strains of high lyrical enthusiasm are not wanting; but what particularly distinguishes his poetry from that of our native writers, and indeed from modern English poets in general, is that vein of playful humor, which occasionally breaks out, seemingly in spite of his efforts to repress it, and always in an exceedingly graceful and happy manner." "We suppose that we might, if we had leisure and disposition," said Bryant in conclusion, "find a little fault with some half dozen lines in the collection. We might, perhaps, detect a false rhyme or two, single out one or two expressions wanting force, mention one or two examples of the injudicious use of metaphorical language, and so forth. We prefer, however, simply to suggest these things to the author, in the confidence that they will be corrected when he comes to republish them, as he will do, without doubt, at no distant time, in company with some more elaborate effort of his genius."[17]

The 1827 edition of Halleck's poems was soon exhausted. "We understand that the greater part of this collection is already sold

16 *Some Notices of the Life and Writings of Fitz-Greene Halleck*, p. 15.
17 II, 8–13.

while we are writing this notice,'' asserted Bryant in his review, ''and we dare say the whole of it will be disposed of before our article issues from the press.''[18] That the possession of a copy of the new book was regarded in the light of a social asset among fashionable *élite* of New York, may be judged from an extract of a letter written at this period by Halleck to his sister:

I sent several dozens of my last published poems to several dozen ladies, at whose houses I had danced or dined. It seems they thought it a becoming compliment to get them elegantly bound, and I have unwittingly put them to the expense of five dollars apiece for binding. No matter, it encourages the bookbinders.[19]

Among those to whom Halleck presented a copy of his volume was Miss Catherine Sedgwick, whose description of the poet, written two years before,[20] we have had occasion to note. ''Miss Sedgwick begs Mr. Halleck's acceptance of a copy of 'Hope Leslie,' ''[21] wrote the novelist in acknowledgment of the book, ''not in exchange as a return for the book Mr. H. was so good as to send her, for Miss S. does not delude herself with the idea that a stone, though it be as big as a rock, is an equivalent for a diamond.''[22]

II

With the publication of the 1827 edition, most of the poetry had been written upon which Halleck's reputation as an artist is to be based. We may, therefore, pause for a time in our record of Halleck's life to consider critically his literary work. Perhaps no one would be more amused at an attempt to discuss Halleck as a man of letters than the poet himself. He shared with other Knickerbocker writers of his day a natural dislike for the man who posed as a *littérateur*. To him the conventional author was something of an anomaly—something more than a *man*. Halleck, indeed, never fully accepted the romantic attitude of the nineteenth century that sought to deify the poet. Standing in thought midway between the eighteenth and nineteenth centuries, he found in the measured standard of the former his ideal of man. Dickens he once praised

[18] *United States Review and Literary Gazette*, II, 8.
[19] Wilson, *Life*, p. 321. The letter is dated May 31, 1827.
[20] See pp. 149–150.
[21] *Hope Leslie, or Early Times in America* (New York, 1827).
[22] Wilson, *Life*, pp. 321–322. The note is undated as printed by Wilson.

as a "thorough good fellow" who had "nothing of the author about him but the reputation,"[23] and the historian, Prescott, possessed, in his opinion, a charm which "consisted in the absence of dignity."[24] If Halleck valued in other authors chiefly their attributes as men, he had no more regard for his own dignity as a poet. Like Irving, he seems to have thought of himself as little more than a "literary idler"[25]—a gentleman writing for his own amusement and that of his friends. Regardless, however, of the curiosity and, perhaps, the scorn with which Halleck would look upon this study of his poetry, we must for a time view him as a man of letters; we must examine the literary influences at work in his poetry, and discover his strength and weakness as an artist.

In appraising the poetry of Halleck, it must first be conceded that he was in large measure dependent for his poetic inspiration upon the works of others. Unlike Wordsworth and Byron, who inaugurated new schools of poetry, he lacked that vital spark of originality which instinctively attracts imitators, and opens up for his generation new paths of poetic endeavor. Thus largely derivative in his poetic thought and style, he always found in reading, a source of profit and inspiration. His knowledge of books was well diversified for a man of his limited formal education. He was a special lover of the anecdote, and his conversation and letters, particularly those of later life, sparkled with the stories of the great he had gleaned from his copious reading.

Varied as was his reading, however, he had one serious limitation; he possessed no first-hand knowledge of the classics. The schooling which his native town afforded, ample in its power to fit one for the practical concerns of life, lacked an appropriate cultural basis. And thus Halleck passed into the world without tasting of the literature of the Greeks and Romans. To be sure, he humorously acknowledged in *Fanny* that

> We owe the ancients something. You have read
> Their works, no doubt—at least in a translation,[26]

[23] *Ibid.*, p. 434. From a letter to Mrs. Rush, dated March 8, 1842.

[24] From a letter addressed to Evert A. Duyckinck, dated March 9, 1864, and preserved in the New York Public Library.

[25] See Prof. S. T. Williams and T. McDowell, *Diedrich Knickerbocker's A History of New York*, p. xiii.

[26] Stanza 46 (1839 ed.)

but there is little evidence that he ever read them to any great extent even in translation.[27] His conversation, correspondence, and poetry are for the most part conspicuously lacking in allusions to the Greek and Roman writers.[28]

If Halleck neglected the classics, he somewhat repaid the debt by a study of several of the languages of modern Europe. Of these he was most familiar with French, in which he was entirely self-taught.[29] "He was a good French scholar," says William A. Jones, the critic, "and of modern writers I heard him speak at length and with high encomium of George Sand (Madame Dudevant) and of Béranger [sic]."[30] General Wilson once heard Halleck repeat "several stanzas of Béranger's 'Lafayette en Amérique' "; and also once saw "in Halleck's handwriting a translation of one of his very popular poems, 'The Garret,' which was a great favorite of his, and a composition from which he often quoted in his letters and conversation both in the original and from Dr. Maginn's admirable translation."[31] Halleck's own paraphrases from the French include lines from Victor Hugo[32] and General Lallemand.[33]

Halleck's knowledge of Italian, though probably inferior to his

---

[27] In 1865, two years before his death, Halleck said, by way of parenthesis, in a letter to Mrs. Botta, "I am reading Lord Derby's 'Homer.' " See *Memoirs of Anne C. L. Botta* (New York, 1894), p. 348. For other references to Halleck's classical reading, done late in life, see the letter to Duyckinck on pp. 415–416. Joel Benton reports Halleck as saying that Pope's *Homer* is "the only readable Homeric translation." (*Frank Leslie's Illustrated Newspaper*, XXV, 243.)

[28] In *Fanny* (stanza 60, 1839 ed.) Halleck refers in passing to Homer, "that blind old man of Scio's rocky isle." [Byron's "Bride of Abydos," II, 2] Prof. Thomas O. Mabbott has pointed out to me an interesting parallel between lines 33–37 of "Marco Bozzaris" and Aeschylus' *Persae*, ll. 402 ff. The parallel can be hardly more than accidental, however, or at best the result of an indirect borrowing through some modern author. If Halleck had been even slightly conversant with the classics in the original, he would probably not have indulged in the tautology—

> One of the few, *immortal* names,
> That were *not born to die.*

[29] See p. 41. [30] Wilson, *Life,* p. 541.

[31] *Ibid.*, p. 304. Maginn's translation of "The Garret" may be found in Rufus Griswold's edition of *The Songs of Béranger* (Philadelphia, 1844), p. 20. The translation of "The Garret" in Halleck's autograph referred to by Wilson is in the collection of Oliver R. Barrett of Chicago, Illinois. Mr. Barrett also possesses some French verses in the poet's hand, entitled "Les Soirées."

[32] *Poetical Writings of Fitz-Greene Halleck* (1869), p. 212.

[33] *Ibid.*, p. 217.

acquaintance with French, was yet sufficient for an appreciation of the literature, which he is said to have loved.[34] His teacher in the language was the celebrated opera librettist, Lorenzo Da Ponte, who became a somewhat intimate friend of the poet.[35] Halleck had at least a passing acquaintance with the works of Ariosto,[36] Dante, and Tasso. "Dante," he once declared, "had never been fairly translated."[37] William Jones relates that "one evening, in his sitting-room, [Halleck] repeated the opening lines of the 'Jerusalem' and dwelt on the music and beauty of the language." "He was a wide reader," added Mr. Jones, "and of catholic liberality of taste and appreciation, ranging from 'Tasso' to the *New-Englander,* and from French novels to works of devotion."[38] Portuguese Halleck also studied "that he might read the Lusiad in the original."[39]

Halleck's proficiency in German was undoubtedly slight, although he produced four paraphrases of poems from German literature, two of which were by Goethe.[40] But Halleck usually dealt severely with Goethe, whom he regarded, as did Wordsworth,[41] as a perverter of morals. " 'Faust' he thought the worst book he had ever read, and if one wished to get the story he should

---

[34] Wilson, *Life,* p. 541.

[35] At the death of Da Ponte in 1838 Halleck was among those who attended the funeral and followed his former master "to the grave" (Wilson, *Life,* p. 406). See also p. 142.

[36] James Lawson, *Southern Literary Messenger,* VIII, [2]43 (April, 1842).

[37] Joel Benton, *Frank Leslie's Illustrated Newspaper,* XXV, 243 (January 4, 1868).

[38] Wilson, *Life,* p. 541.

[39] Bryant, *Some Notices of the Life and Writings of Fitz-Greene Halleck,* p. 33. James Lawson also comments on Halleck's study of Portuguese (*Southern Literary Messenger,* VIII, [2]43, April, 1842).

[40] The source of only two of these it has been possible to discover. Professor Julius Goebel has identified Halleck's lines, "Again ye come, again ye throng around me" (1869 ed., pp. 62–63), "as a rather free translation of the Zueignung of Goethe's *Faust,* Part one." The verses beginning, "All honor to Woman" and labeled "From the German of Goethe" (see 1869 ed., p. 227), remind Prof. Carl Schreiber of one of Goethe's "Roman Elegies," although he is unable positively to identify the lines. Prof. J. T. Hatfield has identified "Forget-Me-Not . . . From the German" (Appendix, p. 433) as a free paraphrase of Hoffmann von Fallersleben's "Vergissmeinnicht" [see *Gedichte* (1874), p. 15]. The verses "Forget Me Not" noted on p. 230 of this biography were also probably suggested by Fallersleben's poem. The original for a "Translation from the German" (1869 ed., p. 242) has not been discovered.

[41] See Ralph W. Emerson, *English Traits,* I (paragraph 23).

take Marlowe's poem. . . . With the exception of Schiller he had little regard for the German poets."[42]

Halleck's most varied reading was, of course, in the English poets. We find him acquainted with the work of Chaucer, Spenser,[43] Cowley, Dryden, Addison, Pope, Gray, and Doctor Johnson.[44] Of Shakespeare he was a "close student"[45] and admirer, and derived unusual pleasure from quoting from the plays.[46] Milton he admired as a poet, but despised as a man.[47] With the poetry of the early nineteenth century, including that of Southey and Hogg, he was especially conversant. Wordsworth he greatly admired.[48] Leigh Hunt's "Rimini" he regarded as "charming poetry" and possessing "much original power of description," but called the story "a silly one."[49] Of the work of three of his English contemporaries, however, Halleck could not approve. His mind, naturally lacking in subtlety, found Robert Browning an enigma.[50] To Joel Benton, who

[42] Joel Benton, *Frank Leslie's Illustrated Newspaper*, XXV, 243 (January 4, 1868). The same sentiment he expressed in a letter to Samuel Ward, dated August 25, 1862: "My dislike to German literature is confined to the 'Faust' of Goethe—the worst book, in the strongest sense of the word *worst* that I have ever read through" (Wilson, *Bryant and His Friends*, p. 266).

[43] Spenser's well-known phrase descriptive of Chaucer, "Well of English undefiled" (*Faerie Queene*, IV, 2, xxxii), was a favorite with Halleck. See Wilson, *Life*, p. 263; and the letter addressed to F. S. Cozzens, and reprinted in the present volume, p. 363.

[44] No attempt is here made to give a complete catalogue of Halleck's reading. The present list is merely suggestive of his knowledge of English literature.

[45] Duyckinck, *Putnam's Magazine*, I, 244 (February, 1868).

[46] Halleck in his poems and correspondence either quotes from or alludes to the following plays: *Hamlet*, *Othello*, *Midsummer Night's Dream*, *Twelfth Night*, *As You Like It*, *Merry Wives of Windsor*, *Much Ado About Nothing*, *King John*, *II Henry IV*, *Henry V*, and *Richard III*.

[47] See p. 287.

[48] F. S. Cozzens, *Fitz-Greene Halleck. A Memorial*, p. 16. Poe has pointed out the possible influence in the first stanza of Halleck's "Lines on the Death of J. R. Drake" of Wordsworth's poem, "She dwelt among the untrodden ways" (*Southern Literary Messenger*, II, 336). H. C. Alexander has pointed out another suggestion of Wordsworth in the stanza from Halleck's "Burns," beginning, "They linger by the Doon's low trees" (*Hours at Home*, VI, 373). But aside from a few verbal echoes of this kind, the influence of Wordsworth on Halleck was small.

[49] Wilson, *Life*, p. 189.

[50] While in America Thackeray once said: "With my friends Irving and Halleck I agree that we do not read Robert Browning because we cannot alto-

had praised "Sordello," Halleck once wrote: "Such stuff nobody
can read. He has not only spoiled his own genius by his odious taste
and style, but he has corrupted Mrs. Browning's poetry also."[51] The
poems of Mrs. Browning and Tennyson he objected to on esthetic
and moral grounds. One of Halleck's favorite tests for good poetry
was the ease with which he could commit to memory the lines he had
been reading.[52] On the poems of Mrs. Browning and Tennyson we
have this comment: "I have read many of them over and over, and
have been told that they are all exceedingly beautiful, and yet I
have not at this moment a single line of them by heart."[53] Mrs.
Browning he found, in fact, "too masculine" and Tennyson "too
feminine."[54] Although there were passages in the work of Tennyson in which he caught the glimmer of genius,[55] in the main he
disliked "the English Laureate, and thought that he had for thirty
years had a most disastrous effect upon English poetry."[56] Toward
the close of his life Halleck lamented keenly "these 'sensation'
times," as he called them, in which "Enoch Arden's story of polygamy (so decent, delicate, and decorous)" should have gained
so strong a hold upon the public.[57] Delightfully whimsical and
illogical, though reflecting a characteristic prejudice, is a passage
from a letter written in 1857, in which he alludes to Mr. Browning
as "the husband of a Lady of that name, whose good taste is equal
to that of the critics that praise her writings, and whose 'Aurora
Leigh' is as free from all that is coarse and vulgar, impious and
impure, licentious and blasphemous, as the 'Faust' of Goethe; and
whose 'Swan's nest among the reeds' is as unwittingly immodest as
the 'Venus' Dove' of Prior,[58] or the very saleable specimens of

gether comprehend him. I have no head above my eyes" (James G. Wilson,
Thackeray in the United States, New York, 1904, I, 118).

[51] *Frank Leslie's Illustrated Newspaper,* XXV, 243 (January 4, 1868).

[52] See p. 204.   [53] Wilson, *Life,* p. 524.

[54] Duyckinck, *Putnam's Magazine,* XI, 246 (February, 1868).

[55] Occasionally Halleck would comment favorably on some felicitous line
of Tennyson that struck his fancy. See F. S. Cozzens, *Fitz-Greene Halleck. A
Memorial,* p. 18; and B. Taylor, *North American Review,* CXXV, 65 (July,
1877).

[56] Joel Benton, *Frank Leslie's Illustrated Newspaper,* XXV, 243 (January
4, 1868).

[57] Wilson, *Life,* p. 533.

[58] Elsewhere Halleck spoke favorably of Matthew Prior, and believed his
poetry should be more generally read. See J. Benton, *Frank Leslie's Illustrated
Newspaper,* XXV, 243.

'Fanny Fern'[59] or a portion of this letter of mine which I beg you to light your cigar with as soon as you have read it.''[60] Prudish one may call all this; yet hardly so when viewed in the light of the poet's innate fear of innovation. Lost in a world growing daily more subtle and scientific, he was powerless to grasp the significance even of the changes which were affecting the art of poetry. "When I find in the lines of your young poets of the day any fancied imperfection,'' wrote Halleck to a friend in 1862, "I do not ascribe them, as you appear to do, to foreign idioms unconsciously adopted, but to the ill-luck of having taken Tennyson and Mrs. Browning as models in place of Spenser and Milton.''[61]

With his face thus irrevocably turned toward the past, Halleck moved, even to the last, in the world of poetry in which he had lived as a youth—a world dominated by Moore, Scott, Campbell, and Byron. Of Halleck's opinion of Moore we cannot be certain. The influence of the Irish poet is distinguishable rather in his early poems than in his later work, and it is probable that Moore was one of his youthful idols. Echoes of Moore's languorous sentimentality are to be found in several of his early poems,[62] and in the later lines,

> I turned a last look to my dear native mountains,
> As the dim blush of sunset grew pale in the sky.[63]

As this boyish enthusiasm for Moore wore away, it is likely that Halleck sickened at his excess of sweetness. At any rate in 1819, he effectively parodied in *Fanny* Moore's "Bendemeer's Stream,''[64] and in 1821 "Araby's Daughter,''[65] both lyrics from *Lalla Rookh*. As time went on, he undoubtedly returned with increasing satisfaction to the more austere poetry of Scott and Campbell.

The influence of Sir Walter Scott, though not so pronounced as

---

[59] Mrs. Sarah Parton, sister to N. P. Willis.

[60] From a letter in the New York Historical Society. See p. 400.

[61] Wilson, *Bryant and His Friends*, p. 265. From a letter of Halleck to Samuel Ward, dated August 25, 1862.

[62] See pp. 23–24.

[63] See p. 45. Published in the 1869 edition under the title "A Farewell to Connecticut,'' p. 247. The "Song by Miss ****'' (1839, p. 111) is written in the same meter as Moore's "To Ladies' Eyes,'' the first line of which Halleck prints below the title of his poem.

[64] See p. 113.   [65] See p. 130.

that of Campbell, cannot be ignored.[66] In speaking of the early years of the nineteenth century, Halleck once remarked, "It is impossible for me to describe to you the delight with which, at that period, we read and committed to memory whole pages of Scott's lyrical romances. I think I could repeat one-half of the 'Lady of the Lake,' and quite as much of 'Marmion.' "[67] Halleck's innate love of chivalry and, in general, of the medieval may have been materially strengthened by a study of Scott's romances. No one can read "Alnwick Castle," and be unimpressed with the fact that its spirit of chivalry was inspired by Scott. The opening lines of the poem bear a close resemblance in tone and meter to the first canto of "Marmion," where the old castle is described. A similar meter Halleck also employed in "Marco Bozzaris."[68] Some years later he recalled in verse for Miss Abbie Flanner, with whom for a time he carried on a flirtatious correspondence,[69] his early enthusiasm for Scott's romances.

> The Scottish Border Minstrel's lay
> Entranced me oft in boyhood's day;
>   His forests, glens, and streams,
> Mountains, and heather blooming fair,
> And Highland lake, and lady, were
>   The playmates of my dreams.[70]

It was Thomas Campbell, however, of all his boyish idols, in whom he gloried most, and whose influence was most salutary and permanent. Halleck's introduction to the poet was early. The first book which he owned, aside from textbooks, was a copy of Camp-

[66] Prof. Charles F. Johnson includes Burns under Halleck's early idols and models. "As a boy he read poetry eagerly and wrote boyish verse. The most genuine poetic influence under which he grew seems to have been that of Burns" (*Proceedings at the Celebration of the 250th Anniversary of the Settlement of Guilford, Conn.*, p. 102). Despite Halleck's praise of the Scottish bard in "Burns," we note but one significant literary influence: The lines "To Ellen" are in a Burnsian stanza.

[67] Wilson, *Life*, p. 162.

[68] For the influence of Scott in *Fanny*, see p. 114 (footnote). H. C. Alexander has also noted an echo of Scott in the lines,

> Nor lives there one,
> Whose infant breath was drawn, etc.
>   [Stanza 99; 1839 ed.] (*Hours at Home*, VI, 371.)

[69] See pp. 267 ff.   [70] "To Ellen" (1869 ed., p. 228).

bell's poems given to him by his teacher.[71] If "to lounge on a rainbow and read Tom Campbell" was his youthful ideal of bliss, the same propensity was, in later life, strengthened and deepened. From many quarters is echoed the esteem in which Halleck held the author of the "Pleasures of Hope." "Among the living poets," remarked James Lawson in 1842, "Campbell is an especial favorite, and on an instant he will repeat from his works almost any passage suggested."[72] And to the same critic Halleck once wrote: "Can you not repeat without book every line which Tom Campbell has published? If not, you have never been as happy a man as you ought to have been."[73] Halleck's phenomenal memory led him, perhaps injudiciously, to commit to memory any poem that pleased his fancy. He loved to repeat "Valedictory Stanzas, to J. P. Kemble, Esq." and "Hallowed Ground";[74] and on one occasion he is said to have recited to a lady "every line of the 'Pleasures of Hope,' "[75] —an indiscretion into which only an uncritical enthusiasm for the poet could have led him.[76]

But with all its absurdity, Halleck's love for Campbell's poetry exerted a healthful influence on the quality of his poetic imagination. And there is perhaps little exaggeration in Halleck's own playful confession that "he stole more [from him] than he did from any other writer."[77] "The Campbell that Halleck so absurdly admired," writes Richard H. Stoddard, "and whom he never ceased to admire, must have been the Campbell of the 'Battle of the Baltic' and 'Ye Mariners of England,' and not the feeble poetaster who wrote 'Gertrude of Wyoming.' "[78] This was un-

---

[71] Wilson, *Life*, p. 52. A copy of Campbell's poems (Philadelphia, 1804), perhaps the one referred to by Wilson, was sold in 1868 with Halleck's library. For a description of the sales catalogue, see the Bibliography in the Appendix.

[72] *Southern Literary Messenger*, VIII, [2]44 (April, 1842).

[73] Wilson, *Life*, p. 349.

[74] Duyckinck, *Putnam's Magazine*, XI, 244 (February, 1868).

[75] Wilson, *Life*, p. 557.

[76] R. H. Stoddard has preserved the following incident illustrative of Halleck's unbounded enthusiasm for Campbell: "Campbell still possessed the early charm for him, and I shall never forget the warmth with which he defended the character of that poet from the aspersions which had been cast upon it by his whilom under-strapper in the management of the *New Monthly Magazine*, Cyrus Redding, to which I somewhat injudiciously drew his attention" (*Lippincott's Monthly Magazine*, XLIII, 895–896, June, 1889).

[77] *New York Evening Mail*, January 9, 1868.

[78] *Lippincott's Monthly Magazine*, XLIII, 890 (June, 1889).

doubtedly true. Although in the notes to his collected editions Halleck refers to "Gertrude of Wyoming" as a "beautiful poem," and once spoke of the vale as "rendered sacred by the muse of Campbell,"[79] his own verses on "Wyoming" do not reflect that romantic reverence for the poem and its characters which an unqualified enthusiasm would have made almost imperative. In the opening stanza of "Wyoming," Halleck in the meter of Campbell recalls the world of romance into which his boyish fancy had been led by the poem.

> Thou com'st, in beauty, on my gaze at last,
> "On Susquehanna's side, fair Wyoming!"[80]
> Image of many a dream, in hours long past,
> When life was in its bud and blossoming,
> And waters, gushing from the fountain-spring
> Of pure enthusiast thought, dimmed my young eyes,
> As by the poet borne, on unseen wing,
> I breathed, in fancy, 'neath thy cloudless skies,
> The summer's air, and heard her echoed harmonies.

But in the third stanza, as he gazes on the scene, he feels a certain disappointment at Campbell's picture, and even ventures to suggest that the Scotch poet might have chosen from the annals of the region a tale of greater pathos than that of Gertrude. To be sure, the disillusionment which follows in the poem can but partly be laid to Campbell's false picture of the scene. Halleck's instinctive protest against excessive illusion and sensibility—the contrast inevitably evoked in his poetry between the romance of the past and the stark reality of the present—is as operative here as in "Alnwick Castle." Still, the protest in this case seems unavoidably to involve Campbell's poem. H. C. Alexander undoubtedly struck upon at least a part of the truth when he said that in "Wyoming," Campbell's "Gertrude" is "at once satirized and excelled."[81]

[79] Wilson, *Life*, p. 174. From an undated letter describing Halleck's visit to Wyoming.

[80] Two other lines from Campbell's poem, acknowledged by quotation marks, are introduced into "Wyoming."

[81] *Hours at Home*, VI, 372 (February, 1868). Even Halleck's reverence for "The Pleasures of Hope" did not prevent him from putting to serio-comic use the lines,

> Beloved of Heaven! the smiling Muse shall shed
> Her moonlight halo on thy beauteous head (Book I).

as the motto for his "Loving Epistle to Mr. William Cobbett."

It was probably the more austere and vigorous poems of Campbell that left a lasting impress on Halleck's style. In contrast to the sentimental lines "To Twilight," which one critic believed were "inspired by Campbell's 'Pleasures of Hope,' "[82] we have the martial vigor of "Marco Bozzaris" and the classic dignity of "The Field of the Grounded Arms." One of the literary influences that went to shape "Marco Bozzaris" was undoubtedly Campbell. "We will not detract from . . . [the] intrinsic claims [of Halleck's poem]," wrote a critic in the *Foreign Quarterly Review*, "by inquiring to what extent Mr. Halleck is indebted to the study of well-known models; for, although in this piece we catch that 'stepping in music' of the rhythm which constitutes the secret charm of 'Hohenlinden,'[83] we are glad to recognize in all his productions, apart from incidental resemblances of this kind, a knowledge as complete, as it is rare amongst his contemporaries, of the musical mysteries of his art."[84] "Marco Bozzaris," asserts Karl Bleibtreu, who has translated the poem, "erinnert in der Knappheit der Dic-

---

[82] G. P. Lathrop, *Atlantic Monthly*, XXXIX, 720 (June, 1877).

[83] Halleck once made the following analysis of "Hohenlinden": "Hohenlinden was one of his favorites,

> On Linden, when the sun was low,
> All *bloodless* lay the untrodden snow.

'There,' he would say, 'I defy any painter to paint that landscape! The poet in one word, *bloodless*, anticipates the coming struggle, the clash of men and arms, the blood-stained field that is to be, the trampled snow,—and in his prophetic vision he paints it all in a word. And now see how the armies are marshalled!—Not by generals and adjutants, but by a supernatural drum at midnight! An inferior poet would have put all the officers in,—pioneers and all—aids and orderlies, to summon the armies to battle,—but Campbell only uses a drum,

> But Linden saw another sight,
> When the *drum* beat at dead of night,
> Commanding *fires of death to light*
> The darkness of the scenery!

And how are these armies brought into line? By officers of squadrons or battalions? No! but by other, supernatural agents—

> By *torch* and *trumpet*, fast arrayed,
> Each horseman drew his battle blade.

By *drum*, by *torch*, and by *trumpet*, the deadly conflict is invoked, and the *fires of death* light up the vivid scenery.' " (F. S. Cozzens, *Fitz-Greene Halleck. A Memorial*, pp. 15-16.)

[84] XXXII, 312 (January, 1844). Two critics, not Halleck's contemporaries, have commented favorably on "Marco Bozzaris." In speaking of the notable English odes, Prof. Charles F. Johnson once said, "Among these, for the dithyrambic quality of ringing music, for rush, fire, and enthusiasm, Halleck's 'Marco Bozzaris' is not the least" (*Proceedings at the Celebration of the 250th Anniversary of the Settlement of Guilford, Conn.*, p. 105). Karl Knortz, the German critic, regarded the poem as "eines der wirksamsten Kriegslieder die jemals geschrieben wurden" (*Geschichte der Nordamerikanischen Literatur*, Berlin, 1891, I, 105).

tion entschieden an 'Hohenlinden' und 'Die baltische Schlacht.' "[85]
The severity of the diction to be found in "Hohenlinden" has been
effectively reproduced in "The Field of the Grounded Arms."
Compare the concluding stanzas of each poem:

Hohenlinden	The Field of the Grounded Arms
Few, few shall part where many meet!	In honorable life her fields they trod,
The snow shall be their winding-sheet,	In honorable death they sleep below;
And every turf beneath their feet	Their sons' proud feelings here
Shall be a soldier's sepulchre.	Their noblest monuments.[86]

A third poem bearing the possible influence of Campbell is
"Burns." Campbell's "Ode to the Memory of Burns" may have
suggested to Halleck his famous lines on the Scotch poet, although
the versification of Campbell's poem is more rugged. Each poet,
too, has conceived of Burns in a different way. Campbell's picture
is of a national poet; Halleck's is of an international character—
who rises above the poet to a representative man. Still, the closing
conception in Campbell's verses of the "grateful pilgrim," who
stops

> To bless the spot that holds thy dust,

may have inspired some of Halleck's finest lines:

> Such graves as his are pilgrim-shrines,
> Shrines to no code or creed confined—
> The Delphian vales, the Palestines,
> The Meccas of the mind.

Another literary influence equal to that of Campbell was Lord
Byron. Of Halleck's debt to Byron in *Fanny* we have already
spoken.[87] That Halleck's serio-comic poem was the outgrowth of his
love of "Beppo" and "Don Juan" there can be little doubt, although the treatment of his subject was not purely Byronic. But
Halleck's admiration for the author of "Don Juan" included also
his more serious verse—an admiration which approached reverence,

---

[85] *Geschichte der Englischen Litteratur in der Renaissance und Klassicität*
(Leipzig [1888]), p. 401.
[86] The concluding stanza, as the poem appears in the collected edition of
Halleck's works. See p. 232.
[87] See pp. 109 ff.

when at a dinner,[88] after Byron's death, Halleck solemnly proposed
a toast to "the memory of Byron—

> For him the voice of festive mirth
> Be hush'd—*his name* the only sound."[89]

And seven years later, with enthusiasm little abated, he undertook
the editing of Byron's works.[90]

In adapting to his use in *Fanny* the *ottava rima* of Byron, Halleck, it will be remembered, modified the original stanza form. In
his fragments on "Connecticut," however, he restored the original
stanza of "Beppo," although attempting little of the serio-comic
manner of Byron's poem, which he had affected in *Fanny*.[91] As for
Halleck's further obligation to Byron, in his humorous style, Prof.
William Ellery Leonard[92] has pointed out that the lines in "The
Recorder" beginning,

> I take the liberty of asking
> Permission, sir, to write your life,

were suggested by a stanza in "The Vision of Judgment."[93] But
even Halleck's contemporaries did not fail to note his indebtedness
to the more serious, heroic verses of Byron. When the *Knickerbocker* in 1834 wrote, "We may mark in Halleck the Byronic spirit
and fire of song," the critic[94] was undoubtedly thinking of "Marco
Bozzaris." Not only the enthusiasm for Greek liberty, but also the
heroic style of Halleck's lyric was derived in large part from

[88] Given in honor of Judge Trumbull. See p. 157.

[89] *New York American*, July 16, 1824. F. S. Cozzens has reported Halleck's
enthusiasm for *Childe Harold*. "When you go to Rome," said the poet, "when
you travel up the Rhine, take Childe Harold with you." (*Fitz-Greene Halleck.
A Memorial*, p. 20.)

[90] See p. 248.

[91] The theme, as well as the meter and manner of "Connecticut," may have
been suggested more immediately by John G. C. Brainard's "Extract from
New Year's Verses for 1825," a Byronic, serio-comic imitation in the *ottava
rima*. It was this poem to which Duyckinck referred when he said that "Connecticut" "appears to be indebted to a happy idea struck out by Brainard, in
his New Year's verse on the same theme" (*Cyclopaedia of American Literature*, II, 209). See *Poems of John G. C. Brainard* (Hartford, 1842), pp. 104–
106.

[92] *Byron and Byronism in America*, p. 41.

[93] Stanza 99.

[94] Willis G. Clark in *The Literary Remains of the Late Willis Gaylord Clark*
(New York, 1844), p. 274. Reprinted from the *Knickerbocker* for July, 1834.

Byron. If the Campbell of "Hohenlinden" influenced the elegiac
quality of "Marco Bozzaris," it was Byron who gave the lyric the
spectacular and melodramatic fire, which made its appeal so universal for two generations. William Allen Butler, "who claimed for
[Halleck] the energy to 'seize the passing moment, the present
scene, the grand event, and make them subservient to use,'[95] hit
unwittingly on Matthew Arnold's analysis[96] of Byron's peculiar
genius.'"[97]

We should pause for a moment in this discussion of Halleck's
literary sources to consider the inspiration of the greatest of all
books. Of the permanent influence of the Bible on the poet's
thought and style, there can be little doubt. Under the guidance of
his mother, he began early to find in the Book of Books a source of
spiritual and literary inspiration. The subjects of several of his
earliest poems were derived from his reading of religious literature.[98] Throughout his life he was a constant student of the Bible;
and it is said that six times after his retirement to Guilford he
completed a reading of the Scriptures. The spiritual consolation
which he found in the Book has been aptly illustrated in a reply,
made a year before his death, to an enthusiast for the writings of
Emanuel Swedenborg. Urged to a study of the works of the great
mystic, he replied in words beautiful alike for their courtesy and
gentle rebuke: "The more I strive to find, in new books on sacred
subjects, food for the soul's health, in the beauty of their prairies,
and their lakes and mountains, the more gladly do I return to the
old pastures amid which my youth was nurtured, and to the One
Book, now many, many centuries old.'"[99]

Of Halleck's admiration for the Bible as literature there can be
no doubt. On one occasion he remarked to Frederic S. Cozzens,
"Study the ancient Hebrew; these be thy Gods, O Israel.'"[100] That

---

[95] [E. A. Duyckinck], *A Memorial of Fitz-Greene Halleck* (New York,
1877), pp. 49–50.
[96] Professor Leonard here refers to the introduction of Arnold's *Poetry of
Byron* (London, 1881). See, for example, p. xxvi.
[97] W. E. Leonard, *Byron and Byronism in America,* p. 42.
[98] See p. 23.
[99] Wilson, *Life,* pp. 537–538. From a letter to the Reverend Solyman Brown,
dated August 25, 1866. The letter originally addressed to Halleck on this occasion has been lost; but another letter urging him to read the works of Swedenborg, and dated August 8, 1864, may be found in the Appendix, pp. 421–422.
[100] *Fitz-Greene Halleck. A Memorial,* p. 23.

Halleck actually put into practice his advice is attested by an extant manuscript[101] consisting of notes on his biblical reading. Sentences possessing special beauty of idea or phrasing are here set down. Thus we find: "My groans are their music"; "Abroad the sword bereaveth"; "Ask for the old paths and walk therein, and ye shall find rest." An unusual cadence or felicitous turn of phrase he has frequently stopped to note: "Amon's son"; "Old and full of days"; "In dark places as the dead of old"; "the footprints of the fox of desolation." The extent of the poet's reading in the Bible may be noted by observing that these excerpts may be traced not only to the canonical books, but to the Apocrypha.

To this intimate study of the Bible is undoubtedly attributable the grace of Halleck's prose style, which gained in beauty and ease of flow, as he matured. His poetry, too, shows the pervasive influence of scriptural diction. Both the purity of idiom and the frequent felicity of phrasing and expression for which his verse is distinguished, may have had their principal source in the Bible. The style of the much-neglected paraphrase of "Psalm CXXXVII," beautiful for its majestic, sonorous swing, is frequently to be found in Halleck's poetry.

> We sat us down and wept,
> Where Babel's waters slept,
> And we thought of home and Zion as a long-gone, happy dream;
> We hung our harps in air
> On the willow-boughs, which there,
> Gloomy as round a sepulchre, were drooping o'er the stream.[102]

A romantic critic after Halleck's death was but slightly betrayed by his own enthusiasm, when he spoke of the poem as "one of the most glorious versions from the Psalms in existence—a version neglecting no inspired statement or suggestion, but displaying an affluence of fancy, a high dramatic and poetic sentiment, and an appropriate, low, melancholy, musical cadence, like the murmur of the 'sad sea-waves,' that have seldom been surpassed, and that

101 This manuscript, dated "Sept. 4, 1831," is preserved in the Henry E. Huntington Library and Art Gallery. It numbers twenty-eight narrow pages (9⅞ x 4 inches), and is unsigned, but the handwriting is unmistakably Halleck's.

102 The meter was perhaps suggested by that of Milton's "On the Morning of Christ's Nativity."

would have added to the reputation of Faber, Keble, Montgomery, or Bishop Heber.''[103] The same dignity is evident in ''The Field of the Grounded Arms.'' The critics who found the poem ''a prosaic article, rather scriptural than poetical''[104] not only overlooked one of the chief sources of beauty in the poem, but disclosed their own blindness to the essentially poetic quality of the King James Version.[105]

III

Halleck's observations on the theory of poetry, though relatively few in number, are sufficient to permit of certain conclusions regarding his own art. It was apparently a poet's ability to emotionalize the fact—to transform events by the subtle power of the imagination—which Halleck regarded as the supreme test of the art. '' 'They are still trying to define poetry,' '' Halleck once remarked in a conversation with Bayard Taylor. '' 'It can be explained in a word: it's simply the opposite of reason! Reason is based on fact; and fact is not poetry. A poet has nothing to do with the facts of things, for he must continually deny them!' 'Will you give me an illustration?' '' asked Taylor. '' 'Certainly,' '' replied the poet, ''and then quoted, not from Campbell, or Byron, or Moore, as I was expecting, but these lines from Wordsworth's 'Song at the Feast of Brougham Castle':

> Armor, rusting on his walls
> On the blood of Clifford calls;—
> 'Quell the Scott!' exclaims the lance—
> 'Bear me to the heart of France!'
> Is the longing of the shield.

'There!' Halleck exclaimed: 'was ever anything more irrational than the lance exclaiming and the shield longing?—but what poetry it is!' ''[106] Though the example here chosen by Halleck was

---

[103] H. C. Alexander, *Hours at Home*, VI, 373 (February, 1868).

[104] See *Emerald and Baltimore Literary Gazette*, II, 15 (January 10, 1829).

[105] Halleck's scriptural allusions were occasionally somewhat hidden. In a letter to Epes Sargent (see pp. 394–395), Halleck referred the lines in ''Marco Bozzaris,''

> Come when the blessed seals
> That close the pestilence are broke—

to the figure of the seals in *Revelation*.

[106] *North American Review*, CXXV, 65 (July, 1877).

somewhat unfortunate, involving no doubt what Ruskin would call the "pathetic fallacy," it illustrates an attitude toward poetry to which Halleck frequently returned. On another occasion he cited the same passage from Wordsworth to indicate the "fusing power of the imagination in blending action with the thought";[107] and at yet another time, in discussing "the criterion of poetry he gave this familiar illustration of the subject. 'Draw your swords,' said he, 'that is prose.' 'Draw your willing swords, that is poetry.' "[108] Admittedly crude as indicating the power of the imagination to vitalize the fact, these examples yet show Halleck, in critical theory, not far from the kingdom of true poetry. Perhaps, however, like some more able critics, he should have left analysis alone, simply insisting, as he once did, that "expression" is "the *attribute* of genius, especially in poetry, 'the vision and the faculty divine.' "[109]

That a power of felicitous expression is one of the distinguishing marks of Halleck's poetry, has frequently been noted. An early reviewer, possibly Bryant, in commenting on the first collection mentioned "a sweetness of versification and a happy command of expression."[110] Poe regarded Halleck's merit as a poet one of expression;[111] and Thomas Powell once noted "the elaborate care with which every thought has been expressed."[112] E. P. Whipple also seems to have referred to this innate gift when he said that Halleck "has more of the faculty than the feeling of the poet."[113] Despite the somewhat imperfect examples which Halleck cited to illustrate the workings of the poetic imagination, he seldom indulged indiscreetly in the "pathetic fallacy." Whether or not Ruskin would have approved of the lines,

> Gaze on the Abbey's ruined pile:
> Does not the succoring ivy, keeping
> Her watch around it seem to smile,
> As o'er a loved one sleeping?[114]

[107] Duyckinck, *Putnam's Magazine*, XI, 244 (February, 1868).
[108] *Ibid.*, XI, 244–245.   [109] Wilson, *Life*, p. 560.
[110] *New York Evening Post*, April 5, 1827.
[111] *Southern Literary Messenger*, II, 335 (April, 1836).
[112] *Living Writers of America* (New York, 1850), p. 223.
[113] *Essays and Reviews* (Boston, 1851), I, 56.
[114] "Alnwick Castle." This passage and the one from the same poem beginning, "One solitary turret gray," Poe regarded as "evincing a degree of

they possess, though somewhat marred by sentimentality, the elements of true poetry. But Halleck's real power undoubtedly lay in an ability to compress meaning into a single line or phrase. Many a verse in his poetry may thus be removed from its context, and made to stand alone—a gem compact with truth. Such phrases as "Meccas of the mind,"[115] "the wild-flower wreath of feeling,"[116] "the half-seen spirit of twilight,"[117] are marvelous in their power of suggestion. So, too, the opening lines of "Album Verses":

> Within a rock, whose shadows linger,
>   At moonlight hours, on Erie's sea,
> Some unseen, Indian spirit's finger
>   Woke in far times sweet minstrelsy.

The pen that could thoughtlessly have written in a lady's album these lines, equal to some of the most imaginative stanzas of Freneau, should not also have squandered on the epistle to Walter Bowne the expressive verses:

> Where are they now? With shapes of air,
> The caravan of things that were,
> Journeying to their nameless home
> Like Mecca's pilgrims from her tomb.

Nor should we forget the lines, thought by Poe to be Halleck's "finest," in which, as in certain of the similes in "Paradise Lost," the imagination is for the moment carried away to some distant vista of romance:

> Thy summons welcome as the cry
> That told the Indian isles were nigh
>   To the world-seeking Genoese.
> When the land wind, from woods of palm,
> And orange-groves, and fields of balm,
>   Blew o'er the Haytian seas.[118]

---

rich imagination not elsewhere perceptible throughout'' Halleck's work. See *Southern Literary Messenger*, II, 334 (April, 1836).

[115] "Burns." Prosper Wetmore in a poem "Greece" (*Lexington, with other Fugitive Poems*, New York, 1830) uses the phrase "The Peru of the mind." The *New York Evening Post* for October 5, 1830, noted Wetmore's indebtedness to Halleck.

[116] "Twilight."

[117] *Fanny* (Lines to the Horseboat).

[118] "Marco Bozzaris."

Next to a characteristic aptness of expression, a quality of simplicity and terseness, already noted, is perhaps the most striking virtue of Halleck's poetry. This directness proceeded from a mind naturally simple in its working. Almost wholly self-taught in intellectual pursuits, he lacked the intricacy and subtlety of thought which a more extended formal education would doubtless have encouraged. The poetry of Browning always troubled him, and indeed "the more recent style of metrical writing, suggestive rather than emphatic, undefined and involved, and borrowed mainly from German idealism, he utterly" repudiated.[119] Here the vigor afforded by his Puritan ancestry stood him in good stead. "The cries and protests, the utterances of 'world pain' with which his contemporaries filled the world," said Bayard Taylor at the dedication of the Halleck monument, "awoke no echo in his sound and sturdy nature."[120] This sturdiness and simplicity which he transferred so effectively to his own poetry, have been frequently noted by critics. "The terseness of Mr. Halleck's language is in admirable harmony with his vivacity of thought and richness of fancy,"[121] wrote a reviewer in *Harper's;* and H. T. Tuckerman ascribed much of the popularity of Halleck's verses "to their spirited, direct, and intelligible character, the absence of all vagueness and mysticism."[122] Karl Bleibtreu, the German critic, in his brief analysis of Halleck's poetry, has also made mention of "eine strenge Reinheit der Diktion und eine gesunde Tendenz."[123]

This tendency may be studied to special advantage in two of Halleck's poems—"On the Death of Joseph Rodman Drake" and "Burns." Of the superiority of the lines on Drake, as an expression of personal grief, to the formal elegies of English literature little need be said. "Lycidas" and "Adonais," greater poems in beauty of figure and breadth of philosophic implication, are inertly cold beside Halleck's simple verses. His bear a universal appeal; they speak an unadorned grief for the loss of a friend. Wordsworth's

[119] H. T. Tuckerman, "A Sketch of American Literature" in Thomas B. Shaw, *A Complete Manual of English Literature* (New York, 1871), p. 515.

[120] *A Memorial of Fitz-Greene Halleck*, edited by E. A. Duyckinck (New York, 1877), p. 20.

[121] *Harper's New Monthly Magazine*, V, 423 (August, 1852).

[122] H. T. Tuckerman, *op. cit.*, p. 515.

[123] *Geschichte der Englischen Litteratur in der Renaissance und Klassicität*, p. 400.

critical theory of diction has seldom been applied to better advantage; here the real language of men carries its message straight to the human heart. One critic has called the poem "superior to Wordsworth's piece[124] of which it seems to be an imitation";[125] and it was also a favorite with Poe, who preferred it "to any of the writings of Halleck. It has that rare merit in compositions of this kind—the union of tender sentiment and simplicity."[126]

Poe's opinion of "Burns" was also high; its "peculiar grace and terseness of expression" he regarded as "remarkable."[127] This poem, which Paulding regarded as Halleck's "noblest,"[128] has had many admirers. In speaking of "Burns" an anonymous critic once attributed to Halleck "a Scott-like faculty . . . of contemplating his theme with a nice severity,—there is a *simplex munditiis* about the objects of his song."[129] And James Lawson believed that "in Burns we have the very man standing before us, in moral and mental grandeur. He is breathing, bloodwarm, alive in healthy vigor and manly strength."[130] In "Burns" the quality of the diction is admirably adjusted to the thought. Burns's genius, in Halleck's conception, rising above that of the poet, is glorified in the man—he

> Lived—died—in form and soul a Man
> The image of his God.

Here excessive poetic adornment has no place. The secret of the power of this representative man is brought home by Halleck with the simple directness of genius.[131]

124 The lyric beginning, "She dwelt among the untrodden ways" is here referred to. Poe mentioned the same parallel in his *Literati* article on Halleck in *Godey's Magazine and Lady's Book*, XXXIII, 14 (July, 1846).

125 H. C. Alexander, *Hours at Home*, VI, 373 (February, 1868).

126 *Southern Literary Messenger*, II, 336 (April, 1836).

127 *Graham's Magazine*, XXIII, 163 (September, 1843).

128 Wilson, *Life*, p. 275.

129 *American Quarterly Review*, XXI, 408 (June, 1837).

130 *Southern Literary Messenger*, VIII, [2]45 (April, 1842).

131 Three literary echoes of Halleck's "Burns" may here be noted. Prof. Thomas O. Mabbott has pointed out that in a copy of Mrs. Emma C. Embury's *Guido* (New York, 1829, p. 80), preserved in the library of the University of Chicago, someone has noted a parallel between her line in "Lament of Camoens," "Then shall my grave become a pilgrim shrine," and Halleck's, "Such graves as his are pilgrim shrines." Another literary parallel between lines in "Burns" and Tennyson's "The Poet" is noted in *Chambers' Cyclopaedia of English Literature*, third edition (London and Edinburgh, 1876), II, 435. A

Halleck always insisted upon the lyrical quality of verse. "There is no poetry," he once remarked, "without music. It must have grace of rhythm and cadence."[132] Closely allied to this, and important, too, in establishing Halleck's criteria for the art is the opinion that good poetry is that most easily committed to memory. Bryant's "Planting of the Apple Tree" Halleck memorized after a single reading,—"an infallible test with me," he asserted, "of true poetry."[133] And yet he did not always intrust a poem entirely to his memory, which, he once said, was "wax to receive and marble to retain."[134] His habit of copying out passages or whole poems which pleased him may have indicated a desire to possess himself of the inner melody of the poem, which verbal commission alone could not give. Thus F. S. Cozzens relates that "when he liked a poem he would copy it off, and get it by heart." "He once gave me a poem," the humorist goes on to say, " 'The Death of Jacob,' an Oxford prize poem, in seventy-seven stanzas of four lines each, with notes, which he had copied from Littell's Living Age."[135]

Halleck, no doubt, possessed toward poetry a lyrical habit of mind, and the critic must inevitably test his work by this standard. "Ein geborener Lyriker," Karl Knortz[136] called him in 1891; and his opinion but echoes the criticism of Halleck's contemporaries. "If we were asked," wrote George S. Hillard in the *New England Magazine,* "what is the peculiar charm of Mr. Halleck's poetry, and what it is that distinguishes him from the other poets of our country, we should answer in one word—Grace"[137]—an honest observa-

---

third curious echo of Halleck's poem may be found in Joaquin Miller's "Burns and Byron"—*Songs of the Sierras* (Boston, 1871), p. 261:

> I seek in vain for name or sign
> Of him who made this mould a shrine,
> A Mecca to the fair and fond
> Beyond the seas, and still beyond.

Miller is here referring to Byron.

[132] W. C. Bryant, *Some Notices of the Life and Writings of Fitz-Greene Halleck,* p. 34.

[133] Wilson, *Life,* p. 557. See also *ibid.,* pp. 221, 526.

[134] *Ibid.,* p. 557.

[135] *Fitz-Greene Halleck. A Memorial,* p. 23. "The Death of Jacob," which originally appeared in the *Dublin University Magazine,* L, 3 (July, 1857), was reprinted in *Living Age,* LIV, 449–452 (August 22, 1857). Wilson also speaks at some length of Halleck's habit of copying poems. See *Life,* pp. 557–558.

[136] *Geschichte der Nordamerikanischen Literatur,* I, 105.

[137] I, 157 (August, 1831).

tion of a Boston critic who might have cited by way of comparison
the crude productions of many a New England versifier of the day.
Henry T. Tuckerman found that Halleck as a poet was "an adept
in that relation of sound to sense which embalms thought in death-
less melody";[138] and James Lawson believed that "one secret of
Halleck's popularity lies in the concord of sweet sounds."[139] "Halleck's poetry, whether serious or sprightly," remarked Bryant, "is
remarkable for the melody of the numbers. It is not the melody of
monotonous and strictly regular measurement. His verse is constructed to please an ear naturally fine, and accustomed to a wide
range of metrical modulation."[140] This gift of melody, which is
distinguishable in even the early verses of the poet, is ever present
in his work. It is to be felt in the carefree, nonchalant meter of
Fanny, in the martial movement of "Marco Bozzaris," and in the
elegiac dignity of the unrhymed "Field of the Grounded Arms."

But it is in his lighter verse that the musical flow of Halleck's
poetry is most in evidence. If his Puritan ancestry was responsible
for the quiet, restrained dignity of his diction, his Cavalier blood
made him the master of compliment. All who knew Halleck agreed
they had "never met with a finer gentleman."[141] His attitude to
all, and especially to women, was one of uncommon gallantry,
which, even in his day, was thought a bit antiquated.[142] A resident
of Guilford, who had several times seen the poet as an old man,
once recalled for me the marked grace with which he removed his
hat to those he addressed. In writing he displayed a like chivalry.
Few have ever been so facile in combining refusal with compliment.
Could a more courteous, engaging manner be found of declining an
irksome task, than that preserved in a letter addressed to Mrs.
Barnes, the actress, who had applied to Halleck for an address to
be spoken at the opening of the Richmond Hill Theatre in 1832?

---

138 Tuckerman, *op. cit.*, p. 516.
139 *Southern Literary Messenger*, VIII, [2]44 (April, 1842).
140 *New York Mirror*, XIV, 97 (September 24, 1836).
141 Wilson, *Life*, p. 467.
142 Compare stanza 104 of "Fanny" (1839 ed.) in which Halleck humorously alludes to the "ill-bred" manners of the age.

> But where is Fanny? She has long been thrown
> Where cheeks and roses wither—in the shade.
> The age of chivalry, you know, is gone. Etc., etc.

Thursday, May 10th.

MR. HALLECK presents his most grateful compliments to Mrs. Barnes, and assures her that nothing could give him greater pleasure than the power of complying with the request with which she honored him in her note of yesterday, but he deeply regrets to be compelled to add that he has been estranged for so long a time from the habit of writing and rhyming, as to find it utterly impossible to frame an Address in the least degree worthy of her who is to speak it, or capable of aiding his own good wishes for the success of herself, and of his excellent friend Mr. Barnes. He therefore begs her to accept those good wishes in place of his bad verses, and to summon to her flattering task some of his youngers and betters. He is himself becoming, like King Lear, "a foolish, fond old man, fourscore and upward," and is broad awake with both eyes from the morning-dream of poetry.[143]

And the same air of grace and compliment is to be found in much of Halleck's verse. Few poets have been more adept in *vers de société*. "By the hackneyed phrase, *sportive elegance*," wrote Poe in 1836, "we might possibly designate at once the general character of his writings."[144] Skilful alike in light verse and in satire, he knew well how to temper the serious with the gay. This faculty, derived from a warring of contrasts within his personality, found frequent expression in his everyday intercourse with men. Evert Duyckinck once said: "As in his poetry, there was frequently a sharp antithesis in his conversation. It was safe not to trust too much to the flow of his compliments, but to look out for the sly parentheses and qualifications."[145] Thus the poet who wrote,

> For thou art Woman—with that word
>   Life's dearest hopes and memories come,
> Truth, Beauty, Love—in her adored,
> And earth's lost Paradise restored
>   In the green bower of home;—[146]

and paid the platonic compliment,

> Be still my worshipped being,
>   In mind and heart—[147]

---

[143] Wilson, *Life*, pp. 347–348.

[144] *Southern Literary Messenger*, II, 334 (April, 1836).

[145] *Putnam's Magazine*, XI, 242 (February, 1868).

[146] "Woman." A similar tone of compliment may be found in "A Poet's Daughter."

[147] "Lines to Her Who Can Understand Them."

could also in "Domestic Happiness" discourse pleasantly on the
infelicity of Mr. and Mrs. Dash; and in "The Winds of March are
Humming" describe the vexation of a disappointed belle.[148] With
sentimental and ironic alike his fancy played with equal charm,
and in which mood the poet was the more sincere it would be hard
to say. Seldom has society verse been written with a greater eye
to contrast.

IV

Yet in this double flash of the poet's wit we glimpse a genius
divided against itself. In Halleck we find intensified the fundamental problem of all reflective men—the adjustment of the ideal
world to the practical. As we have already pointed out, the intensity which the problem assumed with Halleck was, in part, the
result of his ancestry. His paternal inheritance furnished him with
that love of beauty which made him a poet; while the gift of practicality from his mother readily provided for his occupation as an
accountant. To the close of his life he remained a firm devotee of
the beautiful; yet he was no esthete. Clinging as firmly to the pillars of common sense, he found in their support the characteristic
vigor which his nature demanded; yet he was never entirely sub-
dued to what he worked in. As it is hard to think of Halleck as the
littérateur, so it is difficult to picture him entirely the man of business. But however blurred the line that at times separated poet
from banker, we cannot ignore the essential conflict of the two interests which were continually presenting themselves in the poet's
life.

It would be interesting to trace in detail this conflict as it found
expression in the man and the poet. Doubtless present in the pur-

[148] One cannot refrain from quoting the last stanza of this poem:

They tell me there's no hurry
  For Hymen's ring, for Hymen's ring;
And I'm too young to marry:
  'Tis no such thing, 'tis no such thing.
The next spring-tides will dash on
  My eighteenth year, my eighteenth year;
It puts me in a passion,
  Oh dear, oh dear! oh dear, oh dear!
  My second winter's over,
    Alas! and I, alas! and I
  Have no accepted lover:
    Don't ask me why, don't ask me why.

This is perhaps one of the cleverest bits of society verse ever written. One
can almost see the young lady tearing her fan in vexation!

suits of the boy while he was yet in Guilford, it culminated early in an important triumph for the world of reality. Halleck's determination to seek his fortune in New York, instead of preparing himself for a profession whereby he might the more readily indulge his tastes for literature, became curiously representative of the outcome of similar decisions throughout his life. The practical world was invariably the victor, the ideal remaining a beloved but remote realm where he might spend his leisure hours. Thus he came to regard the poet in no false, romantic light; the poet was a man— and no more—who must inevitably submit to the hard-headed practicality of the world. The amusement with which Halleck regarded the poet who needed an artificial stimulus for his imagination is illustrated in a manuscript note appended to Coleridge's famous sonnet to Schiller: "Schiller, it is said, always composed his tragedies at night under the inspiration of three bottles of champagne: Coleridge, I understand, prefers brandy. To see either of them in their inspired moments would be more likely to make one laugh aloud than 'weep aloud.' "[149] Nor was the fame of the poet more sacred than his inspiration, if we are to judge from Halleck's statements. In writing to his sister, he once referred to "some dozen complimentary letters from different parts of the Union, with which I should have been better pleased had the writers paid the postage."[150] Halleck also delighted occasionally in making sly thrusts at the impracticality of poets. He frequently repeated the remark of a "shrewd merchant" who defined the poet as "a man who has soarings after the indefinite, and divings after the unfathomable, *but he never pays cash.*"[151]

Turning to Halleck's poetry, we find that it is this conflict between the ideal and actual about which critics of Halleck's day and since have been most concerned in appraising his work. "He delights in ludicrous contrasts," wrote Bryant in 1836, "produced by bringing the nobleness of the ideal world into comparison with the homeliness of the actual; the beauty and grace of nature with the awkwardness of art. He venerates the past and laughs at the present. He looks at them through the medium which lends to the former the charm of romance, and exaggerates the deformity of the

[149] Wilson, *Life*, p. 229.
[150] *Ibid.*, p. 237.   [151] *Ibid.*, p. 572.

latter.''[152] A similar statement of Halleck's poetic method was
made by James Lawson, who, like Bryant, spoke of the ''strong
contrasts'' which Halleck everywhere finds—a propensity which,
added the critic, ''is not of the highest order; yet we are inclined
to believe that, with his exquisite harmony, it is the true secret of
his popularity.''[153] Henry T. Tuckerman also attributed the success of Halleck's poetry to the love of incongruity. ''An unusual
blending of the animal and intellectual,'' wrote that critic, ''with
that proportion essential to manhood, enables him to utter appeals
that wake the responses in the universal heart. An almost provoking
mixture of irony and sentiment is characteristic of his genius.''[154]
But whereas some critics have been either amused or charmed by
Halleck's habitual love of contrast, which, assert some, makes
''him one of the most uniformly piquant of modern poets,''[155] a
greater number have found in this practice cause for censure. Although the problem as it presents itself in *Fanny* has been thoroughly discussed, we may note in passing a typical bit of sentimental criticism by Mrs. Sarah S. Ellis, who in commenting on the
incongruity of the lyric, ''Young thoughts,''[156] remarked that ''what
could induce the poet to spoil his otherwise pretty verses in this
manner, it is difficult to imagine''[157]—an observation which amused
not a little the editor of the *Knickerbocker*.[158] More genuinely
critical, however, are the comments of E. P. Whipple and G. L.
Lathrop. Edwin P. Whipple at once struck at this literary habit
as a blot upon Halleck's style:

. . . He has few serious thoughts that are not more or less associates
with ludicrous ideas. A laughing imp seems to sit opposite the fountains
of his heart, and dispel with merry flash of his eye every shade and thin
essence which rise in misty beauty from their surface. . . . To produce a
shock of surprise by the sudden intrusion of an incongruous idea into a

[152] *New York Mirror*, XIV, 97 (September 24, 1836).
[153] *Southern Literary Messenger*, VIII, [2]45 (April, 1842).
[154] Tuckerman, *op. cit.*, p. 516.
[155] *Harper's New Monthly Magazine*, V, 423 (August, 1852).
[156] See p. 113.
[157] *Poetry of Life* (New York, 1843), p. 82.
[158] XXII, 181 (August, 1843). The editor's remark was as follows: ''Isn't
this rather rich, friend Halleck? We doubt whether Mrs. Ellis could take a joke
though it were shot at her from a cannon. Indeed, she would doubtless reply to
this remark: 'But how can you shoot a joke out of a cannon? Surely, that can
hardly be feasible!' ''

mournful or sentimental flow of feeling, is but little above the clap-trap of the stage. We are aware that, in Halleck's case, this is done in an inimitable manner, and that the effect on one's risible faculties is irresistible, but still, there are very few who desire to be chocked with a laugh, at the very moment when the tears are starting from their eyes. It introduces a species of scepticism, which is destructive to the enjoyment of poetry.[159]

George L. Lathrop's analysis of Halleck's poetry, contributed ten years after Halleck's death to the *Atlantic Monthly*, though somewhat unsympathetic, is by far the best criticism of his work which appeared in the nineteenth century. After examining in detail Halleck's poetic methods, Lathrop observed: "These various examples which we have reviewed all force us to the conclusion that Halleck instinctively sought, in one way or another, a break in the tune, an abrupt alternation of mood. It was in this clashing of diverse inclinations that he struck out his liveliest sparks of fancy. He sought a certain tantalizing sweetness that floated in the midst of discord."[160] This charm, however, yielding but a momentary pleasure, was symptomatic, Lathrop believed, of an essential poetic weakness which we shall soon consider.

The justice of these critical observations can most readily be tested by an examination of individual poems. Of all Halleck's major productions which admit this contrast between the ideal and actual, "Alnwick Castle" has received most comment. A few typical examples of this criticism may be noted. To Poe "the tone employed in the concluding portions of Alnwick Castle" is "reprehensible and unworthy of Halleck";[161] to Lawson the contrast becomes a fatal anticlimax, leaving with the reader but a sordid impression of human ideals;[162] while to Lathrop, "Alnwick Castle" is an "instance of a sober poem ending in the bitterness of desecrating humor."[163] It may readily be admitted that nothing essentially inartistic lies in the serio-comic style; whatever imperfection attaches to it, has its rise in a lack of adaptation of style to subject matter. In some of Halleck's poems, no doubt, there exists an incongruity of style and subject which results in a loss of artistic power. In *Fanny*, however, we have seen that the style is admirably

[159] *Essays and Reviews* (New York, 1851), I, 57–58.
[160] XXXIX, 724 (June, 1877).
[161] *Southern Literary Messenger*, II, 334 (April, 1836).
[162] *Ibid.*, VIII, [2]48.
[163] *Atlantic Monthly*, XXXIX, 724 (June, 1877).

adjusted to the story—an essential contrast being implied in the absurd and wholly unfounded ambitions of a vulgar merchant and his daughter. And in "Alnwick Castle" we see a similar contrast between the ideal and actual to which Halleck's characteristic style may with justice be applied. There are, we may suppose, two ways for the traveler to view the castle of the Percys—as a monument of old, clothed in medieval romance; or as a building erected centuries ago and now inhabited by modern men, to which no especial romance belongs. Both views are necessary to complete the mental impression of the scene. If Poe was more successful in realizing a sustained romantic vision in "The Coliseum," he presented in that poem less of truth to the generality of men than may be found in "Alnwick Castle." Indeed, we find far more irony than humor in the concluding stanzas of Halleck's poem. Try how we may, we cannot for long recapture the past; and the ideal which we have formed of its beauty and romance, must in the end, for most of us, fade in disillusion—in the light of common day. Thus does the vision of Alnwick as the home of the Percys, suddenly give place to the picture of a modern "market town"— humorous, yes; but how strangely ironic and universal![164]

Several of Halleck's other poems introduce, with more or less success, a similar contrast. "A Poet's Daughter," in its expression of the impingement of the world of business upon that of romance becomes more intimately autobiographical even than "Alnwick Castle." The contrast here is also less abrupt, and, upon the whole we may say, more skilfully handled than in the other poem. But we are again forced to inquire into the fitness of the contrast. Why, we must ask, should Halleck have introduced a personal problem of

---

[164] At least one critic has found in the closing stanzas of "Alnwick Castle" no lack of fitness. Richard Henry Stoddard writes: "It would be difficult, if not impossible, to find in English verse such picturesque suggestions of the pomp and splendor of feudal days as we find in 'Alnwick Castle,' in which the manner of Scott has become a style, and which are suffused with a rich historic light. There is a dignity, not to say distinction in its spirited but careless stanzas, which are needlessly disfigured with imperfect rhymes—a metrical negligence of which Halleck, like Scott and Byron, was too often guilty. Nor is this distinction impaired by the introduction of local and modern allusions, through which, as through a bustling foreground, we are borne back to this stately home of the Percy's high-born race. The poetic, for once, does not suffer from its temporary association with the humorous" (*Lippincott's Monthly Magazine*, XLIII, 894, June, 1889).

this kind into album verses intended for a young lady? We thus observe in the poem a certain incongruity which does not appear in lines like "The Sketch" and "Domestic Happiness," where we enjoy the natural contrast between expectation and fulfilment. An incongruity similar to that in "A Poet's Daughter" and unjustifiable on the grounds of fitness, is practiced in the verses "To Walter Bowne, Esq.," in which Halleck's usual method is reversed,— the mood of play and banter being followed by lines of uncommon beauty. One acknowledges here a unique impression of disillusion, but hardly of sufficient piquancy to warrant the bringing together of moods so totally different. The spirit of mere burlesque evident in these lines is repeated in "The Rhyme of the Ancient Coaster" and "Wyoming." If in the latter poem Halleck had been satisfied, as in "Alnwick Castle," with merely contrasting the romance of anticipation with the reality of experience, he would no doubt have left unviolated the standard of fitness. But such lines as,

> Of the poet-player [Shakespeare]
> The maiden knows no more than Cobbett or Voltaire,

have about them an air of Byronic burlesque, which, though harking back to the days of *Fanny*, is foreign to the subject at hand. To the close of Halleck's life such was the fascination of the poet for this fatal contrast that his last poem, "Young America," is seriously marred by its presence.[165]

So unusual a literary habit, so marked an obsession, suggests an inquiry into the mental cause of the phenomenon. In a word, the reason seems to have lain in an innate *sincerity* of character. Such is always the motive of the genuinely satiric mind. Halleck, whose very face was described by contemporaries as "strongly sarcastic,"[166] found in the foibles of his fellows at once amusement and chagrin. And as in poetry, so in conversation, he sought to prick "the bubbles of conceit and vanity."[167] "No man," notes H. T. Tuckerman, "could be more keenly satirical as to all pseudo-aristocracy";[168] and William Gilmore Simms has mentioned his

---

[165] See pp. 343–344.

[166] See *Journal* of Fanny Kemble (Philadelphia, 1835), I, 122. A similar remark was also made by Abbie Flanner in commenting on Halleck's picture (Wilson, *Life*, p. 369).

[167] William A. Jones in Wilson, *Life*, p. 541.

[168] *Lippincott's Monthly Magazine*, I, 213 (February, 1868).

tone of sarcasm "when speaking of pretense and pretenders."[169] If Carlyle was justified in calling "Don Juan" Byron's most sincere work,[170] we may with equal justice assert *The Croakers* and "Fanny" representative of Halleck's innate sincerity. The parody in "Fanny" of Moore's famous "Bendemeer's Stream" is illustrative of a desire to strip an absurd sentimentalism of its flimsy illusion. Even when the demands of his art require him to realize the romantic vision, the world of reality and experience often rudely intrudes. An instinct, not always artistic, we have found, invariably causes him to pierce through the shell of romance to the core of solid reality.

"Perhaps, in Halleck," remarks E. P. Whipple, "this mischievous spirit is to be referred, in some degree, to that fear of being sentimental which is apt to characterize robust and healthy natures."[171] To his Anglo-Saxon ancestry, or, more particularly to his Puritan, may perhaps be ascribed the critical check which Halleck sought to put upon romance. A lurking fear of emotionalism is a trait of mind for which the Englishman may well be proud, for it has forced him finally, almost in spite of himself, to a dogged loyalty to the truth. In American literature curious elements of disillusion have at times arisen, mention of which may aid in an attempt to interpret the present peculiarity of Halleck's thought. The Knickerbocker tendency to parody, which we have already noted, sprang not alone from a love of humor. Passages of burlesque which disfigure Paulding's *Koningsmarke* and *Westward Ho!* arose, no doubt, from an instinctive distrust of the romantic style the author was attempting to exploit. And to look outside of New York, we find similar effects appearing in Herman Melville's *Moby Dick*. That twist of the imagination which made Melville include among the fraternity of whalers "Perseus, St.

---

[169] Wilson, *Life*, p. 543.

[170] "With longer life," says Carlyle, "all things were to have been hoped for from Byron: for he loved truth in his inmost heart, and would have discovered at last that his Corsairs and Harolds were not true" (*Critical and Miscellaneous Essays*, London, 1894, I, 59). To this statement should be added the one made in "Burns": "Perhaps *Don Juan*, especially the latter parts of it, is the only thing approaching to a *sincere* work he ever wrote; the only work where he showed himself, in any measure, as he was; and seemed so intent on his subject as, for moments, to forget himself" (*Ibid.*, I, 242).

[171] *Essays and Reviews*, I, 58.

George, Hercules, Jonah, and Vishnu,''[172] may be traced to a sub-conscious desire to counteract the overenthusiasm for his subject, which, in the heat of inspiration, was fast gaining control of him.

This sincerity of disposition also led Halleck to a characteristic fairness in appraising men and events. Here again we may note Halleck's English inheritance. Emerson, in commenting on the Anglo-Saxon's dependence upon the logical faculties, adds, ''Into this English logic, however, an infusion of justice enters, not so apparent in other races—a belief in the existence of two sides and the resolution to see fair play.''[173] Although at times curiously narrow and conservative, Halleck often displayed a temper of mind essentially judicial.[174] That inherent love of fair play which prompted him in ''Alnwick Castle'' to present two views of the scene, made him see in Red Jacket both monarch and devil. And the dispassionate poet who shortly before his death called the attribute of the poet's art ''to make the dead on fields of battle, alike the victors and the vanquished, look beautiful in the sunbeams of his song,''[175] had many years before demonstrated the truth of his conviction in ''The Field of the Grounded Arms.''[176] This judicial trend of mind is perhaps most clearly to be seen in the two fragments on ''Connecticut.'' In the first, the narrow prejudice and noble strength of the Yankee character are placed impartially side by side. In the second, the poet presents an intimate portrait of Cotton Mather, wherein the harshness and bigotry of the Puritan divine, though amply acknowledged, are excused because of the ''sour grape-juice in his disposition''; and the pages of his folios, full of wild imaginings and bitter denunciations, gain a childish fascination for the reader, when viewed in the light of poetry. The rugged strength and sly humor of these poems on ''Connecticut'' also contribute to placing them among Halleck's best work.

[172] See Chapter 82.

[173] *English Traits*, V (Paragraph 11).

[174] Vernon Parrington has also recognized this characteristic: ''In Halleck's better work there is sometimes evident a certain critical detachment that permitted him to see both sides of his theme'' (*Main Currents in American Thought*, II, 202).

[175] Wilson, *Life*, p. 524. From a letter to Mrs. Rush dated November 21, 1861.

[176] See pp. 234–235.

V

"We must confess," notes the *Mirror* in reviewing the 1827 edition of Halleck's poems, "we close the work with feelings somewhat akin to disappointment."[177] This comment was far more poignant with meaning than the critic who penned it apparently understood. Whereas he readily explained the disappointment on the grounds of the thinness of the volume, thus implying a compliment to the poet, the remark undoubtedly sprang from a subconscious feeling of genuine discontent. When one has finished reading not only the first collected edition, but the last of 1869, he is left with an indefinable impression of dissatisfaction. Here is a poet, we are forced to conclude, who just missed attaining distinction; one who might have reached the mark had he aimed his arrow with a steadier hand and surer eye.

Whether he could not or would not make the supreme effort remains largely an enigma. Perhaps the popular acclaim which he received in early manhood made him fearful in later life of venturing to extend his fame.[178] Perhaps, as Bayard Taylor has suggested, during the last thirty years of his life Halleck "remained silent because he felt no immediate personal necessity of poetic utterance."[179] And there is much to be said for the opinion of Halleck's contemporaries who laid to his close application to business the reason for the literary inertia that they saw daily growing upon him. But the problem goes deeper than a superficial struggle between a love of poetry and a desire for mundane pleasure. To critics and public alike the contrasts encountered in Halleck's poetry have been irritating or humorous. But to the person who examines critically the poet's personality, they become in a sense tragic; they are seen as the inevitable struggles of a mind seeking rest and finding none. Torn between the ideal world typified by a devotion to the past, and the world of daily experience whose pressure he found inevitable, Halleck moved bewildered yet fascinated by the variety of contrasts presented on every hand. But never a thought did he apparently give to the reconciliation of the two

[177] IV, 263 (March 10, 1827).
[178] Lathrop, *Atlantic Monthly*, XXXIX, 725 (June, 1877).
[179] From Taylor's address at the dedication of the Halleck monument in Guilford. See Duyckinck, *Memorial of Fitz-Greene Halleck* (New York, 1877), p. 21.

worlds; yet in their reconciliation lay his salvation as a man and poet. "Why," justly asks George P. Lathrop, "did he not obey the call of his genius? Why did he not quit trade and, if need were, society, and bring his mind face to face with what struck him as the contradiction between life and poetry, until he should discover how to reconcile them? Then he might have gained for his creative faculty a noble and sustaining confidence. The inevitable conclusion is that his inspiration was not ardent enough, his temperament too much averse to the risk and the effort involved—in a word, that his genius was secondary, and had not the instinct of discovery, which overrules tradition and makes worlds where it was thought none could be."[180]

This judgment is harsh but sound. Halleck's *inspiration was not ardent enough*. Although he was seldom given to self-examination, his lines,

> My spirit's wings are weak; the fire
> Poetic comes but to expire,[181]

suggest the weakness he daily experienced. The "degree of cynicism"[182] and the deficiency in "sensibility"[183] which critics have found in the man and his work, and which undoubtedly made it hard for him to detach himself from this "bank-note world" long enough to feel in all its intensity "the fire poetic," should perhaps be traced to the Puritan strain in his blood. In any case, the Puritan distrust of all things that lie in the uncharted regions beyond the pales of logic found a curious outcropping in the poet, and may in a measure account for the sterility of his genius.

Again, as Lathrop has observed, a deep-seated conservatism, arising perhaps from Halleck's Yankee parentage, played no small part in halting the spontaneity of his imagination. To "a certain persistency of temper"[184] was added a fear of change and innovation. "It was some fifteen or twenty years after he came to live in New York," writes Bryant, "that he said to me, 'I like to go on with the people whom I begin with. I have the same boarding-house

---

[180] Lathrop, *op. cit.*, XXXIX, 726.

[181] "A Poet's Daughter."   [182] Lathrop, *op. cit.*, XXXIX, 726.

[183] R. H. Stoddard, *Lippincott's Monthly Magazine*, XLIII, 889 (June, 1889).

[184] Bryant, *Some Notices of the Life and Writings of Fitz-Greene Halleck*, p. 9.

now that I had when I first came to town; my clothes are made by the same tailor, and I employ the same shoe-maker.' ''[185] And so it was with the favorite poets of his early manhood. Byron and Campbell in youth excited his poetic imagination and gained an ascendancy over him which could not be shaken. Thus the change in taste during the forties and fifties that brought to English literature a delight in poetic subtlety and mysticism left him either cold or completely bewildered. The poet of Byron and Campbell naturally had no relish for Tennyson and Browning. And to a probable realization of this changing taste, and to his inability to follow the new trend of poetic thought and style was, in part, due the silence of his later years.

Perhaps a genius so fragile as that of Halleck should never have come under the influence of the early Knickerbocker school. Avowed literary idlers, Irving and Paulding were not the men to give vitality to a flagging imagination. Setting aside as a test of his poetry Matthew Arnold's dictum of "high seriousness," we none the less regret in Halleck's work the spirit of idling which kept him from that devotion to his art which every great poet must have. Furthermore, he was intellectually shallow. We have seen him frequently lacking in critical judgment, and he often seemed unaware of the existence of human problems—even, be it said, of his own. "His silence," observes Lathrop, "does not appear to have been that of an anguished sorrow too deep for words, but merely the silence of indifference."[186] Finally, Halleck was a confessed literary amateur, and as an amateur he must be judged. "I have published very little," he wrote to a friend in 1859, "and that little almost always anonymously, and have ever been but an amateur in the literary orchestra, playing only upon a pocket flute, and never aspiring, even in a dream, to the dignity of the bâton, the double bass, or the oboe."[187] Lacking the enthusiasm of the artist and scholar, he wrote, in the opinion of contemporaries, "chiefly for amusement,"[188] and was unusually "careless of authorship."[189] There was all in all little of the literary man about him. This, Halleck would heartily have confirmed; and with what greater satis-

---

[185] *Ibid.*, p. 9.
[186] Lathrop, *op. cit.*, p. 729.   [187] Wilson, *Life*, pp. 5–6.
[188] J. Lawson, *Southern Literary Messenger*, VIII, [2]44 (April, 1842).
[189] W. G. Simms in Wilson, *Life*, p. 545.

faction and pride would he have accepted the simple name of gentleman!

It is, then, largely as a gentleman that we shall now view him. To be sure, a few of his best poems were produced during the years immediately following 1827, but they were few indeed, and modified little his contemporary reputation. More and more he rested content with the fame of his early days, finding in the leisure hours spent with friends and acquaintances the social intercourse which was becoming dearer and dearer to him.

IX

FAME AS A POET

1828–32

THE years which immediately followed the publication of the 1827 edition were those of Halleck's greatest popularity as a poet. They represent the culmination of a constantly growing reputation which had its beginning, ten years before, in *The Croakers* and *Fanny*. Starting as a clever wit and playful satirist, he had slowly but with amazing certainty acquired a reputation for poetic versatility. To review this increase in popularity is to observe a new diversity of interest which the public now took in the poet and his work. Halleck had thrown off enough of his natural shyness and reserve to mingle freely in society, and he was soon sought not more for his popularity as a poet than for his polished address and conversation. He now also became a frequent judge at poetical and literary contests; and his poems found their way into anthologies and compilations of the period. Special articles were devoted to criticisms of his poetry, and on every hand he was proclaimed as the literary savior of America. Yet with all this adulation, the public was frankly worried at the scanty output of his work. "What is Halleck about?" became the question on every lip; he must not be allowed to forget his mission. But Halleck cared not for popular praise or censure. Quietly and simply he went about his work, never apparently regarding himself more than a literary idler.

Halleck's popularity which followed in the wake of the new volume is reflected in nothing so clearly as in the demand which society now made upon his time. "The fact is," wrote Halleck to his sister in May, 1827, "that during the past winter I have been, to my own astonishment, quite a ladies' man, a particularly fashionable person. I scarcely know how I got into the whirlpool, but I did get in in the early part of the season, and find it impossible to get out until the season is over. My name is on the visiting-list of all our ultra-fashionables, and I have received, on an average, a dozen invitations per week to parties, balls, etc. They do not interfere either with business or other daily pursuits, for a party does not begin until ten o'clock in the evening. It is pleasant enough while one is there, but, to an indolent person, hardly enough so to compensate for the trouble of dressing. I have become, for it is soon learned, quite *au fait* in the small-talk of society, and can say as much about nothing at all as if I had been taught by a lady-patroness of Almack's. However, the season is nearly over, and I shall, if not forgotten by the next year, invent some excuse for declining all future civilities in this way."[1] It was during the same season, although a month before the publication of the new collection, that Halleck first met Nathaniel Parker Willis. Willis, who was soon to graduate from Yale and issue his first volume of poetry,[2] wrote "to his parents and sisters" concerning Halleck on January 7, 1827. "On Saturday evening," remarked Willis, "I went to a genuine *soirée* at the great Dr. Hosack's.[3] This man is the most luxurious liver in the city, and his house is a perfect palace. You could not lay your hand on the wall for the costly paintings, and the furniture exceeds everything I have seen. I met all the literary characters of the day there, and Halleck, the poet, among them. With him I became quite acquainted, and he is a most glorious fellow. More of him when we meet."[4] Many years later Halleck recalled in a letter to a friend how, as judge in a poetical contest, he had awarded to Willis a prize of fifty dollars, while the young man was still a student at Yale. "I had the honor," wrote Halleck, "of being one of two persons empowered by the publisher of an 'Illustrated Album,' to award a prize of fifty dollars to the author of the best, among several hundred contributed manuscript poems, and saw Mr. Willis smilingly pocket a check for the amount, as our conscientiously declared winner in the contest. My introduction to him at that time—he was then, I think, still a student in Yale College—was the commencement of our long and pleasant intimacy with each other. As soon as I can find access to a volume of his collected poems, I will point

---

[1] Wilson, *Life,* p. 320. The letter is dated May 31, 1827.

[2] *Sketches* (Boston, 1827).

[3] Dr. Hosack was for some years president of the New York Historical Society.

[4] Henry A. Beers, *Nathaniel Parker Willis* (Boston, 1885), p. 56.

out to you the one in question. It was promisingly characteristic of his future poems—the egg to the bird, the acorn to the oak of his renown.''[5]

Another honor which came to Halleck unsought as a probable result of the new volume was his election in 1828 as an honorary member to the Yale Chapter of Phi Beta Kappa.[6] In 1830 he apparently consented to deliver the society poem at the commencement exercises, but, reported the *New York Mirror*, the poet ''was advertised as among the missing. In consequence, the people assembled on the occasion had no poetry with which to wash down the substantial prose delivered to them by Mr. Grimke. The latter was excellent; and perhaps it was better that the digestion of the great moral truths it inculcated was not interfered with by flights of the imagination, or vagabond waggery, which our minstrel can no more avoid, when he stumbles upon a droll association, than Jack Shephard could keep his hands out of a gentleman's fob, when he saw a convenient opportunity of making him carry less weight.''[7] Halleck was also elected substitute poet for ''the commencement of 1852,'' the Reverend John Pierpont acting as the regular poet.[8]

Halleck's eminence as a poet naturally made him a popular judge in literary and dramatic contests. As far back as 1825 the *New York Mirror* had offered a prize of fifty dollars ''to the author of the best prose Essay,'' and Halleck was among those ''literary gentlemen,'' including Verplanck, Paulding, Cooper, and Woodworth, who acted as a committee of award.[9] In the autumn of 1829 Halleck was again called upon to act as one of a committee of six to judge of the merits of a drama submitted in competition for a prize of five hundred dollars, which had been offered by Edwin Forrest, the tragedian. The award was made to John Augustus

[5] This extract from a letter dated March, 1867, appears in some reminiscences of Halleck by ''Barry Gray'' in the *New York Evening Mail* for January 9, 1868. The poem here referred to is probably ''The Soldier's Widow,'' which appeared in the *Token, a Christmas and New Year's Present* (Boston, 1828), pp. 76–77. The prize of one hundred dollars offered by S. G. Goodrich, publisher of the *Token*, was divided between Mrs. Lydia Sigourney and N. P. Willis. See H. A. Beers, *Nathaniel Parker Willis*, pp. 80–81.

[6] See *Phi Beta Kappa General Catalogue. 1776–1922* (Somerville, N. J. [1923]), p. 799.

[7] VIII, 126 (October 23, 1830).   [8] *Yale Banner*, October 6, 1851.

[9] *New York Mirror*, II, 327 (May 7, 1825).

Stone of Philadelphia for his *Metamora*.[10] In 1830 James Hackett, the comedian and a friend of Halleck, offered a prize of three hundred dollars for "an original comedy whereof an American should be the leading character."[11] The judges, who included Bryant, William Leggett, and Halleck, awarded the prize to James K. Paulding for his drama, *The Lion of the West; or a Trip to Washington*.[12]

Among the many literary men of New York whose friendship Halleck enjoyed at this time was Gulian C. Verplanck, a lawyer of unusual intellectual and cultural attainments. Mr. Verplanck was a frequent guest at the home of Henry D. Sedgwick,[13] the brother of Miss Sedgwick, the novelist, where, we have found, Bryant and Halleck were welcome visitors.[14] In 1825 Verplanck was elected to Congress from New York, and for the next eight years sat in the House of Representatives.[15] During this period of public service, he was a faithful advocate of the bill, finally passed in 1831, which extended the term of copyright from fourteen to twenty-eight years. Halleck was among those[16] who signed a letter congratulating Verplanck on his success, and inviting him to a public dinner, "as a testimony of the sense entertained in the district you represent, of the important services rendered by you."[17] The dinner was subsequently held on April 28, 1831, at the City Hotel, and the company, which included many distinguished guests, was described in the quaint idiom of the day, as "numerous, and of the highest respectability."[18] Verplanck, who was an admirer of Halleck's work, twice quoted from his poetry in public addresses;[19]

---

10 *New York Mirror*, VII, 135 (October 31, 1829). The manuscript of *Metamora*, which is incomplete, is preserved in the Forrest Home at Holmesburg, Pennsylvania. The drama was performed at the Park Theatre, December 15, 1829. See A. H. Quinn, *A History of the American Drama, from the Beginning to the Civil War*, p. 443.

11 William Paulding, *Literary Life of James K. Paulding*, p. 218.

12 See the *Morning Courier and New York Enquirer*, November 29, 1830. The drama is not now extant.

13 A. J. Symington, *William Cullen Bryant*, p. 92.

14 See pp. 147–148.

15 Duyckinck, *Cyclopaedia of American Literature*, II, 69.

16 Others who signed were Paulding, Bryant, Sands, Hoffman, and Leggett.

17 *New York Evening Post*, April 30, 1831.

18 *Ibid.*, April 30, 1831.

19 See Verplanck's *Discourses and Addresses* (New York, 1833), p. 120 (quotation from "Marco Bozzaris"); and p. 247 (quotation from "Burns").

while Halleck regarded Verplanck's writings as "American specimens of English literature," which "do honor to our side of the
Atlantic."[20]

The increasing recognition of Halleck as a poet of attainment is
further attested by the inclusion of his verses in anthologies published just after the appearance of his first collected edition.[21] In
1829 Samuel Kettell issued in three volumes his *Specimens of
American Poetry, with Critical and Biographical Notices.* This first
extensive collection of American verse, in which Halleck was amply
represented,[22] found its way to England and France, and thus became the subject of critical comment abroad. By 1829, it should be
observed, the tone of patronage adopted by English critics toward
American poetry had been slightly modified in the light of a few
poets in whom a vein of originality could be discerned. "Bards
have arisen amongst us," asserted the *Critic,* a short-lived periodical conducted by William Leggett, "in whose productions even the
yellow-eyed *collaborateurs* of the London Quarterly find much to
praise."[23] The *Edinburgh Literary Journal,* in discussing in 1829
the condition of poetry in the United States, included Halleck
among the "four poets of greatest eminence which America at
present possesses."[24] "Of Halleck, who is rising into much esteem," went on the critic, "we as yet know little, but the few
things of his we have seen are spirited and good."[25] A review of

[20] Wilson, *Life,* p. 262. From a letter addressed to J. G. Wilson, and dated
September 11, 1867.

[21] Two minor compilations, published in 1831, which contained the work of
Halleck, were the *Academical Speaker* (Boston; edited by B. D. Emerson),
containing "Marco Bozzaris" [see the *New York Mirror,* IX, 66 (September
3, 1831)]; and the *Young Ladies' Class Book* (Boston) [see the *New York
Mirror,* IX, 53 (August 20, 1831)].

[22] Halleck's selections were "Alnwick Castle," "Marco Bozzaris," "To
****" ("The world is bright"), "Love," "Connecticut," "Twilight,"
"Weehawken." The omission of "Burns" is notable. The introductory sketch
of Halleck's life was apparently based upon William Leggett's account of the
poet in the *New York Mirror* for January 26, 1828.

[23] I, 42 (November 16, 1828).

[24] The other three poets were Percival, Bryant, and Paulding.

[25] II, 130–131 (August 8, 1829). The same reviewer was completely ignorant of the authorship of *Fanny,* which he proceeded to discuss thus: "There
is Mr. J. G. Brooks [see Duyckinck, *Cyclopaedia,* II, 323–324], too, of New
York, who, if he is the author of 'Fanny, an American Tale,' in the 'Beppo'
style, is a very clever fellow. This is by far the best specimen of humour in

Kettell's *Specimens* in the *Literary Gazette* accorded special praise to Halleck as the foremost American poet.

Mr. Perceval [*sic*] and Mr. Willis are writers well deserving of praise; but certainly neither of them are first-rate: and the same criticism applies generally:—the stones are bright and sparkling, but they have been set before. One name, however, we do except—one whose fault is truly that with which his countrymen charge him—of having written too little: we need only mention Halleck, in whose compositions there is that originality which marks the true poet: but instead of criticizing, we will quote his very spirited poem of "Alnwick Castle."[26]

Kettell's anthology was less generously handled in France by a critic of the *Revue Encyclopédique,* who, however, singled out Halleck for special mention, "où l'originalité se montre de loin en loin. Dans son *Château d'Alnwick* il y a de la verve et de l'avenir. Il est jeune, qu'il s'affranchisse des traditions littéraires qu'il se confie à ses propres forces, et il aura donné à son pays un poète de plus."[27] A French reviewer again commented on Halleck's verse in noticing George B. Cheever's *Commonplace Book of American Poetry,* which was issued in 1831, and which included several specimens of Halleck's work.[28] "M. Cheever," asserted the critic, "a réuni un considérable de petites pièces, dont plusieurs ont du mérite, mais peut-être pas assez pour traverser l'Océan. 'La Musique sentimentale' de Halleck est une gracieuse chose."[29]

In January, 1828, the *New York Mirror* issued a series of sketches of important American poets, written by William Leggett. The article on Halleck, which was probably the first biographical

verse which America has yet produced, and combines the gay, the grave, the severe, and the pathetic, in a very felicitous manner."

[26] [XIII], 483 (July 25, 1829). "Alnwick Castle" is here quoted entire, as well as "Marco Bozzaris" on the following page. A brief passage from this notice of Halleck was printed with comment in the *New York Evening Post* for September 22, 1829. America at this period naturally welcomed any praise bestowed on her writers by British reviewers. In an editorial in the *New York Mirror* (XI, 311; March 29, 1834), entitled "American Authors Abroad," we find the following remark: "The best of our poets, especially Bryant and Halleck, are duly appreciated in the mother country."

[27] XLIII, 394 (1829). The review was signed "L.Sw.B."

[28] "Marco Bozzaris," "Weehawken," "Burns," "The American Flag" (credited to Halleck), "On the Death of Joseph Rodman Drake," "Wyoming," "Connecticut," "Sentimental Music" ("Young thoughts have music").

[29] *Revue Encyclopédique,* LII, 436 (1831).

account of the poet, was hopelessly inaccurate as to dates.[30] Unfortunately critics for the next few years relied generously upon this sketch for the details of Halleck's life,—a fact which probably accounts for much of the uncertainty among biographers regarding the poet's date of birth. In addition to attempting a sketch of Halleck's life, Leggett indulged in some uncritical remarks on his work, of which the following may serve as a specimen: "As a poet Mr. Halleck ranks very high. He has not written much, but what he has written is faultless. If tenderness and warmth of feeling, playfulness of fancy, imagery, not abundant, but appropriate, and great copiousness, and invariable euphony of language, constitute a claim to excellence, his effusions are excellent. There is one censure—we have already named it—in which all concur; and we most cordially hope that Mr. Halleck will speedily amend the fault that occasions it. But whether he write more or not, as the poet is to be estimated by the quality, and not the quantity of his works, he is entitled to a place which but few can hope to attain."[31] Accompanying this series of articles by Leggett was a group picture of those discussed in the text. Percival occupied a central position, and the others were appropriately grouped about him. This engraving frankly displeased Halleck who commented humorously upon his own picture in a note to Bryant.

Dear Bryant:

MR. MORRIS, the editor of the "Mirror" has asked me to say to you that his engraving of the seven, or nine—I forget which—"Illustrious Obscure" is completed. He has made me what I ought to have been, and very possibly shall be—a Methodist parson. As for the character in which you appear in the plate, he wishes you to call on him, and judge for yourself. The barber-shop sort of immortality with which this engraving honors us is most particularly annoying, but how could we help ourselves? *"Il faut se soumettre,"* as they say in French, or, as that prince of cor-

[30] This inaccuracy is not surprising if we are to credit the anecdote related by General Wilson concerning the writing of this series of sketches. When asked by George Morris, editor of the *Mirror*, to prepare biographies of the American *literati*, Leggett assured the editor of his willingness to undertake the task if he could only be supplied with the facts. Morris replied laconically, "Damn it! write the lives and omit the facts" (*Life*, p. 330).

[31] V, 227 (January 26, 1828). In the body of Leggett's article on Halleck appeared in print for the first time the epistle "To Walter Bowne, Esq." (see p. 130), which had been written as early as 1821. The *New York Evening Post* for January 25, 1828, reprinted the verses.

porals and philosophers, Nym, with his usual brief eloquence, expresses
it, "Things must be as they may."

Y'rs truly,

HALLECK.

Wednesday, 16th Jan'y '28—11 o'clock.[32]

The picture of Halleck used in this group was one painted by John
Wesley Jarvis.[33]

Another portrait of Halleck, done in 1828 by Samuel F. B.
Morse, the president of the National Academy of Arts and Design,
was placed on view at the third annual exhibition of the association.
The *New York Mirror,* however, in reviewing the exhibition, commented unfavorably upon the painting. "Had we never seen the
distinguished poet, of whose features the artist has here attempted
to give a transcript," observed the critic, "we should nevertheless
feel certain that justice had not been done to the subject. There is
no roundness to the head, no projection to the features, no vivacity
in the eye; and the light and shade are so disposed as to inspire the
thought that the subject had occupied a different situation in regard to the light, at every sitting, and that the painter had striven
to transfer to his picture all the different effects thus produced. So
far as mere outline is concerned, the picture certainly bears some
resemblance to Mr. Halleck, but this is so marred and obscured by
the unskillful manner in which the colours have been laid on, that
the placing his name in the catalogue, even by those who are best
acquainted with his appearance, cannot be considered altogether an
act of supererogation."[34] This portrait now hangs in the New York
Public Library.

Three years after the publication of Leggett's sketch of Halleck,
another article, somewhat more critical, appeared in the *New England Magazine.* This was among the earliest attempts to analyze
and appraise the poetry of Halleck. As a medium for Bostonian
thought, this periodical at once observed in Halleck's poetry the
absence of a reflective, philosophical outlook on life. Thus George S.
Hillard, author of the sketch, noted with some justice that Halleck
"has never threaded the mazes of the human heart, nor mused profoundly on the conduct and opinions of men. He does not attempt
to describe the effects of strong passions upon various natures and

32 P. Godwin, *A Biography of William Cullen Bryant,* I, 234–235.
33 See Appendix, p. 384.   34 V, 367 (May 24, 1828).

how they sometimes exalt a low character into sublimity and degrade a great one to the clay of the meanest. He does not seem to have reflected very deeply on the workings of his own mind and the quick impulses that have shot through his own blood. He looks at nature with a poet's eye, and paints its features with a poet's pencil, but he reads in its ample pages none of that deep philosophy, which creates a mysterious union between the mind of man and the mute forms of the external world."[35] The lack of this quality for which the Boston critic sought in vain is perhaps rightly explained by the fact that the poet "has lived in the world and in the fashionable part of it, and has had occasion to observe the carriage and manners of men, rather than the native grain of their natures, and has seen more of the expression of character than of the character itself."[36] But the critic's sectional bias did not prevent him from according to Halleck's poetry due praise. In analyzing more minutely his stylistic qualities, Hillard observed that "the first thing that strikes us in reading his poems is the singular union we find in them of the humorous and pathetic. He seems like 'two single' poets 'rolled into one.' "[37] After commenting upon Halleck's humorous verse, the writer continued: "But while we thus do justice to his humorous poems, we do not in the least forget the admiration which his serious ones challenge for themselves. They present the undying excellence of beautiful and original thoughts, enclosed in language of the most crystal purity. There is nothing diseased in his melancholy, and when he is sentimental, his good genius makes him stop this side of mawkishness. Indeed, there is a very healthy tone about everything he has written; nothing seems the fruit of unnatural excitement."[38]

While the poet was thus enjoying his literary fame in New York, he was not unmindful of the old friends in Guilford. One of these was George Foote, who lived at Nut Plains, a farm situated about two miles outside of Guilford. As a boy, Halleck had been a frequent visitor at Nut Plains, and often submitted his early poetical works to those assembled at the old farmhouse.[39] The hitherto unpublished letter here presented was written by Halleck on the

[35] I, 154 (August, 1831).   [36] *Ibid.*, I, 154.
[37] *Ibid.*, I, 155.   [38] *Ibid.*, I, 157.
[39] John P. Foote, *Memoirs of the Life of Samuel E. Foote*, p. 28. See also pp. 21–22 of the present work.

occasion of Foote's marriage. It is an excellent specimen of Halleck's epistolary style, beaming with graceful humor and playfulness.

New York, May 21, 1829.

My dear George,

I HAVE had the pleasure of receiving your kind and flattering letter of the 18th. To know that after an almost uninterrupted separation of nearly twenty years, I am still remembered, and with affection, by one of the worthiest friends of my boyhood, is a proud and delightful feeling. Maria informed me, some time since, of the wise and happy resolution you had, at length, taken, and of your good fortune in winning as a Cabin Companion for your voyage of life, one of the youngest and loveliest women around you. I beg you to accept my warmest congratulations, make my compliments to your bride, and say to her that I am very anxious to see and be acquainted with her, because in choosing a husband, who, independent of his other estimable qualities, is of a mature age, a ripe apple in the world's orchard, she has proved herself a sound-minded, intelligent, clear-headed girl. No Lady in the full possession of her seven senses ever marries a Boy. It is for "Us Youth" as Fallstaff calls us—"Us Old Batchelors," as the envious nickname us, that all the women really worth having are reserved. Our minds, characters, manners, are formed. In other words if we don't know how to behave ourselves at forty or thereabouts, the chances are one to a hundred that we never shall.

I am very sorry that it will not be in my power to be present at the Bridal, as you have done me the honor and the kindness to request.

I hope and trust that you, & such of my old acquaintances as then and there take a glass of wine to the health and happiness of each other, will, at that moment remember me and mine.

As soon as I can find leisure to make the journey, I shall visit Nut Plains, and make the new Mrs. Foote my newest bow. At any rate, you may expect me at the christening of the son and heir.

Please give my compliments and congratulations to your Mother, your Sister, and family, and believe me,

Your friend & faithful sert,
GREENE HALLECK[40]

The years from 1828 to 1832 when the poet entered the office of John Jacob Astor, were for Halleck a period of relative productiveness in literature. The unusual number of poems written at this time was undoubtedly the result of an enforced idleness that followed

[40] This letter is in the possession of Mrs. Edward Jenkins of New Haven, Connecticut. Mrs. Jenkins is the daughter of George Foote.

the collapse of Jacob Barker's business. Barker, whose financial
resources had been badly crippled by the long series of litigations
in which he had been engaged, was, by the early part of 1829, virtually forced to abandon his business, although continuing for a
time to operate on a very small scale.[41] Halleck left Barker's employ probably toward the close of 1828, and although a portion of
his salary was yet owing him in 1830,[42] he refrained for a time
from seeking new employment, in the hope that Barker might again
be established in business. That Halleck clearly foresaw, however,
the ultimate ruin of Barker's business, but bravely and conscientiously stood at his post, may be clearly seen from an anecdote
related by the poet's friend, Frederic S. Cozzens. "The late Daniel
Embury, formerly President of the Atlantic Bank of Brooklyn, at
that time was Mr. Barker's cashier," remarked the humorist in his
address before the New York Historical Society after the poet's
death. "He always spoke of Halleck with almost boyish affection.
'When I found,' said he, 'that Jacob Barker's affairs were in such
a state that an honest cashier could not remain with him, I spoke to
Halleck about them, for I had determined to leave his office, and
urged him to do so like-wise. But Halleck replied, No! I will not
desert the *sinking ship;* I will remain at my post. When misfortune
comes, that is the very time to stand by one's friends.' "[43] Barker
seems to have duly appreciated the loyalty of his friend. When
asked by General Wilson to contribute some reminiscences to his
biography of Halleck, the banker replied, "I would gladly contribute to the praiseworthy object you are pursuing, if I could say anything which would add to or extend the fame of my lamented friend
Halleck."[44] "Mr. Halleck was so useful," wrote Mr. Barker on
another occasion, "that it would have been difficult for me to have
done without him, and in our long connection of nearly twenty
years not a cool word ever passed between us."[45]

[41] *Incidents in the Life of Jacob Barker*, p. 215.

[42] A small pamphlet of printed letters by Barker (without title-page) in
the New York Public Library explains the financier's attempts to bring to a
satisfactory close the affairs of several companies, including the Dutchess, of
which he had been the head. In one of these, dated April 9, 1830, allusion is
made to the fact that money is still owing to Halleck and several other employees.

[43] *Fitz-Greene Halleck. A Memorial*, pp. 4–5.

[44] Wilson, *Life*, p. 336. The letter is undated.

[45] *Ibid.*, p. 337. The letter is dated April 12, 1868. The following anecdote

In addition to the lines on "The Recorder," three contributions to gift books complete the list of Halleck's compositions for 1828. "Forget Me Not—Imitated from the German" appeared in the *Atlantic Souvenir; a Christmas and New Year's Offering* for 1829. The annual was probably published toward the close of October of the previous year, as Halleck's stanzas were reprinted in the *New York Mirror* for November 1, 1828.[46] The poem, typical of a host of sentimental effusions then appearing in the annuals, was in general not favorably received by reviewers. The public had grown to expect something singular from the pen that had written "Marco Bozzaris," and no trifle, thrown off in an idle hour, could quite satisfy the popular curiosity. "The stanzas contributed by Halleck," wrote William Leggett in the *Critic*, "we must say, we should never have attributed to his pen, had his name not been subscribed to them; for they contain neither the fire of Marco Bozzaris, the fine satire of the Croakers, nor the delicate humor of Fanny. But if the wisest of men are occasionally guilty of folly, if it be allowed that Homer sometimes nods, we know no reason, why the author of *Alnwick Castle* may not be excused for having committed *one* piece of poor poetry. It is his only sin; and we have no fear that it will often be repeated."[47] The *Ladies' Magazine* for November, 1828, in commenting upon "Forget Me Not," called the verses "pretty, though not equal to some productions we have seen from the same fine poet."[48] The *Albion*, however,

---

will illustrate how close and intimate was the relationship between the banker and his clerk. "On one occasion when Halleck was in the employ of Jacob Barker, he was directed to fill out a check in favor of a certain prominent member of the legislature, whose vote Barker required for the passage of a certain important measure. 'I beg your pardon, sir,' said Halleck, 'but doesn't this savor of bribery and corruption?' 'Oh! no sir,' replied Mr. Barker, 'I send it to him merely to enable him to see it's his interest to do what's right!'" This anecdote, hitherto unpublished, accompanies a letter from J. N. Mead, Jr., to E. A. Duyckinck, dated November 29, 1867, now preserved in the Duyckinck Collection of the New York Public Library.

[46] VI, 131. The poem, as it originally appeared, was signed "F.G.Halleck." It was not collected until the edition of 1869, which omitted the following stanza:

> When by the lonely fount we meet,
>   And weep so soon to part,
> The flower springs up beneath our feet,
> And sighs, as if it will'd to greet
>   A kindred broken heart—
>   "Forget me not."

[47] I, 17 (November 1, 1828).   [48] I, 523.

in reprinting the poem, spoke of it as "a very appropriate piece from the pen of Mr. Halleck."[49]

During the spring of 1828 Nathaniel Parker Willis published a miscellany called *The Legendary*. Of this volume the *New York Mirror* said, "We regret that the names of Halleck, Bryant, and Leggett of this city, are not among its contributors, but hope that the second volume will possess the additional value which effusions from their pens would bestow."[50] Whether Willis acted directly upon the suggestion of this reviewer, it would, of course, be difficult to say. In any case, a second volume of the *Legendary* appeared later in the same year, containing Halleck's poem, "The Field of the Grounded Arms." The new volume, the appearance of which was heralded toward the latter part of November,[51] was issued about December first.[52]

"The Field of the Grounded Arms," which was entirely unrhymed, greatly puzzled the reviewers. William Leggett, indeed, found it difficult to call the verses poetry. "As much as we admire the energy of its thoughts, the force and polish of the language," he said, "we should never have suspected it of being a poem, had it not been printed 'in measured file and metrical array.' "[53] In reprinting the lines, Leggett again found it necessary to comment upon the rhymeless structure of the verses, observing that although "poetry does not consist entirely in the

> '. . . union of returning sounds,
> Nor all the pleasing artifice of rhyme,'

yet, however replete with the thoughts that breathe and words that burn, the outpourings of even Halleck's mind are not entitled to that name without them; they may satisfy the understanding, but will not charm the ear, nor warm the heart; they possess all the spirit, but want the form; and in poetry, as in human nature, a rich soul, and a body of fair proportion, are requisite to constitute a perfect creature."[54]

[49] VII, 165 (November 1, 1828).   [50] V, 375 (May 31, 1828).
[51] "A second volume of the Legendary, edited by N. P. Willis, Esq. is soon to appear. Its contents are said to be furnished by writers of great celebrity and merit."—*Critic*, I, 60 (November 22, 1828).
[52] The preface to the second volume of the *Legendary* is dated December 1, 1828. "The Field of the Grounded Arms" is signed "Fitz-Greene Halleck."
[53] *Critic*, I, 129 (December 30, 1828).
[54] *Ibid.*, I, 132.

Charles P. Clinch, who was shocked at Leggett's want of appreciation, wrote to Halleck congratulating him upon the success of his new poem:

It is the most finished poetry that I know of in the English language, and, knowing nothing of any other language but the English, it is to me the most finished poetry in the world. If ever I deliver a course of lectures upon the poetical art, "The Field of the Grounded Arms" shall be my text-book. There is not a line of it but what is an illustration of the spirit of poesy. Your first stanza contains the most beautiful description of thought that ever was conceived, and the entire piece is, in my estimation, perfect. What the devil did Bryant mean by leaving out the last stanza? I have just met with the whole in the *Legendary*. Did he mean to say that it was not in keeping with the rest? or that the piece was complete without it? He is as bad as Leggett, who objected to its want of rhyme! The remembrance of the homely proverb, that "nothing is little or great but by comparison," would have convinced Bryant of the "fitness" of the last stanza. Of its poetical beauty he cannot have doubted, nor —But, pardon me, this is a rhapsody. My excuse is, that "The Field of the Grounded Arms" lies before me.[55]

Bryant's mutilation of the poem[56] is difficult to understand unless it was suggested by Halleck himself, who, when the lines were collected in the edition of 1836, also omitted the final stanza. These concluding verses, suggesting a comparison between the victors of Saratoga and those of Marathon,[57] were not inappropriate, although one feels that the poem gains somewhat in strength by their omission.

Another review of the poem, published in a Baltimore magazine not long after the appearance of the second volume of the *Legendary*, complained that the lines should be called "prosaic," "rather scriptural than poetical," and asserted that the poem "has hardly a line which is not the bed of a poetic gem." After making several quotations from the poem, the reviewer said: "Such are some of the bright thoughts in this poem, which is worthy of any poet who ever lived. Mr. Halleck writes as Washington Allston

[55] Wilson, *Life*, pp. 350–351. The letter is undated.
[56] See *New York Evening Post* for December 16, 1828.
[57] The omitted stanza was as follows:

Feelings as proud as were the Greek's of old,
When in his country's hour of fame he stood,
Happy and bold and free,
Gazing on Marathon.

paints; after an ideal which can never be equalled, while at the same time his production astonishes the world with its undreamt of beauty."[58]

The preceding comments on "The Field of the Grounded Arms" suggest the diversity of opinion which prevailed in Halleck's day regarding the poem. The *American Quarterly Review* in 1837 called the poem "a production which has all the spirit, without any of the poetry, of music around or within it. . . . The sentiment is stirring and patriotic; the conception, fine; but the construction is a species of *composite order,* whose constituents it would be difficult indeed to explain or trace home."[59] A contrary opinion was expressed in 1842 by the *Southern Literary Messenger* who complained they had "scarcely a glimpse of the victors of Saratoga receiving the arms of the conquered enemy," but considered "the language felicitous."[60] The bone of contention was, of course, the stanza-form in which the poem was written. Any familiarity, however, with William Collins' "Ode to Evening" would have made easier an understanding and appreciation of the poem. Collins' verse-form, in which "The Field of the Grounded Arms" is also written, may be regarded as a modified Horatian stanza,[61] achieving

[58] *Emerald and Baltimore Literary Gazette*, II, 5 (January 10, 1829). See also the preliminary notice of the poem in the issue for December 13, 1828. "The Field of the Grounded Arms" was reprinted in the *New York Mirror* for December 20, 1828 (VI, 189), with the final stanza; and in the *New York American* for January 5, 1829, without it. Prosper M. Wetmore in a poem to be found in his anonymous volume, *Lexington, with Other Fugitive Poems* (New York, 1830), used (p. 57) the phrase "plain of the grounded arms," but in a note (p. 86) gracefully acknowledged his borrowing. The borrowing was commented on by the *Post* (October 5, 1830) as "a very adroit and delicate compliment to Halleck." The phrase, "Field of the Grounded Arms," was introduced into an early sketch by Walt Whitman. See Emory Holloway's *Uncollected Poetry and Prose of Walt Whitman* (Garden City, 1921), I, 96. This allusion to Halleck's poem was noted by Prof. Thomas O. Mabbott in *Notes and Queries* for March, 1926. In the *Knickerbocker* for September, 1836 (VIII, 295), a stanza from Halleck's poem was used as a motto for a sketch entitled "Fall of the Alamo."

[59] XXI, 412 (June, 1837).

[60] VIII, [2]46 (April, 1842). Poe found the versification of the poem "disagreeable," but admitted that it contained "some of the finest passages of Halleck." See the *Southern Literary Messenger*, II, 335–336 (April, 1836).

[61] Cf. the so-called "Fifth Asclepiad" meter. See E. C. Wickham's *Horace. The Odes, Carmen Seculare and Epodes* (Oxford, 1887), p. 169. Thomas Powell

in English something of the dignity of blank verse, without the unvaried monotony to which that form is too often prone.[62] Halleck's poem lacks, to be sure, the dramatic fire which gave popularity to "Marco Bozzaris," and the pensive beauty which makes Collins' "Ode" one of the treasured gems of English verse. Yet Halleck's lines, which improve much on second reading, possess a restrained dignity that can be called truly classic.[63] In the opening stanzas the quiet beauty of the landscape is fittingly painted by the poet as a background for the historic memories which the scene evokes. Halleck was never better than when reviving romantic memories of the past. Something of the elegiac tenderness of "Alnwick Castle" and "Burns," with an added martial strength, may be found in this poem on the scene of Burgoyne's surrender. In thought the poem represents an attempt to combine the knightly grace that praises the foe it deigns to strike, with a glorified patriotism which scorns

> the Invader's wrath
> Threatening a gallant land.

Of Halleck's tendency to impartiality of judgment we have already spoken. If the poet's patriotism bade him praise the noble victors of Saratoga, the memory of a father, loyal to the British cause, made him not unmindful of that "gallant army" "disarmed but not dishonored." Halleck's knightly spirit was inborn. Here was no senti-

---

mentions "a critic of some classical taste" who "refused to allow any merit to this poem, and quoted with great energy Horace's ode:

> Quis multa gracilis te puer in rosa,
> Perfusus liquidis urget odoribus
> Grata Pyrrha sub antro?
> Cui flavam religas comam.
> Simplex munditiis."

The Living Writers of America (New York, 1850), p. 237. Halleck, so far as can be ascertained, had no first-hand knowledge of the classics.

[62] This stanza is not unknown elsewhere in English poetry. Henry Kirke White, for example, uses it several times, as in his verses "To an Early Primrose." Thus Halleck in employing the stanza was not making so radical a departure from the standards of conventional English poetry as many of his contemporaries believed. Andrew Marvell's "Horatian Ode Upon Cromwell's Return to Ireland," although rhymed, may also have influenced Halleck in adopting the stanza. See G. P. Lathrop in the *Atlantic Monthly* for June, 1877 (XXXIX, 726).

[63] Thomas Powell says: "It is seldom that a modern touches the Latin harp with any degree of success. We were therefore agreeably surprised with Halleck's verses to the Field of the Grounded Arms." *The Living Writers of America* (New York, 1850), p. 237.

mental drivel, but the honest expression of a nature bathed in the ''autumn tints'' of a noble chivalry.

The third annual to which Halleck contributed in 1828 was the *Talisman*. Edited by William C. Bryant, Gulian C. Verplanck, and Robert C. Sands under the pen name of ''Francis Herbert, Esq.,'' this miscellany treated all its contributors on an equal footing of anonymity. Halleck, who was asked to write for the volume of the annual to appear at the close of 1828, was given two subjects from which to choose.[64] The first of these, ''Weehawken,'' he naturally declined, for his lines in *Fanny* on that romantic spot were already famous, and he would hardly want again to try his pen at a description of the scene. Halleck, therefore, selected Red Jacket, the Indian Chief, as the subject for his poetry. It was, indeed, a timely choice, as Red Jacket was then much in the public eye. In 1828 and the following year the old Indian appeared at various museums and places of public interest, whither he was invited as a special feature of entertainment. He attended in April, 1828, an ''exhibition of Philosophical Experiments'' where he recounted ''the scenes of his early life'';[65] and during the same year, at the request of Dr. John W. Francis, he sat for his portrait in the studio of Robert W. Weir.[66] Using Weir's portrait as a model, Halleck produced his sketch of Red Jacket.[67] Of the poet's contribution to the *Talisman*, Bryant once said: ''For the volume which appeared in 1828, Halleck offered us one of the most remarkable poems, 'Red Jacket,' and I need not say how delighted we were to grace our collection by anything so vigorous, spirited, and original. It was illustrated by an engraving from a striking full length portrait of the old Indian chief, by the elder Wier [*sic*], then in the early maturity of his powers as an artist.''[68]

[64] Wilson, *Life*, pp. 322–323.

[65] Advertisement in the New York *Morning Courier* for April 4, 1828.

[66] William Leete Stone, *Life and Times of Sa-go-ye-what-ha, or Red Jacket* (Albany, 1866), pp. 432–433.

[67] In the *Post* for December 24, 1828, appeared the following advertisement: ''The Talisman for 1829—This day published by Elam Bliss, 128 Broadway, The Talisman, consisting of original pieces, illustrated by engravings, from the entire original drawings, bound in silk.'' Some of the reviews of the *Talisman* appeared a few days before December 24, but were probably written from advanced copies of the volume. In all, three numbers of the *Talisman* were issued, for 1828, 1829, 1830. Halleck contributed only to the volume for 1829, issued at the close of the previous year.

[68] *Some Notices of the Life and Writings of Fitz-Greene Halleck*, p. 17. The

Most of the reviewers of the *Talisman* for 1829 were naturally unaware of the authorship of "Red Jacket." The *New York Mirror,* for example, failed to recognize that Halleck was the author of the poem. "The 'Lament of Romeo,' 'Red Jacket,' the 'Greek Boy,' the 'Hunter's Serenade,' and other pieces of true poetry, are scattered through the volume. The two first, in particular, are gems of the first water. . . . Notwithstanding the length to which this article has unavoidably extended, we cannot refrain from enriching our columns with the following poem."[69] "Red Jacket" was then reprinted. William Leggett in the *Critic,* although alluding to the fact that the poetic style of "Francis Herbert" was like that of Halleck, did not definitely ascribe "Red Jacket" to the poet. "The next article which claims our attention," asserted the reviewer, "is a most beautiful poem. Really this Francis Herbert, Esq. is a surprising writer. He seems to combine in his own individual style the smooth, easy flow of language, sprightliness of fancy, and vivacity of description, which characterize the writings of Verplanck; the tenderness and delicacy of sentiment, the fine relish and appreciation of the beauties of external nature, and the elaborate polish of verse evinced by Bryant, the spirit of gracefulness and energy of Sands, and the delicate humor, rapid transitions from serious to playful, and all that chastened spirit of good-natured satire which distinguish the sweet muse of Halleck. . . . Yet the reader will scarcely believe that the author of *Thor's Hammer* and *Red Jacket* are one and the same. But without wasting our time and space in making useless inquiries in relation to that part of the history of Francis Herbert on which he himself has not chosen to throw any light, we shall proceed to extract a part of his delightful Indian poem, and should be glad to transfer the whole to our columns, did not a sense of duty to the publisher prevent."[70] The reviewer of the volume in the *Evening Post,* who was undoubtedly Bryant, hinted at the authorship of "Red Jacket" as broadly as possible, without actually committing himself. After commenting upon the beauty and elegance of the volume, the critic said, "We offer as an extract the following beautiful lines, which, we think, no reader will be at any loss to ascribe, at once, to the gifted pen of him who possesses

portrait by Weir was engraved for the volume by George W. Hatch. The original painting is now in the New York Historical Society.
    [69] VI, 181 (December 13, 1828).   [70] I, 115 (December 20, 1828).

that peculiar and happy vein of thought that has long distinguished him as one of the most favorite bards the American muse has ever boasted of.''[71]

Subsequent comment on the poem, most of it laudatory, presents a variety of critical opinion. A sentimental writer in the *American Quarterly Review* called ''Red Jacket'' ''one of those lofty and fervid effusions, that one reads to remember,'' but missing entirely the humor of the poem, complained that Halleck should have ''stooped to compare his [Red Jacket's] dress . . . with that of 'George the Fourth at Brighton.' ''[72] Edgar Allan Poe, however, fully appreciated its humor, which he called ''very fine,'' not interfering ''in any degree with the general tone of the poem,'' although he found in the piece, with all its ''power of expression,'' ''little evidence of poetical ability.''[73] Other comments by Halleck's friends are worth noting. Bryant praised the poem as having ''the spirit and variety of a portrait from nature'';[74] and Henry T. Tuckerman found ''Red Jacket'' perhaps ''the most effective Indian portrait''[75] ''in the language.'' Of a similar voice was Dr. John W. Francis, who said that the Indian chief would ''long live by the painting of Weir, the poetry of Halleck, and the fame of his own deeds.''[76]

The opening stanzas of ''Red Jacket,'' which are addressed solely to James Fenimore Cooper, and contribute nothing to the portrait of the Indian chief, have been thought by many an unreserved tribute to the novelist. The author of *The Pioneers* had left America in 1826, and for the next seven years lived chiefly in France and Italy. In 1828 he published *Notions of the Americans; Picked up by a Travelling Bachelor* in answer to the many slanders against America and American society, which were then constantly emanating from the English press. Intended chiefly as propaganda, the book found more to praise than to condemn in the country of

---

[71] January 10, 1829. In a letter of Bryant, dated January 27, 1829, the poet alludes to the popularity of the *Talisman* for 1829. See P. Godwin, *A Biography of William Cullen Bryant*, I, 247.

[72] XXI, 412–413 (June, 1837).

[73] *Southern Literary Messenger*, II, 336 (April, 1836).

[74] *Some Notices of the Life and Writings of Fitz-Greene Halleck*, p. 30.

[75] Thomas Shaw, *A Complete Manual of English Literature . . . with a Sketch of American Literature by Henry T. Tuckerman* (New York, 1871), p. 516.

[76] William Stone, *Life and Times of Sa-go-ye-what-ha, or Red Jacket* (1866), p. 434.

Cooper's birth. In discussing the literature of America, however, Cooper, with customary frankness, mentioned at some length the poetry of Halleck in such a way as not to spare the feelings of the New York poet. Although doing justice to ''Alnwick Castle,'' Cooper treated lightly Halleck's earlier work. As Cooper's comments on Halleck are relatively inaccessible, we here quote them entire:

It is very true there are few young poets now living in this country, who have known how to extract sweets from even these wholesome but scentless native plants. They have, however, been compelled to seek their inspiration in the universal laws of nature, and they have succeeded, precisely in proportion as they have been most general in their application. Among these gifted young men there is one (Halleck) who is remarkable for an exquisite vein of ironical wit, mingled with a fine, poetical, and frequently, a lofty expression. This gentleman commenced his career as a satirist in one of the journals of New York. Heaven knows, his materials were none of the richest; and yet the melody of his verse, the quaintness and force of his comparisons, and the exceeding humour of his strong points, brought him instantly into notice. He then attempted a general satire, by giving the history of the early days of a *belle.* He was again successful, though everybody, at least everybody of any talent, felt that he wrote in leading-strings. But he happened, shortly after the appearance of the little volume just named (Fanny), to visit England. Here his spirit was properly excited, and, probably on a rainy day, he was induced to try his hand at a *jeu d'esprit,* in the mother country. The result was one of the finest semi-heroic ironical descriptions to be found in the English language.[77] This simple fact, in itself, proves the truth of a great deal of what I have just been writing, since it shews the effect a superiority of material can produce on the efforts of a man of true genius.[78]

In the opening lines of ''Red Jacket'' Halleck may, perhaps, be thought of as answering Cooper. These stanzas, hardly an unqualified tribute to the novelist as many have supposed, present him in a somewhat humorous light. The tone of the following verses amply illustrates this spirit of banter.

> And faithful to the Act of Congress, quoted
> As law authority, it passed nem.con.:
> He writes that we are, as ourselves have voted,
> The most enlightened people ever known:

[77] ''This little *morceau* of pleasant irony is called Alnwick Castle'' (Cooper's note).

[78] *Notions of the Americans: Picked up by a Travelling Bachelor* (London, 1828), II, 143–145.

> That all our week is happy as a Sunday
>   In Paris, full of song, and dance, and laugh;
> And that, from Orleans to the Bay of Fundy,
>   There's not a bailiff or an epitaph.

Here, as elsewhere, Halleck's genius for the judicial—his love of nothing in excess asserts itself. The overenthusiasm of Cooper in discussing American institutions thus finds a characteristic check in Halleck's playful sally; and the famous lines become at once a tribute and a rebuke. Cooper himself, it will be remembered, was in later years forced to modify many of his opinions regarding his countrymen; the rebuke of *The American Democrat* (1838), for example, offers a strange contrast to the earlier encomiums of *Notions of the Americans*.

Halleck's frank confession,

> I rhyme for smiles and not for tears,

characterizes not only his remarks on Cooper, but also the portrait of Red Jacket which follows. The Indian chief, dragged from his native haunts to grace museums and lecture platforms, undoubtedly presented to the poet a humorous picture. Halleck was no Boswell ready to glory in "nature's simple plan." He was willing to accept the romance pictured in the dress and painted face of the chief, but saw no simple, guileless soul beneath. He recognized the mind of a monarch naïvely blended with the soul of a savage. In "Red Jacket" the blending of romance and realism in the American Indian has seldom found a more happy expression. When Halleck, after deferring as long as possible the destruction of his romantic dream, finally bursts forth in the lines,

> Thou art, in sober truth, the veriest devil
>   That e'er clinched fingers in a captive's hair!

we know that the world of stark reality has at length come to its own. Romanticist and realist, poet and banker are at last one. This contrast, this paradox, if you will, of Halleck's soul, finds yet another expression in his conception of Red Jacket as king. Halleck's inherent love of the aristocrat and aristocratic institutions was not unmodified by a spirit of pure democracy. Indeed, the two at times found a happy union in the poet's thought. Just as Halleck saw in the chambermaid of Alnwick Castle a member of "Nature's aristocracy,'' so does he present Red Jacket as one of nature's monarchs, a fitting equal of the kings of Europe.

> Well might he [Cooper] boast that we, the Democratic,
> Outrival Europe, even in our Kings!

These lines, though humorous in import, suggest the paradox of an essentially aristocratic mind transplanted to the democratic soil of America, where it has taken firm root.

But with all the broad-mindedness and impartiality often shown in his work, Halleck at times betrayed a mind curiously undemocratic and provincial. Such an attitude may be observed in his "Epistle to Robert Hogbin, Esq.,'' which appeared in the *Evening Post* for November 16, 1830. The verses, obviously intended as a skit on a movement set on foot among the workingmen of New York to form an association for their own improvement, hark back to the days of "The Croakers,''[79] but suggest a snobbishness foreign to the spirit of the original series, and indeed uncommon elsewhere in Halleck's work. Halleck pointed his shaft directly at Robert Hogbin, a tinsmith,[80] described in the subtitle of the poem as "one of the Committee of Working Men, &c., at the Westchester Hotel, Bowery.'' The quality of Halleck's humor is fittingly illustrated in the stanzas:

> Yes, there's much in a name, and a Hogbin so fit is
> For that great moral purpose whose impulse divine
> Bids men leave their own workshops to work in Committees,
> And their own wedded wives to protect yours and mine;

[79] It may here be noted that another poem, published in 1827, carried on the Croaker tradition. "In the graceful humor of the following lines,'' observed the *Post* for August 1, 1827, "our readers will easily recognize the hand of an old and favorite correspondent.'' Then followed the verses beginning, "Dear Tom, I am writing not *to* you but *at* you,'' under the title "Letters from Town—No. I.'' This poem was first collected in the edition of 1839 and printed with the title "To *****.'' George Lathrop has well described the lines as "a sketch of the summer vacation in New York, which though shaded with a pleasant antiquity, presents the city under much the same aspect that it now wears in the hot months'' (*Atlantic Monthly*, XXIX, 722). Unfortunately no more of these "Letters from Town'' made their appearance.

[80] The occupation of Robert Hogbin is given in *Longworth's American Almanac, New York Register, and City Directory* for 1831, as tinsmith. In the *Directory* for the preceding year he had appeared as a turner.

That we Working-Men prophets are sadly mistaken,
  If yours is not, Hogbin, a durable fame,
Immortal as England's philosopher Bacon,
  Whom your ancestors housed, if we judge by his name.

The personality of this jest at Hogbin's expense, lacking the spirit
of righteous indignation which had backed the satire on Richard
Riker, strikes one today as misdirected and spiteful. Not only does
it suggest the aristocratic temper of mind to which Halleck was
slowly yielding, but, as Vernon Parrington has pointed out, doubtless serves to illustrate "the attitude of polite society in New York
a hundred years ago towards the aspirations of the proletariat."[81]
Halleck's lines were signed "A Working Man." Two days later the
Post published the following note:

Several inquiries having been made of us respecting the name of the
author of an Epistle to Mr. Hogbin, published a day or two since in our
paper, we took measures to acquaint him with the fact, in order that, if
there was no objection on his part, we might satisfy the curiosity of those
who had applied to us. This morning we received from him the following
note in reply: "The author of the Epistle to Mr. Hogbin has unfortunately
no name. His father and mother, in that season of life in which children
are generally named, took advantage of his youth and inexperience, and
declined giving him any. He is, therefore, compelled to imitate the minstrel of Yarrow in Leyden's Scenes of Infancy and like him,
    'Saves other names, but leaves his own unsung!' "[82]

Later in the same month Hogbin took up the cudgel in his own defense, and undertook to answer Halleck in some crude verses which
the *Post* prefaced thus: "We have received the following answer
from Mr. Hogbin to the Epistle addressed to him a few days since
by our correspondent without a name. Mr. Hogbin is a manufac-
turer of tin, and professes to have but little skill in the art of
weaving rhyme—an admission of which the reader will no doubt
allow the modesty, as well as the truth. He has for once, however,
turned aside from his pails and kettles to try his ' 'prentice hand'
on verse, and in hammering on rhymes he has produced a sort of
jingle scarcely less agreeable than that which results from his customary pursuit of hammering on tin."[83]

[81] *Main Currents in American Thought*, II, 201.
[82] November 18, 1830.
[83] November 23, 1830. The title of Hogbin's verses was "Reply of Robert

During 1831 and 1832 Halleck contributed four poems to the *New York Mirror*. As early as June, 1830, the readers of the *Mirror* had been promised a poem from the pen of Halleck;[84] but it was not until six months had passed that "The Rhyme of the Ancient Coaster,"[85] written ten years before, made its appearance.[86]

In January, 1831, the *Mirror* published another poem entitled "The Discarded."[87] These verses, also written at an earlier date,[88] made no mention of the person to whom they were addressed. Many years later, however, after the poet's death, *Appleton's Journal*,[89] which printed "The Discarded" as "An Unpublished Poem by F. G. Halleck," referred the verses directly to McDonald Clarke. Clarke was a strange, eccentric poet, who, dressed in a "blue coat" and "cloth cap," found Broadway a pleasant place for his daily promenades, much to the delight and curiosity of the New York populace.[90] His hair or complexion was probably of a sandy hue, as he frequently referred to himself as "sandy Clarke." To his wild, erratic disposition, as well as to many eccentricities of dress and manner, was undoubtedly due his name, the "mad poet." He seems, however, to have been predisposed to madness; "something that was not quite insanity," writes Lydia Maria Child, "but was nigh akin to it, marked his very boyhood."[91] Clarke himself apparently took the appellation in earnest, if we are to judge from one of

Hogbin, workingman, to Rhyme Weaver, in the Evening Post of Tuesday, Nov. 16th." The first four lines will illustrate the style:

> Weaver of Rhyme, now is your time—how long your cloak may last
> Is doubtful, as the march of mind progresses very fast.
> Closed doors by us are not allowed, nor names concealed our plan;
> I therefore must conclude you are a *spurious* working-man.

[84] VII, 383 (June 5, 1830).   [85] See p. 131.

[86] VIII, 220 (January 15, 1831). In noticing this issue of the *Mirror*, the *Morning Courier and New York Enquirer* for January 15, 1831, said: "It also contains an original production—'Rime of the Antient Coaster,' by Halleck, which will be admired. The Commercial says Halleck is a promising *young* Poet; in our opinion he is almost the only man in the country who can lay claim to the appellation, and is certainly entitled to more credit than the Commercial is disposed to give him."

[87] VIII, 233 (January 29, 1831).

[88] The verses were dated "Nov. 1821," and were unsigned. The index to the *Mirror* which was published at the close of volume 8 bore after the entry of the poem the name, "Halleck."

[89] II, 214 (October 2, 1869).

[90] Duyckinck, *Cyclopaedia of American Literature*, II, 261.

[91] L. Maria Child, *Letters from New York* (New York, 1845), p. 101.

his early volumes, *The Elixir of Moonshine, being a Collection of Prose and Poetry by the Mad Poet*.[92] Clarke's verses, full of images of death and references to madness, were, in general, crude and untutored, although occasionally possessed of a naïve beauty. Halleck always displayed a kindly interest in Clarke, and often befriended him in distress.[93] Wilson relates how Clarke once solicited aid of Halleck, who gave him a two-and-a-half-dollar gold piece; but before Clarke could relieve his own wants, he had given the money to an organ-grinder.[94] Halleck on one occasion referred to the mad poet as "my poor friend McDonald Clarke,"[95] and Clarke, who always responded to kindness with a childlike affection, once said, "I would rather have a kind word from that noble man, Fitz-Greene Halleck, than from any emperor."[96] Clarke, who spent the closing days of his life in the insane asylum on Blackwell's Island, died in 1842.[97] Among those who attended the funeral at Grace Church was Fitz-Greene Halleck.[98]

Clarke's "extreme vanity," says the preface to "The Discarded" published in *Appleton's Journal*, "was easily flattered, and the small wits of the town, taking advantage of his weakness, often led him to believe that wealthy young ladies were madly in love with him. A notable instance occurred in the summer of 1821, when poor Clarke was persuaded that the proud and high born Miss Mary —— cherished a passion for him. The cross-gartering of Malvolio was nothing to the pranks they made him perform to win the notice of his lovely *inamorata*. The plot culminated in a forged invitation to visit the lady at her aristocratic mansion. Borrowing a suit for the occasion, and neatly gloved and booted, he proceeded to the residence of the lady, and rang the bell. The damsel, annoyed and forewarned, had given directions, if he ever appeared, to thrust him from the door, which, it is said, was done rudely, and with cruel contumely. The subjoined poem is supposed to have been written by the unfortunate poet, who awakened from his fond dream. Halleck composed it a few days after the event occurred to his brother poet."[99] Such are the traditional circum-

[92] Published in New York in 1822.
[93] Child, *op. cit.*, p. 109.　　　[94] *Life*, p. 466.
[95] *Ibid.*, p. 404.　　　[96] *Ibid.*, p. 430.
[97] L. M. Child, *op. cit.*, pp. 108–109.　　[98] *Ibid.*, p. 109.
[99] II, 214 (October 2, 1869). The same incident is referred to briefly by Lydia M. Child in *Letters from New York*, p. 108.

stances under which the poem was written. The verses, obviously thrown off at an idle moment and never collected by the poet,[100] bear no claim to poetry. Full of grotesque imagery foreign to Halleck's usual mode of expression, they were probably written as much in burlesque of Clarke's own fantastic style[101] as in amusement at his unfortunate predicament.

A third poem published in the *New York Mirror* during 1831 was "A Poet's Daughter, written for Miss ***, at the request of her father by Mr. Halleck." The verses, which were dated "Aug. 22d, 1831," were composed, tradition says,[102] for the album of Harriet Woodworth,[103] the daughter of Samuel Woodworth, the poet. Written in Halleck's happy style of compliment, they nevertheless introduced the habitual contrast between the spirits of the medieval and modern worlds. Again the author confessed his difficulty in realizing the mood of romance demanded of him as a poet.

> "This is no world," so Hotspur said,
> For "titling lips" and "mammets" made,
> No longer in love's myrtle shade
>   My thoughts recline,—
> I'm busy in the cotton trade,
>   And sugar line.

The concluding lines of this stanza, which suggested to the public mind Halleck's employment in Barker's office, excited contemporary comment. Verses, appearing in the *Mirror,* and addressed "to Mr. Halleck, on reading in the Mirror of the tenth instant, among his other verses 'To a Poet's Daughter' the following,"[104]

---

[100] The poem is reprinted in full in the Appendix.

[101] The following verses from a poem entitled "Human Glory" illustrate Clarke's gruesome style:

> Thy music is the low and awful stir
> Of drunken grave-rats, in the lone dark night,
> Whose bold and putrid appetites prefer
> A feast too horrid for a human sight.
>
> (*The Elixir of Moonshine* [1822], p. 37.)

[102] IX, 76 (September 10, 1831). The poem was reprinted in the *New York Evening Post* for September 9, 1831, and in the *New York Commercial Advertiser* for September 10.

[103] See the *Poetical Works of Samuel Woodworth* (New York, 1861), I, 22. In a clipping of the verses in the Duyckinck Collection, however, Mr. Duyckinck has written in above the asterisks "Janet Drake," the daughter of Joseph Rodman Drake. It is now, of course, impossible to determine definitely for whom the verses were written.

[104] The stanza quoted above was then reprinted.

merely embodied the common cry which enjoined Halleck to abandon commerce, and to devote his days and nights to the muse.[105] In republishing the poem in the edition of 1836, Halleck altered the stanza, omitting all reference to the ''cotton trade and sugar line.'' By 1836, when Halleck had become well established in the office of John Jacob Astor, any allusion to his former employer would have been inappropriate, and an alteration in the stanza was consequently essential. Poe, however, objected to the original lines on the score of their vulgarity, and in reviewing the second collected edition of Halleck's works, expressed satisfaction that they had been omitted.[106]

In the summer of 1831 a report became current in literary circles that Halleck was to edit a new periodical. The *Post* was probably the first paper to give substantial form to this report. ''We are requested by Messrs. Peabody & Co.,'' it announced, ''to state that they have entered into arrangements with F. G. Halleck, Esq. to take charge of a monthly magazine, which they propose to publish.''[107] This report, which spread rapidly, cropped out in the article on Halleck, already noted,[108] in the *New England Magazine*. ''We have heard,'' wrote George S. Hillard, ''that Mr. Halleck is to be an editor of a Magazine in the city of New-York. We wish him as much success as he deserves, and we can say nothing more than that. We hope that he may receive *golden* opinions from all men, and exchange his own notes for another sort of notes which have a very magic sound, and which, when properly arranged, form the tune of 'Money in both pockets.' ''[109] The rumor had, indeed, arisen in a misunderstanding, for which the publishers, Messrs. Peabody & Company, were responsible. At the request of Halleck, the Peabodys issued a note of apology in the leading

[105] IX, 87 (September 17, 1831).
[106] *Southern Literary Messenger*, II, 336 (April, 1836). Curiously enough, the *New York Mirror*, XIII, 235 (January 23, 1836), complained that these lines, as well as the whole stanza, were not retained in the collected edition. The phrase, ''busy in the sugar line,'' was used by Walt Whitman in an early sketch (E. Holloway, *Uncollected Poetry and Prose of Walt Whitman*, I, 45). Whitman's borrowing from Halleck was first noted by Prof. Thomas O. Mabbott. See *Notes and Queries*, March, 1926.
[107] July 14, 1831. *Morning Courier and New York Enquirer* for July 14 also commented on the report.
[108] See pp. 226–227.
[109] *New England Magazine*, I, 159 (August, 1831).

New York papers, stating that the announcement of the poet's connection with the new paper "was premature, and without the knowledge of Mr. Halleck."[110] On August 6, 1831, Halleck wrote to his sister who had inquired concerning the rumor: "The report of my intention of editing a magazine was contradicted, by the bookseller who gave rise to it, in all the newspapers. I regret that the contradiction should not have met your eye. The whole thing was a piece of impertinence on his part. He said to me in an accidental conversation that he intended some day or other to get up a magazine. I made some general commonplace remarks expressive of my wish to see such a work established, and my willingness to render it all the aid in my power. On this slight foundation, he immediately advertised, printed a prospectus, and obtained subscribers, without my knowledge or suspicion. He contradicted it a few days after, which was all the atonement he could make me. I was, as you may well suppose, exceedingly annoyed by the affair, particularly at this moment, when I do not wish to appear before the public for reasons which I mentioned in my last."[111] Halleck's unwillingness at this time "to appear before the public" may have been based upon the fact of his recent connection with Mr. Barker, who was then under suspicion owing to his notorious part in the Conspiracy Trials. It should not be overlooked that Halleck was now seeking a new business position, and a report of his intention to edit a new periodical he would undoubtedly have considered injurious to his prospects of finding an employer.

In the fall of the same year Richmond Hill,[112] once the residence of Aaron Burr, was converted into a theater. A prize was offered by Richard Russell,[113] the manager, for the best poem to be spoken at the dedication of the newly equipped building. The committee of award, which consisted of Gulian C. Verplanck, Ogden Hoff-

---

110 *New York Mirror*, IX, 23 (July 24, 1831). The *Post* for July 16 also issued the apology. In the fictitious letter of Halleck which Poe included in his article entitled "Autography," allusion is also made to the report of the new magazine. See the *Southern Literary Messenger*, II, 208 (February, 1836).

111 Wilson, *Life*, pp. 344–345.

112 "Located on the corner of Varick and Charlton streets." See J. G. Wilson, *Memorial History of the City of New York* (New York, 1893), III, 370.

113 J. G. Wilson in the *Independent*, March 7, 1872.

man,[114] and Prosper C. Wetmore,[115] "assembled in one of the old rooms where in Burr's days had gathered Talleyrand, the philosopher Volney, and other celebrities of the time. Gulian C. Verplanck read the successful poem and broke the seal of the envelope containing the name of the successful competitor—Fitz-Greene Halleck."[116] The address beginning, "Where dwells the drama's spirit?"[117] was spoken by Mr. Langton on the opening night, November 14, 1831. On the following day, the *New York Evening Post* published the address,[118] which the *Mirror* rightly called "more poetic than declamatory."[119] Written in heroic couplets, the poem, in its suggestion of a vital relationship between art and life, explains something of Halleck's love of the theater.[120] The following May, 1832, Mrs. Barnes, the actress, applied to Halleck for a similar address to be delivered at the reopening of the theater that spring; but Halleck politely declined.[121]

In February, 1832, Halleck published in the *New York Mirror*[122] his "Lines to Her Who Can Understand Them."[123] These stanzas were written, Wilson asserts, for the album of Miss Lummis, the poet and dramatist, who later married Professor Ellet. While she was on a visit to New York, at the suggestion of a friend, she sent Mr. Halleck a note, asking for an autograph.[124] The complimentary

[114] A well-known New York lawyer, and the half brother of the poet, Charles Fenno Hoffman.

[115] Author of *Lexington, with Other Fugitive Poems* (1830). The names of the three judges are given by Wilson in the *Independent*, March 7, 1872.

[116] Wilson, *Memorial History of the City of New York*, III, 370–371.

[117] First collected in *Fanny, with Other Poems* (1839).

[118] November 15, 1831.

[119] IX, 167 (November 26, 1831). The *Mirror* also reprinted the address in the same issue.

[120] This interest is amply illustrated in Wilson's article "Halleck and His Theatrical Friends" in *Potter's American Monthly*, March, 1875.

[121] Wilson, *Life*, p. 347. A copy of the letter of declension, substantially the same as that printed by Wilson, is preserved in the Duyckinck Collection of the New York Public Library.

[122] IX, 257 (February 18, 1832). The poem was reprinted in the *Morning Courier and New York Enquirer* for February 25. Poe later reprinted the lines in the *Broadway Journal*, II, 319 (November 29, 1845).

[123] Poems with this or similar titles were common at this period. In the *Post* for November 25, 1819, appeared a poem addressed "To Her Who Will Best Understand It"; and in the same paper for December 6, 1826, "Lines for Her Who Understands Them." Verses "To One Who Will Understand Me" were published in the *Southern Literary Messenger* for March, 1835.

[124] Wilson, *Life*, p. 358.

verses written in reply were obviously composed before Halleck came personally to know Mrs. Ellet.

> Yet though unseen, unseeing,
>   We meet and part, we meet and part,
> Be still my worshipped being,
>   In mind and heart, in mind and heart.

Many years later, Mrs. Ellet told General Wilson that Halleck "arranged at the Park Theatre for the production of her first tragedy, 'Teresa Contarini,' "[125] which was acted in 1835.

The only literary labor for which Halleck received any substantial remuneration during the period of his nonemployment, was his editing of the works of Lord Byron.[126] This volume appeared probably at the close of 1832[127] without the editor's name. "In the American edition," states the "Publisher's Advertisement" which was dated "January, 1833," "there is a great number of the Letters of Byron not in the English copy, including his Letters to his mother. There is also in this edition a large collection of Poems not in any previous American one; many blanks are filled up, and explanatory notes added, which will be found of essential service to the reader. The present, therefore, is emphatically the *first* complete edition of the Poetical and Prose works of Lord Byron." The edition of Byron's works which was then being published by Murray in London had but partly appeared at the close of 1832, so that Halleck's volume, as Dearborn, the American publisher, said, was the first edition which aimed at completeness. Unfortunately, however, Halleck's introduction consisted merely of a brief sketch of Byron's life,[128] derived from Moore's biography,[129] and included

[125] Wilson, *Life*, p. 430. Poe's unpleasant experiences with Mrs. Ellet are well known. See Woodberry, *Edgar Allan Poe* (Boston, 1909), II, 183. There is no evidence that Halleck's acquaintance with her was more than casual.

[126] Wilson (*Life*, p. 532) states that Halleck received $1,000 for editing the works of Byron.

[127] The work was copyrighted in 1832, but the date of imprint was 1833. For the complete title, see the Bibliography in Appendix (p. 380).

[128] On January 23, 1836, Halleck wrote to his sister regarding a package of books he had sent her: "It contains a copy of the new edition of my verses, and a copy of the 'Byron' which I edited some years ago. Of the latter, some of the notes, I do not now recollect which, and the sketch of the life, were written by me." (Wilson, *Life*, p. 392.)

[129] Published in 1830.

no criticism of Byron's poetry. The source of the new letters, seventy-four in number, which were not included in Moore's *Life,* remains a mystery, although it is probable that Halleck's publishers in some way or other obtained the new material. Halleck's most considerable editorial services were rendered in connection with the *Hours of Idleness,* for which, in addition to contributing a preface, he collated the various editions, and restored the suppressed poems.[130] In the main, Halleck reproduced faithfully Byron's original notes.

An early review of Halleck's edition, probably by Bryant, appeared in the *New York Evening Post* for February 4, 1833. Here the anonymous editor is praised as one "thoroughly qualified for the undertaking, and one who is himself distinguished by a genius in many respects not unlike that of the great poet whose writings he has supervised." The reviewer for the *Knickerbocker,* however, who probably knew not that Halleck was the editor, called the work "premature." "All the productions of the illustrious poet, with his life and letters, condensed in one volume, would be, perhaps, the most invaluable achievement which encouraged enterprise could offer to the literary world; but it is well known that the great edition of Byron, now publishing by Murray, and edited by Moore, in a manner which has added even to *his* fame a lasting credit, will be extended by an accumulation of materials to three volumes more than were originally contemplated; and many new and interesting details are confidently expected in the supplementary matter. To have an edition, therefore, perfectly complete, these should have been waited for; and we should, moreover, have been presented with a life much more elaborate than a mere chronological sketch which is here prefixed."[131]

Having, no doubt, this criticism in mind, and desiring as com-

---

130 I quote the following extract from the preface to the *Hours of Idleness:* "In the present publication, all those poems from the 'Private Volume,' and the early editions of 'Hours of Idleness' which were suppressed by the author, are reprinted, and all the variations of the different impressions are noticed" (p. 382 [poetry]).

131 I, 182 (March, 1833). In the same issue of the *Knickerbocker* appeared a playlet called "A Peep at the Pow-Wow" in which was a reference to Halleck and his new edition of Byron. The allusion is of value in showing that Halleck's name was generally associated with the volume even before it definitely appeared on the edition of the following year.

plete a collection as possible of Byron's works, Dearborn issued in January, 1834, a second edition, containing the new prose selections and poems[132] which had been added to the London edition, now complete. To the "Advertisement" of this volume Halleck's name was added, thus accurately identifying the editor. In commenting briefly upon the edition in the *New York Mirror* a critic remarked: "Halleck's Byron is well known to be the most complete yet published. Numerous letters, which have not appeared in any other edition are inserted in this, with all the poems in that lately issued by Murray."[133]

Such was the literary work done by Halleck from 1828 to 1832. Three poems, "The Field of the Grounded Arms," "Red Jacket," and the "Address, at the Opening of a New Theatre," together with the edition of Byron's works, may be taken as the sum total of Halleck's literary efforts at this period. The other poems, trifling effusions of an idle hour, may be readily dismissed in appraising his literary output for these years. But however comfortably Halleck rested in the reputation that followed the publication of his 1827 volume, the public, concerned for his fame as a poet, did not overlook the slender body of his work. Indeed, a protest against the curious indifference to verse writing—the inertia literary and artistic[134]—to which the poet was more and more becoming a slave, found frequent expression in the journals of the day. With the appearance of the 1827 edition, the *New York Mirror* complained of Halleck's imprisonment "in the unhallowed office of a broker."[135] Bryant, in reviewing the new volume, was "disposed to expostulate with one who writes so well for writing so little";[136] and Cooper, writing to De Kay from Florence in 1829, observed that he had "heard nothing of Halleck," who, he added, "should not be idle with his genius."[137] A similar protest was made the same

[132] The chief addition to the new volume was a section beginning on page 488, with the heading: "The following poems from manuscripts collected after the death of Lord Byron were first published in London in 1833."

[133] XI, 247 (February 1, 1834).

[134] Robert C. Sands was probably referring to Halleck when he said in the *Atlantic Magazine* for May, 1824 (I, 6), "I know but one man in this city and country who is able to write poetry; and he is lazy to a degree."

[135] IV, 285, March 31, 1827.

[136] *United States Review*, II, 8 (April, 1827).

[137] *Correspondence of James Fenimore-Cooper*, I, 166.

year by an unknown correspondent in the *Post*,[138] who in a "Petition to F. G. Halleck, Esq." called upon the poet for a new edition of *Fanny*—a request in which the editor of that paper heartily concurred. "What is Halleck about?" was the question asked by the *Morning Courier and New York Enquirer* in 1830. "We have found this question put in several distant parts," asserted the editor, "but no echo has replied. . . . The genius of Halleck ought not to be hid under the artificial encrustations of a city life."[139] And a few days later, in renewing the same topic, the editor advanced as a reason for Halleck's inactivity an amiability of disposition, which allowed idlers "to fritter away [his] time."[140] The following year William Snelling, in "Truth, a New Year's Gift for Scribblers,"[141] a satirical poem on contemporary writers, again took up the theme.

> Wilt thou be silent? Wake, O Halleck, wake!
> Thine and thy country's honor are at stake!
> Wake and redeem the pledge—thy vantage keep;
> 'Tis pity one like thee so long should sleep![142]

A few years later the *New York Mirror* also expressed concern at Halleck's silence, once sarcastically asserting that he is "busy, reading everything except the newspapers, and taking care of his cash accounts";[143] and at another time, complaining that he "has written well, but not enough to give him the rank that he deserves."[144] But the poet, apparently indifferent to the voice of critics, to each and all turned a deaf ear.

[138] September 11, 1829.
[139] December 13, 1830.
[141] Boston, 1831.
[143] XI, 375 (May 24, 1834).

[140] December 23, 1830.
[142] P. 32.
[144] XII, 317 (April 4, 1835).

X

THE MAN OF SOCIETY

1832–40

WITH all the reputation that followed the publication of his first collected volume, and the assurances of literary success which the public were constantly urging upon him if only he would abandon commerce for the muse, Halleck could not surrender the thought of financial independence which regular employment affords. Barker once informed General Wilson that after the collapse of his business, Halleck "devoted himself to literature, refusing the employment of others, in the hope that my concerns would assume a more favorable attitude."[1] Thus Halleck's period of nonemployment was one of waiting. His sensitive, conservative nature made painful the thought of readjustment to a new employer, yet he saw clearly that to take up literature for a livelihood was but a hazardous undertaking. To edit a newspaper or periodical was the only employment to which a man of letters might turn with hope of pecuniary success; but Halleck apparently had no taste for the forced demand which the duties of editor would make upon his literary powers. His extreme vexation at having his name heralded as editor of the new periodical which the Peabodys were projecting[2] reflects as much the artistic and literary languor to which he was prone, as a righteous indignation at the imposition. Outside of newspaper work, hope of success for the literary man was small. Editors were more willing to look abroad for material for which they paid nothing than to risk doing their duty by native writers.[3] Halleck must,

---

[1] Wilson, *Life,* pp. 336–337.   [2] See pp. 245–246.

[3] This attitude is well illustrated by the following extract from a prospectus, issued, probably in 1838, by Dr. W. T. Porter and N. P. Willis, of a new periodical called *The Pirate,* which in 1839 was finally published under the title, *The Corsair:* "As to original American productions, we shall, as publishers do, take what we can get for nothing (that is good), holding, as the publishers do, that while we can get Boz and Bulwer for a thank-ye or less, it is not pocket-wise to pay much for Halleck and Irving." Henry Beers, *Nathaniel P. Willis* (Boston, 1885), p. 240.

too, have realized the limited scope of his own literary ability. Unlike Irving, whose powers as an essayist and historian could more easily be turned to profit, Halleck had his sole medium of expression in poetry, which found many admirers, but few purchasers. So after the failure of Barker's business, he waited patiently to see how best he might adjust himself to the new turn which affairs had taken. In the interim he busied himself in writing. Except, however, for the editing of Byron's works, for which Halleck received $1,000, he could have profited little by the writing done at this period. For the contributions to the *Talisman* and the *Legendary* small sums may have been paid the poet; and the prize for the opening address at the Richmond Hill Theatre may have amounted to $100.[4] But very trifling, indeed, must have been the sums, if anything at all, paid for the very trifling pieces contributed to the *Mirror*.[5] It may, therefore, readily be seen that during this period of nonemployment Halleck could not have been self-supporting; and after more than three years of waiting he gladly turned to a financial prospect which at least seemed promising.

In February, 1832, before engaging himself to Astor, Halleck made a visit to Washington with a party of friends. During his stay of several weeks at the capital "he was the recipient of flattering attentions from President Jackson—with whom he dined twice —several members of the Cabinet, and Mr. Vaughan, the British minister, who gave a grand dinner in his honor. During this visit the poet made the acquaintance of Webster, Clay, Calhoun, and many other prominent statesmen of that day."[6]

On May 15, 1832,[7] the period of Halleck's waiting came to an end, and he entered the office of John Jacob Astor, probably in the capacity of a confidential or private secretary. In a letter to his sister, Maria, dated May 29, he mentioned briefly the new duties

[4] The exact cash amount of the prize, if indeed the prize consisted of money, has not been discovered.

[5] It was the usual custom in Halleck's earlier days for newspapers and periodicals to pay nothing for poetical contributions. "You are right," once wrote Bryant to J. G. Wilson, "in supposing that Mr. Halleck received no compensation for anything written for the *Evening Post*. I am quite sure that this is so, for it has never been the practice of the paper to pay anything for verses, which are generally furnished to an extent beyond the space that can be spared for them. Morever, in Mr. Coleman's time the newspapers paid nothing for contributions of any sort" (*Bryant and His Friends*, p. 87).

[6] Wilson, *Life*, p. 353.   [7] *Ibid.*, p. 353.

he had just assumed. ''A few days previous to the receipt of your letter of the 21st.,'' said the poet, ''I accepted a proposition made me by John Jacob Astor, to take a charge in his business here. He himself goes to Europe in two or three weeks. This will probably, if I wish it, be a permanent arrangement, and, possibly a profitable one.''[8]

Astor's country house was situated at Hell Gate, where off and on for several years Halleck appears to have lived with his employer. It was probably here that the poet first met Washington Irving. There is no evidence of an earlier friendship, but during the interval of Irving's residence abroad, Halleck must certainly have come to feel something of the power of Irving's personality, intimate as he was with those who had known the essayist. Paulding and Brevoort[9] may well have served as friendly links between Halleck and the author of the *Sketch Book;* and the sprightly Fairlie sisters—Mary, Louisa, and Julia, called by Halleck the ''Three Graces''—undoubtedly furnished the poet with many a lively anecdote of the Salmagundi days.[10] Upon his return to America in 1832,[11] Irving accepted frequently of Astor's hospitality at Hell Gate. In a letter of Irving, addressed to his nephew, Pierre, on September 15, 1834, the essayist, in alluding to Mr. Astor, spoke of ''Halleck, the poet,'' who ''resides a great deal with him at present, having a handsome salary for conducting his affairs.''[12] Later in the same year, when Irving had in mind the writing of *Astoria,* which Mr. Astor had suggested, he again wrote to his nephew, asking the young man to assist him in the work. Mr. Astor ''has taken a house in town for his winter residence,'' observed Irving, ''and, if you undertake the task, would wish you to reside with him, as long as you may find it agreeable, and has likewise invited Halleck to be his guest. The latter you will find a very

8 Wilson, *Life*, p. 353.

9 Henry Brevoort's son served with Halleck in the Iron Grays. See p. 38.

10 Mary Fairlie was the ''Sophy Sparkle'' of the *Salmagundi* papers. Halleck, however, much preferred Louisa, whose wit he greatly admired. See Wilson, *Life*, pp. 226–227.

11 At a dinner, given to Irving at the City Hall on May 30, 1832 (see Pierre Irving, *Life and Letters of Washington Irving*, II, 486 ff.). Halleck does not seem to have been present. A toast, however, was proposed by Archibald Gracie to ''Croaker & Co.'' (see the *New York Evening Post*, June 2, 1832).

12 Pierre Irving, *op. cit.*, III, 61.

pleasant companion.''¹³ ''For upward of a month past I have been quartered at Hell-Gate, with Mr. Astor,'' wrote Irving again on September 26, 1835, ''and I have not had so quiet and delightful a nest since I have been in America. He has a spacious and well-built house, with a lawn in front of it, and a garden in the rear. The lawn sweeps down to the water's edge, and full in front of the house is the little strait of Hellgate, which forms a constantly moving picture. Here the old gentleman keeps a kind of bachelor hall. Halleck, the poet, lives with him, but goes to town every morning, and comes out to dinner.''¹⁴

This domestic arrangement, which probably lasted for only a few years, if convenient to Astor, who doubtless continued to make good use of Halleck's time at Hell Gate, was naturally boring to the poet. Even his regular duties in town were heavier than a man of Halleck's social inclinations would like; and, of course, the three years of leisure during which he had been waiting for something to turn up, had made it especially hard for him again to settle down to steady employment. His vexation at the business routine to which he was daily subject is reflected in the following extract from a letter written to Miss Maria Halleck.

New York, May 6, 1833.

My dear Sister:

I HAVE received your two last letters, and will endeavor, at some leisure moment, to answer the questions they ask me, particularly. I should be happy to make the acquaintance of Mr. Scoville, but am so much engaged in my "bread-winning" employments in the counting-house, that I can find no time to devote to visits. With the exception of the party you mention, given to Fanny Kemble, and one other party, both of which were so pressed upon me that it was less painful to say "yes" than "no," I have not mingled with the "gay world" for more than two years in a single instance. I hope to be able to be more social some day or other, though I know not on what the hope is founded. But, as Corporal Nym says, "Things must be as they may."¹⁵

The party given to Fanny Kemble to which Halleck here refers is briefly described in the diary of the actress.

¹³ *Ibid.*, III, 63. The letter is dated October 29, 1834.
¹⁴ Pierre Irving, *op. cit.*, III, 78.   ¹⁵ Wilson, *Life*, pp. 359–360.

A pleasant dinner, very. Mr. —— the poet, one Dr. ——, Colonel ——,
and Mr. ——; the only woman was a Miss ——

*   *   *   *   *   *   *   *   *   *

——'s face reminded me of young ——; the countenance was not quite
so good, but there was the same radiant look about the eyes and forehead.
His expression was strongly sarcastic; I liked him very much, notwithstanding.[16]

This cryptic entry is partly elucidated in the course of a letter sent
by the poet to Maria, soon after the appearance of Miss Kemble's
Journal in 1835.

New York, June 22, 1835.

My dear Sister:

PREVIOUS to the receipt of your letter of the 15th, I had written you a
letter, addressed to the care of Mr. Elliot, at New Haven, which you
probably have not yet received. As it enclosed a bank-note, I am anxious
to learn that it reached you. So you wonder what Fanny Kemble could
find to admire in me after a personal acquaintance, and charitably attribute her praises of me to her fears of my reputation as a satirist. Thank
you. Still I cannot but do her the justice to say that you are the first
person that ever accused her of fearing anything. As for her age, about
which you ask, she is probably not far from twenty. She has remarkably
fine eyes, and is, when and where she chooses to be, very agreeable. The
newspapers, whose editors she dislikes, abuse her and hers without mercy.
About them she cares little. Her lot in life is a happy one. She has youth,
health, heart, and intellect, a good husband, a pretty baby, and twenty
thousand dollars a year. I wish all my lady-acquaintances were as fortunate. By the way, she alludes to me in asterisks in the body of her book.
The allusion would doubtless escape your notice. She says of the dinner-
party at which we first met, "It was very pleasant, very." As she was
seated between Mr. Berkeley (a son of the Earl of Berkeley) and myself,
and conversed with us exclusively, I take half the compliment. After
describing my visage, and saying something about "radiancy of eye and
forehead," she closes thus: "The expression of his features is strongly
sarcastic. I liked him very much, notwithstanding." I really care little, at
my age and in my circumstances, about what is thought of my countenance, but such a remark as "strongly sarcastic" from an indifferent
observer made me, when I read it, quite melancholy. You remember me in
my boyhood. You have a miniature of me taken at twenty-one. "Twenty
years," as Southey says, "have wrought strange alteration." Indeed they

[16] *Journal* (Philadelphia, 1835), I, 121–122. From the entry for [October]
6, [1832]. There is nothing to indicate where the dinner was held.

have. The knowledge which I have been compelled, against my will, to acquire of my fellow-men has certainly not raised them in my estimation; and yet I am unwilling to believe that the feelings with which I regard them are written on my features. But I fear it is so. Heaven forgive them and me.

I was not aware that the article about Sachem's Head, in the *Mirror*, was written by George Hill,[17] although the initials might have taught it me had I reflected upon them. I cannot deem it illy written. On the contrary, he is a very clever writer. I always feel a sort of romantic interest in all I hear or see about Guilford, which you, of course, from being on or near the spot, do not appreciate. Still I thought you would be amused by the thing, and sent it accordingly.

Yours affectionately,
F.G.H.[18]

Conspicuous among other dinners which Halleck attended in the early thirties was one in honor of Edwin Forrest, the American actor, who was about to visit Europe. Later, when Forrest was ready to embark, "sixty or seventy of his closest friends went several miles down the harbor in a yacht. Among them were Leggett and Halleck. Leggett, between whom and Forrest had grown a love as ardent and heroic as that of the famed antique examples, threw his arms around him with a tearful 'God bless and keep you!' Halleck said, 'May you have hundreds of beautiful hours in beautiful places, and come back to us the same as you go away, only enriched!' Forrest replied, pressing his hand, 'That is indeed the wish of a poet for his friend. You may be sure when I am at Marathon, at Athens, at Constantinople, I shall often recall your lines on Marco Bozzaris, and be delighted to link with them the memory of this your parting benediction.' "[19]

With the acceptance of a position with Mr. Astor, Halleck's productiveness in poetry came virtually to an end. The pressure of his official duties, together with a desire not to expose himself to the prejudice which business men of the day felt toward the *literati*, was largely responsible for his silence. He is, indeed, reported to have said that "being under the necessity of earning a livelihood, he could not afford to incur the adverse criticism aroused thereby";

17 See the *Mirror*, XII, 373 (May 23, 1835).
18 Wilson, *Life*, pp. 368–370.
19 William R. Alger, *Life of Edwin Forrest* (Philadelphia, 1877), I, 192. The dinner was held on July 25, 1834.

and it is probably true that "he had already more reputation as a poet than was good for him in the esteem of men engaged in business pursuits."[20] Not only did he now largely forego the pleasure of writing and publishing poems at leisure; all requests for occasional poems were also promptly refused.[21] It was probably about the beginning of 1833 that a movement was set on foot for a benefit theatrical performance to be given to William Dunlap, the playwright, "for his long and important services rendered to the Drama and to Literature."[22] On January 21, 1833, a letter was sent to Halleck soliciting from him "a suitable poetical address or prologue to be delivered on the evening of the benefit."[23] It was indeed an interesting commentary on Halleck's reputation at the period that he should have been the first poet selected for the honor. But Halleck declined the offer. In his letter of reply to the committee in charge of the benefit he expressed his "inability to undertake the task." "I do so with the less regret," he went on to say, "because I leave it to others whose names as well as merits, will more essentially serve the good cause you are embarked in, and because there are modes in which I can better aid it. . . . Please tender to the gentlemen of your committee and accept for yourselves individually, my grateful acknowledgment of the honor done me."[24]

[20] William L. Andrews, *Old Booksellers of New York* (New York, 1895), p. 24. See also James H. Hackett's "Reminiscences of the Poet Halleck" in the *Evening Post* for January 31, 1868.

[21] Wilson states (*Life*, p. 360) that during the year 1833 Halleck prepared for the second volume of the *National Portrait Gallery* "a memoir of De Witt Clinton." This task was undertaken, it is said, at the urgent request of the family of the statesman. There is nothing in the memoir itself, however, to indicate it is the work of Halleck. Some of the contributions in the second volume are signed with the initials of the authors; but this is not the case with the sketch of Clinton. The second volume of the *National Portrait Gallery* was copyrighted in 1835, and the title-page bears the same date. Wilson's reasons for assigning the memoir to the year 1833 are not clear. Another uncertain composition of the same date is that mentioned in a notice of a production of the *Magic Flute* given at the Park Theatre: "The music, with the exception of a ballad, with Bayley's poetry and Auber's music, and a song 'Death' with Halleck's poetry and Horn's music, is by Mozart" (*Evening Post*, April 19, 1833). This may be a setting of the lines to Death in "Marco Bozzaris."

[22] *Knickerbocker*, I, 324 (May, 1833).

[23] *Ibid.*, I, 324. The letter is dated January 21, 1833.

[24] *Ibid.*, I, 324. The letter is dated January 28, 1833. Toward the close of the year 1833 a letter was sent to James Fenimore Cooper, congratulating him on his safe return from Europe and inviting him to a complimentary dinner.

Most of Halleck's verses were now of a trivial kind. An example of the poems to which he occasionally turned his hand is the translation, made in 1834, of Piero Maroncelli's Italian verses,

> Primaverìli aurette
> Che Italia sorvolate,
> Voi quì non mai spirate
> Sull' egro prigionier,—

written during the poet's confinement in an Austrian prison. Maroncelli was a companion of Silvio Pellico at Spielberg, where the two poets suffered a most cruel imprisonment from 1822 to 1830. Pellico's prison memoirs, *Le Mie Prigioni*,[25] were translated into English in 1836 under the title, *My Prisons*, and Maroncelli's *Additions to "My Prisons, Memoirs of Silvio Pellico"* was published in the same volume.[26] In Maroncelli's *Additions* appeared the original text of his poem, with Halleck's translation.[27] Halleck had studied Italian under Lorenzo Da Ponte, and it is probable that Maroncelli's text was made accessible to him through the Italian master. Maroncelli was much pleased with the translation, and declared in a flattering letter to the poet: "Consentite, Signor Halleck, ch' io dico di non riconoscere in sì gentili versi le mie *primaveriti aurette*. Certo, quel dolore è fedele, quell' accento è vero; ravviso in esso il dolor mio e la parola del core; ma la grazia onde questa e quello sono abbelliti è tutta vostra."[28]

In 1835 George Dearborn, the publisher, brought out the poems of Drake and Halleck. The works of Drake had never been collected; but "The Culprit Fay," which several periodicals[29] had published in more or less garbled forms, had already become a

Halleck was among the literary men and other citizens of New York to sign the communication (*Correspondence of James Fenimore-Cooper*, I, 327).

[25] Published in Paris in 1833.

[26] Published in Cambridge in 1836. Each part has a separate pagination.

[27] *Additions to My Prisons*, pp. [1]22–123. Poe speaks of Maroncelli's poem as "happily rendered by Mr. Halleck" (see the article on Maroncelli in the "Literati" series, *Godey's Magazine and Lady's Book*, XXXII, 271 [June, 1846]).

[28] Wilson, *Life*, p. 364. The letter is dated "25 Gennaro, 1834." What is probably the original manuscript of Halleck's translation of Maroncelli's poem is preserved in the Biblioteca Comunale of Forlì, Italy.

[29] The following versions of the poem had appeared: *New York Mirror*, II, 22 (August 14, 1824); *ibid.*, XIII, 12 (July 11, 1835); *Athenaeum* [English], February 7, 1835; *Boston Pearl*, IV, 305 (May 30, 1835).

favorite with the public, and a complete edition of the poet's works had long been sought. Halleck was naturally believed the only proper person to edit the works of Drake. In 1830 a local paper issued a report that Halleck was ''seriously thinking of preparing an edition of the 'Croakers' for the press, with a biography of his friend and intellectual partner, the late lamented Doctor Drake'';[30] and the *Mirror,* in publishing a few years later a version of ''The Culprit Fay,'' remarked, ''We have long had a copy of this piece in our possession, but have refrained from publishing it, in the hope that Mr. Halleck would give the entire works of his lamented friend and associate to the publick.'' ''Mr. Halleck, Mr. Halleck! you have much to answer for;'' continued the editor. ''The crime of omission lies heavy at your door.''[31] When in 1835 Drake's daughter, Mrs. Commodore De Kay, finally consented to publish a volume of the more important of her father's poems, fittingly dedicated to Halleck, the poet was asked to prepare a memoir of his friend. It was perhaps a feeling of sadness at the thought of bygone days that made him decline. In mentioning the matter to General Wilson many years later, Halleck observed: ''What could I say about a young poet whose uneventful career was closed at twenty-five? I should have necessarily been almost as brief as Steevens, whose life of Shakespeare was comprised, as you remember, in some half a dozen lines.''[32]

To accompany the volume of Drake's poems, Dearborn issued at the close of the same year a new edition of Halleck's works. As early as August, 1835, the *Southern Literary Messenger* had asserted that ''Halleck's Poems are in press, and will speedily be published. This announcement has been received with universal pleasure. As a writer of light, airy, and graceful things, Halleck is inimitable.''[33] The volume finally made its appearance on December 24.[34] The text of the new edition was substantially a reprint of that of 1827, with the addition of three new poems, which had

[30] *Morning Courier and New York Enquirer,* December 23, 1830.
[31] XIII, 12 (July 11, 1835).   [32] Wilson, *Life,* p. 246.
[33] I, 716 (August, 1835). Other preliminary announcements of the volume appeared in the *Mirror,* XIII, 159 (November 14, 1835); and in the *Knickerbocker,* VI, 578 (December, 1835).
[34] Dearborn's advertisement of the volume appeared in the *Evening Post* for December 24, 1835. The date 1836, however, was placed on the title-page.

previously appeared in periodicals and annuals.[35] There was, thus, little that could be used by critics in revising their estimate of Halleck's work. With the possible exception of the review by Edgar Allan Poe, critical opinion of the volume was quite as laudatory and profuse as it had been nine years before when the first collected edition of his works had been issued. "Mr. Halleck," commented the *Mirror*, "might have made a much larger book had he collected all his works; but he seems to prefer quality to quantity, and has therefore omitted numerous effusions, which, although they would confer an enviable reputation on most native rhymesters, are not worthy, on the whole, perhaps, of the exquisite fancy and inimitable pen of such a true bard as Halleck."[36] An enthusiastic reviewer[37] in the *Knickerbocker* exclaimed: "Fitz-Greene Halleck! Show us an American, with patriotism or poetry in his soul, who does not honor the name. For ourselves, we always feel, when reading his metrical compositions, as if respiring in mountain air"; and after berating Halleck soundly for his reticence, the same critic boasted of having most of the contents of the volume by heart.[38] The *American Quarterly Review*,[39] although eying askance Halleck's frequent lapses into humor, combined all the powers of flowery rhetoric and pious adulation in an attempt to render justice to the beauties of the poet's work. The result, in its fulsome sentimentality, must indeed have amused Halleck. Poe's review of the volume, however, which was made along with that of Drake, was perhaps the earliest rational attempt to evaluate the poetical works of Halleck. Untrammeled by conventional opinion, Poe at once asserted that "Halleck's poetical powers appear to us essentially inferior, upon the whole, to those of his friend, Drake. He has written nothing at all comparable to *Bronx*."[40] In finally estimating Halleck's work, Poe observed: "It will be seen that while we

---

[35] The additional poems were "The Field of the Grounded Arms," "Red Jacket," and "A Poet's Daughter." "A Poet's Daughter" had been reprinted from the *Mirror*, where it originally appeared, in a miscellany entitled the *Atlantic Club Book*, compiled by G. P. Morris and published in two volumes in 1834. Four other pieces, however, copied from the *Mirror* into the same volume—"The Rime of the Ancient Coaster," "Lines to Her Who Can Understand Them," "The Discarded," and "To Walter Bowne, Esq."—Halleck did not include in the new edition.

[36] XIII, 215 (January 2, 1836).　　　　[37] Willis Gaylord Clark.
[38] VII, 88 (January, 1836).　　　　　　[39] XXI, 401 (June, 1837).
[40] *Southern Literary Messenger*, II, 334 (April, 1836).

are willing to admire in many respects the poems before us, we feel obliged to dissent materially from that public opinion (perhaps not fairly ascertained) which would assign them a very brilliant rank in the empire of Poesy. That we have among us poets of the loftiest order we believe—but we do *not* believe that these poets are Drake and Halleck.''[41]

Much more enthusiastic, though far less genuinely critical, was the opinion of the new volume as expressed by Willis Gaylord Clark, brother of Louis G. Clark, who was editor of the *Knickerbocker*. In the following excerpt from a letter in which is introduced the name of Fanny Kemble, whom Halleck had met the previous year, Clark expresses his admiration for the new edition which had recently come into his hands:

Philadelphia, Wednesday, January, 1836.

My Dear Friend:

I was at the opera the other evening with Mrs. Butler,[42] and was surprised to learn that she had written me a letter, enclosing one to you acknowledging the receipt of your beautiful volume of most beautiful poetry. That letter only came to hand yesterday, after the departure of the post. Where it has sojourned since "Fanny" wrote it, "Heaven knows, not I." It is now promptly forwarded, and if its contents should give you half the pleasure that your work has afforded to her or me, you will have a delightsome season in its perusal. For myself, I cannot sufficiently thank you. The best copy of your poems I ever saw before, was one lent me (and religiously returned), by Henry Inman,[43] when he tarried here; but the present edition is beautiful in the extreme. I shall preserve your present—

> "Unto thylke day i' the which I shall creep
> Unto my sepulchre:"

and should I beget children, it shall descend to them, an intellectual heirloom whose warp and woof are of heavenly tinct. There is nothing in the volume which I could not repeat to you, without an error. I said as much in my *Knickerbocker* notice.[44] I like less than any other piece, "The Field of the Grounded Arms." It is full of thought and rich language, but you will forgive me, if I think even harmony would have improved it. *Au reste,*

---

[41] *Southern Literary Messenger*, II, 336. ''Of Poe's review of Halleck and Drake, Paulding says in a private letter: 'I think it one of the finest specimens of criticism ever published in this country' '' (Wilson, *Bryant and His Friends*, pp. 340–341).

[42] Fanny Kemble.

[43] The portrait painter.   [44] See p. 261.

I speak in superlatives. You are the poet for my money, and I do not hesitate to tell the truth to a man who has given me so much delight as you have. "Marco Bozzaris" will be immortal. The passage beginning "An hour passed on," to the close of the next page is magnificent. The thrilling numbers peal into the ear of my spirit, like the very clangor of battle. Such poetry would thrill an oyster, if the march of mind had penetrated the dominions of conchology. By the way, your work will be handsomely reviewed in the next number of the *American Quarterly,* and the part relating particularly to you will be from my pen, dove-tailed into the rest of the article, which is to bear the title "American Lyric Poetry."[45] I tell you this as a *profound secret,* to be repeated to no one,—since you are the only person to whom I shall mention the matter. I shall send you the number as soon as it is published, and shall then give you the name of the author. I do not mention this as likely to please you: for what but damnable iteration, in the way of eulogy, can be said of one whose name has been great so long in mouths of wisest censure.

The elegance of your volume is striking and, for America, unique. I hope it will serve as an example to publishers generally. Half of the works that issue from our native presses look, to use a preacher's phrase, as if they had been printed "with types and figures of the old Testament Dispensation."[46]

The interest which the public now took in Halleck's works, with the publication of the new edition, is reflected both in the frequent reprinting of his poems, and in the renewed comment which the press offered. During the succeeding months, the *Mirror* published four of the poet's lyrics.[47] In printing the last—"On the Death of Lieut. William Howard Allen"—the editor observed: "With the following *monody,* we have published all Mr. Halleck's acknowledged pieces, and many which he has not imbodied in the recent edition of his works. That individual is fortunate, indeed, whose memory is preserved from oblivion by such a poet as Mr. Halleck, whose lines beginning, 'Green be the turf

[45] The article to which Clark here alludes appeared in the *American Quarterly Review* for March, 1836 (XIX, 101 ff.). The special part relating to Halleck's work, of no critical importance, occupies pp. 112–114.

[46] *Potter's American Monthly,* IV, 221–222 (March, 1875). Fanny Kemble's note, to which Clark alludes at the beginning of his letter, is printed in the same magazine, p. 222.

[47] "Musick" (February 13, 1836); "Magdalen" (March 19, 1836); "From the Italian" (April 16, 1836); "On the Death of Lieut. William Howard Allen" (April 30, 1836).

above thee,' and those we now transcribe, may be ranked among
the most beautiful requiems of the time.''[48] A small miscellany of
American poetry, published in Boston the same year with the title
The Laurel: A Gift for all Seasons, included four of the author's
poems.[49] Other journals commented freely on his work. The *New
Yorker,* which in April, 1836, opened a series of sketches of the
"American Poets" with criticisms of the work of Bryant and Halleck, was profuse in its praise of our poet;[50] and Bryant in an
article in the *Mirror,* accompanied by an engraved portrait of Halleck,[51] was no less flattering in his attention.[52] A unique tribute to
Halleck's poetry was paid in 1836 by John Quincy Adams in a
speech delivered before the House of Representatives in which he
mentioned with enthusiasm the beauties of "Alnwick Castle."[53]

The success of his new volume at home now made Halleck hope-
ful of bringing out in England an edition of his works. With this
in mind he solicited aid of Washington Irving, who in turn communicated with Col. Thomas Aspinwall of the American embassy
in England. "Mr. Halleck, whom you must know as one of the
best and most popular of our American poets," wrote Irving,
"is desirous of having a small collection of his works published in
London. It would not be a volume of above a hundred and fifty
pages, for his writings are not voluminous, excelling in quality, not
quantity. Will you ascertain what would be the cost of publishing

[48] XII, 347 (April 30, 1836).

[49] "A Poet's Daughter," "Burns," "Love," "Lines to Her Who Can
Understand Them." The volume was reviewed in the *Mirror,* XIII, 255
(February 6, 1836).

[50] April 16, 1836. The following poems of Halleck also appeared in issues
of the *New Yorker:* "Magdalen" (April 9, 1836); "From the Italian"
(May 7, 1836); "The Recorder" (August 13, 1836).

[51] In 1831 Henry Inman painted a portrait of Halleck which is described
by Wilson (*Life,* p. 591) as "the best likeness ever made of the poet." Of
this portrait G. P. Morris said in the *Mirror:* "We have for some time been in
the possession of the most accurate likeness of this universally popular, accomplished, and eminent native poet ever taken, which we should long since have
published, had we been enabled to find an engraver disengaged who could and
would do justice to the original. At length Mr. Inman employed Mr. Parker,
and it has been transferred to steel under the especial direction of the painter
himself. . . . This will be accompanied with a sketch of his life and writings
from an eminent pen, and will be published in the course of a few weeks"
(XIV, 31 [July 23, 1836]). Three years before, Peabody & Company had
issued proposals for publishing the same portrait to be engraved by Kelly
(*Evening Post,* October 19, 1833), but the project was apparently given up.

[52] XIV, 97 (September 24, 1836).   [53] Wilson, *Life,* pp. 271-272.

a small, but elegant edition of such a volume; and whether Murray
or any other publisher of high standing would undertake to usher
it into circulation; the author taking upon himself all the risque of
cost? You may be able to furnish specimens of Mr. Halleck's writings, as some of them have been republished in England in collections of American poetry.''[54] Colonel Aspinwall often proved himself a friend of Irving and other American authors in his willingness to negotiate with English publishers, but on this occasion his
efforts were apparently unavailing, for no edition of Halleck's
poems was issued in England.

The failure of this effort to bring his works before a British public illustrates beyond a doubt how slender was Halleck's fame
abroad. In 1830 an English journal in reviewing Catherine Sedgwick's novel *Clarence* had noted how strange "the coupling of
Halleck and Bryant with Moore and Byron, as names equally well
known and equally prized, sounds . . . on an Englishman's ear'';[55]
and the following year the London *Monthly Magazine* in quoting
from Halleck's "Burns" innocently prefaced the passage with the
words, "as Wordsworth says."[56] Indeed, we catch but rare glimpses
of Halleck's name in the English periodicals of the period. To N. P.
Willis we owe the tribute paid to his poetry in an issue of the
Athenaeum magazine for 1835;[57] and to an anonymous critic a review of the 1836 edition in the same periodical. Although the latter
confidently asserted that "the principal piece which it contains and
its companion 'Marco Bozzaris' are almost as well known here as on
the other side of the Atlantic,''[58] the fact remains that no other
press notices of Halleck's new volume have been recovered from
English papers.

French comment on the poet at this period was, of course, even
rarer. In 1835, however, the *Revue des deux mondes*, in Philarète
Chasles's article "De la littérature dans l'Amérique du nord,''[59]
spoke of Halleck as a "banquier fort riche, et qui se distingue par

[54] This letter, dated New York, May 20, 1836, is preserved in the Henry E.
Huntington Library and Art Gallery.
[55] *Colburn's New Monthly Magazine*, II, 471 (December, 1830).
[56] See the *New York Mirror*, IX, 87 (September 17, 1831).
[57] February 7, 1835.   [58] October 29, 1836.
[59] III (4e sér.), 169 (1835).

l'humour et la vivacité.''[60] It was probably this reference to Halleck as a wealthy banker to which the poet alluded facetiously in a letter to his sister. In commenting on the fame that had come to him, Halleck remarked:

For my own part, the only instance where I have cared enough for my temporary notoriety, to wish the remarks of reviews, etc., about me true, was some weeks since, on seeing in a Paris paper a paragraph concerning my writings, which stated that I was "une riche banquier qui a fait fortune," a banker who had made himself rich. They probably mistook Bucephalus for his groom. I would give all these "golden opinions of all sorts of people" for a few golden guineas—a very few.[61]

Editors now frequently invited Halleck to contribute poems to their periodicals, but he invariably declined their offers. On June 7, 1836, Edgar Allan Poe addressed a letter to Halleck requesting a contribution for the *Southern Literary Messenger*. ''We wish to issue, if possible,'' he said, ''a number of the *Messenger,* consisting altogether of articles from our most distinguished *literati,* and to this end we have received aid from a variety of high sources. To omit your name in the plan we propose would be not only a negative sin on our part, but a positive injury to our cause. In this dilemma may we not trust to your good-nature for assistance? Send us any little scrap in your portfolio—it will be sure to answer our purpose fully, if it have the name of Halleck affixed.''[62] Halleck's reply to Poe has not been preserved; but it is doubtful, judging from the poet's responses on similar occasions, whether he promised to comply with Poe's request. In any case, Halleck never contributed anything to the *Messenger*. But Poe, fully confident that he would, did not wait for the poet's reply. Upon the same day that he sent the note to Halleck, Poe, in a letter to John P. Kennedy, the author of *Horse-Shoe Robinson,* asking for a contri-

---

[60] *Revue des deux mondes,* III (4e sér.), 179 (1835). In 1851 Philarète Chasles brought out his *Études sur la littérature et les moeurs des Anglo-Americans.* In reviewing the great number of versifiers which America had produced, Chasles found that ''les suels noms que l'on puisse isoler honorablement au milieu de cette forêt de versificateurs sont ceux de Street, Fitz-Greene Halleck, William Cullen Bryant, Henry Wadsworth Longfellow et Emerson.'' Halleck's poems of ''Marco Bozzaris'' and ''Red Jacket,'' Chasles considered ''agréables and purs,'' but he believed Bryant ''de beaucoup supérieur'' to Halleck as a poet (p. 290).

[61] Wilson, *Life,* pp. 392–393.   [62] *Ibid.,* pp. 396–397.

bution, presented a rather formidable list of literary persons who had either promised or given aid, and among these Halleck was included.[63]

At the beginning of the same year began what Halleck afterward described as "one of my life's most cherished romances."[64] The reasons for Halleck's choice of a bachelor's life are, of course, veiled in obscurity; but like many of his Knickerbocker contemporaries,[65] Halleck undoubtedly feared the loss of social liberty which marriage would entail. Indeed, the bachelor spirit of "Cockloft Hall"[66] pervaded much of the early New York life and literature. Never entirely free from the spirit of good-fellowship which in the days of Drake had been the life and soul of his existence, Halleck remained to the end a *bon homme*. But this mood of gaiety had its moments of pathos. He could joke lightly in *Fanny* of his bachelor life,[67] and yet a few years later in mentioning the marriages at which he had assisted, he rather bitterly remarked that he "seemed fated to be present at all weddings except my own."[68] Halleck's bachelor propensities, however, did not prevent his indulging in a romance or two of his own. One of these occurred while Halleck was on a visit to Boston, where he fell in love with a Miss Emily Marshall. To her the poet wished to propose, but left Boston without doing so, because, as he slyly hinted many years later, "he was too poor."[69]

A second and more widely known love story is that told by Halleck's leap year correspondence with Abbie Flanner, a young Quaker lady of Ohio. The earliest available account of this story comes from a letter addressed to the *Evening Post* by a correspondent from Colerain, Ohio, after the poet's death. "On the last evening of the year 1835," asserted the writer, "some ladies and gentlemen were met at the house of a friend in the village of Mount

[63] George Woodberry, *Life of Edgar Allan Poe* (Boston, 1909), I, 165.
[64] Wilson, *Life*, p. 391.
[65] Sands, Hoffman, and Irving were bachelors.
[66] See the *Salmagundi* papers.
[67]
      But if you are a bachelor, like me,
      And spurn all chains, even tho' made of roses,
      I'd recommend segars. (Stanza 24, 1839 ed.)
[68] Wilson, *Life*, p. 305. The letter is dated May 15, 1824.
[69] This information was furnished by Miss L. A. Rice of Springdale, Connecticut, to whose mother Mr. Halleck related the story in 1865 at Guilford Point, Connecticut. The incident is undated.

Pleasant, Jefferson County, Ohio, to watch the 'old year out and
the new year in.' During the evening the writer of this suggested
to one of the ladies (Miss Ellen) the propriety of availing herself
of the privileges of leap-year and challenging some literary gentleman to a correspondence, and mentioned Halleck as likely to relish
the joke.''[70] The ''Miss Ellen,'' here mentioned, who signed herself
''Ellen A. F. Campbell,'' was in reality Miss Abbie Flanner who,
writes William H. Hunter in ''The Pathfinders of Jefferson County,
Ohio,''[71] was ''a teacher in Friends Seminary at Mt. Pleasant. . . .
Miss Flanner was the daughter of a Quaker preacher who was of
the colony from North Carolina. The cottage in which they lived
was christened 'Albi Cottage' by Miss Flanner, and still stands
near the Friends' meeting house, but is not now, as when she lived,
embowered in vines and flowers—when she set the heart of the
bachelor poet aglow with warmth of love by the fire of her genius.
She was not a beautiful woman, those who knew her say she was
very homely,[72] but was possessed of a superior mind and her intellectual qualities, her brilliancy, her marvelous conversational powers, made her the very queen of the circle in which she moved.''[73]

The correspondence was opened by Miss Flanner in some verses
entitled ''New Year's Night, the Merry Mock-Bird's Song,'' which

[70] April 23, 1868. It is probable, however, that the story was current before
this date, judging from a letter sent to the *Post*, and printed in that paper for
April 27, 1868. ''I think your Ohio correspondent is mistaken in supposing
that the poetical epistle to Miss Campbell was never in print. It might not
have been published in any collection of the poet's writings, but probably in
some of the newspapers or periodicals of the day. I was first introduced to it
by a lady in the summer of 1857, who had copied it in her album, and as I
presume, of course from a printed copy. Prefixed to the poem was a letter
from the poet, exhibiting that characteristic modesty for which he was so
remarkable.'' The letter is signed ''F.L.''

[71] This series of articles, one of which deals with the Halleck-Flanner flirtation, was published in volume six of the *Ohio Archaeological and Historical
Publications* (Columbus, 1898). Another article on the affair, using much
material from the Hunter account, but containing a new letter on Miss Flanner from Hunter to the author, was published in the *Pioneer Daughter* for
July 25, 1901, by William H. Safford. Still another account appeared in the
Bookman for July, 1918. Here Stanley M. Ward, in retelling the story, adds
no new facts to this episode in Halleck's life.

[72] This fact is substantiated in a letter written to me by Miss Claire K.
Hague of Wilmington, Ohio, in which she says that when her grandmother
told the story of Abbie Flanner and Halleck, she would invariably close with
the remark, ''And Abbie was the homeliest woman I ever saw.''

[73] Pp. 307–308.

she addressed to Halleck, signing her name, "Ellen A. F. Campbell."

> O'er fields of snow the moonlight falls,
> And softly on the snow-white walls
>   Of Albi Cottage shines;
> And there beneath the breath of June,
> The honeysuckle's gay festoon
>   And multiflora twines.[74]

Halleck sent in reply to Miss Flanner the lines, "To Ellen, the Mocking Bird," which were written in the same verse-form as those submitted to the poet.

> The Scottish Border Minstrel's lay,
> Entranced me oft in boyhood's day;
>   His forests, glens, and streams,
> Mountains and heather blooming fair,
> And highland lake and lady were
>   The playmates of my dreams.[75]

Accompanying these verses was a letter to Miss Flanner in which Halleck alluded pleasantly to the lines she had written.

New York, February 29, 1836.

Dear Miss Campbell:

WERE it not that the delightfully flattering lines with which you have favored me date "Bissextile," I should have taken post-horses for Albi Cottage immediately on receiving them. As it is, I thank you from my heart for your merry mocking song. Though they did not seriously intend to make me a happy man, they have certainly made me a very proud one. I have attempted some verses in the style of your own beautiful lines, and hope you will laugh gently at their imperfections, for they are the first, with a trifling exception, that I have written for years. Would they were better worthy of their subject! A new edition of the humble writings which have been so fortunate to meet with your approbation has recently been published here. It is, to use the printer's phrase, "prettily gotten up." Will you pardon the liberty I take in asking you to accept a copy from me, in consideration of the beauty of the type and the vastness of its margin, and may I hope for a return to this letter,

---

[74] Miss Flanner's verses were first printed, so far as I am aware, in an article by J. M. Kerr entitled "The Bachelor-Poet and the Peasant-Girl," in *The Western* [St. Louis], V (N.S.), 466–477 (September, 1879).

[75] *Poetical Writings of Fitz-Greene Halleck* (New York, 1869), p. 228.

informing me by what conveyance I can have the honor of forwarding it to you?

I am, dear Miss Campbell, very gratefully, or, if you are in good earnest, as I very much fear you are not, I am, dearest Ellen, very affectionately yours,

FITZ-GREENE HALLECK.[76]

Numerous letters passed between the two. Those of the poet's have unfortunately been lost, but several of Miss Flanner's, probably found among Halleck's papers after his death, have been preserved by General Wilson. In a letter dated March 26, 1836, the young Quakeress wrote: "I know not whether to thank you 'Glorious Stranger,' for having created a new era in my existence, or to lament that your goodness and condescension have done me a deep and irreparable injury. I feel that I am no longer the unambitious, contented cottage-maid, with wishes and hopes confined within her humble sphere."[77] In her next letter she remarked: "Though, as a gentleman, it can afford you no gratification to be a subject of personal interest to a simple *paysanne* whom you have never seen, and never will, yet as a poet, you will not scorn the conviction that your tuneful lyre has made your name a word of music and beauty in the rural cottages and beneath the 'Buckeye' shades of the far West. Perhaps a stronger evidence that it breathes the eloquence of truth and nature, than that it is a theme of pride and approbation among the 'savans' of your fair Eastern land."[78] "The term of my privilege will soon expire," observed Miss Flanner on November 20, 1836. "This is probably the last time I shall ever address you, but e'er I make my parting bow, permit me to return my most sincere and cordial thanks for the gentle courtesy with which you have entertained my idle folly, and more than crowned my most ambitious hopes."[79] But the correspondence did not cease with the beginning of the new year. A letter from the young lady, dated February 8, 1837, opened in the following way: "I certainly did suppose I had written to Mr. Halleck for the last time; but you know, before I confess it, that I am but too happy to be convinced by your profound 'logic' that it is not only my privilege, but duty, to acknowledge how much I am indebted to you for your last kind

76 W. H. Hunter, *op. cit.*, p. 311.   77 *Life*, p. 377.
78 *Ibid.*, pp. 381–382. The letter is dated September 25, 1836.
79 *Ibid.*, p. 384.

and humorous epistle."[80] A final letter of Miss Flanner is dated April 18, 1837.[81]

So much of the actual correspondence remains. William H. Hunter, however, asserts that the poet finally announced his intention of visiting Albi Cottage. "This proposal filled Miss Flanner with dismay. Remembering she had commenced the acquaintance, she reflected that a tacit agreement to the poet's wish would place her in the character of a wooer.[82] . . . She absolutely refused him a personal interview and succeeded in eluding his attempts to find her."[83] Thus ended this curiously romantic episode in Halleck's life,—"the beginning, . . . as if directed by Divine inspiration, the ending, so full of pathos that the most austere of the staid Quakers of the village must have been moved to tears by the manifestation of fortitude by this woman of genius, whose sense of honor was so strong, that although she loved him, it would not permit her to entertain the advances of one of America's greatest poets because she herself, in a jest, had opened the way for a proposal."[84] Many years later, after the poet's return to Guilford, he wrote to a friend concerning his romance with Miss Flanner. "Your allusion to the Ohio River alike surprises and delights me," he said, "for it induces me more confidently to hope that you will hasten to give happy tidings of the welfare of the lady you name, the heroine of one of my life's most cherished romances, whose memory has heretofore been numbered among the dearest of my inconsiderable joys."[85] But Miss Flanner, who had married a Mr. Talbot, was already dead.

Despite the tragedy which the sentimental are prone to read into the story, it is doubtful whether Halleck ever took seriously

---

[80] *Ibid.*, p. 385.   [81] *Ibid.*, p. 387.

[82] Some thirty-five years ago a paper, said to have been written by Halleck, was read before a literary society of Guilford on the propriety of women proposing marriage to the other sex. An old resident of Guilford who related this to me, knew nothing of the present location of the paper, if, indeed, it had been preserved.

[83] W. H. Hunter, *op. cit.*, pp. 312–313.   [84] *Ibid.*, pp. 307–308.

[85] Wilson, *Life*, p. 391. The letter is dated August 4, 1858, and was addressed to Richard Lawrence. A brief portion of this letter concerning Halleck's relations with Miss Flanner is contained in the article in the *Post* for April 27, 1868, from which a quotation has already been made in the footnotes. The article, we have noted, was signed "F.L.," who was probably one of the Lawrence family.

this flirtation with Miss Flanner. With his peculiarly chivalric bent of mind, he probably derived for the time a real pleasure from corresponding with her; but at forty-five he had doubtless already shown a similar platonic affection for a score of women. It was perhaps this gallantry of feeling toward all women that made him truly in love with none. But it was a mood too long indulged in now to be easily shaken off. Halleck, who has been described as "a brisk young buck who gently slid into a blasé old buck,"[86] found himself, as the years slipped by, less and less a part of the world about him. Occasional echoes of a lingering sadness come to us as we examine the records of his life at this period. In a letter addressed in 1836 to an unknown correspondent Bryant pictured the poet as a lonely, solitary figure. "I met Mr. Halleck the other day," he wrote, "he enquired about you, as he always does. He says the world is going back; that nothing is talked of but stocks and lots and speculations; that many of his old acquaintances, who were formerly rational companions, are now so sordid in their conversation that it is absolutely intolerable, and therefore he has forsworn society altogether."[87] Three years later, in his published "Translation from the German of Goethe," Halleck may have voiced something of his own loneliness of soul during these years.

> They hear not these my last songs, they whose greeting
>   Gladdened my first; my spring-time friends have gone,
> And gone, fast journeying from that place of meeting,
>   The echoes of their welcome, one by one.
> Though stranger crowds, my listeners since, are beating
>   Time to my music, their applauding tone
> More grieves than glads me, while the tried and true,
> If yet on earth, are wandering far and few.[88]

These retrospections, sad as they doubtless were, Halleck never allowed entirely to take possession of him. If he had at length become weary of a life of "stocks and lots and speculations," he had learned how to dispel his languor. He no longer sought in writing poetry a refuge from this "bank-note world"; it was the society of men to which he now turned. The reticence and shyness of his

---

[86] V. L. Parrington, *Main Currents in American Thought*, II, 200.

[87] P. Godwin, *A Biography of William Cullen Bryant*, I, 317. The letter is dated May 22, 1836.

[88] Third stanza. *The Poetical Works of Fitz-Greene Halleck* (1869), p. 62.

early manhood had gradually given place to a delightful clubable-
ness, which, if it kept him from the art of poetry, made him more
the cheerful companion and gallant gentleman. In spite of the un-
dercurrent of loneliness which seems in part to have saddened his
life, these were years of contentment and freedom from financial
worry. Thus his social instincts were given ample opportunity to
develop. Halleck had learned how, in moments of leisure, to throw
off the pressure of business, and seize the employment which the
moment afforded. "Early in the day," asserts a friend of the poet,
"he looked the man of business, but in the afternoon and evening
he was radiant with wit and fine spirits."[89] His powers as a conversationalist are attested by many a companion of these last years
in New York. H. T. Tuckerman writes: "Halleck's social creed and
sentiment were singularly chivalric: that is the best word I can
summon to express that rare 'heart of courtesy' he possessed—
manliness coalesced with goodfellowship therein.[90] . . . His store
of literary and historical anecdote [he] applied, with singular tact
and original interpretation, to whatever tendency or trait happened to be under consideration. From a very wide and desultory
range of reading, and a social experience rendered vivid by quickness of sensibility and alacrity of insight—fused, as it were, in the
alembic of a mind of active intuitions—these gleanings from life
and lore had with him a certain vitality and significance which
made them impressive. There was no display or pedantry in the
process; the effect was exactly the reverse of that we so often experience at a so-called literary dinner, when 'cut-and-dried' quotations and illustrations are produced like patterns from a shelf—
suggestive of college cramming. Halleck's mind, at such times, was
like a bubbling spring, when the crystal water played forth spon-
taneously bringing now grains of gold, and now a flower's leaf to
the surface. It was this natural richness and spontaneity that made
his talk so charming."[91] "Halleck's word-painting," comments
another friend, "was far more vividly done in conversation than
in verse; and no one of his acquaintances denied his redundancy
of language and exhaustless store of aphorism, which, with his
gems of original ideas, enabled him to throw off sentence after

89 W. A. Jones in Wilson, *Life*, p. 540.
90 *Lippincott's Magazine*, I, 210 (February, 1868).
91 *Ibid.*, I, 212.

sentence, as brilliant as diamonds, surrounding opalescent ideas of a kindly sentiment for every son and daughter of Adam.''[92] ''Though ever attracted to him by the manly sentiment of his poetry,'' writes Evert A. Duyckinck in his memoir of the poet, ''we were not aware, till we knew him personally, of the winning manner which he displayed in intercourse with his companions, and how acquaintanceship ripened into the warmest allegiance of friendship.[93] . . . It may not be easy to convey to those who did not know him the impression of his sparkling, animated look, the zest of his discourse, as his bright eye kindled and the expressive lines of his face wrinkled in unison as the mirthful jest came to his lips. As a wit, he would say sharp things—his manliness found vent in this way—but he would sheathe a sarcasm in the most re-fined of compliments. He did not go about inflicting misery by lying in wait to utter bitter reproaches of his fellows; but if assumption came in his way, his rapier was out and the bladder pricked on the instant. . . . This was the discriminating character of Halleck's humor—infusing a dash of sarcasm into the sentiment to keep it from spoiling. A man of sensibility and not ashamed to display it, he had none of the weakness of a sentimentalist.[94] . . . Halleck's conversational powers were of the first order, not in debate, but in sparkling suggestions, and, in his later years, with the privilege of age and influenced by a partial deafness, a species of monologue. . . . His champagne-talk was fresh and sparkling, bubbling from the fount of his generous nature. For, indeed, whatever he spoke of, he had maturely considered; it was his own reading, his own obser-vation, his own way of thinking. We never heard a talker who em-broidered his discourse with more apposite stories and telling quotations.''[95]

When Halleck told Bryant that he had ''forsworn society alto-gether,''[96] he undoubtedly referred to formal gatherings where he disliked being made the center of attraction. ''He could rarely be prevailed upon to go to evening parties,'' writes James G. Wilson, ''and it was always considered an achievement to obtain the poet's promise to be one of the company on such occasions.''[97] He loved,

[92] Genio C. Scott in Wilson, *Life*, p. 486.
[93] *Putnam's Magazine*, I, 231 (February, 1868).
[94] *Ibid.*, I, 242.   [95] *Ibid.*, I, 243.
[96] See p. 272.   [97] *Life*, p. 480.

however, the quiet *café* and tavern, where alone or with a few friends he could pass a pleasant evening. Much of his time was, of course, spent at Villagrand's, a French establishment visited by many notables from abroad. Here he went to reside during his early years in New York,[98] and probably remained off and on for much of his stay in the city.[99] It was at this place that Halleck dined in company with Joseph Bonaparte,[100] and later with Louis Napoleon.[101] Another French tavern beloved of the poet for its old-world atmosphere is that described by Thomas L. Nichols. "I used to meet him almost every day," writes Dr. Nichols, "at a quiet little French café in Warren Street, opposite the City Hall. He came there to take his *demi tasse* and *petit verre*, and read the evening papers. On the walls hung pictures of the barricades of Paris, surmounted by the tricolor. In the rear were billiards clicking from morning till midnight. At the marble-top tables Frenchmen, Germans, and a few English and Americans who had got into continental habits, played chess and dominoes, and sipped absinthe, or, in warmer weather, iced claret punch and orgeat. It was the stillest public-house, I believe, in New York. You might sit for hours and hear nothing but the click of the billiard balls, the rattle of dominoes, and the 'check!' of the chess-players. The landlord was silence personified. He seldom got beyond a grunt. His face beamed with good-nature, but it never got further expression than some obscure mutterings."[102] The Bohemian atmosphere of the place has been delightfully described by another historian of the day. "In the more or less fashionable boarding-houses of the vicinity," observes Tuckerman, "smoking was deemed objectionable, and, therefore, many gentleman visited the *café* with diurnal regularity, to puff, prose or prophesy, according to the mood. Among them was a Canadian who had been a great traveler; a lawyer whose ambition was to illustrate jurisprudence by belles-lettres; an old native of Holland who wrote Dutch verses and had been decorated by his king; Fenno Hoffman, the stanchest of literary Knickerbockers, fond of descanting, by the hour, upon the scenery, the old society, the bivalves, beauties, and legendary lore of his native State; Henry Inman, fresh from the easel, and the most genial of specula-

---

[98] See p. 41. [99] Wilson, *Life*, p. 296.
[100] See pp. 150–151. [101] See pp. 278–279.
[102] *Forty Years of American Life* (London, 1864), I, 351–352.

tive *raconteurs*. . . . Hither it was Halleck's 'custom of an after-noon' to adjourn, when his clerical duties were over, and here I first knew and often met him: it was exactly the kind of neutral ground whereon most favorably to encounter his special wit and worth; for he had then, in a great measure, cut loose from general society, and, though scrupulous in his *devoirs* to fashionable friends, there was a certain formality in his fulfilment thereof, which precluded much of the old familiar zest; partly, indeed, from want of opportunity, but in a measure, also, because, as the area of New-York society had widened, and new and strange ele-ments mingled there-with, like many others whose hair has begun to silver, the 'favored guest' of the mothers was too much in rela-tion with the past, and too little in personal sympathy with the present, to find satisfaction in the sphere of their daughters, where his own presence and prestige had become a tradition. . . . Ac-cordingly it was in such casual and cosy social nooks as our *café*, and among genial companions, that Halleck then sought and gave social entertainment.''[103]

Another charming account of Halleck's convivial propensities has been preserved by Duyckinck in the words of Richard E. Mount. ''About fifteen years ago,'' writes Mr. Mount, ''an eccen-tric but learned and estimable physician from London, Doctor Banks, who had roamed the world with more heart than purse, settled in this city, lived a few years and died. Him Halleck knew and loved to meet. He imported directly from the London docks wine, in his estimation not to be bought here, also various edible dainties. His sherry was a favorite with our poet, and often have we three met at the old Doctor's office to sup and talk—there were no coarse bacchanalian bumpers there. This same old Banks was also a peripatetic, and I recollect his discovery of an ale-house at Brook-lyn where the English mistress was superior in her choice of barn-yards and their cooking. Halleck appreciated this, and told me that he often went there. Turning my steps thither one day, I met Hal-leck returning from the spot, redolent of its cheer. Anticipating my movement, he hailed me with some rollicking intimation of the crisping duck. I often endeavored to get him to dine with a few friends at the Union Club and elsewhere; but he invariably declined. This, however, was in late years. I fancied that he was afraid of being 'called out'—for of this American propensity he had a horror—or that expectation would be aroused, and the company disappointed.''[104] The poet's love of social retirement and his fear of being ''called out'' are fittingly suggested in an anecdote related by Genio C. Scott. In passing a German tavern in Chatham Street one evening, Halleck was tempted, by a sign of invitation at the door, to partake of its hospitality. ''He therefore entered the room of the society, and quietly took a seat and called for a mug of beer, thinking that no one present knew him, that he could unobtrusively enjoy an hour of music and German anecdote. He sat for half an hour very much interested, when the president of the society arose, and with his gavel called the house to order, stating, 'Gentlemen, please come to order. We are honored to-night by the presence of a distinguished gentleman, who is no less than Fitz-Greene Halleck, the greatest poet of America. I therefore move that he be made an honorary member of our society, and that he be invited to a seat at the right of the president for this evening. Those in favor please signify by saying ay.' The spontaneous burst of welcome took our friend quite aback, as the president named a committee of two to wait upon Mr. Halleck to the seat of honor; but, before being seated, he returned thanks in modest terms, and retired so soon as the meeting adjourned, but he was never seen there again.''[105]

Halleck had several other favorite resorts. One of these was an alehouse kept by William Reynolds, an eccentric Englishman who came from Staffordshire in 1815, and finally retired to Fort Lee, where on many a Sunday afternoon in summer Halleck continued to enjoy his hospitality.[106] Another, called ''Old Shakespeare Tavern,'' stood until 1836 at the corner of Fulton and Nassau Streets. ''Here, De Witt Clinton was wont to discuss his pet project, the Erie Canal; here Fitz-Greene Halleck, and Sands, and Percival, and Paulding, and Willis Gaylord Clark,[107] have met in social converse and passed many a merry and brilliant repartee; here, too,

---

[104] *Putnam's Magazine*, XI, 241.   [105] Wilson, *Life*, pp. 487–488.

[106] *Ibid.*, pp. 411 ff. See also Duyckinck in *Putnam's Magazine*, XI, 240–241; and Bryant in *Some Notices of the Life and Writings of Fitz-Greene Halleck*, p. 20.

[107] Willis G. Clark, twin brother of Louis G. Clark, who was many years editor of the *Knickerbocker*.

McDonald Clarke, the 'Mad Poet,' has often startled the little circle gathered around him by one of his strange outbursts of poetic frenzy.''[108] Occasionally, too, Halleck loved to spend an evening at the tavern of Francis Monteverde in Barclay Street, the gathering place of literary men of the day.[109]

Among the men whose friendship Halleck renewed during these years was Charles Mathews, the English comedian. Halleck had met Mathews on the actor's first visit to America, and had enjoyed his company. He could vividly recall a trip up the Hudson with Mathews, ''on board the Chancellor Livingstone, in the year 1823, on which occasion the mirth-inspiring Matthews [sic] had constantly around him an admiring and amused circle, including the novelist Cooper, Halleck, Dr. De Kay, Dr. John W. Francis, Dunlap, the dramatic author, and other notabilities of the day.'' The group ''sat up nearly the whole night, in the captain's cabin, listening to the inimitable songs, stories, and impersonations, of the . . . actor. On the occasion of Charles Matthews's second visit to this country, in 1835, Halleck gave him a supper at Windust's. Many choice spirits —literary and dramatic—were present. In the words of a survivor, 'It was a great night. I have never seen one like it since. Halleck was called up for a speech, and was succeeded by Matthews, who imitated the poet's manner and voice so successfully that it appeared impossible that we were not listening to Halleck. It was a famous occasion, sir!' ''[110]

Halleck's convivial propensities are further reflected in the acquaintanceship he formed in 1837 with Louis Napoleon, who had been recently shipped to America by the French authorities. For a time Louis occupied a conspicuous place in the society of the city. Among the literary men with whom he was brought in contact were Washington Irving, who entertained him at Sunnyside,[111] and Fitz-Greene Halleck. Louis Napoleon and Halleck seem to have got on well together. The poet sat beside Louis at a dinner party given

---

[108] William L. Stone, *History of New York City* (New York, 1872), pp. 488–490.

[109] Francis Brinley, *Life of William T. Porter* (New York, 1860), p. 92.

[110] Wilson's article ''Halleck and His Theatrical Friends'' in *Potter's American Monthly*, IV, 220 (March, 1875).

[111] See Pierre Irving, *Life and Letters of Washington Irving*, III, 116–117.

by Chancellor Kent of Columbia,[112] and later he and the prince exchanged dinners.[113] Of Louis Napoleon, Halleck once remarked to James Grant Wilson: "'Tis indeed strange. I thought him a dull fellow, which he certainly was while among men, but sprightly enough when surrounded by young ladies. He would sometimes say, 'When I shall be at the head of affairs in France,' or 'When I become emperor,' and I then looked upon him as being as mad as a March hare, or as my poor friend McDonald Clarke.'"[114]

The poet's leisure was further diversified at this time by meetings with friends who would not allow him entirely to forget his literary connections. At the bookstore of Bartlett and Welford Halleck passed many a pleasant evening with acquaintances who were charmed with his conversation;[115] and at the home of Charles M. Leupp, who "derived great pleasure in the society of men of letters," the poet probably met Bryant, Verplanck, and Hackett, the comedian.[116] Philip Hone, at one time mayor of New York, has recorded in his journal for 1836 a meeting of the Book Club, which gathered "every other Thursday evening at Washington Hotel, where they sup, drink champagne and whiskey punch, talk as well as they know how, and run each other good-humoredly." Here Hone spent an evening in company with Halleck and other notables of the city.[117] It was also in April of the following year that several authors of New York organized a club of which Washington Irving was elected president, and Fitz-Greene Halleck vice-president. The club, it is said, included among its members prominent literary men of the city such as Cooper, Hoffman, De Kay, and Morris. Little else, however, is known of the organization, and it is probable it never enjoyed a flourishing existence.[118]

---

[112] Wilson, *Life*, p. 404.   [113] *Ibid.*, p. 405.

[114] *Ibid.*, p. 404. Doctor Thomas L. Nichols in *Forty Years of American Life* (London, 1864) says of Halleck: "He had stories of Napoleon and Wellington, both of whom were his favourites. He knew the present emperor when he was in New York, and thought him 'rather a dull fellow,' as, in fact, he seemed to many persons who did not know what he was up to" (I, 352).

[115] Horace H. Moore in Wilson, *Life*, p. 464.

[116] James Wynne, *Harper's New Monthly Magazine*, XXIV, 639 (April, 1862).

[117] *Diary*, entry for March 16, 1835 (I, 134–135). On October 30, 1834, Hone noted in his journal a family dinner party at which were present, among others, Irving, Halleck, and Charles Mathews, the English comedian (*ibid.*, I, 116). This was during the elder Mathews' second visit to America.

[118] Wilson, *Life*, p. 400. Pierre Irving makes no mention of this club in his

On March 30, 1837, a complimentary dinner was given to the
authors of New York by the booksellers of the city, "at the close
of their semi-annual trade sale."[119] Among those who attended the
affair, which was held at the City Hotel, and has been described by
Philip Hone as "the greatest dinner I was ever at,"[120] were Irving,
Paulding, Poe, Bryant, Inman, Hoffman, Morris, and Halleck.[121]
Halleck at the dinner was twice honored by speakers. John Keese,
the well-known anthologist and editor, who acted as toastmaster,
paid the following compliment to the poet:

We desire still further to explore the mind where mental ore lies buried,
to awaken slumbering genius, and to call into active exercise the dormant
energy and shrinking talent of our young and much-loved land. Why
sleeps the Muse of Drake's twin-brother bard? Why comes not he forth
with fairy wand to silence the scribblers of the day? Who among us would
not esteem it a high honor to be his publisher, and to issue his beautiful
creations in a guise as beautiful as the taste of our best artisans can
exhibit?[122]

Again during the course of the evening Halleck was honored, this
time with a genuine ovation. "Mr. Washington Irving being called
upon for a toast at the late booksellers' jubilee," reported the
Mirror, "rose and observed that he meant to propose the health
of an individual whom he was sure all present would delight to
honour—of Samuel Rogers, the poet. Mr. Irving observed that in
a long intimacy with Mr. Rogers, he had ever found him an en-
lightened and liberal friend of America and Americans. . . . He
had also manifested on all occasions the warmest sympathy in the
success of American writers, and the promptest disposition to
acknowledge and point out their merits. I am led to these remarks,

Life and Letters of Washington Irving. In a catalogue of some "Autograph
Letters and Documents of General James Grant Wilson," issued by the Mer-
win Clayton Sales Company (May 16 and 17, 1905), we note the following
item (No. 255) which is now inaccessible: "Letter of Solyman Brown, Secy.
Author's Club, N. Y. May 17, 1837, to Halleck, informing him of the election
of Washington Irving as President, Halleck and J. Fenimore Cooper as Vice-
Presidents of the Club, with list of members."

[119] *Evening Post*, March 31, 1837.

[120] *Diary*, I, 249.

[121] *Evening Post*, April 3, 1837. See also the *American* and *Commercial
Advertiser* for April 3.

[122] William L. Keese, *John Keese, Wit and Littérateur* (New York, 1883),
p. 22.

added Mr. Irving, by a letter received yesterday from Mr. Rogers, acknowledging the receipt of a volume of Halleck's poems, which I had sent to him, and expressing his opinion of their merits. Mr. Irving here read the following extract from the letter:—'With Mr. Halleck's poems, I was already acquainted—particularly with the two first in the volume; and I cannot say how much I admired them always. They are better than anything we can do just now on our side of the Atlantick (Hear, hear!). I hope he will not be idle, but continue to delight us. When he comes here again he must not content himself with looking on the outside of my house, as I am told he did once, but knock and ring and ask for me as an old acquaintance (cheers). I should say, indeed, if I am here to be found, for if he or you, my dear friend, delay your coming much longer, I shall have no hope of seeing either of you on this side of the grave.' ''[123] Unfortunately, however, Halleck did not answer the burst of applause that followed the reading of the letter, in spite, as Wilson says, of De Kay's remonstrance, ''For God's sake, Fitz, get on your feet.''[124]

The following month[125] Columbia College celebrated the fiftieth anniversary of its founding. On this occasion Halleck received the honorary degree of Master of Arts. ''Never, since the first creation of 'Old Queens' has the college witnessed a scene so impressive,'' said the *New York Mirror* in describing the anniversary exercises. ''The day proved a remarkably fine one, and the library was filled, at an early hour, with citizens and strangers, many of whom had come from a distance to share in the jubilee. At half-past ten, the procession was formed on the college green. . . . The procession passed through several of the publick streets until it reached Hudson Square, where, halting to form anew in St. John's Park, which was thrown open for the occasion, it entered the chapel in reverse order.''[126] During the course of exercises which followed, honorary degrees were conferred upon Fitz-Greene Halleck, William Cullen Bryant, and Charles Fenno Hoffman.

[123] XIV, 359 (May 6, 1837).
[124] *Life*, p. 399. Samuel Rogers was a genuine admirer of Halleck's poetry, as will be further seen from a letter addressed to Halleck by J. G. Cogswell. See Wilson, *Life*, pp. 273–274.
[125] April 13, 1837.
[126] XIV, 351 (April 29, 1837). See also the *New York Commercial Advertiser* for April 14, 1837.

Toward the close of the thirties Halleck resumed for a short time an interest in publication. His "Translation from the German of Goethe,"[127] a paraphrase of the "Dedication" to the first part of *Faust,* to which attention has already been called, appeared in the *New York Mirror* for June 29, 1839. We find no record of Halleck's knowledge of German, and it is probable that he had no first-hand acquaintance with the language. William B. Cairns, in speaking of the influence of German literature in America during the years prior to 1833, has observed that our literature at this period "shows relatively few quotations from German authors, or references to German ideas. The language was little studied. Some of the magazines contain original verses in French and Italian, but none in German."[128] Halleck, we have found, was little in sympathy with German literature, and his antipathy to Goethe's *Faust* is well known, although that antipathy appears not to have included the "Dedication."[129] The chances are that the "Translation" which appeared in the *Mirror* was a paraphrase of a French or even English translation of Goethe's lines. "We are happy to be enabled once more to publish an Original Poem from the pen of Mr. Halleck," commented the editor in presenting the poem. "There is no writer in the United States for whose productions the public clamour is so loud and frequent. The following is not unworthy of the most inspired moments of the author of 'Alnwick Castle' and the lines upon Burns."[130]

In April, 1839, Halleck wrote to his sister concerning new editions of his poems which Harper & Brothers were about to publish. "I have entered into an agreement with Messrs. Harper and Brothers of this city," said the poet, "for the publication of some of my writings, in two parts. First, 'Fanny and other Poems'; second, 'Poems by Fitz-Greene Halleck.' They are to print immediately fifteen hundred copies of each, and give me their note at six months from the completion of the printing, for my proportion, which is to be twenty-five cents per copy. I retain the copyright in my possession, but they are to be allowed to print as many editions hereafter as the market may require, on the same terms."[131]

[127] First collected in the edition of 1845.
[128] *On the Development of American Literature from 1815 to 1833, with Especial Reference to Periodicals* (Madison, Wisconsin, 1898), p. 21.
[129] See pp. 187–188.   [130] XVII, 4 (June 29, 1839).
[131] Wilson, *Life,* p. 409. The letter is dated April 13, 1839.

The first volume mentioned by Halleck—*Fanny with Other Poems*[132]—made its appearance probably about the middle of August, 1839. With the exception of a single pirated edition of *Fanny*,[133] no American edition of the poem had been brought out since 1820. Many of the places and persons to whom allusion had been made twenty years before were still fresh in people's minds, and a new printing of *Fanny* had long been called for. "We wonder that Mr. Halleck has not before listened to the repeated demands of the public for a new edition of this popular poem," commented the *Mirror*. " 'Better late than never,' however. 'Fanny' never appeared in a more becoming dress than that in which she now is to be seen. She has lost none of her charms, and is likely to prove as much of a belle as she was at her first 'coming out.' To drop the language of hyperbole, we will simply inform our readers that an engraved view of Weehawken adorns the volume, which is enriched with a variety of the uncollected poems[134] of Halleck."[135] Curiously enough, the second volume, to which the poet referred in his letter to Miss Halleck, did not appear, for some unknown reason, until 1845.

In 1840 Harper & Brothers also published Halleck's *Selections from the British Poets*,[136] which appeared in two volumes as numbers 112 and 113 of the *Family Library*. This library, which consisted of many standard works of the day, was one of the earliest attempts in America to publish in inexpensive form the best in literature, biography, and history. In preparing this anthology of English poetry it is probable that Halleck did little special reading in connection with the work. He seems to have relied to a considerable

[132] This is the title actually printed,—not "Fanny and other Poems" as mentioned by Halleck in his letter.

[133] See p. 377.

[134] In addition to *Fanny*, the poems included were: "To W*lt*r B*wne, Esq."; "To ******" ("Dear ***, I am writing, not *to* you, but *at* you"); "A Fragment" ("His shop is a grocer's"); "Song, by Miss ***" ("The winds of March are humming"); "Song, for the Drama of the Spy"; "Address at the Opening of a new Theatre"; "The Rhyme of the Ancient Coaster."

[135] XVII, 63 (August 17, 1839). Other reviews of the volume appeared in the *Corsair*, I, 348 (August 10); in the *Knickerbocker*, XIV, 283 (September, 1839); and in the *Ladies' Companion*, XI, 248 (September, 1839).

[136] Wilson states that Halleck received $500 for editing the *Selections* (*Life*, p. 532). In 1840 Bryant also brought out in the same series a volume of *Selections from the American Poets*.

extent upon Thomas Campbell's *Specimens of the British Poets;*[137] and it is likely that he was also indebted to other important anthologies of the day. In the second volume ample space is devoted to his favorites, Moore, Byron, and Campbell. It is to be regretted, however, that Halleck contributed no introduction to the collection.

[137] Halleck's debt to Campbell is particularly evident in the selections from the minor poets.

XI

LAST YEARS IN NEW YORK

1841–48

HALLECK's last years in New York were ones of happiness. The recipient of a good salary from Astor, he was now left free to enjoy the social life which the city afforded. Only partially was he aware of the spiritual struggle that had weakened his life. If there was "something like isolation in his heart,"[1] he was still with hardly a trace of morbid regret for what his life had been. Practicality had been his Puritan inheritance, and to this overmastering principle he had instinctively surrendered himself. Yet at the same time he had pathetically clung to those things that point the way to the ideal world—that feed the hungry imagination. That he was now exhausted by the struggle of the ideal and the practical no one can deny. Years before he had lost the joy of creation, and he had now come to find burdensome any tax put upon his poetic imagination. What he had given to Barker and Astor could never be reclaimed.

If the struggle left him without morbidness and ill temper, it deeply affected his attitude toward the everyday world in which he lived. The inevitable reaction from practicality had brought with it a curious distrust of that very principle.[2] The ideal world in which he sought an escape had blinded him for a *rounded* life in the world of actuality. He could perform through custom the duties laid upon him in Wall Street, but he found it difficult to grasp the meaning of practicality as he daily encountered it in American life. The restless energy of his youth and early manhood had, in fact, settled into a smug conservatism, which, if tempered by a genial whimsicality, was none the less deep seated. Fear of the present—love of the past now became a ruling passion. It is true that he was never entirely free from those qualities which made

---

[1] James Lawson in the *Southern Literary Messenger*, VIII, [2]44.

[2] William Gilmore Simms once wrote: "[Halleck] seemed to me to revolt from all associations of trade, in spite of all his life-long connection with it, and, perhaps, because of that connection" (Wilson, *Life*, p. 545).

him a gentleman rather of the English than of the American mold. "Dislike of change"[3] and a formal courtesy in his dealings with men were doubtless innate; but time had served to strengthen them. During Halleck's last years in New York, he became conspicuous for his dogged insistence upon conservative and reactionary principles. "Halleck would not allow himself to be 'dragged along' in the procession of modern progress, like Lamb," wrote his friend, Tuckerman; "he left it, and stood, in silent protest, a spectator thereof; not without recognition of the good sought and achieved, or sympathy with the humane aspirations and scientific triumphs thereof, but planted firmly on the original instinctive and essential needs and traits of humanity, which he deemed too often overlaid, ignored, and profaned in the rush and presumption bred of material success and arrogant intellectual pretension. He pleaded for the sanctions and the safety of Authority as an element indispensable to the peace and prosperity of the world; of Reverence as a sentiment without which the beauty of human life was desecrated; of Individuality—as to rights, development, and self-respect—constantly invaded by encroachments of what are called popular principles, but which are too often social despotisms. In his isolation, as the champion of such conservative convictions, he would, with a kind of grim jest, overshoot the mark, and startle by extreme statement."[4] The lines of this picture of Halleck have been still further deepened by the pen of the poet, Bayard Taylor: "I can see, now, to what extent his later life was an anachronism,—and utterly without his power to change the fact. No gentleman of Copley's painting, stepped out of his frame into the life of our day, could have found himself more alien to our literary tastes and prevalent political views. Nay, it even seemed that Halleck's nature was an instance of what Darwin terms the 'reversionary tendency' —the sudden reappearance of an original type, after a long course of variation; for he was neither republican, democratic in the ordinary sense, Protestant, nor modern. He was congenitally monarchical, feudal, knightly, Catholic, and mediaeval; but above all, *knightly*. I do not suppose that he had any curious habit of introversion, but a delicate natural instinct told him that he did not

[3] See R. W. Emerson, *English Traits*, Section 6, paragraph 15, "The English power resides also in their dislike of change," etc.

[4] *Lippincott's Magazine*, I, 212–213 (February, 1868).

belong—or had belonged only for a short time—to this century; and he accepted the fact as he would have accepted any fate which did not include degradation."[5]

If Halleck could recognize the possibility of a "nature's aristocracy," he found it difficult to accept a rampant republicanism. "Tell me not," he once exclaimed, "of the blessings of a free country, where any unprincipled blackguard, with money enough to buy types and paper, can blacken my reputation and ruin my fortune, and I have no redress or adequate remedy."[6] This hypothetical case was vividly reduced to the concrete for Halleck by the experiences of his friend, James Fenimore Cooper. The novelist's continued censure of American politics and manners[7] had brought upon his head the vicious attacks of several newspaper editors. His final triumph over his antagonists after a long series of litigations[8] distinctly pleased Halleck, who wrote to Cooper on January 18, 1843, congratulating him on the successful termination of his suits:

I have hoped to have the pleasure of handing you the enclosed in person, but have not been so fortunate as to find you at your lodgings. Allow me to congratulate you upon your success thus far in combating the spirit of Evil, embodied in a work of that evil disposed person John Milton, the author of a defense of "the liberty of *unlicensed* printing."[9]

To the end Halleck retained a disgust for the principles set forth in the *Areopagitica*. Writing to a friend in 1863 he again voiced the same opinion: "The other 'bits' inclosed will also, I think, amuse you as specimens of the liberty taken by our editors with that much-puffed 'Liberty of the Press,' which I have the honour of agreeing with Louis Napoleon in considering a public nuisance."[10]

---

[5] *North American Review*, CXXV, 64 (July, 1877).

[6] Tuckerman in *Lippincott's Magazine*, I, 213.

[7] See *Homeward Bound* (1838) and *Home as Found* (1838).

[8] Cooper once characteristically remarked, "I have beaten every man I have sued who has not retracted his libels" (Duyckinck, *Cyclopaedia of American Literature*, II, 111).

[9] *Correspondence of James Fenimore-Cooper*, II, 490. There can be little doubt of Halleck's dislike of Milton as a man. Note, for example, these lines from "Connecticut" (1869 ed., p. 80):

> Yet Milton, weary of his youth's young wife,
> To her, to king, to church, to law untrue,
> Warred for divorce and discord to the knife,
> And proudest wore his plume of darkest hue.

[10] Wilson, *Bryant and His Friends*, p. 273. The letter is dated March 2, 1863.

Lost amid a growing republicanism whose noisy rabble he could not understand, Halleck had nothing left but to assert his monarchical principles. He was not a snob;[11] his chivalric disposition would have revolted at such a suggestion. His prejudice lay rather in the fact that he had lost contact with the modern world. His mind, grown instinctively to revert to the political and religious institutions of the past, had found in this reversion something of the escape for which his imagination craved. It was no doubt more than a passing sentiment which made him say, on his becoming a Freemason, "that when touched upon the head and knighted by the Grand-Master, who saluted him with these words, 'Arise, Sir Fitz-Greene,' he felt like a knight of old time newly anointed by his sovereign."[12] Although many of his remarks on monarchism were, of course, prompted by the spirit of playfulness, a residuum of truth usually remained after the persiflage had melted away. Somewhat shocked was Bryant, when Halleck and the elder Richard Henry Dana, once his guests at dinner, "talked monarchism," and insisted upon being taken in earnest.[13] And certainly it was more than a momentary prejudice that made Halleck once remark that "the ship of state must be governed and navigated like any other ship, without consulting the crew." "What would become of the stanchest bark in a gale," continued the poet, "if the captain were obliged to call all hands together and say: 'All you who are in favor of taking in sail, will please say, aye.' "[14] If we are to accept Dr. Johnson's definition of a Tory as "one who adheres to the ancient constitution of the state, and the apostolical hierarchy of the Church of England," we are doubtless justified in calling Halleck by that name. He is said to have been "an admirer of the British constitution,"[15] and to have called "her form of govern-

---

[11] The snobbishness suggested by "An Epistle to Robert Hogbin, Esq." (see pp. 240–241) is not a dominant mood in Halleck's writings. Dr. Thomas Nichols relates the following incident of Halleck's meeting with a Negro friend: "I was walking in Broadway one day with the poet Halleck, when he stopped, turned back, took off his hat to, and shook hands with, this negro, then a white-headed old man. After a few words with him, he rejoined me and told me his story" (Forty Years of American Life, II, 240).

[12] Horace H. Moore in Wilson, Life, pp. 469–470.

[13] R. H. Dana in a letter written in August, 1866 (Wilson, Life, p. 542).

[14] Bryant, Some Notices of the Life and Writings of Fitz-Greene Halleck, p. 35.

[15] James Lawson in the Southern Literary Messenger, VIII, [2]44.

ment the best the world has known.''[16] Indeed, late in life Halleck wrote of himself as "an open, frank, outspeaking, and avowed monarchist, devoted to the godly government of the one, and detesting the ungodly government of the many.''[17] To him a king was sacred. He much resented Thackeray's free-handed way of dealing with George the Fourth, whom the poet regarded as "the first gentleman of Europe." After listening a few moments to the lecture, he said to a companion: "I am going. I can't listen any longer to his abuse of a better man than himself"; and they quickly left the hall.[18]

Halleck carefully avoided any participation in American politics. From the days of "The Croakers" to his death he had nothing but contempt for "the solecisms in manners, the vulgar assumptions, the official ignorance, and social incongruities born of, or identified with, the democratic rule."[19] It was partly his natural judicial temper and partly his inherent aristocracy of mind that made possible this aloofness from political issues. Like Irving, weary of "American provinciality,"[20] he stood an impartial spectator of party disputes. Halleck "was a member of neither dominant party," it is said, "and carefully avoided any interference either in local or general elections."[21] He was also "fond of saying that he had never voted for a President."[22] At the close of his life Halleck summed up in a letter to a friend the conclusion to which he had finally come on the subject of American democracy:

With regard to the political topics of your letter, it is proper I should, at the risk of becoming tiresomely egotistical, tell you that, as a Federalist in my boyhood and a monarchist in my manhood, I prefer a government representing property, and, let me add, *probity*, to a government of numbers.

[16] Wilson, *Bryant and His Friends*, p. 274.

[17] Parke Godwin, *A Biography of William C. Bryant*, II, 200. From a letter, addressed to Bryant, dated November 24, 1863. For a further expression of Halleck's monarchical views, see James H. Hackett's "Reminiscences of the Poet Halleck" in the *Evening Post*, January 31, 1868.

[18] Wilson, *Life*, p. 506.

[19] H. T. Tuckerman in *Lippincott's Magazine*, I, 213.

[20] See Irving's *Knickerbocker's History of New York*, edited by Prof. S. T. Williams and Tremaine McDowell (New York [1927]), pp. lxx–lxxi.

[21] James Wynne in *Harper's New Monthly Magazine*, XXIV, 635 (April, 1862).

[22] Joel Benton in *Frank Leslie's Illustrated Newspaper*, XXV, 243 (January 4, 1868).

Under a democracy, a vote is of no value unless given for a candidate of an organized party or faction. To the discipline of such organizations I could not, and cannot submit. It demands the abandonment of the voter's freedom of action and opinion, and sooner or later he degenerates into a mere tool of a few party leaders, a class whom John Randolph used to characterize as "men of seven principles, five loaves and two small fishes."[23]

Democracy in church government pleased Halleck no more than democracy in politics. As he grew older, he leaned more and more toward the Roman Church, although he never formally joined himself to that communion. He took a great delight, however, in defending her faith. "It is a church," he would say, "which saves you a deal of trouble. You leave your salvation to the care of a class of men trained and set apart for the purpose; they have the charge both of your belief and your practice, and so long as you satisfy them on these points you need give yourself no anxiety about either."[24] Although it is true that Halleck's love of discussion and paradox led him, like Dr. Johnson, into absurd extravagances on the subject, there is reason to believe that he deeply respected the Roman creed. "It was not any ritualistic prejudice that induced this declaration of faith," writes H. T. Tuckerman, "but a way of embodying his conviction of the need and the auspicious influence of a church in the old sense of the term—a *Spiritual Power* organized and established on fixed canons for the conversion, the solace, discipline, guidance, and repose of erring, afflicted, wayward, and weary Humanity."[25] If Halleck craved the authority which the Roman faith afforded, he was likewise attracted by her esthetic appeal. "In the grand and imposing ceremonies of the Mass, amidst the peal of the organ, the rich decoration of the altar, and the burning incense," wrote a friend, "he finds a more truthful delineation of his own conceptions of a befitting worship of man to his Maker than in any other."[26] Although it is doubtful that Halleck at any time in his life ever regularly attended the Roman Church, one account of his attendance at service has been

[23] Wilson, *Life,* p. 565. The letter, addressed to Robert G. L. DePeyster, is dated September 12 [1867].

[24] Bryant, *Some Notices of the Life and Writings of Fitz-Greene Halleck,* p. 35.

[25] *Lippincott's Magazine,* I, 213.

[26] J. Wynne in *Harper's New Monthly Magazine,* XXIV, 639 (April, 1862).

preserved. "One Sunday morning," writes William Gowans, an old New York bookseller, "as I was passing a Roman Catholic church in the city of New York, seeing the doors open and throngs of people pressing in, I stepped inside to see what I could see, hear what I could hear, and learn what I could learn. I had not well got inside till I beheld Fitz-Greene Halleck standing uncovered, with reverential attitude, among the crowd, kneeling and standing, of unshorn and unwashed worshippers which can always be seen on Sundays both inside and out of these houses of worship, in irregular confusion, with little or no respect paid to them by the functionaries of the church or those who are wealthy enough to pay for comfortable pews. I remained till I saw him leave. In doing so he made a courteous bow, as is the polite custom by the humblest of these people on taking their departure. I immediately followed, and, on coming up, took the liberty to ask him if he was a member of this church. In reply, he said, '*I am not.*' "[27]

[27] Wilson, *Life*, pp. 432–433. During Halleck's lifetime and since, the question has often arisen whether or not the poet was a Romanist. His frequent declarations in favor of the Church led many to believe that he was. Dr. Thomas L. Nichols, for example, confidently asserted that he "was a zealous Roman Catholic, and maintained that every man who really thought upon the matter must come to the same conviction" (*Forty Years of American Life*, I, 352). Just after the poet's death, the Rev. Dr. Lorenzo Bennett, Rector of Christ Church in Guilford, denied this prevalent report in an open letter to the press. [Copies of this letter were sent to E. A. Duyckinck, who published it in *Putnam's Magazine*, XI, 262 (the original is preserved in the New York Public Library); and to J. G. Wilson, who published it in part in *Hours at Home*, VI, 367, and entire in the *Life*, pp. 591–594.] In spite of Halleck's own denial, as reported by Gowans, and of Dr. Bennett's authoritative statement, confirmed by the poet's sister, the discussion was again renewed by the *Catholic Transcript* (March 29, 1923). The author cast some doubt on Dr. Bennett's assertions, and declared that "it is quite possible . . . that the same piety which he displayed at the early Sunday Mass inspired him and sustained him in his Guilford home, where it would be possible for him, wonderful to relate, to cherish the Bible, and still cling to the tenets of the 'Romish' church." But there is no evidence that he ever accepted in full the tenets of Rome, much less entered the communion of the Church. The truth is that merely certain phases of the creed claimed his respect, or, in the words of Bayard Taylor, Halleck "expressed, in reality, the feeling of an Anglican Catholic who regretted the separation" (*North American Review*, CXXV, 65). It may be of significance to note that Halleck in 1839 contributed the sum of one hundred dollars toward the erection of a new building for the Episcopal Church in Guilford.

Halleck's sister, too, it would seem, was not prejudiced against the Roman Church. A resident of Guilford has informed me that the first time she ever saw the interior of a Catholic church was when Miss Halleck took her, a mere child, within the Guilford edifice.

There can be little doubt that these opinions, expressed without offense to any, made Halleck the more charming and picturesque to those who gathered round him. The moments spent in airing his political and religious views were, of course, but part of the social life which he had now come to love. He still instinctively shrunk from the many, finding his enjoyment in the circle of a few chosen friends. Occasionally, however, he would mingle gaily with the fashionable world. Such an opportunity was afforded by the visit which Charles Dickens made to America in 1842. Leaving Liverpool on the *Britannia* on January 4, 1842, the novelist reached the Boston harbor on the twenty-second of the month. The remaining days of January, Dickens and his lady spent in Boston, enjoying the hospitality which the city had to offer. Passing south by the way of Worcester, Hartford, and New Haven, the novelist arrived in New York on February 13, 1842. The city was prepared in advance for his reception. A public ball, to which he had already given assent, was held in Dickens' honor at the Park Theatre on February 14.[28] Fitz-Greene Halleck was present on the occasion. ''I remember the immense crowd of the 'beauty and fashion' of New York that filled the theatre from its dancing-floor, laid over stage and pit, to the gallery,'' wrote Dr. T. L. Nichols, who was present at the ball. ''I remember the mixed committee, official, fashionable and literary, and some who aspired to all these distinctions. I think Irving and Cooper were there—I am sure of Halleck and Bryant. Willis sported his ringlets there, no doubt; and can I ever forget the beaming, rosy, perspiring face of the American Körner, General George P. Morris?''[29] Dr. Nichols' memory did not fail him; Willis was present at the ball. ''When Mr. and Mrs. Dickens came to America in 1842,'' says Prof. Henry A. Beers, ''Willis ran down to New York to be present at the 'Boz' ball. He wrote to his wife at Glenmary that he had spent an afternoon in showing Mrs. Dickens the splendor of Broadway, and had danced with her at the ball, where encountering Halleck, the two poets 'slipped down about midnight to the ''Cornucopia'' and had rum toddy and broiled oysters.' ''[30]

While Dickens was still in Boston, the citizens of New York had

28 W. Glyde Wilkins, *Charles Dickens in America* (New York, 1912), p. 108.
29 *Forty Years of American Life*, I, 288.
30 *Nathaniel Parker Willis*, p. 264.

addressed a letter to the novelist congratulating him upon his safe arrival in this country, and requesting his presence at a dinner to be given in his honor. Among those who signed the note was Halleck.[31] Dickens accepted the invitation, and the dinner was given on Friday, February 18, 1842. Halleck, who was present, once related to General Wilson how Irving, whose shyness rendered it difficult for him to make after-dinner speeches, broke down before he could complete his address of welcome.[32] In the speech of Dickens which immediately followed, the novelist referred once to Halleck by name. After praising at length the work of Washington Irving, Dickens said, "But these are topics familiar from my boyhood, and which I am apt to pursue, and lest I should be tempted now to talk too long about him, I will in conclusion give you a sentiment— most appropriate, I am sure, in the presence of such writers as Bryant, Halleck, and —— But I suppose I must not mention the ladies here."[33] It may have been of this occasion that Halleck once spoke:

I well remember the night we gave a dinner to Dickens; our limited accommodations were more than full. It was at first designed to invoke the fair sex to grace the occasion; but happily remembering the fact that Boz was an Englishman, and might like to glide under the table "in the sma' wee hours," we dropped the idea altogether. Therefore, when we found that he remained perfectly sober, we regretted the absence of the ladies. We were rather chagrined when he published his Notes[34] and his novel to find no mention of ourselves. I for one was greatly pained at reading Martin Chuzzlewit, but trust in my heart Mr. Dickens will apologize for it before he dies, for the sake of his fame among so many warm friends here. I believe he will yet do so from the depths of his charitable nature.[35]

But Halleck came to know the novelist yet more intimately. Bryant, who was desirous of making the acquaintance of Dickens, had twice called upon him, but on each occasion had found him out. On February 14, 1842, Dickens wrote a note to Bryant, which read in part, "Now, I want to know when you will come and breakfast with me; and I don't call to leave a card at your door asking you,

31 Wilkins, *op. cit.*, pp. 122–123.
32 *Life*, p. 437. 33 Wilkins, *op. cit.*, p. 129.
34 *American Notes for General Circulation*, published in 1842.
35 From an article entitled "An Hour with Halleck" preserved as an unidentified clipping among the *Miscellaneous Papers* in the Manuscript Room of the New York Public Library.

because I love you too well to be ceremonious with you." "They breakfasted together at a time appointed," Parke Godwin, Bryant's biographer, goes on to say, "Halleck and Professor Charles Felton of Cambridge, being of the party, and a lively time they had of it. Felton, writing to Bryant afterward says, 'A breakfast with Bryant, Halleck, and Dickens is a thing to remember forever.' "[36] It may have been to this same breakfast party that Dickens invited Halleck in a very informal note, dated February 14, 1842: "Will you come and breakfast with me on Tuesday, the twenty-second, at half-past ten? Say yes. I should have been truly delighted to have a talk with you to-night (being quite alone), but the doctor says that if I talk to man, woman, or child, this evening, I shall be dumb to-morrow."[37] An interesting anecdote relating perhaps to the same Dickens breakfast at which Halleck was present, is told by Mr. Putnam in his article "Four Months with Charles Dickens," published in the *Atlantic Monthly*. "Mr. Dickens had to breakfast Irving, Bryant, and Halleck. The clerk of the Carleton was himself a great lover of literature, and remarked to me: 'Good Heaven! to think what the four walls of that room now contain! Washington Irving, William Cullen Bryant, Fitz-Greene Halleck, and Charles Dickens.' "[38]

Two other occasions have been recorded on which Halleck was in the company of Charles Dickens—one, a dinner "given at the Astor House by the Novelties Club, composed of New-York actors, artists, and editors";[39] another, a more exclusive affair, in the form of a private dinner at which Louis Gaylord Clark, editor of the *Knickerbocker*, was the host. Of this dinner, at which were present, among others, Bryant, Irving, and Brevoort, Dickens wrote a year later to Clark: "This day twelvemonth I dined at your house; the pleasantest dinner I enjoyed in America. What a company!"[40] Philip Hone also tells of a Dickens dinner given by Charles A. Davis, to which several distinguished guests, including Halleck, were invited. The novelist, however, was obliged through illness to disappoint them, and so, says Hone, "We had to perform the

[36] *A Biography of William Cullen Bryant*, I, 395–396.
[37] Wilson, *Life*, p. 438.
[38] XXVI, 480 (October, 1870).   [39] Wilson, *Life*, p. 438.
[40] See article entitled "Dickens" by L. G. Clark in *Harper's New Monthly Magazine*, XXV, 376 (August, 1862).

tragedy of 'Hamlet,' the part of Hamlet omitted; but we made a good thing of it notwithstanding the hiatus in our ranks.'[41]

Halleck was indeed much delighted with Dickens. In writing to Mrs. Rush on March 8, 1842, the poet said: "You ask about Mr. Boz. I am quite delighted with him. He is a thorough good fellow, with nothing of the author about him but the reputation, and goes through his task as Lion with exemplary grace, patience, and good nature. He has the brilliant face of a man of genius, and a pretty Scottish lassie for a wife, with roses on her cheeks, and 'een sae bonny blue.' His writings you know. I wish you had listened to his eloquence at the dinner here. It was the only specimen of eloquence I have ever witnessed. Its charm was not in its words, but in the manner of saying them.'[42] With the approach of Dickens' second visit to America, Halleck, then in his seventy-seventh year, was looking forward to renewing his acquaintance with the novelist. Only a short time before his death, he remarked to General Wilson, "I must come down and hear him [Dickens], and if he is not too much lionized, perhaps I can capture him, and we three, with Tuckerman, will have a quiet and cosy dinner together.'[43] Dickens also appears to have taken great pleasure in Halleck's company, judging from a letter which General Wilson received from the novelist a few months after Halleck's death. "I too had hoped to see *him!*" wrote Dickens. "My dear Irving being dead, there was scarcely any one in America whom I so looked forward to seeing again as our old friend often thought of.'[44]

Other records throw further light on Halleck's relations at this period with contemporary authors. It was probably during the forties that he came to know Richard Henry Stoddard, the American poet. "When and where I first met Halleck I have forgotten," writes Stoddard; "but it must have been about thirty years after the *annus mirabilis* which inspired this noble trio of Greek, Scot-

41 *Diary*, II, 118 (entry of February 16 [1842]).

42 Wilson, *Life*, p. 434.

43 *New York Daily Tribune*, November 23, 1867.

44 *Life*, p. 440. A brief article on Halleck appeared in *All the Year Round*, XIX, 496 (May 2, 1868), an English magazine "Conducted by Chas. Dickens." Whether or not Dickens was the author we have no means of knowing. Although the article was published after the poet's death, there is no mention of his decease. But the sketch may have been written before Dickens' departure for America (the latter part of January), and before he had heard of Halleck's death.

tish, and English lyrics.[45] It may have been in the editorial room of the *Home Journal,* where the rosy face of General Morris was lighted up with smiles at the unannounced entrance of the author of 'Fanny,' whom he was wont to compliment at the approach of each successive spring by reprinting his airy lines, 'The winds of March are humming.' Or it may have been at a small hotel on Broadway, whither he was brought by Dr. Griswold that he might pay his old-fashioned respects to Miss Alice Cary, whom the anthological doctor of the bards of America had introduced into the literary circles of New York. . . . There was between us, as he once observed, the bond of a clerkly occupation, and he used occasionally to drop in upon me at my room in the Custom-House. I treated him with the deference which was his due, and he treated me with a consideration which was hardly my due, for I was some thirty years his junior. Something about him, I can scarcely say what, reminded me of Lamb, whose odd and fantastic tastes I sometimes fancied I detected in his whimsical talk.'[46]

There were other American writers whose lives Halleck touched at this time. William Gilmore Simms, the novelist, who first visited New York in 1832, found the metropolis full of interest for one who aspired to letters. On several of his visits to the city, he met Irving, Cooper, and Halleck,[47] although his relations with these men were never intimate.[48] Simms, however, was much pleased with the company of Halleck, whom he found "a pleasant companion, genial and sparkling with humor, quick at repartee, and inclining to the sarcastic when speaking of pretension and pretenders."[49] The historian, William Hickling Prescott, was also numbered among the poet's friends. It was young Prescott, one may recall, who had admired the fresh wit of *Fanny,* and had invited Halleck to contribute to the *Club-Room.*[50] Many years elapsed, however, before he met the poet who had aroused his youthful ad-

---

[45] Stoddard had been previously speaking of "Marco Bozzaris," "Burns," and "Alnwick Castle."

[46] *Lippincott's Magazine,* XLIII, 895 (June, 1889).

[47] Simms writes, "We met occasionally during my summer visits annually to the North" (Wilson, *Life,* p. 543).

[48] William P. Trent, *William Gilmore Simms* (Boston, 1892), p. 157.

[49] From Simms's recollections of Halleck contributed to Wilson's *Life,* p. 543.

[50] See p. 92.

miration.[51] If Prescott's impression of Halleck was never committed to writing, Halleck's estimate of the historian's character has fortunately been preserved. The following letter, written three years before the poet's death and alluding pleasantly to his acquaintance with Prescott, was addressed to Evert A. Duyckinck, who had sent Halleck his review[52] of George Ticknor's newly published *Life* of the historian.[53]

Guilford, Connecticut
March 9th 64.

My dear Sir,

PLEASE accept my thanks for your Review of the "Life of Prescott." But for the hope of paying you a visit ere this, I should sooner have expressed them.

The subject is somewhat particularly interesting to me, for I saw a good deal of Mr. Prescott whenever he was in New York in my time, and, I need not add, was delighted with his acquaintance. The charm of his manner consisted in the absence of Dignity, that Owl-like attribute or accomplishment which makes all our political Great Men from a Constable down to a Member of Congress, look so sublimely ridiculous. In conversation he talked hastily and rapidly almost always smiling, and often laughing, and in his bright cheerfulness of look there was the playful simplicity of a child nine years old. The Earl of Carlisle (then Lord Morpeth)[54] used to speak of him here as of one of the best mannered men he had ever known and his Lordship by birth and breeding, ought to be, and is, an excellent judge as well as example of the character.[55]

My antideluvian [*sic*] Eye has found something obscure in your otherwise chrystally clear Article and desires me to ask you why the quotation marks " " are omitted where Shakespeare is quoted? and why the "The" is omitted before the "Reverend Mr. Greenwood" and admitted before the "learned Mr. Pickering"? and why the former for being a Clergyman should be deprived the dignity of the definite article? and moreover, assuming that, like Mr. President Lincoln and myself, you are well read

---

[51] Prescott's first visit to New York mentioned in George Ticknor's *Life of Prescott* was in 1838 (p. 153). He made another important visit in 1842 (p. 188).

[52] *New York Times,* February 20, 1864.

[53] Published in 1864.

[54] Lord Morpeth, who visited the United States in 1841, and who became acquainted with Prescott, entertained a high opinion of the historian (see Ticknor, *Life*, pp. 186–188).

[55] Lord Morpeth must, indeed, have represented to Halleck the ideal of a gentleman. Prescott once wrote of his Lordship that he was "a beautiful specimen of British aristocracy in mind and manners" (see Ticknor, *Life*, p. 188).

in Jo. Miller, is the so doing your own hare [*sic*] or a wig? in other words is its merit or demerit your own or your Printer's?

Aware that questions of such vast importance require cogitation, I beg you to be in no hurry to answer them in writing, but to be prepared to enlighten me in regard to them when I have the pleasure of meeting you, which I hope and trust will be on the *first* day of April coming, an appropriate day for the controversy. In the meantime, believe me, My dear Sir,

Truly yours

FITZ-GREENE HALLECK.

E. A. Duyckinck Esq.[56]

Unfortunately, Halleck never came intimately to know Nathaniel Hawthorne. To a single meeting with the novelist, however, Halleck once referred with characteristic humor. "We happened to sit together at dinner," he remarked to a friend, "and I assure you that for an hour we talked incessantly, although *Hawthorne said nothing.*"[57] Somewhat more intimate, however, were his relations with Maria Gowen Brooks, the eccentric author of *Idomen.*[58] During the summer of 1841 Halleck called upon Mrs. Brooks at the American and Astor Houses, but found her out. When in the spring of the following year Mrs. Brooks was about to publish her *Idomen,* she discovered that a part of her only copy was missing. As she had heard indirectly that Halleck had once had the copy and knew of the missing part, she consequently applied to him in the hope that he could find it. Unfortunately Halleck's reply has not been preserved, but from Mrs. Brooks's letter which followed we may infer that he was unsuccessful.[59] It is to be hoped, however, that Halleck accepted Mrs. Brooks's charming invitation to dine with her some Sunday afternoon at Governor's Island where her distinguished son, Lieutenant Brooks, was first in command.

It was also during the forties that Halleck met many literary friends at the receptions given by Miss Anne Lynch, who in 1855

[56] This letter is preserved in the Duyckinck Collection of the New York Public Library.

[57] Joel Benton in *Frank Leslie's Illustrated Newspaper*, XXV, 243.

[58] For the biography of Mrs. Brooks see Miss Ruth S. Granniss' *An American Friend of Southey*, privately printed at the De Vinne Press in 1913. An intimate picture of Mrs. Brooks from the pen of Prof. Thomas O. Mabbott appeared in the *American Collector* for August, 1926.

[59] Both these letters of Mrs. Brooks are preserved in the Yale Collection of American Literature. See Appendix, pp. 419 ff.

married Vincenzo Botta. Here Halleck might have conversed with the poet and essayist, Henry Tuckerman, with Charles Fenno Hoffman, Dr. John Francis, and Edgar Allan Poe.[60] Rufus Griswold, who also accepted of Miss Lynch's hospitality, in recalling those whom he had seen on those memorable evenings, mentioned Halleck, Bryant, and George P. Morris.[61] Sara Jane Lippincott,[62] also a friend of Miss Lynch, was undoubtedly among her guests. Miss Lynch, who was herself an admirer of Halleck, sent to the poet on Saint Valentine's Day, 1847, a tribute in verse which began,

> I see the sons of Genius rise,
>   The nobles of our land,
> And foremost in the gathering ranks
>   I see the poet-band.[63]

Even after Halleck had retired to Guilford, he kept up a correspondence with Mrs. Botta.[64]

It is probable that Halleck first made the acquaintance of Rufus Griswold in 1842.[65] About a year later, after Griswold had succeeded Poe as editor of *Graham's Magazine*, he wrote to Halleck regarding a portrait of the poet that was soon to appear in the periodical. The engraving had been done by Mr. Parker from the portrait made by Henry Inman in 1831. Griswold requested in particular that Halleck send him a poem to accompany the portrait. "Anything by you," observed the editor, "will, of course, be gladly received and promptly paid for at the highest rates ever paid for contributions to periodicals in America. Mr. Bryant, Mr. Dana, Mr. Longfellow receive from Mr. Graham fifty dollars an

---

[60] D. G. Mitchell, *American Lands and Letters*, II, 388.

[61] *Passages from the Correspondence and Other Papers of Rufus Griswold* (Cambridge, 1898), p. 217. See also *Memoirs of Anne C. L. Botta* (New York, 1894), p. 16. For another account of Miss Lynch's receptions, see Hervey Allen, *Israfel, the Life and Times of E. A. Poe* (New York, 1926), pp. 677 ff.

[62] Mrs. Lippincott, popularly known as Grace Greenwood, once addressed some verses to Halleck. See Wilson, *Life*, pp. 472–473.

[63] Wilson, *Life*, pp. 471–472. The verses were reprinted in *Memoirs of Anne C. L. Botta*.

[64] See pp. 352–353 and 416–417.

[65] In a letter addressed to James T. Fields, dated July 10, 1842, Griswold refers to having "smoked with Halleck" while on a short trip to New York (*Passages from the Correspondence and Other Papers of Rufus Griswold*, p. 113).

article, and that sum, or one yet larger, will be paid to you.'' Griswold concluded his letter by informing Halleck that he had engaged Poe to prepare a sketch of the poet's life and work.[66]

When Poe had once prepared for a magazine a critical or biographical study, he would seldom write an entirely new article, if requested a sketch on the same subject for another periodical. It was his custom to recast his earlier article, adding, of course, what he considered necessary to meet the demands of the moment, but in the main allowing his opinions, and, indeed, much of his earlier phrasing, to stand substantially as he had first set them down. Such was the case with Poe's article on Halleck which appeared with Inman's portrait in the September number of *Graham's Magazine*.[67] As a whole, however, Poe displayed a somewhat more lenient and appreciative attitude to Halleck's work than he had done in his review of the edition of 1836.[68] This change in attitude is revealed near the opening of the article where Poe states that ''no name in the American poetical world is more firmly established than that of Fitz–Greene Halleck, and yet few of our poets— none, indeed, of eminence—have accomplished less, if we regard the quantity without the quality of his compositions. That he has written so little, becomes, thus, proof positive that he has written that little well.''[69] As for ''Marco Bozzaris,'' we note a distinct change in critical attitude. That poem which the critic had once called scarcely ''anything more than an ordinary matter,'' he now designated as ''by far the best of the poems of Halleck. It is not very highly ideal, but is skillfully constructed, abounds in the true lyrical spirit, and, with slight exception, is admirably versified.''[70]

When or where Halleck first met Edgar Allan Poe it would be difficult to say. As early as 1836 Poe, we have noted, had asked Halleck to contribute to the *Southern Literary Messenger*.[71] And on June 24, 1841, Poe (then editor of *Graham's Magazine*) applied to Halleck for support in the establishment of a new magazine which he and Graham were planning.[72] But these overtures resemble those made to other *literati*, and were based, no doubt, rather upon Hal-

---

[66] Wilson, *Life*, pp. 441–442. The letter is dated July 25, 1843.

[67] XXIII, 160. Halleck, of course, made no contribution.

[68] *Southern Literary Messenger*, II, 326 (April, 1836). See pp. 261–262.

[69] *Graham's Magazine*, XXIII, 160.

[70] *Ibid.*, XXIII, 163. [71] See p. 266.

[72] Harrison's edition of Poe's *Works* (1903), XVII, 89–91.

leck's literary reputation than upon personal friendship. It was perhaps toward the close of 1843 that Halleck made Poe's acquaintance. Poe's change in attitude toward Halleck's poems as expressed in the article in *Graham's* may thus have been the result of a cordial meeting between the two. During the closing months of 1843, before his connection with the *Evening Mirror,* Poe was probably a frequent visitor in New York;[73] and it was supposedly on one of these visits that Halleck met the author of "The Raven." To a meeting of Poe and Halleck, which took place probably in the early part of 1844, and which presupposed an acquaintance of the two, Gabriel Harrison refers in some reminiscences once published in the *Brooklyn Daily Eagle.* Harrison, a young actor who had given up the stage for the tea and tobacco business, had as an occasional visitor at his store Edgar Allan Poe, who always gave his name as Thaddeus K. Peasley. Another welcome guest was Fitz-Greene Halleck. "In the evenings Mr. Halleck frequently visited me," writes Harrison, "and behind a pile of tea chests with which I had partitioned off a little room, we would sit in company with old Grant Thorburn,[74] who kept a floral depot next door to me, and would listen to his stories of old New York. Incidentally, we three lords of the hour, snugly ensconced behind our China walls, would embellish our evening's entertainment with occasional tastes of my several wines. . . . On one of these occasions when Mr. Halleck was leaving my store, he met the so-called Peasly [*sic*] entering it, whom he hailed as Poe. An explanation was soon made, and in a few moments we were behind those blessed walls, smiling over the *nom de plume* of Thaddeus K. Peasley."[75] Later in the evening "Poe left with Halleck and stopped at his house that night."[76]

Toward the close of 1844 followed Poe's appointment as a "paragraphist" on the *Evening Mirror,* and the next year the publication of "The Raven," with his withdrawal from the paper. In March, 1845, Poe became one of the editors of the *Broadway*

73 George E. Woodberry, *Life of Edgar Allan Poe* (Boston, 1909), II, 422.
74 See his *Fifty Years' Reminiscences of New York* (New York [1845]).
75 November 18, 1875.
76 *New York Times Saturday Review of Books and Art,* March 4, 1899. Here Harrison repeats with some minor changes the story of the meeting of Poe and Halleck. This time Poe's assumed name is Thaddeus K. *Perley.*

Journal, and finally the sole proprietor and owner. But he soon
found himself involved in financial difficulties. On December 1,
1845, shortly before the demise of the paper, Poe directed a letter
to Halleck asking for assistance. He indicated that there were "one
or two persons" who were making a "deliberate attempt" to ruin
him, and that a loan of one hundred dollars for three months would
be most acceptable.[77] Halleck was apparently one of a few friends
who were willing to assist Poe in so difficult a crisis. The money
was, of course, never returned, for at the beginning of 1846 the
Broadway Journal was numbered among defunct periodicals.

In 1846 Poe contributed to *Godey's Magazine and Lady's Book*
a series of critical sketches entitled "The Literati of New York
City." In writing the article on Halleck, Poe, according to his
usual method, drew largely upon his previous criticisms of the
poet. "The name of *Halleck* is at least as well established in the
poetical world as that of any American," observed the critic in an
attempt to rank Halleck among his contemporaries. "Our principal
poets are, perhaps, most frequently named in this order—Bryant,
Halleck, Dana, Sprague, Longfellow, Willis, and so on,—Halleck
coming second in this series, but holding, in fact, a rank in the
public opinion quite equal to that of Bryant. The accuracy of the
arrangement as above made may, indeed, be questioned. For my own
part, I should have it thus—Longfellow, Bryant, Halleck, Willis,
Sprague, Dana; and, estimating rather the poetic capacity than the
poems actually accomplished, there are three or four comparatively
unknown writers whom I would place in the series between Bryant
and Halleck, while there are about a dozen whom I should assign
a position between Willis and Sprague."[78] Several specimens of
criticism from the "Literati" essay have already been quoted, and
we shall not further comment upon the article other than to note
a curious strain of perversity in Poe's nature, as exhibited in his
opinion of "Marco Bozzaris." Three years before, we have noted,
Poe had pronounced "Marco Bozzaris" "by far the best of the
poems of Halleck."[79] In the present article he reverted substantially
to the opinion of the poem as expressed in the review of the 1836
edition of Halleck's works. "Marco Bozzaris," he noted, "has
much lyrical, without any great amount of *ideal* beauty. Force is

[77] Wilson, *Life,* p. 431.   [78] XXXIII, 13 (July, 1846).
[79] *Graham's Magazine,* XXIII, 163 (September, 1843).

its prevailing feature. . . . I should do my conscience great wrong," he continued, "were I to speak of 'Marco Bozzaris' as it is the fashion to speak of it, at least in print. Even as a lyric or ode it is surpassed by many American, and a multitude of foreign compositions of a similar character."[80]

Poe might at this time have ranked Halleck third among the poets of America, but to the New Yorker of that day Halleck represented the glory of a great literary tradition. He was still the author of "Marco Bozzaris" and "Burns." During the early months of 1842 a Burns anniversary was held in New York City at the Waverly House. Halleck, who was unable to attend the celebration, sent a letter to be read at the gathering. This "characteristic letter," reported the *Knickerbocker*, "was received and read with applause."[81] Four years later, while on a professional tour in England, Edwin Forrest, the American actor, recited Halleck's "Burns" at a Sheffield banquet given in honor of the Scotch poet. The recitation of the verses, it is said, "was received with vociferous cheering."[82]

But in vain during these last years in New York do we search for a revival of Halleck's former interest in writing. His days as a man of letters had indeed gone forever. It was not that he lacked encouragement; on every hand, critics and public alike clamored for him to resume his pen. But neither entreaty nor sarcasm could now move him. It was true that

> . . . in his eye yet glows the light
> Of the celestial fire,
> But cast beside him on the earth
> Is his neglected lyre.[83]

"We hope," wrote the editor of the *Mirror* with quiet rebuke, "that there is truth in the buzz that Halleck has roused himself from his long devotion to the affairs of the counting house, and is about to complete his innumerable unfinished poems."[84] But certainly Morris knew Halleck too well ever to credit such a rumor.

80 *Godey's Magazine*, XXXIII, 14.
81 XIX, 283–284 (March, 1842).
82 William R. Alger, *Life of Edwin Forrest*, I, 403.
83 From Mrs. Botta's verses addressed to Halleck on Saint Valentine's Day, 1847 (Wilson, *Life*, p. 471).
84 XX, 247 (July 30, 1842).

Not infrequently was old Jacob Astor made responsible for the poet's silence. One writer in the *Knickerbocker,* for example, was shocked

> To think that e'en a millionaire
>
> . . . .
>
> Should have withal the hard assurance
> To hold a Son of Song in durance.[85]

But it was not the silence of Halleck alone that in the forties troubled the public. The truth is that the palmy days of Knickerbocker literature had now passed. Looking back upon the buoyant humor of *Knickerbocker's History* and the racy satire of *The Croakers* and *Fanny,* critics could but regret the old age that had slowly crept upon literary New York. The forties were in truth an age of transition. Not until the next decade did the works of Frederic Cozzens, John Saxe, and William Butler help to revive in New York letters something of the earlier *gaieté de coeur.* "The literary arena is now unoccupied," lamented the *New Mirror* in 1843, "and it could be wished that some of our own knights out of practice would don their armour for a tilt—that Wetmore[86] would come away from his crockery and Halleck from his ledger, Bryant from his scissors and politics, and Sprague[87] from his cerberus post at the Hades of Discount—and give us some poetry." A year later the same journal was more daring in its accusation. "Give up the blood horses harnessed into your dull drays, oh Wall-street and Pearl!" it demanded. "Untie your fetters of red tape and let loose your enslaved poets and novelists, oh Nassau and Pine! Discharge Halleck, oh Astor, and give up Wetmore, oh crates of crockery."[88]

With all this urging and prompting, Halleck published, so far as is known, but two[89] new lyrics during the forties; and these had doubtless been previously written in the albums of lady friends. In

---

[85] From a poem on Halleck, entitled "Epistle to the Editor" and signed "W.P.P.," in the *Knickerbocker,* XXIII, 437 (May, 1844).

[86] Prosper Wetmore, engaged in mercantile business in New York City, published in 1830 *Lexington, with Other Fugitive Poems.*

[87] Although Charles Sprague, the poet, was not a Knickerbocker, his name was frequently mentioned along with the group of early New York writers. For many years Sprague was the cashier of the Globe Bank in Boston.

[88] I, 351 (September 2, 1843); III, 176 (June 15, 1844).

[89] To the year 1844 Wilson assigned the lines, "The Winds of March Are Humming," which, he says, first appeared in the *Evening Mirror* (*Life,* p. 444). This statement, however, is an error, as the poem was first collected in

the *Knickerbocker* for January, 1841,[90] appeared his "Translation from the French of Victor Hugo." Halleck, we have noted, acquired a knowledge of French during his early days in New York, and later in 1822, at the time of his trip to Europe, strengthened his acquaintance with the language. The French text of Hugo's poem appeared with the translation made by Halleck. The *New York Mirror*, in reprinting the lines, said that they preferred Halleck's paraphrase to the original.[91]

Two years later the *Knickerbocker*[92] published another set of Halleck's verses entitled "Forget-Me-Not: 'Myosotis Avensis,'" which were described in a subtitle as coming "From the German." In commenting upon the poem, the editor said: "We derive from a lady-friend, to whose kindness our readers have therefore been indebted, the stanzas translated from the German by Fitz-Greene Halleck, Esq., in the preceding pages. They were withheld originally from publication; the fastidious taste of the writer suggesting infelicities, which we are certain will escape the scrutiny of less refined critics of 'the gentle art of song.' "[93] Charlotte Cushman, the actress, answered these verses in "Lines to Fitz-Greene Halleck, on Reading 'Forget-Me-Not' in the July Knickerbocker."[94]

Although Halleck's creative days were now over, his name and the spirit of his earlier work were kept alive at this time by the publication of two new editions of his poems. The second volume of his works, which was scheduled to appear in 1839 or 1840,[95] for some unknown reason was not given to the public until 1845.[96] It was probably toward the close of March or the first of April that

the 1839 edition of Halleck's works, under the title of "Song, by Miss ***." The *Evening Mirror*, it may be observed, was not founded by George P. Morris until 1844. No magazine publication of the poem prior to its appearance in the 1839 edition has been noted.

90 XVII, 59. Wilson states that these lines were written in November, 1838, for the album of Mrs. J. J. Roosevelt (*Life*, pp. 406–407). They were first collected in the edition of 1869.

91 XIX, 18 (January 16, 1841).   92 XXII, 48 (July, 1843).

93 *Ibid.*, p. 92. The poem, which has never appeared in any collected edition of Halleck's works, is reprinted in full in the Appendix.

94 *Ibid.*, p. 364 (October, 1843).

95 See pp. 282–283.

96 As far back as 1841, the edition had been prophesied. The *Southern Literary Messenger* for November, 1841 (VII, 816), basing its statement on literary gossip, reported that "the collection will embrace all Mr. Halleck's more serious poems, hitherto published, and 'The Minute Men,' and other original pieces."

the volume actually made its appearance. The *Knickerbocker* for March noted briefly that "Harpers have also in press a *complete edition* of Halleck's poems, beautifully executed, which has been long waited for and which will speedily make way for a *second* edition";[97] and the *Broadway Journal* for April 5 announced that the volume had been issued.[98] The main title-page read *Alnwick Castle with Other Poems by Fitz-Greene Halleck;* an engraved title which preceded was simply inscribed *Poems by Fitz-Greene Halleck.*

The edition, which was substantially a reprint of the text of 1836, with the single addition of the "Translation from the German of Goethe," attracted but little attention from critics. The comment by the editor of the *Knickerbocker* was brief: "This is one of those books concerning which, at this day, anything beyond a mere announcement of its accessibility would be wholly adscititious. Everybody has read, everybody *will* read Halleck's poetry. His is the kind of poetry that finds buyers."[99] A review in the *Broadway Journal*, however, was conspicuous for its obtuse estimate of Halleck's verse. With the battering ram of logic the critic was doubtless able to demolish certain obvious absurdities in Halleck's work, but failed utterly to appreciate the poet's finer touches.[100]

It was probably during the latter part of October or the early days of November, 1847, that the first illustrated edition of Halleck's poems appeared.[101] It was issued by D. Appleton & Company, and was distinctly an elegant production. Bound in red cloth and stamped with gold, it was regarded as one of the most salable books of the Christmas season.[102] The volume was further adorned by

[97] XXV, 282.

[98] I, 211. Another announcement of the publication of the edition appeared in the *United States Magazine and Democratic Review* for April, 1845 (XVI, 409).

[99] XXV, 470 (May, 1845). A rambling, uncritical estimate of Halleck's poetry also appeared in the *Knickerbocker* for December, 1845 (XXVI, 553).

[100] I, 281 (May 3, 1845). A brief review of the volume by Charles Fenno Hoffman was published in the *Evening Gazette* for April 3, 1845.

[101] The earliest available review is the one in the *Knickerbocker* for November, 1847. For various subsequent editions of the volume see the Bibliography in the Appendix.

[102] The reason for Halleck's change in publishers at this time is not clear. It is obvious, however, that after 1845 or 1846 Halleck severed his relations

At the age of fifty-seven.

From an engraving by John Cheney after the Elliott portrait.

engraved illustrations suggested by scenes in the poet's works. Mr. Charles L. Elliott had early in 1847 painted a portrait of Halleck expressly for the firm of Appleton.[103] This portrait, engraved by John Cheney, who was much in demand at this period as an illustrator of annuals and gift books, was published in the new edition of Halleck's poems.

The contents of this volume included the poet's works as contained in the two editions of 1839 and 1845, which had been previously published by Harper Brothers. That is, no new poems were added. The volume was, however, the most complete single edition which had yet appeared of Halleck's works. As no new material had been admitted, contemporary periodicals gave little space to extended notices of the book. The *Knickerbocker,* for example, merely remarked that "we should as soon think of sitting down to write a review, with illustrative extracts, of John Bunyan's 'Pilgrim's Progress,' as of the poems of Halleck"; and were satisfied with describing briefly, and commenting with praise upon the elegant appearance of the book, and the appropriateness of the illustrations.[104] A longer and somewhat more critical notice of the volume appeared in the *Southern Literary Messenger.* "Since Halleck achieved his renown," observed the critic, "a change has occurred in public taste. There is now a manifest love of the dreamy and fanciful school of poetry to which German literature has given birth. We recognise the merits and acknowledge the claims of this order of verse. It has its place and its mission. At the same time its most delectable specimens have never won us from an early attachment to the direct appeal, the clear expression and the rhetorical fire which distinguishes the genuine Anglo-Saxon

with the Harpers, for from 1847 on, Appleton and Redfield issued his works. An illustrated edition of Halleck's poems had been expected at least two years before its publication by Appleton. The *Broadway Journal* noted in its number for January 25, 1845 (I, 62), that "Lea and Blanchard . . . are going to issue illustrated editions of Bryant's, Longfellow's, Halleck's, and Dana's Poems."

103 Wilson relates that Elliott once told him "that Miss Sedgwick and Mrs. Kirkland would call at his studio and chat with Halleck while he was sitting for his portrait, and that he had rarely, if ever, enjoyed a greater intellectual treat than in listening to the conversation of these gifted friends" (*Life,* p. 478).

104 XXX, 449 (November, 1847).

poet—which gives fervor to the noblest of Byron's heroics and has enshrined the lyrics of Campbell in the hearts of two nations. In our country, Halleck and Whittier have best illustrated this school. It is refreshing to turn over the beautiful pages of this exquisite volume and con the familiar and eloquent verses.''[105] In mentioning Halleck's portrait, the reviewer said: ''It seems to us inimitable. It is perfect as a likeness and the engraving has admirably copied the very detail of expression from Elliott's pencil. It is the most satisfactorily engraved head of an American we have ever seen.''[106]

An amusing comment on the new volume is preserved in James Russell Lowell's description of Halleck in *A Fable for Critics*, published in 1848.

> There goes Halleck, whose Fanny's a pseudo Don Juan
> With the wickedness out that gave salt to the true one,
> He's a wit, though, I hear of the very first order,
> And once made a pun on the words soft Recorder.[107]
> More than this, he's a very good poet, I'm told,
> And has had his works published in crimson and gold,
> With something they call "Illustrations" to wit,
> Like those with which Chapman obscured Holy Writ,
> Which are said to illustrate, because as I view it,
> Like *lucus a non,* they precisely don't do it;
> Let a man who can write what himself understands
> Keep clear, if he can, of designing men's hands,
> Who bury the sense, if there's any worth having,
> And then very honestly call it engraving.[108]

The rarity of English comment on Halleck gives special interest to the single extant reference to his work during the forties. In 1842 Rufus Griswold had published his well-known anthology, *The Poets and Poetry of America*. In reviewing the book two years later, a critic in the *Foreign Quarterly Review* discussed the general question of American poetry. His tone in dealing with Hal-

---

[105] XIII, 762 (December, 1847).

[106] *Ibid.*, p. 762. Another review containing significant comment appeared in *Graham's American Monthly Magazine*, XXXII, 70 (January, 1848).

[107] The reference here is to the lines from Milton (*Paradise Lost*, I, 549–551) which were prefixed to ''The Recorder.''

> On they move
> In perfect phalanx to the Dorian mood
> Of flutes and soft Recorders.

[108] 1848 ed., p. 69.

leck's poetry was throughout one of praise. "Marco Bozzaris" the
reviewer called a "noble lyric," and asserted that had the author
"written nothing more he must have earned a high popularity; but
he has written much more equally distinguished by a refined taste
and cultivated judgment." In continuing his praises of "Marco
Bozzaris," the critic called the poem "one of the most perfect
specimens of versification we are acquainted with in American
literature."[109] The poet's verse was then commended for its "melo-
diousness of structure"; and the "freedom and airiness" of its
versification were illustrated by an extract from "Red Jacket."[110]

Another comment on Halleck suggested by Griswold's anthology
was that included in the brochure, *The Poets and Poetry of
America; a Satire,* which was published in Philadelphia in 1847.[111]
In a passage of the satire addressed to Halleck, the author embodied the criticism, then current in literary circles, which emphasized the poet's indifference to writing. After commenting on Halleck's immortality derived from "Marco Bozzaris," the author
concluded:

> Grant that thy palm of praise is fairly won,
> Is all achieved that mortal might have done?
> Call not beneath thee song so just and great,
> Which mightier bards in loftier verse relate!
> Scorn the vile throng, as if in vengeance set
> To write for each vile monthly and gazette;
> Extend thy sphere, thy native powers expand
> And as confess'd, immortal poet stand.[112]

[109] XXXII, 312 (January, 1844).

[110] *Ibid.,* p. 313. In 1850 Halleck's poems were again reviewed by an
English periodical. A critic in *Fraser's Magazine* for July (XLII, 13) found
Fanny largely an enigma because of its local allusions. "What we can judge of
in *Fanny,*" he said, "are one or two graceful lyrics interspersed in it, though
even these are marred by untimely comicality and local allusions." The lines "On
the Death of Drake," "Burns," and "Marco Bozzaris" are then praised, and
passages quoted from the poems.

[111] This pamphlet was signed "Lavante." For many years no effort was
made to identify the author. In 1887, however, a certain "Geoffrey Quarles,"
who later issued a book entitled *Poe, the Man, the Master, the Martyr,* under
his real name, Oliver Leigh, published a brochure containing a reprint of the
satire, together with an elaborate argument to prove Edgar Allan Poe the
author. The argument, probably too ingenious to be valid, is, in the opinion
of Prof. T. O. Mabbott, the well-known Poe scholar, "altogether absurd."
The author of the poem is still unknown, although it has been ascribed to
Lambert A. Wilmer, a satirical writer of Poe's generation.

[112] 1847 ed., p. 14.

For sixteen years Halleck had served John Jacob Astor as a confidential secretary. On March 29, 1848, the financier died. "I give to my friend Fitz-Greene Halleck," read the fifth section of a "Further Codicil" to Astor's will, *an annuity of two hundred dollars,* commencing at my decease, and payable half-yearly for his life, to be secured by setting apart so much of my personal estate as may be necessary; which I intend as a mark of regard to Mr. Halleck."[113] A "Third Codicil," dated August 22, 1839, which referred to the establishment of the Astor Library, also designated Halleck as one of the trustees of the institution. Washington Irving was named first on the list of trustees, and the other members included Joseph G. Cogswell, Henry Brevoort, Jr., and Samuel Ward, Jr.[114] Thus Astor chose to honor Halleck.

Mr. Astor's phrasing of his bequest to Halleck showed clearly the respect which he had for the poet. Halleck's business ability can be undoubted. Mr. Astor's son once informed Wilson that the poet "was an excellent man of business—rapid, and always reliable in figures, with an excellent memory for all transactions that came under his notice."[115] But we may surely believe that in using the word "friend" Mr. Astor referred alike to Halleck's personal qualities of faithfulness and good fellowship. Astor could not long have lived under the same roof with the poet without feeling the charm that impressed all who knew him. That Astor remembered Halleck at all with an annuity was ample proof of his regard for the poet. But the meager bequest became the subject of comment both among Halleck's friends and the press. One periodical called it "a shabby affair,"[116] and it is said that many of the poet's friends "expressed the hope that he would reject it with indignation."[117] Halleck's replies to these suggestions were characteristic of the gentleman. "I had no claim on Mr. Astor," he said; "I was not of his blood; I had rendered him services and he had paid me for them. If he had any bequest to make, it was for him to judge of its magnitude, not me; and the annuity is as acceptable as it would have been, had it been ten times its present size. It evidenced the respect of Mr. Astor; and it does not become me to denounce it."[118]

113 James Parton, *Life of John Jacob Astor* (New York, 1865), p. 117.
114 *Ibid.*, p. 113.   115 Wilson, *Life,* p. 478.
116 *National Magazine,* I, 483 (December, 1852).
117 *New York Atlas,* July 25, 1852 [?].   118 *Ibid.*

On another occasion he replied to those who sought to cast doubt upon Mr. Astor's kindness, "Mr. Astor treated me like a gentleman. For years he remunerated me handsomely for my services,[119] and now he pays me the compliment of remembering me as a friend in his will by a trusteeship and a bequest."[120] Frederic S. Cozzens once asked Daniel Embury, a fellow clerk of Halleck, "why it was that John Jacob Astor had left Halleck, his faithful clerk, only this trifling sum. 'I think I can explain that,' he said. 'Halleck often used to joke Mr. Astor about his accumulating income, and perhaps rather rashly said, "Mr. Astor, of what use is all this money to you? I would be content to live upon a couple of hundreds a-year for the rest of my life, if I was only sure of it." 'The old man remembered that,' said Mr. Embury, 'and with a bitter satire, reminded Halleck of it in his will.' "[121]

Report says that Astor's son, William, added to the bequest which his father had made to Halleck; but there is no consensus of opinion as to the amount. Wilson states definitely that the poet was made an additional gift of ten thousand dollars.[122] The *Life of John Jacob Astor,* published in 1865, commented thus upon the bequest: "To his old friend and manager, Fitz-Greene Halleck, he [Astor] left the somewhat ridiculous annuity of two hundred dollars, which Mr. William Astor voluntarily increased to fifteen hundred."[123] Whether this was a direct gift or an increase in the annuity itself, is not made clear. Further light is thrown on the situation, only to increase its complexity, by a letter written to Evert A. Duyckinck by the Rev. Lorenzo Bennett, rector of the Christ Church in Guilford. After Halleck's death, Doctor Bennett inquired of Maria, the poet's sister, whether "the common report that Wm. B. Astor conveyed to her brother ten thousand dollars, some years ago, was true. She replied that she had no information to that effect." "Next to Mr. H[alleck]'s sister," Dr. Bennett goes on to say, "a cousin of fourscore years is the nearest relative. A daughter of this cousin, an intelligent lady, who was intimate with Miss Halleck and her brother, assures me confidently that Mr. H[alleck] did receive $10,000 from Wm. B. Astor, and

---

[119] A New York lawyer, who requested that his name be withheld, has informed me that Halleck received from Mr. Astor a salary of $5,000.

[120] Wilson, *Life,* p. 477. [121] *Fitz-Greene Halleck,* pp. 5–6.

[122] *Life,* p. 477. [123] Parton, *op. cit.,* p. 83.

loaned it to a friend, without security, and in that manner lost it.''[124] There is no comment to be made on these conflicting reports other than to say that the simplicity and indeed the frugality of the poet's home life with Maria after his return to Guilford indicate that he never had the use of the substantial sum which Astor's son is reported to have given him.

Halleck soon resigned his post as trustee of the Astor Library.[125] His resignation, in favor of Reverend Doctor Taylor of Grace Church, was probably caused by his retirement in 1849 to his native town. While living in Guilford, Halleck doubtless felt this trusteeship would be a burden, and believed that someone residing in the city could better perform the duties for which he had been selected.

In concluding this record of Halleck's last years in New York, we may profitably pause for a moment over two descriptions, made by contemporaries, of the poet's personal appearance at this period. "He was stiff, angular, and clean-shaved," observes Maunsell B. Field; "wore a high, standing shirt collar, and in the finest weather carried a green cotton umbrella under his arm.''[126] This umbrella, it may be noted, was an inseparable companion of the poet in later life. Frederic S. Cozzens has described Halleck as "of medium stature; his real height was probably five feet nine inches, although a slight inclination of the body forward, in what might be called a deferential attitude, made him appear less tall than he really was. He was always scrupulously neat in his dress and person—never over-dressed—and his manners were equally plain and unpretending. . . . But the real characteristics of our dear friend appeared when he was talking with some congenial companion about the great poets he loved, with all the fervor of his soul. Then the domous head would seem to have gathered electric fire from the words that poured from his heart, the branching veins on his

---

[124] This letter, dated December 20, 1867, is preserved in the Duyckinck Collection of the New York Public Library.

[125] Wilson, *Life*, p. 476. The trustees of the Astor Library were apparently made known to the public some years before the death of the financier. James Lawson in the *Southern Literary Messenger* for April, 1842 (VIII, [2]43), wrote: "In conjunction with Irving, Brevoort, and others, Mr. Astor has selected Halleck as one of the trustees of a noble public library, which he has appropriated a large sum of money to establish:—and the trustees, we understand, are now engaged in the selection of books, etc.''

[126] *Memories of Many Men and of Some Women* (New York, 1874), p. 223.

temples would suddenly shoot out, and swell, and enlarge. Then his blue eyes would dart out gleams of intellectual light, the projecting lower jaw would tremble with passion, the lips would quiver, one hand would pound another with expressive vehemence, and the foot, not less expressive, would respond, and when the heroic sentiment was reached, or pathos had carried all before it, then the voice would falter, the eyes fill, and you felt that the spell of living genius was upon you.''[127]

[127] *Fitz-Greene Halleck. A Memorial,* pp. 26–28.

XII

RETIREMENT IN GUILFORD

1849–67

The concluding period of Halleck's life was noticeably lacking in outward incident. During his last years in New York the poet had settled down to a simple, uneventful existence, living in the afterglow of a poetic reputation acquired many years before. The remainder of his life, now spent in his native Guilford, Halleck passed in simple retirement with his maiden sister. He could not, however, wholly sever himself from the society which for so many years had afforded him the keenest pleasure. Frequent trips to New York kept the poet in touch with the old friends who were now becoming fewer and fewer, and with new friends whom he welcomed with simple affection. Correspondence with former literary associates also helped to keep Halleck from social and mental atrophy. The letters written after his retirement to Guilford are of interest both for their store of literary and personal anecdote, and for the keenness of intellect and quiet humor which they evince even to the last year of the poet's life. From these epistles, many of which are now published for the first time, we may glimpse something of the pleasant fancy and charming quaintness which fascinated all who knew him.

It was in the spring of 1849 that Halleck left the employ of the Astor firm.[1] He had planned, after retiring from business, once again to visit Europe. With this trip in mind, the poet went so far as to secure a passport, "which was the last document signed by James Buchanan as Secretary of State, before retiring from office, March 7, 1849."[2] But Halleck never made use of the passport. It is probable that ill health and lack of resources prevented his making the journey. That he was not in the best of health at the time of his retirement from Astor's employ is evidenced by the letter which the Rev. Dr. Lorenzo Bennett sent to the press relating to the poet's

---

[1] Wilson, *Life*, p. 478.   [2] *Ibid.*, p. 482.

alleged connection with the Roman church. "Mr. Halleck," said Doctor Bennett, "returned to this, his native town, in 1849, quite enfeebled in health."[3]

Halleck was at first undecided whether he would retire to Fort Lee or to Guilford. Fort Lee, situated on the Jersey coast across the Hudson from New York, offered many attractions to the poet. During his life in the city he had there spent many leisure hours with his friends, and in the presence of General Wilson once called the spot his "country seat."[4] To his acquaintances at Fort Lee Halleck wrote many charming epistles which show how dear the place must have been to him, even after his return to Guilford. "I declined Mr. Duer's invitation to drive with him from Highwood [Hoboken] to Fort Lee on the new road now completed along the banks of the river," wrote the poet to Adrian Dunning in 1858, "because I could not assist in desecrating, in such a manner, my old romantic walks."[5] And in another letter written a year later to the same gentleman, he again bemoaned the improvements that had overtaken his beloved retreat. "I have now been and returned without seeing Fort Lee except from the Bloomingdale side of the river, from whence I satisfied myself that so vividly and indelibly were its scenes of beauty and its old associations impressed upon my memory as to render a nearer view of it unnecessary for enjoyment, and resolved not to risk what I have been long fearing, the sight of some villanous alteration, miscalled *Improvement*, which might sadden all my future recollections of so many of my pleasantest hours and pleasantest acquaintances."[6] "It is now a long time since I have been seen at Fort Lee," wrote Halleck to a lady in 1863, "but I am in all my moments of real enjoyment invisibly there in mind and in heart, living over its past pleasantness, and revelling in the memory of its beautiful scenery and the associations so delightfully blended with it."[7]

It is probable that if Halleck had been given the opportunity, he would have retired to Fort Lee. But the state of his resources undoubtedly prevented such an indulgence of his wishes. Some-

---

[3] *Ibid.*, p. 591. [4] *Ibid.*, p. 411.
[5] *Ibid.*, p. 418. The letter is dated December 13, 1858.
[6] *Ibid.*, p. 420. The letter is dated November 19, 1859.
[7] *Ibid.*, p. 422. The letter, addressed to Miss Fanny Wake, is dated February 21, 1863.

thing has already been said of the poet's meager income after his return to Guilford. Halleck's care and personal integrity had made him invaluable to Mr. Astor; but it is doubtful whether he ever possessed sufficient audacity for a successful business man. Had he been less conservative, he might, through his constant intercourse with financiers, have invested to advantage a portion of his income. But there is little evidence that he gave much thought to the future. In early life he had doubtless been extravagant; and as time went on, if he had learned economy, his resources must have been appreciably diminished by the money frequently sent home to his sister.[8] To a man of Halleck's amiability and generosity the yearly salary of five thousand dollars said to have been paid by Mr. Astor, would not have been large; and the annuity of two hundred, which he received on retirement, by no means sufficient to support him for the rest of his life.[9] Upon his return to Guilford in June, 1849,[10] he took up his residence in an old house with a broad veranda, facing the southwest corner of the village green.[11] In this house which he rented, the poet lived with his sister. Halleck frequently intimated to his rector that he was "quite impoverished." "Mr. and Miss Halleck constituted a family by themselves," wrote Doctor Bennett to Duyckinck after the poet's death, "with no domestic to assist in the household affairs; & all appearances indicating straitened circumstances." Again Doctor Bennett said: "George Elliott, Esq. of Erie, Pa., a gentleman of wealth . . . was disposed to extend liberal assistance to Mr. and Miss H.,—

[8] See in the Appendix, pp. 392–393, the brief notes written to Miss Halleck regarding her financial affairs.

[9] The proceeds from the sale of his works were, of course, not large. "The whole sum received by Mr. Halleck for the various editions of his poems, including his poetical contributions to periodicals was sixteen thousand dollars" (Wilson, *Life*, p. 532).

[10] *Ibid.*, p. 482.

[11] This house, according to an old resident of Guilford, Halleck did not own, and he rented only a portion of it for his apartment. There are, in fact, no records in the office of the town clerk in Guilford to show that the property was ever in the possession of the Halleck family. About 1865 the landlord of the house wished to convert the premises into an inn, and Halleck and his sister were forced to vacate (see Wilson, *Bryant and His Friends*, p. 255). Many years after Halleck's death the old house was torn down, and a modern building—a hotel—which now stands on the corner, was erected. Up to a very few years ago this hotel was called "The Halleck House," but now simply bears the sign "Hotel Guilford."

but, in response to his offer, no representation was made to call it into exercise. Miss H. had a small income,[12] & I presume her brother had a small income also; but I have not information to give a nearer statement."[13] James Wynne in 1862 described Halleck's home life as "simple and unostentatious."[14] Joel Benton likewise commented on its simplicity, but added that "the utter lack of pretension in both its comforts and adornments gave it a charm quite undescribable and irresistible. Mr. Halleck's maiden sister, who is near his own age, was the presiding spirit of the interior."[15] The mutual love of brother and sister, both now well past the prime of life, must indeed have been beautiful. "It was a most grateful sight to me," writes the critic, William A. Jones, who first met the poet in Guilford in 1849, "to witness the fond pride of his affectionate sister in him and in his conversational powers. She seemed to enjoy his jests, and stories, and quotations, as if for the first time, and with an original relish."[16]

The monotony of Halleck's life in the quiet town of Guilford was broken by frequent trips to the city. On one of these visits in 1851 Halleck first met James Grant Wilson who was presented to the poet by Mr. Charles M. Leupp. "The recollection is still fresh in my mind," writes General Wilson, "of the mingled awe and admiration with which I gazed upon the author of lines I revered only less than those of Shakespeare and Milton, and how quickly he placed me at my ease and won my heart by his gracious and genial manner."[17] The meeting took place at Bixby's hotel, located at the corner of Broadway and Park Place. At this hotel many prominent men of letters stopped on their visits to the city. The

---

[12] What was probably the original Halleck property mentioned in the first chapter was no doubt in Maria's hands at this time. This was also at the west of the green, although not on the corner. A quitclaim deed, transferring all the poet's interest in this property (and three other parcels of land in Guilford) to his sister, was filed on October 9, 1837 (see town records, v. 31, p. 471). A similar deed had been filed nine years before (January 14, 1828) by the father, Israel Hallock, releasing all his claims to the property in favor of Maria (v. 29, p. 383). It is probably the small income derived from the rental of this property to which Doctor Bennett here referred.

[13] This letter, preserved in the New York Public Library, is dated December 20, 1867.

[14] *Harper's New Monthly Magazine*, XXIV, 634 (April, 1862).

[15] *Frank Leslie's Illustrated Newspaper*, XXV, 243 (January 4, 1868).

[16] Wilson, *Life*, p. 539.   [17] *Ibid.*, p. 484.

proprietor of Bixby's was well known to James Fenimore Cooper; and it was the novelist who introduced Halleck to the inn. "Since my acquaintance with Halleck," wrote James Wynne in his reminiscences of the poet, "he has always, when in town, occupied apartments at Bixby's. Now Bixby's is just the place for a bachelor, and certainly it is for a poet. Everybody calls in at Bixby's. Poor Charles Leupp[18] used to go to Bixby's, Verplanck goes to Bixby's, the author of 'Sparrowgrass Papers'[19] goes to Bixby's. 'Ik Marvel,'[20] when in town, is to be found at Bixby's. Bayard Taylor, whenever he can find rest for his weary feet, settles down at Bixby's; and last but not least, Halleck, whether uptown or downtown, whenever in town, is sure to be found at Bixby's."[21] In 1858 Bixby was obliged to change his establishment to upper Broadway. The following graceful note Halleck sent to the proprietor on receiving an announcement of the change.

Guilford, Connecticut,
May 3rd, 1858.

My dear Mr. Bixby:

On my return home I am favored with the circular announcing your intention of taking for your establishment a more aristocratic position, and placing it among the "Upper ten." I take pleasure for your sake in congratulating you upon this removal, and I hope and trust that it will be advantageous to you in all respects. Still, for my own sake, I cannot but regret it, for I fear that you will be too far "up" for my purpose while I am a visitor in your city, and I am certain to be the loser of a good home which your old and favorite house has so often and so agreeably proved itself to be for me during the seven or eight years past.

The experience of our late friend, Mr. Cooper, the novelist, which preceded mine, enabled him to recommend it highly to me, and he as you know had a very high standard of domestic comfort, and never willingly overpraised anything; and my own experience has most pleasantly confirmed his opinion of its merits.

Allow me to add that I feel greatly indebted to your personal courtesy for frequent introductions to the gentlemen, your guests, among whom I am now proud to number many of my most valuable acquaintances.

[18] Charles M. Leupp, a lover of art and literature, and an active member of the Century Club.
[19] Frederic S. Cozzens, the humorist.
[20] Donald G. Mitchell, author of *Reveries of a Bachelor*.
[21] *Harper's New Monthly Magazine*, XXIV, 638.

Repeating best wishes for your perfect success in your new enterprise, I beg you to believe me, my dear sir,

Truly yours,
FITZ-GREENE HALLECK.[22]

James Fenimore Cooper, who had once recommended to Halleck the hotel of Mr. Bixby, died at Cooperstown, New York, on September 14, 1851. The friends of the novelist met a few days later[23] at the City Hotel to consider the erection of a suitable memorial to his memory. To carry out this project, a committee was elected, of which Washington Irving was chosen chairman, and Fitz-Greene Halleck and Rufus Griswold, secretaries.[24] The committee proposed that a monument be erected in one of the public squares of New York. With this memorial in mind, the officers called another meeting of the novelist's friends which was held on March 25, 1852, and which resulted in the formation of a Cooper Monument Association. But the attempt to raise the necessary funds was unsuccessful, and the money which was collected was ultimately used in the erection of a monument at the novelist's grave at Cooperstown.[25] For Cooper, Halleck entertained the greatest respect. "I had the honor of knowing Mr. Cooper well, and of esteeming him very highly," wrote the poet a month before his own death in 1867. "He was a remarkable model of Sincerity. His regard for truth in the most minute things as in the most important, excelled that of any man I have ever known, and his life, in its controversies with those he deemed in the wrong, was a long martyrdom to his principles."[26]

Among the new friends which Halleck made during the early fifties was the poet and traveler, Bayard Taylor. "My acquaint-

---

[22] James C. Derby, *Fifty Years among Authors, Books, and Publishers* (New York, 1886), p. 593. Derby mentions among others who frequented Bixby's Ralph Waldo Emerson, Nathaniel Hawthorne, Oliver Wendell Holmes, George P. Morris, N. P. Willis, Rufus Griswold, and Alice and Phoebe Cary (p. 591). Wilson states that Bixby abandoned his business altogether in 1862 (*Life*, p. 484).

[23] On September 25, 1851.

[24] *Memorial of James Fenimore Cooper* (New York, 1852), p. 7. At the first meeting Halleck was present in person. See the *New-York Daily Times* for September 25, 1851.

[25] Wilson, *Life*, p. 490.

[26] From a letter of Halleck to T. A. Cheney dated October 26, 1867, and now in the possession of Mr. W. W. Lange, president of the Southside Malleable Casting Company, Milwaukee, Wisconsin. For the entire letter see the Appendix, pp. 417–418.

ance with him," writes Taylor, "extended over the last fifteen years of his life. Although the intolerance of youth still clung to me, and his tastes and opinions were sometimes so divergent from mine as to seem incredible, they were always expressed so simply and with such manly gentleness that I never ventured to dispute them.[27] . . . I saw him last, about the beginning of the war, on one of his visits to New York. Calling with a friend at the quiet hotel where he was wont to lodge, I found that he was ill, and would have withdrawn; but he sent down a request that we should go to his room. With unnecessary courtesy, he had risen from his bed and taken an arm-chair: he looked weak and suffering; but his kindliness and gentle grace were so perfect as to be really touching. It was impossible to detect how much effort he made to converse cheerfully; the spirit of the knightly gentleman controlled his body, and gave him a factitious ease, which I trust we did not abuse."[28]

Only occasionally after his return to Guilford did Halleck take up his poetic pen. A silence of almost ten years, however, was broken in 1852 by the publication in the *Knickerbocker*[29] of the second part of the poem "Connecticut." The first fragment of this work, begun as early as 1826, had appeared in the *New York Review and Athenaeum Magazine* as an extract from "The Minute Men."[30] Halleck had by now, of course, given up all hope of completing the poem which he had planned in early manhood, and, in publishing the new fragment, wisely refrained from all mention of "The Minute Men." That Halleck, however, intended this new extract as a part of a larger whole may be easily inferred from the fact that the two fragments were written in the same verse-form. In publishing the two parts in the edition of 1852, Halleck further indicated by means of cross references that the fragments were mutually related. The new poem was in no way inferior to Halleck's earlier sketch on "Connecticut." The rugged lines bespoke something of the strength and energy that had conceived "Marco Bozzaris"; while frequent lapses into the language of prose suggested that the old interest in Byron's "Don Juan" still survived.

[27] *North American Review*, CXXV, 63–64 (July, 1877).
[28] *Ibid.*, CXXV, 66.
[29] XXXIX, 409 (May, 1852). The verses were first published under the title "Extract from an Unpublished Poem."
[30] See pp. 165–167.

The new poem, presenting a fair and indeed striking portrait of Cotton Mather, epitomized two antithetical traits of character, peculiar not only to Mather himself[31] but to the Puritan mind. "No finer study of Mather has appeared," wrote Evert Duyckinck in his sketch of Halleck; "and certainly, alongside of the bitterest denunciation of evil doing, no more genial praise of the virtues of New England."[32] George Hill, the poet's friend, once related to General Wilson that while "Halleck composed this portion of the poem during his walks in and around Guilford, . . . he would repeat the lines aloud, and as he occasionally emphasized a line by swinging his umbrella (without which he never left his home for a walk) in the air, the good people of Guilford" were given grounds for believing that the poet was quite out of his mind.[33]

It was probably in July of the same year that J. S. Redfield issued a new edition of Halleck's poems. As far as the contents were concerned, the edition was but a reprint of the text of 1847, with the single addition of the "Extract from an Unpublished Poem," contributed to the *Knickerbocker* two months before. No unusual excitement was, of course, produced in the literary world by the appearance of the volume. "We congratulate the admirers of Fitz-Greene Halleck, and what reader of American poetry is not his admirer," observed *Harper's New Monthly Magazine*, "on a new edition of his *Poetical Works* recently issued by Redfield, containing the old, familiar, and cherished pieces, with some extracts from a hitherto unpublished poem. . . . Combining a profuse wealth of fancy with a strong and keen intellect, he tempers the passages in which he most freely indulges in a sweet and tender pathos, with an elastic vigor of thought, and dries the tears which he tempts forth, by sudden flashes of gayety, making him one of the most uniformly piquant of modern poets."[34] The *Southern Literary Messenger* was much more conventional and perfunctory in its notice of the volume. "Halleck is a poet after our own heart," observed the critic, "though the Tennysonian taste of the day has exalted others above him, who are more psychological (or more egotistical) than he, and throw around their ideas a cloudier drapery of language. We therefore thank Mr. Redfield for this seasonable and

[31] See p. 214.
[32] *Putnam's Magazine*, XI, 235 (February, 1868).
[33] *Life*, p. 490.   [34] V, 423 (August, 1852).

handsome edition of his poems. In looking over it, we find our old favorite pieces as delightful as ever, and recognize in the 'Extract from an Unpublished Poem' a new candidate for our admiration.''[35]

Although the publication of the new volume caused little sensation in the literary world, the name of Halleck still recalled to many the palmy days of New York letters. When in September, 1853, a ''Fruit Festival'' was given to the authors of America, a special invitation was sent to Halleck,[36] who was finally prevailed upon to attend. Here he had the privilege of meeting many of the distinguished *literati* of the country, who also enjoyed the hospitality of the New York booksellers. It was ''the most delightful occasion which I can recall in my publishing career,'' writes J. C. Derby. ''The gathering took place at the Crystal Palace, which had been erected in Reservoir Square, under the direction of the American Institute, through whose courtesy the exceptional accommodations for the festival were secured. The whole scene itself was one of great splendor, and will linger long in the memory of those who participated.''[37]

In November, 1853, several of Halleck's literary friends conceived the idea of giving the poet a complimentary dinner at the Century Club in New York. This club had been founded in 1847, having for its objects ''the cultivation of a taste for letters and the arts and social enjoyment.''[38] The organization was composed of most of the important literary men residing at that time in the city. Halleck had at first been a member,[39] but on his retirement to Guilford had probably withdrawn. Wishing to honor an old friend whose name and poetry had now become a cherished memory in the city, the club sent to Halleck a note signed by many of his former companions, including Verplanck, Leupp, and Bryant, ask-

---

[35] XVIII, 511 (August, 1852). Another brief review of the volume appeared in the *Knickerbocker* for August (XL, 164).

[36] George Haven Putnam, *George Palmer Putnam. A Memoir* (New York, 1912), p. 409.

[37] *Fifty Years among Authors*, pp. 34–35. Among those who attended the festival were Bryant, L. M. Child, Alice and Phoebe Cary, Cozzens, Holmes, Irving, Lowell, Lossing, Longfellow, and Catherine Sedgwick. Derby gives the date of the festival incorrectly as 1855.

[38] Francis G. Fairfield, *The Clubs of New York* (New York, 1873), p. 32.

[39] *Ibid.*, p. 36.

ing him to set a date on which he might conveniently meet them at the Century.[40] In reply to their invitation the poet stated his inability at that time to make a definite engagement for the future, but expressed his intention to Mr. Verplanck and the others of calling upon them "ere long, in New York, in order to place myself at your disposal."[41] On January 18, 1854, the dinner was finally held. "No account was published in the *Evening Post* of the dinner given to Halleck at the Century Club, at which I presided," wrote Bryant to General Wilson after the poet's death. "Mr. George B. Butler was present and a communication giving a brief account of the dinner, written, as I was told, by him, appeared in the *Journal of Commerce.*"[42] The account in the *Journal* read in part:

Many eminent gentlemen were present on the occasion. Mr. Bryant made one of the elegant speeches for which he is distinguished, and called out Mr. Halleck, who delighted the audience with a brilliant response, but retained his chair, giving as a reason for it that Mr. Gardiner, who was spoken of by John Randolph as a great orator, was completely overwhelmed by attempting to express his sentiments without rising, and stating that Mr. Gardiner could only regain his self-possession by getting on his feet, and that he, on the contrary, did not dare to rise. Mr. Verplanck responded in a most delightful manner to a toast offered by Mr. Bryant to the Bucktail Bards. The dinner will long be remembered as one of the most pleasant and elegant ever given in the city.[43]

"It fell to me to preside," wrote Bryant in recalling the dinner some fifteen years later, "and in toasting our guest I first spoke, in such terms as I was able to command, of the merits of his poetry, as occupying a place in our literature like the poetry of Horace in the literature of ancient Rome. I dwelt upon the playfulness and grace of his satire, and the sweetness and fervor of his lyrical vein. Halleck answered very happily. 'I do not rise to speak,' he said, 'for if I were to stand up I could say nothing. I must keep my seat

[40] Wilson, *Life*, pp. 496–497. The note is dated November 22, 1853.
[41] *Ibid.*, pp. 497–498. The note is dated November 26, 1853. In the New York Historical Society is preserved a leaflet which reprints both the invitation of the Century Club and Halleck's note written in reply, from which we have just quoted.
[42] *Bryant and His Friends*, p. 88.   [43] January 19, 1854.

and talk to you without ceremony.' And then he went on, speaking modestly and charmingly of his own writings.''[44]

In the same year a movement was set on foot by the friends and admirers of Louis Gaylord Clark, the editor of the *Knickerbocker*, to produce for his benefit a volume, the contents of which should be furnished gratuitously by ''the surviving writers for the *Knickerbocker*.''[45] It was planned that the proceeds from the sale of the book should be used ''in building, on the margin of the Hudson, a cottage, suitable for the home of a man of letters, who, like Mr. Clark, is also a lover of nature and of rural life.''[46] The volume, called the *Knickerbocker Gallery*, and issued in 1855, was a large book of 505 pages, elaborately embellished with engraved portraits of all the contributors. The writers included many of the most distinguished *literati* of America—Bayard Taylor, Tuckerman, Morris, Longfellow, Cozzens, Willis, and Griswold being among the number. Aware of his now almost habitual silence,

> (From long-neglected garden-bowers
> Come these, my songs' memorial flowers),[47]

Halleck nevertheless turned in pleasant memory to honor a friend of his early manhood. The concluding poem of the volume—''To Louis Gaylord Clark, Esquire''—was written by Halleck at Fort Lee during the summer of 1854.[48] The verses, unusually personal in their allusion to Clark's marriage at which Halleck had been present, were most gratifying to the editor of the *Knickerbocker*. ''My heart is in my mouth,'' wrote Clark to the poet in acknowledgment of the verses, ''and most grateful tears are in my wife's eyes, and I don't know how to express to you my fervent thanks, my most deep gratitude, for the noble, the *proud* lines you have been so good as to address to my humble name. To have had your world-known Muse represented in the testimonial to me was of itself an honor, and a high one; but to have me and mine person-

---

[44] *Some Notices of the Life and Writings of Fitz-Greene Halleck*, p. 23. The Century Club four years later invited Halleck again to partake of their hospitality. The New York Historical Society possesses a formal note written by Halleck on January 2, 1858, expressing his regret that he could not attend.

[45] *Knickerbocker Gallery* (New York, 1855), p. xiv.

[46] *Ibid.*, p. xiv.

[47] ''To Louis Gaylord Clark, Esquire.'' See 1869 ed., p. 252.

[48] The printed poem was dated ''Fort-Lee, N. J., *July*, 1854.''

ally remembered in words of such exquisite beauty and power—to know and feel what a legacy this will be to our children when we have 'gone hence'—*this* overflows my cup of gratitude, of pride, and of joy. If it be happiness to make others supremely happy, that happiness should be yours this blessed night.'[49]

Accompanying the poem addressed to Clark was an engraving of Halleck made after the Elliott portrait painted in 1847.[50] Another portrait of the poet was painted in 1855 by Thomas Hicks, "at the request," says Wilson, "of his friend and former colleague at Jacob Barker's, Benjamin R. Winthrop."[51] While Halleck was "sitting to Mr. Hicks for his portrait . . .," writes Bayard Taylor in his reminiscences of the poet, "I called several times, at the artist's request, to make his hours of service a little more endurable, by inciting him to talk."[52] Whether Halleck was ever entirely pleased with the painting, it would be difficult to say. A slight feeling of dissatisfaction and bitterness may have prompted the remark recorded by Cozzens, "I see he [Hicks] has caught that peculiar expression of my mouth, which some of my friends say is like Voltaire's, half smile, half sneer."[53]

Halleck was again in New York to meet Thackeray when the novelist made his tour of America in 1855–56. The poet was chosen to serve on a committee to make arrangements for a dinner at Delmonico's, to which Thackeray was invited by many distinguished literary and social figures of the city.[54] Halleck had several opportunities to meet the novelist. He attended a dinner given to Thackeray by Charles M. Leupp, who, in inviting the poet, said, "Thackeray had an engagement for Monday, but cancelled it for the pleasure of meeting you."[55] "No one," Halleck once remarked, "could be in Thackeray's company without the positive feeling that they were in the presence of a gentleman."[56] But in spite of Halleck's respect for Thackeray, the poet did not hold him in the high regard that he held Dickens. We have already recounted the anecdote concerning Halleck, who, with his friend

---

[49] Wilson, *Life*, p. 501.
[50] See pp. 307 and 385–386.   [51] *Life*, p. 501.
[52] *North American Review*, CXXV, 64 (July, 1877).
[53] *Fitz-Greene Halleck. A Memorial*, pp. 23–24.
[54] J. G. Wilson, *Thackeray in the United States* (New York, 1904), I, 46.
[55] Wilson, *Life*, p. 505.
[56] Wilson, *Thackeray in the United States*, I, 208.

Doctor Ludlow, attended Thackeray's lecture on George the Fourth. Halleck "was so much displeased with what he considered a caricature of the man, for whom, with all his faults, he entertained a regard as 'the first gentleman of Europe,' that sitting for a few minutes, he said to his companion, 'I am going. I can't listen any longer to his abuse of a better man than himself,' and the friends accordingly arose and left the hall.''[57]

Occasionally Halleck's friends persuaded him to go beyond the limits of New York City. It was during these years that he made rare visits to Fort Lee, on one of which he composed the lines "To Louis Gaylord Clark.''[58] At the invitation of Nathaniel Parker Willis, Halleck once visited Idlewild,[59] which "lay upon a shelf or terrace of the Hudson, lifted some two hundred feet above the level of the river, at the point where its waters received the slender tribute of Moodna Creek.''[60] But usually Halleck confined himself to the city. In September, 1857, he and James Grant Wilson attended the performance of a comedy, *Married for Money*. On the following morning, Halleck breakfasted with Wilson, and the two set out together to visit St. Paul's and Trinity's churchyards. "After pointing out the graves of some of the 'old familiar faces,' friends of his early and later years,'' says Wilson, "he led me to the last resting-place of the celebrated actor, George Frederick Cooke, and pointed out the tomb erected by the liberality of Edmund Kean in 1821.''[61] Passing on to the graveyard of old Trinity, the poet in a similar manner sought out the tomb of Alexander Hamilton, and entertained his companion "with eulogistic remarks on that eminent statesman.''[62]

The following month Halleck was again in New York where he put up, as usual, at Bixby's. On the occasion of this visit he was introduced by a friend to Robert Barry Coffin, the author of *Cakes and Ale* and other novels, who preferred the somewhat less forbidding pseudonym of "Barry Gray.'' Halleck "received me with great cordiality,'' wrote Barry Gray some years later in recalling

---

57 Wilson, *Life*, p. 506.　　58 See pp. 324–325.

59 Wilson, *Bryant and His Friends*, pp. 314–315.

60 H. A. Beers, *Willis*, p. 326. Willis took up his residence at Idlewild in 1853 (*ibid.*, p. 328).

61 Halleck, it will be remembered, wrote the inscription for Cooke's monument. See pp. 132–133.

62 Wilson, *Life*, pp. 511–512.

the meeting, "and as we drew our chairs up before the glowing fire in the grate—for it was a chilly night out of doors—he spoke of the cheerfulness of an open fire, and alluded complimentally [*sic*] to certain sketches of mine, which had just then appeared in the *Home Journal*, wherein I had uttered approving words of an old-fashioned wood fire. It was a small matter in itself, but one which I fully appreciated, for it assured me in a very pretty way, that Mr. Halleck not only knew me, but had done me the honor of reading my writings."[63]

Halleck, if possible, always visited New York on the Fourth of July. "I am gradually lessening the number of my visits to your city," wrote the poet to a friend on October 2, 1858, "and becoming more and more 'a stranger and sojourner' there. I was there, as usual, to see my favorite day, the 'Fourth of July,' which I found as noisy and as merry as ever."[64] Of Halleck's frequent visits to the city Duyckinck has observed: "He never forgot the old holiday of his youth, the 'Fourth of July!' When every citizen who could escape had fled from the noise and tumult of that boisterous celebration, Halleck might be seen making his way in the throng, regardless of the tumult and the explosions. He liked, he said, 'the life of the scene.' It was something in the spirit of the retired tallow-chandler, who came to town on 'melting' days."[65]

On his annual Fourth of July excursion in the summer of 1858 Halleck met at Bixby's hotel Professor Canale, the translator of "Marco Bozzaris."[66] In the following excerpt from a letter written to Charles W. Sandford, Halleck refers to his meeting with Canale, and playfully alludes to his own service, many years before, in company with General Sanford in the Iron Grays:[67] "I intended to have availed myself of your always so kindly proffered hospitality on the 5th instant, but I was detained at the critical moment by a young Greek, who called on me with a letter of introduction. I had, however, the pleasure of seeing him delighted while gazing

---

[63] See "Fitz-Greene Halleck—Reminiscences of Barry Gray" in the *New York Evening Mail* for January 9, 1868. Barry Gray reprinted a letter he once received from Halleck in *Cakes and Ale at Woodbine* (New York, 1868), pp. 177–178. See also Evert Duyckinck's comment on the letter in *Putnam's Magazine*, XI, 241–242.

[64] Wilson, *Life*, p. 512.

[65] *Putnam's Magazine*, XI, 233–234 (February, 1868).

[66] See p. 163.   [67] See p. 39.

with me from Bixby's windows upon the 'pomp and circumstance' of your military display, and he spoke of the discipline and the brilliant appearance of the troops, and of their leader, in such flattering terms, that I could not refrain from telling him that but for the wound that I received while fighting by your side, in one of our battles, during our last war, on the day when you were decorated with the Cross of the Legion of Honor, I should myself have remained in the army! That young man now knows something of American history, which is more than I can say of any other European of my acquaintance.''[68]

In January, 1859, Halleck again visited New York, this time to attend a centenary dinner in honor of Burns. To this dinner, given by the Burns Club at the Astor House, many noted men, including Bryant, Verplanck, Dr. Francis, Peter Cooper, and Horace Greeley, were invited. Halleck's poem on Burns, as Duyckinck has said, ''justly entitled him to be free of the guild.''[69] During the celebration both Bryant and Halleck were honored by Charles Gould, ex-President of the organization. ''Gentlemen of the Burns Club,'' he said: ''It is a pleasure to you and to me to greet, on this proud centennial, the two great poets of America, presiding in pleasant fellowship over our pleasant festival. Bryant and Halleck: God bless you both, now and forever! and when your centennial shall come, the lovers of Nature's Great Poet will love your memories and embalm your names.''[70] In Scotland, also, Halleck was honored by having his poem to Burns featured in the centennial celebration. ''To a Rose, Brought from near Alloway Kirk'' was printed as the leading poem in a small pamphlet entitled *The Genius of Burns,* to which the following prefatory letter was added:

Hundreds of poets, or rhymsters, have written tributes to Burns within the last century, but I consider this to be one of the finest, if not the very best that has appeared in that time. Among other fine touches his prophetic genius saw the rising popularity and enthusiasm with which the name of Burns would be greeted by all succeeding generations. And as I know there are thousands who are great admirers and lovers of Burns who

---

[68] Wilson, *Life,* pp. 516–517. The letter is dated July 19, 1858. On Halleck's sixty-ninth birthday, Canale addressed to the poet some verses which Wilson prints on page 517 of the *Life.*

[69] *Putnam's Magazine,* XI, 241.   [70] *Evening Post,* January 26, 1859.

have never come across this fine poem, I take the liberty of publishing it in this centenary year, when the minds of thousands—I might say millions —the wide world over are turned towards the shrine of the Immortal Bard. I have also added two short pieces of my own, which may interest some into whose hands this leaflet may fall.—I am respectfully yours,

JOHN COOK, PRESTWICK, AYR.[71]

It was also about this time, probably early in the year 1859, that Halleck met Thomas Bailey Aldrich, who had just published *Babie Bell and Other Poems*. James Derby relates that on the appearance of the poem "Mr. Frederic S. Cozzens (whose Sparrowgrass Papers I had recently published) . . . made an appointment with the young poet to come to his place of business in Warren St., and meet Fitz-Greene Halleck, who had read the poem, and had written to Mr. Cozzens, expressing a desire to know the author. Aldrich said that Halleck was most delightfully kind and complimentary."[72]

While Halleck was thus forming friendships with literary men of a new generation, he was frequently called upon to mourn the death of his older companions. In 1851 Cooper had died, and eight years later Irving passed away. In the following letter, written to Charles A. Davis,[73] the author of *Letters of Jack Downing*, Halleck comments gracefully on an account,[74] from the pen of Davis, of "the closing scenes at Sunnyside," the beloved home of Irving.

[71] A copy of this very rare pamphlet was sent to me by the late Dr. D. McNaught, author of *The Truth about Burns*. For complete title, see Bibliography in Appendix, p. 378.

[72] *Fifty Years among Authors*, p. 229. To Cozzens, Halleck wrote regarding Aldrich: "I am happy to agree with you in your estimate of the young poet. He is much more than promising, and I hope you will persuade him to work on" (*Fitz-Greene Halleck. A Memorial*, p. 17).

[73] In a letter to Samuel Ward, dated June 3, 1865, Halleck writes thus regarding Davis: "Mr. Seba Smith, alluded to in the *Spectator*, was the creator of the first 'Jack Downing,' a droll narrator of droll stories in the Yankee dialect. Our wise and witty friend Charles Augustus Davis took him under his protection, made him a major in the Downingville Militia and a leading politician, unequalled in fun if not in fame" (J. G. Wilson, *Bryant and His Friends*, p. 278).

[74] The account here mentioned has unfortunately not been recovered. Romantic pictures, however, presenting the funeral observances at Sunnyside in a manner similar to that referred to by Halleck, were more or less common at the time. See, for example, the accounts to be found in *Irvingiana* (New York, 1860).

Guilford, Connecticut
Decemb 19th '59

My dear Sir

YOUR kind letter, so especially welcome at the moment, ought to have been and would have been immediately answered but for my expectation, from day to day, of being with you in New York, and I now address you for the single purpose of craving your permission to defer the Much I have to say and to ask on the subject which prompted it, a subject so deeply interesting to us both, until I am enabled to call upon you as I hope to do in the course of two or three weeks. It is highly gratifying to know that the perfect propriety of feeling and of language characterizing your description of the closing scenes at Sunnyside has influenced, in a greater or less degree, all similar publications that have, thus far, met my eye, and that your happy expression of a graceful thought, blending, as it does, the summer beauty of the day of burial with the beauty of Irvings character, has already become inseparable from his fame.

Believe me, My dear Sir,
Truly yours
FITZ-GREENE HALLECK

Charles Aug. Davis, Esq.[75]

Halleck was now nearing the age of seventy, but he had grown old gracefully. The poet of the late fifties has been described by one who once saw him as "a man of medium stature, neither short nor tall, stout nor lean, with handsome gray hair inclined to curl, and worn rather long, as was the fashion in those days. He stood so erect, with head slightly thrown back, that he looked taller than he really was. I noticed that, like most men of his generation, he turned his toes out (like a French dancing master), so that his gait had something pedantic, as of a former time. His dress bespoke a serious interest in the subject, as became an earlier day, before carelessness of attire grew from an affectation to a fad. He seemed, notwithstanding his defiant erectness, to be about seventy years of age."[76]

But if his physical strength was somewhat abated, his mind was yet alert, responding eagerly to the advances of those who were wise enough to claim his friendship. The warmth of his address and the good humor of his conversation at once bespoke the days when

[75] Preserved in the New York Public Library.
[76] "A Morning with Fitz-Greene Halleck" in the *Atlantic Monthly*, LXXXIX, 722 (May, 1902). The author of the sketch is not given.

as a young man he had startled New York with *The Croakers* and *Fanny*—only the boisterous, racy wit displayed in *The Croakers* had now grown into the charming playfulness of old age. The social spirit of the early Knickerbockers still stirred in his veins. "Age seems to have come upon him with such a genial touch," wrote James Wynne in 1862, "that few can be found so versatile in conversation, so witty, and yet withal so considerate of the feelings of others."[77] Halleck had lost nothing of his chivalry; nothing of his inherent devotion to the past. "We have been charmed by his conversational ease and fullness," Professor Johnson once observed, "and have listened to his reminiscences of men and things belonging like himself to an older social world that was passing away."[78] But if conservatism had become more and more a part of the very stuff of his thoughts, it did not make the world about him less beautiful either for himself or for others with whom he was brought in contact. The contrast between the worlds of Yesterday and Today still constantly presented itself to him, only to make the present more engaging and piquant. Tuckerman has expressed the regret that Halleck left no book of "Recollections." "The peculiar features of such a work," he observes, "would have been, aside from its incidents and characters, a rare contrast between the Romance and Reality of life in this age: no one felt this more keenly than Halleck, or illustrated it with such amusing zest. That 'ours are the days of fact, not fable,' was a text that awakened his wit and pensiveness to the last; few have loved the poetry of the Past more truly, or perceived the disenchantment of the Present more keenly."[79]

In lieu of such a volume of "Recollections," we may turn to the poet's correspondence during the closing years of his life. With advancing age Halleck found it difficult to visit so often the city where the best part of his life had been spent, and to which his heart even now turned with longing. More and more confined to his native Guilford, he turned as a solace to letter writing. No one who has had the pleasure of examining the poet's letters written at this period can fail to be struck with the truth of Tuckerman's

[77] *Harper's New Monthly Magazine*, XXIV, 638–639.
[78] *Proceedings at the Celebration of the 250th Anniversary of the Settlement of Guilford, Conn.*, p. 128.
[79] *Lippincott's Magazine*, I, 215.

observation: "As a correspondent, his courtesy and tact were extreme: his most casual notes are models of neatness and epigrammatic English, not seldom elaborated into charming epistles. His skill in compliment belonged to a past age; it had an old-world flavor and a graceful kindliness, which few have time—to say nothing of the heart—to fashion now into agreeable phrases."[80] Thus in the correspondence of these last years is reflected the personality of an old man living essentially in the past, but still alert and cheerful at threescore years and ten.

Halleck's exceptional alertness to questions of historic and literary importance[81] is exemplified in the following hitherto unpublished letter which he wrote to Brantz Mayer, the historian. In 1851 Mr. Mayer had delivered before the Maryland Historical Society a lecture discussing the authenticity of Logan's famous speech, as set forth in Thomas Jefferson's *Notes on the State of Virginia* (1784); and defending Captain Michael Cresap against the charges of the Indian chief.[82] The lecture was subsequently published,[83] a copy of which Mr. Mayer appears to have sent to Halleck.

Guilford, Connecticut
Oct. 23^d '58

Dear Sir,

On my return here from a visit to New York I have the honor of receiving your favor of the 11th inst. I am grateful for the pleasure and profit derived from the perusal of the two presents your kindness has sent me.

We have never, in this quarter, attached any importance to the charges of Logan against Colonel Cresap, it being deemed by us, as complete a fiction as the Speech itself, which we have always considered wholly the production of Mr Jeffersons imagination. I am glad to learn from your researches that its merits are truly and substantially Indian, independent[?] of the beautiful language in which he has clothed it, and that the renown it has secured is due really, and nobly to our old School Boy friend Logan, whom his worst foe must admit to have been as powerfully eloquent, and as seldom sober,[84] as Pitt, or Fox, or Sheridan. We are all

---

[80] *Lippincott's Magazine*, I, 211.

[81] For further examples of Halleck's interest in subjects of this kind, see the letter addressed to Thurlow Weed discussing the mystery of Junius (Wilson, *Life*, pp. 551–553); and the letter to W. H. H. Murray in which the poet outlines the pedigree of Alexandre Dumas (see p. 404 of the present work).

[82] Logan accused Cresap of murdering in cold blood his entire family.

[83] *Tah-gah-jute or Logan and Captain Michael Cresap*, Baltimore, 1851. A revised edition of the work was published in Albany in 1867.

[84] Toward the close of his life Logan was a victim of intemperance.

largely indebted to you for relieving, so decidedly, the gallant memory of
Colonel Cresap from unmerited reproach, while we cannot but deem
Logans error in naming him, considering the Colonels high position as
Leader in our rough Border wars, a very natural error, and one appealing
strongly to the magnanimity of the sufferers by it.

Believe me   Dear Sir
gratefully yours
FITZ-GREENE HALLECK

B. Mayer, Esqr[85]

One of the more recent friends of whom Halleck was now becoming fond was Evert A. Duyckinck, who with his brother George had
brought out in 1855 the *Cyclopaedia of American Literature*. The
friendship between Duyckinck and Halleck resulted in a rather
extensive correspondence.[86] In the earliest available letter the poet
expresses his thanks to Duyckinck and his brother who have probably offered him a subscription to the *Century*;[87] and in addition
discourses playfully on a favorite subject of the "Queen's English," which, he always insisted, must be kept "undefiled."

Guilford, Connecticut
Feby. 15th '59

Dear Sir,
I HAVE had the pleasure of receiving your note of the 11th. Please say to
Mr. McElrath that I am very grateful for his courtesy and for the prom-
ised benefits to be derived from so much good reading.

For your part as Editor, I intend to be pleased with everything you
insert, with the following exceptions, one of which has truly annoyed me
sadly in your present numbers.

First, I beg you never to write Honorable John Smith without giving
him the benefit of the definite article. Always say *The* Honorable John
Smith. Secondly, never admit that vile new-born and ill bred phrase *"in
our midst,"* and Thirdly, never admit that still newer and still more ill
bred phrase *"in this connexion."* Like Shylock, I have but few antipathies,

---

[85] Preserved in the Historical Society of Pennsylvania.

[86] A series of fourteen letters of Halleck to Duyckinck is preserved in the
Duyckinck Collection of the New York Public Library.

[87] *The Century; A National Newspaper of Politics, Commerce, Finance,
Economy, Literature, Science and Art*, published weekly by Thomas McElrath,
who for some years had been associated with Horace Greeley on the *Tribune*,
is probably the paper here referred to. In the first issue (December 25, 1858)
it is stated that "the Editorship of *The Century* will be impersonal." Thus no
mention either of the Duyckincks or of any other writers appears in the paper;
but it is probable that the Duyckincks were intimately connected with its editorial management.

but like Tony Lumpkin's companion, the Barnum of his time, who kept a dancing Bear, "I cannot bear anything that's low."

Please give my kind regards to your brother. I meant, as he did me the honor to proffer me the paper, to address my letter to him, but luckily blundered into blending your names in a brotherly manner, and am happy, therefore, in luring two birds from the tree with one whistle. Still, in the strict etiquette of propriety I ought to have placed your brother's name first. With cordial remembrances to our good friend M[r] Panton,[88] I am, Dear Sir

Truly yours

FITZ-GREENE HALLECK.

Evert A. Duyckinck, Esq.[89]

In another letter addressed to Mr. Duyckinck a few days later, Halleck again alludes to the "Queen's English," and also speaks briefly of the articles on himself and Drake in the *Cyclopaedia of American Literature*, which the Duyckincks were planning to issue in a second edition.[90]

Guilford, Connecticut
Feb. 21, '59

Dear Sir,

I HAVE your favor of the 17th and hasten to beg your pardon for my "aspersion," to quote from Mrs. Malaprop, "of your parts of speech," and for preferring the Queen's English of "in connexion with this subject," to the provincialism of our own "in this connexion." I presume that, hereafter, in place of "in compliance with this request," we must write "in this compliance," and for "in pursuance of this object" "in this pursuance," and so on.

After looking over the papers[91] enclosed in your letter, I deem it right and best to ask you to allow me to hold them, in their present state, subject to your order. The alterations in question would be at most very unimportant and the benefit to be derived from them a very inadequate compensation for the time and labor your desire to be strictly accurate has induced you to proffer. The parties to the Biography ought to be, and one of them gratefully is, more than satisfied with the honorable position in which they have been placed in the earliest Edition by the courteous

---

[88] An unidentified friend of Halleck. See also pp. 397–398.

[89] In the Duyckinck Collection of the New York Public Library.

[90] In another letter to Duyckinck (in the New York Public Library), dated May 13, 1866, Halleck again speaks of the articles and suggests two alterations to be made in the text. See letter on p. 355.

[91] Proof sheets of the articles.

partiality of its Authors. Should I have the pleasure of seeing you in time
to make you suggestions for a second Edition available for your purposes,
I shall be happy to be guided by your wishes in relation to it. In the
meantime, pray believe me,

Dear Sir

Truly yours

FITZ-GREENE HALLECK

E. A. Duyckinck, Esq.[92]

In October, 1859, Halleck visited New York. One morning General Wilson breakfasted with him, and was much charmed with the
poet's fund of anecdote. "He conversed on twenty topics in the
course of two hours," relates the biographer. On the following day,
the two planned a trip to Weehawken, and had dinner together
upon their return.[93]

During April of the following year, the poet was again in the
city. The frequency with which he undertook these trips is sufficient evidence, one may believe, of the monotony of Halleck's life
in Guilford. "That he was ever contented with his simple life at
Guilford," wrote Richard Henry Stoddard, "I can no more believe
than that Lamb was content with *his* simple life at Enfield, whither
he retired after leaving the India House. . . . For like Lamb, Halleck was a person of clerkly habits, and was most himself in the
sweet security of the streets. The banishment of men like these
from great cities is seldom voluntary and never consolatory."[94]
Unlike Paulding, who once said, "I have been down [to New York]
but once in ten years, and rarely go farther from home than to
Poughkeepsie,"[95] Halleck derived the keenest of pleasure from
these frequent excursions to the city. But Halleck's visit in April,
1860, was attended with illness, and he was confined to his hotel
during most of his stay.[96] In a letter to John Bigelow, which
alluded pleasantly to the receipt of M. de Chatelain's translation
of "Alnwick Castle," the poet said, "During my recent illness in
New York, Mr. Bryant did me the honor to make my sick room a
pleasant one, by frequently calling upon me. I wish you had been

[92] In the Duyckinck Collection of the New York Public Library.
[93] Wilson, *Life*, p. 518.
[94] *Lippincott's Magazine*, XLIII, 895 (June, 1889).
[95] *Knickerbocker*, LXI, 261 (March, 1863).
[96] Wilson, *Life*, p. 521.

present when he read the translation. His appreciation of the fun of the thing was visible in his eyes. They sparkled like stars in a frosty sky, in the absence of moon or cloud; a study for an artist.''[97]

In 1860 Charles C. Moreau, the friend of the poet, published under the auspices of the Bradford Club the first complete edition of *The Croakers*.[98] The text followed with creditable accuracy the reading of the original versions,—the only considerable change being the substitution of the entire forms of the proper names in place of the dashes and stars of the original—a change entirely within the bounds of propriety. As for the notes accompanying the edition, which consisted largely of commentary upon the men and events mentioned in the satires, so favorable an opinion cannot be expressed. Halleck, who had nothing to do with their preparation, was frankly shocked at their inaccuracy. In writing to Wilson in 1861, the poet remarked, ''I am highly flattered by your expressed wish for the volume you name, but I cannot regret having put it out of my power to present you with it. I have not been willing to send it, for fear of your finding old and new errors innumerable, which it is now too late to correct, and which if corrected would but leave the 'original sins' less excusable.''[99] Again, almost two years after this, Halleck wrote to Benjamin Winthrop: ''With regard to the notes, in the compiling of which, as in the collecting together and publishing for private distribution the Rhymes, you are aware, I was not consulted. I have looked over but the first leaf, and find so many errors, trivial and otherwise, that I have sadly and carefully refrained from throwing a single glance over the remaining leaves.''[100]

The words, these, of an old man, unwilling to disturb the memories of the past. But even during these last years of Halleck's retirement in Guilford, echoes of his old literary fame were wafted to him; he was still counted among the literary celebrities of America. Early in the sixties Halleck was included in a group pic-

---

[97] Wilson, *Life*, p. 523. The letter is dated May 24, 1860. A copy of this letter is preserved in the Duyckinck Collection of the New York Public Library. Of de Chatelain's translation, mention has already been made (see pp. 146–147).

[98] The edition was limited to 250 copies.

[99] *Life*, p. 221. The letter is dated January 28, 1861.

[100] *Ibid.*, p. 223. The letter is dated December 29, 1862. The manuscript sheets from which the Bradford edition was printed are now preserved in the Yale Collection of American Literature.

ture entitled "Washington Irving and his Literary Friends."[101] To this group, designed by the famous illustrator, F. O. C. Darley and painted by C. Schussele of Philadelphia,[102] Halleck playfully refers in a note to Pierre Irving: "It is now nearly a year since I visited New York, and I, thus far, have not yet had the pleasure of seeing the painting of your uncle's friends, in which I am honored with a place; but I understand that its artist has considerately made me the ugliest-looking fellow of the group. Remembering, as I do, the boast of the backwoodsman that he had the swiftest horse, the surest rifle, the prettiest sister, and the ugliest dog in all Kentucky, meaning a compliment to each, I feel highly flattered in being portrayed as 'Poor Tray,' who, you know, is renowned as the ugliest, the fondest, and the most faithful of all dogs in story and song."[103] "We did not see all Irving's literary friends . . .," remarked the editor of the *Knickerbocker* in commenting on the painting, "but Cooper, Prescott, Longfellow, Bancroft, Hawthorne, Willis, Simms, Bryant, Halleck, and a few more were there naturally grouped without being caricatured."[104] An engraving[105] was later made after the painting, a copy of which the publishers sent to Halleck. The following note, addressed to Evert Duyckinck, relates to another copy of the engraving in the hands of one of Halleck's friends in Guilford, who had desired the poet to find for it a purchaser.

Guilford, Connecticut
April 18, '66

My dear Sir,

In ungrateful return for your kind letter of the 15th, I am about to bother you with a request.

A neighbor of mine, here in the country, has the control, in the way of trade, of a copy of the Engraving of "Washington Irving's Friends," for which he is desirous of finding a sale in New York. It is in good condition, and equal, if not superior in appearance, to the Copy in my Possession, Presented me by its publishers. Will you please endeavor, if opportunity

---

[101] It was exhibited at the Derby Galleries in New York, 625 Broadway.

[102] *Knickerbocker*, LXIII, 94 (January, 1864).

[103] Wilson, *Life*, pp. 528–529. The letter is undated.

[104] LXIII, 94 (January, 1864).

[105] Made by Thomas Oldham Barlow of London. See *Sketches of Distinguished American Authors, Represented in Darley's New National Picture, entitled Washington Irving and his Literary Friends, at Sunnyside* (New York, 1863).

offers, to procure an offer for it from some responsible Picture dealer, advising me of the amount, and oblige

My dear Sir   Yours truly

F. G. HALLECK

E. A. Duyckinck, Esq.[106]

Thus Halleck seems to have taken a friendly interest in the affairs of his neighbors. But the inhabitants of Guilford were often disturbed by the poet's bohemian ways. Long accustomed to indulgence in wines while in New York, he never gave up the enjoyment which he found in their use. For this reason he frequently shocked the Puritan sensibilities of many of the villagers, who often failed to respond to the poet's addresses.[107] But Halleck had his friends in Guilford who were charmed by his courteous manners and innate chivalry. Henry P. Robinson of Guilford in 1889, at the two hundred and fiftieth anniversary of the town, thus recalled Halleck as an old man: "We see still the surtouted, pliant figure of this gifted man, moving with gentle bearing through our streets, giving us the cue of courtesy while lifting his hat with kindly grace to all."[108] William A. Jones, the critic, who spent July, 1866, in Guilford, gives us a similar picture of Halleck's winning manners. The poet several times waited upon Mr. Jones, and "made good long calls, enlivened by his charming vivacity, anecdote, ready illustration and brilliant fancy; by his ever apt and agreeable reminiscences; by his playful satire and wit; by his fine sense and admirable taste and temper."[109] "Owing to the increasing deafness which accompanied his later years, Mr. Halleck's conversation, by tacit agreement with his interlocutors, was suffered to take quite largely the form of monologue; and no one who has ever

[106] In the Duyckinck Collection of the New York Public Library.

[107] See Wilson, *Life*, p. 58. The following unpolished comment of an old Guilford inhabitant at once suggests the prejudice of some of Halleck's townsmen. "I went often to his [Halleck's] home, attended the dedication of his monument, heard Bayard Taylor read his *Connecticut*, saw the bunch of natives who kept away back in the grave yard at the dedication services, because they thought they had not ought to honor Halleck because he drank whiskey!" It is of interest to note that Bayard Taylor was also more than once annoyed by the prejudices of his Quaker neighbors at Kennett. See Hanson-Taylor and Scudder, *Life and Letters of Bayard Taylor* (Boston, 1884), II, 514-515.

[108] *Proceedings at the Celebration of the 250th Anniversary of the Settlement of Guilford, Conn.*, p. 128.

[109] Wilson, *Life*, p. 539.

heard him on these occasions will forget the brilliant fund of anecdote with which he was endowed, or the animated manner which
illumined his whole face and enlivened his slightest gestures as he
talked.''[110] One of Halleck's chief diversions, after his return to
Guilford, was walking. ''He was a great walker for a man of
seventy-six,'' writes Jones, ''and took his daily stroll to the hotel
at the Point, chatted with the visitors, his old and new acquaintances. He was regularly at the post-office when the New-York mail
came in, and almost always had a budget. His New-York friends
kept him supplied with magazines, papers, pamphlets, etc., etc. I
often accompanied him in these walks, and became more his admirer than ever. He had a fine, quaint nature, evinced in many
ways; always had a kind word for children, and sometimes for
favorite canine acquaintances; nodded, or bowed, or smiled, salut-
ing every one most appropriately, according to his degree and sta-
tion—a truly courteous, gallant and chivalric gentleman, in the
best sense of that abused word.''[111] Not only at Guilford Point, a
near-by seaside resort, was the poet often to be found, but also at
Sachem's Head, an even more popular retreat for vacationists.
''At the 'Head' Halleck is always a welcome visitor,'' observed
James Wynne in 1862, ''and his arrival is ever sure to produce
some little bustle among the inmates of this retired but really
beautiful watering-place. Indeed, he is here looked upon as in
some sort a part of their property—a kind of local lion, which
they have a right to include among the attractions of the place.
Halleck submits good-humoredly to all this, and talks so pleasantly
that no one regrets a tarry at the 'Head' if, during his sojourn, he
happens to make his acquaintance.''[112]

With 1861 came the outbreak of the Civil War. Halleck's attitude to the Rebellion is reflected at this period in his correspondence. His earliest reference to the conflict is made in a letter addressed to Mrs. John Rush who had asked the poet to write a war
lyric. ''Moreover, sadly and seriously,'' replied the poet, ''is this
Southern, this sin-born war of ours, worthy of a poet's consecra-
tion? a poet, whose art, whose attribute it is to make the dead on

[110] Joel Benton, *Frank Leslie's Illustrated Newspaper*, XXV, 243.
[111] Wilson, *Life*, pp. 539–540.
[112] *Harper's New Monthly Magazine*, XXIV, 634. It was at the ''Head''
that Wynne first met Halleck.

fields of battle, alike the victors and the vanquished, look beautiful in the sunbeams of his song. On the contrary, it is but a mutiny, a monster mutiny, whose ring-leaders are a dozen crime-worn politicians, determined to keep themselves in power, and will sooner or later find its Nemesis in the blood and tears of a servile insurrection."[113] Henry T. Tuckerman recalls "the inexpressible sadness of his expressive features when he spoke of the war for the Union as one too sternly sad to inspire a native minstrel. 'A necessary war, waged,' he said, 'to put down a base mutiny.' "[114] In reply to a note written to the poet by Samuel Ward, enclosing some verses which the latter had written, evidently as a satire upon Gen. Benjamin Butler, Halleck said: "Your lines delight my anti-Lincoln neighbours, to whom I have lent them. As a lover of fair-play I have tried to induce them to read Butler's 'Farewell,' but in vain. A party-man like Irving's Dutch Justice always refuses to be bothered by hearing both sides. For my part, Butler is one of my heroes, of which this deplorable war has produced at least four, viz., Jefferson Davis, General Butler, John Van Buren, and Captain Rynders."[115] Such was the fairness, the broad-mindedness of the poet's soul, as to consider impartially both sides of the struggle that had divided the nation. Thus he did not scruple to place Davis first upon his list of heroes. Stonewall Jackson also claimed his admiration. Upon one occasion the poet wrote: "I refrain from alluding to this deplorable and never-to-be-ended war. Would to God we could have my old friend Jackson back again to put down this accursed rebellion and restore the blessings of peace to our bleeding country."[116] But in spite of Halleck's love of fair play, an instinct inherent in his nature to recognize ability and bravery wherever encountered, Halleck preserved his loyalty to the North. Of the poet's attitude to the Southern cause, Joel Benton has written:

During the late rebellion he was heartily with the Government. He told me, the last time I met him, he thought the war had cured the South of two things—"the crime of Slavery, and the folly of State Sovereignty."

[113] Wilson, *Life*, p. 524. The letter is dated November 21, 1861.

[114] *Lippincott's Magazine*, I, 215.

[115] Wilson, *Bryant and His Friends*, pp. 269–270. The letter is dated January 3, 1863.

[116] Wilson, *Life*, p. 529. The letter is undated.

At about the age of seventy-five.

South Carolina, he considered, had made herself utterly ridiculous, when, in attempting to achieve her State independence, she had, by joining the Confederacy, put her neck directly under the foot of a Mississippi autocrat. Mr. Halleck had known Mr. Calhoun, and considered him a rather second-rate man in many respects.[117]

During the month of August, 1863, subsequent to the fall of Vicksburg, James Grant Wilson, who was serving in the Union army, obtained a furlough and visited his friends in the North. In calling upon the poet, Wilson found him "much changed in appearance." His beard had now grown white, and he whimsically remarked to his friend, "I was afraid I should be taken for twenty-five, and so I have white-washed my beard *to avoid the draft.*"[118] But Joel Benton, to whom the poet similarly commented on his white beard, found less change in Halleck's appearance at this period. "Accosting him soon after the close of the war," Benton relates, "when I had not seen him for three years, I remarked how little he had changed. To which he replied, with singularly playful humor, 'Oh yes; but you see I have white-washed my beard, so that I should not be taken for twenty-five and be drafted.' "[119]

Not infrequently, during these years of retirement, must Halleck have been gratified with the special honors which fellow poets were pleased to bestow upon him. About a decade before, in 1852, Mrs. Lydia Huntley Sigourney addressed to Halleck a poetic epistle, which concluded:

> Halleck! beneath your natal sky
> Still do you link in classic numbers
> That humor, quiet, quaint, and fine
> Which few like you are skilled to twine?
> Or with Bozzaris' battle-cry,
> Startle the mermaids from their slumbers,
> Where Guilford, like a well-set pin,
> Stands *"Head"* and *"Point"* the sea within?
> Please solve these doubts, when inclination
> And leisure blend,
> And count me still, in every station,
> Truly, your friend.[120]

[117] *Frank Leslie's Illustrated Newspaper*, XXV, 243 (January 4, 1868).
[118] *Life*, p. 530.
[119] *Frank Leslie's Illustrated Newspaper*, XXV, 243 (January 4, 1868).
[120] Wilson, *Life*, pp. 493–494. Wilson dates these verses "June, 1852."

It should not be supposed that Halleck was so ungracious as to neglect to answer this charming epistle. Unfortunately, however, no reply has been found—and, indeed, no correspondence between the two for a period of about ten years. The following letter of Halleck to Mrs. Sigourney, written in 1863, when both were well over seventy,[121] is full of that youthful, courtly dalliance in addressing women, which Halleck had never lost.

> Guilford, Connecticut,
> November 21, 1863

My dear Mrs. Sigourney,

I TAKE much pleasure in thanking you for your very courteous letter of remembrance, and for the high compliment your expressions of regret for the failure of my anticipated visit you so gracefully pay me, and I am glad to find that, in one respect, my list has had the good sense to model itself after yours by its habit of "early rising," for the music of Shakespeare's line, "Rise with the lark to-morrow, young Norfolk," has nightly accompanied my evening Song since Childhood. The gentlemen, however, who have so kindly reminded you of me, have slightly misunderstood my remark. I did not mean to say that I was told that you were not *up,* but that you were not *down;* in other words, were not in the Drawing Room, and fancying that a Lady's absence from her Moted [?] Morning Seat was, in the etiquette of Watering places, a silent and civil manner of saying "Not at home." I sadly submitted accordingly, and requested a gentleman there of your acquaintance, to present to you my compliments and good wishes, in his best style, but it now appears, that he neglected to do so, being inclined to bear, like the Turk, "no brother near the throne," and keep himself and his own interests solely in view during all his conversations with you—like a sensible man.

I open our friend Mr. Bonner's Ledger weekly, in the hope, and I am glad to say often in the certainty of finding you and yours there, always in their Autumn re-opening, fulfilling the promise of the bud and the blossom, to delight of his readers. H—[?] has, more than once, kindly expressed his willingness to number me among his contributors, and I have recently half promised to avail myself of it, but my pen has so long been out of print that I fear it can do nothing capable of pleasing him, and I find it very difficult indeed to weave a web of song, or of story which he can conscientiously deem worthy of a place on the same page with the verse of Mrs. Sigourney, and the prose of Edward Everett.

Repeating my thanks for your kind letter, and hoping that it will form

---

[121] As Mrs. Sigourney was born in 1791, she was but one year younger than Halleck.

the prelude to many others, equally gracious and gratifying, I beg you to believe me, Dear Lady,

Very gratefully and respectfully yours,

FITZ-GREENE HALLECK.

Mrs. L. H. Sigourney[122]

Although courteously pleading his inability to contribute anything to Mr. Bonner's paper that should be deemed "worthy of a place on the same page with the verse of Mrs. Sigourney, and the prose of Edward Everett," Halleck was at this time unquestionably preparing a poem for the columns of the *New York Ledger*. His "Young America" appeared in the *Ledger* for January 23, 1864. Joel Benton, in commenting on the poem, observed that "for many years Mr. Halleck had abandoned writing. No poem had appeared from his pen during a long interval, until Mr. Bonner (how, I never could exactly tell) induced him to contribute to the *Ledger*."[123] Mr. Benton need not have inquired deeply into the reasons for Halleck's capitulation to Bonner's request, had he considered the fact that the poet received for his verses the sum of five hundred dollars.[124] Halleck, who was undoubtedly at this time sorely pressed for money, probably embraced this means of repairing his resources.

The poem, a belated and feeble attempt at satire, portrays Young America,[125] a boy of fifteen, rejecting the idealistic callings of Preacher, Soldier, and Teacher, to marry in the end "A Rich Wife." Halleck had never surrendered his preoccupation in the contrast presented by romance and reality; and his inherent dislike of America's commercialism, to which so much of his life had been devoted, thus found a final expression, four years before the poet's death. But the execution of the idea was feeble. In "Young

[122] In the Hoadley Collection of the Connecticut Historical Society, Hartford, Connecticut.

[123] *Frank Leslie's Illustrated Newspaper*, XXV, 243 (January 4, 1868).

[124] Cozzens, *Fitz-Greene Halleck. A Memorial*, p. 19.

[125] The phrase "Young America" was in frequent use at this period. As early as 1845 a New York paper bore the phrase as a title. Concerning its adoption as a slogan by a group of New York Democrats in the election of 1852, see M. E. Curti's article "Young America" in the *American History Review*, XXXII, 34–55 (October, 1926). The theme of Halleck's poem may have been suggested by a parody of "Hiawatha" entitled "Plu-Ri-Bus-Tah," which was written by Mortimer Thompson and published in 1856. Here "Yunga-Merrekah" perishes, seeking the "Almighty dollar."

America'' we have neither the well-balanced contrast of the medieval and modern worlds which we find in ''Alnwick Castle,'' nor the consistent serio-comic manner of *Fanny*. Thus ''Young America'' lacks artistic balance. Whereas two thirds of the poem is devoted to a sentimental picturing of the idealistic possibilities open to Young America, the conclusion, suggestive of the serio-comic, and bearing little relation in style to the previous portion of the poem, is obviously forced and incongruous. To be sure, a few passages suggest the charm of Halleck's earlier verse; and the introduction of a war lyric must have given the poem a certain contemporary interest; but the work as a whole could hardly have been identified as Halleck's had not his name been attached.

Halleck was apparently pleased with his latest effort at verse, although he modestly wrote to Wilson, ''I took the liberty, some time since, of shipping by mail to New Orleans a package of weak rhymes. Had they sufficient strength to reach you alive?''[126] To his disappointment, however, at the silence of Mrs. Rush of Philadelphia, a lady whose friendship he highly valued, the poet alludes in the following extract from a letter written probably in January, 1865:

I am very grateful to the two pre-Raphaelite pictures which embellish my "Young America,"[127] partly because they have uplifted its price from five cents to fifty, and particularly because they have upwaked your friendly recollections of me, and have added one more to your always-wished-for and welcome letters.

I was not disappointed by your silence on the subject of the verses when I sent them to you a year ago. In these "sensation" times I cannot expect them to be liked, or even tolerated. There is, I am aware, nothing in them resembling Miss Braddon's exciting themes in prose, or Enoch Arden's story of polygamy (so decent, delicate, and decorous) in verse. Yet there is "balm in Gilead," for, to soothe and strengthen me against your so deeply-lamented disapproval of them, your neighbor, Mr. Allibone,[128] the author of the best book of its kind in any language, and with whom, although I have never yet met him, I have the honor of corresponding, has sent me a notice of them, written by a relation of his, and pub-

---

[126] *Life*, p. 533. Letter dated February, 1864.

[127] At the close of 1864 an illustrated edition of the poem was brought out by Appleton. The date on the title-page was 1865.

[128] The author of *A Critical Dictionary of English Literature and British and American Authors* (Lippincott, 1858–71; 4 vols.).

lished in your *City Item* newspaper of 31st December last. Pray borrow a copy, and you will learn how much of all that is good and graceful, etc., etc., you have missed finding in them, and (he blushes as he writes it) in their ingenious and ingenuous author![129]

Many of Halleck's friends, however, were pleased with "Young America." Joel Benton believed that in this poem Halleck had "struck the final chords of his melodious verse. The choice of 'Young America' gave him a characteristic theme, one happily suited to his genial fancy, and sunny, lambent humor. It was handled in his own peculiar inimitable vein, and I know that the author looked upon it ever after as worthy to rank among his best works."[130] Another friend, William H. H. Murray,[131] wrote Halleck the following note in regard to his new poem:

> Washington
> Conn—
> Jan–18–64[132]

Fitz-Greene Halleck
Dear Sir,
NOTHING but the fear of taxing your good nature by trespassing upon the time required by your other and more entertaining correspondents has restrained me from writing you long ago. Nor [can] I ever conceive that you still remember one kindly who is grateful to you for whatever of correct taste he may have in regard to polite literature—especial [sic] in that branch which your own writings adorn. And perhaps even now, a fear of troubling you would have kept me silent were it not for the fact that by resuming your pen after so long a lapse you have, as it were, given a certain license for your admirers to address you. In common with many others I presume I hasten to improve the opportunity.

Your "Young America" reached me a day after it was published. I have read it with much carefulness, and pardon me when I say with some anxiety—for being one who takes an honest pride in your reputation present & future I feared lest your long cessation from composition (say nothing about the increasing weight of your many years) would make it difficult for you to equal the excellence of your earlier productions. Allow

---

129 Wilson, *Life*, pp. 533–534.

130 *Frank Leslie's Illustrated Newspaper*, XXV, 243.

131 Born in Guilford in 1840, and graduated from Yale in 1862. He was subsequently noted as a clergyman, and as the author of numerous prose works.

132 "Young America" appeared in the *Ledger* for January 23, 1864. As this was a weekly paper, it was probably issued some days in advance of its actual date. This fact probably accounts for the discrepancy suggested by the date of this letter.

me to say I find myself happily disappointed. It seems to me you have written in ten stanzas[133] the best war lyric our country has yet produced. I feel it in my heart to thank [you] not so much as a personal friend as an American. And taking the poem as a whole I cannot tell you how much I am pleased with it. May God give you life and health to produce another and another before you lay down your pen forever. My Lady joins me heartily in all that I have written especially in the closing sentence. If your leisure and health permit will you not please send me the pedigree of Alex. Dumas.[134]

Please remember me kindly to your amiable sister as I remain

Yours Truly—W. H. H. MURRAY[135]

Frederic S. Cozzens, the humorist, was another friend who was enthusiastic in his praise of the poem.

Chestnut College, Jany 24, 1863.[136]

My dear Mr. Halleck

I AM much obliged to you for your courtesy in sending me a copy of your new poem. It went to Washington where I was not, then returned to New York, and finally reached me here, where I am spending a few brief happy days. Well Sir I read it over three or four times, and the more I read it, the better I liked it. Excuse me for telling you my own impressions about it. At first it seemed not well put together, the changes seemed too abrupt, but then I recollected that "extreme exactitude is the sublime of fools," and began to consider whether I should mete your poem by the standards of my mind, or measure my mind by the genius of your poem. Following the last course I began to read with renewed delight and certain passages with renewed relish. I cannot compare it to anything else for it is not like anything else. But I recognize in it the touch of a master's hand. Something that may be enjoyed but cannot be defined. Light-hearted, joyous, exuberant, here and anon a touch of pathos that unveils the secret urn of tears. But one thing—one line I do not see the truth of :—

"But my ambitious leaves no more are green."[137]

I should prefer to amend it thus,

In ages hence thy laurels will be seen,
And every leaflet won will be Fitz-Greene.

---

[133] "Young America": "Nearer the bugle's echo comes" (1869 ed., p. 181).

[134] For Halleck's answer to this question, see the letter dated January 29, 1864, on p. 404.

[135] In the Chamberlain Collection of the Boston Public Library.

[136] This date, which should, of course, be 1864, is obviously an error due to an inadvertence only too common at the opening of a new year.

[137] "Young America" (1869 edition of Halleck's poems, p. 192).

Oh you will have a wreath of laurel when that old Puritan[138] who has more brain than heart, will fade away in the effulgence of Wordsworth's fame. Did you ever read Wordsworth, and after him Bryant? Why it is a penny trumpet after a full orchestra.

How shocked I was to hear of the death of Thackeray.[139] He was a great man and a kindly one. As you know they have deposed Verplanck[140] at the Century[141] and elected Bancroft[142] in his place. One of the members who voted against Verplanck told me he considered him *socially* as superior to his successor, but he did not like his politics.[143] So a club for the promotion of social enjoyment and literary and artistic taste abjures its original intentions and places upon its pedestal the image of Lincoln!— or Bancroft. I am writing a few notes on Irving.[144] Some anecdotes of him which I derived from you I suppose I may repeat? Be assured the last will be done with proper delicacy. I leave Yonkers for Washington tomorrow and if you can bestow a few lines on me there I shall be proud and happy.

Truly your much obliged
FRED^k S. COZZENS[145]

William Cullen Bryant, however, was more equivocal in his praise. "*Young America*," he once observed, is "a poem, which, though not by any means to be placed among his best, contains, as Mr. Cozzens,[146] in a paper read before this society justly remarks, passages which remind us of his earlier vigor and grace."[147] Evert A. Duyckinck, in a review of the poem published in the *New York Times*, correctly described "Young America" as "a poem of some three hundred lines, or rather a series of lyrics in varied measure, held together by a running comment in airy, rhymed iambics." Duyckinck, however, seems largely to have missed the satiric touch with which the poem concludes. After bestowing due praise upon the verses in general, he comments thus upon the abrupt ending:

[138] Bryant.
[139] Thackeray died December 24, 1863.
[140] See pp. 222–223.
[141] The Century Club. See p. 322.
[142] George Bancroft, the historian.
[143] Verplanck was a Democrat.
[144] So far as can be ascertained, these notes were never published. To the *New York Ledger* for December 17, 1859, Cozzens contributed a brief article on Irving which was reprinted in *Irvingiana* (New York, 1859), p. lvi; but no later article has come to light.
[145] In the collection of Captain Frank L. Pleadwell, Medical Corps, United States Navy.
[146] Of this poem Cozzens had said in *Fitz-Greene Halleck. A Memorial* (p. 29), "It is a spirited production, with many very beautiful lines, whose music recalls some of his earliest and best verses."
[147] *Some Notices of the Life and Writings of Fitz-Greene Halleck*, p. 18.

"Most lame and impotent conclusion to this finely touched poem. We can appreciate the author's difficulty, after getting the young sleeping hero so magnificently on the stage, to get him creditably off again. But that was his look out. He introduced him, and is responsible for his exit. It is an old affectation of Halleck, this 'art of sinking,' as the Scriblerus Club called it, originating, possibly, in his desire to escape the semblance of sentimentality, somewhat redeemed by the felicity of his verse and its occasional humor, but a doubtful aid to his genius. In the present case the poet has lost a golden opportunity of building a truly heroic poem, and has dragged down one of the finest of modern lyrics at the end to the level of that questionable form of composition, a humorous (?) college anniversary 'Poem.' We cannot help comparing this conclusion with the simple, exquisite early sketch by Hawthorne, entitled 'David Swan,'[148] who is also a youth asleep by the roadside in a 'grassy lair' where various personages brush against him, with different designs of good or evil for his fortunes, illustrating the events which may nearly happen to a man without his being conscious of them.'[149]

In the following letter addressed to Mr. Duyckinck, Halleck comments at length upon the preceding review of "Young America":

Guilford, Connecticut,
Feby. 2^d 64

My dear Sir,

I HAVE had the honor of receiving your kind letter, and I hasten to thank you very much for placing my name in such good company, and, in behalf of Mr. Bonner's purse and my own poetry, for saving him the expense of a Page of Advertisements in the "Times" and me from the mortification of being unnoticed in its Pages.

In the words of our old and gentlemanly acquaintance, Mr. Recorder Riker, addressed to me on a certain occasion, "You have made me immortal."[150] You, doubtless, remember the case of Assault and Battery, wherein the Sufferer's Lawyer so eloquently depicted his Client's wrongs, that the poor fellow burst into tears, and declared that until then he had had no idea how terribly he had been beaten; so in my case, I had not the slight-

---

[148] This sketch of Hawthorne's in *Twice-Told Tales*, similar in design to Halleck's poem, may have suggested the plan of "Young America."
[149] January 30, 1864.   [150] See p. 174.

est idea of my own exalted merits, until your eloquence of thought and expression convinced me of the fact.

Hereafter I shall, like King Richard, esteem myself "a marvelous proper man," entitled like Mr. Justice Dogberry to have "two gowns and everything handsome about me," and you, by the beauty and power of your style as a writer of unsurpassable prose, are now wearing the Mantle of Sir Philip Sidney, renowned in song as the delightful "warbler of Poetic prose." Long may you live to tread in the footsteps of your Illustrious predecessor.

Seriously, I am truly happy to learn, and to have so gracefully conveyed to me, your good opinion of the dignified part of the poem and as I am, myself, delighted with the undignified part of it, all is well between us.

When I again visit New York, it is now nearly a year since my last visit, I shall hasten to express more fully in person my share of your courtesies. In the meantime, please remember me kindly to your brother in Law, and quoting from Farquar [sic] in his "Beaux Stratagem" "to all friends round this [Wrekin?]"[151] and believe me,—My dear Sir

gratefully yours

FITZ-GREENE HALLECK.

Evert Duykink [sic] Esq.[152]

A little later in the same month, Duyckinck wrote to Halleck with the request, "If you have not an oath in heaven against such impertinences, may I put your good nature to the trouble of copying for me,—that I may rejoice in the autograph—the lyric of 'Young America' commencing,

Hark! a bugles' Echo comes."[153]

Halleck's reply, which accompanied the autograph, relates in part to "Young America."

---

[151] This word is illegible in the manuscript, and I have been unable to find anything like the quotation given, in the editions of *The Beaux' Stratagem* which I have examined. Halleck may here have confused Farquhar's play with another.

[152] In the Duyckinck Collection.

[153] A copy of Duyckinck's letter, dated February 5, 1864, is in the Duyckinck Collection.

This lyric, which was much admired, appeared, among other places, in *Autograph Leaves of Our Country's Authors* (Baltimore, 1864), edited by John P. Kennedy and Alexander Bliss. Halleck's letter of transmittal to Mr. Kennedy, accompanying the copy of the verses, is now in the Peabody Institute of the City of Baltimore.

Guilford, Connecticut
Feby 17 '64

My dear Sir,

I OWE you an apology for so long delaying my grateful acknowledgments of the receipt of your letter, of the request with which it honored me, and of the very curious and interesting presents it enclosed, for all which please accept my best thanks.

The truth is that your recent notice of me has, allow me to repeat, made me, for the moment, a man of mark, a sort of Target for Ladies and others aiding Sanitary fairs,[154] &c., to shoot their letters at, and I have been so much occupied, of late, in answering and obliging those of the gentler sex, as to be compelled to rely upon the gallantry of the rougher, and their principle of *place aux dames* for pardon and forbearance.

Moreover, I have deemed it proper, with reference to the Enclosed, to obtain Mr. Bonner's permission in the premises, the copyright, for the present, being his. He consents, very gracefully, and adds, by the way, that he intends making a donation of the Original Manuscript to your City's Sanitary Fair.[155] Ought it not (the Manuscript, I mean, not the City) to be very proud? I have assured him that you mean to keep the Copy exclusively to yourself until you can find a purchaser. Hoping often to hear from you and of your welfare I am

My dear Sir, truly yours
FITZ-GREENE HALLECK.[156]

On the seventieth anniversary of Bryant's birth, November 5, 1864,[157] the members of the Century Club gave the poet a dinner. Halleck, who was confined to his home because of illness, was unable to be present. Like several who could not attend, however, he sent a note to those in charge of the dinner, expressing his disappointment, and asking them "to assure Mr. Bryant that, although far off in body, I shall be this evening near him in spirit, repeating the homage which with heart, and voice, and pen, I have during more than forty years of his 'three score and ten' been delighted

---

[154] Preserved in the library of the Long Island Historical Society (Brooklyn, New York) is a manuscript containing twelve lines of Halleck's verses to Lieutenant Allen copied by the poet for "the Brooklyn Sanitary Fair," and dated "Feby. 6, 1864."

[155] During April, 1864, the Sanitary Fair issued a periodical called the *Spirit of the Fair*, to which many American writers contributed original selections. Halleck, it was thought, would make a contribution, but unfortunately failed to do so.

[156] In the Duyckinck Collection.

[157] Bryant was born November 3, 1794; the "Bryant Festival" was held November 5, 1864.

to pay him.''[158] In speaking at the dinner of those whose faces he missed, Bryant said, ''I miss Pierpont,[159] venerable in years, yet vigorous in mind and body, and with an undimmed fancy; and him whose pages are wet with the tears of maidens who read the story of 'Evangeline'; and the author of 'Fanny' and the 'Croakers,' no less renowned for the fiery spirit which animated his 'Marco Bozzaris'; and him to whose wit we owe the 'Biglow Papers,' who made a lowly flower of the wayside as classical as the rose of Anacreon.''[160]

Thus were reminders of the ''good old days'' constantly being brought back to Halleck, who, in his retreat at Guilford, responded with whole-hearted interest to the efforts of friends to make his last years happy. The following letters—one, retrospective in its mention of the former president of the New York Historical Society; the other, full of that playful gallantry that marked his address to women—were written in October, 1865. The name of Mrs. Botta must have recalled to the poet many a social evening spent years before in her salon in company with distinguished *literati* of the city.[161]

Guilford, Connecticut
Oct. 16, 65

Dear Sir,
I CANNOT refrain from accepting the very courteous proffer conveyed in

---

[158] *The Bryant Festival at ''The Century.''* November 5, MDCCCLXIV (New York, 1865), pp. 71–72.

[159] John Pierpont (1785–1866), a Boston clergyman, was the author of *Airs of Palestine,* first published in 1816.

[160] P. Godwin, *A Biography of William Cullen Bryant,* II, 215. The mutual admiration of Bryant and Halleck lasted to the end. Of Bryant's ''The Planting of the Apple Tree,'' published in *Thirty Poems* (New York, 1864), Halleck was an admirer. He knew the poem by heart, and once made a copy of the verses, which General Wilson later sent to Bryant (see *Some Notices of the Life and Writings of Fitz-Greene Halleck,* p. 19; and Wilson, *Bryant and His Friends,* p. 86). Concerning Bryant's poetry Halleck once made the following remark, the last sentence of which displays a critical acumen unusual with the poet: ''His genius is almost the only instance of a high order of thought becoming popular; not that the people do not prize literary worth, but because they are unable to comprehend obscure poetry. Bryant's pieces seem to be fragments of one and the same poem, and require only a common plot to constitute a unique epic'' (*The Family Library of Poetry and Song. . . . Edited by William Cullen Bryant. . . . also containing the Biographical Memoir of Bryant by James Grant Wilson,* New York [1880], p. 19).

[161] See pp. 298–299.

your letter of the 13th of a copy of the Engraving of Mr. Bradish,[162] an intimacy of more than forty years with that accomplished scholar and gentleman having rendered his memory particularly dear to me,—a proffer for which I beg you to believe me very grateful. My only regret is that in placing it in my obscure Cabinet, I am depriving its merits as a Work of art from being known to a wider circle of admirers, than I am well assured they eminently deserve.

Pray let it be sent me at the least possible trouble and expense to you, and with my kindest remembrances and acknowledgments to your Brother, believe me, Dear Sir

Truly yours
FITZ-GREENE HALLECK

Charles C. Moreau, Esq.[163]

October 17, 1865.

My dear Mrs. Botta:

AMONG the "winged words" (I am reading Lord Derby's "Homer") and winning words of yours that made our recent interview so pleasant to me, were those expressing your willingness to possess the inclosed portrait of mine. I trust that its beard, being more flowing and picturesque and Bryant-like than mine is since its last reaping, will have the honor to meet your generous and gracious approval.

When Madame Catalani, at Weimar, was proffered an introduction to Goethe, she innocently asked: "Who is *he?* What instrument does he play upon?" I find myself fast becoming as ignorant of books and of their authors as a dozen opera-singers, for until I saw (since seeing you) at Appleton's your husband's very handsome volume,[164] I had no idea that he was an author, even in his own language, still less that he was so complete a master of ours as a glance over the volume so convincingly showed me. I look forward to great pleasure and profit from its perusal.

Why did you not, my dear lady, mention it to me the other day when we talking about Dante? Why did you allow me to utter such superficial nonsense about his writings, translations, etc., when you were brimful of all his beautiful thoughts and still more beautiful expressions, and could have set me right when I was wrong, and made me knowing when I was

---

[162] Luther Bradish (1783–1863). Well known as a lawyer and philanthropist. He held several political positions in New York state. From 1845 to 1849 Vice-President of the New York Historical Society; from 1850 to 1863 President.

[163] In the Henry E. Huntington Library and Art Gallery, San Gabriel, California.

[164] Vincenzo Botta, *Dante as Philosopher, Patriot, and Poet* (New York, 1865).

ignorant? O woman! woman! how you must have laughed at me in both your sleeves!

I am not quite sure that I thanked you in voice, at the time you gave it, for your "Handbook."[165] If I did, twice over can do no harm. I wish I had had access to such a work in my boyhood. It would have saved me from becoming tired of getting by heart all the quartos and octavos composing such a library as Charles Lamb says "no gentleman is without"— such works as Tom Campbell defines many of the Elizabethan dramas to be—a bucket of water containing a single glass of whiskey. Your well-brewed and delicately flavored bowl of punch is worth them all.

Pray oblige me by saying that this inclosed has reached you, and that you are, as usual, "healthy, wealthy, and wise"; and believe me, dear Mrs. Botta, Truly yours,

FITZ-GREENE HALLECK[166]

Though somewhat enfeebled in health, Halleck, during the closing years of his life, it may readily be seen, possessed a mind almost as keenly alive to the world about him, as it had ever been at any time in his younger days. Richard Henry Dana, author of "The Buccaneer," himself a man of eighty, in writing to William A. Jones in August, 1860, said: "Your account of Mr. Halleck put new life in me, or rather, renewed my old. What a blessing to be in full possession of such a cheerful old age, with all the faculties wide awake, and so many too, as his!"[167] The vigor of Halleck's mind at

---

[165] Mrs. Anne C. Lynch Botta published the *Handbook of Universal Literature* in 1860.

[166] *Memoirs of Anne C. L. Botta* (New York, 1894), pp. 348–349.

[167] Wilson, *Life*, p. 542. Halleck had no intimate acquaintance with Dana, who once wrote to General Wilson: "I greatly regret my acquaintance with Mr. Halleck having been too slight for me to tell you anything new about him. I well remember dining with him, many years ago, at our friend Bryant's, and how frank and genial he was. I took to him at once, but never saw him after" (*Bryant and His Friends*, pp. 204–205). Of this meeting Parke Godwin has spoken. Once when Dana and Longfellow "were Mr. Bryant's guests at a dinner, they were joined by Halleck, and thus the four most famous poets that our literature had yet produced were brought together, and their conversations, we may well suppose, if they could have been reported, would have added a lively chapter to the best chronicles of table-talk. Dana and Halleck were men of the past in politics and religion; Bryant and Longfellow men of the present and future" (*A Biography of William Cullen Bryant*, I, 376). Toward the close of Halleck's life Dana wrote, probably to Wilson: "You tell me wonders of Halleck. Why, I thought he was on his last legs! I should indeed like to see him, and especially in his Connecticut village. One would be at home with him there, if I understand him. I have met with very few professedly literary men so much to my liking, so natural and easy and self-forgetful" (*Bryant and His Friends*, p. 204).

the age of seventy-six is further attested by the following sheaf of
letters addressed to Mr. Duyckinck a year before the poet's death.
With the aid of annotation, they tell their own story of Halleck's
life for 1866, and reflect throughout that "cheerful old age," so
much admired by Dana.

Guilford, Connecticut
April 11 '66

My dear Sir,

I AM very grateful to you, and to the Publishers[168] named in your letter
of yesterday for your intention to introduce me to Posterity in such good
company, and I hope that you will enable me to appear, not like the ghost
of the elder Hamlet, in his habit as he *died,* my beard a silver sabled, but
in the beauty of his "Counterfeit presentment," with "a grace seated on my
brow," "Hyperion curls," and so forth, and that your Artist will prove
the Poetry of his Art by lifting the real up to the ideal, and picturing me
"not as I am but as I ought to be." As for standing up in a Photo-
graphical Pillory for a "full length," my consent cannot be won for any
money. To be Pillored in a sitting posture is torture sufficient, and a deed
I have sometime since done for the last time, to give being to the Enclosed,
which is said to resemble me as I now am, and to which your Artist has
only to add a pair of trousers and Patent leathers from the work shop of
his imagination to form a complete & concrete "full length" of his Patient.

I have ventured to blend before it my name with yours in the harmony
of old acquaintanceship, in the hope that you will accept them as a Token
of our long and, to me, very gratifying intimacy. I hope you will agree
with me in thinking it as a Work of Art, and considering his lack of materials, very creditable to Mr. Fredericks [*sic*].[169]

---

[168] In 1861–1862 Johnson, Fry & Company of New York published in two
volumes the *National Portrait Gallery of Eminent Americans*. The portraits
were engraved from paintings made by Alonzo Chappel, and accompanied by
biographical sketches prepared by Evert A. Duyckinck. During the next few
years new editions of the *Gallery* appeared which contained additional portraits. In the letter here published Halleck replies to Duyckinck who has asked
the poet to sit for a photograph to be used by Chappel in the making of a
painting. Halleck's portrait finally appeared in an edition of the *Gallery* issued
probably in 1867, the year in which the engraving was copyrighted.

[169] Of the firm of Charles D. Fredricks & Company, situated at 587 Broadway. The photograph which Halleck sent to Duyckinck on this occasion is
preserved in the Print Room of the New York Public Library. It is inscribed: "To Evert A. Duyckinck, Esq. from his friend and servant, Fitz-
Greene Halleck. April, 11th, 1866."

I am preparing to be in town for a few days within next week or the week after and shall hasten to call upon you, as of old, at an early morning hour. I have, in relation to our good friend Mr. Andrews,[170] much to say, and much to praise. Such men are not met with every day, at the Corners of the streets. Believe me

My dear Sir
Truly yours
FITZ-GREENE HALLECK

Evert A. Duyckinck, Esq.[171]

Guilford, C[t] May 13, 1866

My dear Sir,

I HAVE had the pleasure of receiving the Volume devoted to our old friend, Doctor Francis.[172] For your two fold kindness in presenting me this and your "Freneau" Volume,[173] I beg you to believe me deeply grateful.

The interest which your Biography of the latter has given to his memory induces me to hope that a collected edition of his Poems, distinct from his patriotic, may soon appear under your auspices. For I, sadly, miss many life long remembered lines of his, including those honored by the Patronage and pilfering, "convey the wise it call," of Sir Walter and Campbell.[174]

In acknowledgment of the compliment you are paying to the writings of Doct. Drake and myself,[175] I have looked over the proof sheets you sent me some years ago, which I have kept subject to your order, and hand you herewith two Extracts, for the purpose of explanation.

The preface to "Simon"[176] was Coleman's nonsense, not mine. Pray let it be omitted. The "Culprit Fay"[177] was written in 1816. De Kay was then in Europe. Drake was never acquainted personally with Cooper. The whole paragraph is a fiction. I have searched in vain for the Greek

[170] William Loring Andrews, see pp. 359–360.

[171] Preserved in the Duyckinck Collection of the New York Public Library.

[172] Dr. John Francis, *Old New York*, issued in 1865, with an introduction by Henry T. Tuckerman, is here probably referred to.

[173] In 1865 E. A. Duyckinck published his *Poems Relating to the American Revolution by Philip Freneau.*

[174] The pilferings of Scott and Campbell from the riches of Freneau have been conveniently noted by F. S. Cozzens in his *Fitz-Greene Halleck. A Memorial*, pp. 9–10.

[175] The changes were not made in the subsequent editions of the *Cyclopaedia*. Duyckinck, however, noted the changes in his own interleaved copy of the work, now preserved in the New York Public Library.

[176] See p. 65.   [177] See p. 43.

Translation of Marco Batzaris, which I promised to send you. When found or returned, I will hasten to keep my word.[178]

Believe me My dear Sir,
gratefully yours

FITZ-GREENE HALLECK

E. A. Duyckinck, Esq.

P.S. Have you ever looked at the Notice taken of me in Appleton's Biographical Work edited by Ripley,[179] &c. It was shown to me before publication, and, so far as I recollect, contains the few incidents of my uneventful life correctly stated. Perhaps it may aid you in your new labors.

H.[180]

Guilford Connecticut
May 23d '66

My dear Sir,

IN order to prove myself entitled to the exclamation of Peter Quince in the "Midsummer Nights Dream," Bless thee, bless thee, Bottom! thou art translated, and to gratify your love of literary curiosities, I send you herewith, not only the promised Greek translation of "Marco Batzaris,"[181] but also a French translation of "Alnwick Castle."[182]

The former has, today, been returned to me by a Yale College Professor of Greek, to whom I had lent it. I presume from the cudgelled appearance of its outside that its inside must have cudgelled his Brains not a little, a proof, either that he knows little of the ancient Greek he professes, or that my Greek-born friend Mr Canale's favorite theory, that the difference between the ancient and the modern is very slight, cannot be, as he fancies, sustained. Are you a sufficiently "Learned Pundit" to enlighten me on the subject?

The French translation was sent me some five or six years since, from London, by Mr Bigelow our present Ambassador at Paris "at the request," as he says in his letter enclosing it, "of its Author, Monsieur de Chatelaine, a French gentleman of some distinction in the world of letters as the translator of Chaucer."

You will observe that I am indebted to the Translators genius for many ideas exclusively his own. Among them should you find any sufficiently Picturesque, the "Centaure amical," for instance for Illustrations,

[178] See the letter which follows.
[179] *The New American Cyclopaedia.* Edited by G. Ripley and C. A. Dana. New York, 1859–63. 15 v.
[180] In the Duyckinck Collection of the New York Public Library.
[181] See p. 163.   [182] See pp. 146–147.

please point them out to our friend Mr Andrews, the Moreau Brothers, &c, for their benefit.

I also fulfil my promise by sending you herewith two fairly written Autographs to be used at your pleasure. My failures in Autographs are as frequent as those of Beau Brummell in Neckties. These specimens will I hope prove presentable.

Am I encroaching too much upon your good nature by asking you for the loan of your Copy of the Bradford Club Croakers? It can be sent to me safely by Mail, and will be very soon returned in same conveyance. I am desirous as I have told you, of adding Notes to the verses, and have not a single Copy nearer me than yours.[183] If you are unwilling to part with it for a short time, please say so frankly, and kindly tell me by what means I can most readily procure one.

I am still waiting for a copy of the newly ennobled "Fanny"[184] but hope for it soon. When you see Mr Andrews please give him my best regards, and with them the information he desires concerning the Christian name &c of Mr. Rogers, the miniature painter.[185]

As I have no copies of the enclosed translations please keep them carefully under your own eye, and return them to me per mail at your future convenience, and oblige,—

My dear Sir, yours very truly

FITZ-GREENE HALLECK

E. A. Duyckinck, Esq.[186]

Guilford, Connecticut
Nov. 17, '66

Dear Sir,

YOUR favor of the 24 Ult. would have been sooner answered but for the hope derived from it of a speedy decision on the part of our friend, Mr Hurd,[187] a decision now so long delayed as to amount to a negative one, expressed by a revival of the old proverb that "Silence means consent."

---

[183] There was apparently some discussion at this time about issuing a new volume of *The Croakers*, perhaps in a limited edition, as *Fanny* was then being published. Halleck, it will be remembered, was much dissatisfied with the notes accompanying the Bradford Club edition. As the following letter suggests, however, the project was not realized.

[184] In 1866 William Loring Andrews issued the poem *Fanny* in a private edition, to which Halleck contributed notes. See pp. 359–360.

[185] In 1820 Nathaniel Rogers painted a miniature of Halleck. The edition of *Fanny* issued by Mr. Andrews included an engraving of this miniature executed by Charles Burt.

[186] In the Duyckinck Collection of the New York Public Library.

[187] Melancthon M. Hurd, coming to New York in 1864, joined H. O. Houghton in the book-publishing business. See J. C. Derby, *Fifty Years among Authors, Books, and Publishers*, p. 276.

A similar silence on your part leads to a similar conclusion as to your application to Mr Widdleton[188] concerning a separate edition of the Croakers. For your truly kind exertions, on this and on so many occasions, pray believe me very grateful.

I ought also to be very grateful to Mr Hurd for deeming my verses (including my Vesper Song) worthy of a Cabinet consultation, a compliment pleasantly modified by his hint that they are, and are to be, salable only at a particular season of the year, like Sleigh bells and canvas back ducks.[189]

With further regard to the new collection,[190] the Messrs. Appleton, my publishers, notwithstanding that it would lessen the sale of the remaining copies of their old volume, and render its old types valueless, continue to express their wish to undertake it as soon, they say, as the price of paper, &c., &c., will promise them a profit; an event that may happen, in common with the Millennium and the payment of Mr Macawber's Notes at 3–6 and 9 Months. In the meantime, some one of his "somethings may turn up."

Have you read the Life of Percival?[191] It has added greatly to my previous high opinion of his genius and acquirements. Had his career been more in Europe, especially on the Continent of Europe, he would have ranked among the ablest of her learned and lettered men. Even here in America, where a Geologist is the embodied wonder and wisdom of the home, the man whom Sir Charles Lyell pronounced to be "one of the most remarkable men he had ever seen" ought to be known and esteemed wherever Sir Charles himself is.[192]

The only weekly papers I read from New York are the Albion[193] and the Home Journal.[194] Can you tell me who is the literary critic of the former, and who is the Mr Fairfield,[195] a contributor to the latter?

[188] W. J. Widdleton, a New York book publisher of the period, who issued in 1865 an edition of Praed's poems, mentioned by Halleck in a letter to Samuel Ward, dated February 25, 1865. See p. 405.

[189] Probably *The Croakers* are here referred to; but the allusion to the ''Vesper Song'' is an enigma.

[190] This was the edition which was finally brought out in 1869 under the editorship of J. G. Wilson.

[191] Julius H. Ward's *Life and Letters of James Gates Percival* (Boston, 1866).

[192] See Ward's *Life*, p. 374.

[193] A weekly newspaper published in New York and devoted to foreign news.

[194] A weekly periodical begun in 1846 under the editorship of G. P. Morris and N. P. Willis.

[195] Francis Gerry Fairfield (1844–87). A New York journalist, and author of *The Clubs of New York* (New York, 1873). See *Appletons' Cyclopaedia of American Biography* (New York, 1900), II, 403.

I should be happy to aid your friend Mr Gould[196] in his task of keeping the "Well of English" undefiled, and will search some of my old antipathies, & send them to him. For the present, I beg him to doom, as Sir Walter Scott's favorite seven year old girl used to say, to "unquestionable fire" the following. In our midst, in this connection, going to Europe *on* a Steam Boat, writing a letter *on* Chamber S^t and delivering it *on* 5th Avenue, being mounted *on* the Times Newspaper, our Father who art *on* Heaven, omitting the *The* before the name of the Reverend Mr Sturgeon &c &c.   Yours my dear sir,

Very truly

F. G. HALLECK.[197]

Halleck's comments, made in the preceding letters, on the prospective publication of his works had a far more practical basis than a desire to perpetuate his name. They reflect without doubt the low state of the poet's financial resources at this time, and the wish to be self-supporting. His pride as a gentleman would not allow him to accept of help from a relative[198]—much less from strangers. What he received must be the fruit of his own labors. It was with this attitude that he approached the project, kindly suggested and no doubt largely financed by William Loring Andrews, to issue a privately printed edition of *Fanny*, which should be disposed of by subscription. The edition, to which Halleck contributed notes, was limited to seventy copies. Halleck's first reaction to Mr. Andrews' plan was purely commercial. "Allow me," wrote the poet, "to address you a few lines, exclusively with 'an eye to business.' When an Irish beggar in the streets of Dublin was told that the person from whom he was seen asking charity was 'Sir Walter Scott, the Great Poet,' he said, 'the divil a bit of a poet is he, but a *real gentleman*, for he gave me half a crown.' In order, therefore, that I who rank among the *small* poets may be allowed to pass now and then for a *real gentleman*, by having a half crown in my pocket, I should much like to know our prospects of making money by the work we have in hand, and when and to what amount I am to give a receipt for my share in the premises.'"[199] When, however, as Duyckinck relates, "the anticipated proceeds were sent to him in

---

[196] Edward Sherman Gould (1808–85). Author of *Good English, or Popular Errors in Language* (New York, 1867).
[197] In the Duyckinck Collection of the New York Public Library.
[198] See pp. 316–317.
[199] Duyckinck, *Putnam's Magazine*, XI, 237.

advance, and without regard to the subscription, he expressed his gratitude in the warmest terms for the attention which had been paid him.''[200]

Two years before the poet's death, Halleck left the large house facing the southwest corner of the village green, where he had lived since his retirement in Guilford. He was now forced to change his residence because the landlord desired ''to convert the old mansion into an inn.''[201] The poet subsequently moved to a smaller house situated a short distance down the adjoining street which runs south.[202] This house, where Halleck died, is still standing, and is appropriately marked with a placard.

Not only meager financial resources, but the death of many old friends cast their shadow upon the closing years of the poet's life. Several years before, Halleck had begun to feel heavily the loss of those friends whose lives had been linked so closely with his in the social and literary affairs of the metropolis. ''Almost every letter I receive now,'' he wrote to a friend in 1862, ''comes to me with crape on its left arm.''[203] One of the last of his old companions to go was Nathaniel Parker Willis, whose friendship Halleck had enjoyed since the late twenties. In a note to ''Barry Gray,'' dated February 4, 1867, Halleck remarked: ''Although the long illness of our friend, Mr. Willis, had prepared me for the sad tidings of his death, I feel it not the less sensibly and deeply. You and I have lost a most pleasant and gentlemanly companion, and the admirers of his many able and admirable writings, will, in vain, seek among his survivors for his equal in his peculiarly graceful and courtly style.''[204]

During the last year of his life Halleck was three times in New York. In April, 1867, he spent several evenings in company with James Grant Wilson, who has reported many characteristic anecdotes told by the poet.[205] On returning home, Halleck wrote to Mr. Duyckinck, playfully mentioning his inability, while he was in

---

[200] Duyckinck, *Putnam's Magazine*, XI, 236. The same year Mr. Andrews also issued privately the *Lines to the Recorder*, with notes by Halleck, in an edition of seventy copies.

[201] Wilson, *Bryant and His Friends*, p. 255.

[202] Water Street.

[203] Wilson, *Bryant and His Friends*, p. 263. The letter, written to Samuel Ward, is dated July 14, 1862.

[204] *New York Evening Mail*, January 9, 1868.

[205] *Life*, p. 546.

town, to call upon his friend. The whimsical turn of thought in the first paragraph, which hovers neatly between apology and compliment, shows there yet lingered in the old man something of the same wit, now softened and mellowed by age, that went into the making of many an earlier poem.

Guilford, Connecticut
April 13, '67[206]

Dear Sir,

I WRITE you, not to apologize for neglecting to call upon you when I was in Town last week, but to claim your approval and applause of my self-sacrifice in refraining from calling; and your sympathy in the suffering it has cost me.

For a visitant Cold, what Falstaffs recruit Bullcalf calls a "Whoreson Cold" had made me, for the time being, as deaf and as disagreeable a companion as any person distinguished in that time in history, from Julius Caesar to Miss Martineau, and quite unfitted me for endurable conversation.

As soon as the coming mild weather restores me to the use of my voice and ears, I shall hasten to again seek the pleasure of knocking at your hospitable door. Until then, believe me, My dear Sir, Truly yours,

FITZ-GREENE HALLECK

Evert A. Duyckinck[207]

It was not until June that Halleck made his promised trip to the city.[208] In August, Wilson visited the poet at his home in Guilford. On this occasion Halleck discoursed pleasantly of many things, mentioning in particular the delight which he took in Bryant's poem, "The Planting of the Apple Tree," of which he remarked, "I knew those lines after a single reading, an infallible test with me of true poetry."[209] Wilson states that Halleck was "then in excellent health," and "in our rambles around Guilford he entertained me with much pleasant gossip about his native town."[210]

In a letter to General Wilson, written the following month, Halleck mentioned a gift he had just received from Frederic S. Cozzens of his recently published book, *The Sayings of Dr. Bushwhacker.*[211] Of this volume the poet wrote, "In thanking Mr. Coz-

---

206 Another letter was written on the same day to Mrs. Botta. See p. 416.
207 In the Duyckinck Collection of the New York Public Library.
208 *Life,* p. 554.
209 See also p. 204.   210 *Life,* p. 561.
211 Dr. John Francis (1789–1861), a physician of note and one of the early

zens for the present of the book, I told him that it proved him to have drunk of the waters of the 'well of English undefiled,' even if he had stolen the bottles in which they were imported!''[212] This letter of acknowledgment to Mr. Cozzens, has fortunately been preserved, and is here published for the first time.

Guilford, Connecticut
August 21^d 67

My dear Sir,

WHEN John Keats, whom Lord Byron used to call John Ketch, said that "a thing of Beauty is a joy forever" he must have had, in his prophetic eye, the Volume, for your kind gift of which I am now so delightfully your debtor.

Since the dropping of the Swan's quill that wrote "the Knickerbocker" (a bolder and a funnier book than that of "the Sketch Book,") there has not appeared among us a quill equal to yours in its rare Rabelaisian power & pathos, purified for modern libraries by a delicate sense of propriety.

I have, therefore, often told you so, as now your rarely [?] printed pages are witnessing, swearing, or if Quakers, solemnly affirming, to the truth of my assertions. Like the fact that Jack Cades father "had built a chimney in Smith's fathers house, the bricks are alive at this day to testify it, therefore, deny it not."

When our clever and cordial friend Hacket [*sic*][213] is again in town, pray

---

Knickerbockers associated with Halleck, was apparently the prototype of Cozzens' "Dr. Bushwhacker." In the same letter to Wilson, Halleck says: "I am very thankful for your kind offer to send me the 'Old New York' of my old favorite, Dr. Francis; but I have already the pleasure of possessing a copy, the gift of our friend Mr. Tuckerman. It is especially interesting to me, more so than it can well be to you, a younger man, from my personal intimacy with him, and with many of the persons and events it memorializes. In connection with it, allow me to beg you to read Mr. F. S. Cozzens' recently published volume, 'The Sayings of Dr. Bushwhacker,' etc., where you will see and hear the doctor (assuming that you have known him more or less intimately) alive and speaking before you. The 'faculty divine,' the power of invention, the wit, the wisdom, the stores of miscellaneous literature, the doctor did not possess. Your admiration of all these belongs to Mr. Cozzens; but the doctor dramatically represents them to your perfect delight'' (*Life*, p. 262). Almost no records remain to indicate the intimacy once existing between Dr. Francis and Halleck. In Tuckerman's memoir of Francis published in *Old New York* (New York, 1865), we find this brief note among others which describe the Doctor's characteristic manner in conversation, "Here he would invoke the hero of one of Halleck's Croaker lyrics, and quote a jest or describe a caricature'' (pp. xx–xxi). Halleck was, of course, associated with Francis in the Bread and Cheese Club (see p. 153).

[212] Wilson, *Life*, p. 263. The letter is dated September 11, 1867.

[213] James Hackett, the comedian, of whom Halleck was a friend and admirer. For letters addressed to Hackett, see pp. 407 and 412.

let me know and I will be there purposely to hear you and him read the "Sayings" to Page 68 in Dialogue,—you in person, and he in the Doctor. I have seen and heard him imitate the latter to the life, and with your marvellously choice words, and his marvellously choice manner of saying them, it will be a treat for the gods. How well you have pictured your odd and excellent original. I can hear him breathe and laugh and chuckle before me. It is his hand [?] and the shake of it; his "my dear friend," "my dear Doctor" &c, all are perfect!

I had not the pleasure of seeing Mr. Verplancks admirable contributions to "the Wine Press,"[214] when they originally appeared, and they come to me alike in their freshness, and their finish, to my exceeding amusement and instruction. He is full as familiar with the classics as if he were still at School drinking them in with the mothers milk of his Alma Mater, and he makes their wit and wisdom subservient to his own in a way that must be very pleasant to him as well as to his reader.

I wish you could prevail upon him to gather together, in a Volume or two, the scattered-abroad children of his pen. As American specimens of English Literature his writings and yours (I will say it and you cannot help yourselves), are proofs, that the "waters of the well of English undefiled" can be drunk here in all their purity, although we steal from England the bottles in which they are imported.[215]

Repeating my thanks for your so patiently continued courtesies, I am, My dear Sir

ever truly yours
FITZ-GREENE HALLECK

Fred. S. Cozzens, Esq.[216]

In October, 1867,[217] Halleck paid a last visit to his beloved New York. He had left Guilford with a cold, which was not improved by his stay in the city. While in New York the poet was compelled to remain indoors for a part of the time, only twice venturing out, —once, for a visit to Dr. Carnochan, and again, for a short walk with General Wilson on Broadway and the Bowery. "He never came to New York," observes Wilson, "without taking a glimpse of 'the substantial beauties of the Bowery,' as he termed the rosy-cheeked damsels to be met with in that Germanized thorough-

---

214 A periodical once edited by Cozzens. See The Sayings of Dr. Bush-whacker (New York, 1867), p. 4.

215 This is no doubt a sly allusion to the fact that Mr. Cozzens, besides being a humorist, was a wine merchant of note.

216 In the Yale Collection of American Literature.

217 Wilson, Life, p. 566. The poet arrived in New York on October 7.

fare."[218] But the poet's visit to the city was not accompanied by his usual cheerfulness. He spoke to Wilson of his increasing ill health,[219] and of his many friends who had lately died. "The only survivors among the prominent New-Yorkers" of the very early days "whom he could then . . . recall, were his friends, Jacob Barker, now of New Orleans, and Gulian C. Verplanck, then a member of the Historical Society and a trustee of the Society Library."[220] "This was the only occasion," remarks Wilson, "on which I ever saw the poet in other than a cheerful mood, for it was characteristic of Halleck that he said nothing of his troubles, even to his intimate friends."[221] Halleck felt, indeed, that the end was near, and could not conceal the heavy weight that pressed upon his mind. "If we never meet again," he said sadly to his friend, "come and see me laid under the sod of my native village."[222] On the morning of October 14 Halleck left New York, arriving in Guilford that evening.[223]

This was the last time that Halleck saw New York. But in his unfailing love of the good old days he thought once more to meet his friends in the city. "In one of the last letters I received from him," writes Cozzens, "he spoke of Mr. James H. Hackett, and proposed coming to the city especially to see him.[224] . . . It was proposed by Mr. Hackett to invite Mr. Halleck, Mr. Verplanck, and one or two other old friends to meet together, and have a good old-fashioned dinner. . . . But the projected dinner was unhappily interrupted by the decease of the poet, in whose honor it was intended to be given. I met Mr. Hackett and Mr. Verplanck, and agreed upon the day when I was to notify Halleck—and an hour after that meeting, I heard the sad news of his death."[225]

The circumstances attending the death of the poet were described by a correspondent, probably General Wilson, in a letter written on the day of Halleck's funeral, to a New York newspaper. "On Sunday morning," November 17, the account runs, "Mr. Halleck

---

[218] Wilson, *Life*, p. 566. [219] *Ibid.*, p. 568.
[220] *Ibid.*, p. 104. [221] *Ibid.*, p. 569.
[222] *Ibid.*, p. 572. [223] *Ibid.*, p. 572.
[224] The letter of Halleck's to which Cozzens here alludes may, of course, be the one printed on p. 362, although Halleck's proposal to see Mr. Hackett is not made very definite.
[225] *Fitz-Greene Halleck. A Memorial*, pp. 29–30. Bryant also alludes to this proposed dinner. See *Some Notices of the Life and Writings of Halleck*, p. 38.

walked out for the last time, his object being to consult his physician, Dr. Canfield.[226] The medicine prescribed afforded him temporary relief, but on Monday and Tuesday he complained of feeling very unwell, and during that period he received several visits from his physician. He retired earlier than usual on Tuesday, saying to his sister, Miss Halleck, 'I am afraid I shall not live till morning.' A few minutes before 11 o'clock she went to his bedroom, and found him sitting up in his bed. He said, 'Maria, hand me my pantaloons, if you please.' She turned to the other side of the room to get them, but before she reached her brother's bedside, he had fallen back dead—expiring without a groan or struggle.'[227] It was the custom in Guilford, when anyone died, wrote the Rev. Lorenzo Bennett to Mr. Duyckinck, "to have the bell strike the number of his years. This leads the villagers to inquire who has departed this life. Miss Halleck declined having the bell tolled, in her brother's case, & as he had no previous illness, I presume very many of our villagers were uninformed of his decease, till they heard the funeral bell."[228]

On the following Friday, November 22, the poet's funeral was held at Christ Church in Guilford. The service was performed by the rector of the church, the Rev. Dr. Lorenzo Bennett, assisted by the Rev. C. W. Everest[229] of Hamden. The funeral was not largely attended. The indifference and prejudice of many of the villagers doubtless thinned the audience, and few of the poet's friends in New York knew of his death in time to be present at the services. In writing of the funeral to Duyckinck, Dr. Bennett said: "You state that, had a definite notice been given respecting Mr. Halleck's funeral, 'it would doubtless have been largely attended.' I was of that opinion, & thought it due to his position, & to his friends

[226] Bryant states that during the latter part of his life Halleck "was subject to a painful disease, from which he seems to have suffered only in occasional paroxysms" (*Some Notices of the Life and Writings of Fitz-Greene Halleck*, p. 38). Of this "painful disease" nothing is known. Dr. Canfield, Halleck's physician in Guilford, informed General Wilson that the poet's "death was caused by bronchial disease, terminating in effusion of the lungs" (*Life*, p. 574).

[227] *New-York Daily Tribune*, November 23, 1867.

[228] From a letter preserved in the Duyckinck Collection of the New York Public Library, and dated November 30, 1867.

[229] The author of *The Poets of Connecticut* (Hartford, 1843), and of several volumes of original verse.

in N[ew] Y[ork] that such notice should be given; & mentioned to his sister that I would send despatches accordingly. She, however, declined my offer—wishing all practicable quietness to be observed."[230] The body was borne from the Church, and the Burial Service of the Episcopal faith read at the grave in Alderbrook Cemetery. The coffin was simply marked, "Fitz-Greene Halleck, aged 77 years."[231]

[230] From the same letter above cited. An article in the *New Haven Daily Palladium* just after the poet's death commented on the small number who attended the funeral exercises—a fact, thought the writer, which reflected upon Halleck as a man and poet. Dr. Lorenzo Bennett, Rector of Christ Church in Guilford, who was indignant at this aspersion cast upon the poet's character, wrote a letter to Duyckinck, a portion of which we have just quoted.

[231] Wilson, *Life*, p. 574.

XIII

MONUMENT AND STATUE

H ALLECK'S posthumous reputation may be briefly related. The poet had been too long removed from the active world of letters for his death to create a stir among the critics and the general public. Only his friends, only the few who had known the man and had felt the charm of his personality could understand the loss they sustained in his death. It was Halleck's friends who now came forward with tributes and reminiscences. Bryant in a brief obituary notice in the *Post* spoke of Halleck as "personally a most agreeable man, and one of the pleasantest companions in the world."[1] Frederic S. Cozzens delivered substantially the same verdict in his address, early the following January, before the New York Historical Society.[2] This address, full of ready wit and sprightly anecdote, is of particular importance to the biographer in recapturing the poet's personality. At the meeting of the Historical Society at which Cozzens delivered his oration, resolutions were passed in memory of Halleck. One of these indicated that Bryant should be invited "to prepare a memorial paper on the life and genius" of the poet.[3] The address which Bryant gave before the society on February 3, 1869,[4] most fittingly recalled a friendship with Halleck of almost forty-five years. With the exception of Gulian C. Verplanck, Bryant was the only one now left of Halleck's literary associates who could revive memories of the good old days of "Marco Bozzaris" and "Red Jacket." To Bryant, who had earlier prepared memorial addresses on Cooper and Irving, we are indebted for much bio-

---

[1] November 20, 1867.

[2] *Fitz-Greene Halleck. A Memorial* (New York, 1868). Reviewed in *Putnam's Magazine*, XI, 768.

[3] *Ibid.*, p. 30.

[4] Bryant's address first appeared in the *New York Evening Post* for February 3, 1869. It was later reprinted in the *Living Age*, C, 515 (February 27, 1869), and also appeared as a separate pamphlet under the title, *Some Notices of the Life and Writings of Fitz-Greene Halleck* (New York, 1869). The address was briefly reviewed in *Harper's New Monthly Magazine*, XXXVIII, 704 (April, 1869).

368 FITZ-GREENE HALLECK

graphical and anecdotal matter which would otherwise have been lost.

In the meantime other friends had contributed their reminiscences. Of particular biographical significance may be noted those articles by Evert A. Duyckinck[5] and Henry T. Tuckerman[6] which have been frequently quoted in the course of the present work. Interesting too in showing the charm which Halleck exerted over his friends are personal sketches from the pen of the comedian, James H. Hackett;[7] of the novelist, "Barry Gray";[8] and of the essayist, Joel Benton.[9] In 1869 appeared General James Grant Wilson's *Life and Letters of Fitz-Greene Halleck*,[10] which, in view of the loss of most of the manuscript material which went into the making of the volume,[11] remains indispensable to every student of Halleck as a source book of biographical data.

For a year or two previous to his death Halleck had contem-

[5] *Putnam's Magazine*, XI, 231 (February, 1868).
[6] *Lippincott's Magazine*, I, 208 (February, 1868).
[7] *New York Evening Post*, January 31, 1868.
[8] *New York Evening Mail*, January 9, 1868.
[9] *Frank Leslie's Illustrated Newspaper*, XXV, 243 (January 4, 1868). Among other articles on Halleck which appeared just after his death may be noted George W. Curtis' brief note ("Editor's Easy Chair") in *Harper's New Monthly Magazine*, XXXVI, 261 (January, 1868); J. G. Wilson's biographical sketch in *Hours at Home*, VI, 362 (February, 1868); H. C. Alexander's critical sketch in *ibid.*, VI, 367; and brief biographical notices in the *Eclectic Magazine*, VII (N.S.), 257 (February, 1868), and in *Appleton's Annual Encyclopedia* for 1867.

It should be noted, however, that not all of the obituary comment on Halleck was laudatory. A writer in the *Nation* (American) for December 5, 1867, in commenting at length on Halleck and the literary group to which he belonged, found the work of the early Knickerbocker authors completely out of date and forgotten. Although acknowledging that these writers were once "very eminent," the critic insisted that "they have since so thoroughly lost their distinction that we do not know where to look for a case parallel to theirs. . . . They were our first crop—to borrow a figure—and very properly were ploughed in, and though nothing of just the same sort has come up since, and we may be permitted to hope that nothing of just the same sort will ever again come up, yet certainly they did something toward fertilizing the soil from the products of which we are now getting a part of our food."

[10] Reviewed in the *Eclectic Magazine*, IX (N.S.), 506 (April, 1869); and in *Harper's New Monthly Magazine*, XXXVIII, 707 (April, 1869).

[11] See the Preface to the present work, p. viii. Other important biographical articles on Halleck by Wilson are those in the *Independent* for February 29 and March 7, 1872; and in *Bryant and His Friends* (New York, 1886).

plated the publishing of a new edition of his poems. The Appletons, who had already brought out several volumes for the poet, hesitated at that time, for business reasons, to issue a new collection.[12] But Halleck, probably in need of the financial aid he hoped to derive from a sale of the book, now negotiated with Ticknor & Fields, who went so far in the transaction as to engage William Cullen Bryant to write the preface. This plan had been completed by the first of January, 1867, for Bryant in a letter to Frederic S. Cozzens makes reference to the projected edition, and to the introduction which he had been asked to contribute.[13] Halleck now undertook the task of preparing the new work for the press;[14] but before he could complete the arrangements for its publication, he died. Still Ticknor & Fields expected to bring out the new work, if we may judge from a newspaper note which probably had a wide circulation. "Fitz-Greene Halleck about a month before he died," ran the report, "prepared his poems with a final revision to be issued in one volume by Messrs. Ticknor & Fields. The notes are said to be very elaborate and full of interesting material. It is understood that the volume will be prefaced with some introductory matter, biographical and critical, from the pen of the poet's friend, William Cullen Bryant."[15] Dr. Lorenzo Bennett also referred to the same edition in writing to Duyckinck a few days after the poet's death. "Ticknor and Fields had requested Mr. Halleck to prepare an Edition of his Works for them to publish, and a fortnight before his decease, he had forwarded the papers,—with additional Notes— stating his terms, &c. No reply has as yet been rec[superscript d]. General Wilson promised Miss H[alleck] that he would write a biographical paper to be published with the edition here alluded to.'"[16] The conclusion of Dr. Bennett's remarks shows that the original plan, which arranged for a preface to the work by Bryant, had been modified, and that General Wilson now expected to prepare the

[12] See on p. 358 Halleck's letter to Duyckinck dated November 17, 1866.

[13] This letter, dated January 3, 1867, is preserved in the Yale Collection of American Literature.

[14] See Preface to the 1869 edition of Halleck's works, pp. xiii–xi[x].

[15] From an unidentified clipping in the Manuscript Division of the New York Public Library, giving this quotation as coming from the *Boston Transcript*.

[16] This letter, dated November 27, 1867, is preserved in the Duyckinck Collection of the New York Public Library.

introduction. In fact, it is evident that before his death, Halleck had in part intrusted to Wilson the publication of his poems;[17] and that before many months had passed the original scheme for bringing out the volume was entirely altered.[18] The book finally appeared toward the close of 1868[19] with a biographical introduction by General Wilson. It was published, however, not by Ticknor & Fields, as originally announced, but by D. Appleton & Company, with whom Halleck had first made his overtures. The reason for the change is not at first evident, although it was no doubt some insuperable difficulty over the copyright that made Ticknor & Fields relinquish the undertaking. The new volume was well printed, and containing as it did a full text of *The Croakers*, together with Halleck's other works, is the most complete and authentic edition which we have.[20]

Shortly after the death of the poet, a movement was set on foot by General Wilson for the erection of a monument over Halleck's grave in Guilford. By January 1, 1868, one thousand dollars had been subscribed for the memorial;[21] and in the summer of the same year[22] the monument, designed by Douglas Smythe of New York City,[23] was erected which still marks the final resting place of the poet. At the eightieth anniversary of Halleck's birth, a formal dedication of the monument took place. Bryant was at first chosen to deliver an oration at the ceremony. "I like the design of the Halleck monument, a photograph of which you have been so kind as to send me," said Bryant in writing to General Wilson in December, 1868. "It is in good taste, as I think; and I am glad that the place of the poet's rest is now marked by so fitting a memorial.

[17] See Preface to the 1869 edition of Halleck's works, p. xiii.

[18] It was even rumored that Evert Duyckinck was to edit the new edition. See a letter addressed by Robert Barry Coffin ("Barry Gray") to Duyckinck, dated January 21, 1868, and preserved in the Duyckinck Collection of the New York Public Library.

[19] The date on the title-page was 1869. That it was published, however, at the close of the previous year may be seen from a letter dated November, 1868, which Bryant wrote to Wilson, thanking him for a copy of the new edition of Halleck's poems (see *Bryant and His Friends*, p. 86).

[20] Brief notices of the new volume appeared in *Harper's New Monthly Magazine*, XXXVIII, 420 (February, 1869), and in the *Eclectic Magazine*, IX (N.S.), 248 (February, 1869).

[21] See letter of Dr. Bennett to Duyckinck, dated January 17, 1868, and preserved in the Duyckinck Collection of the New York Public Library.

[22] Wilson, *Life*, p. 579.   [23] *Ibid.*, p. 594.

But I must be excused from delivering any address on the occasion of its erection. I have consented to read a paper before the Historical Society on the writings of Halleck, and having done this, it appears to me that I shall have fulfilled my duty to his memory, much as I cherish it. Some more eloquent speaker must perform the office of which you speak, at the burial ground."[24] Bayard Taylor finally consented to perform the duties of orator on the occasion. "I prefer to make a short address," wrote Taylor to General Wilson on June 18, 1869, "not only because the time is brief, but because I think long-winded orations—however excellent the theme —have become an American vice. I can say everything needful in half an hour, and an audience cannot keep freshly attentive and receptive longer than that."[25] On July 8 the dedicatory exercises were held. The oration was given by Bayard Taylor,[26] and a poem, composed by Oliver Wendell Holmes, was read by General Wilson.

> He sleeps; he cannot die!
> As evening's long-drawn sigh,
> Lifting the rose-leaves on his peaceful mound
> Spreads all their sweet around,
> So, laden with his song, the breezes blow
> From where the rustling sedge
> Frets our rude ocean's edge
> To the smooth sea beyond the peaks of snow.
> His soul the air enshrines, and leaves but dust below![27]

Before the formal dedication of the monument at Alderbrook Cemetery, Wilson was again active in raising money for a bronze statue of the poet to be erected in Central Park, New York. The first hint which we have of such a plan is given in a letter of Bryant to General Wilson in November, 1868. "The idea of erecting a bronze statue to Halleck in the Central Park," observed the

---

[24] Wilson, *Bryant and His Friends*, pp. 87–88.

[25] *Ibid.*, p. 364.

[26] Some interesting reminiscences of the occasion are given by Bayard Taylor in his article on Halleck in the *North American Review*, CXXV, 60 (July, 1877).

[27] The last stanza of Holmes's poem, to be found in the complete collected editions of Holmes's works. The poem was also published separately as a four-page leaflet. See item 524 in the catalogue of the *Stephen H. Wakeman Collection of Nineteenth Century American Writers*, sold by the American Art Galleries, April 28–29, 1924. A facsimile of the manuscript of Holmes's poem appeared in the *Criterion* for July, 1901.

poet, "is one which I approve with all my heart; but I am so little in town, and have so little time at my command, that I cannot consent to be the chairman of the executive committee appointed to carry the plan into effect, although I have no objection to being put on the committee. Mr. Verplanck should be the chairman. He was a special and life-long friend of Halleck, and a far better judge in matters connected with the fine arts than I can pretend to be."[28] Samuel F. B. Morse finally accepted the post of chairman, and it was probably upon his death in 1872 that Bryant was prevailed upon to take Morse's place. Efforts were at once made to raise the ten thousand dollars proposed for the erection of the statue. In 1869 an amateur entertainment was held in aid of the statue fund at the residence of Dr. Ward.[29] Several prospectuses are preserved in the New York Public Library, some unfortunately without date, describing the character of the project, giving the names of the officers of the association, and requesting further contributors.[30]

The sculptor chosen was Wilson MacDonald who by 1874 had completed the statue in clay. In writing of the model Bryant said: "I have seen the statue of the late Fitz-Greene Halleck in the clay, as modelled by the sculptor, Mr. Wilson MacDonald, and examined it with care. I am quite pleased with the general effect and the execution. The likeness is good and pleasing, the attitude dignified and graceful, and the accessories well imagined. The artist appears to me to have been successful and the statue will prove a worthy ornament of the Central Park of this city."[31] But the funds had not yet all been raised. Evert A. Duyckinck, who was upon the executive committee, received a letter from MacDonald, which alluded both to the foregoing note of Bryant, and to the amount yet to be raised for the fund. "I send you a Copy of a letter written by Mr. Bryant in my studio yesterday. I fear to send you the original for the reason that it might be lost in transit. The old Gentleman was very much pleased and was in splendid spirits.

[28] Wilson, *Bryant and His Friends*, p. 87.

[29] A copy of the program of this entertainment may be found in the Duyckinck Collection of the New York Public Library.

[30] The last of the prospectuses in the Duyckinck Collection is dated October 30, 1873.

[31] A copy of this letter addressed to MacDonald and dated June 18, 1874, may be found in the Duyckinck Collection.

Now will you not be good enough to write me out your impressions on the statue, and if you please, say that there is not enough money raised yet to pay for the work, and recommend that the present subs[cribers] double or add to their subscription enough to complete the work according to the original intention; in this way I guess I can get some of the 'older boys' to double up.''[32]

By the summer of 1876 the statue was virtually completed.[33] Bryant, who had succeeded Prof. Samuel Morse as chairman of the Halleck Statue Committee, wrote to the Park Commissioner of New York City, requesting that the statue "should not be placed in the Mall, where it would be scarcely observed among the more showy and imposing statues already there," but should be granted some special "picturesque nook of the grounds.''[34] But in this the poet was disappointed. In writing to Wilson, Bryant said: "I am sorry that the Park Commissioners do not see the propriety of allowing the statue of Halleck to be placed in some particular and characteristic nook of the Park. But their decision is made, and I suppose there is no contending against it.''[35]

On May 1, 1877, printed invitations were issued for the ceremony of dedication,[36] and on the fifteenth of the month the exercises were held.[37] William Cullen Bryant called the assembly to order, and made a brief address, which was followed by the unveiling of the statue by President Hayes. The orator of the occasion was William A. Butler. A poem commemorating the event was composed by

[32] Duyckinck Collection.

[33] When the statue was nearing completion, the sculptor was in need of a model for the eyes. A drawing teacher of his acquaintance, who was engaged by the Marguerite Institute as an instructor, took a girl of nine years from the school to the sculptor's studio. This child, whose name was Bartholomew, furnished the model for the eyes as desired. The model, who herself provided me with this anecdote, is now Mrs. Emma Wyckoff and lives in Brooklyn.

[34] Wilson, *Bryant and His Friends*, p. 90.

[35] *Ibid.*, p. 90.

[36] A copy of this invitation may be found in the Duyckinck Collection.

[37] For the complete details (including speeches, poems, etc.) regarding the dedication of the monument in 1869 and the statue in 1877, see *A Memorial of Fitz-Greene Halleck. A Description of the Dedication of the Monument Erected to His Memory at Guilford, Connecticut; and of the Proceedings Connected with the Unveiling of the Poet's Statue in the Central Park, New York* (New York, 1877), edited by E. A. Duyckinck. Various newspaper and magazine clippings relating to both celebrations are preserved in the Duyckinck Collection.

Whittier, but as the Quaker poet was unable to be present, the
verses were read by General Wilson.

> Too late, alas!—of all who knew
>   The living man to-day
> Before his unveiled face, how few
>   Make bare their locks of gray!
>
> Our lips of praise must soon be dumb
>   Our grateful eyes be dim;
> O, brothers of the day to come,
>   Take tender charge of him!
>
> New hands the wires of song may sweep,
>   New voices challenge fame;
> But let no moss of years o'er creep
>   The lines of Halleck's name.[38]

The dedication of Halleck's statue, the first erected to an American poet, was the occasion of widespread comment. Few of these
remarks, however, concern intimately the subject of the present
biography. The honor paid to the memory of Halleck in the erection of a statue, was due, as the *New York Tribune* aptly pointed
out, "less to the intrinsic quality of his achievement as poet, than
to the unchanging personal regard which he enjoyed for half a
century."[39] To Halleck's social genius—to Halleck, the gentleman
—we must inevitably recur in a final appraisal of the man. It was
this side of his character which made Halleck live in the memory
of such friends as Bayard Taylor[40] and Richard Henry Stoddard,[41]
who were among the last to pay their tributes to the dead poet. Ten
years after Halleck's death, his poetry had quite slipped from the
memory of critics and public alike. In George P. Lathrop's critical
article on Halleck's work, contributed to the *Atlantic Monthly* just
after the erection of the statue, we have an unsympathetic though
in many respects a fair estimate of the poet's genius. His work, of

[38] The last three stanzas of Whittier's poem. The poem may be found in
any collected edition of Whittier's works. It was also issued separately as a
four-page leaflet.

[39] May 15, 1877. Among the articles which the erection of the statue called
forth may be noted those by A. J. Symington in the *Glasgow Herald* (April
14, 1877), and by George W. Curtis in *Harper's Weekly* (June 2, 1877).

[40] *North American Review*, CXXV, 60 (July, 1877).

[41] *Lippincott's Magazine*, XLIII, 886 (June, 1889).

which "Marco Bozzaris" may be taken as typical, was brilliant but amateurish. An artist at moments, he too easily sank to the level of poetaster. "From one point of view, how versatile and susceptible was this man!" observes Lathrop, "from another, how chilly and limited! But his self-divided genius causes him to stand forward as a peculiarly apt representative of that large class of minds that are potentially poet-minds, but never find means of expression."[42]

[42] XXXIX, 729 (June, 1877).

APPENDICES

A. BIBLIOGRAPHIES

A. THE SEPARATE PUBLICATIONS OF FITZ-GREENE HALLECK

POEMS, / By / Croaker, Croaker & Co. / and / Croaker, Jun. / As Published / In the Evening Post. /

"Mine were the very cipher of a function, to find / the faults and let the actors go." /

"I am Sir Oracle, and when I ope my lips, let no dog bark!" / *Shakspeare* /

Published for the Reader / New-York—1819.

1 p.l., [3]–36 p. 14cm.

This unauthorized edition of *The Croakers* is very rare. Copies in the Yale Collection of American Literature, in the Harris Collection of American Literature at Brown University, and in the library of the American Antiquarian Society.

FANNY. /

A fairy vision
Of some gay creatures of the element,
That in the colours of the rainbow live—
And play in the plighted clouds.—*Milton* /

New-York: / Published by C. Wiley & Co. No. 3 Wall-Street. / Clayton and Kingsland, Printers. / 1819.

2 p.l., [5]–49 p. 23cm. Issued in wrappers.
Copies at Yale, Brown, New York Public Library, etc.

FANNY. /

A fairy vision
Of some gay creatures of the element,
That in the colours of the rainbow live—
And play in the plighted clouds.—*Milton* /

Second Edition. / New-York: / Published by Wiley & Halsted. No. 3, Wall-Street. / William Grattan Printer. / 1821.

2 p.l., [5]–67 p. 23cm. Issued in wrappers.
Copies at Yale, Brown, New York Public Library, etc.[1]

[1] There is evidence for the existence of the following editions of *Fanny*, but no copies have come to light: (a) London, 1821. (The *Monthly Review* for November, 1821, in reviewing the volume, prefaced their comments with the words, "Printed at New York, and republished in London by Whittakers. 1821."); (b) Greenock [1821?]. (See E. A. Duyckinck in *Putnam's Magazine* for February, 1868; and p. 137 of the present work.); (c) Edinburgh [1821?]. (See E. A. Duyckinck, *A Memorial of Fitz-Greene Halleck*, p. 70. This reference may be to the same edition as the preceding.); (d) *Fanny; a Satiric Tale*,

ALNWICK CASTLE, / WITH OTHER POEMS. / New-York: / Published by G. & C. Carvill, 108 Broadway. / Elliott & Palmer, Printers. / 1827.

1 p.l., [3]–64 p. 22cm. Issued in light-weight cardboard covers.
Copies in all the important collections of American literature.

FANNY. /

> A fairy vision
> Of some gay creatures of the elements,
> That in the colours of the rainbow live—
> And play in the plighted clouds.—Milton/

By Fitz Green Helleck [*sic*]. / New York: / 1833.

1 p.l., [3]–48 p. 13½cm.
The only known copy of this unauthorized edition is in the Harris Collection at Brown University.

THE / RECORDER: / WITH OTHER POEMS. / By / F.G.H. / New-York: / Henry Ludwig, Printer, / Corner of Greenwich and Vesey-streets. / MDCCCXXXIII.

8 pp. +. 23cm. Marble boards.
Only known copy, in the New York Historical Society, is incomplete.

ALNWICK CASTLE, / WITH OTHER POEMS. / New-York: / George Dearborn, Publisher, / No. 38 Gold Street. / MDCCCXXXVI.

2 p.l., [9]–98 p., 1 l. 24½cm.

FANNY: A Poem. /

> A fairy vision
> Of some gay creatures of the element,
> That in the colours of the rainbow live,
> And play in the plighted clouds.—Milton./

London / T. Tickler & Co. Picadilly. / 1837.

52 p. 13½cm. Brown paper covers.
The only known copy is in the Harris Collection.

FANNY, / WITH / OTHER POEMS. / [Vignette of Weehawken] / New-York / Harper & Brothers / 1839.

2 p.l., [5]–130 p., 1 l., engraved title-page. 19½cm.
Edition reprinted in 1846.

ALNWICK CASTLE, / WITH / OTHER POEMS. / By / Fitz-Greene Halleck. / New-York: / Harper & Brothers, 82 Cliff-St. / 1845.

1 p.l., [9]–104 p., 1 l., extra-engraved title-page. 19½cm.

THE / POETICAL WORKS / OF / FITZ-GREENE HALLECK. / Now First Collected. / Illustrated with Steel Engravings, / From Drawings by American Artists. / New York: / D. Appleton & Company, 200 Broadway. /

Glasgow, 1835. (This item is noted on page 211 of the *Systematic Catalogue of Books in the Collection of the Mercantile Library Association of the City of New-York* [1837].)

Philadelphia: / Geo. S. A. Appleton, 148 Chestnut Street. / MDCCC-XLVII.

1 p.l., [5]–280 p., 5 pl., 1 port., extra-engraved title-page. 21½cm.
Reprints appeared in 1848 (''Second Edition'') and in 1850 (''Third Edition'').

The / Poetical Works / of / Fitz-Greene Halleck. / New Edition / [Ornament] / Redfield, / Clinton Hall, New York. / 1852.

2 p.l., [iii]–iv p., [9]–232 p. 19½cm.
Edition reprinted in 1853 and in 1855.

The / Poetical Works / of / Fitz-Greene Halleck. / New Edition. / [Ornament] / New York: / D. Appleton and Company, / 346 & 348 Broadway. / M.DCCC.LVIII.

2 p.l., [iii]–iv p., [9]–238 p. 19cm. Printed from the plates of the 1852 edition, but with ''Marco Bozzaris'' as the first poem instead of ''Alnwick Castle.'' The 1858 edition adds the lines ''To Louis Gaylord Clark, Esq.''
Edition reprinted in 1859.

The / Poetical Works / of / Fitz-Greene Halleck. / Now First Collected / Illustrated with Steel Engravings, / From Drawings by American Artists. / Third Edition. / New York: / D. Appleton and Company, / 346 & 348 Broadway. / M.DCCC.LVIII.

1 p.l., [5]–286 p., 5 pl., 1 port., extra-engraved title-page. 21½cm. This edition is the same as that of 1847, except for the addition of the lines ''To Louis Gaylord Clark, Esq.''
Rare. Copy in the New York Public Library.

Halleck's / Marco Botzares, / in Modern Greek / by / George D. Canale, / A Zacynthian. / Cambridge: / Welch, Bigelow, and Company, / Printers to the University. / 1859.

2 p.l., [5]–9 p. 23½cm.
Copy in the New York Public Library.

The / Poetical Works / of / Fitz-Greene Halleck. / New Edition / New York: / D. Appleton and Company, / 346 & 348 Broadway. / M.DCCC.LIX.

2 p.l., [5]–238 p. 14½cm. Issued in blue and gold binding.
Edition reprinted in 1861 and 1865.

The Genius of / Burns. / [Cut of Burns] / Fitz-Greene Halleck, / an American Poet, / To a Rose, brought from near Alloway Kirk, in / Ayrshire, in the Autumn of 1822. [Ayr, 1859]

7 p. 20½cm. Unbound.
For an account of this reprinting of Halleck's ''Burns,'' see the letter of Dr. D. McNaught on pages 437 and 438; see also pages 328–329.

THE / CROAKERS / by / Joseph Rodman Drake / and / Fitz-Greene Halleck. / First Collected Edition / New York / MDCCCLX.

2 p.l., [v]–viii p., [1]–191 p., 2 ports. 27cm.
One Hundred and Fifty Copies for the Bradford Club. A special Club Edition, limited to one hundred copies, was also issued. For further bibliographical details regarding the Bradford *Croakers*, see A. Growoll, *American Book Clubs* (New York, 1897), pp. 51–52.

YOUNG AMERICA: / A POEM. / by / Fitz-Greene Halleck. / New York: / D. Appleton and Company. / 443 & 445 Broadway. / 1865.

1 p.l., [11]–49 p., front. 18cm. Issued in Pictorial Boards.

FANNY: / A POEM. / by / Fitz-Greene Halleck / New York: / 1866.

3 p.l., [7]–84 p., 1 port. 27cm.
"Edition of Seventy Copies Printed for W. L. Andrews."

LINES / TO / THE RECORDER. / by / Fitz-Greene Halleck / New York: / 1866.

2 p.l., [5]–31 p., 1 port. 27cm.
"Edition of Seventy Copies Printed for W. L. Andrews."

ΜΑΡΚΟΣ ΒΟΤΣΑΡΗΣ / ΠΟΙΗΜΑ / ΑΛΛΕΚΟΥ (Halleck) (*) / (Μετάφρασις ἐκ τοῦ Ἀγγλικοῦ) [by A. P. Rangabe]

No title-page. The above serves as a caption. [1]–7 p. 15cm.
This translation of "Marco Bozzaris" was made in 1868. See Wilson, *Life*, p. 295; and p. 163 of the present work. The star appearing in the third line of the caption refers to a footnote which gives a brief account of the poet's life, and makes mention of his poem.

THE / POETICAL WRITINGS / OF / FITZ-GREENE HALLECK. / WITH EXTRACTS FROM THOSE OF / JOSEPH RODMAN DRAKE. / Edited by / James Grant Wilson. / New York: D. Appleton and Company, / 90, 92 & 94 Grand Street. / 1869.

2 p.l., [v]–xviii p., 1 l., [13]–389 p., 1 port., extra-engraved title-page. 19½cm.
This edition was reprinted in 1873 and in 1885. A large paper edition, limited to 150 copies, was also issued in 1869.

THE / POETICAL WRITINGS / OF / FITZ-GREENE HALLECK. / Edited by / James Grant Wilson. / New York: / D. Appleton and Company. / 90, 92 & 94 Grand Street. / 1869.

2 p.l., [v]–x p., [7]–272 p., 1 port. 15cm.
Edition reprinted in 1873.

POEMS / by / Fitz-Greene Halleck / New York / Hurst & Company / Publishers

1 p.l., [3]–158 p. 19cm. Uncopyrighted.
This edition of Halleck contains his chief works and several poems never before

collected. The latter were probably reprinted from Wilson's *Life and Letters of Fitz-Greene Halleck*. The edition was probably issued in the early nineties. An autograph inscription in a copy in my possession bears the date ''1892.''

Poems / by / Fitz-Greene Halleck / New York / T. Y. Crowell & Co. / Publishers

1 p.l., [3]–158 p. 19cm. Uncopyrighted. Printed from the plates of the preceding edition. Pages surrounded by a border line in red.

A / Letter / Written by / Fitz-Greene Halleck / to / Joel Lewis Griffing / in / Guilford, Connecticut / in 1814 / 31 Copies Printed for / Charles F. Heartman and his Friends / Rutland, 1921.

5 unnumbered leaves. Unbound.

WORKS EDITED BY FITZ–GREENE HALLECK

The / Works of Lord Byron, / in Verse and Prose, / [Engraving of Lord Byron on India paper mounted on title-page] / Including his Letters, Journals, etc. / with a Sketch of his Life. / Stereotype of A. Pell & Brother. / New York: / George Dearborn, Publisher, / 71 John-Street, Corner of Gold. / Sold by Collins and Hannay, New York—Grigg and Elliott, Philadelphia; / and Carter, Hendee and Co., Boston. / MDCCC-XXXIII.

3 p.l., [vii]–xxviii p., [1]–302 p., [1]–619 p., 2 facsims. 25½cm.
An enlarged edition of *The Works of Lord Byron* appeared in 1834 with the following collation:
3 p.l., [vii]–xxviii p., [1]–319 p., [1]–627 p., 2 facsims., extra-engraved title-page. 25½cm. See pp. 249–250 of the present work. This edition was reprinted in 1835, 1836, 1837, 1839.
About 1840 the plates of the work passed into the hands of Alexander V. Blake (New York) who issued an edition in 1844. Later in the forties Silas Andrus & Son of Hartford, Connecticut, bought the plates, and published editions in 1847 and 1851. In 1855 Phillips, Sampson & Co. of Boston issued a volume entitled *The Works of Lord Byron: Embracing his Suppressed Poems, and a Sketch of his Life*. The text of this work was based upon that of Halleck. The more important changes in the new edition were the substitution of a fresh biographical sketch of Byron for Halleck's earlier one, and the placing of the poetry of Byron before the prose. There is no evidence that Halleck was consulted in the preparation of this volume. Subsequent issues of the work appeared in 1856, 1857, and 1860.

Selections / from / the British Poets. / In Two Volumes. / Vol. I. / New York: / Harper & Brothers, 82 Cliff Street / 1840.

Volume I: 2 p.l., [v]–ix p., 1 l., [13]–359 p.
Volume II: 2 p.l., [v]–x p., 1 l., [13]–360 p.
Reprints were issued in 1841, 1843, and 1870, and one appeared without date.

B. WORKS HAVING PARTICULAR REFERENCE TO FITZ-GREENE HALLECK

Bryant, William C., *Some Notices of the Life and Writings of Fitz-Greene Halleck* [New York], 1869.

Catalogue of the Private Library of the Late Fitz-Greene Halleck, Esq. To Be Sold by Auction at the Book Sale Rooms & Art Galleries, Clinton Hall, New York. Leavitt, Strebeigh & Co., Auctioneers, Monday, Oct. 12, 1868. [New York, 1868.]

Cozzens, Frederic S., *Fitz-Greene Halleck. A Memorial*, New York, 1868.

Duyckinck, Evert A., *Fitz-Greene Halleck*, New York, 1868. Privately printed for William Loring Andrews. Reprinted from an article in *Putnam's Magazine* for February, 1868.

[Duyckinck, Evert A.], *A Memorial of Fitz-Greene Halleck. A Description of the Dedication of the Monument Erected to His Memory at Guilford, Connecticut; and of the Proceedings Connected with the Unveiling of the Poet's Statue in the Central Park, New York*, New York, 1877. A special privately printed edition of this work with extra portraits and the author's name on the title-page appeared in 1879.

A Memorial of the American Poet Fitz-Greene Halleck, with a Translation of Marco Botzares also in the Modern Greek, by Prof. George D. Canale, Athens, 1870. See E. Duyckinck, *A Memorial of Fitz-Greene Halleck*, p. 72. No copy of this work has been discovered.

Wilson, James G., *The Life and Letters of Fitz-Greene Halleck*, New York, 1869. A large paper edition, limited to 100 copies, was issued the same year.

[Wilson, James G.], *A Description of the Dedication of the Monument Erected at Guilford, Connecticut, in Honor of Fitz-Greene Halleck*, New York, 1869.

C. BOOKS (NOT MENTIONED IN THE TEXT), WITH PASSING REFERENCES TO HALLECK

[Ashmead, Catherine Forrester], *Fallings from a Lady's Pen* (Philadelphia, 1849).

Contains poem "To Halleck."

Duganne, Augustine, *The Poetical Works* (Philadelphia, 1855).

Reference to Halleck in the satire, "Parnassus in Pillory," p. 192.

Follen, The Works of Charles, with a Memoir of his Life (Boston, 1841), 5 v.

See I, 228.

Hawthorne, Nathaniel, *Mosses from an Old Manse* (New York, 1846), 2 v.

Brief reference in "P's Correspondence" (v. 2).

Hows, John A., *Forest Scenes by William Cullen Bryant, Henry Wadsworth Longfellow, Fitz-Greene Halleck, Alfred B. Street, Illustrated by J. A. Hows* (Boston, 1864).

Reprints Halleck's "Wyoming."

Hows, John A., *In the Woods with Bryant, Longfellow, and Halleck* (New York, 1863).

Reprints Halleck's "Wyoming."

Longfellow, Samuel, *Life of Henry Wadsworth Longfellow* (Boston, 1886), 2 v.

In praising Longfellow's "Skeleton in Armor," Halleck remarked that "there was nothing like it in the language" (I, 367).

Loper, Samuel Ward, *Echoes from the Home of Halleck and Other Poems* (Boston, 1904).

Morris, George P., *Poems . . . Fourth Edition* (New York [1860]).

Passing reference in "New York in 1826," p. 191.

Radford, Harry V., *Adirondack Murray. A Biographical Appreciation* (New York, 1905).

Halleck's relations with W. H. H. Murray, pp. 49–50.

Richardsiana; or Hits at the Style of Popular American Writers (New York, 1841).

Brief reference in the parody entitled "Bunkum Stanzas, from *Boots*, an Unpublished Poem by M'D. C[larke]."

Speeches and Essays . . . with Poems on Burns by Montgomery, Halleck, Campbell, Mrs. William Smith, and Others (Washington, 1902).

Reprints Halleck's "Burns."

Tricks of the Times (The), or, the World of Quacks; A Farce of Domestic Origin. In Two Acts (New York, 1819).

Contains several interesting references to *The Croakers*. See *The Albert A. Bieber Collection of American Plays, Poetry and Songsters* sold by the American Art Association, Inc., November 13, 1923; Item 118.

Wallace, Horace Binney, *Literary Criticisms and Other Papers* (Philadelphia, 1856).

Unimportant review of "The Poems of Fitz-Greene Halleck, New York, Harpers" (1845), pp. 60–63.

Woodworth, Samuel, *Melodies, Duets, Trios, Songs, and Ballads* (New York, 1831).

Brief reference to Halleck in "An Epistle Addressed to my Friend G. P. Morris, Esq.," p. 259.

D. ENGLISH ANTHOLOGIES CONTAINING POEMS OF HALLECK

(Arranged Chronologically)

Specimens of the American Poets; with Critical Notices, and a Preface (London, 1822).

Contains *Fanny*. See p. 127.

Gems from American Poets (London, 1836).

Contains "Marco Bozzaris."

Mitford, Mary Russell, *Recollections of a Literary Life* (London, 1853), 2 v.

Though not strictly an anthology, this volume of Miss Mitford's contains selections from many poems which impressed her in the course of her reading. From the work of Halleck are included the lines, "Young thoughts have music in them" (*Fanny*) and those to Drake. Of the latter she says: "This is a true and manly record of a true and manly friendship. There is no doubting the sorrow, honourable alike to the Departed and the Survivor" (II, 70–72).

Hows, John W. S., *Golden Leaves from the American Poets . . . With an Introductory Essay by Alexander Smith* (London, 1866).

Contains "Marco Bozzaris," "Connecticut," and "The World is Bright before Thee."

Rossetti, William Michael, *American Poems* (London [1872]).

This volume, which is dedicated to Walt Whitman, contains "Marco Bozzaris," "A Poet's Daughter," and "To Louis Gaylord Clark."

Linton, W. J., *Poetry of America, Selections from One Hundred American Poets from 1776 to 1876* (London, 1878).

Contains "Marco Bozzaris." Of this collection Mr. Linton says in his preface, "I claim precedence for it as the first fair and comprehensive sample of American Poetry given to the old country. The *American Poems* of my friend Mr. W. M. Rossetti may not claim to be this, as he omits Longfellow and all humorous verse, as, not having had before him the last edition of Griswold (prepared by Mr. Stoddard in '72 but published only in the Fall of last year), he was apparently unacquainted with much of the best poetry of the last twenty years."

Humorous Poems by English and American Writers (London [1878]).
Contains "Red Jacket," and "Alnwick Castle."

Ross, John D., *Round Burns's Grave: the Poems and Dirges of Many Bards* (Paisley [Scotland], 1892).
Contains "Burns."

B. LIST OF HALLECK PORTRAITS AND ENGRAVINGS

Miniature painted on ivory in 1811.

J. G. Wilson in his *Life and Letters of Fitz-Greene Halleck* (p. 126) credited this miniature to a certain "Mysterious Brown," an English artist residing in New York in 1811. When Wilson brought out his *Memorial History of the City of New York* in 1893, however, he ascribed the miniature to Nathaniel Rogers, a well-known New York artist who is said to have been instructed by "Brown." See IV, 225. The reason for this change in the artist's name is not clear, nor has other evidence on the subject come to light.
Unfortunately the present location of this miniature is unknown. After Halleck's death, this portrait came into the possession of James G. Wilson, who willed it to the Metropolitan Museum of Art. The secretary of that institution, however, assures me that the miniature is not in their collection.
This portrait was reproduced in photograph by J. G. Wilson. A copy appears in a large paper edition of the *Poetical Works of Fitz-Greene Halleck* (1869), now in the New York Public Library. A woodcut of the same miniature was also published in Wilson's *Memorial History of the City of New York*, IV, 225. A reproduction of the photograph noted above appears in the present work, facing p. 30.

Miniature painted by Nathaniel Rogers about 1820.

See Wilson's *Life*, p. 591. Now in the possession of Mrs. William Loring Andrews of New York City. When William Loring Andrews printed in 1866 an edition of *Fanny* (see p. 359 of the present work), he had this miniature engraved by Burt. A copy of the engraving on India paper was inserted as the frontispiece to the volume. An "artist's proof," of which only twenty-five were printed, is preserved in the Print Room of the New York Public Library. The same engraving was used as one of the illustrations in E. A. Duyckinck's *A Memorial of Fitz-Greene Halleck*, privately printed in 1879. A reproduction of this portrait from the Burt engraving appears in this work, facing p. 116.

Portrait painted by John Wesley Jarvis between 1820 and 1825.

See E. A. Duyckinck, *A Memorial of Fitz-Greene Halleck* (1877), p. 67. Present location unknown. It was probably from this painting that an engraving was made for the group picture of American poets which was published in the *New York Mirror* for January 26, 1828. See Wilson, *Life*, pp. 330 ff., and pp. 225–226 of the present work. A half-tone print of the entire group appeared in the *Bookman* for June, 1897.

Portrait painted by Prof. S. F. B. Morse about 1828.

See p. 226 of the present work. Now in the New York Public Library.

Portrait done in crayon by Henry Inman about 1831.

In the New York Historical Society.

Portrait painted by Henry Inman in 1828.

This portrait, painted for George P. Morris of the *New York Mirror*, is in the New York Historical Society. See p. 264 (note) of the present work. A copy of this portrait, smaller than the original and done by G. W. Twibill, Jr., about 1836, is also in the New York Historical Society. Three engravings have been made after the original portrait.

(a) By G. Parker. This engraving originally appeared in the issue of the *New York Mirror* for September 24, 1836. Copies were later inserted in F. S. Cozzens, *Fitz-Greene Halleck. A Memorial* (1868); and in E. A. Duyckinck, *A Memorial of Fitz-Greene Halleck* (1879). A lithograph, made probably from the first Parker engraving, appears as the frontispiece to *Gems of Poetry from Forty-Eight American Poets*, published in Hartford in 1848 (c1838). A half-tone from this engraving was published in the *Bookman* for June, 1897; and in M. A. De Wolfe Howe, *American Bookmen* (New York, 1898), p. 106.

(b) By G. Parker. See p. 299 and p. 391 of the present work. This engraving may easily be distinguished from the preceding by its lack of shading in the poet's coat. It was first published in *Graham's Lady's and Gentleman's Magazine* for September, 1843. A copy of the engraving was later used as one of the illustrations in E. A. Duyckinck, *A Memorial of Fitz-Greene Halleck* (1879). A half-tone, made probably from this engraving, appears on page 283 of Donald G. Mitchell's *American Lands and Letters. The Mayflower to Rip Van Winkle* (New York, 1897).

(c) By H. R. Hall, Jr. Used as the frontispiece to J. G. Wilson, *Life and Letters of Fitz-Greene Halleck*. This engraving found its way into E. A. Duyckinck, *A Memorial of Fitz-Greene Halleck* (1879), and into the *New York Genealogical and Biographical Record* for January, 1893.

Miniature painted in 1842 by Mary Ann Hardy.

In the New York Historical Society.

Portrait painted by Charles Loring Elliott in 1847.

Painted for D. Appleton & Co., and now in their possession. See p. 307 of the present work. A copy of this painting done in oil by John G. Taggart is now in the New York Historical Society. Two engravings have been made after the original painting.

(a) By J. Cheney. Inserted in the 1847 and 1869 editions of Halleck's works, published by Appleton. The engraving also appeared in *The Bryant Festival at "The Century,"* Illustrated Edition (New York, 1865); and in E. A. Duyckinck, *A Memorial of Fitz-Greene Halleck* (1877 and 1879). This engraving has been reproduced in the present work, facing p. 307.

(b) By E. Teel. This engraving appeared in the *Knickerbocker Gallery* (New York, 1855); in the *Knickerbocker* for March, 1857; and in the *At-*

lantic Souvenir (New York, 1859). A half-tone print of the engraving was published in the *Bookman* for June, 1897. A line background was later added to the original engraved plate, from which were struck the prints inserted in F. S. Cozzens, *Fitz-Greene Halleck. A Memorial* (1868); in the *American Portrait Gallery*, published by J. C. Buttre (New York [1877]), volume 1; and in E. A. Duyckinck, *A Memorial of Fitz-Greene Halleck* (1879).

Crude woodcuts after the Elliott portrait were printed in the *International Magazine* for July 1, 1851; in the *National Magazine* for December, 1852; and in E. A. and G. L. Duyckinck, *Cyclopaedia of American Literature* (1855), II, 208.

Portrait painted by Thomas Hicks in 1855.

See p. 325 of the present work. This portrait, which was painted for Benjamin R. Winthrop, a fellow clerk of Halleck in the office of Jacob Barker, is now in the New York Historical Society. An engraving was made after this painting by H. Wright Smith, and India paper impressions inserted in the edition of *The Croakers* published by the Bradford Club in 1860. The same engraving was also used as an illustration in the large paper edition of James G. Wilson, *Life and Letters of Fitz-Greene Halleck* (1869), and the privately printed *Memorial of Fitz-Greene Halleck*, edited by E. A. Duyckinck (1879). Crude woodcuts of the Hicks portrait appeared in the *New England Magazine* for December, 1889; and in the *Critic* for January, 1900.

Drawing of Halleck's head done in bas-relief style by Horatio Greenough.

Of the original drawing nothing is known. An engraving was made after the original by Charles Burt for *Putnam's Magazine*, and appeared in the issue of that periodical for February, 1868, to accompany an article on Halleck by E. A. Duyckinck. An India paper print of the engraving, without the magazine imprint at bottom, was used as the frontispiece of the privately printed edition of Duyckinck's article issued by William Loring Andrews in 1868.

Photograph (*daguerreotype*). Taken at about the age of 65.

The original, once owned by Wilson, is not now available. See *Century Magazine* of July, 1910, for half-tone reproduction.

Photograph (*carte de visite*). Poet seated in chair; body turned to right; probably taken between the ages of 65 and 70. Reverse side reads: "Published by E. Anthony, 501 Broadway, New York. From Photographic Negative by M. B. Brady."

Copy in the Print Room of the New York Public Library. An enlarged reproduction of the photograph appears as the frontispiece to this volume.

Photograph (*carte de visite*). Bust only; head turned slightly to left; with beard; probably taken at 75 years of age.

The copy in the Print Room of the New York Public Library has no mark identifying the photographer. A steel engraving made after this photograph, and also preserved in the New York Public Library collection, is signed "H. B. Hall's Sons, 22 Park Place, New York." A reproduction of this engraving appears in the present work, facing p. 341. Half-tone prints of the photograph appeared in the *Bookman* for June, 1897; and in M. A. De Wolfe Howe, *American Bookmen* (New York, 1898), p. 118. The last-mentioned volume identifies the picture as taken "from an engraving of a photograph by Brady."

Photograph (*carte de visite*). Bust only; head turned to left; with beard; probably taken at 75 years of age. Signed, "C. D. Fredricks & Co. N. Y."

Copy in the Print Room of the New York Public Library. After this presentation copy to E. A. Duyckinck (see p. 354 of the present work) a painting of the poet seated in a chair was made in 1867 by Chappel (location unknown). From this painting an engraving was produced, and inserted in an edition of *National Portrait Gallery of Eminent Americans* (volume 1), edited by E. A. Duyckinck and brought out by Johnson, Fry & Company, probably in 1868. "The Portrait in the Gallery," wrote the Rev. Lorenzo Bennett of Guilford to E. A. Duyckinck, "is very life-like, & an excellent production of art." (See letter dated January 17, 1868, in the New York Public Library.)

For the following prints of Halleck as an old man no original photographs have been discovered:

Steel engraving published in the *Eclectic Magazine* for February, 1868.

Woodcut from a photograph by "Brady, 785 Broadway," published in *Harper's Weekly* for December 7, 1867. Head turned to right.

Woodcut in *Potter's American Monthly* for March, 1875. Head turned slightly to left.

Half-tone in H. P. Robinson, *Guilford Portraits* (New Haven, 1907), p. 84. Full length.

A wood engraving of the Halleck statue erected in Central Park in 1877 appeared in the *Art Journal* [New York] for January, 1877; and in E. A. Duyckinck, *A Memorial of Fitz-Greene Halleck* (1877), p. 31.

Attention should be called to the excellent collection of Halleck engravings and photographs in the Print Room of the New York Public Library. In this collection are many separate prints, some proofs in various states, which were never used as book illustrations.

C. UNCOLLECTED LETTERS OF FITZ-GREENE HALLECK

THESE letters, some fifty in number, represent a portion of Halleck's correspondence which for one reason or another was not included in the body of the biography. Of the earlier letters written during the poet's stay in New York, few are included in this collection. It was to his sister, Maria, that Halleck in his early and middle manhood revealed himself most fully in writing; but all these family letters soon after the poet's death fell into the hands of James Grant Wilson, who published many of them in his life of the poet (see Preface of the present work, p. viii). Only a few of the present letters of this earlier period possess more than a passing interest for the reader.

It was with Halleck's retirement to Guilford that he found the time and leisure for letter writing; and to this period most of the present collection belong. In many different moods, and addressed to a variety of persons, these letters, most of them unknown to Wilson, possess an undoubted value to the student of Halleck in throwing side lights on his character, interests, and works. In addition to illustrating various epistolary styles, they suggest Halleck's relations with many of his contemporaries, particularly the minor *literati*, with a surprising number of whom the poet was acquainted. Though Halleck is said to have been irritated at the frequent demands of autograph hunters, few authors have been more facile in fulfilling their requests in terms of graceful compliment. Other correspondents, slightly more tactful, engaged his attention, we may believe, simply to receive the dainty notes which fell from his pen. It was to his intimate friends, however, that Halleck during these years of retirement most perfectly revealed his genial and engaging personality. The cloak of dignity removed, the poet now stood beaming in his graceful humor, which played pleasantly on men and events of the period. To these intimate letters we must turn for the most perfect reflection of Halleck's personality during the final years.

Wherever possible, Halleck's orthography and punctuation have been retained. In but few cases is the poet's original punctuation so irregular as to be unworthy of preservation; and here we have taken the liberty of making it conform to standard usage. But in no instance have we wittingly changed a mark that might lead to confusion or ambiguity. Generally the poet's practice of capitalizing important words, though contrary to present usage, has been followed. Indeed, it has been thought best to reproduce the letters, so far as common sense will allow, just as the poet wrote them.

Most of these letters are here published for the first time. A few that have been taken from printed sources have been deemed of sufficient interest to include in this collection. Of the many letters that must have been written to the poet only a few have been recovered. Several of these, hitherto unpublished, appear at the close of this Appendix.

To T. M. Olcott[2]

Dutchess Co. in C[t].
New York Dec.–29, 1826

T. M. Olcott Esq[r] Cash—
Sir,
IF George R. Barker should require any specie, you will oblige this Company by furnishing it—and his draft at sight for 3000 dollars shall meet due honor. I have sent B. F. Butler Esq. this day a post note for 2000 dollars, which will probably pay for as much specie as will be wanted.

Very Respectfully
Yr. Ob. Ser.
F. G. HALLECK Sec[y].

To Thomas H. Barker[3]

Philadelphia, March 20, 1831.

Dear Sir,
I HAVE recovered the two Trunks and the Bag. As the Steam Boat does not run to day (Sunday) I shall leave here tomorrow morning. I thought for a moment of taking the mail, but the road is too bad, the weather too cold, the night too long, and moreover, my passage in the Steam Boat Line is paid through, so that two important considerations, Cash & Comfort, induce me to remain here till tomorrow. I trust you all arrived in safety and in good time yesterday, as the afternoon proved pleasant.

Yours truly
F. G. HALLECK

Tho[s] H. Barker, Esq[r]

[2] This note, the only extant letter of Halleck written in 1826, will serve as a specimen of the poet's epistolary style in business. The original is owned by Prof. Thomas O. Mabbott.

[3] Thomas Barker was a relative of Jacob Barker—probably the one with whom Halleck for a short time was associated in an unsuccessful business enterprise. The letter is preserved in the Henry E. Huntington Library and Art Gallery.

To John Alonzo Clark[4]

New York, 10th Dec. '36

Reverend & Dear Sir,

I HAVE the honor to acknowledge the receipt of your favor of the 18th Ulto. It would be very gratifying to me to avail myself of the opportunity you allow me of contributing to the laudable work you have undertaken, but my engagements do not permit me, at present, to attempt ought connected with literature. With confident hope in the success of your endeavors to promote the most important of all objects, I am,

> Very respectfully
> Your obt servt.
> FITZ-GREENE HALLECK

To Joseph B. Boyd[5]

New York 31 Jany. '38

Dear Sir,

I HAVE received, via Boston, your favor of the 19th Ulto & hasten to avail myself of the honor it, in so flattering a manner, allows me.

> Very respectfully
> Your obt servt
> FITZ-GREENE HALLECK

To Joseph B. Boyd[6]

New York 22d May, '39

Dear Sir,

YOUR favor of the 31 March last did not reach its destination till yesterday. I take great pleasure in availing myself of the honor it allows me, and regret the accident that has given you so much trouble.

> Very respectfully yours
> FITZ-GREENE HALLECK

Joseph B. Boyd Esqr

To George Roberts[7]

New York 9th Jany. '41

Dear Sir,

I HAVE received your favor of the 28th Ulto and I thank you for the "No-

---

4 J. A. Clark (1801–1843) was an Episcopal clergyman of Philadelphia, and the author of several religious works. In what project he had solicited Halleck's aid has not come to light. The original letter is preserved in the library of the University of Amsterdam.

5 The original letter is preserved in the library of the University of Amsterdam.

6 Preserved in the Historical Society of Pennsylvania.

7 Editor or proprietor of the Boston *Notion*. The letter is preserved in the library of Brown University.

tion" which followed it. It would give me pleasure to avail myself of your courtesy in offering me a place in your next "Double," but my mind is so much occupied with matters foreign to literature that I can furnish you with nothing creditible [*sic*], either to your paper or to myself. I read your weekly sheet always with much gratification, and, as I procure it here without difficulty, I do not feel myself justified in putting you to the expense & trouble of forwarding it to me as you so kindly propose.

I am Dear Sir,
Very gratefully yours
FITZ-GREENE HALLECK

George Roberts Esqr

To W. E. Robinson[8]

New York May 31, '41

Dear Sir,

I HAVE had the honor of receiving your favor of the 12th ins^t and am made proud and grateful by the high compliment paid me by the gentlemen of your Society. It would have given me great pleasure were it in my power to avail myself of your offer to hear a poem from me at your coming Commencement, but my engagements, I regret to say, do not allow me to undertake the task.

I am Dear Sir,
very respectfully
Y^r ob. Servt
FITZ-GREENE HALLECK

To W. E. Robinson Esqr
  President of the Society of
    "Brothers in Unity"
      Yale College

To Rufus W. Griswold[9]

New York Dec. 28, '41

Dear Sir,

GENERAL MORRIS has kindly consented to loan the portrait as you re-

---

[8] This letter was first called to my attention by Mr. Walter R. Benjamin of New York City, who kindly provided me with a copy of it. The note is now owned by Prof. Stanley T. Williams of Yale University.

[9] Preserved in the Historical Society of Pennsylvania. R. W. Griswold, one of the editors of *Graham's Magazine*, desired Henry Inman's portrait of Halleck, then in the possession of George P. Morris of the *Mirror*, that an engraving might be made from the painting to accompany an article on Halleck in *Graham's*. An engraving from the same portrait had been published in the *Mirror* for September 24, 1836 (see p. 264). Two years later (1843), Griswold wrote to Halleck for a contribution to *Graham's* (see p. 299), and in mention-

quested. It is at N° 87 Prince St.[10] Will you do me the favor to send for it as soon as possible & see that it is well taken care of.

Very respectfully
Your Ob^t Ser^t
FITZ-GREENE HALLECK

R. W. Griswold, Esqr

To Richard Henry Wilde[11]

New York December 26. 1844

My dear Sir,

I HAVE had the pleasure of receiving your favor of the 17th ult°, and have conversed with Mr Astor on the subject it refers to, but he informs me that he has not now, and has never had any interest in the lands you mention. I hope that your determination to make New Orleans your home in future will not prevent you from occasionally visiting New York, where no one would be more warmly welcomed than your good self. Believe me My dear Sir,

Most truly yours
FITZ-GREENE HALLECK

To the Honorable R. H. Wilde
New Orleans.

To Miss Maria Halleck[12]

N. Yk. Oct° 27 45

My dear Sister,

I ENCLOSE renewal Certificate—please see that the Number is right. In your answer please let me know the state of your money affairs.

affectionately

[Unsigned][13]

ing the new engraving which had recently been completed, said, ''Mr. Inman expressed to me his perfect satisfaction with the execution of the plate, and I think it will generally be deemed better even than that of the *Mirror*'' (Wilson, *Life*, p. 441). The engraving and an article by Poe finally appeared in *Graham's* for September, 1843. See list of Halleck portraits, p. 385.

[10] The address of John Jacob Astor, Halleck's employer.

[11] R. H. Wilde (1789–1847), Italian scholar and poet. Toward the close of his life he was a resident of New Orleans, where in 1844 he was admitted to the Bar, and practiced law until his death. As a poet, he is best known for his delicate verses, ''My Life is like the Summer Rose.'' The letter is in the Yale Collection of American Literature.

[12] Preserved among the *Miscellaneous Papers* in the Manuscript Room of the New York Public Library.

[13] This letter and the one addressed to his sister on May 2, 1848, Halleck probably left unsigned, so that no one would be tempted to preserve them as autograph notes.

To George H. Graham[14]

New York Nov. 28, 1846.

George H. Graham, Esq[r]
    Philadelphia,

Dear Sir,

I ADDRESSED you a letter last Week in which I asked whether, you were willing to receive as a Contribution to your Magazine, a Translation of "The Bell" of Schiller, & some other lines which I have in hand. I fear, having received no answer, that my letter has not reached you. Allow me to request a reply at your convenience, & believe me

Yours truly

FITZ-GREENE HALLECK

To Rufus W. Griswold[15]

Dear Sir,

I HAVE this day rec[d] your favor of the 27th Ult[o] and am grateful for your kindness in so promptly attending to my request. I can do better in this Market with the merchandise in question.

I hope soon to see your Book of the prosers,[16] and I wish it a rapid sale.

Most truly Dear Sir
Yours—

FITZ-GREENE HALLECK

R. W. Griswold, Esq[r]   New York 3[d] March '47.

To Miss Maria Halleck[17]

My dear Sister,

I ENCLOSE $50 which should have accompanied my Letter of yesterday. Have you sold the hydrate [?] yet?

Yours opportunely [?]

[Unsigned]

Thursday, May 2, '48.

---

14 This letter, preserved in the Historical Society of Pennsylvania, was addressed probably to the publisher of *Graham's Lady's and Gentleman's Magazine.* Graham's middle initial, however, was "R." Halleck's use of "H" was undoubtedly due to inadvertence. The poems here referred to never appeared in the *Magazine;* or have we any other record of a translation by Halleck of Schiller's "The Bell." Concerning Halleck's slight knowledge of German see p. 187. It is, of course, possible that Halleck was here attempting to find a publisher for poems of another author. This seems especially likely in view of the fact that at this period Halleck was himself writing almost no poetry.

15 Preserved in the Historical Society of Pennsylvania. Griswold was one of the editors of *Graham's Magazine,* and later became Poe's literary executor.

16 Griswold's *Prose Writers of America* was published in Philadelphia in 1847.

17 In the library of Yale University.

To Epes Sargent[18]

Guilford, Connecticut,
October 18 1851.

My dear Sir,

YOUR favor of the 10th inst addressed to me at New Haven, has reached me here, where I now reside. I am grateful for your kind remembrance of me, after so long a seperation [sic], and for the promise you make me of giving me so honored a place in your coming book. As you request, I have corrected the proof, so far as it goes. Many lines have been, I observe, omitted, the want of which seems to me to break the unity &c of the whole, but, as the omissions give a value to the poem by making it shorter and less tedious, I am greatly obliged to them. What a question you do put, in asking a rhymer what his rhymes mean! Were you not poet yourself,[19] and, moreover, almost a *prize* poet, I would not attempt an answer. But I think I meant in the lines you quote

> "Come when the blessed seals
> "That close the Pestilence are broke"

to speak of one of the Instruments of Heavens wrath towards man, named in the Litany—"Plague, Pestilence and Famine," kept bottled up,

---

[18] This letter, preserved in the Historical Society of Pennsylvania, concerns in part the insertion of ''Marco Bozzaris'' in Epes Sargent's *Standard Reader*, published in 1852. As the letter was printed with certain unnoted omissions in Wilson's *Life*, p. 298, it has been thought best here to reproduce it entire. In 1856 Mr. Sargent sent the letter to his uncle, Arthur G. Coffin, with the following note, also in the Historical Society of Pennsylvania:

Boston, Dec. 16th, 1856.

My dear uncle,

I SEND you another contribution for your collection of autographs. It is a letter from Halleck, the poet, and has reference to his poem of Marco Bozzaris, a poem which has been in half of the Speakers and Readers for the last twenty years, and will probably be in half of those published during the next two centuries. I wrote Halleck asking him what he meant by the two lines which I have underlined in the following:

> Come to the bridal-chamber, Death!
> Come to the mother's when she feels
> For the first time her first born's breath;
> *Come when the blessed seals*
> *Which* [sic] *close the pestilence are broke,*—&c.

His answer will be found in the accompanying letter, and may be interesting to some poetical antiquarian of the year 1975—for that Halleck's poem will be *alive* then I fully believe.

I have other letters in store for you, which will doubtless turn up as soon as I have time to reduce my papers to some order.

With affectionate regards to aunt Matilda, I remain,

Yours sincerely,
dear uncle,

EPES SARGENT.

Arthur G. Coffin Esq.
Philadelphia
Pa.

[19] Mr. Sargent had published in 1849 *Songs of the Sea and Other Poems.*

corked up, *sealed* up, for use, and only opened on important occasions, a sort of Torpedo enclosed in a letter which explodes when you *break the seal*. I do not recollect where I stole the idea. There is something very like it in the Revelations chap[t] 5th and 6th.

As John Wilson said when he knocked a man down at Ambleside, "I hope I make myself understood now."

Pray let me hear from you often, and believe me,

My dear Sir,
Most truly yours,
FITZ-GREENE HALLECK.

E. Sargeant [*sic*] Esq[r]

To Clement C. Cline[20]

Guilford, Connecticut
November 29th 1852.

Dear Sir,

I CRAVE your pardon for my long delay in answering your kind favor, but I have been for some time absent from home, and it was, by mistake, kept here waiting for me. I am most grateful to you, and to the other Gentlemen of your Society, for the high honor so courteously proffered me. In availing myself of your request, I have taken the liberty to substitute the enclosed lines in place of the "Marco Bozzaris," you name, and I hope that their Nationality will cause them to be the more acceptable to you. Believe me,

Dear Sir,
Very respectfully yours,
FITZ-GREENE HALLECK

Clement C. Cline Esq[r]
  Corres. Sec[y] New York
    Rhetorical Society

To Charles C. Moreau[21]

Guilford Connecticut
May 24th 1853.

Dear Sir,

LET me hope that you will cease to accuse me of neglecting your kind letter when you learn that, by some sad mistake, it was kept for weeks at

---

[20] Preserved in the Henry E. Huntington Library and Art Gallery.

[21] This letter, preserved in the Henry E. Huntington Library and Art Gallery, refers to an extra-illustrated edition of Halleck's poems (probably that of 1847) made by C. C. Moreau. Whether or not Moreau presented the volumes to Halleck, is not entirely clear. A portion of this letter was reprinted by Evert A. Duyckinck in his article on Halleck in *Putnam's Magazine*, XI, 236 (February, 1868).

Bixbys Hotel, and then sent on here during my absence, where it has long waited my return. I hasten to beg you to accept my most grateful acknowledgements of the high compliment you have paid me in your collection of Illustrations; proving as it does, in a manner so flattering to me, a devotedness of your time and taste and treasure that has given a real life like existence to subjects of which my all unworthy verses only dreamed. Henceforth I shall scorn the simplicity of print, and refer to your splendid volumes in the pride of Prior's Chameleon, who, after borrowing beauty from the plumes of the Peacock, strutted

"As if the rainbow were *in Tail*
"Settled on him and his heirs male."

Let me further hope that, when I again visit New York, I may be allowed the pleasure of calling upon you, and of expressing more becomingly, in person, my sense of the honor you have so gracefully bestowed on me. In the meantime believe me, Dear Sir,

Very faithfully yours,
Fitz-Greene Halleck

C. C. Moreau, Esqr
&c. &c.

To Henry Stephens Randall[22]

Guilford, Connecticut
Nov. 29, 1853

Dear Sir,

I am happy to say that the Books have been received in good order, & do repeat my most earnest thanks for your courtesy.

With great regard & respect
Your ob. serv^t
Fitz-Greene Halleck

The Honor. H. S. Randall

To William Pitt Palmer[23]

Guilford, Connecticut
February 18th '56

Dear Sir:

One of my acquaintances here owns New Grenada Bonds, issued at

22 H. S. Randall (1811–76), the author of several works on agriculture and of the *Life of Thomas Jefferson* (New York, 1857). The letter is in the Yale Collection of American Literature.

23 W. P. Palmer (1805–84), an insurance president of New York City, and a writer of verse. See Rufus Griswold, *Poets and Poetry of America* (1855), p. 325. The letter is preserved among the *Miscellaneous Papers* in the Manuscript Room of the New York Public Library.

Bogata some thirty years since, for Interest on the old Colombia debt. Will you do me the kindness to endeavor to ascertain from your Wall Street neighbors their present and probable future value, and, when quite convenient, let me know the results of your enquiries? The Newspapers are beginning to tell us that New Grenada is fast becoming rich, but of her intention to pay her old debts they say nothing. Let me hope that you will pardon the annoyance, I am giving you, and believe me,

Dear Sir,
Most truly yours,
FITZ-GREENE HALLECK

Wm Pitt Palmer, Esqr

To ————————[24]

Guilford, Connecticut
December 13, '56

Dear Sir,

I HAVE had the honor of receiving your highly poetical letter. Mine is not the Autograph of a Statesman or a Governor (is not a Governor always a Statesman?) or a poetess. I therefore cannot add as you ask, one more to your collection, but "such as I have give unto thee."

Yours truly,
FITZ-GREENE HALLECK

To Gulian C. Verplanck[25]

Guilford, Connecticut
Octo. 3^d '57

Dear Sir,

I HAVE been informed that Mr Henry Panton is an Applicant for the place of Librarian in the New York Society Library[26] of which you are one of the Trustees.[27]

A long acquaintance with that gentleman has prompted me to take the

[24] This graceful autographic note was probably addressed either to C. J. Hoadly, from 1855 to 1900 librarian of the Connecticut State Library, or to his brother, George E. Hoadley [*sic*], also a resident of Hartford. The letter is preserved in the Hoadley Collection of the Connecticut Historical Society.

[25] A lawyer by profession, Mr. Verplanck (1786–1876) devoted himself freely to a study of the fine arts, and was much in demand as a lecturer. His relations with Halleck, although undoubtedly cordial (see pp. 222–223), were probably never of an intimate nature, judging from the formal language in which the present letter is couched. The note is preserved in the New York Historical Society.

[26] This historic New York library, now located at number 109 University Place, was founded in 1754.

[27] Verplanck was elected Trustee in 1810.

liberty of addressing you in his behalf, and has enabled me to say to you that I deem him well qualified for the duties of such a position, not only from his general ability, but from his knowledge of Books, alike as a "Constant Reader," and as a man of business, accustomed to the purchase and sale of them, and, moreover, from his uniform courtesy of manner, so important in the officers of Institutions like yours, desirous, in some degree, of public favor in aid of their usefulness. Should this expression of my high sense of his merits induce you to inform yourself of them from other and better sources, and help to give him the benefit of your support at the coming election, I shall have assisted you in doing a good deed for all parties; and shall be anxious, at all times, to prove my gratitude for your kindness. Believe me,

Dear Sir,
truly yours,
FITZ-GREENE HALLECK

Gulian C. Verplanck, Esqʳ

To ——————————²⁸

Guilford, Connecticut
Octᵒ 3ᵈ '57

My dear Sir,

You have once more to repeat the old story of *"Monsieur Tonson come again."*²⁹ This is what your character for goodness and kindness subjects you to, and you can only make up your mind to endure. So let me hope that you will, as usual, do the needful with the enclosed Receipt, and forward the check at your convenience.

I hope, in your answer, that you will tell me that all is well with you and yours, and that the present storm among *"men of credit"* in Wall Street &c., &c., is all the better for you *"men of money"* & that so long as Uncle Sam is as he was when we last talked on the subject, your Debtor to the amnᵗ of his Taxes, in your name, you sleep quietly & independently. Please give me all the information about yourself & the others in whom you are interested that you may fancy will gratify me & believe me My dear Sir

Most truly yours
FITZ-GREENE HALLECK

It is so very long since I have had the pleasure of seeing you, that I must be pardoned for looking you up & bothering you with a visit the

---

²⁸ The address has been lost. The letter is preserved in the library of Brown University.

²⁹ A proverbial remark taken from William T. Moncrieff's play of *Monsieur Tonson* (London, 1821 [?]). The performance of the play in New York (1822) by the elder Mathews, Halleck's friend, was very popular.

next time I come to New York, probably in the course of the coming month. I will not ask very much of your valuable time.

H

I addressed a letter to my former Tailor Mr B. M. Noe, N° 673 Broadway Lafarge Hotel, a few days since, to which I have rec^d no answer. Can you without too much trouble ascertain whether & where he has removed or if he has not, whether he has received & will attend to the letter I wrote him—and let me know in your reply to this.

To Charles J. Hoadly[30]

Guilford, Connecticut,
November 15, 1857.

Dear Sir,

I MOST sincerely beg your pardon for my long delay in answering your favor of the 7th Aug., but I have been absent from home during a great part of the last three months, and your letter was, in consequence, mislaid, and not until to-day recovered. I well remember your grandfather and grandmother, as among my earliest acquaintances, and am glad to claim you as, to some extent, a brother townsman. Your wish to preserve my Autograph makes me quite proud. Let me hope that you will visit Guilford, and do me the kindness to call on me.

Very truly yours,
FITZ-GREENE HALLECK

Charles J. Hoadly Esq.
Hartford.

To Frederic S. Cozzens [?][31]

Guilford, Connecticut
Decem. 22^d '57

My dear Sir,

I GLADLY hasten to thank you for the present of your charming poem, "a

[30] C. J. Hoadly was for many years librarian of the Connecticut State Library. See also p. 397. The letter is preserved in the Hoadley Collection of the Connecticut Historical Society.

[31] Although the address of this letter, now in the New York Historical Society, has been lost, it is probable, from the allusion to Mrs. Sparrowgrass in the first paragraph, that it was written to Frederic S. Cozzens, the humorist. In 1855 Cozzens had published *The Sparrowgrass Papers*, a series of humorous sketches in which the chief character speaks in the first person and frequently alludes to his wife as Mrs. Sparrowgrass. Thus Halleck, in his playful way, might have referred to Cozzens' wife as Mrs. Sparrowgrass. The first paragraph as a whole, however, is an enigma.

beautiful thought and sweetly bodied forth," and for the pleasure which its good sense, good feeling, good music, and good English have given me. But oh! that for such healthy and promising offspring, *possibly* its only offspring, a Golden wedding should be indebted to a *third* person! How shocking! and what an example you are setting; and what will Mrs. Sparrowgrass say?

You were very fortunate in being absent when I called twice upon you lately in New York, for I had a thousand questions on a thousand themes to bother you with, but do not flatter yourself;—for you may not be able to escape me the next time, and sooner or later I shall win from you the compliment which my friend Horace Greeley, in his Lecture, pays to the Spenser of "The Fairy Queen"; that of being written down a *Bore*—Apropos. you are no doubt delighted, like me, to learn that our old favorite, Shakespeare, so long infamous as a vagabond preacher and poet, is becoming respectable. A maiden Lady, a Miss Bacon, one of the murderers of Putnams Magazine and the Queens English; recently ascertained that he was, in his time, Lord High Chancellor of England;[32] and now Mr Greely [sic] denounces his religious and political opinions as those of a Christian and a Gentleman! He, however, kindly exonerates him from the charge of being a poet, and transfers that somewhat equivocal distinction to a Mr. Browning, the husband of a Lady of that name, whose good taste is equal to that of the critics that praise her writings, and whose "Aurora Leigh" is as free from all that is coarse and vulgar, impious and impure, licentious and blasphemous, as the *"Faust"* of Goethe;[33] and whose "Swans nest among the reeds" is as unwittingly [?] immodest as the "Venus' Dove" of Prior, or the very saleable specimens of "Fanny Fern"[34] or a portion of this letter of mine which I beg you to light your cigar with as soon as you have read it.

Please accept my truest and kindest good wishes of the "the Season" and of all pleasant seasons, and believe me,

My dear Sir

gratefully yours.

FITZ-GREENE HALLECK

[32] Miss Delia Bacon first suggested her Shakespeare-Bacon theory in an article in *Putnam's Magazine* for January, 1856. The theory was subsequently elaborated in her volume entitled *Philosophy of the Plays of Shakspere Unfolded* (London and Boston, 1857).

[33] For Halleck's antipathy to the poetry of the Brownings and to the *Faust* of Goethe, see pp. 188–190.

[34] The pseudonym of Mrs. Sarah P. Parton, sister to Nathaniel P. Willis, and author of *Ruth Hall, Fern Leaves*, etc.

To Charles C. Moreau[35]

Guilford Conn.
May 9, 1859

Dear Sir:—

I TAKE great pleasure in acknowledging the receipt of your favor of the 5th inst and in thanking you most sincerely for your choice and cherished present.

I was not until now aware that your "Ballantyne" Club had republished the Soldier's Journal you mention. It has long been a favorite of mine and I delight in recollecting the brave fellow's story so simply told, of the arrival at Perth Amboy of himself and his comrades on their return from captivity and of the *"as one man"* kiss of affection with which they greeted kneeling their "Mother Land" the only instance of kissing by *Platoons* within my memory.

There was more woman in their great Leader and Teacher, General Arnold, than we are willing to believe.

I am Dear Sir
Very truly yours
FITZ-GREENE HALLECK

Charles C. Moreau, Esq.

---

[35] In the library of the University of Chicago. Halleck here refers without doubt to a volume published in 1857 by ''The Club'' of which Charles Moreau and his brother, John, were among the original members. In 1859 the Moreau brothers withdrew from the organization and founded the ''Bradford Club.'' (See A. Growoll, *American Book Clubs,* New York, 1897, pp. 35 ff.) In referring to ''your 'Ballantyne' Club,'' the poet probably had in mind not the famous Ballantyne Press, founded by James Ballantyne in Scotland in 1796, but the ''Bannatyne Club,'' organized in Edinburgh in 1823, and named after George Bannatyne (1545–1608?), the Scotch antiquary. Halleck had apparently confused the two names. The volume alluded to in this letter, and published by ''The Club'' was *A Journal of the Expedition to Quebec, in the year 1775, under the Command of Colonel Benedict Arnold. By James Melvin, a Private in Captain Dearborn's Company.* New York, 1857. But here we must note another confusion on Halleck's part. Evidently the poet had not seen the volume to which Moreau referred, for the incident which Halleck mentions cannot be found in the work. Such a story, however, is given in another record of this Revolutionary episode —John Joseph Henry's *Campaign against Quebec* (Watertown, New York, 1844). As a group of the soldiers who were returning from captivity in Canada neared Elizabethtown Point, New Jersey, ''the intelligence,'' says Henry, ''caused a sparkling in every eye. On the next day about noon we were in the boats. Adverse winds retarded us. It was ten or eleven at night, before we landed; the moon shone beautifully. Morgan stood in the bow of the boat; making a spring not easily surpassed, and falling on the earth as it were to grasp it, cried 'Oh my country.' We that were near him, pursued his example. Now a race commenced, which in quickness could scarcely be exceeded, and soon brought us to Elizabethtown'' (p. 202). It was in all probability this incident to which Halleck referred, and Henry's book which he believed Moreau's club to have published.

To Frederic S. Cozzens[36]

Guilford, Connecticut,
Aug. 10th '59.

My dear Sir,

I HAD not the pleasure of receiving your kind present, (for which please accept my best thanks) until many days after your letter reached me.

I once asked one of your admirers if he had ever read Wheaton's History of the Northmen.[37] He answered, with his pleasantest *Sunnyside* smile, "I cannot say that I have read it, but I have *reviewed* it."

With such an example before me, I did not wait for your Volume,[38] but, in compliance with your so sincerely expressed wish to be admonished for its faults, I wrote a review of it, embracing a list of them which I deemed sufficiently long, and, by way of proving that there is "balm" in Criticism as well as "in Gilead," I admitted a few, very few beauties.

But after perusing the Book itself, I found its faults so many more than I could have imagined that I abandoned the task, and, having learnt, from the Knickerbocker, that our good friend Mr Clark[39] had much improved your work since its original appearance, I at once discovered to whom it owed its few beauties, notwithstanding the real authors purchased silence on the subject.

That such "a thing of spreads and patches" should *sell,* as it does, (60th thousandth on the title page) is no wonder. Like Peter Pindars razors, "it was *made* to sell."!!

Will the foregoing do? and is not its perusal a delightful pastime for you? There are others, besides Sir Peter Teazle, whose motto is—"It is a damned bad world and the fewer we praise the better," and, when you hereafter think of appealing to a good friends sincerity remember me, and this, my lesson.

Now that I have d'offd my critic mask and domino (they fitted me very badly) I hurry, as the Free Masons say, "from labor to refreshment," from fiction to the truth I love.

I am delighted with the Book. It was not Strange to me, to be sure, but there is more in it than of old, and I have read it more carefully and consecutively. I skip the Historical past, of course, agreeing with a certain renowned painter of our acquaintance, who, in his group of men of

---

[36] This letter to Frederic S. Cozzens, the humorist, is here published through the courtesy of Mr. Thomas E. Madigan of New York City.

[37] Published in London in 1831.

[38] Probably Cozzens' *Acadia; or, A Month with the Blue Noses* (New York, 1859), which had previously appeared as a serial in the *Knickerbocker.*

[39] Louis Gaylord Clark, editor of the *Knickerbocker.* A brief review of *Acadia* appeared in the *Knickerbocker* for July, 1859.

Genius, has placed the Historians in the background, as persons who, like words in a parenthesis, can be omitted without injury to the sense or the scene. They are just now, the fashion, but wait! This is the age of Poet *Laureates,* "Pye[40] &c," that of Poets will come, again, ere long.

I have reserved for another letter a remark or two, or, rather, a query or two, for our mutual benefit. For the present, I think it was Roland, the husband of Madam Roland, who insulted his Queen by wearing strings in his Shoes at her Levee and not Mirabeau. Mirabeau was a gentleman.

Believe me,   My dear Sir,
truly yours,
FITZ-GREENE HALLECK

Fred^k S. Cozzens, Esqr.

To Alfred Hudson Guernsey[41]

Guilford, Connecticut
Feby. 13th '62

Dear Sir,
I HAVE again the pleasure of receiving a letter from you.

It is now generally believed that the "Man with the Iron Mask" was of the Blood Royal of England, and I am, today, very glad to find, in an Editor unmasked, one of the Blood Royal of Literature.

You doubtless recollect that Miller, the printer, in sending to Doctor Johnson the last proofs of his Dictionary, wrote "Mr. Miller presents his compliments to Doctor Johnson and thanks Heaven he has done with him." Allow me to hope that you will, in my case, refrain from a similar act of piety, until I have the honor of calling upon you in Town; and thanking you, in person, for your many kindnesses, and for placing my translation in such good company. Could not your compliments be extended to two of our Versions of Homer's "Saffron-robed Morning," to Pope's "Aurora, daughter of the dawn," and Chapman's "Cheerful Lady of the Light"?

Believe me, Dear Sir
briefly and truly yours,
FITZ-GREENE HALLECK

Be assured of my entire satisfaction in referring to your arrangement of the two lines you mention & to all your proceedings "in the premises."

A. H. Guernsey, Esq.

[40] Henry J. Pye preceded Robert Southey as Poet Laureate of England.

[41] A. H. Guernsey (1818–1902), author of several prose works including *Emerson, Poet and Philosopher* (New York, 1882). From 1863 to 1869 he was also editor of *Harper's.* Unfortunately the volume here referred to, which Guernsey is apparently editing, and to which Halleck is contributing a translation, has not been identified. The letter is preserved in the Chamberlain Collection of the Boston Public Library.

To William H. H. Murray[42]

Guilford, Connecticut
Janʸ 29. '64

My dear Sir,

Herewith I beg leave to hand you the reply, from the Astor Library, to your question as to the pedigree of Alexander Dumas. It appears that his father was a General of Artillery highly distinguished in the French service, a favorite of the First Emperor Napoleon, a blood relation of the Empress Josephine, and a Mulatto of the first generation. That the Son is a Quadroon of the second generation, and, as it happens, resembles in front, complexion &c, his Negro Grandmother. He is, moreover, one of the most eminent literary Men in Europe, and he and the present Emperor are considered in France as two of the cleverest persons in their way, now living. If the object of your inquiry, therefore, is to determine what proportion of Black and White is necessary to the making up a Man of Genius, you have now the materials before you enabling you to come to a decision.

With my best regards to your good Lady, I beg you to believe me, My dear sir, truly yours

Fitz-Greene Halleck

The Revᵈ W. H. H. Murray

I shall be glad to know that this letter is so fortunate as to reach you.

H.

To William Alfred Jones[43]

Guilford, Connecticut
Dec. 29, 1864.

My dear Sir

An illness of several weeks, called here a lung fever, has so enfeebled me that, until now my fingers have lost their power over a pen. With their returning strength I hasten to say that I am happy to find that the College Library is still under your care and that you would like to point out to me in person its attractions. You know how much I like Books, & when

---

42 W. H. H. Murray (1840–1904), a Congregational clergyman and the author of the well-known *Adventures in the Wilderness* (1868). This letter was written in reply to a request of Mr. Murray for information regarding the ancestry of Alexandre Dumas. See p. 346. I have had the opportunity of examining the original letter through the kindness of Mr. Alfred E. Hammer of Branford, Connecticut.

43 William A. Jones (1817–1900), the author of various critical works, was librarian of Columbia College from 1851 to 1865. This letter is preserved in the "Columbia University Library Collections of Autograph Letters and Other MSS."

to my liking for them you add my regard for your comments and remarks upon and concerning them, the inducements on my part to accept and enjoy your kind invitation are manifest. It is uncertain how soon I can again be in New York, but at my next visit I hope to be enabled to call upon you and to thank you in person for your many pleasant and profitable courtesies towards me. In the meantime, pray excuse the illegibility of my penmanship and believe me, my dear Sir

Very truly yours

FITZ-GREENE HALLECK.

To Samuel Ward[44]

Guilford, Connecticut
Feby 25– '65

My dear Sir,

I HASTEN to assure you of my regret that a fortnights absence from home has, until now, deprived me of the pleasure of thanking you for your kind letter, and for the long-looked-and hoped-for Volume,[45] its welcome and cherished companion.

A glance over it gladdens me with the sight of many of my old manuscript favorites, enshrined among your old letters, and of more whose merits claim a relationship with them, and I am, particularly, delighted to find that the example of the leading Poets, those "Cynthias of the minute," on the other side of the Atlantic, has not prevented you from blending, with graver and grander themes, the gentle and the genial, from entwining Wit with Wisdom, good humour with good sense, and good fellowship with them all. Hoping that your Volume & Praed's,[46] recently [?] republished from his enlarged Edition, may win the popularity they deserve, and make their readers, healthier and happier, than they can ever become by the study of such themes for song as the unwedded Mother in "Aurora Leigh" the unclothed Lady in Peeping "Tom of Coventry," and the sentimental Lady Paligamist [sic] and her perspiring [?] first husband, in "Enoth [sic] Arden;"[47] I beg you to believe me   my dear Sir

ever gratefully yours

FITZ-GREENE HALLECK.

Samuel Ward, Esq.

[44] Halleck carried on with Samuel Ward, the banker-poet of New York (1814–84), a rather extensive correspondence, much of which has been printed in James G. Wilson's *Bryant and His Friends.* The present letter, hitherto unpublished, is here printed through the kindness of Mr. Thomas E. Madigan of New York City.

[45] Probably Samuel Ward's *Lyrical Recreations* (New York and London, 1865).

[46] *The Poems of W. M. Praed . . . Enlarged Edition. With a Memoir by Rev. Derwent Coleridge.* Published in two volumes by W. J. Widdleton in 1865.

[47] For Halleck's dislike of the work of Mrs. Browning and Tennyson, see pp. 188–190.

To Samuel Austin Allibone[48]

Guilford, Connecticut
Feby 28th '65

My dear Sir,

My desire to grant any request of yours causes me sadly to regret my inability to comply with that conveyed in your favor of the 23^d inst. The Volume you name has been compiled from sources beyond my controul. I have but slightly glanced over its Text, and, of its Notes I am wholly ignorant, having, in the fear of their possible incorrectness, refrained from reading them.

The Verses have never desired or deserved any other than a short life and a "merry one," and those most interested in their welfare have, hitherto, let them, and intend hereafter to let them, "sleep the sleep that knows no waking."

The gentlemen of the "Bradford Club" have paid them a very high compliment by placing them, so richly enrobed, in their Library of literary curiosities; to them the Volume exclusively belongs; and it is to them that your friend should be referred for such aid in his contemplated work as he thinks useful.

Trusting to your clemency for pardoning my dereliction from duty in this, I hope, solitary instance, I beg you to believe me,

My dear Sir   truly yours

FITZ-GREENE HALLECK

S. Austin Allibone, Esqr

To William Loring Andrews[49]

Guilford, Connecticut
June 7. '65.

Dear Sir,

Your generous present, the beautiful "Crawford" Volume,[50] has reached me, and added largely to my indebtedness to your courtesy. With our friend Mr Hicks[51] eloquent Eulogy, I have long been familiar and my intimacy with the family of Mrs Crawford gave me the honour of a per-

---

[48] S. A. Allibone (1816–89), editor of *A Critical Dictionary of English Literature and British and American Authors* (Philadelphia, 1858–71; 4 vols.). This interesting letter, preserved in the Historical Society of Pennsylvania, concerns the edition of *The Croakers* issued by the Bradford Club in 1860. See p. 336.

[49] This letter to William L. Andrews, the New York bibliophile, is preserved in the Waterston Collection of the Massachusetts Historical Society.

[50] Thomas Hicks, *Eulogy on Thomas Crawford* (New York, 1865). Crawford (1814–57) was an American sculptor, who lived much abroad.

[51] Thomas Hicks painted Halleck's portrait in 1855.

sonal acquaintance with her distinguished husband during his last visit to this country. I need not, therefore, assure you how trebly interesting the Volume has become to me. Do not ask me to exchange it for the bound one you mention. I have always preferred the single leafed simplicity of our way-side Rose to the many-flounced attractions of her garden cousin.

Hoping soon to be enabled to thank you in person for your continued remembrance of me, I am, My dear sir

truly yours

FITZ: GREENE HALLECK

Wm L. Andrews, Esq.

To James Henry Hackett[52]

Guilford, Conn.
August 14, 1865.

My dear Sir:

I AM very glad, indeed, to learn from your kind letter of remembrance that there are other sensible young women besides Mrs. Enoch (See Genesis 5, 21st) and the late Lady Leicester, who believe that it takes sixty-five years to make a good husband. Mrs. Enoch became the mother of Methusalem, a millionaire in years, and Lady Leicester the mother of five sons, each a millionaire in money. May your marriage destiny be the long life of the one, and the long purses of the other.

For my own part, I still continue to fancy that Methusalem's resolution —not to marry until he was one hundred and eighty-one—was wise and prudent as a general rule. I am fast approaching that interesting period; and, unless Mrs. Hackett when I have the pleasure of conversing with her, shall, by reference to her own pleasant example, persuade me into an early marriage, I shall wait patiently another century for the happy day.

Please accept my best thanks for the Shakespeare pamphlet.[53] I have kept pace admiringly with your progress in an enterprise so honorable to

[52] This graceful letter, in which Halleck indulges in his customary vein of quiet humor, was written to James H. Hackett (1800–1871), the well-known comedian. Hackett first made Halleck's acquaintance in 1818 through John Buchanan Burr, a fellow clerk of the poet's. Hackett's first wife was Miss Catherine Lee Sugg, an actress, whom Halleck mentioned in his epistle ''To Mr. Simpson'' (1869 ed., p. 267). At the age of sixty-five Hackett was married a second time to a Miss Morgan. It was on the occasion of this marriage that Halleck wrote the letter which appears among Hackett's reminiscences of the poet in the *New York Evening Post* for January 31, 1868. It was later reprinted in Wilson, *Life*, pp. 494–496.

[53] Hackett was one of a committee appointed for the erection of a Shakespeare monument at the three hundredth anniversary of the dramatist's birth. Hackett had sent to Halleck a circular describing the enterprise.

you and your associates, and well acquainted as I have so long been with your own special energy and perseverance in every species of well-doing, I have great expectation of your ultimate success. Thus far our climate and that of England do not seem congenial to such "out-of-doors" undertakings.

Our flattering and facetious friend Chas. Augustus Davis[54] once promised if I would die, to impedestal a statue of me in some one of your city's triangular parks, and when I objected, for fear of taking cold with the park gates open, he kindly assured me that I should stand with an umbrella over my head. Whether he has found a sculptor cunning enough in carving stone umbrellas and has patronized his genius, I have not yet been told.

Repeating my acknowledgments of your pleasant recollections of me, I am, my dear Sir,

most truly yours,
FITZ-GREENE HALLECK

Jas. H. Hackett, Esq., New York.

To Evert A. Duyckinck[55]

Guilford, Conn^t
Aug. 24, '65

My dear Sir:

I FIND myself fast becoming as ignorant of Books and of their writers as the President of a College or the Regent of a University. Will you kindly inform me who is John Esten Cooke[56] and what and about what he has written? I wish to answer a very gentlemanly letter I have received from him, and to avoid treading upon any provincial or partizan toes.

Please fancy yourself my Father Confessor, & believe me

My dear Sir
Truly yours
FITZ-GREENE HALLECK

E. Duyckinck, Esq.

If quite convenient, let me have your reply by return of mail, and oblige me

H

---

[54] C. A. Davis (1795–1867), author of the *Letters of Jack Downing* (1834). See p. 329 of this biography.

[55] Preserved in the Duyckinck Collection of the New York Public Library.

[56] A Virginia novelist (1830–86) who served in the Confederate army during the Civil War. *The Virginia Comedians* and *Leather Stocking and Silk* are his best-known novels.

To Evert A. Duyckinck[57]

Guilford, Connecticut
Aug. 27, '65

My dear Sir,

I HASTEN to thank you for your prompt attention to my request and for your highly valued present of the Photograph of your Brother.[58]

Have you ever seen the original or an Engraving from the portrait of Pope, by Jervas.[59] If so, have you not observed a very striking resemblance between the intellectual look of your Brothers countenance and that of the Poet?[60]

Hoping soon to have the pleasure of calling upon you in Town, I am,
My dear sir   Truly yours

FITZ-GREENE HALLECK

E. A. Duyckinck

To Evert A. Duyckinck[61]

Guilford, Connecticut
Sept. 14, '65

My dear Sir,

I ONCE more beg leave to annoy you, in the character of "your petitioner who will ever pray," by asking that when you again write to our friend Mr. J. E. Cooke,[62] you will do me the kindness to say that I wrote him some three weeks since in a letter addressed as he directed, to which I have not yet had the pleasure of receiving an answer.

The unsettled state of things in Virginia at present, extending, I presume, to the Mail routes, induces me to fear that it has not reached and may not reach him, and I am anxious to preserve his good opinion by causing him to be assured of my prompt and grateful attention to the request with which he has honored me.

[57] In the Duyckinck Collection of the New York Public Library.

[58] George L. Duyckinck, coeditor of *The Cyclopaedia of American Literature*, died 1863.

[59] Charles Jervas (1675?–1739), English portrait painter.

[60] On another occasion Halleck called attention to the same resemblance. A memorandum in Duyckinck's hand, preserved in the Duyckinck Collection, reads: "Insisted upon a resemblance in my brother's engraved portrait to Jervas' painting of Pope in the full length engraving which he called for."

[61] Preserved in a copy of Duyckinck's *Fitz-Greene Halleck* (privately printed by William Loring Andrews) in the Reserve Room of the New York Public Library.

[62] See the letter addressed to Duyckinck (dated August 24, 1865) in regard to John Esten Cooke, p. 408.

Begging you not be "weary in well doing," however severely I try your patience, I am

My dear Sir,   truly yours

FITZ-GREENE HALLECK

Evert A. Duykinck [*sic*], Esq.

To William Loring Andrews[63]

Guilford, Connecticut

Jany 13, '66

My dear Sir,

YOUR letter of yesterday telling me that you have found an old copy of the poem you had done me the honor to wish for, and had placed it, clothed in "Purple and fine linen" in your library, gratifies me greatly, especially as our friends, the Publishers, have decided not to issue the new edition, in favor of which you have kindly devoted so much time and pains. Should a new edition appear in any shape hereafter, I shall hasten to ask your acceptance of a copy.

I am seeking to avoid the cold weather by making a journey to the South, in the course of which I hope to have the pleasure of calling upon you in New York.

In the meantime, pray believe me, My dear Sir

Truly yours

FITZ: GREENE HALLECK

Wm. L. Andrews, Esq.

To Lewis Jacob Cist[64]

Guilford, Connecticut

Feby, 1866.

Dear Sir,

YOUR favor of the 12th inst with its very interesting catalogue of curiosi-

---

[63] Preserved in an extra-illustrated copy of Duyckinck's *Cyclopaedia of American Literature* in the Manuscript Room of the New York Public Library. About this time Halleck was concerned in negotiating with publishers regarding new editions of his poems (see pp. 357–358). This letter, addressed to William Loring Andrews, the New York bibliophile, was written probably with reference to *Fanny*, which the publishers had apparently decided they could not bring out in spite of Mr. Andrews' efforts in Halleck's behalf. It was perhaps this failure to find a publisher for *Fanny* that made Mr. Andrews, later in the same year, himself issue a privately printed edition of the poem (see p. 359).

[64] L. J. Cist (1818–85), a western banker who published in Cincinnati, 1845, a volume of verse entitled *Trifles in Verse*. Cist was also a collector of autographs and portraits, of which he had a large and valuable collection. The "catalogue of curiosities" to which Halleck here alludes may be a list of some of the autographs in Cist's collection. The letter is preserved in the library of Haverford College, Haverford, Pennsylvania.

ties, and the letter of our patriarchal friend, Mr. Pierpont,[65] has given me great pleasure. It is gladdening to learn from the letter which, as you request I return herewith that his genius still flourishes at fourscore in the long-lifed beauty of a Cedar of Lebanon.

I hasten to avail myself of your so kindly expressed willingness to place the enclosed "Greenback" to my credit in the book of such a Treasury of gold and diamonds, as you propose at par. It has made me, I need not add, exceedingly proud.[66]

Pray let me know soon that this has reached you, and for your many courtesies, past and present, believe me,

My dear Sir,

Gratefully yours

FITZ-GREENE HALLECK

Lewis J. Cist Esq.

To Charles C. Moreau[67]

Guilford, Connecticut

March 5th. 1866

Dear Sir,

I HAVE had the pleasure of receiving, with your letter of the 28th Ulto your generous and dearly valued Present. Please, kindly, accept my very best thanks.

As a work of Art, it has great Merit, and the more I look at it, the more exact the likeness appears to me.

Please present my truest regards to your Brother,[68] and believe me Dear Sir

gratefully yours

FITZ-GREENE HALLECK

Charles C. Moreau, Esqr

[65] John Pierpont (b. 1785), a Unitarian clergyman of Boston, who was famous in his day as the author of *Airs of Palestine*, a collection of verse first published in Baltimore in 1816. Pierpont died later in the year 1866, at the age of eighty-one.

[66] Cist had apparently asked Halleck for his autograph, which is the "Greenback" named.

[67] This letter, preserved in the Henry E. Huntington Library and Art Gallery, was probably written in acknowledgment of the engraving of Luther Bradish which C. C. Moreau had promised the poet the previous October. See the letter addressed to Moreau, pp. 351–352.

[68] John B. Moreau and his brother, Charles, author of this letter, were among the original members of "The Club," founded in 1857. In 1859 the Moreau brothers and one or two other members withdrew from "The Club," and founded the "Bradford Club," which in 1860 issued an edition of *The Croakers*. See A. Growoll, *American Book Clubs* (New York, 1897), pp. 35 ff.

To James H. Hackett[69]

Guilford, August 21 1866

My dear Sir,

I TAKE great pleasure in acknowledging the receipt of another kind letter of remembrance from you and in learning that your good lady[70] (to whom please present my very best good wishes) and yourself are merrily and wisely enjoying life in the pleasant village home of your boyhood—a summer Sunday home of my own, by the way, "lang syne."

I need not tell you how gladly I would serve you in the way you name if in my power; but I have never in my life been able to make a speech, either political or *post prandial,* on my own account; and my attempt at one to be spoken by another would be a sure failure. I am moreover wholly wanting in the knowledge of the party watchwords and the war cries of the period you mention—so necessary in their slang eloquence to win the "screeches" (Mathews'[71] great desideratum)—to which you have been so long accustomed from hearty and happy audiences.

All I can do for you is to refer you to your friend Gulian C. Verplanck,[72] with whose admiration of the Falstaff of Shakespeare and of your own (creating a sort of Humbold & Hopkins partnership) you are doubtless acquainted. I know no person more minutely informed in the colonial and general history of his own state—a history with which his own name has so long and so honorably been blended; and his success in making an excellent speech at sight is as certain as that of Captain

---

[69] This letter James H. Hackett, the comedian, printed among his reminiscences of Halleck in the *New York Evening Post* for January 31, 1868. The occasion which called forth the letter may best be described in Hackett's own words. ''In 1866, being urged by the manager of a New York theatre to revive my standard dramatic version of Washington Irving's story of 'Rip Van Winkle' (by Bayle Bernard in 1833), and which, owing to the burning, some eighteen years by-gone, of the Park Theatre, together with its appropriate and indispensable scenery, could not be acted in New York since, I wrote to Halleck that I was inclined to listen to a proposal for arranging the getting up of it afresh, and was very desirous that the Yankee part of 'Peaskill,' the tavern-keeper, and that of the Knickerbocker lawyer Brom Van Brunt, in the second act, should be enlivened by the addition of an 'Election scene at Catskill, 1783,' and the introduction by them respectively of speeches on the occasion, which should be characteristic of their distinct races, and though ludicrous, yet should bear historical reference to political subjects agitated at that period; and that I had great confidence in his (Halleck's) ability, and of his friendly inclination to aid the effect of such scene, by writing for each of those characters a short speech.''

[70] See the letter of Halleck (dated August 14, 1865) addressed to Hackett on the occasion of his second marriage, p. 407.

[71] Probably the younger Charles Mathews is here referred to.

[72] For Halleck's relations with Verplanck, see p. 222 and pp. 397–398.

Scott's rifle in winning its raccoon. I hope you will find him willing to aid you effectually.

When I was, some time since, in New York, I had the gratification of paying my personal homage to your "Tall Son of York,"[73] and of congratulating the city in possessing in one of her party-chosen-chief-magistrates,[74] that rare bird in the political aviary, a scholar and a gentleman. The grace of his brow, as our wine glasses touched each other, proved him to be a genial "chip of the old block."

Believe me my dear sir, as of old, faithfully yours,

FITZ-GREENE HALLECK

Jas. H. Hackett, Esq.

To William Alfred Jones[75]

Guilford, Connecticut
Sept. 15, '66

Dear Sir,

I HAVE your kind favor of the 10th, and the Magazine, which appears to be one of a series of interesting compilations, useful as *"memoirs pour Servir."* For both please accept my best thanks.

M[r] Dawson's[76] propensities and acquirements, as an Antiquary, peppered, as they are, by his Mitford-like "wrath and partiality," make his writings very valuable. He knows vastly more of the personages of my Story than its Story teller does, and I shall not fail, in my future editions, to profit by his friendly criticism.

His kind hint that I exercise a poets license to deal in fiction, (in other words, the "faculty divine" of lying), equally well in prose as in verse, is a compliment paid to my "Heaven of Invention" of which I ought to be proud. I only regret that his fault-finding impulses compel him to abuse M[r] Alford's [sic][77] printing and paper, both of which, to my eye, are far superior to those of the Bradford Club Volume.[78]

[73] For the origin of this phrase (usually ''York's tall son''), first applied to William T. Porter (1802?–58), for many years editor of the *Spirit of the Times*, see Francis Brinley, *Life of William T. Porter* (New York, 1860), pp. 48 ff.

[74] Halleck here refers to Recorder John H. Hackett of New York City.

[75] This letter, written to William A. Jones, the critic, apparently concerns a review, which is now lost, of the privately printed *Fanny* of 1866 (see p. 359). The letter is here published for the first time through the courtesy of Thomas E. Madigan of New York City.

[76] Possibly George Dawson, who, in 1862, succeeded Thurlow Weed (a friend of Halleck) as editor and proprietor of the *Albany Evening Journal*.

[77] The colophon on verso p. 84 of *Fanny* (1866) reads ''Alvord Printer, N. Y.''

[78] *The Croakers*, issued by the Bradford Club in 1860.

It is possible that I am mistaken in the name or the place of residence of the Senator you mention, although I am almost quite sure that he hailed, as the Sailors say, from Norwich. It is more than probable that, able and eloquent as I found him in the Senate Chamber two or three years since, he has already met the fate of our Party Politicians, and is utterly forgotten by his former constituents. Are there three men in the country more contemptibly insignificant in the eye of the Public than Millard Fillmore, Franklin Pierce, and James Buchanan? Pray let their doom be a solemn warning to you not to accept the nomination for the Presidency of the United States two years hence.

But for a slight attack of fever and ague from which I am fast recovering, I would undertake at once the defense of "Pope versus Fletcher," to which you challenge me in one of your late pleasant letters.[79] For the present, I will only quote the line, "Wait the Great Teacher, Death and God adore,"[80] a line embracing in eight words the whole moral of the Book of Job, and one of the most expressively poetical images in our language—and the line "Grove nods at grove each alley has its brother,"[81] as equally imaginative in its way.

With my most respectful regards to your good Lady, and gratitude to you both for the pleasure and profit derived from your visit among us, in which my Sister most cordially unites with me, I am

Dear Sir, very truly yours
FITZ-GREENE HALLECK

W. A. Jones Esq.

To John Bell Bouton[82]

Guilford Connecticut
March 27. '67

Dear Sir,

I AM highly honored by the request conveyed in your letter of the 23d inst of which our friend, Mr. Fowler, had, previously advised me, and regret that I cannot, at this moment, promise to avail myself of its courtesy. If, at some future moment, I can, in the Sailors phrase, "Spin a Yarn" deemed worthy of being listened to in or out of the Central Park, I shall be most happy to forward it to you, but I have so long left the

---

[79] Probably the one on pp. 423–424 in which Jones discusses the question of fancy and imagination.

[80] Pope's *Essay on Man*, I, 92.   [81] Pope's *Moral Essays*, IV, 117.

[82] J. B. Bouton (1830–1902), author of a volume of essays, *Loved and Lost*, and other prose works. The letter is preserved in the Yale Collection of American Literature.

Forecastle for an idle life on shore, that I am doubtful of my ability to do you good service.

Believe me Dear Sir

very respectfully yours,

Fitz-Greene Halleck

Jn. B. Bouton, Esq.

To Evert A. Duyckinck[83]

Guilford, C^t March 29, '67

Dear Sir,

Your two kind presents have added largely to my old debt. Please accept my grateful acknowledgements.

The likeness of Mr Paulding[84] does not remind me of him either in his youth, or age. I saw him for the first time in, I think, 1813. He was then one of the literary Lions of my admiration. In his after life, he honored me with his acquaintance and hospitality.

I am very glad to learn that his collected writings[85] are soon to appear. He had great honors as a writer, and great merit as a man. He thought clearly and bravely, and spoke as he thought. His two lines alluding to our old revolutionary soldiers wherein he says they "Saved this good land and when this tug was o'er—Begged their way home at every Scoundrels door" are a specimen of his manner of expression when indignantly battling for the right against the wrong.

I prophesy and hope for the Translation of Virgil a great sale, present and future. It lacks our old friend Drydens "varying Verse, his full resounding line, His long majestic march and energy divine," nor has Gray's Fancy, "bright-eyed Fancy, hovering o'er" Mr Connington[86] "scattered from her pictured Urn, Thoughts that breathe or words that burn," and, as has been said of Lord Derby's Iliad,[87] it is the Eniad with the poetry left out, and its place supplied by a sort of prose-versification; still it will be popular and salable among young beginners in Latin— giving them Virgils *meaning* without the trouble of a Grammar or dictionary, and helping [?] them, in the absence of his *music,* to "sing him

[83] Preserved in the Duyckinck Collection of the New York Public Library.

[84] This paragraph and the next, relating to James K. Paulding, have been reprinted on pp. 97–98.

[85] *The Literary Life of James K. Paulding* and four volumes of his collected works, edited by his son, William, were published by Scribners in 1867–68.

[86] John Connington's (1825–69) translation of the *Aeneid* appeared in 1866.

[87] Edward G. S. S. Derby's (1799–1869) translation of the *Iliad* appeared in 1864.

to their tune." I have, as yet, only read the first Canto, very likely it will improve, as it goes on.

As soon as this stormy March weather, almost hitherto unexampled in furosity, allows, I shall hope for the pleasure of calling upon you and of finding you at leisure to answer a thousand inquiries about Books and their Authors and sellers. In the meantime believe me,

Dear Sir, Truly yours
FITZ-GREENE HALLECK

Evert A. Duyckinck, Esq

To Mrs. Anne C. L. Botta[88]

April 13, 1867.

Dear Mrs. Botta,

SINCE viewing very gratefully your twofold gift, the sonnet and the letter, I have passed a week in New-York. "Indeed!" you say, "and did not call on me, Mr. Halleck?"

Strike! my dear madam, but hear me!

A violent cold—my penance, I presume, for preferring a hot chop to a smoked herring during Lent—caused me during the whole week to be as deaf as any personage the most distinguished in that line of calamity in history, from Julius Caesar to Miss Martineau, and consequently to be such a disagreeable and unendurable conversationalist as you would walk a dozen miles to miss.

Therefore, in denying myself the pleasure of seeing you, I have done you a great kindness, and may justly claim your thanks for my self-sacrifice and your sympathy in the suffering it has caused me. As soon as I recover the possession of all my seven senses, I shall hasten once more to ring at your door.

In the meantime, should you be on your way across the water, I bid you and yours *bon voyage* out and home. I hope you will be delighted with Europe, and I know that when she knows you as well as I do, she will be delighted with you.

Pray, why should your dear mother (to whom please kindly remember me) be the obstacle you mention? Why does she not go with you? The change from shore to sea, and from sea to shore will add years to her life, and if she declines going, you know that the request, "Ye gods! annihilate both time and space, and make two lovers happy!" has been granted—may say per telegraph "Good morning" to each other as punctually as you have ever done.

---

[88] For Halleck's friendship with Mrs. Vincenzo Botta (Miss Anne C. Lynch), see pp. 298–299 and 352–353. This letter appears in Vincenzo Botta's *Memoirs of Anne C. L. Botta* (New York, 1894), pp. 349–350.

You have added a pure and lasting source of pleasure to Mr. Peabody's[89] honorable consciousness of well doing, by the graceful sanction of your song, so briefly and beautifully anticipating the expression of "the thanks of millions yet to be." That you have made it a compliment to me is very kind on your part, and as it has reminded you of me and given me the lines and the letter, I thank you from my heart.

With my kindest regards to Mr. Botta and your good mother, believe me, dear lady, Very respectfully yours,

FITZ-GREENE HALLECK

To S. P. Lewis[90]

Guilford, Connecticut
Aug[t] 24, '67

Dear Sir,

I AM very grateful for the compliments paid and promised me in your letter of yesterday. To avoid blotting, I send the photograph separately— to be annexed or attached at your pleasure. The full size at Brady's taken several years since, was said to be a likeness at the time when taken. The miniature copy[91] seems to me a faithful one. It is the first copy I have seen, and is less of a Caricature of me than others that have been shown me.

Believe me   Dear Sir
Truly Yours
FITZ-GREENE HALLECK

S. P. Lewis
    Esq.

To Theseus Apoleon Cheney[92]

Guilford Connecticut
Oct 26 '67.

Dear Sir,

WITH the exception of the grief caused by hearing that your health still continues imperfect, your letter of the 23[d] inst and its companion have given me much pleasure. The Poetry is among your best and most musical

---

[89] Halleck here refers to Mrs. Botta's sonnet "To George Peabody," the American philanthropist. See *Memoirs of Anne C. L. Botta* (New York, 1894), p. 443. Mrs. Botta had apparently sent a copy of the verses to Halleck. See first paragraph of this letter.

[90] Copied from the original with the kind permission of the proprietor of the Pegasus Book Shop, New York City.

[91] For the Brady photographs taken of Halleck, see pp. 386–387. It is impossible to determine to which one of the photographs Halleck here refers.

[92] T. A. Cheney (1830–78), a historian whose special field was western New York State. This letter refers to some portions either of the manuscript or of the proof sheets of Cheney's *Historical Sketch of the Chemung Valley*,

and the Sketch of Wyoming, and of the character &c of Mr. Cooper are very ably written. I had the honor of knowing Mr. Cooper well, and of esteeming him very highly. He was a remarkable model of Sincerity. His regard for truth in the most minute things as in the most important, excelled that of any man I have ever known, and his life, in its controversies with those he deemed in the wrong, was a long martyrdom to his principles.

Your complimentary desire that my Autograph should have been attached to the Photograph of me you so kindly accepted can easily be gratified by your placing the signature to this letter glued to the foot of it. I must crave your pardon for humbly declining the attempt to improve your contemplated Poem as you so flatteringly suggest. An Author knows his own meaning better and can better express it than his critic can. Critics like noxious weeds do but cumber the ground they spring up on. Never let your fear of them influence you. In the words of Beattie's Minstril "Know your own worth and reverence the Lyre." With regard to the success of the poem with the Publishers and Public it will depend more upon what is called "accidental" than upon the intrinsic merit of the work. " 'Tis not in mortals," says Addison, "to command success,"—you can only do your best to desire it.

Hoping soon to be assured of better tidings as to your health, and begging you, not to endanger it by overthinking or overworking I am

Dear Sir   truly yours

FITZ-GREENE HALLECK

T. Apoleon Cheney Esq.

To L. Stanislaus[93]

Monday, Nov. 18

My dear Sir,

I HAVE your note of Saturday. Madame Villagrands[94] address in her last

which apparently he had sent to Halleck for his approval. The sketch, which was published the following year (1868) in Watkins, New York, contains both a historical description of Wyoming, in which a stanza from Halleck's poem on the valley has been included, and an account of James F. Cooper. Of the poem mentioned in this letter nothing has come to light. Halleck's estimate of Cooper's character given here has been quoted on p. 319. The original letter is the property of W. W. Lange, President of the Southside Malleable Casting Company, Milwaukee, Wisconsin.

[93] This letter is preserved in the library of Haverford College, Haverford, Pennsylvania.

[94] It was at Villagrand's that Halleck boarded for many years during his stay in New York. See Wilson, *Life*, pp. 175, 296, 405. Apparently at the time this letter was written Monsieur Villagrand was dead, and his wife had moved South.

letter to me was "Care of E. W. Johnston—Post Master, Botetourt Springs, Bonvalle Co., Virginia." Hoping that you are in good health and good spirits, I am

Yours truly,

F. G. HALLECK
187 Astor House

L. Stanislaus, Esq.,
72 Broadway.

From Maria Gowen Brooks[95]

Fort Columbus, (New York Harbour) Governor's Island. *Sir/* Having received from the Messrs. Harper my only entire copy of *"Idomen; or, The Vale of Yumuri,"* I find that the first & second parts, or chapters, are wanting (with the exception of six pages which I have found scattered & detached on looking the leaves carefully over.)

One of the Brothers Harper, who delivered the same copy to Lieut. Brooks, said it had been, Sir, in your possession;—that you had expressed a fear that some of it might be wanting; & that you were so good as to say that you would look for it.

If, Sir, you can easily find what is wanting it will much oblige me as I have no other copy by me, & cannot get one without referring to the files of a newspaper, more than two hundred & fifty miles from this place, where the principal part of the work was published more than three years ago. My object in sending the pages, as I wrote them, to a Newspaper was merely to obtain copies. That object, however, was not accomplished; for tho' I had a promise of the preservation of both proofs & M.S. a large part of both was lost.

Last summer, Sir, soon after my arrival from Cuba, I learned that you had been so kind as to call for the purpose of seeing me, both at the American & Astor Houses; if so, my evil genius contrived that I should be absent when your visits were made.

At present, I have an establishment sufficient for many of the little rites of hospitality, and many of my evenings are spent entirely "de-soeuvéed"[96] [*sic*].

[95] This letter of Maria Gowen Brooks and the one following concern Mrs. Brooks's only copy of her prose tale *Idomen; or, The Vale of Yumuri*, a portion of which had been lost. She now needed the entire copy in bringing out a privately printed edition of the work, which appeared the following year (1843). See p. 298. Both letters, which are in the Yale Collection of American Literature, were printed in Miss Ruth S. Granniss' *An American Friend of Southey*, privately issued by the De Vinne Press in 1913.

[96] Sometimes entirely alone [Mrs. Brooks's own footnote].

On Sunday I usually go, in the afternoon, to the chapel of the soldiers, & dine, on my return at five.

The officer's barge leaves this islet, at nine on Sunday morning, & returns soon after divine service, at New York; & besides this conveyance, private boats, (I think they are called "White Hall boats") may be had at almost any hour.

If you can find, Sir, the pages I miss, I shall be happy to share with you my repast on Sunday next (if not before) & entertain you in the best way according to my means.

Lieut. Brooks being now absent, I have full time to write & converse on the subject in question; & your company, even tho' without the lost pages, will be a great favour to

Sir, your obedient servant,

MARIA BROOKS.

To

    Fitz Greene Haleck [*sic*] Esq.

P.S. We live within the walls of the fort;—almost any one on the island will know where are the rooms of Lieut. Brooks & myself.

From Maria Gowen Brooks

Fort Columbus Governor's Island. June 15, '42.

Sir

I AM sorry that the too-late receipt of my letter deprived us of the pleasure of your company on Sunday; but can only repeat, that, we keep always, at our frugal table, a plate for hospitality.

Sunday, in this busy country, is the only day given to rest & to heaven, & is therefore, on every account the best for any calm and harmless interview. On that day, as I have said, I frequently dine entirely alone. We shall be happy, however, to see you, "sans cérémonie," on any day that may be convenient to yourself.

Our windows overlook Brooklyn, & also the avenue where the boats are accustomed to land; one must cross a bridge; enter a gate, or, (as they call it here) a "Sally Porte;" & the first flight of steps on the left (after entering this gate) conducts to the piazza in front of our rooms. During the afternoon service our apartments may possibly be locked; but there is a seat on the piazza, & shade, air, shelter, & a "buena vista" over the same gate by which you enter, near the grassy parapet.

"Idomen" was published in the "Boston Saturday Evening Gazette"— either in the year 37 – 8 – or 9–.

I forwarded the parts or chapters from West Point as fast as I could get them done, accompanied by letters directing, a little, how to print them, postage for the whole.

Mr. Clapp the editor of the paper, was so obliging as to inform me that he never sold so many numbers of his papers, severally as he did while "Idomen" was coming out; that several persons to his knowledge had cut out the columns containing it & pasted them into books; & that persons had said "the work was such a one as did not appear more than once in a hundred years."

This information, (if its sincerity may be taken for granted,) together with the little expense I have mentioned, may make it less indelicate & more practicable to obtain the lost pages than I at first feared, & even, now, fear.

As I have an almost unconquerable repugnance to the business of such affairs, any little assistance will be gratefully received by

Sir, your obedient servant,

MARIA BROOKS

[The two following notes appear on the back of the letter:]

[1] My letters &c are usually directed to the care of Lieut. Horace Brooks, now second in command at this islet.

[2] I have reasons for wishing the publication, in one or two volumes, of this story, the like of which I never can write again—but the task to me is one of extreme difficulty.

From Solyman Brown[97]

Danby

Tompkins Co. N.Y.

8th August 1864

Dear friend Halleck,

THE receipt of a copy of your beautiful poem entitled "Young America," was a gratifying token of your remembrance not only of me but of the Muses. I had signified to you my desire to see some of your most mature conversations with the Muses. My wish has been fully gratified, and I see now what the tree of genius can produce in the "sere and yellow" of its leaf.

I take pleasure in hailing you from the elevated sources of the streams which flow into the St. Lawrence and the Susquehannah, which Symbolize the two kindred Nations whose common language you have elevated to its highest musical cadence, on the Summit of Parnassus. Some few of my literary friends during the past 30 years have regarded another hon-

---

[97] Solyman Brown (1790–1876), a Swedenborgian clergyman. As may be seen from this letter, the works of the Swedish mystic have strangely affected the literary style of a too fond disciple. Fortunately Halleck found no inspiration in Swedenborg, and preferred "the old pastures amid which my youth was nurtured, and . . . the One Book, now many, many centuries old" (see p. 197). Mr. Brown's letter is preserved in the Chamberlain Collection of the Boston Public Library.

ored name as the rival of your own as *Poet Laureate* of young America. But as for myself *"I cannot see it"*; and in this respect, I have found myself agreeing with a very large majority of my friends.

I will confidently challenge any Poet of America, & I might almost or altogether include England during the last half century, to produce equal matches to *"Connecticut," "Burns," Red Jacket, Bozzaris, & Alnwick Castle;* to say nothing of minor gems.

But, you are aware of your own position among the Bards of Columbia, without this statement as to my own judgment & and that of my many acquaintances.

Yet, with all this unrivalled exaltation, on the natural plane, you must not be surprised when I recur to an idea in one of my former letters, that a perusal of some of the best works of Emanuel Swedenborg, such as his, *"True Christian Religion,"* his *"Wisdom of the Angels,"* his *"Conjugial [sic] Love,"* his *"Divine Providence,"* his treatise on *"Heaven and Hell,"* & his *"Celestial Arcana,"* would elevate your thoughts and your affection to a plane of life far above "Ossa piled upon Pelion," in the natural sphere.

I most devoutly wish that I could excite the attention of your leisure hours, to this great theme; to the descent of the N. Jerusalem from God out of heaven, effected *initially* by the incomparable writings of the Swedish Scribe, and now making its way rapidly in the hearts and understandings of mankind. I know nothing in all the treasuries of science that could afford such aliment to a mind like yours blessed with leisure, as the development of spiritual knowledge from the scriptures, & the illumined pen of Swedenborg. All the books in the world pale before the Scriptures illustrated by the *"Science of Correspondence"* which enfolds their genuine sense.

In a literal sense the writings of The Law, the Prophets, the Gospels, & the Apocalypse, are disjointed, strange, unaccountable, inexplicable, and in most part absurd; whereas in the spiritual sense, they are beautiful, instructive, scientific, harmonious and divine. This great fact is being developed more and more from day to day, and the *World* will soon learn to stand abashed at the presence of the *"Word."*

Yours always   SOLYMAN BROWN

From John Williamson Palmer[98]

Elizabeth, New Jersey,
May 30th /66

Dear Mr. Halleck,

I AM the compiler of an illustrated collection of poetry, entitled "Folk-

[98] The letter is preserved in the Chamberlain Collection of the Boston Public Library. No edition of Palmer's *Folk Songs* has been discovered that contains Halleck's lines on Drake.

Songs," which you may have seen—published by Scribner & Co of New York. I am now preparing for the next holiday season a new edition, thoroughly revised and very much enlarged; there will be one hundred new poems and twenty new pictures; and we are bestowing every care upon it, to make it the most elegant collection, internally and externally, ever published in this country. Will you do me the favor to send me an *autograph* copy, with your signature attached, of the Lines on the death of the Poet Drake. I cannot account for the oversight by which a poem so universally admired was omitted from the first editions; and shall feel truly obliged to you if you will afford me the opportunity now, while I am reading the proofs, to supply the omission.

I am,   Sir,

Most respectfully yours,

J. W. PALMER

My address is
   "Care of David Williams Esq.
      Elizabeth,
         N. J."

From William Alfred Jones[99]

Dear Sir,

I DON'T think I can add anything of my own to the acute and gossiping criticism of Leigh Hunt, & your own felicitous notes—Coleridge in his Biog Literaria & throughout his Literary Remains & Table Talk (passing), has said the finest & justest things on the topic of Imagination & Fancy—Wordsworth, also, in his critical prefaces has gone over the ground, pretty thoroughly. Hazlitt, in his 1st Lecture, of the course on the English Poets, has also made some just and fine remarks. Keats, if I am not mistaken in the preface to his Endymion, has displayed a fine critical tact in his distinctions.

My own poor page of distinctions[100] is a meagre note on the matter— Nothing, I believe, was *written* about these matters, before the present century, in English—The german critics, probably have done more than any continental writers. The whole subject appears to me to be summed up in your foot notes pp 20 & 21. Your confirmation and censure of Hunt in different places occur to me as entirely just & correct: eg. notes on

99 This interesting letter concerns a copy of Leigh Hunt's *Imagination and Fancy* (New York, 1852) to which Halleck had added manuscript notes of his own. The poet had apparently sent the volume to the critic, William A. Jones, for his comment. Mr. Jones's reply is contained in this letter now in the Chamberlain Collection of the Boston Public Library.

100 Mr. Jones probably refers here to one of his "Aesthetical Fragments" entitled "Imagination and Fancy" and contained in his volume of *Essays Upon Authors and Books* (New York, 1849), p. 177.

page 3, 4, 5, 7, 45, 46, 23, in particular—But under corrections, may I beg to hint, that your praise of Campbell[101] appears to me to err in the degree of generosity (p. 6)—and, (p 24) Is the stanza from Suckling an instance of Fancy *and* Imagination? It certainly is a capital specimen of Fancy—Is not the next half stanza on the same page an example of fine *poetical* description tho' also literal fact? As the Dramatist, is commonly ranked the *first,* in the poetical Peerage, does not Fletcher tho 2d or 3d rate, as compared with Shakespeare rank above the first rate, in satire, compliment, moral painting, eloquence like Pope.—Could Pope have written the finest passages in the Faithful Shepherdess & the Two Noble Kinsmen &, the Elder Brother &c?—Pope comes nearer to me, as a writer, but as Lamb & Coleridge & Hazlitt, I think, all agree, his finest things are Horatian, whereas Fletcher in a few (perhaps) of his finest flights, is Shakespearian or Miltonic[102]—Imagination is creative, gives a life & soul, to inanimate Nature. This is one of its many powers or phases, while Fancy, is more purely illustrative & limited.—But—you have doubtless read all I refer to, have thought it all over, continually—and have done what not even my Masters in Criticism, of whom I am but an Apprentice, could do, given admirable instances of but fine qualities of genius in your choice lyrical and descriptive poetical works.

Pray pardon my presumption in discussing the question at all to which your courtesy and condescension tempts me.—"The words of (even) Mercury, (much less those of one of his humblest followers) are harsh, after the Songs of Apollo"—

My wife begs your acceptance of the bookmark as a slight token of remembrance.

I am, Very Respectfully & cordially

Yr obliged Servt

W. A. JONES[103]

Fitz Greene Halleck Esqr

From Drake De Kay[104]

THIRTY NINTH CONGRESS, U. S.

HOUSE OF REPRESENTATIVES.

Washington, D. C. Jany 16th 1867

Dear Mr Halleck:

THE bill to pension the survivors of the War of 1812 was referred to the

[101] Concerning Halleck's reverence for Campbell's poetry, see pp. 191 ff.

[102] Halleck in his letter to Mr. Jones, dated September 15, 1866, defends briefly the poetry of Pope. See p. 414.

[103] Mr. Jones, the critic, was from 1851 to 1865 librarian of Columbia College. See Halleck's letter to Mr. Jones, pp. 404–405.

[104] This letter suggests well the state of the poet's finances during the

Committee of the House on Invalid Pensions and the Chairman informs me that in all probability action will be taken upon it within the next ten days.

I fear however that the action will be unfavorable from the fact that it will necessitate an appropriation of One hundred & fifty millions to pension liberally the Estimated Survivors of the War.

The Young Ladies of Guilford will have to await the reduction of the War Debt of the present decade if they are so mercenary as to calculate upon your pension.

The Columbian Minister has gone to N. York where I will see him next week and report upon value of your bond.

Most respectfully yours
DRAKE DE KAY

Mr. Fitz Greene Halleck

D. UNCOLLECTED POEMS OF FITZ-GREENE HALLECK

SOME of the poems which we here present are now published for the first time. Others, which were never included in any of Halleck's collected editions, have been obtained from periodical sources generally inaccessible.

INVOCATION TO SLEEP

[THESE verses were probably written before Halleck left Guilford. They are in a style wholly different from that of any of his later work, and were obviously composed during his poetic apprenticeship. They may have been suggested by the opening lines of Young's *Night Thoughts*. The manuscript is owned by Mrs. Edward Jenkins of New Haven, Connecticut.]

O, come sweet sleep, thy balmy influence shed,
And o'er my soul, th' oblivious mantle spread.
Here, on this lovely bank, whilst I recline
Do thou my brows with opiate wreaths entwine.
Light o'er my senses draw thy lethen band
And close my eyelids, with a gentle hand.
With thy gay Visions hover round my head,
With thy soft Pinions soften still my bed.
Thy welcome presence brings a sweet relief,
Lightens the heart and shuts the springs of grief.

closing years of his life. Halleck had apparently sought information from Drake De Kay, grandson of Joseph Rodman Drake, regarding a proposed pension for the survivors of the War of 1812. In the event of the passing of the bill, Halleck would undoubtedly have based his claim for pension on his service in the Iron Grays (see pp. 38 ff.). The letter is in the collection of Captain Frank L. Pleadwell.

Thy Magic Power dissolves the pris'ner's chain.
With Thee worn Labour quite forgets her pain.
The lowly Poor, by fortune's frown oppressed,
In Thee find refuge, balmy peace and rest.
Thou wert to man in boundless mercy given—
The richest boon, the choicest gift of Heaven.
Then come, thou friend of man, Tired Nature's Friend,
And in thy Arms my song and sorrows end.

G.

[INVITATION AND REPLY]

[THIS invitation written by Mrs. Mary Ward Foote Hubbard and Halleck's reply have been mentioned on p. 22. I have been furnished with copies of these through the courtesy of Mrs. Edward Jenkins of New Haven and of Miss Lilly G. Foote of Hartford, Connecticut.]

TO F. G. H.

OUR birds sing sweet, our scenes are fair
And fresh and fragrant is the air,
And Sarah smiles with every grace,
And Catherine wears a pensive face.
And who is here to feel her smile?
What swain can Catherine's griefs beguile?
Can'st thou not come at evening hour
And try at least thy wonted power?
Then far more sweet shall Sarah's smile appear
Nor Catherine think of grief when thou art here.

TO MRS. M. W. H.

AH, well I know your scenes are fair
And nature's fairest forms are there—
And do you think I can deny
What e'er you ask so prettily?
Yet much I fear no art of mine
Can lift the grief of Catherine,
And Sarah's smile too oft, I feel,
It leaves a wound that does not heal.
But I'll exert my feeble power
To cheer the lonely evening hour,
And Catherine's sorrows to beguile
I'll share in Sarah's sweetest smile
And all that decks your rural home.
Yes,—yes, with all my heart I'll come.

SOFT AS THE FALLING DEWS OF NIGHT

[THESE youthful verses of Halleck were printed by James G. Wilson in the *Independent* for February 29, 1872. They were written, says Wilson, "during the winter of 1809–10 for one of the young poet's female friends."]

Soft as the falling dews of night
   The tear of pity flows;
Bright as the moon's returning light
   That gilds the opening rose.

Sweet as the fragrant breeze of May
   Her sympathetic sigh;
Mild as the morning tint of day,
   The beam that lights her eye.

Still, gentle spirit, o'er my heart
   Preserve thy wonted sway;
Teach me to blunt Affliction's dart,
   And soothe her cares away.

Or, if thy anxious efforts fail,
   While sorrows still pursue;
I'll wish, while listening to the tale,
   That good I cannot do.

THE WILD-FLOWER WREATH

[THESE verses of Halleck were printed by James G. Wilson in the *Independent* for February 29, 1872. "During his first summer in New York," says Wilson, Halleck "received a gift of flowers from a young lady in Connecticut, to whom he sent the following verses."]

The wild-flower wreath, though faded, love,
   Which you have sent to me,
A bright remembrance still doth prove
   Of hours I've past with thee.

O, dear to me their native fields,
   And valleys ever green;
There Nature every beauty yields
   To deck her sylvan scene.

How often on their banks we've strayed,
   Or sought the shady grove,
When the lake's bright sunbeams played,
   And fragrant garlands wove.

In Memory's eye their bloom shall last,
   Preserved with fondest care,
Secure from ev'ry wintry blast,
   Till I to thee repair.

Then love shall weave a brighter wreath,
   Of flowers which ne'er shall fade;
And sighs which we in absence breathe
   By joy shall be o'erpaid.

LINES

[THIS poem was originally published in the *Columbian* for July 14, 1814. See p. 37. It was reprinted in *Appleton's Journal*, I, 181 (May 8, 1869), which called it "an unpublished poem by Fitz-Greene Halleck, written in camp at Greenwich, 1814." A manuscript of this poem is preserved in the Yale Collection of American Literature.]

Flag of my country! proudly wave!
   High to the favoring breeze of Heaven;
The rallying point that forms the brave,
   Whene'er the battle-word is given.

As when at evening on the deep,
  From their lov'd firesides distant far,
Their anxious eyes, the sailors keep
  Fix'd on their guide, the northern star—

So, on thy stars, in danger's day,
  The warrior turns his daring eye,
And dauntless treads the crimson'd way,
  Through honor's path, to victory!

Where first their eagle met the gale,
  Our fathers bade these shores be free,
And long, where slaughter strew'd the vale,
  They fearless fought and bled for thee.

Till England's banner-cross was furled,
  And Peace her olive branch display'd;
Then 'mid the plaudits of a world,
  They sheath'd the consecrated blade.

Yet once again the trump of war
  Has bid the dream of peace be o'er;
Again Invasion's crimson car
  Drives threatening round our hallow'd shore.

But shall that flag which on the billow,
  So late has won Fame's laurel wreath,
Which formed a hero's[105] dying pillow,
  And wrapt his pallid corse in death?

Say, shall that flag e'er share the fate
  Of Gallia's fallen *tri-color?*
Shall history say, "It once was great,
  But soon it fell to rise no more"?

No! while within each manly breast
  Burns one faint spark of valor's flame;
While glory lifts its glittering crest,
  And honor points the path to fame.

While spring adorns with flow'rets fair,
  The grave[106] where low our fathers lie,
So long its stars shall blaze in air,
  So long to Heaven's breezes fly!

Flag of my country! proudly wave!
  Nor dread the invader's bold command;
While nobly fight the good and brave
  For freedom and their native land.
                                        Y. H. S.
New York, July, 1814.

---

[105] A footnote in the Yale manuscript says that the hero here referred to is
Captain James Lawrence of the *Chesapeake.*
[106] The Yale manuscript reads "graves."

To Margaret

Written Some Time In 1814

[THESE lines are preserved in an extra-illustrated copy of Halleck's poems to which I was
kindly given access by the proprietor of the Pegasus Book Shop, Inc., New York City. They
are not in Halleck's autograph, but were probably copied from an album by another hand.
The style of compliment, however, is unmistakably Halleck's.]

You told me, Margaret, that in time
  You might, perhaps, be learned to love me;
But 'twas because that I can rhyme
  A little—if the spirit move me.

Ah, had the lyre that winning art
  I well might call its skill divine
And were I sure 'twould make your heart
  Beat in congenial throbs with mine

Again I'd seek the Muses' bowers,
  Which long I've passed neglected by,
Again invoke the fairy powers
  To aid my harp's wild melody.

But ah! I fear 'twere fruitless toil—
  Experience has the lesson taught,
That woman's fond, enrapturing smile
  Can never be so cheaply bought.

And I would spurn, however dear,
  The heart that verse had power of stealing,
Its passion could not be sincere—
  Love claims a purer test of feeling.

Yet I had hoped that, ere 'twas known
  That I could pen a song or sonnet,
Your bosom's little guest had flown
  On Cupid's wing, and I had won it.

Come, tell me, is it so or not,
  Whate'er my fate I beg to know it;
Say—and the Muses all forgot—
  You love the Man, and not the Poet.
                  FITZ-GREENE HALLECK

Were the Whole Ocean Ink

[THESE lines, printed by James G. Wilson in the *Independent* for March 7, 1872, were written in a commonplace book of Francis R. Tillou, the brother-in-law of Drake. It was probably the same volume from which C. Graham Tillou, the son, copied other poems of Halleck
for Evert A. Duyckinck. See pp. 37 and 436. Wilson believes these verses to have been composed "before the year 1823."]

Were the whole ocean ink,
  And every stick a quill,
Were the whole earth of parchment made,
  And every man a scribe by trade,

To write the love of God on high,
It would drain the ocean dry;
Nor would the scroll contain the whole,
Though it were stretched from pole to pole.

ASKS SHE MY NAME

[THERE is no evidence to whom these verses were addressed, but judging from the context, they were probably written in the album of a lady of England. The manuscript is preserved in the Yale Collection of American Literature.]

Asks she my name, with hers to rest,
Among the blessing and the blest,
    In these her pages of the heart?
There needs no second call—I come,
Be this my autographic home,
My name no more in blight or bloom,
    From hers to part.

Lady of England! for her cheek's
Bright rose her island birth place speaks,
    Her cradle clime of smiles and tears;
Not in this sunset land of mine
Are poets born like hers, divine,
Their fame her pride, their graves her shrine
    A thousand years.

Yet, though the song-bird of an hour,
I win not with a poet's power
    A couch in fame's sepulchral hall,
A nation's anthem, proud and solemn,
Or breathing bust, or storied column
I've won this leaf in beauty's volume
    Well worth them all.

                    FITZ-GREENE HALLECK
New York Dec. 28, 1829.

THE DISCARDED

[THIS poem was originally published in the *New York Mirror* for January 29, 1831 (VIII, 233). It has since been republished several times. Important among these reprintings is that in *Appleton's Journal* for October 2, 1869 (II, 214), stating the circumstances of composition. See pp. 242 ff.]

"No doubt, she was right in rejecting my suit;
    But why did she kick me down stairs?"—*Ballad*

I live, as lives a withered bough,
    Blossomless, leafless, and alone;
There are none left to love me now,
    Or shed one tear when I am gone.

When I am gone—no matter where;
    I dread no other world but this;
To leave it is my only prayer,
    That hope my only happiness.

For I am weary of it—black
   Are sun and stars and sky to me;
And my own thoughts are made the rack
   That wrings my nerves in agony.

There's not a wretched one that lives,
   And loathes like me the light of day;
And I shall bless the hour that gives
   My body to its kindred clay.

And yet at times, I know not why,
   There comes a foolish, feverish thought,
Of where these shrivelled limbs shall lie,
   And where this dead, cold flesh shall rot—

When the quick throbbing of my brain
   That now is maddening me is o'er,
And the hot fire in each swoln [*sic*] vein
   Is quench'd at last to burn no more.

And then I shudder at the tone
   Of my heart's hymn and seem to hear
The shrieking of my dying groan,
   The rattling clod upon my bier;

And feel the pang which he who dies
   Welcomes—the pang which gives me rest,
Ere the lead-weights are on my eyes,
   Or the white shroud is on my breast;

When the death-foam is on my lip,
   And the death-dews are in my hair,
And my clinch'd fingers in the grip
   Of agony, are clinging there!

And then I feel how sad it is
   To know there's none my fate to weep,
Print on my lip the unanswered kiss,
   Or close my eyes in their last sleep.

For all unheard the damp earth flung
   Upon my coffin-lid must be;
By strangers will the bell be rung,
   That tolls in mockery for me.

And he who tolls will laugh the while,
   And whistle his light song of mirth;
And he who digs my grave will smile
   As senseless as its senseless earth.

Some dark-robed priest, perhaps, will pray
　　Beside my bier because he must;
And some hoarse voices sing, or say,
　　The unfeeling adage ''Dust to dust.''

And if perchance I leave behind
　　Enough of wordly pelf to raise
A marble tomb, my name, enshrined
　　In prodigality of praise,

May meet the passing stranger's eye;
　　A sculptor's monument and pride,
Telling that man was born to die,
　　And I—was born, and lived, and died.

And men will trample on my grave,
　　And keep the grass from growing there,
And not even one poor flower will wave
　　Above me in the summer air;

For there are none to plant it—none
　　To water it with patient tears;
My cradle-watchers, they are gone;
　　The monitors of my young years

Are silent now. There was a time—
　　It is a long, long time ago—
When in a pure and holy clime
　　I breathed—and if the clouds of woe

Dimm'd the blue heaven of my thought,
　　Like summer storms they flitted by,
And when they vanish'd, there were wrought
　　Bright rainbows in the twilight sky,

On which my wild gaze linger'd till
　　Their colours faded far away,
Those clouds—I feel their dampness still;
　　But the bright rainbows—where are they?

And she I loved? I must not think
　　Of her—''for that way madness lies!''
Boy, start that champaigne-cork—I'll drink,
　　And dream no more of Mary's eyes.
Nov. 1821

ODE TO THE PENSIONED PRESSES

[REGARDING Halleck's possible authorship of this "Ode" on political bribery of the public press, see p. 138. The poem appeared in the *Evening Post* for April 7, 1834.]

For the Evening Post

Growl! minions of mammon, growl on ye hired hounds
　　Of an infamous cause, at Democracy's name:
For long as that name in vassal-ears sounds,
　　It must crimson your cheeks with the blushes of shame!

Foam! foam at the mouth, while your venom'd pens write
    The falsehoods ye utter, still thicker and faster!
It is wiser and safer to slander than fight
    The party that *limits the life* of your master.

You have dared us to battle, and twice have we met,
    And beat you, alike in the field and the forum,
And as your false hearts are not satisfied yet,
    There's a coming defeat hanging up in terrorem!

Scribble on! let your efforts to ages disclose
    That your impotent stabs at the patriot Jackson,
And the spirit that prompts[107] your assassin-like blows
    Were *contracted for,* in "a fair business transaction!"

And wear on your foreheads the *brand* you have sought!
    Prove that yours is the task of the hireling and slave,
Whose honour and conscience are sold and are bought,
    And who toils in the ditch of his own freedom's grave.

But think not there's one in The Party so base
    As to truckle, or tremble, or pale at your ire!
No! No! let it burn 'till the last of your race
    In the war-fires you've kindled, in torture, expire!

For our fathers have taught us forever to cherish
    A hatred of bribery, heart-rooted and deep!
If that vow is ere broke, may the perjured one perish!
    And accursed be the spot where his traitor-bones sleep!
                    THE PEOPLE

FORGET-ME-NOT: "MYOSOTIS AVENSIS"
FROM THE GERMAN: BY FITZ-GREENE HALLECK

[THIS poem appeared originally in the *Knickerbocker* for July, 1843 (**XXII**, 48), and, so far as can be ascertained, has never been republished. See p. 305.]

I
There is a flower, a lovely flower
    Tinged deep with Faith's unchanging hue;
Pure as the ether in its hour
    Of loveliest and serenest blue.
The streamlet's gentle side it seeks,
    The silent fount, the shaded grot,
And sweetly to the heart it speaks,
    Forget-me-not, forget-me-not.

II
Wild as the azure of thine eyes,
    Soft as the halo-beam above,
In tender whispers still it sighs,
    Forget me not, my life, my love!

---

[107] The *Post* printed *pompts.*

There where thy last steps turned away,
  Wet eyes shall watch the sacred spot,
And this sweet flower be heard to say,
  Forget! ah, no! forget-me-not!

III

Yet deep its azure leaves within
  Is seen the blighting hue of care;
And what that secret grief hath been,
  The drooping stem may well declare.
The dew-drops on its leaves are tears,
  That ask, ''Am I so soon forgot?''
Repeating still, amidst their fears,
  My life, my love! forget-me-not!

[CHARADE]

[THIS charade, the manuscript of which is preserved in the Yale Collection of American Literature, is unmistakably in the autograph of Halleck, although unsigned. An indorsement at the close in another hand (in pencil) indicates the author as Fitz-Greene Halleck, and the date of the poem as 1864.]

Come from my First, ah, Come!
  The Battledawn is nigh
And the screaming trump and the thundering drum
  Are calling thee to die.
Fight as thy fathers fought
  Fall as thy fathers fell
Thy task is taught thy shroud is wrought
  So forward and farewell!

Toll for my Second, toll
  Fling high the flambeaus light,
And sing the hymn for a parted soul
  Beneath the silent night.
The wreath upon his head,
  The cross upon his breast
Let the prayer be said and the tear be shed
  So take him to his rest.

Call for my Whole, ah Call,
  The Lord of lute and lay
And let him greet the sable pall
  With a noble song to-day.
Yea call him by his name
  No fitter hand may crave
To light the flame of the Soldier's fame
  On the turf of a Soldiers grave.

WOODWORTH

[THE following humorous lines are preserved in the Duyckinck Collection of the New York Public Library. They are here described as "Lines by Halleck, written from his dictation," and were probably taken down by Mr. Duyckinck himself. The date given is May 7, 1866.

The verses refer to the well-known portrait of Samuel Woodworth (author of "The Old Oaken Bucket") engraved by Thomas Gimbrede, a copy of which appears as the frontispiece to volume one of *Woodworth's Literary Casket and Pocket Magazine* (1821).]

> Thanks to Gimbrede his phyz has been neatly engraven,
> The poet should thank him a thousand times o'er;
> His cravat is quite clean, and his beard newly shaven,
> 'Tis a type that he never appeared in before.

TRANSLATION FROM THE GERMAN

[HALLECK once owned a scrapbook in which he pasted letters he had received from famous men, and other mementos including some manuscripts of his own. After the poet's death, this volume found its way into the library of J. H. V. Arnold, and was sold with his books in 1879.[108] The anonymous purchaser of the volume wrote an article entitled "Poet Halleck's Great Scrap-Book," which he contributed to a newspaper unfortunately not identified.[109] In this article appears a version of the lines printed in the 1869 edition (pp. 242–243) as "Translation from the German." As the version of the *Scrap-Book* differs materially from that of 1869, we are here printing in the footnotes the variants appearing in the *Scrap-Book* text, which is obviously the earlier one. As few preliminary drafts of Halleck's poems have survived, the present collation should prove of interest in showing the poet's manner of revising his work. From what German original the stanzas were translated has not been discovered.]

> There's one who long will think[110] of thee,
>   Though thou art cold in death's last sleep;[111]
> There's one will love thy memory
>   Till his own grave the night-dews steep.
> And if[112] no outward tears he weep,
>   And none his silent sorrows[113] know,
> Still doth his heart its vigils keep[114]
>   Beside the spot where thou art[115] low.
>
> Sad was thy mortal[116] pilgrimage,
>   And bitter tears thine eyes have shed;
> But now the storm hath[117] spent its rage;
>   The turf is green above thy head,[118]
> And, loveliest of the buried dead,
>   Sweet may thy dreamless slumbers be;
> Thy grave the summer's bridal bed,[119]
>   Her evening winds thy minstrelsy.[120]

[108] See item 1439 in the *Catalogue of the Library of J. H. V. Arnold, Esq.* (New York, 1879), where the *Scrap-Book* is described.

[109] A clipping of this article may be found among the *Miscellaneous Papers* on Halleck in the Manuscript Room of the New York Public Library.

[110] *dream.*

[111] *Now thou'rt at rest in death's dark sleep.*

[112] *though.*   [113] *sorrow.*

[114] *Long will his heart her vigils keep.*

[115] *liest.*

[116] *earthly.*   [117] *has.*

[118] *The blue of heaven is o'er thy head.*

[119] *A grave of summer's flowers thy bed.*

[120] *You sleep in beauty's purity. A winter's snow born purity* was a still earlier version of the line which the poet deleted.

As withered on thy cheek the rose,
  I cursed[121] the hour when love betrayed thee;
'Twas mine,[122] in death, thine eyes to close,
  And watch till on the bier they laid thee.
No gloomy cypress-boughs shall shade thee,
  No marble thy sad story tell;
The cruel world shall ne'er upbraid thee
  With having loved—and loved too well.

To a Piece of Plumb-Cake

[This poem and the one following were sent to Evert A. Duyckinck by C. Graham Tillou, the nephew of Joseph Rodman Drake, on December 6, 1867. They had been copied into a commonplace-book once owned by Tillou's father. In sending the poems to Mr. Duyckinck, Tillou stated that he had been unsuccessful in finding the original "autograph copies" but that he had "an indistinct recollection of having seen" them. The copies of the poems with the accompanying letter by Mr. Tillou are preserved in the Duyckinck Collection of the New York Public Library. "To a Piece of Plumb-Cake" is here published for the first time. "A Valentine" was printed in the *Independent* for March 7, 1872. See p. 131.]

Some folks like pleasant sights to please the eye;
  Some like to charm the scene by gentle smell;
And some to court the ear with music's sigh;
But I with Epicurean sages wise
  Love the delights that on the palate dwell.

Sweet piece of cake! to thee the bard shall raise
  The tuneful notes from his devoted lyre;
And as I chaunt oh! charming cake, thy praise,
I'll cut a little bit between my lays,
  My pen with magic ardor to inspire.

But yet, dear bit of cake, I'd have thee know
  It is not for thy taste alone, I woo thee;
For Emma's gentle finger well I trow
Hath mused among thee when thou wert but dough
  And that imparted thy sweet flavor to thee.

And yet perhaps that Emma's lily hands
  Were dirty gentle cake, when thou wast made;
I'll never mind it, for by God's command,
Each man must eat his peck of dirt or sand;
  At least by ancient proverb so 'tis said.

And Emma, since I've sweetly sung thy praise,
  In strains that might have charmed the bards of Greece,
Oh! then reward your minstrels charming lays,—
Perchance again to you his song he'll raise,
  And humbly ask you for another piece.

---

[121] *He banned.*   [122] *his.*

A Valentine

Given *to* Miss Caroline M. Drake (Mrs. F. N. Tillou) the evening of her wedding, 14 Feby: 1821.

Beside the nuptial curtain bright
    The bard of Eden sings;
Young Love his constant lamp will light,
    And wave his purple wings;
But rain-drops from the clouds of care,
    May bid that lamp be dim;
And little Love will pout and swear,
    'Tis then no place for him.[123]

But Cara dear, when we are wed,
    Tho' dim at times may be
The lamp beside our nuptial bed,
    We will not weep; for we
Have better light around our bower,
    The moonbeam smiles within it;
There love will linger many an hour,
    And deem them but a minute.

And should the moonbeam melt away,
    There still are stars above;
And were they gone, the firefly's ray
    Is bright enough for love;
Even in the dark his wing will wear
    Unseen, its purple hue,
And but to dream he hovers there
    Be bliss for me and you.

E. LETTER OF DOCTOR D. McNAUGHT ON HALLECK'S LINES TO "BURNS"

[The following letter was addressed to me by the late Dr. D. McNaught, author of the volume *The Truth About Burns*, in reply to an inquiry regarding Halleck's poem on the Scotch bard. Doctor McNaught's comments are based upon the following remarks of James G. Wilson, which I had submitted to him for verification: "I only know that they (the verses on Burns) were written and published anonymously in Great Britain before his (Halleck's) departure for the United States. The poem attracted much attention in England and in Scotland, and a copy of it, printed in large type and neatly framed, has ever since hung on the walls of the principal room of Burns' birthplace" (*Life*, pp. 274–275).]

Benrig,
Kilmaurs [Ayrshire], 6th April 1925

Nelson F. Adkins Esqr
My Dear Sir,
I have to apologise for being so long in answering yours of 7th Feby., my reasons being indifferent health for some weeks, and the necessity of

---

[123] The first stanza was originally used as the opening lines of one of *The Croakers* (see p. 71), which was later included in Halleck's works under the title, "Domestic Happiness."

being accurate in my information I might forward on the subject of your queries. I have not found any trace of Halleck's poem on Burns being published before 1827, by G. and C. Carvill, New York, in 8vo. size, entitled "Alnwick Castle, with other poems, by Fitz-Greene Halleck." A friend of mine in Glasgow, who is a very reliable Bibliographer of Burns *"thinks"* that he had seen it in a magazine before that date, but does not remember title of same, consequently it is a "think" and nothing more. I have seen a stanza from the poem quoted on at least two pretty early editions of Burns or Burnsiana, but never the whole poem. Of course this is of no value to you. Mr Grant Wilson must have made a mistake about the poem he refers to as being in the Cottage Museum, at Alloway. I never saw it there, but I made particular inquiries regarding it, addressed to the proper authorities, and found that no such thing was there, nor ever had been so far as their knowledge went. This, in my opinion, is conclusive, for if such a thing had ever come into their hands, it wd [sic] not have been parted with. Mr Grant Wilson may have confounded it with Colonel Ingersoll's "Poem on the birthplace of Robt Burns," a framed facsimile of the M.S. of that poem (large size) still hangs in the Cottage Museum. I have recovered a copy of a Centenary (1859) publication,[124] with no imprint or date, but which was evidently printed at Ayr about that date. It contains the *whole poem* and therefore may be of interest to you. If so, you need not return it—it is perhaps the first Scots publication of the poem entire, that is, if the "think" magazine does not materialise. You might try the *London Burns Club* which has greater facilities for reference than Glasgow even, and see what they may have to say. The most direct way is to address Mr Will,[125] the editor of the "Graphic," which you doubtless have seen, and whose business address can be got from the newspaper.

Hoping I have communicated something that may be useful to you, I am,

Yours truly

D McNaught

[124] See pp. 328–329.

[125] Mr. William Will, although generously furnishing other data regarding Halleck, could find no early printing of ''Burns.''

GENERAL INDEX

INDEX OF SOURCES

I. BOOKS

Album, The (1824), 146

Alger, William R., *Life of Edwin Forrest* (1877), 257, 303

Allen, Hervey, *Israfel, the Life and Times of Edgar Allan Poe* (1926), 299

American Portrait Gallery (1877), 386

Andrews, William L., *Old Booksellers of New York* (1895), 258

Appleton's Annual Encyclopedia (1867), 368

[Ashmead, Catherine Forrester], *Fallings from a Lady's Pen* (1849), 381

Atlantic Souvenir (1859), 386

Atlantic Souvenir; a Christmas and New Year's Offering (1829), 230

[Barker, Jacob], *Disclosure of the Real Parties to the Purchase and Sale of the Tradesmen's Bank* (1828), 171, 172

[Barker, Jacob], *Incidents in the Life of Jacob Barker* (1855), 133, 143, 167, 168, 169, 170, 171, 229

[Barker, Jacob], *Jacob Barker's Letters, Developing the Conspiracy Formed in 1826 for His Ruin* (1826?), 167, 170

[Barker, Jacob], *Speeches of Mr. Jacob Barker and his Counsel* (1826), 170

[Barker, Jacob], *Trial of Jacob Barker, Thomas Vermilya, and Matthew Davis for Alleged Conspiracy* (1827), 170

Beers, Henry, *Nathaniel Parker Willis* (1885), 220, 221, 252, 292, 326

Bertin, George, *Joseph Bonaparte en Amérique, 1815–1832* (1893), 150

[Bigelow, Jacob], *Eolopoesis. American Rejected Addresses* (1855), 147

Bleibtreu, Karl, *Geschichte der Englischen Litteratur in Neunzehnten Jahrhundert* (1888), 162, 194–195, 202

[Botta, Vincenzo, ed.], *Memoirs of Anne C. L. Botta* (1894), 186, 299, 353, 416, 417

Brainard, The Poems of John G. C. (1842), 196

Brinley, Francis, *Life of William T. Porter* (1860), 278, 413

Bryant, William C., ed., *The Family Library of Poetry and Song* (1880), 351

Bryant, William C., *Some Notices of the Life and Writings of Fitz-Greene Halleck* (1869), 13, 54, 67, 98, 112, 148, 159, 165, 172, 174, 180, 181, 183, 187. 204, 216, 217, 235, 237, 277, 288, 290, 324, 347, 351, 364, 365, 367, 381

Bryant Festival at "The Century," The (1865), 351, 385

Cairns, William B., *British Criticisms of American Writings, 1815–1833* (1922), 127

Cairns, William B., *On the Development of American Literature from 1815 to 1833 with Especial Reference to Periodicals* (1898), 282

Canale, George, *Halleck's Marco Botzares in Modern Greek* (1859), 163, 378

Canale, George, *A Memorial of the American Poet Fitz-Greene Halleck* (1870), 163, 381

Catalogue of the Library of J. H. V. Arnold, Esq. (1879), 435

Catalogue of the Private Library of the Late Fitz-Greene Halleck, 93, 130, 381

Chambers' Cyclopaedia of English Literature (1876), 203

II. PERIODICALS

(All periodicals and newspapers are published in New York unless otherwise noted)

III. NEWSPAPERS